THE WESTERN HERITAGE

Eleventh Edition

VOLUME B: 1300–1815

Donald Kagan
YALE UNIVERSITY

Steven Ozment
HARVARD UNIVERSITY

Frank M. Turner
YALE UNIVERSITY

Alison Frank
HARVARD UNIVERSITY

PEARSON

Boston   Columbus   Indianapolis   New York   San Francisco   Upper Saddle River   Amsterdam
Cape Town   Dubai   London   Madrid   Milan   Munich   Paris   Montréal   Toronto   Delhi   Mexico City
São Paulo   Sydney   Hong Kong   Seoul   Singapore   Taipei   Tokyo

Editorial Director: Craig Campanella
Editor-in-Chief: Dickson Musslewhite
Executive Editor: Jeff Lasser
Associate Editor: Rob DeGeorge
Director of Marketing: Brandy Dawson
Senior Marketing Manager: Maureen E. Prado Roberts
Marketing Coordinator: Samantha Bennett
Marketing Assistant: Cristina Liva
Senior Digital Media Editor: Paul DeLuca
Digital Media Editor: Lisa M. Dotson
Digital Media Project Manager: Claudine Bellanton
Managing Editor: Ann Marie McCarthy

Production/Project Manager: Barbara Mack
Full-Service Project Management and Composition:
    Laserwords
Art Director: Maria Lange
Interior Designer: Liz Harasymcuk
Cover Designer: Liz Harasymcuk
Cover Photo: The Four Conditions of Society: Work (vellum),
    Bourdichon, Jean (1457–1521)/Bibliotheque de l'Ecole des Beaux-
    Arts, Paris, France/Giraudon/The Bridgeman Art Library
Operations Manager: Mary Fischer
Operations Specialist: Alan Fischer

Credits and acknowledgments borrowed from other sources and reproduced, with permission, in this textbook appear on the appropriate page within text.

Library of Congress Cataloging-in-Publication Data
Library of Congress Control Number: Cataloging in Publishing Data is on record at the Library of Congress.

10 9 8 7 6 5 4 3 2 1 V092 13 14 15

ISBN 10: 0205962424

BRIEF CONTENTS

CONTENTS

DOCUMENTS

*Documents preceded by an asterisk appear in the printed book. Documents without asterisks are referenced throughout the text by title and are available at MyHistoryLab.com.

MAPS

PREFACE

The years since the publication of the Tenth Edition of *The Western Heritage* have produced significant changes that present new and serious challenges to the West and the rest of the world. The most striking of these changes is in the economy. In 2008, a serious financial crisis produced a deep recession that diminished the widespread economic growth and prosperity of the West and much of the world and threatened to produce the political instability that usually accompanies economic upheaval. By 2012, the European Union, long an economic powerhouse, felt the threat to its currency and the solvency of its weaker members. The United States also suffered a severe setback, and the recovery from its recession was the slowest in decades. There seems to be little agreement as to solutions to the problem within or among the nations of the West and even less willingness to make the sacrifices that might be necessary.

In the realms of international relations and politics, the United States and its European friends and allies pursued mixed policies. The war in Iraq, which some had thought lost, took a sharp turn in 2008 when the Americans changed their approach, that was popularly called "the surge," introducing a sharply increased military force and a new counter-insurgence strategy. It was so successful that the Western allies chose to withdraw their combat troops and leave the remaining fighting to the new Iraqi government. With fewer troops and a less clear commitment the Americans undertook a similar "surge" using a similar plan in Afghanistan. The effort met with considerable success, but the prospect of continued fighting and diminishing support by the engaged Western powers left the future of their efforts to clear the region of terrorist bases uncertain.

New challenges arose in still another area involving important Western interests: the Middle East. Insurrections against well-established autocracies in Libya and Egypt drew support in different degrees from members of NATO. Both nations succeeded in removing dictatorial rulers, but the character of the new regimes and their relationship with the West remains uncertain.

The authors of this volume continue to believe that the heritage of Western civilization remains a major point of departure for understanding and defining the challenges of our time. The spread of its interests and influence throughout the world has made the West a crucial part of the world's economy and a major player on the international scene. This book aims to introduce its readers to the Western heritage so that they may be better-informed and more culturally sensitive citizens of the increasingly troubled and challenging global age.

Since *The Western Heritage* first appeared, we have sought to provide our readers with a work that does justice to the richness and variety of Western civilization and its many complexities. We hope that such an understanding of the West will foster lively debate about its character, values, institutions, and global influence. Indeed, we believe such a critical outlook on their own culture has characterized the peoples of the West since the dawn of history. Through such debates we define ourselves and the values of our culture. Consequently, we welcome the debate and hope that *The Western Heritage*, Eleventh Edition, can help foster an informed discussion through its history of the West's strengths and weaknesses and the controversies surrounding Western history. To further that debate, we have included an introductory essay entitled "What Is the Western Heritage?" to introduce students to the concept of the West and to allow instructors and students to have a point of departure for debating this concept in their course of study.

We also believe that any book addressing the experience of the West must also look beyond its historical European borders. Students reading this book come from a wide variety of cultures and experiences. They live in a world of highly interconnected economies and instant communication between cultures. In this emerging multicultural society it seems both appropriate and necessary to recognize how Western civilization has throughout its history interacted with other cultures, both influencing and being influenced by them. For this reason, there is a chapter that focuses on the nineteenth-century European age of imperialism. Further examples of Western interaction with other parts of the world, such as with Islam, appear throughout the text. To further highlight the theme of cultural interaction, *The Western Heritage* includes a series of comparative essays, "The West & the World."

In this edition, as in past editions, our goal has been to present Western civilization fairly, accurately, and in a way that does justice to this great, diverse legacy of human enterprise. History has many facets, no single one of which can alone account for the others. Any attempt to tell the story of the West from a single overarching perspective, no matter how timely, is bound to neglect or suppress some important parts of this story. Like all other authors of introductory texts, we have had to make choices, but we have attempted to provide the broadest possible introduction to Western civilization.

▼ Goals of the Text

Our primary goal has been to present a strong, clear, narrative account of the central developments in Western history. We have also sought to call attention to certain critical themes:

- The capacity of Western civilization, from the time of the Greeks to the present, to transform itself through self-criticism.
- The development in the West of political freedom, constitutional government, and concern for the rule of law and individual rights.
- The shifting relations among religion, society, and the state.
- The development of science and technology and their expanding impact on Western thought, social institutions, and everyday life.
- The major religious and intellectual currents that have shaped Western culture.

We believe that these themes have been fundamental in Western civilization, shaping the past and exerting a continuing influence on the present.

Flexible Presentation *The Western Heritage*, Eleventh Edition, is designed to accommodate a variety of approaches to a course in Western civilization, allowing instructors to stress what is most important to them. Some instructors will ask students to read all the chapters. Others will select among them to reinforce assigned readings and lectures. We believe the documents as well as the "Encountering the Past" and "A Closer Look" features may also be adopted selectively by instructors for purposes of classroom presentation and debate and as the basis for short written assignments.

Integrated Social, Cultural, and Political History *The Western Heritage* provides one of the richest accounts of the social history of the West available today, with strong coverage of family life, the changing roles of women, and the place of the family in relation to broader economic, political, and social developments. This coverage reflects the explosive growth in social historical research in the past half-century, which has enriched virtually all areas of historical study.

We have also been told repeatedly by instructors that no matter what their own historical specialization, they believe that a political narrative gives students an effective tool to begin to understand the past. Consequently, we have sought to integrate such a strong political narrative with our treatment of the social, cultural, and intellectual factors in Western history.

We also believe that religious faith and religious institutions have been fundamental to the development of the West. No other survey text presents so full an account of the religious and intellectual development of the West. People may be political and social beings, but they are also reasoning and spiritual beings. What they think and believe are among the most important things we can know about them. Their ideas about God, society, law, gender, human nature, and the physical world have changed over the centuries and continue to change. We cannot fully grasp our own approach to the world without understanding the religious and intellectual currents of the past and how they have influenced our thoughts and conceptual categories. We seek to recognize the impact of religion in the expansion of the West, including the settlement of the Americas in the sixteenth century and the role of missionaries in nineteenth-century Western imperialism.

Clarity and Accessibility Good narrative history requires clear, vigorous prose. As with earlier editions, we have paid careful attention to our writing, subjecting every paragraph to critical scrutiny. Our goal has been to make the history of the West accessible to students without compromising vocabulary or conceptual level. We hope this effort will benefit both instructors and students.

▼ The Eleventh Edition

New to This Edition

- This edition is closely tied to the innovative website, the New MyHistoryLab, which helps you save time and improve results as you study history (www.myhistorylab.com). MyHistoryLab icons connect the main narrative in each chapter of the book to a powerful array of MyHistoryLab resources, including primary source documents, analytical video segments, interactive maps, and more. A MyHistoryLab Media Assignments feature now appears at the end of each chapter, capping off the study resources for the chapter. The New MyHistoryLab also includes both eBook and Audio Book versions of *The Western Heritage*, Eleventh Edition, so that you can read or listen to your textbook any time you have access to the Internet.
- New with this Eleventh Edition: *The Western Heritage* now uses the latest release of the New MyHistoryLab, which offers the most advanced Study Plan ever. You get personalized Study Plans for each chapter, with content arranged from less complex thinking—like remembering facts—to more complex critical thinking—like understanding connections in history and analyzing primary sources. Assessments and learning applications in the Study Plan link you directly to *The Western Heritage* eBook for reading and review.
- For the Eleventh Edition, the authors welcome Alison Frank, professor of history at Harvard University. Alison Frank is interested in transnational approaches to the history of Central and Eastern Europe, particularly the Habsburg Empire and its successor states in the nineteenth and twentieth centuries. Other interests include the Eastern Alps, the Mediterranean slave trade, and environmental history.

Here are just some of the changes that can be found in the Eleventh Edition of *The Western Heritage:*

Chapter 1

- **Expanded coverage** of the eventual demise of the Hittite kingdom.
- **New Closer Look:** Babylonian World Map

Chapter 2

- **New Document:** Husband and Wife in Homer's Troy

Chapter 3

- **New Document:** Plutarch Cites Archimedes and Hellenistic Science

Chapter 5

- **New Document:** Mark Describes the Resurrection of Jesus

Chapter 6

- **Revised and reorganized the sections** on "The Byzantine Empire," "Islam and the Islamic World," and "On the Eve of the Frankish Ascendancy" to create a narrative flow that is more logical from a historical perspective.
- **Expanded coverage** of the Byzantine Empire.
- **Revised introductions** to the sections on "Islam and the Islamic World" and "Western Society and the Church" in accordance with the overall reorganization of the chapter.
- **New Documents:** Justinian on Slavery, The Carolingian Manor, The Character and "Innovations" of Justinian and Theodora

Chapter 7

- **New Document:** The English Nobility Imposes Restraints on King John
- **New feature** comparing Romanesque and Gothic architecture

Chapter 8

- **Section on schools and universities in the 12th century** has been revised with additional detail included.
- **Coverage of medieval parenting** has been revised in accordance with the most recent scholarship.
- **New Documents:** The Services of a Serf, Philip II Augustus Orders Jews out of France, Student Life at the University of Paris

Chapter 9

- **Expanded coverage** of the Black Death.
- **New Documents:** Boccaccio Describes the Ravages of the Black Death in Florence, Propositions of John Wycliffe Condemned at London, 1382, and at the Council of Constance, 1415

- **New Closer Look** feature examining a burial scene for Black Death victims from a 1349 manuscript entitled *Annals of Gilles de Muisit*

Chapter 10

- **Expanded coverage** of the art and culture of the Italian Renaissance.
- **Expanded coverage** of Northern Renaissance art.
- **Expanded coverage** of Machiavelli.
- **New Documents:** Vasari's Description of Leonardo da Vinci, Machiavelli Discusses the Most Important Trait for a Ruler, Erasmus Describes the Philosophy of Christ

Chapter 11

- **New Documents:** Calvin on Predestination, The Obedience and Power of the Jesuits

Chapter 12

- **New Document:** The Destruction of Magdeburg, May 1631

Chapter 13

- **New Document:** An Account of the Execution of Charles I

Chapter 14

- **New Document:** Man: A Mean between Nothing and Everything

Chapter 16

- **Expanded coverage** of slavery and racism as well as the wars of the mid-eighteenth century.
- **New Document:** Thomas Paine's "Common Sense"

Chapter 17

- **Extensive new coverage** of Enlightenment attitudes toward Islam and a new discussion of Immanuel Kant and his ideas.
- **Expanded coverage** of the philosophes, particularly in regard to patronage.
- **Revised discussion** of the Jewish Enlightenment.
- **New Document:** Du Châtelet Explains Happiness Scientifically

Chapter 18

- **New coverage** of U.S. attitudes toward the French Revolution.
- **Expanded coverage** of taxation by the monarchy, particularly in regard to its impact on peasants.
- **New Closer Look** feature focusing on a late eighteenth-century cartoon satirizing the French social and political structure
- **New Document:** A Nation at Arms

Chapter 19

- **Coverage of the Haitian Revolution was moved** from Chapter 20 to Chapter 19 in the new edition.
- **A new discussion** of Mary Godwin Shelley.
- **Expanded coverage** of the Romantic movement and its origins, with a particular focus on writers of the period, and expanded coverage of British naval supremacy as evidenced during the Battle of Trafalgar.
- **New Documents:** Napoleon Announces His Seizure of Power, Mary Shelley Remembers the Birth of a Monster, A Polish Legionnaire Recalls Guerilla Warfare in Spain [part of the **Compare & Connect** feature]

Chapter 20

- **The entire chapter** has been completely reorganized to create a more logical sequence of topics.
- **Coverage of Classical Economics was moved** from Chapter 21 to Chapter 20 in the new edition.
- **New coverage** of the relationship of nationalism to liberalism.
- **New Document:** John Stuart Mill Advocates Independence
- **New Closer Look** feature focusing on the painting titled *The Insurrection of the Decembrists at Senate Square, St. Petersburg on 14th December, 1825,* by Karl Kolman

Chapter 21

- **Expanded coverage** of the revolutions that occurred in 1848 and of nationalist movements.
- **New Document:** A Czech Nationalist Defends the Austrian Empire

Chapter 22

- **Expanded coverage** of the aftermath of the Crimean War and of Italian and German unification, and greatly expanded coverage of the Habsburg Empire.
- **New Map** of Crimea has been added to the chapter
- **New Map** showing nationalities within the Habsburg Empire has been added to the chapter
- **New Document:** Mark Twain Describes the Austrian Parliament
- **New Closer Look** feature focusing on a painting by Albert Rieger titled *The Suez Canal*

Chapter 23

- **New subsection** on the influence of the British Suffrage movement abroad, particularly in the United States.
- **Expanded coverage** of women and gender.
- **New Documents:** Praise and Concerns Regarding Railway Travel, A Doctor Learns How to Prevent Childbed Fever

Chapter 24

- Darwin's significance in regard to thought about **evolution and natural selection** is placed within a more realistic context by emphasizing predecessors and contemporaries that arrived at similar conclusions.
- **Expanded coverage** of the *Kulturkampf* in Germany.
- **Coverage of the Dreyfus Affair** was moved from Chapter 22 to Chapter 24 in the new edition.
- **New Document:** Herzl Advocates Jewish Nationalism
- **New Closer Look** feature examining the 19th century revival in popular religiosity, and in particular in the practice of pilgrimage

Chapter 25

- **New section on** women's involvement in missionary activity.
- **Expanded coverage** of the Berlin Conference and of U.S. efforts to acquire the rights to build and control the Panama Canal.
- **New Document:** Gandhi Questions the Value of English Civilization

Chapter 26

- **Greatly expanded coverage of World War I,** including new military technology used during the war, increased opportunities for women on the home front, and increased government involvement in domestic economies to address shortages and inflation.
- **New Document:** The Austrian Ambassador Gets a "Blank Check" from the Kaiser

Chapter 27

- **New Document:** Hitler Denounces the Versailles Treaty

Chapter 28

- **Greatly expanded coverage of the domestic front** during World War II, particularly regarding government involvement in private affairs.
- **New Document:** Winston Churchill Warns of the Effects of the Munich Agreement

Chapter 29

- **Expanded coverage** of the ideological differences between the Soviet Union and the United States that formed the basis of the Cold War.

Chapter 30

- **New section** on the European debt crisis.
- **Increased focus on women** throughout the chapter.
- **Greater emphasis** on social issues after 1991
- **Updated and expanded coverage** of European population trends.
- **New Document:** Voices from Chernobyl

- **New Compare & Connect** feature: Muslim Women Debate France's Ban on the Veil—Mona Eltahawy Argues Women's Rights Trump Cultural Relativism and Kenza Drider Defends Her Right to Wear the Veil in Public
- **New Closer Look** feature focuses on the Nameless Library in Vienna
- A list of **Learning Objectives** now opens each chapter.
- A list of **Key Terms** has been added at the end of each chapter. These are important terms that are bold in the narrative and defined in the Glossary at the end of the book.
- **Suggested Readings were updated** throughout the text.

▼ A Note on Dates and Transliterations

This edition of *The Western Heritage* continues the practice of using B.C.E. (before the common era) and C.E. (common era) instead of B.C. (before Christ) and A.D. (anno Domini, the year of the Lord) to designate dates. We also follow the most accurate currently accepted English transliterations of Arabic words. For example, today *Koran* has been replaced by the more accurate *Qur'an*; similarly *Muhammad* is preferable to *Mohammed* and *Muslim* to *Moslem*.

▼ Ancillary Instructional Materials

Instructors using this text can visit the Instructor's Resource Center online at www.pearsonhighered.com/irc in order to download text-specific materials, such as the Instructor's Resource Manual, Test Item File, MyTest, and PowerPoint™ presentations.

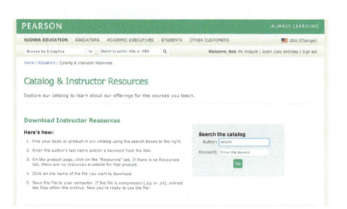

▼ Acknowledgments

We are grateful to the scholars and instructors whose thoughtful and often detailed comments helped shape this revision: Patricia Behre, Fairfield University; Hans Broedel, University of North Dakota; Dorothea Browder, Western Kentucky University; Edward Cade, Lakeland Community College; Amy Colon, Sullivan County Community College; Jean Glockler, Moraine Valley Community College; Joseph Gonzalez, Truckee Meadows Community College; Derrick Griffey, Gadsden State Community College; Sigrun Haude, University of Cincinnati; David Mock, Tallahassee Community College; Patricia O'Neill, Central Oregon Community College; Sonia Tandon, Forsyth Technical Community College; and Margarita Youngo, Pima Community College.

We would like to thank the dedicated people who helped produce this new edition. Our acquisitions editor, Jeff Lasser; our project manager, Rob DeGeorge; our production liaison, Barbara Mack; Maria Lange, our art director, and Liz Harasymcuk, who created the beautiful new interior and cover design of this edition; Alan Fischer, our operations specialist; and Karen Berry, production editor.

D.K.
S.O.
F.M.T.
A.F.

MyHistoryLab™

MyHistoryLab (www.myhistorylab.com)

The moment you know

Educators know it. Students know it. It's that inspired moment when something that was difficult to understand suddenly makes perfect sense. Our MyLab products have been designed and refined with a single purpose in mind: to help educators create that moment of understanding with their students.

Annotated Instructor's eText

Housed in the instructor's space within MyHistoryLab, the Annotated Instructor's eText for *The Western Heritage*, Eleventh Edition, leverages the powerful Pearson eText platform to make it easier than ever for instructors to access subject-specific resources for class preparation, providing access to the resources below:

CourseSmart www.coursesmart.com

CourseSmart is an exciting new choice for students looking to save money. As an alternative to purchasing the printed textbook, students can purchase an electronic version of the same content. With a CourseSmart eTextbook, students can search the text, make notes online, print out reading assignments that incorporate lecture notes, and bookmark important passages for later review. For more information, or to purchase access to the CourseSmart eTextbook, visit www.coursesmart.com

The Instructor's Resource Manual

Available at the Instructor's Resource Center, at www.pearsonhighered.com/irc, the Instructor's Resource Manual contains a chapter summary, a chapter outline with references to the MyHistoryLab resources cited in the text, learning objectives from the text, key topics, class discussion questions, lecture topics, information on audiovisual resources that can be used in developing and preparing lecture presentations, and the MyHistoryLab Media Assignments feature found at the end of each chapter in the text.

Books à la Carte

Books à la Carte editions feature the exact same content as the traditional printed text in a convenient, three-hole-punched, loose-leaf version at a discounted price—allowing you to take only what you need to class. Books à la Carte editions are available both with and without access to MyHistoryLab.

The Test Item File

Available at the Instructor's Resource Center, at www.pearsonhighered.com/irc, the Test-Item File contains a diverse set of 2,400 multiple choice, short answer, and essay questions, supporting a variety of assessment strategies. The large pool of multiple-choice questions for each chapter includes factual, conceptual, and analytical questions, so that instructors may assess students on basic information as well as critical thinking.

Primary Source: Documents in Western Civilization DVD

This DVD-ROM offers a rich collection of textual and visual—many never before available to a wide audience—and serves as an indispensable tool for working with sources. Extensively developed with the guidance of historians and teachers, *Primary Source: Documents in Western Civilization* includes over 800 sources in Western civilization history—from cave art, to text documents, to satellite images of Earth from space. All sources are accompanied by headnotes and focus questions and are searchable by topic, region, or theme. In addition, a built-in tutorial guides students through the process of working with documents. The DVD can be bundled with *The Western Heritage*, Eleventh Edition, at no charge. Please contact your Pearson sales representative for ordering information. (ISBN 0-13-134407-2)

MyTest

Available at www.pearsonmytest.com, the MyTest program helps instructors easily create and print quizzes and exams. Questions and tests can be authored online, allowing instructors ultimate flexibility and the ability to manage assessments anytime, anywhere! Instructors can easily access existing questions and edit, create, and store using simple drag-and-drop and Word-like controls.

Titles from the renowned **Penguin Classics** series can be bundled with *The Western Heritage*, Eleventh Edition, for a nominal charge. Please contact your Pearson sales representative for details.

SUPPLEMENTS FOR QUALIFIED COLLEGE ADOPTERS	SUPPLEMENTS FOR STUDENTS
PowerPoint Presentations Available at the Instructor's Resource Center, at www.pearsonhighered.com/irc, the PowerPoint slides to accompany *The Western Heritage*, Eleventh Edition, include a lecture outline for each chapter and full-color illustrations and maps from the textbook. All images from the textbook have captions from the book that provide background information about the image.	*Library of World Biography Series* www.pearsonhighered.com/educator/series/Library-of-World-Biography/10492.page Each interpretive biography in the Library of World Biography Series focuses on a person whose actions and ideas either significantly influenced world events or whose life reflects important themes and developments in global history. Titles from the series can be bundled with *The Western Heritage*, Eleventh Edition, for a nominal charge. Please contact your Pearson sales representative for details.
	***The Prentice Hall Atlas of Western Civilization,* Second Edition** Produced in collaboration with Dorling Kindersley, the leader in cartographic publishing, the updated second edition of *The Prentice Hall Atlas of Western Civilization* applies the most innovative cartographic techniques to present western civilization in all of its complexity and diversity. Copies of the atlas can be bundled with *The Western Heritage*, Eleventh Edition, for a nominal charge. Contact your Pearson Arts and Sciences sales representative for details. (ISBN 0-13-604246-5)
	***Lives and Legacies: Biographies in Western Civilization,* Second Edition** Extensively revised, *Lives and Legacies* includes brief, focused biographies of 60 individuals whose lives provide insight into the key developments of *Western Civilization*. Each biography includes an introduction, pre-reading questions, and suggestions for additional reading.
	A Guide to Your History Course: What Every Student Needs to Know Written by Vincent A. Clark, this concise, spiral-bound guidebook orients students to the issues and problems they will face in the history classroom. Available at a discount when bundled with *The Western Heritage*, Eleventh Edition. (ISBN 0-13-185087-3)
	***A Short Guide to Writing about History*, Seventh Edition** Written by Richard Marius, late of Harvard University, and Melvin E. Page, Eastern Tennessee State University, this engaging and practical text helps students get beyond merely compiling dates and facts. Covering both brief essays and the documented resource paper, the text explores the writing and researching processes, identifies different modes of historical writing, including argument, and concludes with guidelines for improving style. (ISBN 0-13-205-67370-8)

ABOUT THE AUTHORS

DONALD KAGAN is Sterling Professor of History and Classics at Yale University, where he has taught since 1969. He received his A.B. degree in history from Brooklyn College, his M.A. in classics from Brown University, and his Ph.D. in history from Ohio State University. During 1958 to 1959 he studied at the American School of Classical Studies as a Fulbright Scholar. He has received three awards for undergraduate teaching at Cornell and Yale. He is the author of a history of Greek political thought, *The Great Dialogue* (1965); a four-volume history of the Peloponnesian war, *The Origins of the Peloponnesian War* (1969); *The Archidamian War* (1974); *The Peace of Nicias and the Sicilian Expedition* (1981); *The Fall of the Athenian Empire* (1987); a biography of Pericles, *Pericles of Athens and the Birth of Democracy* (1991); *On the Origins of War* (1995); and *The Peloponnesian War* (2003). He is coauthor, with Frederick W. Kagan, of *While America Sleeps* (2000). With Brian Tierney and L. Pearce Williams, he is the editor of *Great Issues in Western Civilization*, a collection of readings. He was awarded the National Humanities Medal for 2002 and was chosen by the National Endowment for the Humanities to deliver the Jefferson Lecture in 2004.

STEVEN OZMENT is McLean Professor of Ancient and Modern History at Harvard University. He has taught Western Civilization at Yale, Stanford, and Harvard. He is the author of twelve books, including *When Fathers Ruled: Family Life in Reformation Europe* (1983). *The Age of Reform, 1250–1550* (1980) won the Schaff Prize and was nominated for the 1981 National Book Award. Five of his books have been selections of the History Book Club: *Magdalena and Balthasar: An Intimate Portrait of Life in Sixteenth Century Europe* (1986), *Three Behaim Boys: Growing Up in Early Modern Germany* (1990), *Protestants: The Birth of a Revolution* (1992), *The Burgermeister's Daughter: Scandal in a Sixteenth Century German Town* (1996), and *Flesh and Spirit: Private Life in Early Modern Germany* (1999). His most recent publications are *Ancestors: The Loving Family of Old Europe* (2001), *A Mighty Fortress: A New History of the German People* (2004), "Why We Study Western Civ," *The Public Interest, 158* (2005), and *The Serpent and the Lamb: Cranach, Luther, and the Making of the Reformation* (2011).

FRANK M. TURNER was John Hay Whitney Professor of History at Yale University and Director of the Beinecke Rare Book and Manuscript Library at Yale University, where he served as University Provost from 1988 to 1992. He received his B.A. degree from the College of William and Mary and his Ph.D. from Yale. He received the Yale College Award for Distinguished Undergraduate Teaching. He directed a National Endowment for the Humanities Summer Institute. His scholarly research received the support of fellowships from the National Endowment for the Humanities, the Guggenheim Foundation, and the Woodrow Wilson Center. He is the author of *Between Science and Religion: The Reaction to Scientific Naturalism in Late Victorian England* (1974); *The Greek Heritage in Victorian Britain* (1981), which received the British Council Prize of the Conference on British Studies and the Yale Press Governors Award; *Contesting Cultural Authority: Essays in Victorian Intellectual Life* (1993); and *John Henry Newman: The Challenge to Evangelical Religion* (2002). He also contributed numerous articles to journals and served on the editorial advisory boards of *The Journal of Modern History, Isis,* and *Victorian Studies*. He edited *The Idea of a University,* by John Henry Newman (1996), *Reflections on the Revolution in France by Edmund Burke* (2003), and *Apologia Pro Vita Sua and Six Sermons* by John Henry Newman (2008). He served as a Trustee of Connecticut College from 1996–2006. In 2003, Professor Turner was appointed Director of the Beinecke Rare Book and Manuscript Library at Yale University.

ALISON FRANK is Professor of History at Harvard University. She is interested in transnational approaches to the history of Central and Eastern Europe, particularly the Habsburg Empire and its successor states in the nineteenth and twentieth centuries. Her first book, *Oil Empire: Visions of Prosperity in Austrian Galicia* (2005), was awarded the Barbara Jelavich Book Prize, the Austrian Cultural Forum Book Prize, and was co-winner of the Polish Studies Association's Orbis Prize in Polish Studies. Her current book project, *Invisible Empire: A New Global History of Austria*, focuses on the Adriatic port city of Trieste and the Habsburg monarchy's participation in global commerce in the long nineteenth century. Other interests include the Eastern Alps, the Mediterranean slave trade, and environmental history. She is Associate Director of the Center for History and Economics at Harvard University.

WHAT IS THE WESTERN HERITAGE?

This book invites students and instructors to explore the Western Heritage. What is that heritage? The Western Heritage emerges from an evolved and evolving story of human actions and interactions, peaceful and violent, that arose in the eastern Mediterranean, then spread across the western Mediterranean into northern Europe, and eventually to the American continents, and in their broadest impact, to the peoples of Africa and Asia as well.

The Western Heritage as a distinct portion of world history descends from the ancient Greeks. They saw their own political life based on open discussion of law and policy as different from that of Mesopotamia, Persia, and Egypt, where kings ruled without regard to public opinion. The Greeks invented the concept of citizenship, defining it as engagement in some form of self-government. Furthermore, through their literature and philosophy, the Greeks established the conviction, which became characteristic of the West, that reason can shape and analyze physical nature, politics, and morality.

The city of Rome, spreading its authority through military conquest across the Mediterranean world, embraced Greek literature and philosophy. Through their conquests and imposition of their law, the Romans created the Western world as a vast empire stretching from Egypt and Syria in the east to Britain in the west. Although the Roman Republic, governed by a Senate and popular political institutions, gave way after civil wars to the autocratic rule of the Roman Empire, the idea of a free republic of engaged citizens governed by public law and constitutional arrangements limiting political authority survived centuries of arbitrary rule by emperors. As in the rest of the world, the Greeks, the Romans, and virtually all other ancient peoples excluded women and slaves from political life and tolerated considerable social inequality.

In the early fourth century C.E., the Emperor Constantine reorganized the Roman Empire in two fundamental ways that reshaped the West. First, he moved the imperial capital from Rome to Constantinople (Istanbul), establishing separate emperors in the East and West. Thereafter, large portions of the Western empire became subject to the rulers of Germanic tribes. In the confusion of these times, most of the texts embodying ancient philosophy, literature, and history became lost in the West, and for centuries Western Europeans were intellectually severed from that ancient heritage, which would later be recovered in a series of renaissances, or cultural rebirths, beginning in the eighth century.

Constantine's second fateful major reshaping of the West was his recognition of Christianity as the official religion of the empire. Christianity had grown out of the ancient monotheistic religion of the Hebrew people living in ancient Palestine. With the ministry of Jesus of Nazareth and the spread of his teachings by the Apostle Paul, Christianity had established itself as one of many religions in the empire. Because Christianity was monotheistic, Constantine's official embrace of it led to the eradication of pagan polytheism. Thereafter, the West became more or less coterminous with Latin Christianity, or that portion of the Christian Church acknowledging the Bishop of Rome as its head.

As the emperors' rule broke down, bishops became the effective political rulers in many parts of Western Europe. But the Christian Church in the West never governed without negotiation or conflict with secular rulers, and religious law never replaced secular law. Nor could secular rulers govern if they ignored the influence of the church. Hence from the fourth century C.E. to the present day, rival claims to political and moral authority between ecclesiastical and political officials have characterized the West.

In the seventh century the Christian West faced a new challenge from the rise of Islam. This new monotheistic religion originating in the teachings of the prophet Muhammad arose on the Arabian Peninsula and spread through rapid conquests across North Africa and eventually into Spain, turning the Mediterranean into what one historian has termed "a Muslim lake." Between the eleventh and the thirteenth centuries, Christians attempted to reclaim the Holy Land from Muslim control in church-inspired military crusades that still resonate negatively in the Islamic world.

It was, however, in the Muslim world that most of the texts of ancient Greek and Latin learning survived and were studied, while intellectual life languished in the West. Commencing in the twelfth century, knowledge of those texts began to work its way back into Western Europe. By the fourteenth century, European thinkers redefined themselves and their intellectual ambitions by recovering the literature and science from the ancient world, reuniting Europe with its Graeco-Roman past.

From the twelfth through the eighteenth centuries, a new European political system slowly arose based on centralized monarchies characterized by large armies, navies, and bureaucracies loyal to the monarch, and by the capacity to raise revenues. Whatever the personal ambitions of individual rulers, for the most part these monarchies recognized both the political role of local or national assemblies drawn from the propertied elites and the binding power of constitutional law on themselves. Also, in each of these monarchies, church officials and church law played important roles in public life. The monarchies, their military, and their expanding commercial economies became the basis for the extension of European and Western influence around the globe.

In his painting *The School of Athens*, the great Italian Renaissance painter Raphael portrayed the ancient Greek philosopher Plato and his student, Aristotle, engaged in debate. Plato, who points to the heavens, believed in a set of ideal truths that exist in their own realm distinct from the earth. Aristotle urged that all philosophy must be in touch with lived reality and confirms this position by pointing to the earth. Such debate has characterized the intellectual, political, and social experience of the West. Indeed, the very concept of "Western Civilization" has itself been subject to debate, criticism, and change over the centuries. © Scala/ Art Resource, NY

In the late fifteenth and early sixteenth centuries, two transforming events occurred. The first was the European discovery and conquest of the American continents, thus opening the Americas to Western institutions, religion, and economic exploitation. Over time the labor shortages of the Americas led to the forced migration of millions of Africans as slaves to the "New World." By the mid-seventeenth century, the West consequently embraced the entire transatlantic world and its multiracial societies.

Second, shortly after the American encounter, a religious schism erupted within Latin Christianity. Reformers rejecting both many medieval Christian doctrines as unbiblical and the primacy of the Pope in Rome established Protestant churches across much of northern Europe. As a consequence, for almost two centuries religious warfare between Protestants and Roman Catholics overwhelmed the continent as monarchies chose to defend one side or the other. This religious turmoil meant that the Europeans who conquered and settled the Americas carried with them particularly energized religious convictions, with Roman Catholics dominating Latin America and English Protestants most of North America.

By the late eighteenth century, the idea of the West denoted a culture increasingly dominated by two new forces. First, science arising from a new understanding of nature achieved during the sixteenth and seventeenth centuries persuaded growing numbers of the educated elite that human beings can rationally master nature for ever-expanding productive purposes improving the health and well-being of humankind. From this era to the present, the West has been associated with advances in technology, medicine, and scientific research. Second, during the eighteenth century, a drive for economic improvement that vastly increased agricultural production and then industrial manufacturing transformed economic life, especially in Western Europe and later the United States. Both of these economic developments went hand in hand with urbanization and the movement of the industrial economy into cities where the new urban populations experienced major social dislocation.

During these decades certain West European elites came to regard advances in agricultural and manufacturing economies that were based on science and tied to commercial expansion as "civilized" in contrast to cultures that lacked those characteristics. From these ideas emerged the concept of Western Civilization defined to suggest that peoples dwelling outside Europe or inside Europe east of the Elbe River were less than civilized. Whereas Europeans had once defined themselves against the rest of the world as free citizens and then later as Christians, they now defined themselves as "civilized." Europeans would carry this self-assured superiority into their nineteenth- and early twentieth-century encounters with the peoples of Asia, Africa, and the Pacific.

During the last quarter of the eighteenth century, political revolution erupted across the transatlantic world. The British colonies of North America revolted. Then revolution occurred in France and spread across much of Europe. From 1791 through 1830, the Wars of Independence liberated Latin America from its European conquerors. These revolutions created bold new modes of political life, rooting the legitimacy of the state in some form of popular government and generally written constitutions. Thereafter, despite the presence of authoritarian governments on the European continent, the idea of the West, now including the new republics of the United States and Latin America, became associated with liberal democratic governments.

Furthermore, during the nineteenth century, most major European states came to identify themselves in terms of nationality—language, history, and ethnicity—rather than loyalty to a monarch. Nationalism eventually inflamed popular opinion and unloosed unprecedented political ambition by European governments.

These ambitions led to imperialism and the creation of new overseas European empires in the late nineteenth century. For the peoples living in European-administered Asian and African colonies, the idea and reality of the West embodied foreign domination and often disadvantageous involvement in a world economy. When in 1945 the close of World War II led to a sharp decline in European imperial authority, colonial peoples around the globe challenged that authority and gained independence. These former colonial peoples, however, often still suspected the West of seeking to control them. Hence, anticolonialism like colonialism before it redefined definitions of the West far from its borders.

Late nineteenth-century nationalism and imperialism also unleashed with World War I in 1914 unprecedented military hostilities among European nations that spread around the globe, followed a quarter century later by an even greater world war. As one result of World War I, revolution occurred in Russia with the establishment of the communist Soviet Union. During the interwar years a Fascist Party seized power in Italy and a Nazi Party took control of Germany. In response to these new authoritarian regimes, West European powers and the United States identified themselves with liberal democratic constitutionalism, individual freedom, commercial capitalism, science and learning freely pursued, and religious liberty, all of which they defined as the Western Heritage. During the Cold War, conceived of as an East-West, democratic versus communist struggle that concluded with the collapse of the Soviet Union in 1991, the Western Powers led by the United States continued to embrace those values in conscious opposition to the Soviet government, which since 1945 had also dominated much of Eastern Europe.

Since 1991 the West has again become redefined in the minds of many people as a world political and economic order dominated by the United States. Europe clearly remains the West, but political leadership has moved to North America. That American domination and recent American foreign policy have led throughout the West and elsewhere to much criticism of the United States.

Such self-criticism itself embodies one of the most important and persistent parts of the Western Heritage. From the Hebrew prophets and Socrates to the critics of European imperialism, American foreign policy, social inequality, and environmental devastation, voices in the West have again and again been raised to criticize often in the most strident manner the policies of Western governments and the thought, values, social conditions, and inequalities of Western societies.

Consequently, we study the Western Heritage not because the subject always or even primarily presents an admirable picture, but because the study of the Western Heritage like the study of all history calls us to an integrity of research, observation, and analysis that clarifies our minds and challenges our moral sensibilities. The challenge of history is the challenge of thinking, and it is to that challenge that this book invites its readers.

QUESTIONS

1. How have people in the West defined themselves in contrast with civilizations of the ancient East, and later in contrast with Islamic civilization, and still later in contrast with less economically developed regions of the world? Have people in the West historically viewed their own civilization to be superior to civilizations in other parts of the world? Why or why not?

2. How did the Emperor Constantine's adoption of Christianity as the official religion of the Roman Empire change the concept of the West? Is the presence of Christianity still a determining characteristic of the West?

3. How has the geographical location of what has been understood as the West changed over the centuries?

4. In the past two centuries Western nations established empires around the globe. How did these imperial ventures and the local resistance to them give rise to critical definitions of the West that contrasted with the definitions that had developed in Europe and the United States? How have those non-Western definitions of the West contributed to self-criticism within Western nations?

5. How useful is the concept of Western civilization in understanding today's global economy and global communications made possible by the Internet? Is the idea of Western civilization synonymous with the concept of modern civilization? Do you think the concept of the West will once again be redefined ten years from now?

To view a video of the authors discussing the Western heritage, go to www.myhistorylab.com

A procession of flagellants at Tournai in Flanders in 1349, marching with the crucified Christ and scourging themselves in imitation of his suffering. © ARPL/HIP/The Image Works

((•—[**Listen** to the **Chapter Audio** on **MyHistoryLab.com**

9

The Late Middle Ages: Social and Political Breakdown (1300–1453)

▼ **The Black Death**
Preconditions and Causes of the Plague • Popular Remedies • Social and Economic Consequences • New Conflicts and Opportunities

▼ **The Hundred Years' War and the Rise of National Sentiment**
The Causes of the War • Progress of the War

▼ **Ecclesiastical Breakdown and Revival: The Late Medieval Church**
The Thirteenth-Century Papacy • Boniface VIII and Philip the Fair • The Avignon Papacy (1309–1377) • John Wycliffe and John Huss • The Great Schism (1378–1417) and the Conciliar Movement in the Church to 1449

▼ **Medieval Russia**
Politics and Society • Mongol Rule (1243–1480)

▼ **In Perspective**

LEARNING OBJECTIVES

What were the social and economic consequences of "The Black Death"?

How did the Hundred Years' War contribute to a growing sense of national identity in France and England?

How did secular rulers challenge papal authority in the fourteenth and fifteenth centuries?

How did Mongol rule shape Russia's development?

DURING THE LATE Middle Ages epidemic plagues contributed to almost unprecedented political, social, and ecclesiastical calamity. Sweeping over almost all of Europe, the great pandemic that struck between 1346 and 1353 left two-fifths of the population dead. No one then, however, called it "The **Black Death**," a term invented in the sixteenth century. In these same years, France and England grappled with each other in a prolonged conflict known as the Hundred Years' War (1337–1453). In the war's later stages, mutual, willful self-destruction was made even more horrible by the introduction of gunpowder and the invention of heavy artillery. If those two events were not calamity enough, a great Schism erupted in the Church (1378–1417), creating the spectacle of three elected competing popes and colleges of cardinals.

In 1453, the Turks marched invincibly through Constantinople into the West. As political and religious institutions buckled, disease, bandits, wolves, and Islamic armies gathered on the borders. Confronting overwhelming calamities Europeans beheld what seemed to be the imminent collapse of their civilization. These centuries saw rulers resist wisdom, nature strain mercy, and the clergy turn its back on its flock.

▼ The Black Death

Preconditions and Causes of the Plague

The virulent plagues struck Europe at a time of overpopulation and malnutrition. Nine-tenths of the population lived and worked in the countryside. Over time, the three-field system of crop production increased the amount of arable land and with it the food supply. As the latter grew again, so did the population, now estimated to have doubled over the two centuries between 1000 and 1300. Now again there were more people than there was food to feed them and jobs to employ them.

Watch the **Video**
"Video Lectures: The Plague" on
MyHistoryLab.com

The average European could then face the probability of extreme hunger at least once in an expected thirty-five-year lifespan. Between 1315 and 1317, crop failures produced the greatest famine of the Middle Ages. Densely populated urban areas, such as the industrial towns of the Netherlands, suffered the most. Decades of overpopulation, economic depression, famine, and bad health weakened Europe's population, leaving it highly vulnerable to a bubonic plague that struck with full force in 1348. The description of the plague as "The Black Death" referenced the discoloration of its victims. Riding the backs of rats, plague-infested fleas from the Black Sea area boarded the sailing ships on the trade routes from Asia to Europe, thereby planting the plague in Western Europe. Appearing in Constantinople in 1346 and in Sicily a year later (1347), it entered Europe through the ports of Venice, Genoa, and Pisa by 1347, sweeping rapidly through Spain and southern France into northern Europe. (See Map 9–1.)

Popular Remedies

Plague reached many a victim's lungs during the course of the disease. The sneezing and wheezing of victims spread the plague by direct contact from person to person. Despite the plague's power, physicians, academics, and educated laypeople found effective ways to cope with and defend themselves against the plague. The advice

This illustration from the *Canon of Medicine* by the Persian physician and philosopher Avicenna (980–1037), whose Arabic name was Ibn Sina, shows him visiting the homes of rich patients. In the High Middle Ages, the *Canon of Medicine* was the standard medical textbook in the Middle East and Europe.   Biblioteca Universitaria, Bologna, Italy. Scala/Art Resource, NY

literature described the plague as punishment for sin and recommended penance as the best resolution. Physicians had numerous guidelines to health. They applied natural, herbal medications in good conscience and often to good effect. There were also "green" measures, such as fumigating rooms and aerating city spaces with herbs and smoke, a remedy that lowered the number of fleas. Other measures were washing and cleansing with scented waters.

Read the **Document**
"University of Paris Medical Faculty, Writings on the Plague" on
MyHistoryLab.com

Popular speculation held that corruptions in the atmosphere caused the plague. Some blamed poisonous fumes released by earthquakes, which moved many to seek protection in aromatic amulets. Eyewitness Giovanni Boccaccio, an Italian, recorded the different reactions to the plague in a famous collection of tales of the plague, titled *The Decameron* (1358). Some of the afflicted sought an escape in moderation and a temperate life, while more fatalistic minds gave themselves over entirely to their passions. In the stricken areas, sexual promiscuity ran high. "The best remedy perhaps," wrote Boccaccio, "was flight and seclusion, migration to non-infected lands, and keeping faith."

Map 9–1 SPREAD OF THE BLACK DEATH Apparently introduced by seaborne rats from Black Sea areas where plague-infested rodents had long been known, the Black Death brought huge human, social, and economic consequences. One of the lower estimates of Europeans dying is 25 million. The map charts the plague's spread in the mid-fourteenth century. Generally following trade routes, the plague reached Scandinavia by 1350, and some believe it then went on to Iceland and even Greenland. Areas off the main trade routes were largely spared.

One extreme reaction was the procession of flagellants, religious fanatics who beat themselves in ritual penance in the belief that it would bring divine help. More likely, their dirty, bleeding bodies both increased the terror and spread the disease. So socially disruptive and threatening did they become that the church outlawed all such processions. In some places Jews were cast as scapegoats, the result of centuries of Christian propaganda that bred hatred toward Jews, as did also their own role as society's moneylenders. Pogroms occurred in several cities, sometimes incited by the flagellants.

■○─ **Read the Document**
"Flagellants Attempt to Ward Off the Black Death, 1349" on **MyHistoryLab.com**

BOCCACCIO DESCRIBES THE RAVAGES OF THE BLACK DEATH IN FLORENCE

The Black Death provided an excuse to the poet, humanist, and storyteller Giovanni Boccaccio (1313–1375) to assemble his great collection of tales, The Decameron. *Ten congenial men and women flee Florence to escape the plague and pass the time telling stories. In the Introduction, Boccaccio embeds a fine clinical description of plague symptoms as seen in Florence in 1348 and of the powerlessness of physicians and the lack of remedies.*

What did people do to escape the plague? Was any of it sound medical practice? What does the study of calamities like the Black Death tell us about the people of the past?

In Florence, despite all that human wisdom and forethought could devise to avert it, even as the cleansing of the city from many impurities by officials appointed for the purpose, the refusal of entrance to all sick folk, and the adoption of many precautions for the preservation of health; despite also humble supplications addressed to God, and often repeated both in public procession and otherwise, by the devout; towards the beginning of the spring of the said year [1348] the doleful effects of the pestilence began to be horribly apparent by symptoms that [appeared] as if miraculous.

Not such were these symptoms as in the East, where an issue of blood from the nose was a manifest sign of inevitable death; but in men and women alike it first betrayed itself by the emergence of certain tumours in the groin or the armpits, some of which grew as large as a common apple, others as an egg, some more, some less, which the common folk called gavoccioli. From the two said parts of the body this deadly gavoccioli soon began to propagate and spread itself in all directions indifferently; after which the form of the malady began to change, spots black or livid making their appearance in many cases on the arm or the thigh or elsewhere, now few and large, now minute and numerous. And as the gavoccioli had been and still were an infallible token of approaching death, such also were these spots on whomsoever they shewed themselves. Which maladies seemed to set entirely at naught both the art of the physician and the virtues of physic; indeed, whether it was that the disorder was of a nature to defy such treatment, or that the physicians were at fault . . . and, being in ignorance of its source, failed to apply the proper remedies; in either case, not merely were those that recovered few, but almost all died within three days of the appearance of the said symptoms . . . and in most cases without any fever or other attendant malady.

From *The Decameron of Giovanni Boccaccio*, trans. J. M. Rigg (New York, 1930), p. 5.

Modern DNA studies of plagues past are shedding new light on the medieval epidemics. The exploration of ancient burial pits across Europe confirm the bacterium, *Yersinia pestis*, to have been the cause of the plague, while research continues to study unknown strains of the bacterium. The debate today continues over whether bubonic plague was the sole lethal agent. Were there more disease agents in the mix, such as anthrax, typhus, smallpox, dysentery, or an ebola-like virus? Still to be resolved is the question of how the bacillus, the fleas, the rats, and humans interacted at the various temperatures, humidity, and geographical locations to spread the epidemic across Europe.

Social and Economic Consequences

Whole villages vanished in the wake of the plague. Among the social and economic consequences of such high depopulation were a shrunken labor supply and a decline in the value of the estates of the nobility.

Farms Decline As the number of farm laborers decreased, wages increased and those of skilled artisans soared. Many serfs chose to commute their labor services into money payments and pursue more interesting and rewarding jobs in skilled craft industries in the cities. Agricultural prices fell because of waning

A Closer LOOK

View the Closer Look on MyHistoryLab.com

A BURIAL SCENE FROM THE BLACK DEATH

ORIGINATING IN ASIA, the Black Death reached Europe around 1347. Raging for close to four years in some areas, the disease affected every class in European society and destroyed between a quarter to a third of the population. This illustration, *The Burying of Plague Victims in Tournai*, is from a 1349 manuscript entitled *Annals of Gilles de Muisit*. Tournai was a thriving trading center in Belgium at the time of the plague. The entire image is filled with those burying the dead and the many that wait to be buried. Approximately 7500 people died from the disease every day.

Children were especially vulnerable. Jean de Venette, a Carmelite friar in Paris, noted that many men "left many inheritances and temporal goods to churches and monastic orders, for in many cases they had seen their close heirs and children die before them."

Snark/Art Resource, NY

There was often a shortage of coffins, and it was impractical to wait until they could be built before burying the deceased. As a result, large, makeshift graves were common.

This image illustrates the necessity of a quick burial, and there seems to be little to no orderliness in the process. The objective was to dispose of bodies as quickly as possible in order to prevent the spread of the disease. In the rush to bury the dead, graves were dug with little attention to detail or ritual.

How does this rendition depict the enormity of the disease? How did the plague impact towns such as Tournai?

What might be deduced about the spiritual and emotional toll the pandemic took on the population of Europe?

DEALING WITH DEATH

DEATH WAS ALL too familiar in the late Middle Ages, and not just in the time of the plague, when both princes and the simple folk buried their children in the same communal pits. In popular art and literature, the living and the dead embraced in the "Dance of Death," reminding rich and poor, young and old, of their mortality. In the fourteenth century, death divided the Middle Ages from the Renaissance: On one side of the divide was an overpopulated medieval society devastated by the four horsemen of the Apocalypse. On the other side, a newly disciplined Renaissance society learned to forestall famine, plague, war, and conquest by abstinence, late marriage, birth control, and diplomacy.

Yet death rates in the past were three times those of the modern West and life expectancy only half as long. Life was a progressive dying, and death a promise of everlasting life. In sixteenth-century Florence, fully a third of newborns died in infancy. In seventeenth-century England, infant mortality was 2 percent on the day of birth, 4 percent at the first week, 9 percent by the first month, and 13 percent at the end of the first year. By their teens and adulthood almost everyone had suffered from some chronic illness (tuberculosis), debilitating condition (arthritis, gout), and/or life-threatening infection (streptococci).

In Renaissance Italy, Lorenzo de' Medici, duke of Urbino (d. 1519), was plagued with leg ulcers and syphilis in his early twenties. At twenty-five, he received a head wound that was treated by trephination (i.e., the boring of holes in his skull). The poor man also developed an abscessed foot that never healed. At twenty-six, he fell prey to chills, fever, diarrhea, vomiting, joint pains, and anorexia, and was dead at twenty-seven. His physicians identified the cause of death as a catarrhal phlegm, or "suffocation of the heart."

Looking ahead, in Reformation Germany, at the age of sixty-two Saxon Elector Frederick the Wise of Saxony (d. 1525), who was Martin Luther's protector, spent the last year of his life enclosed in his favorite residence. When his strength permitted, he rolled about the castle on a specially made stool with wheels. Cursed with kidney stones, he died from septic infection and kidney failure when the stones became too many and too large to pass through his urethra. An autopsy discovered stones "almost two finger joints long and spiked."

Those who suffered from such afflictions found themselves, in the words of a sixteenth-century merchant, "between God and the physicians," a precarious position for the chronically ill in any age. The clergy and the physicians profited greatly from the age's great mortality. People feared both dying and dying out of God's grace. Together, the physician and the priest prepared the way to a good temporal death, while the priest guided the dead through purgatory and into heaven, assisted by the laity's purchase of indulgences and commemorative masses. Like the physicians' bleedings and herbal potions, the church's sacraments and commemorations exploited and eased the passage into eternity that every Christian soul had to make.

Sources: Bruce Gordon and Peter Marshall, eds. *The Place of the Dead: Death and Remembrance in Late Medieval and Early Modern Europe* (Cambridge, UK: Cambridge University Press, 2008), chaps. 2, 14; Ann C. Carmichael, "The Health Status of Florentines in the Fifteenth Century," in M. Tetel et al., eds. *Life and Death in Fifteenth-Century Florence* (Durham, NC: Duke University Press, 1989), chap. 3.

How do illness and death shape history and culture?

How well prepared were the physicians and the clergy to address and heal the stricken?

Were the afflicted only wasting their time with herbal remedies and prayers?

Name some contemporary medicines and procedures that might have given the afflicted at least some relief, comfort, and hope?

Death and the Physician, from the series Dance of Death. Death leads an old man to a physician and, standing between physician and patient, hands the physician a urine sample for examination. This 1545 woodcut by Hans Lützelburger, after Hans Holbein the Younger, can be seen as a commentary on the futility of the medical profession in its attempts to ward off the inevitable.

demand, and the price of luxury and manufactured goods—the work of skilled artisans—rose. The noble landholders suffered the greatest decline in power. They were forced to pay more for finished products and for farm labor, while receiving a smaller return on their agricultural produce. Everywhere rents declined after the plague.

Peasants Revolt To recoup their losses, some landowners converted arable land to sheep pasture, substituting more profitable wool production for labor-intensive grains. Others abandoned the farms, leasing them to the highest bidder. Landowners also sought to reverse their misfortune by new repressive legislation that forced peasants to stay on their farms while freezing their wages at low levels. In 1351, the English Parliament passed a Statute of Laborers, which limited wages to pre-plague levels and restricted the ability of peasants to leave their masters' land. Opposition to such legislation sparked the English peasants' revolt in 1381. In France the direct tax on the peasantry, the *taille*, was increased, and opposition to it helped ignite the French peasant uprising known as the Jacquerie.

View the **Map** "Map Discovery: The Spread of the Black Death and Peasant Revolts" on **MyHistoryLab.com**

Cities Rebound Although the plague hit urban populations hard, the cities and their skilled industries came in time to prosper from its effects. Cities had always protected their own interests, passing legislation as they grew to regulate competition from outside rural areas and to control immigration. After the plague, the reach of such laws extended beyond the cities to include the surrounding lands of nobles and landlords, many of whom now peacefully integrated into urban life.

The omnipresence of death also whetted the appetite for goods that only skilled industries could produce. Expensive clothes and jewelry, furs from the north, and silks from the south were in great demand in the decades after the plague. Initially this new demand could not be met. The basic unit of urban industry, the master and his apprentices (usually one or two), purposely kept its numbers low, jealously guarding its privileges. The first wave of plague turned this already restricted supply of skilled artisans into a shortage almost overnight. As a result, the prices of manufactured and luxury items rose to new heights, which, in turn, encouraged workers to migrate from the countryside to the city and learn the skills of artisans. Townspeople profited coming and going. As wealth poured into the cities and per capita income rose, the prices of agricultural products from the countryside, now less in demand, declined.

New Conflicts and Opportunities

By increasing the demand for skilled artisans, the plague contributed to social conflicts within the cities. The economic and political power of local artisans and trade guilds grew steadily in the late Middle Ages, along with the demand for goods and services. The strong merchant and patrician classes found it increasingly difficult to maintain their traditional dominance and only grudgingly gave guild masters a voice in city government. As the guilds won political power, they lobbied for restrictive legislation to protect local industries. The restrictions, in turn, caused conflict between master artisans, who wanted to keep their own numbers low and expand their industries at a snail's pace, thereby denying many a journeyman a chance to rise to the rank of master.

After 1350, the results of the plague put the two traditional "containers" of monarchy—the landed nobility and the Church—on the defensive. Kings now exploited growing national sentiment in an effort to centralize their governments and economies. At this same time, the battles of the Hundred Years' War demonstrated the superiority of paid professional armies over the old noble cavalry, thus bringing the latter's future role into question. The plague also killed many members of the clergy—perhaps one-third of the German clergy fell victim as they dutifully attended to the sick and the dying. The reduction in clerical ranks occurred in the same century that saw the pope move from Rome to Avignon in southeastern France (1309–1377) and the Great Schism (1378–1417) divide the Church into new warring factions.

▼ The Hundred Years' War and the Rise of National Sentiment

Medieval governments were by no means all-powerful and secure. The rivalry of petty lords kept lands in constant turmoil, allowing dynastic rivalries to plunge entire lands into war, especially when power was being transferred to a new ruler. This doubled the woes of the ruling dynasty that failed to produce a male heir.

To field the armies and collect the revenues that made their existence possible, late medieval rulers depended on carefully negotiated alliances among a wide range of lesser powers. Like kings and queens in earlier centuries they, too, practiced the art of feudal government, but on a grander scale and with greater sophistication. To maintain the order they required, the Norman kings of England and the Capetian kings of France fine-tuned traditional feudal relationships by stressing the sacred duties of lesser powers to higher ones, and the unquestioning loyalty noble vassals owed to their king.

The result was a degree of centralized royal power unseen before in these lands, accompanied by a growing national consciousness that prepared both France and England for a prolonged, international war.

The Causes of the War

The great conflict came to be known as the Hundred Years' War because it began in May 1337 and extended off and on to October 1453. English king Edward III (r. 1327–1377), the grandson of Philip the Fair of France (r. 1285–1314), may have started the war by asserting his claim to the French throne after the French king Charles IV (r. 1322–1328), the last of Philip the Fair's surviving sons, died without a male heir. The French barons had no intention of placing the then fifteen-year-old Edward on the French throne. They chose instead the first cousin of Charles IV, Philip VI of Valois (r. 1328–1350), the first of a new French dynasty that would rule into the sixteenth century.

View the **Map**
"Interactive Map: The Hundred Years' War" on **MyHistoryLab.com**

There was of course more to the war than just an English king's assertion of a claim to the French throne. England and France were then two emergent territorial powers in close proximity to one another. Edward, a vassal of Philip VI, actually controlled several sizable French territories as fiefs from the king of France, a relationship dating back to the days of the Norman conquest. English possession of any French land was repugnant to the French because it threatened the royal policy of centralization. The two lands also quarreled over control of Flanders, which, although a French fief, was subject to political influence from England because its principal industry, the manufacture of cloth, depended on supplies of imported English wool. Compounding these frictions was a long history of animosity between the French and English people, who constantly confronted one another on the high seas and in ports. Taken altogether, these factors made the Hundred Years' War a struggle for national identity as well as for control of territory.

French Weakness France had three times the population of England, was far the wealthier of the two lands, and fought on its own soil. Yet, for most of the conflict before 1415, the major battles ended in often stunning English victories. (See Map 9–2.) The primary reason for these French failures was the internal disunity brought on by endemic social conflict. Unlike England, fourteenth-century France was still struggling to make the transition from a splintered feudal society to a centralized "modern" state.

Desperate to raise money for the war, French kings resorted to such financial policies as depreciating the currency and borrowing heavily from Italian bankers, which aggravated internal conflicts. In 1355, in a bid to secure funds, the king turned to the **Estates General**, a representative council of townspeople, clergy, and nobles. Although it levied taxes at the king's request, its independent members exploited the king's plight to broaden their own regional sovereignty, thereby deepening territorial divisions.

France's defeats also reflected English military superiority. The English infantry was more disciplined than the French, and the English archers mastered a formidable weapon, the longbow, capable of firing six arrows a

Edward III pays homage to his feudal lord Philip VI of France. Legally, Edward was a vassal of the king of France. Archives Snark International/Art Resource, NY

Map 9–2 THE HUNDRED YEARS' WAR The Hundred Years' War went on intermittently from the late 1330s until 1453. These maps show the remarkable English territorial gains up to the sudden and decisive turning of the tide of battle in favor of the French by the forces of Joan of Arc in 1429.

minute with enough force to pierce an inch of wood or the armor of a knight at two hundred yards. French weakness during the long war was also due in no small degree to the mediocrity of its rulers. The English kings were far the shrewder in state building.

Progress of the War

The war had three major stages of development, each ending with seemingly decisive victory by one side or the other.

The Conflict During the Reign of Edward III In the first stage of the war, Edward embargoed English wool to Flanders, sparking urban rebellions by merchants and the trade guilds. Inspired by a rich merchant, Jacob van Artevelde, the Flemish cities, led by Ghent, revolted against the French and in 1340 signed an alliance with England acknowledging Edward as king of France. On June 23 of the same year, in the first great battle of the war, Edward defeated the French fleet in the Bay of Sluys, but his subsequent effort to invade France by way of Flanders failed.

In 1346, Edward attacked Normandy and after a series of easy victories culminating in the Battle of Crécy, he seized the port of Calais. Exhaustion on both sides and the onset of the Black Death forced a truce in late 1347, as the war entered a brief lull. In 1356, the English won their greatest victory, routing the French cavalry and taking the French king captive back to England after a complete breakdown of the political order in France.

Power in France now lay with the Estates General. Led by the powerful merchants of Paris, that governing body took advantage of royal weakness, demanding and receiving rights similar to those Magna Carta had granted to the English privileged classes. Yet, unlike the English Parliament, which represented the interests of a comparatively unified English nobility, the French Estates General was too divided to be an instrument for effective government.

To secure their rights, the French privileged classes forced the peasantry to pay ever-increasing taxes and to repair their war-damaged properties without compensation. This bullying was more than the simple folk could bear, and they rose up in several regions in a series of bloody rebellions known as the **Jacquerie** of 1358. The name was taken from the peasant revolutionary known popularly as Jacques Bonhomme, or "simple Jack." The nobility quickly put his revolt down, matching the rebels atrocity for atrocity.

On May 9, 1360, another milestone of the war was reached when England forced the Peace of Brétigny-Calais on the French. This agreement declared an end to Edward's vassalage to the king of France and affirmed his sovereignty over English territories in France. Such a partition was unrealistic, and sober observers on both sides knew it could not last. France struck back in the late 1360s and, by the time of Edward's death in 1377, had beaten the English back into their coastal enclaves.

French Defeat and the Treaty of Troyes During the reign of Richard II (r. 1377–1399), England had its own version of the Jacquerie. In June 1381, long-oppressed peasants and artisans joined in a great revolt of the underprivileged classes led by John Ball, a secular priest, and Wat Tyler, a journeyman. As in France, the revolt was brutally crushed within the year, and the country divided for decades.

Read the **Document**
"Peasant Revolt in England: The John Ball Sermon, 1381" on
MyHistoryLab.com

England recommenced the war under Henry V (r. 1413–1422), whose army routed the French at Agincourt on October 25, 1415. In the years thereafter, the Burgundians closed ranks with French royal forces, another coalition promising to bring victory over the English, only to see the dream shattered in September 1419, when the duke of Burgundy was assassinated.

France was now Henry V's for the taking, at least in the short run. The Treaty of Troyes (1420) disinherited the legitimate heir to the French throne and proclaimed Henry V successor to the French king, Charles VI. When Henry and Charles died within months of each other (1422), the infant king Henry VI of England was proclaimed king of both France and England in Paris. Therein, Edward III's dream set the great war in motion, the goal of making the ruler of England also the ruler of France.

The story did not end here because the son of Charles VI now became, upon the death of his father, King Charles VII to most French people, who ignored the Treaty of Troyes. Displaying unprecedented national feeling inspired by the remarkable Joan of Arc, Charles VII now rallied to his cause and put together a victorious coalition.

Joan of Arc and the War's Conclusion Joan of Arc (1412–1431), a peasant from Domrémy in Lorraine in eastern France, presented herself to Charles VII in March 1429, declaring that the King of Heaven had called her to deliver the besieged city of Orléans from the English. Charles was skeptical, but being in retreat from what seemed to be a hopeless war, he was willing to roll the dice to reverse French fortunes. The deliverance of Orléans, a key city that controlled the territory south of the Loire River, would indeed be a godsend for him. So King Charles's desperation overcame his skepticism, and he gave Joan his leave.

Circumstances worked perfectly to her advantage. The English force was exhausted by a six-month siege and at the point of withdrawal when Joan arrived with fresh French troops. After driving the English from Orléans, the French enjoyed a succession of victories popularly attributed to her. She did indeed deserve much

A contemporary portrait of Joan of Arc (1412–1431). Anonymous, 15th century. "Joan of Arc." Franco-Flemish miniature. Archives Nationales, Paris, France. Photograph copyright Bridgeman-Giraudon/Art Resource, NY

credit, but not because she was a military genius. She gave the French soldiers something military experts could not: a proud, enraged sense of national identity and destiny. Within a few months of the liberation of Orléans, Charles VII received his crown in Rheims, ending the nine-year "disinheritance" prescribed by the Treaty of Troyes.

The new king forgot his liberator (Joan) as quickly as he had embraced her. When the Burgundians took her captive in May 1430, he could have secured her release, but chose to do little to help her. The Burgundians and the English wanted her publicly discredited, believing this would also discredit King Charles VII and demoralize French resistance.

In the end, Joan was turned over to the Inquisition in English-held Rouen. The inquisitors broke the courageous "Maid of Orléans" after ten weeks of interrogation. She was executed as a relapsed heretic on May 30, 1431. Twenty-five years later, in 1456, Charles reopened her trial, as the French state and church moved to get on history's side. She was now declared innocent of all the charges against her. In 1920, the Roman Catholic Church declared her a saint. In 1435, the duke of Burgundy made peace with Charles, allowing France to force the English back. By 1453, the war now ended, the English held only their coastal enclave of Calais.

The Hundred Years' War saw sixty-eight years of nominal peace and forty-four of hot war, and left lasting political and social consequences. It devastated France, but it also awakened French nationalism, which in turn hastened the transition of France from a feudal monarchy to a centralized state. The outcome also made Burgundy a major European political power.

THE HUNDRED YEARS' WAR (1337–1453)

1340	English victory at Bay of Sluys
1346	English victory at Crécy and seizure of Calais
1347	Black Death strikes
1356	English victory at Poitiers
1358	Jacquerie disrupts France
1360	Peace of Brétigny-Calais recognizes English holdings in France
1381	English peasants revolt
1415	English victory at Agincourt
1420	Treaty of Troyes recognizes the English king as heir to the French throne
1422	Henry VI proclaimed king of both England and France
1429	Joan of Arc leads French to victory at Orléans
1431	Joan of Arc executed as a heretic
1453	War ends; English retain only Calais

▼ Ecclesiastical Breakdown and Revival: The Late Medieval Church

At first glance, the popes may appear to have been in a favorable position in the latter thirteenth century. Frederick II had been vanquished and imperial pressure on Rome had been removed. (See Chapter 8.) The French king, Louis IX, was an enthusiastic supporter of the church, as evidenced by his two disastrous Crusades, which won him sainthood. Although it would last for only seven years, a reunion of the Eastern and Roman churches was proclaimed by the Council of Lyons in 1274, after the Western Church took advantage of Byzantine Emperor Michael VII Palaeologus's (r. 1261–1282) request for aid against the Turks. Despite these positive events, Rome's position would turn out to be less favorable than it appeared.

The Thirteenth-Century Papacy

As early as the reign of Pope Innocent III (r. 1198–1216), when papal power had reached its height, there were ominous developments. Innocent elaborated the doctrine of papal *plenitude of power* and on that authority declared the Church's saints, disposed benefices to clergy, and created a centralized papal monarchy with a strong political mission. His transformation of the papacy into a great secular power weakened the church spiritually even as it strengthened it politically. Thereafter, the church as a papal monarchy increasingly parted company with the church as the "body of the faithful."

What Innocent began, his successors perfected. Under Urban IV (r. 1261–1264), the papacy established its own court, the *Rota Romana*, which tightened and centralized the church's legal proceedings. The last half of the thirteenth century saw a new elaboration of the system of clerical taxation. Although a reform that had begun in the twelfth century as an emergency measure to raise funds for the Crusaders, it instantly became a fixed institution. In this same period, papal power determined all appointments to major and minor church offices—the so-called "reservation of *benefices*"—was greatly broadened. By the thirteenth century the papal office had become a powerful, political institution governed by its own laws and courts and serviced by an efficient international bureaucracy, thoroughly preoccupied with secular tasks and goals.

Papal centralization of the church undermined both diocesan authority and popular support. Rome's interests, not local needs, controlled church appointments, policies, and discipline. Discontented lower clergy turned to Rome to address the lax discipline of local bishops. In the second half of the thirteenth century, bishops and abbots protested undercutting of their powers. To its critics, the church in Rome was hardly more than a legalized, fiscalized, bureaucratic institution. As early as the late twelfth century, heretical movements of Cathars and Waldensians had appealed to the biblical ideal of simplicity and separation from the world. Other reformers who were unquestionably loyal to the church, such as Saint Francis of Assisi, also protested perceived materialism in official religious garb.

Political Fragmentation More disturbing than internal religious quarreling was the spiritual undermining of the thirteenth-century church. The demise of imperial power meant the papacy in Rome was no longer the leader of anti-imperial (Guelf, or pro-papal) sentiment in Italy. Instead of being the center of Italian resistance to the emperor, popes now found themselves on the defensive against their old allies. That was the ironic price the papacy paid to vanquish the Hohenstaufen rulers. Now having a large stake in Italian politics, rulers directed intrigue formerly aimed at the emperor toward the College of Cardinals.

Boniface VIII and Philip the Fair

Boniface came to rule when England and France were maturing as nation-states. In England, a long tradition of consultation between the king and powerful members of English society evolved into formal parliaments during the reigns of Henry III (r. 1216–1272) and Edward I (r. 1272–1307), and these meetings helped create a unified kingdom. The reign of the French king Philip IV the Fair (r. 1285–1314) saw France become an efficient, centralized monarchy. Philip was no St. Louis, but a ruthless politician. He was determined to end England's continental holdings, control wealthy Flanders, and establish French hegemony within the Holy Roman Empire.

Boniface had the further misfortune of bringing to the papal throne memories of the way earlier popes had brought kings and emperors to their knees. Painfully he discovered that the papal monarchy of the early thirteenth century was no match for the new political juggernauts of the late thirteenth century.

The Royal Challenge to Papal Authority France and England were on the brink of all-out war when Boniface became pope in 1294. Only Edward I's preoccupation with rebellion in Scotland, which the French encouraged, prevented him from invading France and starting the Hundred Years' War a half century earlier. As both countries mobilized for war, they used the pretext of preparing for a Crusade to tax the clergy heavily. In 1215, Pope Innocent III had decreed that the clergy were to pay no taxes to rulers without papal consent. Viewing English and French taxation of the clergy as an assault on traditional clerical rights, Boniface took a strong stand against it. On February 5, 1296, he issued a bull, *Clericis laicos*, which forbade lay taxation of the clergy without papal approval and revoked all previous papal dispensations in this regard.

In England, Edward I retaliated by denying the clergy the right to be heard in royal court, in effect denying them the protection of the king. Philip the Fair struck back with a vengeance: In August 1296, he forbade the exportation of money from France to Rome, thereby denying the papacy the revenues it needed to operate. Boniface had no choice but to come to terms quickly with Philip.

Pope Boniface VIII (r. 1294–1303), depicted here, opposed the taxation of the clergy by the kings of France and England and issued one of the strongest declarations of papal authority over rulers, the bull *Unam Sanctam*. This statue is in the Museo Civico, Bologna, Italy. Statue of Pope Boniface VIII. Museo Civico, Bologna. Scala/Art Resource, NY

Boniface was at this time also under siege by powerful Italian enemies, whom Philip did not fail to patronize. A noble family (the Colonnas), rivals of Boniface's family (the Gaetani) and radical followers of Saint Francis of Assisi (the Spiritual Franciscans), were seeking to invalidate Boniface's election as pope on the grounds that Celestine V had been forced to resign the office. Charges of heresy, simony, and even the murder of Celestine were now hurled against Boniface.

Boniface's fortunes appeared to revive in 1300, a so-called "Jubilee year." In such a year, all Catholics who visited Rome and fulfilled certain conditions had the penalties for their unrepented sins remitted. Tens of thousands of pilgrims flocked to Rome, and Boniface, heady with this display of popular religiosity, reinserted himself into international politics. He championed Scottish resistance to England, for which he received a firm rebuke from an outraged Edward I and the English Parliament.

But again a confrontation with the king of France proved too costly. Seemingly eager for another fight with the pope, Philip arrested Boniface's Parisian legate, Bernard Saisset, whose independence Philip had opposed. Accused of heresy and treason, Saisset was tried and convicted in the king's court. Thereafter, Philip demanded that Boniface recognize the royal process against Saisset, something Boniface could do only if he was prepared to surrender his jurisdiction over the French episcopate. Unable to sidestep this challenge, Boniface acted swiftly to champion Saisset as a defender of clerical, political independence within France. Demanding Saisset's unconditional release, he revoked all previous agreements with Philip regarding clerical taxation, and ordered the French bishops to convene in Rome within a year. A bull, titled *Ausculta fili*, or "Listen, My Son," was sent to Philip in December 1301, pointedly informing the French king that "God has set popes over kings and kingdoms."

Unam Sanctam (1302) Philip now unleashed a ruthless antipapal campaign. Two royal apologists, Pierre Dubois and John of Paris, rebutted papal claims to the right to intervene in temporal (secular) matters. Increasingly placed on the defensive, Boniface made a last-ditch stand against state control of national churches. On November 18, 1302, he issued the bull *Unam Sanctam*. This famous statement of papal power declared royal, temporal authority to be "subject" to the spiritual power of the church. On its face a bold assertion, *Unam Sanctam* was, in truth, a desperate act of a besieged papacy. (See "Compare and Connect: Who Runs the World: Priests or Princes?," pages 278–279.)

Read the Document
"Unam Sanctam (1302) Pope Boniface VIII" on **MyHistoryLab.com**

After *Unam Sanctam*, the French and their allies moved against Boniface with force. Philip's chief minister, Guillaume de Nogaret, denounced Boniface to the French clergy as a heretic and common criminal. In mid-August 1303, his army surprised the pope at his retreat in Anagni, beat him up, and almost executed him before an aroused populace returned him safely to Rome. The ordeal, however, proved to be too much, and Boniface died in October 1303.

Boniface's immediate successor, Pope Benedict XI (r. 1303–1304), excommunicated Nogaret for his deed, but there was to be no lasting papal retaliation. Benedict's successor, Clement V (r. 1305–1314), was forced into French subservience. A former archbishop of Bordeaux, Pope Clement had declared that *Unam Sanctam* should not be understood as in any way diminishing French royal authority. He released Nogaret from excommunication and pliantly condemned the Knights Templars, whose treasure Philip thereafter seized.

In 1309, Clement moved the papal court to Avignon, an imperial city on the southeastern border of France. Situated on land that belonged to the pope, the city maintained its independence from the French king. In 1311, Clement made it his permanent residence to escape a strife-ridden Rome and further pressure from Philip. There the papacy would remain until 1377.

After Boniface's humiliation, popes never again seriously threatened kings and emperors, despite continuing papal excommunications and political intrigue. The relationship between church and state now tilted in favor of the state, and the control of religion fell into the hands of powerful monarchies. Ecclesiastical authority now became subordinate to larger secular political policies.

The Avignon Papacy (1309–1377)

The Avignon papacy was in appearance, although not always in fact, under strong French influence. Under Pope Clement V, the French dominated the College of Cardinals, testing the papacy's agility politically and economically. Finding itself cut off from its Roman estates, the papacy had to innovate to get needed funds. Clement expanded papal taxes, especially *annates*, the first year's revenue of a church office, or *benefice*, bestowed by the pope. Clement VI (r. 1342–1352) began the practice of selling *indulgences*, or pardons, for unrepented sins. To make the purchase of indulgences more compelling, church doctrine on purgatory—the place of punishment where souls would atone for venial sins—developed enterprisingly during this period. By the fifteenth century, the church had extended indulgences to cover the souls of people already dead, allowing the living to buy a reduced sentence in purgatory for deceased loved ones. Such practices contributed to the Avignon papacy's reputation for materialism and political scheming and gave reformers new ammunition against the Church.

Who Runs the World: Priests or Princes?

📖 Read the **Compare and Connect** on MyHistoryLab.com

IN ONE OF the boldest papal bulls in the history of Christianity, Pope Boniface VIII declared the temporal authority of rulers to be subject to papal authority. Behind that ideology lay a long, bitter dispute between the papacy and the kings of France and England. Despite the strained scholastic arguments from each side's apologists, the issue was paramount and kingdoms were at stake. The debaters were Giles of Rome, a philosopher and papal adviser, and John of Paris, a French Dominican and Aristotle expert. Quoting ecclesiastical authorities, Giles defended a papal theocracy, while John made the royal case for secular authority.

QUESTIONS

1. Are the arguments pro and con logical and transparent?

2. How is history invoked to support the opposing sides?

3. Which of the two men have the better authorities behind his arguments?

I. Giles of Rome, *On Ecclesiastical Power* (1301)

Hugh of St. Victor . . . declares that the spiritual power has to institute the earthly power and to judge it if it has not been good. . . . We can clearly prove from the order of the universe that the church is set above nations and kingdoms [Jeremiah 1:10]. . . . It is the law of divinity that the lowest are led to the highest through intermediaries. . . . At Romans 13 . . . the Apostle, having said that there is no power except from God, immediately added: "And those that are, are ordained of God." If then there are two swords [governments], one spiritual, the other temporal, as can be gathered from the words of the Gospel, "Behold, here are two swords" (Luke 22:38), [to which] the Lord at once added, "It is enough" because these two swords suffice for the church, [then] it follows that these two swords, these two powers and authorities, are [both] from God, since there is no power except from God. But, therefore they must be rightly ordered since, what is from God must be ordered. [And] they would not be so ordered unless one sword was led by the other and one was under the other since, as Dionysius said, the law of divinity which God gave to all created things requires this. . . . Therefore the temporal sword, as being inferior, is led by the spiritual sword, as being superior, and the one is set below the other as an inferior below a superior.

It may be said that kings and princes ought to be subject spiritually but not temporally. . . . But those who speak thus have not grasped the force of the argument. For if kings and princes were only spiritually subject to the church, one sword would not be below the other, nor temporalities below spiritualities; there would be no order in the powers, the lowest would not be led to the highest through intermediaries. If they *are* ordered, the temporal sword must be below the spiritual, and [royal] kingdoms below the vicar of Christ, and that by law . . . [then] the vicar of Christ must hold dominion over temporal affairs. ■

II. John of Paris, *Treatise on Royal and Papal Power* (1302–1303)

It is easy to see which is first in dignity, the kingship, or the priesthood. . . . A kingdom is ordered to this end, that an assembled multitude may live virtuously . . . and it is further ordered to a higher end which is the enjoyment of God; and responsibility for this end belongs to Christ, whose ministers and vicars are the priests. Therefore, the priestly power is of greater dignity than the secular power and this is commonly conceded . . .

But if the priest is greater in himself than the prince and also greater in dignity, it does not follow

Papal ring: gold with an engraving on each side and set with a square stone.   Dorling Kindersley Media Library. Geoff Dann © The British Museum

that he is greater in all respects. For the lesser secular power is not related to the greater spiritual power as having its origin from it or being derived from it as the power of a proconsul is related to that of the emperor, which is greater in all respects since the power of the former is derived from the latter. The relationship is rather like that of a head of a household to a general of armies, since one is not derived from the other but *both* from a superior power. And so the secular power is greater than the spiritual in some things, namely, temporal affairs, and in such affairs it is not subject to the spiritual power in any way because it does not have its origin from it, but rather both have their origin immediately from the one supreme power, namely, the divine. Accordingly the inferior power is not subject to the superior in all things, but only in those where the supreme power has subordinated it to the greater. [For example] a teacher of literature or an instructor in morals directs the members of a household to a very noble end, namely, the knowledge of truth. [That] end is more noble than [that] of a doctor who is concerned with a lower end, namely, the health of bodies. But who would say therefore that the doctor should be subjected to the teacher in preparing his medicines . . . ? Therefore, the priest is greater than the prince in spiritual affairs and, on the other hand, the prince is greater in temporal affairs. ■

Pope John XXII Pope John XXII (r. 1316–1334), the most powerful Avignon pope, tried to restore papal independence and return to Italy. This goal led him into war with the Visconti, the powerful ruling family of Milan, and a costly contest with Emperor Louis IV (r. 1314–1347). John challenged Louis's election as emperor in 1314 in favor of the rival Habsburg candidate. The result was a minor replay of the confrontation between Philip the Fair and Boniface VIII. When John obstinately and without legal justification refused to recognize Louis's election, the emperor declared him deposed and put in his place an antipope. As Philip the Fair had also done, Louis enlisted the support of the Spiritual Franciscans, whose views on absolute poverty John condemned as heretical. Two outstanding pamphleteers wrote lasting tracts for the royal cause: William of Ockham, whom John excommunicated in 1328, and Marsilius of Padua (ca. 1290–1342), whose teaching John declared heretical in 1327.

In his *Defender of Peace* (1324), Marsilius stressed the independent origins and autonomy of secular government. Clergy were to be subjected to the strictest apostolic ideals and confined to purely spiritual functions, and the pope was denied all power of coercive judgment. In the clerical judgment of kings, so wrote Marsilius, spiritual crimes must await an eternal punishment. Transgressions of divine law, over which the pope held jurisdiction, were to be punished in the next life, not in the present one, unless the secular ruler should declare a divine law also a secular law. This assertion directly challenged the power of the pope to excommunicate rulers and place countries under interdict. The *Defender of Peace* depicted the pope to be a subordinate member of a society over which the emperor ruled supreme and in which temporal peace was the highest good.

Pope John XXII made the papacy a sophisticated international agency and adroitly adjusted it to the growing European money economy. The more the **Curia**, or papal court, mastered the latter, the more vulnerable it became to secular criticism. Under John's successor, Benedict XII (r. 1334–1342), the papacy became entrenched in the city of Avignon. Seemingly forgetting Rome altogether, Benedict began to build the great Palace of the Popes from which he attempted to reform both papal government and the religious life. His high-living French successor, Pope Clement VI (r. 1342–1352), placed papal policy in lockstep with the French. In this period the cardinals became barely more than lobbyists for policies their secular patrons favored.

National Opposition to the Avignon Papacy As Avignon's fiscal tentacles probed new areas, monarchies took strong action to protect their interests. The latter half of the fourteenth century saw new legislation restricting papal jurisdiction and taxation in France, England, and Germany. In England, Parliament several times passed statutes that restricted payments and appeals to Rome along with the pope's power to make high ecclesiastical appointments.

In France, the so-called Gallican, or "French liberties," regulated ecclesiastical appointments and taxation. These national rights over religion had long been exercised, and the church legally acknowledged them in the *Pragmatic Sanction of Bourges* in 1438. This agreement recognized the right of the French church to elect its own clergy without papal interference, prohibited the payment of *annates* to Rome, and limited the right of appeals from French courts to the Curia in Rome. In Germany and Switzerland local city governments also limited and overturned traditional clerical privileges and immunities.

John Wycliffe and John Huss

The popular lay religious movements that assailed the late medieval church most successfully were the **Lollards** in England and the **Hussites** in Bohemia. The Lollards looked to the writings of John Wycliffe (d. 1384) to justify their demands, while moderate and extreme Hussites turned to those of John Huss (d. 1415), although both men would have disclaimed the extremists who revolted in their names.

Wycliffe was an Oxford theologian and a philosopher of high standing. His work initially served the anticlerical policies of the English government. He became within England what William of Ockham and Marsilius of Padua had been for Emperor Louis IV: a major intellectual spokesman for the rights of royalty against the secular pretensions of popes. After 1350, English kings greatly reduced the power of the Avignon papacy to make ecclesiastical appointments and to collect taxes within England, a position Wycliffe strongly supported. His views on clerical poverty followed original Franciscan ideals and, more by accident than by design, gave justification to government restriction and even confiscation of church properties within England. Wycliffe also argued that the clergy "ought to be content with food and clothing."

For Wycliffe, personal merit and morality, not rank and office, was the true basis of religious authority. The allegedly good people rightly deserved the money and power of the allegedly immoral people. This was a dangerous teaching for all governments because it raised allegedly pious laypeople above allegedly corrupt ecclesiastics regardless of their official stature. It directly threatened civic-secular dominion and governance, as well as that of the church. At his posthumous condemnation by the pope, Wycliffe was accused of the ancient heresy of **Donatism**—the teaching that the efficacy of the church's sacraments did not only lie in their true performance but also depended on the moral character of the clergy who administered them. Wycliffe also

A portrayal of John Huss as he was led to the stake at Constance. After his execution, his bones and ashes were scattered in the Rhine River to prevent his followers from claiming them as relics. This pen-and-ink drawing is from Ulrich von Richenthal's *Chronicle of the Council of Constance* (ca. 1450). CORBIS/Bettmann

the most famous of whom was John Huss, the rector of the university after 1403.

The Czech reformers supported vernacular translations of the Bible and were critical of traditional ceremonies and alleged superstitious practices, particularly those accompanying the sacrament of the Eucharist. They advocated lay communion with cup as well as bread, which had traditionally been reserved for the clergy as a sign of their spiritual superiority over the laity. The Hussites taught that bread and wine remained bread and wine after priestly consecration, and they questioned the validity of sacraments performed by priests in mortal sin.

Wycliffe's teaching appears to have influenced the movement early. Regular traffic between England and Bohemia had existed since the marriage of Anne of Bohemia to King Richard II in 1318. Bohemian students studied at Oxford and returned home with Wycliffe's writings.

John Huss became the leader of the pro-Wycliffe faction at the University of Prague. In 1410, his activities brought about his excommunication, and Prague was placed under papal interdict. In 1414, Huss won an audience with the newly assembled Council of Constance. He journeyed to the council eagerly under a safe-conduct pass from Emperor Sigismund (r. 1410–1437), naïvely believing he would convince his strongest critics of the truth of his teaching. Within weeks of his arrival in early November 1414, he was accused of heresy and imprisoned. He died at the stake on July 6, 1415, and was followed there less than a year later by his colleague Jerome of Prague.

The reaction in Bohemia to the execution of these national heroes was a fierce revolt. Militant Hussites and Taborites set out to transform Bohemia by force into a religious and social paradise under the military leadership of one John Ziska. After a decade of belligerent protest, the Hussites won significant religious reforms and control over the Bohemian church from the Council of Basel.

anticipated certain Protestant criticisms of the medieval church by challenging papal infallibility, the sale of indulgences, the authority of Scripture, and the dogma of transubstantiation.

The Lollards were the English advocates of Wycliffe's teaching. They preached in the vernacular, disseminated translations of Holy Scripture, and championed clerical poverty. They also joined with the nobility and the gentry in confiscating clerical properties. After the English peasants' revolt of 1381, an uprising filled with egalitarian notions, Lollardy was officially viewed as subversive. Opposed by an alliance of church and crown, the heresy became a capital offense in England in 1401.

▶ Read the **Document**
"The Lollard
Conclusions, 1394" on
MyHistoryLab.com

Heresy was less easily brought to heel in Bohemia, where it coalesced with a strong national movement. The University of Prague, founded in 1348, became the center for both Bohemian nationalism and a new religious reform movement. The latter began within the bounds of orthodoxy. It was led by local intellectuals and preachers,

The Great Schism (1378–1417) and the Conciliar Movement in the Church to 1449

Pope Gregory XI (r. 1370–1378) reestablished the papacy in Rome in January 1377, ending what had come to be known as the "Babylonian Captivity" of the church in Avignon, a reference to the biblical bondage of the

Document

PROPOSITIONS OF JOHN WYCLIFFE CONDEMNED AT LONDON, 1382, AND AT THE COUNCIL OF CONSTANCE, 1415

Wycliffe was the leading scholar of the University of Oxford, where he spent most of his life. One of the most notable points in his teaching was the theory of "dominion by grace"—that is, lordship, spiritual or temporal, was derived directly from God, as opposed to the feudal conception of derivation through intermediaries, which was paralleled by the conception of grace derived through the Pope and the church hierarchy.

Does the Bible really sanction all of the propositions of Wycliffe? Are certain teachings of Wycliffe brazenly anarchic? Do so-called "good people" rightly deserve the money and power of "immoral people"?

That the material substance of bread and . . . wine remain in the Sacrament of the altar.

That Christ is not in the Sacrament essentially . . . in his own corporeal presence.

That if a bishop or priest be in mortal sin he does not [effectively] ordain, consecrate, or baptise . . .

That it is contrary to Holy Scripture that ecclesiastics should have possessions.

That any deacon or priest may preach the word of God apart from the authority of the Apostolic See, or a Catholic bishop.

That no one is a civil lord, or a prelate, or a bishop when he is in mortal sin.

That temporal lords can at their will take away temporal goods from the church, when those who hold them are habitually sinful.

That the people can at their own will correct sinful lords.

That tithes are mere alms, and that parishioners can withdraw them at their will because of the misdeeds of their curates.

That friars are bound to gain their livelihood by the labor of their hands, and not by begging.

That . . . the ordination of clerics [and] the consecration of [holy] places are reserved for the Pope and bishops on account of their desire for temporal gain and honor.

That the excommunication of the Pope or any prelate is not to be feared, because it is the censure of antichrist.

It is fatuous to believe in the indulgences of the Pope and the bishops.

From *Documents of the Christian Church*, ed. Henry Bettenson (New York: Oxford University Press, 1947).

Israelites. The return to Rome proved to be short lived, however.

Urban VI and Clement VII On Gregory's death, the cardinals, in Rome, elected an Italian archbishop as Pope Urban VI (r. 1378–1389), who immediately announced his intention to reform the Curia. The cardinals, most of whom were French, responded by calling for the return of the papacy to Avignon. The French king, Charles V (r. 1364–1380), wanting to keep the papacy within the sphere of French influence, lent his support to what came to be known as the **Great Schism**.

View the Map
"Map Discovery: The Great Schism" on
MyHistoryLab.com

On September 20, 1378, five months after Urban's election, thirteen cardinals, all but one of them French, formed their own conclave and elected Pope Clement VII (r. 1378–1397), a cousin of the French king. They insisted they had voted for Urban in fear of their lives, having been surrounded by a Roman mob demanding the election of an Italian pope. Be that as it may, the papacy had now become a "two-headed thing" and a scandal to Christendom. Allegiance to the two papal courts divided along political lines. England and its allies acknowledged Urban VI, while France and its orbit supported Clement VII. Subsequent church history has recognized the Roman line of popes as legitimate.

Justice in the late Middle Ages. Depicted are the most common forms of corporal and capital punishment in Europe in the late Middle Ages and the Renaissance. At top: burning, hanging, drowning. At center: blinding, quartering, the wheel, cutting of hair (a mark of great shame for a freeman). At bottom: thrashing, decapitation, amputation of hand (for thieves).   Herzog August Bibliothek

Two approaches were initially taken to end the schism. The first attempted to win the mutual cession of both popes, thereby clearing the way for the election of a new one. The other sought to secure the resignation of the one in favor of the other. Both approaches failed. Each pope considered himself fully legitimate, and too much was at stake for either to make a magnanimous concession. Only one way remained: a special church council empowered to depose them both. Legally, only a pope could convene and dissolve a church

council, and the competing popes were not about to summon a council they knew would depose them both. Also, the removal of a legitimate pope against his will by a council of the church was as serious as the deposition of a monarch by a representative assembly.

The correctness of a conciliar deposition of a pope was debated a full thirty years before any action was taken. Advocates of the **conciliar theory** sought to fashion a church in which a representative council could effectively regulate the actions of the pope. To that end the conciliarists defined the church as the whole body of the faithful, of which the elected head, the pope, was only one part. The sole purpose was to maintain the unity and well-being of the church—something the schismatic popes were far from doing. The conciliarists argued that a council of the church acted with greater authority than the pope alone. In the eyes of the pope(s), such a concept of the church threatened both its political and religious unity.

On the basis of the arguments of the conciliarists, cardinals representing both popes convened another council on their own authority in Pisa in 1409. There they deposed both the Roman and the Avignon popes, and elected a singular pope, Alexander V. To the council's consternation, neither pope accepted its action, and Christendom suddenly faced the spectacle of three contending popes. Although most of Latin Christendom accepted Alexander and his Pisan successor John XXIII (r. 1410–1415), the popes of Rome and Avignon refused to step down.

The intolerable situation ended when Emperor Sigismund prevailed on John XXIII to summon a new council in Constance in 1414, which the Roman pope Gregory XII also recognized. In a famous declaration entitled *Sacrosancta*, the council asserted its supremacy and elected a new pope, Martin V (r. 1417–1431), after the three contending popes had either resigned or been deposed. The council then made provisions for regular meetings of church councils, within five, then seven, and thereafter every ten years.

The Council of Basel (r. 1431–1449)   Conciliar government of the church peaked at the Council of Basel (1431–1449), when the council directly negotiated church doctrine with heretics. In 1432, the Hussites of Bohemia presented the *Four Articles of Prague* to the council as a basis for negotiations. This document contained requests for (1) giving the laity the Eucharist with cup as well as bread; (2) free, itinerant preaching; (3) the exclusion of the clergy from holding secular offices and owning property; and (4) just punishment of clergy who commit mortal sins.

In November 1433, an agreement among the emperor, the council, and the Hussites gave the Bohemians jurisdiction over their church. Three of the four Prague articles were conceded: communion with cup, free preaching by ordained clergy, and similar punishment of clergy and laity for mortal sins.

The exercise of such powers by a council did not please the pope, and in 1438, he upstaged the Council of Basel by negotiating a reunion with the Eastern church. Although the agreement, signed in Florence in 1439, was short lived, it restored papal prestige and signaled the demise of the conciliar movement. Having overreached itself, the Council of Basel collapsed in 1449. A decade later, Pope Pius II (r. 1458–1464) issued the papal bull *Execrabilis* (1460) condemning appeals to councils as "erroneous and abominable" and "completely null and void."

A major consequence of the short-lived conciliar movement was the devolving of greater religious responsibility onto the laity and secular governments. Without effective papal authority and leadership, secular control of national or territorial churches increased. Kings asserted their power over the church in England and France, while in German, Swiss, and Italian cities, magistrates and city councils reformed and regulated religious life. The High Renaissance did not reverse this development. On the contrary, as the papacy became a limited, Italian territorial regime, national control of the church ran apace. Perceived as just one among several Italian states, the Papal States could now be opposed as much on grounds of "national" policy as for religious reasons.

▼ Medieval Russia

In the late tenth century, Prince Vladimir of Kiev (r. 980–1015), then Russia's dominant city, received delegations of Muslims, Roman Catholics, Jews, and Greek Orthodox Christians, each of which hoped to persuade the Russians to embrace their religion. Vladimir chose Greek Orthodoxy, which became the religion of Russia, adding strong cultural bonds to the close commercial ties that had long linked Russia to the Byzantine Empire. Here, we find the late Byzantine centuries after their magnificent earlier reigns, now to be only a shadow of what had been, and still a potent force among the cultures of the world after the passage of almost a century.

▶ Read the Document
"Vladimir of Kiev's Acceptance of Christianity (989)" on **MyHistoryLab.com**

Politics and Society

Vladimir's successor, Yaroslav the Wise (r. 1016–1054), developed Kiev into a magnificent political and cultural center, with architecture rivaling that of Constantinople. He also pursued contacts with the West in an unsuccessful effort to counter the political influence of the Byzantine emperors. After his death, rivalry among their princes slowly divided Russians into three cultural groups: the Great Russians, the White Russians, and the Little Russians (Ukrainians). Autonomous principalities also challenged Kiev's dominance, and it became just one of several national centers. Government in the principalities combined monarchy (the prince), aristocracy (the prince's council of noblemen), and democracy (a popular assembly of all free adult males). The broadest social division was between freemen and slaves. Freemen included the clergy, army officers, **boyars** (wealthy landowners), townspeople, and peasants. Slaves were mostly prisoners of war. Debtors working off their debts made up a large, semifree, group.

Mongol Rule (1243–1480)

In the thirteenth century, Mongol, or Tatar, armies swept through China, much of the Islamic world, and Russia. These were steppe peoples with strongholds in the south, whence they raided the north, devastating Russia and compelling the obedience of Moscow for a while. Genghis Khan (1155–1227) invaded Russia in 1223, and Kiev fell to his grandson Batu Khan in 1240. Russian cities became dependent, tribute-paying principalities of the segment of the Mongol Empire known as the *Golden Horde* (the Tatar words for the color of Batu Khan's tent). Geographically, the Golden Horde included the steppe region of what is today southern Russia and its capital at Sarai on the lower Volga. The conquerors stationed their own officials in all the principal Russian towns to oversee taxation and the conscription of Russians into Tatar armies. The Mongols filled their harems with Russian women and sold Russians who resisted into slavery in foreign lands. Russian women—under the influence of Islam, which became the religion of the Golden Horde—began to wear veils and lead more secluded lives. This forced integration of Mongols and Russians created further cultural divisions between Russia and the West. The Mongols, however, left Russian political and religious institutions largely intact and, thanks to their far-flung trade, brought most Russians greater prosperity. Princes of Moscow collected tribute for their overlords and grew wealthy under Mongol rule. As that rule weakened, the Moscow princes took control of the territory surrounding the city in what was called "the gathering of the Russian Land." Gradually the principality of Moscow expanded through land purchases, colonization, and conquest. In 1380, Grand Duke Dimitri of Moscow (r. 1350–1389) defeated Tatar forces at Kulikov Meadow, a victory that marked the beginning of the decline of the Mongol hegemony. Another century would pass, however, before Ivan III, the Great (d. 1505), would bring all of northern Russia under Moscow's control and end Mongol rule (1480). Moscow replaced Kiev as the political and religious center of Russia. After Constantinople fell to the Turks in 1453, the city became, in Russian eyes, the "third Rome."

View the **Closer Look**
"A Mongol Passport" on
MyHistoryLab.com

View the **Map**
"Interactive Map: The Rise of Moscow" on
MyHistoryLab.com

In Perspective

Plague, war, and schism convulsed much of late medieval Europe throughout the fourteenth and into the fifteenth centuries. Two-fifths of the population, particularly along the major trade routes, died from plague in the fourteenth century. War and famine continued to take untold numbers after the plague had passed. Revolts erupted in town and countryside as ordinary people attempted to defend their traditional communal rights and privileges against the new autocratic territorial regimes. Even God's house seemed to be in shambles in 1409, when three popes came to rule simultaneously.

There is, however, another side to the late Middle Ages. By the end of the fifteenth century, the population losses were rapidly being made up. Between 1300 and 1500, education had become far more accessible, especially to laypeople. The number of universities increased from twenty to seventy, and the rise in the number of residential colleges was even more impressive, especially in France, where sixty-three were built. The

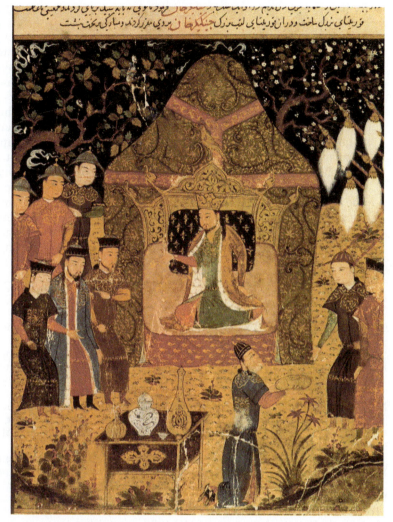

Genghis Khan holding an audience. This Persian miniature shows the great conqueror and founder of the Mongol empire with members of his army and entourage as well as an apparent supplicant (lower right). © Sonia Halliday Photographs/Alamy

fourteenth century saw the birth of humanism, and the fifteenth century gave us the printing press. Most impressive were the artistic and cultural achievements of the Italian Renaissance during the fifteenth century. The later Middle Ages were thus a period of growth and creativity, as well as one of waning and decline.

KEY TERMS

Black Death (p. 265)	Curia (p. 280)	Great Schism (p. 282)	Lollards (p. 280)
boyars (p. 284)	Donatism (p. 280)	Hussites (p. 280)	*taille* (p. 271)
conciliar theory (p. 283)	Estates General (p. 272)	Jacquerie (p. 273)	

REVIEW QUESTIONS

1. What were the underlying and precipitating causes of the Hundred Years' War? What advantages did each side have? Why were the French finally able to drive the English almost entirely out of France?

2. What were the causes of the Black Death, and why did it spread so quickly throughout Western Europe? Where was it most virulent? How did it affect European society? How important do you think disease is in changing the course of history?

3. Why did Pope Boniface VIII quarrel with King Philip the Fair? Why was Boniface so impotent in the conflict? How had political conditions changed since the reign of Pope Innocent III in the late twelfth century, and what did that mean for the papacy?

4. How did the church change from 1200 to 1450? What was its response to the growing power of monarchs? How great an influence did the church have on secular events?

5. What was the Avignon papacy, and why did it occur? How did it affect the papacy? What relationship did it have to the Great Schism? How did the church become divided and how was it reunited? Why was the conciliar movement a setback for the papacy?

6. Why were kings in the late thirteenth and early fourteenth centuries able to control the church more than the church could control the kings? How did kings attack the church during this period?

SUGGESTED READINGS

C. Allmand, *The Hundred Years' War: England and France at War, c. 1300–c. 1450* (1988). Overview of the war's development and consequences.

R. Barber, ed., *The Pastons: Letters of a Family in the War of the Roses* (1984). Rare revelations of English family life in an age of crisis.

N. F. Cantor, *In the Wake of the Plague* (2002). A postmortem of the plague.

E. H. Gillett et al., *Life and Times of John Huss: The Bohemian Reformation of the Fifteenth Century* (2001). Most recent biography.

R. Horrox, ed. and trans., *The Black Death* (1994). Focus on contemporary responses to plague in scientific and medical terms.

J. Huizinga, *The Waning of the Middle Ages: A Study of the Forms of Life, Thought, and Art in France and the Netherlands in the Dawn of the Renaissance* (1924). Exaggerated, but engrossing, study of mentality at the end of the Middle Ages.

P. Kahn et al., *Secret History of the Mongols: The Origins of Ghingis Kahn* (1998). Introduction to the greatest Mongol ruler.

D. Kruger, ed., *Byzantine Christianity* (2006). A people's history of Christianity.

M. Lindemann, *Medicine and Society in Early Modern Europe* (2010). Broad social and cultural approach guided by medical anthropology, sociology, and ethics.

V. Nutton, ed., *Pestilential Complexities: Understanding Medieval Plague* (2008). Widely praised and recommended.

S. Ozment, *The Age of Reform, 1250–1550* (1980). Highlights of late medieval intellectual and religious history.

C. Platt, *King Death: The Black Death and its Aftermath in Late-Medieval England* (1996). A comprehensive "You Are There."

D. Seward, *The Hundred Years War, 1337–1453* (1999). A compact and highly praised book.

M. Spinka, *John Huss's Concept of the Church* (1966). Lucid account of Hussite theology.

J. Sumption, *The Hundred Years War*, Vols. I–III. (2011). The standard account of the war.

L. J. Taylor, *The Virgin Warrior: The Life and Death of Joan of Arc* (2010). A recent, in-depth, flesh and spirit biography of the famous saint.

W. R. Trask, ed. and trans., *Joan of Arc in Her Own Words* (1996). Joan's interrogation and self-defense.

MyHistoryLab™ MEDIA ASSIGNMENTS

Find these resources in the Media Assignment folder for Chapter 9 on **MyHistoryLab**.

QUESTIONS FOR ANALYSIS

1. How can you explain the patterns that emerged during the Great Schism, with some rulers supporting Rome, and some Avignon?

   Section: **Ecclesiastical Breakdown and Revival: The Late Medieval Church**

   ◉─┤View the **Map** Map Discovery: The Great Schism, p. 282

2. How has our understanding of the plague and responses to it changed in recent decades?

   Section: **The Black Death**

   ◉─┤Watch the **Video** Video Lectures: The Plague, p. 266

3. What is the significance of Ball's remarks about Adam and Eve?

   Section: **The Hundred Years' War and the Rise of National Sentiment**

   ▢●┤Read the **Document** Peasant Revolt in England: The John Ball Sermon, 1381, p. 274

4. What powers and authority are claimed by Boniface VIII?

   Section: **Ecclesiastical Breakdown and Revival: The Late Medieval Church**

   📖 Read the **Document** *Unam Sanctam* (1302) Pope Boniface VIII, p. 277

5. Whether legend or fact, what are the important points concerning the Russian adoption of Greek Orthodoxy?

   Section: **Medieval Russia**

   📖 Read the **Document** Vladimir of Kiev's Acceptance of Christianity (989), p. 284

OTHER RESOURCES FROM THIS CHAPTER

The Black Death

📖 Read the **Document** University of Paris Medical Faculty, Writings on the Plague, p. 266

📖 Read the **Document** Flagellants Attempt to Ward Off the Black Death, 1349, p. 267

🔍 View the **Map** Map Discovery: The Spread of the Black Death and Peasant Revolts, p. 271

The Hundred Years' War and the Rise of National Sentiment

🔍 View the **Map** Interactive Map: The Hundred Years' War, p. 272

Ecclesiastical Breakdown and Revival: The Late Medieval Church

📖 Read the **Compare and Connect** Who Runs the World: Priests or Princes?, p. 278

📖 Read the **Document** The Lollard Conclusions, 1394, p. 281

Medieval Russia

🔍 View the **Closer Look** A Mongol Passport, p. 285

🔍 View the **Map** Interactive Map: The Rise of Moscow, p. 285

The Renaissance celebrated human beauty and dignity. Here Flemish painter Rogier van der Weyden (1400–1464) portrays an ordinary woman more perfectly on canvas than she could ever have appeared in real life.   Rogier van der Weyden (Netherlandish, 1399.1400–1464), "Portrait of a Lady." 1460. .370 × .270 [14¹⁄₁₆ × 10⅝] framed: .609 × .533 × .114 [24 × 21 × 4½]. Photo: Bob Grove. Andrew W. Mellon Collection. Photograph © Board of Trustees, National Gallery of Art, Washington, DC

((•—[Listen to the **Chapter Audio** on **MyHistoryLab.com**

10

Renaissance and Discovery

LEARNING OBJECTIVES

How did humanism affect culture and the arts in fourteenth- and fifteenth-century Italy?

What were the causes of Italy's political decline?

How were the powerful monarchies of northern Europe different from their predecessors?

How did the northern Renaissance affect culture in Germany, England, France, and Spain?

What were the motives for European voyages of discovery, and what were the consequences?

IF THE LATE Middle Ages saw unprecedented chaos, it also witnessed a recovery that continued into the seventeenth century. There was both a waning and a harvest; much was dying away, while new fruit was being gathered and seed grain sown. The late Middle Ages were a time of creative fragmentation and new synthesis.

By the late fifteenth century, Europe was recovering from two of the three crises of the times: the demographic and the political. The great losses in population were being replenished, and able monarchs and rulers were imposing a new political order. A solution to the growing religious crisis would have to await the Reformation and Counter-Reformation of the sixteenth century.

The city-states of Italy survived a century and a half (1300–1450) better than the territorial states of northern Europe. This was due to Italy's strategic location between East and West and its lucrative Eurasian trade. Great wealth gave the rulers and merchants the ability to impose their will on both society and culture. They were now the grand patrons of government, education, and the arts both by self-aggrandizement and benevolence. Whether the patron was a family, firm, government, or the church, their endowments enhanced their reputation and power. The result of such patronage was a cultural Renaissance in the Italian cities unmatched elsewhere.

With the fall of Constantinople to the Turks in 1453, Italy's once unlimited trading empire began to shrink. City-state now turned against city-state, warring that opened the door to French armies in the 1490s. Within a quarter century, Italy's great Renaissance had peaked.

The fifteenth century also saw an unprecedented scholarly renaissance. Italian and northern humanists recovered classical knowledge and languages that set educational reforms and cultural changes in motion that spread throughout Europe in the fifteenth and sixteenth centuries. In the process Italian humanists invented, for all practical purposes what we today call critical historical scholarship, which was widely disseminated by a new fifteenth-century invention, the art of printing with movable type.

In this period the vernacular—the local language—began to take its place alongside Latin, the international language, as a widely used literary and political means of communication. European states also progressively superseded the Church as the community of highest allegiance, as patriotism and incipient nationalism captured hearts and minds as strongly as did religion. States and nations henceforth "transcended" themselves not only by journeys to Rome, but by competitive voyages to the Far East and the Americas, opening the age of lucrative, global exploration.

For Europe, the late fifteenth and sixteenth centuries were a period of unprecedented expansion and experimentation. Permanent colonies were established within the Americas, and the exploitation of the New World's human and mineral resources never stopped after it began. Imported American gold and silver spurred scientific invention and a new weapons industry. The new bullion helped create the international traffic in African slaves, as rival African tribes sold their captives to the Portuguese. Transported in ever-increasing numbers, these slaves worked the mines and plantations of the New World, taking the place of American natives whose population declined precipitously following the conquest.

The period also saw social engineering and political planning on a large scale, as newly centralized governments began to put long-range economic policies into practice, a development that came to be called *mercantilism*.

▼ The Renaissance in Italy (1375–1527)

Jacob Burckhardt, an influential nineteenth-century Swiss historian, famously described the Renaissance as the "prototype of the modern world." In his book, *Civilization of the Renaissance in Italy* (1860), he argued that the revival of ancient learning in fourteenth- and fifteenth-century Italy gave rise to new secular and scientific values. This was a period in which people began to adopt rational, empirical, and statistical approaches to the world around them, and in the process discovered their latent creativity. The result, in Burckhardt's words, was the gradual release of the "full, whole nature of man."

Most scholars today find Burckhardt's description exaggerated and accuse him of overlooking the continuity between the Middle Ages and the Renaissance. His critics point to the strong Christian character of Renaissance humanism. Earlier "renaissances," such as that of the twelfth century, had also embraced the revival of the ancient classics showing a new interest in Latin language and Greek science and a new appreciation of the creativity of individuals.

Medieval Europe before the twelfth century was a fragmented feudal society with an agricultural economy, whose thought and culture was largely dominated by the church. By contrast, Renaissance Europe after the fourteenth century displayed a growing national consciousness and political centralization. The new urban economy, based on organized commerce and capitalism, brought lay control of thought and culture independently from the clergy and religious authorities.

This creative expansion was threatened around 1527, when Spanish-imperial soldiers looted and torched Renaissance Rome, recalling the sacking of ancient Rome by the Visigoths and Vandals. At this time, the French king, Francis I, joined with the Holy Roman Emperor, Charles V, in making Italy the battleground for their mutual dynastic claims on Burgundy and parts of Italy. For many scholars, that was the beginning of the end of the cultured Italian Renaissance.

The Italian City-States

Renaissance society first took shape within the merchant cities of late medieval Italy. Italy had always had a cultural advantage over the rest of Europe because its geography made it the natural gateway between East and West. Venice, Genoa, and Pisa traded with the Near East throughout the Middle Ages, growing vibrant, urban societies. When in the eleventh century commerce revived on a grand scale, Italian merchants quickly mastered the business skills of organizing, bookkeeping, developing new markets, and securing monopolies. The trade-rich cities became powerful city-states, dominating the political and economic life of their surrounding countryside. By the fifteenth century, those cities were the bankers for much of Europe.

Growth of City-States The endemic warfare between the pope and the emperor, both the Guelf (pro-papal) and Ghibelline (pro-imperial) factions, assisted the expansion of Italian cities and urban culture. Either one of these factions might have subdued the cities, if only they had permitted each other to do so. Instead, they weakened one another, thereby strengthening the merchant oligarchies. Unlike the great cities of northern Europe, where kings and regional princes utterly dominated, the large Italian cities remained free to expand on their own. Becoming independent states, they absorbed the surrounding countryside and assimilated the local nobility in an urban meld of old and new rich. Five major competitive states evolved at this time: the duchy of Milan, the republics of Florence and Venice, the Papal States, and the kingdom of Naples. (See Map 10–1.)

Social strife and competition for political power were so intense within the cities that most evolved into despotisms to survive. A notable exception was Venice, which was ruled by a merchant oligarchy. The Venetian government controlled a patrician senate of three hundred members and a ruthless judicial body, known as the Council of Ten, who were quick to suppress rival groups.

Social Class and Conflict Florence was the most striking example of social division and anarchy. Four distinguishable social groups existed within the great city: (1) the old rich, or *grandi*, the noblemen and merchants who ruled the city; (2) the newly rich merchant class, the capitalists and bankers known as the *popolo grosso*, "the fat people," who in the late thirteenth and early fourteenth centuries, challenged the old rich for political power; (3) the middling burgher ranks of the guild masters, shop owners, and professionals, the small business people who in Florence, as elsewhere, sided with the new rich against the conservative policies of

Map 10–1 RENAISSANCE ITALY The city-states of Renaissance Italy were self-contained principalities whose internal strife was monitored by their despots and whose external aggression was long successfully controlled by treaty.

the old; and (4) the *popolo minuto*, or the "little people," the bottom of society, the lower socioeconomic classes. In 1457, one-third of the population of Florence, about 30,000, were officially listed as paupers, having no wealth at all.

These social divisions produced conflict at every level of society. In 1378, a great uprising of the poor, known as the Ciompi Revolt, occurred. It resulted from a combination of three factors that made life unbearable for the unfortunate: the feuding between the old rich and the new rich; the social anarchy created when the Black Death cut the city's population almost in half; and, last but not least, the collapse of the great banking houses of Bardi and Peruzzi, which left the poor more vulnerable

Florentine women doing needlework, spinning, and weaving. These activities took up much of a woman's time and contributed to the elegance of dress for which Florentine men and women were famed. Palazzo Schifanoia, Ferrara. Alinari/Art Resource, NY

brother in 1478 by a rival family, the Pazzi, who had long plotted with the pope against the Medicis, made Lorenzo a cautious and determined ruler.

Despotism elsewhere was even less subtle. To prevent internal social conflict and foreign intrigue from paralyzing their cities, the dominant groups cooperated to install hired strongmen, or despots. Known as a *podestà*, the despot's sole purpose was to maintain law and order. He held executive, military, and judicial authority, and his mandate was direct and simple: to permit, by whatever means required, the normal flow of business activity without which neither the old rich and new rich, nor the poor of a city, could long survive, much less prosper. Because despots could not count on the loyalty of the divided populace, they operated through mercenary armies obtained through military brokers known as **condottieri**.

It was a hazardous job. Not only was a despot subject to dismissal by the oligarchies that hired him, he was also a popular object of assassination attempts. The spoils of success, however, were great. In Milan, it was as despots that the Visconti family came to power in 1278 and the Sforza family in 1450, both ruling without constitutional restraints or serious political competition.

Mercifully, the political turbulence and warfare of the times also gave birth to the art of diplomacy. Through skilled diplomats, the city-states stayed abreast of foreign military developments and, when shrewd, gained power and advantage over their enemies without actually going to war. Most city-states established resident embassies in the fifteenth century for that very purpose. Their ambassadors not only represented them in ceremonies and at negotiations, they also became their watchful eyes and ears at rival courts.

Whether within the comparatively tranquil republic of Venice, the strong-arm democracy of Florence, or the undisguised despotism of Milan, the disciplined Italian city proved a congenial climate for an unprecedented flowering of thought and culture. Italian Renaissance culture was promoted vigorously by both despots and republicans, and as enthusiastically by secularized popes as by spiritually minded ones. Such widespread

than ever. The Ciompi Revolt established a chaotic four-year reign of power by the lower Florentine classes. After the Ciompi Revolt real stability did not return to Florence until the ascent to power of the fabled Florentine banker and statesman Cosimo de' Medici (1389–1464) in 1434.

Despotism and Diplomacy Cosimo de' Medici was the wealthiest Florentine and a natural statesman. He controlled the city internally from behind the scenes, manipulating the constitution and influencing elections. A council, first of six and later of eight members, known as the *Signoria*, governed the city. These men were chosen from the most powerful guilds, those representing the major clothing industries (cloth, wool, fur, and silk) and such other strong groups as bankers, judges, and doctors. Through informal, cordial relations with the electors, Cosimo kept councilors loyal to him in the *Signoria*. From his position as the head of the Office of Public Debt, he favored congenial factions. His grandson, Lorenzo the Magnificent (1449–1492; r. 1478–1492), ruled Florence in almost totalitarian fashion during the last, chaotic quarter of the fifteenth century. The assassination of his support occurred because the main requirement for patronage of the arts and letters was the one thing Italian cities of the High Renaissance had in abundance: very great wealth.

Humanism

Scholars still debate the meaning of the term *humanism*. Some see the Italian Renaissance as the birth of modernity, a cultural and educational movement driven by a philosophy that stressed the dignity of humankind, individualism, and secular values. Others argue that the humanists were actually the champions of Catholic Christianity, opposing the pagan teaching of the ancient Greek philosopher Aristotle and the Scholasticism his writings nurtured. For still others, humanism was a neutral form of empirical-minded historical scholarship adopted to promote political liberty and a sense of civic responsibility.

By the scholarly study of the Latin and Greek classics and the works of the ancient Church Fathers, the Humanists advocated the **studia humanitatis**, a liberal arts program of study that embraced grammar, rhetoric, poetry, history, politics, and moral philosophy. The Florentine humanist Leonardo Bruni (ca. 1370–1444) was the first to give the name *humanitas*, or "humanity," to the learning that resulted from such studies. Bruni was a star student of Manuel Chrysoloras (ca. 1355–1415), the great Byzantine scholar who opened the world of Greek scholarship to Italian humanists when he taught in Florence between 1397 and 1403.

The first humanists were orators and poets who wrote original literature in both classical and vernacular languages inspired by the ancients. They also taught rhetoric in the universities, and when they were not so employed, royal and papal courts hired them as secretaries, speechwriters, and diplomats.

Petrarch, Dante, and Boccaccio Francesco Petrarch (1304–1374) was the "father of humanism." He left the legal profession to pursue letters and poetry. Most of his life was spent in and around Avignon. He was involved in a popular revolt in Rome (1347–1349) and, in his later years, he served the Visconti family in Milan.

Petrarch celebrated ancient Rome in his *Letters to the Ancient Dead*, fancied personal letters to Cicero, Livy, Vergil, and Horace. He also wrote a Latin epic poem (*Africa*, a poetic historical tribute to the Roman general Scipio Africanus) and biographies of famous Roman men (*Lives of Illustrious Men*). His most famous contemporary work was a collection of highly introspective love sonnets to a certain Laura, a married woman he admired romantically from a safe distance.

▣▶ **Read** the **Document** "Petrarch, Letter to Cicero (14th c.)" on **MyHistoryLab.com**

His critical textual studies, elitism, and contempt for the learning of the Scholastics were features many later humanists also shared. As with many later humanists, Classical and Christian values coexist uneasily in his work. Medieval Christian values can be seen in his imagined dialogues with Saint Augustine and in tracts he wrote to defend the personal immortality of the soul against the Aristotelians.

Petrarch was, however, far more secular in orientation than his famous near-contemporary Dante Alighieri (1265–1321), whose *Vita Nuova* and *Divine Comedy* form, with Petrarch's sonnets, the cornerstones of Italian vernacular literature. Petrarch's student and friend Giovanni Boccaccio (1313–1375) was also a pioneer of humanist studies. His *Decameron*—one hundred often bawdy tales told by three men and seven women in a safe country retreat away from the plague that ravaged Florence in 1348 (see Chapter 9)—is both a stinging social commentary (it exposes sexual and economic misconduct) and a sympathetic look at human behavior. An avid collector of manuscripts, Boccaccio also assembled an encyclopedia of Greek and Roman mythology.

▣▶ **Read** the **Document** "*Divine Comedy* (1321)" on **MyHistoryLab.com**

Educational Reforms and Goals Humanists took their mastery of ancient languages directly to the past, refusing to be slaves to their own times. Such an attitude made them not only innovative educators, but also kept them in search of new sources of information that addressed the ills of contemporary society. In their searches, they assembled magnificent manuscript collections brimming with the history of the past, potent remedies for contemporaries, and sound advice to politicians and rulers wherever they were.

The goal of humanist studies was wisdom eloquently spoken, both knowledge of the good and the ability to move others to desire it. Learning was not meant to remain abstract and unpracticed. "It is better to will the good than to know the truth," Petrarch taught. That became a motto of many later humanists, who, like Petrarch, believed learning always ennobled people. Pietro Paolo Vergerio (1349–1420), the author of the most influential Renaissance tract on education (*On the Morals That Befit a Free Man*), left a classic summary of the humanist concept of a liberal education:

We call those studies liberal which are worthy of a free man; those studies by which we attain and practice virtue and wisdom; that education which calls forth, trains, and develops those highest gifts of body and mind which ennoble men and which are rightly judged to rank next in dignity to virtue only. For a vulgar temper, gain and pleasure are the one aim of existence, but to a lofty nature, moral worth and fame.[1]

[1]Cited by De Lamar Jensen, *Renaissance Europe: Age of Recovery and Reconciliation* (Lexington, MA: D. C. Health, 1981), p. 111.

THE RENAISSANCE GARDEN

IN THE MIDDLE Ages and early Renaissance, few possessions were as prized, or as vital, as a garden. Within that enclosed space grew both ornamental and medicinal flowers and herbs. The more common kitchen garden existed in every manor, castle, monastery, guildhall, and small household. In addition to their large, elaborate gardens, the rich also had orchards and vineyards to grow the fruit from which they made sweet drinks and wine. Behind their shops and guildhalls, apothecaries and barber-surgeons cultivated the curative flowers and herbs from which they concocted the medicines of their trades. Beyond manor and guildhall walls, small householders and cottagers hoed the small, narrow plots behind their houses in which they grew the basic herbs and vegetables of their diet. Although the grandeur and variety of a garden reflected the prestige of its owner, every garden's main purpose was to serve the immediate needs of the household.

Versatility and pungency distinguished the most popular flowers and herbs. The violet was admired for its beauty, fragrance, and utility. Medieval people put violets in baths, oils, and syrups, prizing its soft scent and healing power as well as its ability to color, flavor, and garnish dishes. Nonetheless, subtlety and delicacy were not as important to the medieval palate as they are to ours. An herb or flower was only as good as its impact on the senses. Potent scents and flavors were loved for their ability to bring an otherwise starchy and lackluster meal to life. Fruit, although it was the main ingredient for sweet drinks, rarely appeared on a medieval plate, and vegetables were only slightly more common. Cabbage, lentils, peas, beans, onions, leeks, beets, and parsnips were the most often served vegetables at the medieval table, made palatable by heavy application of the sharpest and bitterest spices.

Beyond its practical function as a source of food and medicine, the medieval garden was a space of social and religious significance. In Christian history, gardens represented sacred places on earth. During the Middle Ages and early Renaissance, it was not the sprawling paradise of the Garden of Eden that captured the imagination, but rather the closed garden of the Bible's Song of Songs (4:12): "A garden enclosed is my sister, my spouse; a spring shut up, a fountain sealed." Such sensuous imagery symbolized the soul's union with God, Christ's union with the Catholic Church, and the bond of love between a man and a woman.

Although enclosed behind walls, fences, or hedges to protect them as vital food sources, gardens were also the private places of dreamers and lovers. Pleasure gardens bloomed around the homes of the wealthy. There, amid grottoes and fountains, lovers breathed the warm scents of roses and lilies and pursued the romantic trysts popularized in court poetry. The stories of courtly love were cautionary as well as titillating, for as the catechism reminded every medieval Christian, the garden was also a place of temptation and lost innocence.

Sources: Teresa McClean, *Medieval English Gardens* (New York: Viking Press, 1980), pp. 64, 133; Marilyn Stokstad and Jerry Stannard, *Gardens of the Middle Ages* (Lawrence, KS: Spencer Museum, 1983), pp. 19–21, 61.

What kinds of gardens existed in the Middle Ages and the early Renaissance?

How did religion give meaning to gardens?

How were gardens maintained and what were the nature of their fruits and vegetables?

A wealthy man oversees apple picking at harvest time in a fifteenth-century French orchard. In the town below, individual house gardens can be seen. Protective fences, made of woven sticks, keep out predatory animals. In the right foreground, a boar can be seen overturning an apple barrel. The British Library

The ideal of a useful education and well-rounded people inspired far-reaching reforms in traditional education. The Roman orator Quintilian's (ca. 35–100) *Education of the Orator*, the complete text of which was discovered in 1416, became the basic classical guide for the humanist curriculum. Vittorino da Feltre (d. 1446) exemplified those ideals. Not only did he have his students read the difficult works of Pliny, Ptolemy, Terence, Plautus, Livy, and Plutarch, he also subjected them to vigorous physical exercise and games.

Despite the grinding process of acquiring ancient knowledge, humanistic studies were not confined to the classroom. As Baldassare Castiglione's (1478–1529) *Book of the Courtier* illustrates, the rediscovered knowledge of the past was both a model and a challenge to the present. Written as a practical guide for the nobility at the court of Urbino, a small duchy in central Italy, the book embodies the highest ideals of Italian humanism. The successful courtier is said to be one who knows how to integrate knowledge of ancient languages and history with athletic, military, and musical skills, while at the same time practicing good manners and exhibiting a high moral character.

Privileged, educated noblewomen also promoted the new education and culture at royal courts. Among them was Christine de Pisan (1363?–1434), the Italian-born daughter of the physician and astrologer of French king Charles V. She became an expert in classical, French, and Italian languages and literature. Married at fifteen and the widowed mother of three at twenty-seven, she wrote lyric poetry to support herself and was much read throughout the courts of Europe. Her most famous work, *The Treasure of the City of Ladies*, is a chronicle of the accomplishments of the great women of history. (See "Christine de Pisan Instructs Women on How to Handle Their Husbands," page 295.)

The Florentine "Academy" and the Revival of Platonism Of all the important recoveries of the past made during the Italian Renaissance, none stands out more than the revival of Greek studies—especially the works of Plato—in fifteenth-century Florence. Many factors combined to bring this revival about. A foundation, mentioned above, was laid in 1397 when the city invited Manuel Chrysoloras to come from Constantinople to promote Greek learning. A half century later (1439), the ecumenical Council of Ferrara-Florence, convened to negotiate the reunion of the Eastern and Western churches, opened the door for many Greek scholars and manuscripts to pour into the West. After the fall of Constantinople to the Turks in 1453, many

◐─ **View** the **Closer Look** *"Primavera"* on **MyHistoryLab.com**

Greek scholars fled to Florence for refuge. This was the background against which the Florentine Platonic Academy evolved under the patronage of Cosimo de' Medici and the supervision of Marsilio Ficino (1433–1499) and Pico della Mirandola (1463–1494).

Renaissance thinkers were especially attracted to the Platonic tradition and to those Church Fathers who tried to synthesize Platonic philosophy with Christian teaching. The Florentine Academy was actually not a formal school, but an informal gathering of influential Florentine humanists devoted to the revival of the works of Plato and the Neoplatonists: Plotinus, Proclus, Porphyry, and Dionysius the Areopagite. To this end, Ficino edited and published the complete works of Plato.

The appeal of **Platonism** lay in its flattering view of human nature. It distinguished between an eternal sphere of being and a perishable world in which humans actually live. Human reason was believed to have pre-existed in the pristine world and still commune with it, a theory supported by human knowledge of eternal mathematical and moral truths.

Strong Platonic influence is evident in Pico's *Oration on the Dignity of Man*, perhaps the most famous Renaissance statement on the nature of humankind. (See "Compare and Connect: Is the 'Renaissance Man' a Myth?," page 298.) Pico wrote the *Oration* as an introduction to his pretentious collection of nine hundred theses. Published in Rome in December 1486, these theses were intended to serve as the basis for a public debate on all of life's important topics. The *Oration* drew on Platonic teaching to depict humans as the only creatures in the world who possess the freedom to do and to be whatever they chose, to fly with angels or wallow with pigs.

Critical Work of the Humanists: Lorenzo Valla

Because they were guided by scholarly ideals of philological accuracy and historical truth, learned humanists could become critics of tradition. Their dispassionate critical scholarship shook long-standing foundations, not the least of which were those of the medieval church. The works of Lorenzo Valla (1406–1457), author of the standard Renaissance text on Latin philology, the *Elegances of the Latin Language* (1444), reveal the explosive character of the new learning. Although a good Catholic, Valla became a hero to later Protestant reformers. His popularity among them stemmed from his brilliant exposé of the *Donation of Constantine* (see Chapter 6) and his defense of predestination against the advocates of free will.

The fraudulent *Donation*, written in the eighth century, purported to be a good-faith grant of vast territories to the pope and the church by the Roman emperor Constantine (r. 307–337). Valla did not intend the exposé of the *Donation* to have the devastating force that

CHRISTINE DE PISAN INSTRUCTS WOMEN ON HOW TO HANDLE THEIR HUSBANDS

Renowned Renaissance noblewoman Christine de Pisan has the modern reputation of being perhaps the first feminist, and her book, The Treasure of the City of Ladies *(also known as* The Book of Three Virtues*), has been described as the Renaissance woman's survival manual. Here she gives advice to the wives of artisans.*

How does Christine de Pisan's image of husband and wife compare with other medieval views? Would the church question her advice? As a noblewoman commenting on the married life of artisans, does her high social standing influence her advice? Would she give similar advice to women of her own social class?

All wives of artisans should be very painstaking and diligent if they wish to have the necessities of life. They should encourage their husbands or their workmen to get to work early in the morning and work until late. . . . [And] the wife herself should [also] be involved in the work to the extent that she knows all about it, so that she may know how to oversee his workers if her husband is absent, and to reprove them if they do not do well. . . . And when customers come to her husband and try to drive a hard bargain, she ought to warn him solicitously to take care that he does not make a bad deal. She should advise him to be chary of giving too much credit if he does not know precisely where and to whom it is going, for in this way many come to poverty. . . .

In addition, she ought to keep her husband's love as much as she can, to this end: that he will stay at home more willingly and that he may not have any reason to join the foolish crowds of other young men in taverns and indulge in unnecessary and extravagant expense, as many tradesmen do, especially in Paris. By treating him kindly she should protect him as well as she can from this. It is said that three things drive a man from his home: a quarrelsome wife, a smoking fireplace, and a leaking roof. She too ought to stay at home gladly and

Christine de Pisan, who has the modern reputation of being the first European feminist, presents her internationally famous book *The Treasure of the City of Ladies*, also known as *The Book of Three Virtues*, to Isabella of Bavaria amid her ladies in waiting.   Philip de Bay/Historical Picture Archive/Corbis

not go off every day traipsing hither and yon gossiping with the neighbours and visiting her chums to find out what everyone is doing. That is done by slovenly housewives roaming about the town in groups. Nor should she go off on these pilgrimages got up for no good reason and involving a lot of needless expense.

Protestants later attributed to it. He had only proved in a careful, scholarly way what others had long suspected. Using textual analysis and historical logic, Valla demonstrated that the document was filled with anachronistic terms, such as *fief*, and also contained information that could not have existed in a fourth-century document, hence a fraud. In the same dispassionate way, he also pointed out errors in the Latin Vulgate, then the authorized version of the Bible for Western Christendom.

Such discoveries did not make Valla any less loyal to the church, nor did they prevent his faithful fulfillment of the office of apostolic secretary in Rome under Pope Nicholas V (r. 1447–1455). Nonetheless, historical humanistic criticism of this type also served those far less loyal to the medieval church. Young humanists formed the first identifiable group of Martin Luther's supporters.

Civic Humanism   A basic humanist criticism of Scholastic education was the uselessness of so much of its content. The humanists believed education should promote individual virtue and self-sacrificing public service, hence the designation, civic humanism. The most striking examples of this were found in Florence, where three humanists served as chancellors of the city: Coluccio Salutati (1331–1406), Leonardo Bruni (ca. 1370–1444), and Poggio Bracciolini (1380–1459). Each used his rhetorical skills to rally the Florentines against their aggressors. However, many modern scholars doubt that humanistic scholarship accounted for such civic activity and rather view the famous humanist chancellors of Florence as men who simply wanted to exercise great power.

Toward the end of the Renaissance, many humanists became cliquish and snobbish intellectual elites more concerned about narrow Latin scholarly interests than with revitalizing civic and social life. In reaction to this elitist trend, the humanist historians Niccolò Machiavelli (1469–1527) and Francesco Guicciardini (1483–1540) wrote in Italian and made contemporary history their primary source and subject matter. Here, arguably, we can see the two sides of humanism: deep historical scholarship and practical transparent politics.

High Renaissance Art

In Renaissance Italy, as in Reformation Europe, the values and interests of the laity were no longer subordinated to those of the clergy. In education, culture, and religion, the laity now assumed a leading role and established models for the clergy to emulate. This development was due in part to the church's loss of international power during the great crises of the late Middle Ages. The rise of national sentiment and the emergence of national bureaucracies staffed by laymen, rather than clerics, encouraged the rapid growth of lay education over the fourteenth and fifteenth centuries. And medieval Christians adjusted to a more this-worldly spirit and mission.

◉ **Watch** the **Video** "The Italian Renaissance" on **MyHistoryLab.com**

This new perspective on life is prominent in the painting and sculpture of the High Renaissance (1450–1527), when art and sculpture reached their full maturity. Whereas medieval art had tended to be abstract and formulaic, Renaissance art emphatically embraced the natural world and human emotions. Renaissance artists gave their works a rational, even mathematical, order—perfect symmetry and proportionality reflecting a belief in the harmony of the universe.

High Renaissance artists were helped by the development of new technical skills during the fifteenth century. In addition to the availability of oil paints, two special techniques gave them an edge: the use of shading to enhance naturalness (**chiaroscuro**) and the adjustment of the size of figures to give the viewer a feeling of continuity with the painting (*linear perspective*). These techniques enabled the artist to portray space realistically and to paint a more natural world. The result, compared to their flat Byzantine and Gothic counterparts, was a three-dimensional canvas filled with energy and life.

Giotto (1266–1336), the father of Renaissance painting, signaled the new direction. An admirer of Saint Francis of Assisi, whose love of nature he shared, he painted a more natural world. Though still filled with religious seriousness, his work was no longer an abstract and unnatural depiction of the world. The painter Masaccio (1401–1428) and the sculptor Donatello (1386–1466) also portrayed the world around them literally and naturally. The great masters of the High Renaissance, Leonardo da Vinci (1452–1519), Raphael (1483–1520), and Michelangelo Buonarroti (1475–1564), reached the heights of such painting.

Leonardo da Vinci   A master of many skills, Leonardo exhibited the Renaissance ideal of the universal person. One of the greatest painters of all time, he also advised Italian princes and the French king Francis I (r. 1515–1547) on military engineering. He approached his work empirically, as a modern scientist, dissecting corpses to learn anatomy, and was a self-taught botanist. His inventive mind foresaw such modern machines as airplanes and submarines. The variety of his interests was so great that it could shorten his attention span. His great skill in conveying inner moods through complex facial expression is apparent not only in his most famous painting, the *Mona Lisa*, but also in his self-portrait as well.

A Closer LOOK

View the Closer Look on MyHistoryLab.com

LEONARDO PLOTS THE PERFECT MAN

VITRUVIAN MAN BY Leonardo da Vinci, c. 1490. The name "Vitruvian" is taken from that of a first-century C.E. Roman architect and engineer, Marcus Pollio Vitruvius, who used squares and circles to demonstrate the human body's symmetry and proportionality. Vitruvius' commentary reads counter-clockwise in three paragraphs that highlight Leonardo's scientific portrayal.

And just as the human body yields a circular outline, so too a square figure may be found from it. For if we measure the distance from the soles of the feet to the top of the head, and then apply that measure to the outstretched arms, the breadth will be found to be the same as the height.

Leonardo, like most artists of his time, shared this classical ideal of human perfection even in his gloomiest etchings and paintings. With few exceptions, the great painters of the age wanted to portray men and women in a more than human beauty and glory. Even the rabbits of the German painter Albrecht Dürer, who shared this ideal, were superior to any rabbit one might see in the wild.

If a man be placed flat on his back, with his hands and feet extended, and a pair of compasses centered at his navel, the fingers and toes of his two hands and feet will touch the circumference of a circle described therefrom.

CORBIS/Bettmann

From Marilyn Stokstad and David Cateforis, *Art History* (New York: Pearson, 2005), p. 651.

Compare Leonardo's nude body painting of "the perfect man" with those of Adam and Eve at the hand of the northern Renaissance painter, Lucas Cranach, the Elder (see page 309). Which of these images is truer to real life?

Is Leonardo's "Vitruvian Man" a true, perfect human being, or body worship of man as a perfect machine?

Is the "Renaissance Man" a Myth?

📖 Read the **Compare and Connect** on **MyHistoryLab.com**

AS SEVERAL ILLUSTRATIONS in this chapter attest, the great artists of the Renaissance (Raphael, Leonardo da Vinci, Albrecht Dürer) romanticized their human subjects and made them larger than life. Not only was the iconic "Renaissance man" perfectly proportioned physically, he was also effective in what he undertook, endowed with the divine freedom and power to be and to do whatever he chose.

QUESTIONS

1. Who or what are Pico's and Dürer's glorified humans? Is the vaunted "Renaissance man" real or fictional?

2. What is one to make of an era fixated on the perfect body and mind?

3. Is Martin Luther's rejoinder (the bondage of the human will) truer to life, or religious misanthropy?

I. Pico della Mirandola, *Oration on the Dignity of Man* (ca. 1486)

One of the most eloquent descriptions of the Renaissance image of human beings comes from Italian humanist Pico della Mirandola (1463–1494). In his famed Oration on the Dignity of Man *(ca. 1486), Pico describes humans as free to become whatever they choose.*

Pico's "Renaissance Man" stands in stark contrast to the devout Christian pilgrim of the Middle Ages. The latter found himself always at the crossroads of heaven and hell, in constant fear of sin, death, and the devil, regularly confessing his sins and receiving forgiveness in an unending penitential cycle. Had the Middle Ages misjudged human nature? Was there a great transformation in human nature between the Middle Ages and the Renaissance?

The best of artisans [God] ordained that that creature (man) to whom He had been able to give nothing proper to himself should have joint possession of whatever had been peculiar to each of the different kinds of being. He therefore took man as a creature of indeterminate nature and, assigning him a place in the middle of the world, addressed him thus: "Neither a fixed abode nor a form that is thine alone nor any function peculiar to thyself have we given thee, Adam, to the end that according to thy longing and according to thy judgment thou mayest have and possess what abode, what form, and what functions thou thyself shalt desire. The nature of all other beings is limited and constrained within the bounds of laws prescribed by Us. Thou, constrained by no limits, in accordance with thine own free will, in whose hand We have placed thee, shalt ordain for thyself the limits of thy nature. We have set thee at the world's center that thou mayest from thence more easily observe whatever is in the world. We have made thee neither of heaven nor of earth, neither mortal nor immortal, so that with freedom of choice and with honor, as though the maker and molder of thyself, thou mayest fashion thyself in whatever shape thou shalt prefer. Thou shalt have the power to degenerate into the lower forms of life, which are brutish. Thou shalt have the power, out of thy soul's judgment, to be reborn into the higher forms, which are divine." O supreme generosity of God the Father, O highest and most marvelous felicity of man! To him it is granted to have whatever he chooses, to be whatever he wills. ∎

From Giovanni Pico della Mirandola, *Oration on the Dignity of Man*, in *The Renaissance Philosophy of Man*, ed. by E. Cassirer et al. (Chicago: Phoenix Books, 1961), pp. 224–225.

II. Albrecht Dürer

In 1500, Albrecht Dürer, then 28, painted the most famous self-portrait of the European Renaissance and Reformation, one that celebrated his own beauty and genius by imposing his face on a portrayal of Christ, a work of art that has been called "the birth of the modern artist."

Fourteen years later (1514), on the occasion of his mother's death, Dürer engraved another famous image of himself, only now as a man in deep depression, or melancholy, his mind darkened and his creativity throttled.

In this self-portrait he is neither effective nor handsome, much less heroic and divine, not a self-portrait of a Renaissance man.

Albrecht Dürer (1471–1528). *Self-portrait at Age 28 with Fur Coat.* 1500. Oil on wood, 67 × 49 cm. Alte Pinakothek, Munich, Germany. Photograph © Scala/Art Resource, NY

Albrecht Dürer. *Melencolia I.* 1514. Engraving. 23.8 × 18.9 cm. Courtesy of the ary of Congress. ■

III. Martin Luther, *The Bondage of the Will* (1525)

The greater challenge to the Renaissance man came from Martin Luther, who met his "Pico" in northern humanist Desiderius Erasmus. Like Pico, Erasmus, flying in the face of Reformation theology, conceived free will to be "a power of the human will by which a man may apply himself to those things that lead to eternal salvation, or turn away from the same." Of such thinking, Luther made short-shift.

It is in the highest degree wholesome and necessary for a Christian to know whether or not his will has anything to do in matters pertaining to salvation. . . . We need to have in mind a clear-cut distinction between God's power and ours and God's work and ours, if we would live a godly life. . . . The will, be it God's or man's, does what it does, good or bad, under no compulsion, but just as it wants or pleases, as if totally free. . . . Wise men know what experience of life proves, that no man's purposes ever go forward as planned, but events overtake all men contrary to their expectation. . . . Who among us always lives and behaves as he should? But duty and doctrine are not therefore condemned, rather they condemn us.

God has promised His grace to the humbled, that is, to those who mourn over and despair of themselves. But a man cannot be thoroughly humbled till he realizes that his salvation is utterly beyond his own powers, counsels, efforts, will and works, and depends absolutely on the will, counsel, pleasure, and work of Another: GOD ALONE. As long as he is persuaded that he can make even the smallest contribution to his salvation, he . . . does not utterly despair of himself, and so is not humbled before God, but plans for himself a position, an occasion, a work, which shall bring him final salvation. But he who [no longer] doubts that his destiny depends entirely only on the will of God . . . waits for God to work in him, and such a man is very near to grace for his salvation. So if we want to drop this term ("free will") altogether, which would be the safest and most Christian thing to do, we may, still in good faith, teach people to use it to credit man with 'free will' in respect not of what is above him, but of what is below him. . . . However, with regard to God and in all that bears on salvation or damnation, he has no 'free will' but is a captive, prisoner and bond-slave, either to the will of God, or to the will of Satan. ■

From Martin Luther, *On the Bondage of the Will*, ed. by J. I. Packer and O. R. Johnston (Westwood, NJ: Fleming H. Fevell Co., 1957), pp. 79, 81, 83, 87, 100, 104, 107, 137.

Document

VASARI'S DESCRIPTION OF LEONARDO DA VINCI

In this passage, Giorgio Vasari (1512–1574), friend and biographer of the great Renaissance painters, sculptors, and architects, claims Leonardo da Vinci's versatility was actually a handicap.

According to Vasari, how does Leonardo's genius work against him? Why do you suppose so many scholars have pointed to Leonardo as the prototypical "Renaissance man"?

The richest gifts are occasionally seen to be showered, as by celestial influence, upon certain human beings; nay, they sometimes supernaturally and marvelously gather in a single person—beauty, grace, and talent united in such a manner that to whatever the man thus favored may turn himself, his every action is so divine as to leave all other men far behind. . . . This was . . . the case of Leonardo da Vinci . . . who had . . . so rare a gift of talent and ability that to whatever subject he turned his attention . . . he presently made himself absolute master of it. . . .

He would without doubt have made great progress in the learning and knowledge of the sciences had he not been so versatile and changeful. The instability of his character led him to undertake many things, which, having commenced, he afterwards abandoned. In arithmetic, for example, he made such rapid progress in the short time he gave his attention to it, that he often confounded the master who was teaching him. . . . He also commenced the study of music and resolved to acquire the art of playing the lute . . . singing to the instrument most divinely. . . .

Being also an excellent geometrician, Leonardo not only worked in sculpture but also in architecture; likewise, he prepared . . . designs for entire buildings. . . . While only a youth, he first suggested the formation of a canal from Pisa to Florence by means of certain changes . . . in the river Arno. He made designs for mills, fulling machines, and other engines run by water. But as he had resolved to make painting his profession, he gave the greater part of his time to drawing from nature.

From J. H. Robinson, ed., *Readings in European History*, Vol. 1 (Boston: Athenaeum, 1904), pp. 535–536.

Raphael A man of great kindness and a painter of great sensitivity, Raphael was loved by his contemporaries as much for his person as for his work. He is most famous for his tender madonnas and the great fresco in the Vatican, *The School of Athens*, a virtually perfect example of Renaissance technique. It depicts Plato and Aristotle surrounded by other great philosophers and scientists of antiquity who bear the features of Raphael's famous contemporaries.

Michelangelo The melancholy genius Michelangelo also excelled in a variety of arts and crafts. His eighteen-foot sculpture of David, which long stood majestically in the great square of Florence, is a perfect example of Renaissance devotion to harmony, symmetry, and proportion, all serving the glorification of the human form. Four different popes commissioned works by Michelangelo. The frescoes in the Vatican's Sistine Chapel are the most famous, painted during the pontificate of Pope Julius II (r. 1503–1513), who also set Michelangelo to work on his own magnificent tomb. The Sistine frescoes originally covered 10,000 square feet and involved 343 figures, over half of which exceeded ten feet in height, but it is their originality and perfection as works of art that impress one most. This labor of love and piety took four years to complete.

Read the **Document** "Giorgio Vasari on the Life of Michelangelo, 1550" on **MyHistoryLab.com**

His later works are more complex and suggest deep personal changes. They mark, artistically and philosophically, the passing of High Renaissance painting and the advent of a new style known as **mannerism**, which reached its peak in the late sixteenth and early seventeenth centuries. A reaction to the simplicity and symmetry of High Renaissance art, which also had a parallel in contemporary music and literature, mannerism made room for the strange and the abnormal, giving freer rein to the individual perceptions and feelings of the artist, who now felt free to paint, compose, or write in a "mannered," or "affected," way. Tintoretto (d. 1594) and El Greco (d. 1614) are mannerism's supreme representatives.

Slavery in the Renaissance

Throughout Renaissance Italy, slavery flourished as extravagantly as art and culture. A thriving western slave market existed as early as the twelfth century, when the Spanish sold Muslim slaves captured in raids and war to wealthy Italians and other buyers. Contemporaries looked on such slavery as a merciful act, since their captors would otherwise have killed the captives. In addition to widespread household or domestic slavery, collective plantation slavery, following East Asian models, also developed in the eastern Mediterranean during the High Middle Ages. In the savannas of Sudan and the Venetian estates on the islands of Cyprus and Crete, gangs of slaves cut sugarcane, setting the model for later slave plantations in the Mediterranean and the New World.

Combining the painterly qualities of all the Renaissance masters, Raphael created scenes of tender beauty and subjects sublime in both flesh and spirit.   Musée du Louvre, Paris/Giraudon, Paris/ Bridgeman Art Library/SuperStock

---

Document

VASARI'S DESCRIPTION OF RAPHAEL'S PERSONALITY

In this passage, Vasari describes the painter Raphael as a person with an extraordinary ability to create an atmosphere of harmony among those who worked with him.

Do you find the personal traits of Raphael, as described by Vasari, also reflected in his paintings? Is the author romanticizing the artist? Compare this with his description of Leonardo in the preceding document.

There was among his many extraordinary gifts one of such value and importance that I can never sufficiently admire it and always think thereof with astonishment. This was the power accorded him by heaven of bringing all who approached his presence into harmony, an effect . . . contrary to the nature of our artists. Yet all . . . became as of one mind once they began to labor in the society of Raphael, and they continued in such unity and concord that all harsh feelings and evil dispositions became subdued and disappeared at the sight of him . . . This happened because all were surpassed by him in friendly courtesy as well as in art. All confessed the influence of his sweet and gracious nature. . . . Not only was he honored by men, but even by the very animals who would constantly follow his steps and always loved him.

From J. H. Robinson, *Readings in European History*, Vol. 1 (Boston: Athenaeum, 1904), pp. 538–539.

This portrait of Katharina, by Albrecht Dürer, provides evidence of African slavery in Europe during the sixteenth century. Katharina was in the service of one João Bradao, a Portuguese economic minister living in Antwerp, then the financial center of Europe. Dürer became friends with Bradao during his stay in the Low Countries in the winter of 1520–1521. Albrecht Dürer (1471–1528), *Portrait of the Moorish Woman Katharina*. Drawing. Uffizi Florence, Italy. Photograph © Foto Marburg/Art Resource, NY

MAJOR POLITICAL EVENTS OF THE ITALIAN RENAISSANCE (1375–1527)

1378–1382	The Ciompi Revolt in Florence
1434	Medici rule in Florence established by Cosimo de' Medici
1454–1455	Treaty of Lodi allies Milan, Naples, and Florence (in effect until 1494)
1494	Charles VIII of France invades Italy
1494–1498	Savonarola controls Florence
1495	League of Venice unites Venice, Milan, the Papal States, the Holy Roman Empire, and Spain against France
1499	Louis XII invades Milan (the second French invasion of Italy)
1500	The Borgias conquer Romagna
1512–1513	The Holy League (Pope Julius II, Ferdinand of Aragon, Emperor Maximilian, and Venice) defeats the French
1513	Machiavelli writes *The Prince*
1515	Francis I leads the third French invasion of Italy
1516	Concordat of Bologna between France and the papacy
1527	Sack of Rome by imperial soldiers

After the Black Death (1348–1350) reduced the supply of laborers everywhere in Western Europe, the demand for slaves soared. Slaves were imported from Africa, the Balkans, Constantinople, Cyprus, Crete, and the lands surrounding the Black Sea. Taken randomly from conquered people, they consisted of many races: Tatars, Circassians, Greeks, Russians, Georgians, and Iranians as well as Asians and Africans. According to one source, "By the end of the fourteenth century, there was hardly a well-to-do household in Tuscany without at least one slave: brides brought them [to their marriages] as part of their dowry, doctors accepted them from their patients in lieu of fees—and it was not unusual to find them even in the service of a priest."[2]

Owners had complete dominion over their slaves; in Italian law, this meant the "[power] to have, hold, sell, alienate, exchange, enjoy, rent or unrent, dispose of in [their] will[s], judge soul and body, and do with in perpetuity whatsoever may please [them] and [their] heirs and no man may gainsay [them]."[3] A strong, young, healthy slave cost the equivalent of the wages paid a free servant over several years. Considering the lifespan of free service thereafter, slaves were well worth the price.

Tatars and Africans appear to have been the worst treated, but as in ancient Greece and Rome, slaves at this time were generally accepted as family members and integrated into households. Not a few women slaves became mothers of their masters' children. Fathers often adopted children of such unions and raised them as their legitimate heirs. It was also in the interest of their owners to keep slaves healthy and happy; otherwise they would be of little use and even become a threat. Slaves

[2]Iris Origo, *The Merchant of Prato: Francesco di Marco Datini, 1335–1410* (New York: David Godine, 1986), pp. 90–91.
[3]Origo, *The Merchant of Prato*, p. 209.

nonetheless remained a foreign and suspected presence in Italian society; they were, as all knew, uprooted and resentful people.

Italy's Political Decline: The French Invasions (1494–1527)

As a land of autonomous city-states, Italy had always relied on internal cooperation for its peace and safety from foreign invasion—especially by the Turks. Such cooperation was maintained during the second half of the fifteenth century, thanks to a political alliance known as the Treaty of Lodi (1454–1455). Its terms brought Milan and Naples, long traditional enemies, into the alliance with Florence. These three stood together for decades against Venice, which frequently joined the Papal States to maintain an internal balance of power. However, when a foreign enemy threatened Italy, the five states could also present a united front.

Around 1490, after the rise to power of the Milanese despot Ludovico il Moro, hostilities between Milan and Naples resumed. The peace that the Treaty of Lodi made possible ended in 1494 when Naples threatened Milan. Ludovico made a fatal response to these new political alignments: He appealed to the French for aid. French kings had ruled Naples from 1266 to 1442 before being driven out by Duke Alfonso of Sicily. Breaking a wise Italian rule, Ludovico invited the French to reenter Italy and revive their dynastic claim to Naples. In his haste to check rival Naples, Ludovico did not recognize sufficiently that France also had dynastic claims to Milan. Nor did he foresee how insatiable the French appetite for new territory would become once French armies had crossed the Alps and encamped in Italy.

Charles VIII's March Through Italy

The French king Louis XI had resisted the temptation to invade Italy while nonetheless keeping French dynastic claims in Italy alive. His successor, Charles VIII (r. 1483–1498), an eager youth in his twenties, responded to the call with lightning speed. Within five months, he had crossed the Alps (August 1494) and raced as conqueror through Florence and the Papal States into Naples. As Charles approached Florence, its Florentine ruler, Piero de' Medici, tried to placate the French king by handing over Pisa and other Florentine possessions. Such appeasement only brought about Piero's exile by a citizenry that was being revolutionized by a radical Dominican preacher named Girolamo Savonarola (1452–1498). Savonarola convinced the fearful Florentines that the French king's arrival was a long-delayed and fully justified divine vengeance on their immorality.

That allowed Charles to enter Florence without resistance. Between Savonarola's fatal flattery and the payment of a large ransom, the city escaped destruction. After Charles's departure, Savonarola exercised virtual rule over Florence for four years. In the end, the Florentines proved not to be the stuff theocracies are made of. Savonarola's moral rigor and antipapal policies made it impossible for him to survive indefinitely in Italy. After the Italian cities reunited and ousted the French invader, Savonarola's days were numbered. In May 1498, he was imprisoned and executed.

Charles's lightning march through Italy also struck terror in non-Italian hearts. Ferdinand of Aragon (r. 1479–1516), who had hoped to expand his own possessions in Italy from his base in Sicily, now found himself vulnerable to a French–Italian axis. In response he created a new counteralliance—the League of Venice. Formed in March 1495, it brought Venice, the Papal States, and Emperor Maximilian I (r. 1493–1519) together with Ferdinand against the French. The stage was now set for a conflict between France and Spain that would not end until 1559.

Meanwhile, the Milanese despot who had brought these ill winds, Ludovico il Moro, recognized that he had sown the wind. Having desired a French invasion only as long as it weakened his enemies, he now saw a whirlwind of events he had himself created threaten Milan. In reaction, he joined the League of Venice, which was now strong enough to send Charles into retreat and to end the menace he posed to Italy.

Pope Alexander VI and the Borgia Family

The French returned to Italy under Charles's successor, Louis XII (r. 1498–1515). This time a new Italian ally, the Borgia pope, Alexander VI, assisted them. Probably the most corrupt pope who ever sat on the papal throne, he openly promoted the political careers of Cesare and Lucrezia Borgia, the children he had had before he became pope. He placed papal policy in tandem with the efforts of his powerful family to secure a political base in Romagna in north central Italy.

In Romagna, several principalities had fallen away from the church during the Avignon papacy. Venice, the pope's ally within the League of Venice, continued to contest the Papal States for their loyalty. Seeing that a French alliance would allow him to reestablish control over the region, Alexander took steps to secure French favor. He annulled Louis XII's marriage to Charles VIII's sister so Louis could marry Charles's widow, Anne of Brittany—a popular political move designed to keep Brittany French. The pope also bestowed a cardinal's hat on the archbishop of Rouen, Louis's favorite cleric. Most important, Alexander agreed to abandon the League of Venice, a withdrawal of support that made the league too weak to resist a French reconquest of Milan.

All in all it was a scandalous trade-off, but one that made it possible for both the French king and the pope to realize their ambitions within Italy. Louis invaded Milan in August 1499. Ludovico il Moro, who had originally opened the Pandora's box of French invasion, spent his last years languishing in a French prison. In 1500, Louis and Ferdinand of Aragon divided Naples between them, and the pope and Cesare Borgia conquered the cities of Romagna without opposition. Alexander's victorious son was given the title "duke of Romagna."

Pope Julius II

Cardinal Giuliano della Rovere, a strong opponent of the Borgia family, succeeded Alexander VI as Pope Julius II (r. 1503–1513). He suppressed the Borgias and placed their newly conquered lands in Romagna under papal jurisdiction. Julius raised the Renaissance papacy to its peak of military prowess and diplomatic intrigue, gaining him the title of "warrior pope." Shocked, as were other contemporaries, by this thoroughly secular papacy, the humanist Erasmus (1466?–1536), who had witnessed in disbelief a bullfight in the papal palace during a visit to Rome, wrote a popular anonymous satire titled *Julius Excluded from Heaven*. This humorous account purported to describe the pope's unsuccessful efforts to convince Saint Peter that he was worthy of admission to heaven.

Read the **Document**
"Desiderius Erasmus, 'Pope Julius Excluded from Heaven,' 1513–1514" on **MyHistoryLab.com**

Assisted by his powerful allies, Pope Julius drove the Venetians out of Romagna in 1509 and fully secured the Papal States. Having realized this long-sought papal goal, Julius turned to the second major undertaking of his pontificate: ridding Italy of his former ally, the French invader. Julius, Ferdinand of Aragon, and Venice formed a second Holy League in October 1511 and were joined by Emperor Maximilian I and the Swiss. In 1512, the league had the French in full retreat, and the Swiss defeated them in 1513 at Novara.

The French were nothing if not persistent. They invaded Italy a third time under Louis's successor, Francis I (r. 1515–1547). This time French armies massacred Swiss soldiers of the Holy League at Marignano in September 1515, avenging the earlier defeat at Novara. The victory won the Concordat of Bologna from the pope in August 1516, an agreement that gave the French king control over the French clergy in exchange for French recognition of the pope's superiority over church councils and his right to collect annates in France. This concordat helped keep France Catholic after the outbreak of the Protestant Reformation, but the new French entry into Italy set the stage for the first of four major wars with Spain in the first half of the sixteenth century: the Habsburg-Valois wars, none of which France won.

Niccolò Machiavelli

The foreign invasions made a shambles of Italy. The same period that saw Italy's cultural peak in the work of Leonardo, Raphael, and Michelangelo also witnessed Italy's political tragedy. One who watched as French, Spanish, and German armies wreaked havoc on Italy was Niccolò Machiavelli (1469–1527). The more he saw, the more convinced he became that Italian political unity and independence were ends that justified any means.

A humanist and a careful student of ancient Rome, Machiavelli was impressed by the way Roman rulers and citizens had then defended their homeland. They possessed *virtù*, the ability to act decisively and heroically for the good of their country. Stories of ancient Roman patriotism and self-sacrifice were Machiavelli's favorites, and he lamented the absence of such traits among his compatriots. Such romanticizing of the Roman past exaggerated both ancient virtue and contemporary failings. His Florentine contemporary, Francesco Guicciardini (1483–1540), a more sober historian less given to idealizing antiquity, wrote truer chronicles of Florentine and Italian history.

Machiavelli also held republican ideals, which he did not want to see vanish from Italy. He believed a strong and determined people could struggle successfully with fortune. He scolded the Italian people for the self-destruction their own internal feuding was causing. He wanted an end to that behavior above all, so a reunited Italy could drive all foreign armies out.

His fellow citizens were not up to such a challenge. The juxtaposition of what Machiavelli believed the ancient Romans had been, with the failure of his contemporaries to attain such high ideals, made him the famous cynic whose name—in the epithet "Machiavellian"—has become synonymous with ruthless political expediency. Only a strongman, he concluded, could impose order on so divided and selfish a people; the salvation of Italy required, for the present, cunning dictators.

It has been argued that Machiavelli wrote *The Prince* in 1513 as a cynical satire on the way rulers actually do behave and not as a serious recommendation of unprincipled despotic rule. To take his advocacy of tyranny literally, it is argued, contradicts both his earlier works and his own strong family tradition of republican service. But Machiavelli seems to have been in earnest when he advised rulers to discover the advantages of fraud and brutality, at least as a temporary means to the higher end of a unified Italy. He apparently hoped to see a strong ruler emerge from the Medici family, which had captured the papacy in 1513 with the pontificate of Leo X (r. 1513–1521). At the same time, the Medici family retained control over the powerful territorial state of Florence. *The Prince*, his famous book, was pointedly dedicated to Lorenzo de' Medici, duke of Urbino and grandson of Lorenzo the Magnificent.

Read the **Document**
"*The Prince* (1519) Machiavelli" on **MyHistoryLab.com**

MACHIAVELLI DISCUSSES THE MOST IMPORTANT TRAIT FOR A RULER

Machiavelli believed that the most important personality trait of a successful ruler was the ability to instill fear in his subjects.

Why does Machiavelli think so little of his fellow man? Is he a humanist? Does history bear out his description of humankind? Is fear the best way to hold a state together? Who in the present-day world would you describe as a modern Machiavellian?

Here the question arises; whether it is better to be loved than feared or feared than loved. The answer is that it would be desirable to be both but, since that is difficult, it is much safer to be feared than to be loved, if one must choose. For on men in general this observation may be made: they are ungrateful, fickle, and deceitful, eager to avoid dangers, and avid for gain, and while you are useful to them they are all with you, offering you their blood, their property, their lives, and their sons so long as danger is remote, as we noted above, but when it approaches they turn on you. Any prince, trusting only in their words and having no other preparations made, will fall to his ruin, for friendships that are bought at a price and not by greatness and nobility of soul are paid for indeed, but they are not owned and cannot be called upon in time of need. Men have less hesitation in offending a man who is loved than one who is feared, for love is held by a bond of obligation which, as men are wicked, is broken whenever personal advantage suggests it, but fear is accompanied by the dread of punishment which never relaxes.

From Niccolo Machiavelli, *The Prince* (1513), trans. and ed. by Thomas G. Bergin (New York: Appleton-Century-Crofts, 1947).

Whatever Machiavelli's hopes may have been, the Medicis proved not to be Italy's deliverers. The second Medici pope, Clement VII (r. 1523–1534), watched helplessly as the army of Emperor Charles V sacked Rome in 1527, also the year of Machiavelli's death.

▼ Revival of Monarchy in Northern Europe

After 1450, sovereign rulers set in motion a shift from divided feudal monarchy to unified national monarchies. Dynastic and chivalric ideals of feudal monarchy did not, however, vanish. Territorial princes remained on the scene and representative bodies persisted and even grew in influence.

View the **Map** "Geographical Tour: Europe in 1500" on **MyHistoryLab.com**

The feudal monarchy of the High Middle Ages was characterized by the division of the basic powers of government between the king and his semiautonomous vassals. The nobility and the towns then acted with varying degrees of unity and success through evolving representative assemblies, such as the English Parliament, the French Estates General, and the Spanish *Cortés*, to thwart the centralization of royal power into a united nation. But after the Hundred Years' War and the Great Schism in the church, the nobility and the clergy were in decline and less able to block growing national monarchies.

The increasingly important towns now began to ally with the king. Loyal, business-wise townspeople, not the nobility and the clergy, increasingly staffed royal offices and became the king's lawyers, bookkeepers, military tacticians, and foreign diplomats. This new alliance between king and town broke the bonds of feudal society and made possible the rise of sovereign states.

In a sovereign state, the powers of taxation, war-making, and law enforcement no longer belong to semiautonomous vassals but are concentrated in the monarch and exercised by his or her chosen agents. Taxes, wars, and laws become national, rather than merely regional, matters. Only as monarchs became able to act independently of the nobility and representative assemblies could they overcome the decentralization that impeded nation-building. Ferdinand and Isabella of Spain rarely called the *Cortés* into session. The French Estates General met irregularly, mostly in time of crisis, but was never essential to royal governance. Henry VII (r. 1485–1509) of England managed to raise revenues without going begging to Parliament, which had voted him customs revenues for life in 1485. Brilliant theorists, from Marsilius of Padua in the fourteenth century to Machiavelli in the fifteenth to Jean Bodin (1530–1596) in the sixteenth, emphatically defended the sovereign rights of monarchy.

📖 **Read** the **Document**
"Jean Bodin, *Six Books of the Commonwealth*" on
MyHistoryLab.com

The many were, of course, never totally subjugated to the one. But in the last half of the fifteenth century, rulers demonstrated that the law was their creature. They appointed civil servants whose vision was no longer merely local or regional. In Castile they were the *corregidores*, in England the justices of the peace, and in France bailiffs operating through well-drilled lieutenants. These royal ministers and agents became closely attached to the localities they administered in the ruler's name. Throughout England, for example, local magnates represented the Tudor dynasty that seized the throne in 1485. These new executives remained royal bureaucrats whose outlook was "national" and loyal to the "state."

Monarchies also created standing national armies in the fifteenth century. The noble cavalry receded as the infantry and the artillery became the backbone of royal armies. Mercenary soldiers from Switzerland and Germany became the major part of the "king's army." Professional soldiers who fought for pay and booty were far more efficient than feudal vassals. However, monarchs who failed to meet their payrolls now faced a new danger of mutiny and banditry by foreign troops.

The growing cost of warfare in the fifteenth and sixteenth centuries increased the monarch's need for new national sources of income. The great obstacle was the stubborn belief of the highest social classes that they were immune from government taxation. The nobility guarded their properties and traditional rights and despised taxation as an insult and a humiliation. Royal revenues accordingly had to grow at the expense of those least able to resist and least able to pay.

The monarchs had several options when it came to raising money. As feudal lords, they could collect rents from their royal domains. They could also levy national taxes on basic food and clothing, such as the salt tax (*gabelle*) in France and the 10 percent sales tax (*alcabala*) on commercial transactions in Spain. The rulers could also levy direct taxes on the peasantry, which they did through agreeable representative assemblies of the privileged classes in which the peasantry did not sit. The *taille*, which the French kings determined independently from year to year after the Estates General was suspended in 1484, was such a tax. Innovative fundraising devices in the fifteenth century included the sale of public offices and the issuance of high-interest government bonds.

Rulers still did not levy taxes on the powerful nobility, but instead, they borrowed from rich nobles and the great bankers of Italy and Germany. In money matters, the privileged classes remained as much the kings' creditors and competitors as their subjects.

France

Charles VII (r. 1422–1461) was a king made great by those who served him. His ministers created a permanent professional army, which—thanks initially to the inspiration of Joan of Arc—drove the English out of France. In addition, the enterprise of an independent merchant banker named Jacques Coeur helped develop a strong economy, diplomatic corps, and national administration throughout Charles's reign. These sturdy tools in turn enabled Charles's son and successor, the ruthless Louis XI (1461–1483), to make France a great power.

French nation-building had two political cornerstones in the fifteenth century. The first was the collapse of the English Empire in France following the Hundred Years' War. The second was the defeat of Charles the Bold (r. 1467–1477) and his duchy of Burgundy. Perhaps Europe's strongest political power in the mid-fifteenth century, Burgundy aspired to dwarf both France and the Holy Roman Empire as the leader of a dominant middle kingdom, which it might have done had not the continental powers joined to prevent it. When Charles the Bold died in defeat in a battle at Nancy in 1477, the dream of a Burgundian Empire died with him. Louis XI and Habsburg emperor Maximilian I divided the conquered Burgundian lands between them, with the treaty-wise Habsburgs getting the better part. The dissolution of Burgundy ended its constant intrigue against the French king and left Louis XI free to secure the monarchy. Between the newly acquired Burgundian lands and his own inheritance the king was able to end his reign with a kingdom almost twice the size of that he had inherited. Louis successfully harnessed the nobility, expanded the trade and industry that Jacques Coeur so carefully had nurtured, created a national postal system, and even established a lucrative silk industry.

A strong nation is a two-edged sword. Because Louis's successors inherited a secure and efficient government, they felt free to pursue what proved ultimately to be bad foreign policy. Conquests in Italy in the 1490s and a long series of losing wars with the Habsburgs in the first half of the sixteenth century left France, by the mid-sixteenth century, once again a defeated nation almost as divided as it had been during the Hundred Years' War.

Spain

Both Castile and Aragon had been poorly ruled and divided kingdoms in the mid-fifteenth century, but the union of Isabella of Castile (r. 1474–1504) and Ferdinand of Aragon (r. 1479–1516) changed that situation. The two future sovereigns married in 1469, despite strong protests from neighboring Portugal and France, both of which foresaw the formidable European power the marriage would create. Castile was by far the richer and more populous of the two, having an estimated 5 million inhabitants to Aragon's population of under 1 million. Castile was also distinguished by its lucrative sheep-farming industry, run by a government-backed organization called the *Mesta*, another example of developing centralized economic planning. Although the marriage of Ferdinand and Isabella dynastically united the two kingdoms, they remained constitutionally separated. Each retained its respective government agencies—separate laws, armies, coinage, and taxation—and cultural traditions.

Ferdinand and Isabella could do together what neither was able to accomplish alone: subdue their realms, secure their borders, venture abroad militarily, and Christianize the whole of Spain. Between 1482 and 1492 they conquered the Moors in Granada. Naples became a Spanish possession in 1504. By 1512, Ferdinand had secured his northern borders by conquering the kingdom of Navarre. Internally, the Spanish king and queen won the allegiance of the *Hermandad*, a powerful league of cities and towns that served them against stubborn noble landowners.

Spain had long been remarkable among European lands as a place where three religions—Islam, Judaism, and Christianity—coexisted with a certain degree of toleration. That toleration was to end dramatically under Ferdinand and Isabella, who made Spain the prime exemplar of state-controlled religion.

Ferdinand and Isabella exercised almost total control over the Spanish church. They appointed the higher clergy and the officers of the Inquisition. The latter, run by Tomás de Torquemada (d. 1498), Isabella's confessor, was a key national agency established in 1479 to monitor the activity of converted Jews (*conversos*) and Muslims (*Moriscos*) in Spain. In 1492, the Jews were exiled and their properties confiscated. In 1502, nonconverting Moors in Granada were driven into exile by Cardinal Francisco Jiménez de Cisneros (1437–1517), under whom Spanish spiritual life was successfully conformed. This was a major reason why Spain remained a loyal Catholic country throughout the sixteenth century and provided a secure base of operation for the European Counter-Reformation.

Ferdinand and Isabella were rulers with wide horizons. They contracted anti-French marriage alliances that came to determine a large part of European history in the sixteenth century. In 1496, their eldest daughter, Joanna, later known as "the Mad," married Archduke Philip, the son of Emperor Maximilian I. The fruit of this union, Charles I, was the first to rule over a united Spain; because of his inheritance and election as emperor in 1519, his empire almost equaled in size that of Charlemagne. A second daughter, Catherine of Aragon, wed Arthur, the son of the English king Henry VII. After Arthur's premature death, she was betrothed to his brother, the future King Henry VIII (r. 1509–1547), whom she married eight years later, in 1509. The failure of this marriage became the key factor in the emergence of the Anglican church and the English Reformation.

The new power of Spain was also revealed in Ferdinand and Isabella's promotion of overseas exploration. They sponsored the Genoese adventurer Christopher Columbus (1451–1506), who arrived at the islands of the Caribbean while sailing west in search of a shorter route to the spice markets of the Far East. This patronage led to the creation of the Spanish Empire in Mexico and Peru, whose gold and silver mines helped make Spain Europe's dominant power in the sixteenth century.

England

The latter half of the fifteenth century was a period of especially difficult political trial for the English. Following the Hundred Years' War, civil warfare broke out between two rival branches of the royal family: the House of York and the House of Lancaster. The roots of the war lay in succession irregularities after the forced deposition of the erratic king Richard II (r. 1377–1399). This conflict, known to us today as the Wars of the Roses (because York's symbol, according to legend, was a white rose and Lancaster's a red rose), kept England in turmoil from 1455 to 1485.

The duke of York and his supporters in the prosperous southern towns challenged the Lancastrian monarchy of Henry VI (r. 1422–1461). In 1461, Edward IV (r. 1461–1483), son of the duke of York, seized power and instituted a strong-arm rule that lasted more than twenty years; it was only briefly interrupted, in 1470–1471, by Henry VI's short-lived restoration. Assisted by able ministers, Edward effectively increased the power and finances of the monarchy.

His brother, Richard III (r. 1483–1485), usurped the throne from Edward's son, and after Richard's death, the new Tudor dynasty portrayed him as an unprincipled villain who had also murdered Edward's sons in the Tower of London to secure his hold on the throne. Shakespeare's *Richard III* is the best-known version of this characterization—unjust according to some. Be that as it may, Richard's reign saw the growth of support for the exiled Lancastrian Henry Tudor, who returned to England to defeat Richard on Bosworth Field in August 1485.

Henry Tudor ruled as Henry VII (r. 1485–1509), the first of the new Tudor dynasty that would dominate England throughout the sixteenth century. To bring the rival royal families together and to make the hereditary claim of his offspring to the throne uncontestable, Henry married Edward IV's daughter, Elizabeth of York. He succeeded in disciplining the English nobility through a special instrument of the royal will known as the

Court of Star Chamber. Created with the sanction of Parliament in 1487, the court was intended to end the perversion of English justice by "over-mighty subjects," that is, powerful nobles who used intimidation and bribery to win favorable verdicts in court cases. In the Court of Star Chamber, the king's councilors sat as judges, and such tactics did not sway them. The result was a more equitable court system.

It was also a court more amenable to the royal will. Henry shrewdly used English law to further the ends of the monarchy. He managed to confiscate lands and fortunes of nobles with such success that he was able to govern without dependence on Parliament for royal funds, always a cornerstone of a strong monarchy. In these ways, Henry began to shape a monarchy that would develop into one of early modern Europe's most exemplary governments during the reign of his granddaughter, Elizabeth I (r. 1558–1603).

The Holy Roman Empire

Germany and Italy were the striking exceptions to the steady development of politically centralized lands in the last half of the fifteenth century. Unlike England, France, and Spain, the Holy Roman Empire saw the many thoroughly repulse the one. In Germany, territorial rulers and cities resisted every effort at national consolidation and unity. As in Carolingian times, rulers continued to partition their kingdoms, however small, among their sons. By the late fifteenth century, Germany was hopelessly divided into some three hundred autonomous political entities.

The princes and the cities did work together to create the machinery of law and order, if not of union, within the divided empire. Emperor Charles IV (r. 1346–1378) and the major German territorial rulers reached an agreement in 1356 known as the **Golden Bull**. It established a seven-member electoral college consisting of the archbishops of Mainz, Trier, and Cologne; the duke of Saxony; the margrave of Brandenburg; the count Palatine; and the king of Bohemia. This group also functioned as an administrative body. They elected the emperor and, in cooperation with him, provided what transregional unity and administration existed.

The figure of the emperor gave the empire a single ruler in law if not in fact. The conditions of his rule and the extent of his powers over his subjects, especially the seven electors, were renegotiated with every imperial election. Therefore, the rights of the many (the princes) were always balanced against the power of the one (the emperor).

In the fifteenth century, an effort was made to control incessant feuding by the creation of an imperial diet known as the *Reichstag*. This was a national assembly of the seven electors, the nonelectoral princes, and representatives from the sixty-five imperial free cities. The cities were the weakest of the three bodies represented in the diet. During such an assembly in Worms in 1495, the members won from Emperor Maximilian I an imperial ban on private warfare, the creation of a Supreme Court of Justice to enforce internal peace, and an imperial Council of Regency to coordinate imperial and internal German policy. The emperor only grudgingly conceded the latter because it gave the princes a share in executive power.

These reforms were still a poor substitute for true national unity. In the sixteenth and seventeenth centuries, the territorial princes became virtually sovereign rulers in their various domains. Such disunity aided religious dissent and conflict. It was in the cities and territories of still feudal, fractionalized, backward Germany that the Protestant Reformation broke out in the sixteenth century.

▼ The Northern Renaissance

The scholarly works of northern humanists created a climate favorable to religious and educational reforms on the eve of the Reformation. Northern humanism was initially stimulated by the importation of Italian learning through such varied intermediaries as students who had studied in Italy, merchants who traded there, and the Brothers of the Common Life. This last was an influential lay religious movement that began in the Netherlands and permitted men and women to live a shared religious life without making formal vows of poverty, chastity, and obedience.

The northern humanists, however, developed their own distinctive culture. They tended to come from more diverse social backgrounds and to be more devoted to religious reforms than their Italian counterparts. They were also more willing to write for lay audiences as well as for a narrow intelligentsia. Thanks to the invention of printing with movable type, it became possible for humanists to convey their educational ideals to laypeople and clerics alike. Printing gave new power and influence to elites in both church and state, who now could popularize their viewpoints freely and widely.

View the **Closer Look** "Rogier Van Der Weyden, *Deposition*" on **MyHistoryLab.com**

The Printing Press

A variety of forces converged in the fourteenth and fifteenth centuries to give rise to the invention of the printing press. Since the days of Charlemagne, kings and princes had encouraged schools and literacy to help provide educated bureaucrats to staff the offices of their kingdoms. Without people who could read, think critically, and write reliable reports, no kingdom, large or small, could be properly governed. By the fifteenth century, a new literate lay

Lucas Cranach the Elder, *Adam and Eve*, 1513–1515. Compare Lucas Cranach, the Elder's rendering of Adam and Eve with the nude body depicted in Leonardo's *Vitruvian Man* (see page 297). Which of these images is truer to real life? © INTERFOTO/Alamy

of Western Europe. Thereafter, books were rapidly and handsomely produced on topics both profound and practical and were intended for ordinary lay readers, scholars, and clerics alike. Especially popular in the early decades of print were books of piety and religion, calendars and almanacs, and how-to books (for example, on childrearing, making brandies and liquors, curing animals, and farming).

The new technology proved enormously profitable to printers, whose numbers exploded. By 1500, within just fifty years of Gutenberg's press, printing presses operated in at least sixty German cities and in more than two hundred cities throughout Europe. The printing press was a boon to the careers of humanists, who now gained international audiences.

View the **Image**
"Gutenberg Bible" on
MyHistoryLab.com

Literacy deeply affected people everywhere, nurturing self-esteem and a critical frame of mind. By standardizing texts, the print revolution made anyone who could read an instant authority. Rulers in church and state now had to deal with a less credulous and less docile laity. Print was also a powerful tool for political and religious propaganda. Kings could now indoctrinate people as never before, and clergymen found themselves able to mass-produce both indulgences and pamphlets. (See "The West & The World: The Invention of Printing in China and Europe," on page 260.)

public had been created, thanks to the enormous expansion of schools and universities during the late Middle Ages.

The invention of a cheap way to manufacture paper also helped make books economical as well as broaden their content. Manuscript books had been inscribed on vellum, a cumbersome and expensive medium (170 calfskins or 300 sheepskins were required to make a single vellum Bible). Single-sheet woodcuts had long been printed. The process involved carving words and pictures on a block of wood, inking it, and then stamping out as many copies as possible before the wood deteriorated. The end product was much like a cheap modern poster.

In response to the demand for books that the expansion of lay education and literacy created, Johann Gutenberg (d. 1468) invented printing with movable type in the mid-fifteenth century in the German city of Mainz, the center of printing for the whole

The printing press made possible the diffusion of Renaissance learning, but no book stimulated thought more at this time than did the Bible. With Gutenberg's publication of a printed Bible in 1454, scholars gained access to a dependable, standardized text, so Scripture could be discussed and debated as never before. Reproduced by permission of The Huntington Library, San Marino, California

Erasmus

The far-reaching influence of Desiderius Erasmus (1466?–1536), the most famous northern humanist, illustrates the impact of the printing press. Through his printed works, Erasmus gained fame both as an educational and as a religious reformer. A lifelong Catholic, Erasmus, through his life and work, made clear that many loyal Catholics wanted major reforms in the church long before the Reformation made them a reality.

When patronage was scarce (authors received no royalties and had to rely on private patrons for their livelihood), Erasmus earned his living by tutoring well-to-do youths. He prepared short Latin dialogues for his students, intended to teach them how to speak and live well, inculcating good manners and language by internalizing what they read.

These dialogues were entitled *Colloquies*. In consecutive editions, they grew in number and length, including anticlerical dialogues and satires on religious dogmatism and superstition. Erasmus also collected ancient and contemporary proverbs, which appeared under the title *Adages*. Beginning with 800 examples, the final edition included more than 5,000. Among the locutions the *Adages* popularized are such common expressions as "Leave no stone unturned" and "Where there is smoke, there is fire."

Erasmus aspired to unite classical ideals of humanity and civic virtue with the Christian ideals of love and piety. He believed disciplined study of the classics and the Bible, if begun early enough, was the best way to reform individuals and society. He summarized his own beliefs with the phrase *philosophia Christi*, a simple, ethical piety in imitation of Christ. He set this ideal in stark contrast to what he believed to be the dogmatic, ceremonial, and bullying religious practices of the later Middle Ages. What most offended him about the Scholastics, both the old authorities of the Middle Ages and the new Protestant ones, was their letting dogma and argument overshadow Christian piety and practice.

Erasmus was a true idealist, who expected more from people than the age's theologians believed them capable of doing. To promote what he deemed to be the essence of Christianity, he made ancient Christian sources available in their original versions, believing that if people would only imbibe the pure sources of the faith, they would recover the moral and religious health the New Testament promises. To this end, Erasmus edited the works of the Church Fathers and produced a Greek edition of the New Testament (1516), later adding a new Latin translation of the latter (1519). Martin Luther used both of those works when he translated the New Testament into German in 1522.

These various enterprises did not please the church authorities. They remained unhappy with Erasmus's "improvements" on the Vulgate, Christendom's Bible for over a thousand years, and his popular anticlerical writings. At one point in the mid-sixteenth century, all of Erasmus's works were on the church's *Index of Forbidden Books*. Luther also condemned Erasmus for his views on the freedom of human will. Still, Erasmus's works put sturdy tools of reform in the hands of both Protestant and Catholic reformers. Already in the 1520s, there was a popular saying: "Erasmus laid the egg that Luther hatched."

Humanism and Reform

In Germany, England, France, and Spain, humanism stirred both educational and religious reform.

Germany Rudolf Agricola (1443–1485), the "father of German humanism," spent ten years in Italy and introduced Italian learning to Germany when he returned. Conrad Celtis (d. 1508), the first German poet laureate, and Ulrich von Hutten (1488–1523), a fiery knight, gave German humanism a nationalist coloring hostile to non-German cultures, particularly Roman culture. Von Hutten especially illustrates the union of humanism, German nationalism, and Luther's religious reform. A poet who admired Erasmus, he attacked indulgences and published an edition of Valla's exposé of the *Donation of Constantine*. He died in 1523, the victim of a hopeless knights' revolt against the princes.

The controversy that brought von Hutten onto the historical stage and unified reform-minded German humanists was the Reuchlin affair. Johann Reuchlin (1455–1522) was Europe's foremost Christian authority on Hebrew and Jewish learning. He wrote the first reliable Hebrew grammar by a Christian scholar and was attracted to Jewish mysticism. Around 1506, supported by the Dominican order in Cologne, a Christian who had converted from Judaism began a movement to suppress Jewish writings. When this man, whose name was Pfefferkorn, attacked Reuchlin, many German humanists, in the name of academic freedom and good scholarship—not for any pro-Jewish sentiment—rushed to Reuchlin's defense. The controversy lasted for years and produced one of the great satires of the period, the *Letters of Obscure Men* (1515), a merciless satire of monks and Scholastics to which von Hutten contributed. When Martin Luther came under attack in 1517 for his famous ninety-five theses against indulgences, many German humanists saw a repetition of the Scholastic attack on Reuchlin and rushed to his side.

England Italian learning came to England by way of English scholars and merchants and visiting Italian prelates. Lectures by William Grocyn (d. 1519) and Thomas Linacre (d. 1524) at Oxford and those of Erasmus at Cambridge marked the scholarly maturation of English humanism. John Colet (1467–1519), dean of Saint Paul's Cathedral, patronized humanist studies for the young and promoted religious reform.

Document

ERASMUS DESCRIBES THE PHILOSOPHY OF CHRIST

Although Erasmus called his ideal of how people should live the "philosophy of Christ," he found it taught by classical authors as well. In this selection he comments on its main features, with obvious polemic against the philosophy of the Scholastics.

How does the "philosophy of Christ" differ from eloquent debate? What kind of philosophy is Erasmus preaching? If life is more than debate, inspiration more than erudition, is the religious transformation of life beyond intellectual comprehension? What is the good life beyond the present one according to Erasmus? Is he speaking mumbo-jumbo?

This kind of philosophy [the philosophy of Christ] is located more truly in the disposition of the mind than in syllogisms. Here life means more than debate, inspiration is preferable to erudition, transformation [of life] a more important matter than intellectual comprehension. Only a very few can be learned, but all can be Christian, all can be devout, and—I shall boldly add—all can be theologians. Indeed, this philosophy easily penetrates into the minds of all; it is an action in special accord with human nature. What else is the philosophy of Christ, which he himself calls a rebirth, than the restoration of human nature . . . ? Although no one has taught this more perfectly . . . than Christ, nevertheless one may find in the books of the pagans very much which does not agree with it. There was never so coarse a school of philosophy that taught that money rendered a man happy. Nor has there ever been one so shameless that fixed the chief good in vulgar honors and pleasures. The Stoics understood that no one was wise unless he was good. . . . According to Plato, Socrates teaches . . . that a wrong must not be repaid with a wrong, and also that since the soul is immortal, those should not be lamented who depart this life for a happier one with the assurance of having led an upright life. . . . And Aristotle has written in the *Politics* that nothing can be a delight to us . . . except virtue alone. . . . If there are things that belong particularly to Christianity in these ancient writers, let us follow them.

From *The Paraclesis in Christian Humanism and the Reformation: Desiderius Erasmus*, ed. and trans. by John C. Olin (New York: Harper, 1965), pp. 100–101.

Thomas More (1478–1535), a close friend of Erasmus, is the best-known English humanist. His *Utopia* (1516), a conservative criticism of contemporary society, rivals the plays of Shakespeare as the most read sixteenth-century English work. *Utopia* depicted an imaginary society based on reason and tolerance that overcame social and political injustice by holding all property and goods in common and requiring everyone to earn their bread by their own work.

Read the Document
"Utopia (1516)" on
MyHistoryLab.com

More became one of Henry VIII's most trusted diplomats. His repudiation of the Act of Supremacy (1534), which made the king of England head of the English church in place of the pope (see Chapter 11), and his refusal to recognize the king's marriage to Anne Boleyn, however, led to his execution in July 1535. Although More remained Catholic, humanism in England, as also in Germany, helped prepare the way for the English Reformation.

France The French invasions of Italy made it possible for Italian learning to penetrate France, stirring both educational and religious reform. Guillaume Budé (1468–1540), an accomplished Greek scholar, and Jacques Lefèvre d'Etaples (1454–1536), a biblical authority, were the leaders of French humanism. Lefèvre's scholarly works exemplified the new critical scholarship and influenced Martin Luther. Guillaume Briçonnet (1470–1533), the bishop of Meaux, and Marguerite d'Angoulême (1492–1549), sister of King Francis I, the future queen of Navarre, and a successful spiritual writer in her own right, cultivated a generation of young reform-minded humanists. The future Protestant reformer John Calvin was a product of this native reform circle.

Spain Whereas in England, France, and Germany humanism prepared the way for Protestant reforms, in Spain it entered the service of the Catholic Church. Here the key figure was Francisco Jiménez de Cisneros

(1437–1517), a confessor to Queen Isabella and, after 1508, the "Grand Inquisitor"—a position that allowed him to enforce the strictest religious orthodoxy. Jiménez founded the University of Alcalá near Madrid in 1509, printed a Greek edition of the New Testament, and translated many religious tracts designed to reform clerical life and better direct lay piety. His great achievement, taking fifteen years to complete, was the *Complutensian Polyglot Bible*, a six-volume work that placed the Hebrew, Greek, and Latin versions of the Bible in parallel columns. Such scholarly projects and internal church reforms joined with the repressive measures of Ferdinand and Isabella to keep Spain strictly Catholic throughout the Age of Reformation.

▼ Voyages of Discovery and the New Empires in the West and East

The discovery of the Americas dramatically expanded the horizons of Europeans, both geographically and intellectually. Knowledge of the New World's inhabitants and the exploitation of its mineral and human wealth set new cultural and economic forces in motion throughout Western Europe.

Beginning with the voyages of the Portuguese and Spanish in the fifteenth century, commercial supremacy progressively shifted from the Mediterranean and Baltic seas to the Atlantic seaboard, setting the stage for global expansion. (See Map 10–2.)

The Portuguese Chart the Course

Seventy-seven years before Columbus, who sailed under the flag of Spain, set foot in the Americas, Prince Henry "the Navigator" (1394–1460), brother of the king of Portugal, captured the North African Muslim city of Ceuta. His motives were mercenary and religious, both a quest for gold and spices and the pious work of saving the souls of Muslims and pagans who had no knowledge of Christ. Thus began the Portuguese exploration of the African coast, first in search of gold and slaves, and then by century's end, of a sea route around Africa to Asia's spice markets. Pepper and cloves topped the list of spices, as they both preserved and enhanced the dull diet of most Europeans. Initially the catch of raiders, African slaves were soon taken by Portuguese traders in direct commerce with tribal chiefs, who readily swapped captives for horses, grain, and finished goods (cloth and brassware). Over the second half of the fifteenth century, Portuguese ships delivered 150,000 slaves to Europe.

Before there was a sea route to the East, Europeans could only get spices through the Venetians, who bought or bartered them from Muslim merchants in Egypt and the Ottoman Empire. The Portuguese resolved to beat this powerful Venetian–Muslim monopoly by sailing directly to the source. Overland routes to India and China had long existed, but their transit had become too difficult and unprofitable by the fifteenth century. The route by sea posed a different obstacle and risk: fear of the unknown, making the first voyages of exploration slow and tentative. Venturing down the African coast, the Portuguese ships were turned out into the deep ocean by every protruding cape, and the farther out they sailed to round them, the greater the sailors' fear that the winds would not return them to land. Each cape rounded became a victory and a lesson, giving the crews the skills they needed to cross the oceans to the Americas and East Asia.

In addition to spice markets, the voyagers also gained new allies against Western Europe's archenemies, the Muslims. In 1455, a self-interested pope granted the Portuguese explorers all the spoils of war—land, goods, and slaves—from the coast of Guinea in West Africa to the Indies in East Asia. The church expected exploration to lead to mass conversions, a Christian coup as well as a mercantile advantage. The explorers also kept an eye out for a legendary Eastern Christian ruler known as Prester John.

Bartholomew Dias (ca. 1450–1500) pioneered the eastern Portuguese Empire after safely rounding the Cape of Good Hope at the tip of Africa in 1487. A decade later, in 1498, Vasco da Gama (1469–1525) stood on the shores of India. When he returned to Portugal, he carried a cargo of spices worth sixty times the cost of the voyage. Later, the Portuguese established colonies in Goa and Calcutta on the coast of India, whence they challenged the Arabs and the Venetians for control of the spice trade.

The Portuguese had concentrated their explorations on the Indian Ocean. The Spanish turned west, believing they could find a shorter route to the East Indies by sailing across the Atlantic. Instead, Christopher Columbus (1451–1506) discovered the Americas.

The Spanish Voyages of Columbus

Thirty-three days after departing the Canary Islands, on October 12, 1492, Columbus landed in San Salvador (Watlings Island) in the eastern Bahamas. Thinking he was in the East Indies, he mistook his first landfall as an outer island of Japan. The error was understandable given the information he relied on, namely, Marco Polo's thirteenth-century account of his years in China and Martin Behaim's spherical map of the presumed world. That map showed only ocean and Cipangu (Japan) between the west coast of Europe and the east coast of Asia. (See Martin Behaim's map, page 314.) Not until his third voyage to the Caribbean in 1498 did Columbus realize that Cuba was not Japan and South America was not China.

Naked, friendly natives met Columbus and his crew on the beaches of the New World. They were Taino Indians, who spoke a variant of a language known as Arawak.

VOYAGES OF DISCOVERY

▨	Portuguese Claims
▨	Spanish Claims
– – –	Line of Demarcation, 1494

Map 10–2 **European Voyages of Discovery and the Colonial Claims of Spain and Portugal in the Fifteenth and Sixteenth Centuries** The map dramatizes Europe's global expansion in the fifteenth and sixteenth centuries.

Die beiden Erdkugeln nach dem Globus Behaim's.
(Vergl. die Karte Toscanelli's S. 39.)

What Columbus knew of the world in 1492 was contained in a map by Nuremberg geographer Martin Behaim, creator of the first spherical globe of the earth. Departing the Canary Islands, Columbus expected his first major landfall to be Japan. When he landed at San Salvador, he thought he was on the outer island of Japan. Thus, when he arrived in Cuba, he thought he was in Japan.   © Mary Evans Picture Library/Alamy

Believing the island on which he landed to be the East Indies, Columbus called these people Indians, a name that stuck with Europeans even after they realized he had actually discovered a new continent. The natives' generosity amazed Columbus, as they freely gave his men all the corn, yams, and sexual favors they desired. "They never say no," Columbus marveled. He also observed how easily the Spanish could enslave them.

On the heels of Columbus, Amerigo Vespucci (1451–1512), after whom America is named, and Ferdinand Magellan (1480–1521) explored the coastline of South America. Their travels proved that the new lands Columbus had discovered were an entirely unknown continent that opened on the still greater Pacific Ocean. Magellan, who was continuing the search for a westward route to the Indies, made it all the way around South America and across the Pacific to the Philippines, where he was killed in a skirmish with the inhabitants. The remnants of his squadron eventually sailed on to Spain, making them the first sailors to circumnavigate the globe.

Intended and Unintended Consequences Columbus's first voyage marked the beginning of more than three centuries of a vast Spanish empire in the Americas. What began as voyages of discovery became expeditions of conquest, not unlike the warfare Christian Aragon and Castile waged against Islamic Moors. Those wars had just ended in 1492, and their conclusion imbued the early Spanish explorers with a zeal for conquering and converting non-Christian peoples.

Much to the benefit of Spain, the voyages of discovery created Europe's largest and longest surviving trading bloc and spurred other European countries to undertake their own colonial ventures. The wealth extracted from its American possessions financed Spain's commanding role in the religious and political wars of the sixteenth and seventeenth centuries, while fueling a Europe-wide economic expansion.

European expansion also had a profound biological impact. Europeans introduced numerous new species of fruits, vegetables, and animals into the Americas and brought American species back to Europe. European expansion also spread European diseases. Vast numbers of Native Americans died from measles and smallpox epidemics, while Europeans died from a virulent form of syphilis that may have originated in the Americas.

For the Native Americans, the voyages of discovery were the beginning of a long history of conquest, disease, and slave labor they could neither evade nor survive. In both South and North America, Spanish rule left a lasting imprint of Roman Catholicism, economic dependency, and hierarchical social structure, all still visible today. (See Chapter 18.)

The Spanish Empire in the New World

When the first Spanish explorers arrived, the Aztec Empire dominated Mesoamerica, which stretches from Central Mexico to Guatemala, and the Inca Empire dominated Andean South America. Both were rich, and their conquest promised the Spanish the possibility of acquiring large quantities of gold.

The Aztecs in Mexico The forebears of the Aztecs had arrived in the Valley of Mexico early in the twelfth century, where they lived as a subservient people. In 1428, however, they began a period of imperial expansion. By the time of Spanish conquest, the Aztecs ruled almost all of central Mexico from their capital Tenochtitlán (modern-day Mexico City). The Aztecs demanded heavy tribute in goods and labor from their subjects and, believing the gods must literally be fed with human blood to guarantee sunshine and fertility, they also took thousands of captives each year for human sacrifice. These policies bred resentment and fear among the subject peoples.

In 1519, Hernán Cortés (1485–1547) landed in Mexico with about five hundred men and a few horses. He opened communication with Moctezuma II (1466–1520), the Aztec emperor. Moctezuma may initially have believed Cortés to be the god Quetzalcoatl, who, according to legend, had been driven away centuries earlier but had promised to return. Whatever the reason, Moctezuma hesitated to confront Cortés, attempting at first to appease him with gold, which only whetted Spanish appetites. Cortés forged alliances with the Aztecs' subject peoples, most importantly, with Tlaxcala, an independent state and traditional enemy of the Aztecs. His forces then marched on Tenochtitlán, where Moctezuma welcomed him. Cortés soon seized Moctezuma, who died in unexplained circumstances. The Aztecs' wary acceptance of the Spaniards turned to open hostility. The Spaniards were driven from Tenochtitlán and were nearly wiped out, but they returned and laid siege to the city. The Aztecs, under their last ruler, Cuauhtemoc (ca. 1495–1525), resisted fiercely but were finally defeated in 1521. Cortés razed Tenochtitlán, building his own capital over its ruins, and proclaimed the Aztec Empire to be New Spain.

The Incas in Peru The second great Native American civilization the Spanish conquered was that of the Incas in the highlands of Peru. Like the Aztecs, the Incas also began to expand rapidly in the fifteenth century and, by the time of the Spanish conquest, controlled an enormous empire. Unlike the Aztecs, who extracted tribute from their subject peoples, the Incas compelled their subjects to work for the state on a regular basis.

In 1532, largely inspired by Cortés's example in Mexico, Francisco Pizarro (c. 1478–1541) landed on the western coast of South America with about two hundred men to take on the Inca Empire. Pizarro lured Atahualpa (ca. 1500–1533), the Inca ruler, into a conference and then seized him, killing hundreds of Atahualpa's followers in the process. The imprisoned Atahualpa tried to ransom himself with a hoard of gold, but instead of releasing him, Pizarro executed him in 1533. The Spaniards then captured Cuzco, the Inca capital, but Inca resistance did not end until the 1570s.

The conquests of Mexico and Peru are among the most dramatic and brutal events in modern history. Small military forces armed with advanced weapons subdued, in a remarkably brief time, two powerful peoples. The spread of European diseases, especially smallpox, among the Native Americans also aided the conquest. But beyond the drama and bloodshed, these conquests, as well as those of other Native American peoples, marked a fundamental turning point. Whole civilizations with long histories and enormous social, architectural, and technological achievements were destroyed. Native American cultures endured, accommodating themselves to European dominance, but there was never any doubt about which culture had the upper hand. In that sense, the Spanish conquests of the early sixteenth century marked the beginning of the transformation of South America into Latin America.

Armored Spanish soldiers, under the command of Pedro de Alvarado (d. 1541) and bearing crossbows, engage unprotected and crudely armed Aztecs, who are nonetheless portrayed as larger than life by Spanish artist Diego Duran (sixteenth century). Codex Duran: Pedro de Alvarado (c. 1485–1541), companion-at-arms of Hernando Cortés (1845–1547) besieged by Aztec warriors (vellum) by Diego Duran (16th century), Codex Duran, Historia De Las Indias (16th century). Biblioteca Nacional, Madrid, Spain. The Bridgeman Art Library International Ltd.

The Church in Spanish America

Roman Catholic priests had accompanied the earliest explorers and the conquerors of the Native Americans. Steeped with the social and religious ideals of Christian humanism, these first clergy members believed they could foster Erasmus's concept of the "philosophy of Christ" in the New World. They were filled with zeal not only to convert the inhabitants to Christianity, but also to bring to them European learning and civilization.

Tension, however, existed between the early Spanish conquerors and the mendicant friars who sought to minister to the Native Americans. Without conquest, the church could not convert the Native Americans, but the priests often deplored the harsh conditions imposed on the native peoples. By far the most effective and outspoken clerical critic of the Spanish conquerors was Bartolomé de Las Casas (1474–1566), a Dominican. He contended that conquest was not necessary for conversion. One result of his campaign was new royal regulations to protect the Indians after 1550.

Another result of Las Casas's criticism was the emergence of the "Black Legend," according to which all Spanish treatment of the Native Americans was unprincipled and inhumane. Those who created this view of Spanish behavior drew heavily on Las Casas's writings. Although substantially true, the "Black Legend" exaggerated the case against Spain. Certainly the rulers of the native empires—as the Aztec demands for sacrificial victims attest—had often themselves been exceedingly cruel to their subjects.

By the end of the sixteenth century, the church in Spanish America had become largely an institution upholding the colonial status quo. Although individual priests defended the communal rights of Indian peoples, the colonial church prospered as the Spanish elite prospered by exploiting the resources and peoples of the New World. The church became a great landowner through crown grants and bequests from Catholics who died in the New World. The monasteries took on an economic as well as a spiritual life of their own. Whatever its concern for the spiritual welfare of the Native Americans, the church remained one of the indications that Spanish America was a conquered world. Those who spoke for the church did not challenge Spanish domination or any but the most extreme modes of Spanish economic exploitation. By the end of the colonial era in the late eighteenth century, the Roman Catholic Church had become one of the most conservative forces in Latin America.

The Economy of Exploitation

From the beginning, both the Native Americans and their lands were drawn into the Atlantic economy and the world of competitive European commercialism. For the Indians of Latin America and, somewhat later, the black peoples of Africa, that drive for gain meant forced labor.

The colonial economy of Latin America had three major components: mining, agriculture, and shipping. Each involved labor, servitude, and the intertwining of the New World economy with that of Spain.

Mining

The early **conquistadores**, or "conquerors," were primarily interested in gold, but by the mid-sixteenth century, silver mining provided the chief source of metallic wealth. The great mining centers were Potosí in Peru and somewhat smaller sites in northern Mexico. The Spanish crown received one-fifth (the *quinto*) of all mining revenues. For this reason, the crown maintained a monopoly over the production and sale of mercury, required in the silver-smelting process. Exploring for silver continued throughout the colonial era. Its production by forced labor for the benefit of Spaniards and the

◉ Watch the Video
"Video Lectures: The Columbian Exchange" on
MyHistoryLab.com

Spanish crown epitomized the wholly extractive economy that stood at the foundation of colonial life.

Agriculture   The major rural and agricultural institution of the Spanish colonies was the **hacienda**, a large landed estate owned by persons originally born in Spain (*peninsulares*) or persons of Spanish descent born in America (*creoles*). Laborers on the *hacienda* were usually subject in some legal way to the owner and were rarely free to move from working for one landowner to another.

The *hacienda* economy produced two major products: foodstuffs for mining areas and urban centers and leather goods used in mining machinery. Both farming and ranching were subordinate to the mining economy.

In the West Indies, the basic agricultural unit was the plantation. In Cuba, Hispaniola, Puerto Rico, and other islands, the labor of black slaves from Africa produced sugar to supply an almost insatiable demand for the product in Europe.

A final major area of economic activity in the Spanish colonies was urban service occupations, including government offices, the legal profession, and shipping. Those who worked in these occupations were either *peninsulares* or *creoles*, with the former dominating more often than not.

Labor Servitude   All of this extractive and exploitive economic activity required labor, and the Spanish in the New World decided early that the native population would supply it. A series of social devices was used to draw them into the new economic life the Spanish imposed.

The first of these was the **encomienda**, a formal grant of the right to the labor of a specific number of Indians, usually a few hundred, but sometimes thousands, for a particular period of time. The *encomienda* was in decline by the mid-sixteenth century because the Spanish monarchs feared its holders might become too powerful. There were also humanitarian objections to this particular kind of exploitation of the Indians.

The passing of the *encomienda* led to a new arrangement of labor servitude: the *repartimiento*. This device required adult male Indians to devote a certain number of days of labor annually to Spanish economic enterprises. In the mines of Peru, the *repartimiento* was known as the *mita*, the Inca term for their labor tax. *Repartimiento* service was often harsh, and some Indians did not survive their stint. The limitation on labor time led some Spanish managers to abuse their workers on the assumption that fresh workers would soon replace them.

The eventual shortage of workers and the crown's pressure against extreme versions of forced labor led to the use of free labor. The freedom, however, was more in appearance than reality. Free Indian laborers were required to purchase goods from the landowner or mine owner, to whom they became forever indebted. This form of exploitation, known as *debt peonage*, continued in Latin America long after the nineteenth-century wars of liberation.

Black slavery was the final mode of forced or subservient labor in the New World. Both the Spanish and the Portuguese had earlier used African slaves in Europe. The sugar plantations of the West Indies and Brazil now became the major center of black slavery.

The conquest, the forced labor of the economy of exploitation, and the introduction of European diseases had devastating demographic consequences for the Native Americans. For centuries, Europeans had lived in a far more complex human and animal environment than Native Americans did. They had frequent contact with different ethnic and racial groups and with a variety of domestic animals. Such interaction helped them develop strong immune systems that enabled them to survive measles, smallpox, and typhoid. Native Americans, by contrast, grew up in a simpler and more sterile environment and were defenseless against these diseases. Within a generation, the native population of New Spain (Mexico) was reduced to an estimated 8 percent of its numbers, from 25 million to 2 million.

The Impact on Europe

Among contemporary European intellectuals, Columbus's discovery increased skepticism about the wisdom of the ancients. If traditional knowledge about the world had been so wrong geographically, how trustworthy was it on other matters? For many, Columbus's discovery demonstrated the folly of relying on any fixed body of presumed authoritative knowledge. Both in Europe and in the New World, there were those who condemned the explorers' treatment of American natives, as more was learned about their cruelty. Three centuries later, however, on the third centenary of Columbus's discovery (1792), the great thinkers of the age lionized Columbus for having opened up new possibilities for civilization and morality. By establishing new commercial contacts among different peoples of the world, Columbus was said to have made cooperation, civility, and peace among them indispensable. Enlightenment thinkers drew parallels between the discovery of America and the invention of the printing press—both portrayed as world historical events opening new eras in communication and globalization, an early multicultural experiment.[4]

On the material side, the influx of spices and precious metals into Europe from the new Portuguese and Spanish Empires was a mixed blessing. It contributed to a steady rise in prices during the sixteenth century that created an inflation rate estimated at 2 percent a year. The new supply of bullion from the Americas joined with enlarged European production to increase greatly the amount of coinage in circulation, and this increase, in turn, fed inflation. Fortunately, the increase in prices was by and large spread over a long period and was not sudden. Prices doubled in Spain by 1550, quadrupled by 1600. In Luther's Wittenberg in Germany, the cost of basic food and clothing increased almost 100 percent between 1519 and 1540. Generally, wages and rents remained well behind the rise in prices.

The new wealth enabled governments and private entrepreneurs to sponsor basic research and expansion in the printing, shipping, mining, textile, and weapons industries. There is also evidence of large-scale government planning in such ventures as the French silk industry and the Habsburg-Fugger development of mines in Austria and Hungary.

In the thirteenth and fourteenth centuries, capitalist institutions and practices had already begun to develop in the rich Italian cities (for example, the Florentine banking houses of Bardi and Peruzzi). Those who owned the means of production, either privately or corporately, were clearly distinguished from the workers who operated them. Wherever possible, entrepreneurs created monopolies in basic goods. High interest was charged on loans—actual, if not legal, usury. The "capitalist" virtues of thrift, industry, and orderly planning were everywhere in evidence—all intended to permit the free and efficient accumulation of wealth.

The late fifteenth and the sixteenth centuries saw the maturation of this type of capitalism together with its attendant social problems. The Medicis of Florence grew rich as bankers of the pope, as did the Fuggers of Augsburg, who bankrolled Habsburg rulers. The Fuggers lent Charles I of Spain more than 500,000 florins to buy his election as the Holy Roman Emperor in 1519 and boasted they had created the emperor. The new wealth and industrial expansion also raised the expectations of the poor and the ambitious and heightened the reactionary tendencies of the wealthy. This effect, in turn, aggravated the traditional social divisions between the clergy and the laity, the urban patriciate and the guilds, and the landed nobility and the agrarian peasantry.

These divisions indirectly prepared the way for the Reformation as well, by making many people critical of traditional institutions and open to new ideas—especially those that seemed to promise greater freedom and a chance at a better life.

In Perspective

As it recovered from national wars during the late Middle Ages, Europe saw the establishment of permanent centralized states and regional governments. The foundations of modern France, Spain, England, Germany, and Italy were laid at this time. As rulers imposed their will

---

[4]Cf. Anthony Pagden, "The Impact of the New World on the Old: The History of an Idea," *Renaissance and Modern Studies* 30 (1986): pp. 1–11.

on regions outside their immediate domains, the "one" progressively took control of the "many," and previously divided lands came together as nations.

Thanks to the work of Byzantine and Islamic scholars, ancient Greek science and scholarship found its way into the West in these centuries. Europeans had been separated from their classical cultural heritage for almost eight centuries. No other world civilization had experienced such a disjunction from its cultural past. The discovery of classical civilization occasioned a rebirth of intellectual and artistic activity in both southern and northern Europe. One result was the splendor of the Italian Renaissance, whose scholarship, painting, and sculpture remain among Western Europe's most impressive achievements.

Ancient learning was not the only discovery of the era. New political unity spurred both royal greed and national ambition. By the late fifteenth century, Europeans were in a position to venture far away to the shores of Africa, the southern and eastern coasts of Asia, and the New World of the Americas. European discovery was not the only outcome of these voyages: The exploitation of the peoples and lands of the New World revealed a dark side of Western civilization. Some penalties were paid even then. The influx of New World gold and silver created new human and economic problems on the European mainland. Some Europeans even began to question their civilization's traditional values.

KEY TERMS

chiaroscuro (p. 296)
condottieri (p. 291)
conquistadores (p. 316)

encomienda (p. 316)
Golden Bull (p. 308)
hacienda (p. 316)

mannerism (p. 300)
Platonism (p. 294)
studia humanitatis (p. 292)

REVIEW QUESTIONS

1. What was Jacob Burckhardt's interpretation of the Renaissance? What criticisms have been leveled against it? What did the term mean in the context of fifteenth- and sixteenth-century Italy?
2. How would you define Renaissance humanism? In what ways was the Renaissance a break with the Middle Ages, and in what ways did it owe its existence to medieval civilization?
3. Who were some of the famous literary and artistic figures of the Italian Renaissance? What did they have in common that might be described as "the spirit of the Renaissance"?
4. Why did the French invade Italy in 1494? How did this event trigger Italy's political decline? How did

the actions of Pope Julius II and the ideas of Niccolò Machiavelli signify a new era in Italian civilization?
5. A common assumption is that creative work proceeds best in periods of calm and peace. Given the combination of political instability and cultural productivity in Renaissance Italy, do you think this assumption is valid?
6. How did the Renaissance in the north differ from the Italian Renaissance? In what ways was Erasmus the embodiment of the northern Renaissance?
7. What factors led to the voyages of discovery? Why were the Portuguese interested in finding a route to the East? Why did Columbus sail west across the Atlantic in 1492?

SUGGESTED READINGS

D. Abulafia, *The Discovery of Mankind: Atlantic Encounters in the Age of Columbus* (2008). The latest telling of the European invasion of the New World.

L. B. Alberti, *The Family in Renaissance Florence*, trans. by R. N. Watkins (1962). A contemporary humanist, who never married, explains how a family should behave.

K. Atchity, ed., *The Renaissance Reader* (1996). The Renaissance in its own words.

H. Baron, *The Crisis of the Early Italian Renaissance*, Vols. 1 and 2 (1966). A major work on the civic dimension of Italian humanism.

G. A. Brucker, *Giovanni and Lusanna: Love and Marriage in Renaissance Florence* (1986). Love in the Renaissance shown to be more Bergman than Fellini.

J. Burckhardt, *The Civilization of the Renaissance in Italy* (1958). Modern edition of an old nineteenth-century classic that still has as many defenders as detractors.

R. E. Conrad, *Children of God's Fire: A Documentary History of Black Slavery in Brazil* (1983). Not for the squeamish.

L. Hanke, *Bartholomé de Las Casas: An Interpretation of His Life and Writings* (1951). Biography of the great Dominican critic of Spanish exploitation of Native Americans.

J. Hankins, *Plato in the Renaissance* (1992). A magisterial study of how Plato was read and interpreted by Renaissance scholars.

D. Herlihy and C. Klapisch-Zuber, *Tuscans and Their Families* (1985). Important work based on unique demographic data that give the reader a new appreciation of quantitative history.

J. C. Hutchison, *Albrecht Dürer: A Biography* (1990).

L. Martines, *Power and Imagination: City States in Renaissance Italy* (1980). Stimulating account of cultural and political history.

S. E. Morrison, *Admiral of the Ocean Sea: A Life of Christopher Columbus* (1946). Still the best Columbus read.

E. Panofsky, *Meaning in the Visual Arts* (1955). Eloquent treatment of Renaissance art.

J. H. Parry, *The Age of Reconnaissance* (1964). A comprehensive account of exploration in the years 1450 to 1650.

I. A. Richter, ed., *The Notebooks of Leonardo da Vinci* (1985). The master in his own words.

A. Wheatcroft, *The Habsburgs* (1995). The dynasty that ruled the center of late medieval and early modern Europe.

C. C. Willard, *Christine de Pizan* (1984). Demonstration of what an educated woman could accomplish in the Renaissance.

MyHistoryLab™ MEDIA ASSIGNMENTS

Find these resources in the Media Assignments folder for Chapter 10 on **MyHistoryLab**.

QUESTIONS FOR ANALYSIS

1. What aspects of Humanism and the Renaissance are illustrated by these letters?

   Section: **The Renaissance in Italy (1375–1527)**

   Read the **Document** Petrarch, *Letter to Cicero* (14th c.), p. 292

2. How did the ideas of Platonism influence Botticelli's work?

   Section: **The Renaissance in Italy (1375–1527)**

   View the **Closer Look** *Primavera*, p. 294

3. How does this brief dialog illustrate some of the elements of Humanism, particularly those of Northern Europe?

   Section: **Italy's Political Decline: The French Invasions (1494–1527)**

   Read the **Document** Desiderius Erasmus, "Pope Julius Excluded from Heaven," 1513–1514, p. 304

4. How do the powers and rights of Bodin's sovereign differ from those of monarchs of the Middle Ages?

   Section: **Revival of Monarchy in Northern Europe**

   Read the **Document** Jean Bodin, *Six Books of the Commonwealth*, p. 306

5. What was the impact of the silver trade on world economies in the sixteenth century?

   Section: **Voyages of Discovery and the New Empires in the West and East**

   Watch the **Video** Video Lectures: The Columbian Exchange, p. 316

OTHER RESOURCES FROM THIS CHAPTER

The Renaissance in Italy (1375–1527)

Read the **Document** *Divine Comedy* (1321), p. 292

Watch the **Video** The Italian Renaissance, p. 296

View the **Closer Look** Leonardo Plots the Perfect Man, p. 297

Read the **Compare and Connect** Is the "Renaissance Man" a Myth?, p. 298

Read the **Document** Giorgio Vasari on the Life of Michelangelo, 1550, p. 300

Italy's Political Decline: The French Invasions (1494–1527)

Read the **Document** *The Prince* (1519) Machiavelli, p. 304

Revival of Monarchy in Northern Europe

View the **Map** Geographical Tour: Europe in 1500, p. 305

The Northern Renaissance

View the **Closer Look** Rogier Van Der Weyden, *Deposition*, p. 308

View the **Image** Gutenberg Bible, p. 309

Read the **Document** *Utopia* (1516), p. 311

Painted on the eve of the Reformation, Matthias Grunewald's (ca. 1480–1528) *Crucifixion* shows a Christ who takes all the sins of the world into his own body, as his mother, Mary Magdalene, and John the Baptist share the pain of his afflictions.   Musée Unterlinden, Colmar, France/The Art Archive/SuperStock

((•—[**Listen** to the **Chapter Audio** on **MyHistoryLab.com**

11

The Age of Reformation

LEARNING OBJECTIVES

What was the social and religious background of the Reformation?

Why did Martin Luther challenge the church?

Where did other reform movements develop and how were they different from Luther's?

What were the political ramifications of the Reformation?

How did royal dynastic concerns shape the Reformation in England?

What was the Counter-Reformation and how successful was it?

What was the social significance of the Reformation and how did it affect family life?

What was family life like in early modern Europe?

How was the transition from medieval to modern reflected in the works of the great literary figures of the era?

IN THE SECOND decade of the sixteenth century, a long-building, powerful religious movement began in Saxony in Germany and spread rapidly throughout northern Europe, deeply affecting society and politics, as well as the spiritual lives of men and women. Attacking what they believed to be burdensome superstitions that robbed people of both their money and their peace of mind, Protestant reformers led a broad revolt against the medieval church. In a short time, hundreds of thousands of people from all social classes set aside the beliefs of centuries and adopted a more simplified religious practice.

The Protestant Reformation also challenged aspects of the Renaissance, especially its tendency to glorify human nature and its loyalty to Rome. Protestants were more impressed by the human potential for evil than by the inclination to do good. They encouraged parents, teachers, and magistrates to be firm disciplinarians, but they also embraced much of the Renaissance, especially its educational reforms and the training of students in ancient history and languages. Like the Italian humanists, the Protestant reformers prized the tools that allowed them to go directly to original sources, both biblical and classical. It was especially the study of the Hebrew and Greek scriptures that enabled them to root their challenge to Rome in the authority of biblical antiquity.

▼ Society and Religion

The Protestant **Reformation** occurred at a time of sharp conflict between the emerging nation-states of Europe bent on conformity and centralization within their realms and the self-governing towns and villages long accustomed to running their own affairs. Since the late fourteenth century, the territorial ruler's law and custom had progressively overridden local law and custom almost everywhere. The towns remained keenly sensitive to the loss of traditional rights and freedoms. Many townspeople and village folk perceived in the Protestant revolt an ally in their struggle to remain politically free and independent.

Social and Political Conflict

The Reformation broke out first in the free imperial cities of Germany and Switzerland, and the basic tenets of Lutheran and Zwinglian Protestantism remained visible in subsequent Protestant movements. There were sixty-five free imperial cities, each a small kingdom unto itself. Most had Protestant movements but with mixed success and duration. Some quickly turned Protestant and remained so. Some were Protestant only for a short time. Still others developed mixed confessions. Frowning on sectarianism and aggressive proselytizing, they made it possible for Catholics and Protestants to live side by side with appropriate barriers between them.

A seeming life-and-death struggle with higher princely or royal authority was not the only conflict late medieval cities were experiencing. They also coped with deep social and political divisions. Certain groups favored the Reformation more than others. In many places, the guilds, whose members were socially rising and economically prospering, were in the forefront of the Reformation. The printers' guild is a prominent example. Its members were literate, sophisticated about the world, and belonged to a rapidly growing industry. They also had an economic stake in fanning religious conflict with Protestant propaganda. Guilds with a history of opposition to reigning governmental authority also stood out among early Protestant supporters, regardless of education level. Evidence also suggests that people who felt pushed around and bullied by either local or distant authority—a guild by an autocratic local government, or a city or region by a powerful prince or king—could perceive an ally in the Protestant movement.

Social and political experience also influenced religious change in town and countryside. A Protestant sermon or pamphlet praising religious freedom seemed directly relevant, for example, to the townspeople of German and Swiss cities who faced incorporation into the territory of a powerful local prince, who looked on them as his subjects rather than as free citizens. When Martin Luther and his followers wrote, preached, and sang about a priesthood of all believers, while ridiculing papal laws as arbitrary human inventions, they touched both political and religious nerves. This was also true in the villages and in the towns. Like city dwellers, the peasants on the land heard in Protestant sermons and read in Protestant pamphlets promises of political liberation, even a degree of social betterment. More so than the townspeople, the peasants found their traditional liberties—from fishing and hunting rights to representation in local diets—progressively being chipped away by the secular and ecclesiastical landlords of the age.

Popular Religious Movements and Criticism of the Church

The Protestant Reformation could not have occurred without the challenges to the medieval church during its "exile" in Avignon, the Great Schism, the Conciliar period, and the Renaissance papacy. For a great too many, the medieval church had ceased to provide a viable foundation for religious piety. Many intellectuals and laypeople felt a sense of spiritual crisis. At the Diet of Worms in 1521 (see page 325), the German nobility presented the emperor with a list of 102 "oppressive [church] burdens and abuses" said to be corrupting the care of German souls. Between the secular pretensions of the papacy and the dry teaching of Scholastic theologians, laity and clerics alike sought a more heartfelt religious piety.

A Closer ▶ LOOK

⌕ View the Closer Look on MyHistoryLab.com

A SAINT AT PEACE IN THE GRASP OF TEMPTATION

MARTIN SCHONGAUER (c. 1430–1491), the best engraver in the Upper Rhine, portrays the devil's temptation of St. Anthony in the wilderness as a robust physical attack by demons rather than the traditional melancholic introspection.

Unlike the saint, the demons look perplexed and disbelieving, as their every thrust fails to penetrate.

Although the demons are all over him, Anthony remains untouched. The artist's remarkably distinct lines keep saint and demons apart, reinforcing the saint's inner peace and serenity.

This rendering of faith as serenity amid the most brutal assault anticipates Martin Luther's great hymn of the Reformation: "A Mighty Fortress is Our God," in which it is said that "one little word" (i.e., belief in Christ) slays the devil and his minions.

Martin Schongauer/National Gallery of Art, Washington, DC

What in this image might turn late medieval Christians to the Protestant gospel?

Is the caricature more humorous than fearful?

How effective was art in winning hearts and minds to the Reformation?

What is the role of faith here? Asked what the Christian should do if he finds himself face to face with the Devil and his entourage, Luther replied: "Spit in his Face!"

A variety of factors contributed to the growing lay criticism of the church. Urban laypeople were increasingly knowledgeable about the world around them and the rulers who controlled their lives. They had traveled widely—as soldiers, pilgrims, explorers, and traders. New postal systems and the printing press increased the information at their disposal. A new age of books and libraries raised literacy and heightened curiosity. Laypeople were free to shape the cultural and religious life of their communities.

View the Map
"Map Discovery: The Spread of Printing" on **MyHistoryLab.com**

From the Albigensians, Waldensians, Beguines, and Beghards in the thirteenth century to the Lollards and Hussites in the fifteenth, lay religious movements shared a common goal of religious simplicity in the imitation of Jesus. The laity were inspired by a simple religion of love and self-sacrifice like that of Jesus and the disciples. To that end, the laity sought a more egalitarian church—one that gave its members a voice.

Lay Control over Religious Life   On the eve of the Reformation, Rome's international network of church offices, which had unified Europe religiously during the Middle Ages, was falling apart in many areas. The collapse was hurried along by a growing sense of regional identity, an increasingly competent local secular administration, and a newly emerging nationalism. The long-entrenched *benefice* system of the medieval church had permitted ecclesiastical posts to be sold to the highest bidders and had often failed to enforce the requirement that priests and bishops had to live in their parishes and dioceses. Such a system threatened a vibrant, lay spiritual life. The substitutes hired by nonresident, clerical holders of *benefices* frequently lived elsewhere, many in Rome. They milked the revenues of their offices, performed their clerical chores mechanically, and had neither firsthand knowledge of, nor much sympathy for, local spiritual needs and problems. Rare was the late medieval German town that did not have complaints about the maladministration, concubinage, and financial greed of its clergy—especially the higher clergy (bishops, abbots, and prelates).

Communities loudly protested the financial and spiritual abuses of the medieval church long before Luther published his summary of economic grievances in a treatise titled *Address to the Christian Nobility of the German Nation* (1520). The sale of indulgences, in particular, had been repeatedly attacked before Luther came on the scene. On the eve of the Reformation, this practice had expanded to permit people to buy release from time in purgatory for both themselves and their deceased loved ones!

Rulers and magistrates had little objection to their sale as long as a portion of the income from the sales remained in the local coffers. Yet when an indulgence was offered primarily for the benefit of distant interests, as with the sale of indulgences to raise money for a new Saint Peter's basilica in Rome, resistance arose for strictly financial reasons: their sale drained away local revenues.

The sale of indulgences could not end until rulers found new ways to profit from religion and the laity discover more effective remedies for religious anxiety. City governments also acted to improve local religious life on the eve of the Reformation by endowing preacherships. These positions, supported by *benefices*, made possible the hiring of well-trained priests who provided regular preaching and pastoral care beyond the performance of the Mass. These preacherships often became platforms for Protestants.

Magistrates carefully restricted the growth of ecclesiastical properties and clerical privileges. During the Middle Ages, canon and civil law had recognized special clerical rights in both property and person. Because they were holy places of "sacral peace" and asylum, churches and monasteries were exempted from the taxes and laws that affected others. Church law also deemed it inappropriate for holy persons (clergy) to burden themselves with such "dirty jobs" as military service, compulsory labor, standing watch at city gates, and other ordinary civic obligations. Nor was it thought right that the laity should sit in judgment on those who were their shepherds and intermediaries with God. The clergy, accordingly, came to enjoy an immunity from the jurisdiction of civil courts.

Already on the eve of the Reformation, the medieval church passed measures to restrict these clerical privileges and to end their abuses. Governments also grew tired of church interference in what to them were strictly secular political spheres of competence and authority. Secular authorities accordingly began to scrutinize the church's acquisition of new properties, finding ways to get around its right of asylum when it interrupted the secular administration of justice, generally bringing the clergy under local tax codes.

▼ Martin Luther and the German Reformation to 1525

Unlike England and France, late medieval Germany lacked the political unity to enforce "national" reforms during the late Middle Ages. There were no lasting Statutes of Provisors and Praemunire, as in England, nor a Pragmatic Sanction of Bourges, as in France, limiting papal jurisdiction and taxation on a national scale. What happened on a unified national level in England and France occurred only locally and piecemeal within German territories and towns. As popular resentment of clerical immunities and ecclesiastical abuses spread among German cities and towns, an unorganized "national" opposition to Rome formed. German humanists had long given voice to such criticism, and by 1517 it was pervasive enough to provide a solid foundation for Luther's protest of indulgences and the theology that legitimated them.

The son of a successful Thüringian miner, Luther (1483–1546) was educated in Mansfeld, Magdeburg (where the Brothers of the Common Life had been his teachers), and Eisenach. Between 1501 and 1505, he attended the University of Erfurt, where the nominalist teachings of William of Ockham and Gabriel Biel (d. 1495) prevailed. (See Chapter 8.) After receiving his master-of-arts degree in 1505, Luther registered with the law faculty in accordance with his parents' wishes. He never began the study of law. To the disappointment of his family, he instead entered the Order of the Hermits of Saint Augustine in Erfurt on July 17, 1505. That decision had apparently been building for some time and was resolved by a lightning storm in which a terrified young Luther cried out to Saint Anne, the patron saint of travelers in distress, promising her that he would enter a monastery if he escaped death.

Ordained in 1507, Luther pursued a traditional course of study. In 1510, he journeyed to Rome on the business of his order, finding there justification for the many criticisms of the church he had heard in Germany. In 1511, he moved to the Augustinian monastery in Wittenberg, where he earned his doctorate in theology in 1512, thereafter to become a leader within the monastery, the new university, and the spiritual life of the city.

Luther was especially plagued by the disproportion between his own sense of sinfulness and the perfect righteousness God required for salvation, according to traditional church teaching. He came to despise the phrase "righteousness of God" because it demanded of him a perfection neither he nor any other human being could attain. His insight into the meaning of "justification by faith alone" (*sola fide*) was a gradual process between 1513 and 1518. The righteousness that God demands, he concluded, did not result from charitable acts and religious ceremonies but was given in full measure to any and all who believed in and trusted Jesus Christ as their perfect righteousness satisfying to God.

The medieval church had always taught that salvation was a joint venture, a combination of divine mercy and human good works, what God alone could do and what man was expected to do in return. Luther also taught that faith without charitable service to one's neighbor was dead. A Christian did not fulfill all of his due obligations by simply saying, "I believe," and thereafter doing as he pleased. The big issue was not whether good works should be done, but how those works should be regarded. It was unbiblical, Luther argued, to treat works as contributing to one's eternal salvation, something only an almighty God could bestow. He also believed that the Roman church's conditioning of salvation on good works left many Christians only counting their merits and demerits, unable to act selflessly and struggling to maintain inner peace of mind.

Good works were expected over a lifetime, Luther taught, but not because they earned salvation. The believer who is bound to Christ by faith already possesses God's perfect righteousness. It is this knowledge of faith that sets narcissistic souls free to serve their neighbors selflessly. Such service is ethical, not soteriological—a good work, not a saving work. Inspired by the security faith conveys, such works belong to one's neighbor, who needs help, not to God in heaven, who has everything. God is pleased when those who believe in him do good works, and he expects his people always to do them, but he does not take those works into account when he is merciful and bestows eternal life, which would make God a puppet of man.

The Attack on Indulgences

An **indulgence** was a remission of the temporal penalty imposed on penitents by priests as a "work of satisfaction" for their confessed mortal sins. According to medieval theology, after the priest absolved a penitent of guilt for sin, the penitent still remained under an eternal penalty, a punishment God justly imposed. Priestly absolution, however, was said to transform this eternal penalty into a temporal penalty, a manageable "work of satisfaction" a penitent might perform here and now by prayers, fasting, almsgiving, retreats, and/or pilgrimages. Penitents who defaulted on such prescribed works of satisfaction could expect to suffer for them in purgatory for an indefinite period of time before entering heaven.

Indulgences had originally been given to Crusaders who could not complete their penances because they had fallen in battle. By the late Middle Ages, indulgences had become an aid to laypeople anxious over future suffering in purgatory for neglected penances or unrepented sins. In 1343, a clever Pope Clement VI (r. 1342–1352) proclaimed the existence of a "treasury of merit," an infinite reservoir of good works in the church's possession that could be dispensed at the pope's discretion. On the basis of this alleged treasury, Rome sold "letters of indulgence," which made good on the works of satisfaction owed by penitents. In 1476, Pope Sixtus IV (r. 1471–1484) extended indulgences to the unrepented sins of all Christians in purgatory.

By Luther's time, indulgences were regularly dispensed for small cash payments, modest sums that were regarded as a good work of almsgiving. Indulgence preachers presented them to the laity as remitting not only their own future punishments, but also those of dead relatives presumed still to be suffering in purgatory.

In 1517, Pope Leo X (r. 1513–1521) revived a plenary Jubilee Indulgence that had first been issued by Pope Julius II (r. 1503–1513), the proceeds of which were to rebuild St. Peter's Basilica in Rome. Such an indulgence promised forgiveness of all outstanding unrepented sins upon the completion of certain acts. That indulgence was subsequently preached on the borders of Saxony in the territories of the future Archbishop Albrecht of Mainz, who was much in need of revenues because of the large debts he had incurred to gain a papal dispensation to hold three ecclesiastical appointments at the same time.

Johannes Tezelius Dominicaner Müuch/mit sei-
nen Römischen Ablaßtram/welchen er im Jahr Christi 1517. in Deutschen-
landen zu marckt gebracht/wie er in der Kirchen zu Pirn in seinem
Vaterland abgemahlet ist.

O ihr deutschen mercket mich recht/
Des heiligen Vaters Papstes Knecht/
Bin ich/vnd br ingeuch ist allein/
Zehn tausent vnd neun hundert care in/
Gnad vnd Ablaß von einer Sünd/
Vor euch/ewer Eltern/Weib vnd Kind/
Sol ein jeder gewehret sein
So viel ihr legt ins Kästelein/
So bald der Gülden im Becken klingt/
Im hun die Seel im Himel springt/

A contemporary caricature depicts John Tetzel, the famous indulgence preacher. The last lines of the jingle read, "As soon as gold in the basin rings, right then the soul to Heaven springs." It was Tetzel's preaching that spurred Luther to publish his ninety-five theses. akg-images

The selling of the indulgence became a joint venture by Albrecht, the Augsburg banking house of Fugger, and Pope Leo X, with half the proceeds going to the pope and half to Albrecht and his creditors. The famous indulgence preacher John Tetzel (d. 1519) was enlisted to preach the indulgence in Albrecht's territories. A seasoned professional, he knew how to stir ordinary people to action. Here is an example of his oratory:

Don't you hear the voices of your dead parents and other relatives crying out, "Have mercy on us, for we suffer great punishment and pain. From this you could release us with a few alms. . . . We have created you, fed you, cared for you, and left you our temporal goods. Why do you treat us so cruelly and leave us to suffer in the flames, when it takes only a little to save us?"[1]

View the **Image**
"Johann Tetzel Selling Indulgences" on
MyHistoryLab.com

When Luther posted his ninety-five theses against indulgences on the door of Castle Church in Wittenberg

[1]*Die Reformation in Augenzeugen berichten*, ed. by Helmar Junghaus (Düsseldorf: Karl Rauch Verlag, 1967), p. 44.

(October 31, 1517), he protested especially the impression Tetzel created that indulgences remitted sins and released unrepentant sinners from punishment in purgatory. Luther believed these claims went far beyond the traditional practice and seemed to make salvation something that could be bought and sold.

Read the **Document**
"Martin Luther, 'Ninety-Five Theses' (Holy Roman Empire), 1517" on
MyHistoryLab.com

Election of Charles V

The ninety-five theses were embraced by Nuremberg humanists, who translated and widely circulated them. This made Luther a central figure in an already organized national German cultural movement against foreign influence and competition, particularly on the part of the Italians. In October, he was summoned before the general of the Dominican order in Augsburg to answer for his criticism of the church. Yet as sanctions were being prepared against him, Emperor Maximilian I died (January 12, 1519)—a fortunate event for the budding Reformation as it turned attention away from heresy in Saxony to the contest for a new Holy Roman Emperor.

In that contest, the pope backed the French king, Francis I. However, Charles I of Spain, a youth of nineteen, successfully succeeded his grandfather as Emperor Charles V. (See Map 11–1, p. 326.) Charles was blessed by both the long tradition of the Habsburg imperial rule and a massive Fugger campaign chest that secured the votes of the seven imperial **electors**. The most prominent among the seven was Frederick the Wise, Luther's lord and protector. Frederick took great pride in his new University of Wittenberg, and he was not about to let any harm come to his famous court preacher.

In exchange for their votes, the electors wrung new concessions from the Spanish favorable to the Germans. Before becoming emperor, Charles I agreed to revive the German-based Imperial Supreme Court and the Council of Regency and also promised to consult with a diet of the empire on all major domestic and foreign affairs affecting the empire. These measures also helped the development of the Reformation by preventing unilateral imperial action against the Germans.

Luther's Excommunication and the Diet of Worms

In the same month in which Charles was elected emperor, Luther debated Ingolstadt Professor John Eck in Leipzig (June 27, 1519). During this contest, Luther

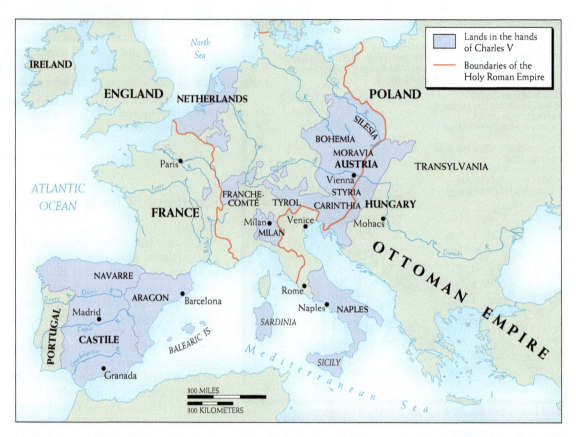

Map 11–1 **THE EMPIRE OF CHARLES V** Dynastic marriages and simple chance concentrated into Charles's hands rule over the lands shown here, plus Spain's overseas possessions. Crowns and titles rained down on him; his election in 1519 as emperor gave him new distractions and responsibilities.

challenged the infallibility of the pope and the inerrancy of church councils, appealing, for the first time, to the sovereign authority of Scripture alone. He burned all his bridges to the old church when he further defended certain teachings of John Huss, who had been condemned to death for heresy at the Council of Constance.

In 1520, Luther signaled his new direction with three famous pamphlets. The *Address to the Christian Nobility of the German Nation* urged the German princes to force reforms on the Roman church, especially to curtail its political and economic power in Germany. The *Babylonian Captivity of the Church* attacked the traditional seven sacraments, arguing that only two, baptism and the Eucharist, were unquestionably biblical, and it exalted the authority of Scripture, church councils, and secular princes over that of the pope. The eloquent *Freedom of a Christian* summarized the new teaching of salvation by faith alone.

On June 15, 1520, Leo's papal bull *Exsurge Domine* ("Arise, O Lord") condemned Luther for heresy and gave him sixty days to retract. The final bull of excommunication was issued on January 3, 1521.

In April 1521, Luther presented his views before the Diet of Worms, over which the newly elected Emperor Charles V presided. Ordered to recant, Luther declared that to do so would be to act against Scripture, reason, and

his conscience. On May 26, 1521, he was placed under the imperial ban, which made him an "outlaw" to secular as well as religious authority. For his own protection, friends disguised and hid him in Wartburg Castle at the instruction of Elector Frederick. There, he spent almost a year, from April 1521 to March 1522. During his stay, he translated the New Testament into German using Erasmus's new Greek text and Latin translation, while directing by correspondence the first steps of the Reformation in Wittenberg.

Imperial Distractions: War with France and the Turks

The Reformation was greatly helped in these early years by the emperor's war with France and the advance of the Ottoman Turks into eastern Europe. Against both adversaries Charles V, who remained a Spanish king with dynastic responsibilities in Spain and Austria, needed loyal German troops, to which end he sought friendly relations with the German princes. Between 1521 and 1559, Spain (the Habsburg dynasty) and France (the Valois dynasty) fought four

View the **Map** "The Hapsburgs in Europe After the Peace of Augsburg, 1555" on MyHistoryLab.com

ÆTHERNA IPSE SVAE MENTIS SIMVLACHRA LVTHERVS
EXPRIMIT·AT VVLTVS CERA LVCAE OCCIDVOS.

M·D·XX·

In 1520, Luther's first portrait, shown here, depicted him as a tough, steely-eyed monk. Afraid that this portrayal might convey defiance rather than reform to Emperor Charles V, Elector Frederick the Wise of Saxony, Luther's protector, ordered court painter Lucas Cranach to soften the image. The result was a Luther placed within a traditional monk's niche reading an open Bible, a reformer, unlike the one depicted here, who was prepared to listen as well as to instruct. © Foto Marburg/Art Resource, NY

major wars over disputed territories within Italy and along their respective borders.

Thus preoccupied, the emperor agreed through his representatives at the German Diet of Speyer (1526) that each German territory was free to enforce the Edict of Worms (1521) against Luther "so as to be able to answer in good conscience to God and the emperor." That concession in effect gave the German princes, who five years earlier had refused to publish the emperor's condemnation of Luther, territorial sovereignty in their religious matters. It also bought the Reformation some time to put down deep roots in Germany and Switzerland. Speyer proved to be a true precedent for the final settlement of religious conflict in the empire. Later, the Peace of Augsburg (1555) would enshrine regional princely control over religion in imperial law.

How the Reformation Spread

In the late 1520s and 1530s, the Reformation passed from the free hands of the theologians and pamphleteers into the firmer ones of the magistrates and princes. In many cities, the latter quickly mandated new religious reforms. Many rulers had themselves worked for decades to bring about basic church reforms, and they welcomed Lutheran preachers as new allies. Reform now ceased to be merely slogans and was transformed into laws all townspeople had to obey.

The elector of Saxony and the prince of Hesse, the two most powerful German Protestant rulers, led the politicization of religious reform within their territories. Like the urban magistrates, the German princes recognized the political and economic opportunities offered them by the demise of the Roman Catholic Church in their lands. Soon they were pushing Protestant faith and politics onto their neighbors. In the 1530s, German Protestant lands formed a powerful defensive alliance, the Schmaldkaldic League, and prepared for war with the Catholic emperor.

The Peasants' Revolt

In its first decade, the Reformation suffered more from internal division than from imperial interference. By 1525, Luther had become almost as much an object of protest within Germany as was the pope. Original allies, sympathizers, and fellow travelers increasingly declared their independence from Wittenberg.

The punishment of a peasant leader in a village near Heilbronn. After the defeat of rebellious peasants in and around the city of Heilbronn, Jacob Rorbach, a well-to-do peasant leader from a nearby village, was tied to a stake and slowly roasted to death. Courtesy of the Library of Congress

Like the German humanists, the German peasantry also had at first believed Luther to be an ally. Since the late fifteenth century, the peasantry had opposed the efforts of their secular and ecclesiastical lords to override their traditional laws and customs and to subject them to new territorial regulations and taxes. Peasant leaders, several of whom had been Lutherans, saw in Luther's teaching about Christian freedom and his criticism of monastic landowners a point of view close to their own. They

📖● **Read** the **Document**
"Martin Luther, *Against the Murderous, Thieving Hordes of Peasants* (1525)" on
MyHistoryLab.com

openly solicited Luther's support of their alleged "Christian" political and economic rights, including a revolutionary demand of release from serfdom.

Luther had initially sympathized with the peasants, while condemning the tyranny of the princes and urging them to meet the just demands of the peasants. Lutheran pamphleteers made Karsthans ('Hans with a hoe'), the burly, hard-working peasant who earned his bread by the sweat of his brow, a model of the honest life God wanted all people to live.

The Lutherans, however, were not social revolutionaries and they saw no hope for their movement if it

became intertwined with a peasant revolution. When the peasants revolted against their landlords in 1524–1525, invoking Luther's name, Luther predictably condemned them as "un-Christian" and urged the princes to crush the revolt mercilessly. Tens of thousands of peasants (estimates run between 70,000 and 100,000) died by the time the revolt was suppressed.

For Luther, the freedom of the Christian lay in inner spiritual release from guilt and anxiety, not in revolutionary politics. Had the reformers joined the peasants' revolt, Luther would have contradicted his own teaching and likely shared the fate of former Lutherans who died as leaders of peasant revolts. In that scenario the German Reformation would not have survived beyond the 1520s. Still, many critics believe that Luther's decision ended the promise of the Reformation as a social and moral force in history.

▼ The Reformation Elsewhere

Although the German Reformation was the first, Switzerland and France had their own independent church reform movements almost simultaneously with Germany's.

Map 11–2 **THE SWISS CONFEDERATION** Although nominally still a part of the Holy Roman Empire, Switzerland grew from a loose defensive union of the central "forest cantons" in the thirteenth century into a fiercely independent association of regions with different languages, histories, and, finally, religions.

From them developed new churches as prominent and lasting as the Lutheran.

Zwingli and the Swiss Reformation

Switzerland was a loose confederacy of thirteen autonomous *cantons*, or states, and their allied areas. (See Map 11–2.) Some cantons became Protestant, some remained Catholic, and a few others managed to effect a compromise. There were two main preconditions of the Swiss Reformation. First was the growth of national sentiment occasioned by popular opposition to foreign mercenary service. (Providing mercenaries for Europe's warring nations was a major source of Switzerland's livelihood.) Second was a desire for church reform that had persisted in Switzerland since the councils of Constance (1414–1417) and Basel (1431–1449).

The Reformation in Zurich Ulrich Zwingli (1484–1531), the leader of the Swiss Reformation, had been humanistically educated. He credited Erasmus over Luther with having set him on the path to reform. He served as a chaplain with Swiss mercenaries who were on the losing side in the disastrous Battle of Marignano in Italy in 1515. Thereafter he became an eloquent critic of Swiss mercenary service, believing it threatened both the political sovereignty and the moral fiber of the Swiss

This 1525 woodcut shows Swiss peasants hanging a seller of indulgences during the Reformation.   The Granger Collection, NYC—All rights reserved

A Raw Deal for the Common Man, or Just Desserts?

📖 Read the **Compare and Connect** on MyHistoryLab.com

BEGINNING IN THE late fifteenth century, German feudal lords, both secular and ecclesiastical, increased labor and crop quotas on their peasant tenants, while restricting their freedoms and overriding their customary laws as well. In 1525 massive revolts occurred in southern Germany, in what became the largest social uprising before the French Revolution. Among those responding directly to the revolt were two highly respected authorities: Wittenberg theologian Martin Luther and Nuremberg artist Albrecht Dürer.

QUESTIONS

1. What is there in Luther's religious teaching that might have led the peasants to think he would support their revolt? What personal interest might he have had in turning them his way? What does he advise them to do to address their grievances properly?

2. Does Dürer's 1527 sketch of a "Memorial to the Peasants' Revolt," depicting a peasant sitting atop a chicken coop with a sword thrust through his back, suggest sympathy for the peasants? Or can it be read as agreement with Luther that the peasants received their just desserts for rebelling against lawful authority?

3. Does Dürer's monument support or condemn the rebellious peasants?

I. Martin Luther, *An Admonition to Peace* (1525)

ON STOPPING THE WAR

This matter is great and perilous, concerning both the kingdom of God and the kingdom of the world; if this rebellion gets the upper hand, both kingdoms will be destroyed and there will be neither world government nor Word of God; there will rather result the permanent destruction of all of Germany, therefore, it is necessary . . . to speak boldly. . . . Since there is nothing Christian on either side and nothing Christian is at issue between you . . . let yourselves be advised and attack these matters with justice, not with force or strife, and do not start an endless bloodshed in Germany!

We have no one on earth to thank for this mischievous rebellion, except you lords and princes, especially you blind bishops and mad priests and monks. . . . In your government you do nothing but flay and rob your subjects in order that you may lead a life of splendor and pride, until the poor common folk can bear it no longer . . .

[As for] the peasants, they must take the name and title of a people who fight because they will not and ought not endure wrong or evil, according to the teaching of nature. You should have that name, and let the name of Christ alone. . . . [As for your so-called 'Christian' demands for] freedom of game, birds, fish, wood, forests, labor services, tithes, imposts, excises, and release from the death tax, these I leave to the lawyers, for they are things that do not concern a Christian who is a martyr on this earth. . . . Let the name of Christian alone and act in some other name, as men and women who want human and natural rights. ■

From *A Sincere Admonition to Peace*, cited by Ozment, *Age of Reform*, p. 283 [first paragraph]; cited by Steven Ozment, *The Age of Reform* (New Haven, CT:, Yale University Press, 1980), pp. 280–282 [second and third paragraphs].

II. Martin Luther, *Against the Robbing and Murdering Peasants* (1525)

FINAL WORDS

[The princes] should have no mercy on obstinate, hardened, blinded peasants who refuse to listen to reason. Let everyone, as he is able, strike, hew, stab, and slay, as though among mad dogs, so that by doing so he may show mercy to those [nonrebelling peasants] who have been ruined, put to flight, and led astray by these rebelling peasants [so that] peace and safety may return . . . ■

From Ozment, *The Age of Reform*, p. 284.

III. *An Open Letter Concerning the Hard Book Against the Peasants* (1525)

FINAL WORDS

Suppose I were to break into a man's house, rape his wife and daughters, break open his coffers, take his money, set a sword to his breast and say: 'If you will not put up with this, I shall run you through, for you are a godless wretch.' Then if a crowd gathered and were about to kill me for doing this, or if the judge ordered my head off, suppose I were to cry out: 'But Christ teaches that you are to be merciful and not kill me.' What would people say then? Well, that is exactly what my peasants and their advocates are doing now. The kingdom of this world is nothing else than the servant of God's wrath upon the wicked and it is a real precursor of hell and everlasting death. It should not be merciful, but strict, severe, and wrathful in the fulfillment of its works and duty. Its tool is not a wreath or roses or a flower of love, but a naked sword.

From the start I had two fears. If the peasants became lords, the devil would become abbot; if these tyrants became lords, the devil's dam would become abbess. Therefore I wanted to do two things: quiet the peasants and instruct the lords. The peasants were unwilling, and now they have their reward. The lords will not hear, and they shall have their reward also. ■

From *An Open Letter Concerning the Hard Book Against the Peasants*, cited by Ozment, *Age of Reform*, pp. 286–287 [first paragraph]; Ozment, *The Age of Reform*, p. 287 [second and third paragraphs].

IV. Albrecht Dürer, *Memorial to the Peasants' Revolt* (1527)

Dürer's "Memorial to the Peasants," drawn in 1527, the year before his death, appeared in a book devoted to 'perspective in art.' Fearing that Protestant iconoclasm (destruction of icons) and the coming of religious wars would remove decorative art from the churches, his book was to be a primer for artists who in the aftermath of such destruction would have to learn the art of painting all over again. The sketch shows a peasant sitting atop a chicken coop with a sword thrust through his back, the classic iconography of betrayal.

At this time Dürer's peers, friends, and associates condemned the Peasants' Revolt as strongly as Luther. During the war Dürer painted portraits of the Fuggers, the great merchant family the peasants despised, and also Margrave Casimir of Brandenburg-Ansbach, a brutal slayer of peasants and Anabaptists. Within this context might Dürer's slain rebellious peasant, like Luther's, have gotten his just due? ■

From Joseph Leo Koerner, *The Moment of Self-Portraiture in Renaissance Art* (Chicago: University of Chicago Press, 1993), p. 235.

10.

The caption reads: "He who wants to commemorate his victory over the rebellious peasants might use to that end a structure such as I portray here." Foto Marburg/Art Resource, NY

331

confederacy. By 1518, Zwingli was also widely known for his opposition to the sale of indulgences and to religious superstition.

In 1519, he competed for the post of people's priest in the main church of Zurich. His candidacy was initially questioned after he acknowledged fornicating with a barber's daughter, who had since delivered a child. Zwingli successfully minimized the affair, claiming the woman in question had been a skilled seducer, and denying any paternity as she had had affairs with other men as well. Zwingli's conduct was not so scandalous to contemporaries, who sympathized with the plight of a celibate clergy. One of Zwingli's first acts as a reformer was to petition for an end to clerical celibacy and for the right of clergy legally to marry, a practice accepted in all Protestant lands.

From his new position as people's priest in Zurich, Zwingli engineered the Swiss Reformation. In March 1522, he was party to the breaking of the Lenten fast—then an act of protest analogous to burning one's national flag today. Zwingli's reform guideline was simple and effective: Whatever lacked literal support in Scripture was to be neither believed nor practiced. As had also happened with Luther, that test soon raised questions about such honored traditional teachings and practices as fasting, transubstantiation, the worship of saints, pilgrimages, purgatory, clerical celibacy, and certain sacraments. A disputation held on January 29, 1523, concluded with the city government's sanction of Zwingli's Scripture test. (See "Zwingli Lists the Errors of the Roman Church," page 333.) Thereafter Zurich became the center of the Swiss Reformation. The new regime imposed a harsh discipline that made the city one of the first examples of puritanical Protestantism.

The Marburg Colloquy Landgrave Philip of Hesse (1504–1567) sought to unite Swiss and German Protestants in a mutual defense pact. However, Luther's and Zwingli's bitter theological differences, especially over the nature of Christ's presence in the Eucharist, spoiled his efforts. Zwingli favored a symbolic interpretation of Christ's words, "This is my body." Christ, he argued, was spiritually, not bodily, present in the bread and wine of the Eucharist. Luther, to the contrary, insisted that Christ's human nature was such that it shared the properties of his divine nature. Hence, where Christ was spiritually present, he could also be bodily present, for such was his special human nature. Luther wanted no part of an abstract, spiritualized Christ, while Zwingli feared Luther was still mired in medieval sacramental theology.

Philip of Hesse brought the two Protestant leaders together in his castle in Marburg in early October 1529 to work out their differences. However, the effort proved to be in vain. Luther left thinking Zwingli a dangerous fanatic, forevermore to paint him black. Although cooperation between the two Protestant sides did not cease altogether, the disagreement splintered the Protestant movement theologically and politically. Separate defense leagues formed, and semi-Zwinglian theological views came to be embodied in the non-Lutheran *Tetrapolitan Confession* prepared by the Strasbourg reformers Martin Bucer and Caspar Hedio in 1530.

Swiss Civil Wars As the Swiss cantons divided themselves between Protestantism and Catholicism, civil wars erupted. There were two major battles, both at Kappel, one in June 1529 and a second in October 1531. The first ended in a Protestant victory, which forced the Catholic cantons to break their foreign alliances and to recognize the rights of Swiss Protestants. After the second battle, Zwingli lay wounded on the battlefield, and when discovered, he was unceremoniously executed, his remains thereafter hacked into pieces and scattered to the four winds so his followers would have no relics to console and inspire them. The subsequent treaty confirmed the right of each canton to determine its own religion. Heinrich Bullinger (1504–1575), Zwingli's protégé and later son-in-law, became the new leader of the Swiss Reformation and guided its development into an established religion, eventually to merge with Calvinism.

Anabaptists and Radical Protestants

The moderate pace and seemingly low ethical results of the Lutheran and Zwinglian reformations discontented many people, among them some of the original followers of Luther and Zwingli. These were devout fundamentalist Protestants who desired a more rapid and thorough implementation of Apostolic Christianity. They accused the reform movements that went before them of having gone only halfway. The most important of these radical groups were the **Anabaptists**, the sixteenth-century ancestors of the modern Mennonites and Amish. The Anabaptists were especially distinguished by their rejection of infant baptism and their insistence on only adult baptism, as was the case with Jesus, who was baptized as an adult. (The term *Anabaptism* derives from the Greek word meaning "to rebaptize.") Only a thoughtful consenting adult, able to understand the Scriptures and what the biblical way of life required, could enter the covenant of faith.

Although Luther and Zwingli also taught that believers must believe for themselves (Luther called it the "priesthood of all believers"), they retained the historical practice of infant baptism, despite the absence of any clear biblical mandate. They argued that the congregation "believed for the infant," stood in his or her place, and pledged to raise the baptized infant in the faith. Here, the communal nature and responsibility of the church was deemed to be more basic to Christianity than the radical individualism the Anabaptists asserted.

Document

ZWINGLI LISTS THE ERRORS OF THE ROMAN CHURCH

Prior to the first Zurich Disputation (1523), which effectually introduced the Protestant Reformation in Zurich, the reformer Zwingli prepared such a summary of the errors of the Roman Church known as the Sixty-Seven Articles. *Here are some of them.*

How do Zwingli's basic religious views compare with those of Martin Luther?

All who consider other teachings equal to or higher than the Gospel err, and they do not know what the Gospel is.

In the faith rests our salvation, and in unbelief our damnation; for all truth is clear in Christ.

In the Gospel one learns that human doctrines and decrees do not aid in salvation.

That Christ, having sacrificed himself once, is to eternity a certain and valid sacrifice for the sins of all faithful, wherefrom it follows that the Mass is not a sacrifice, but is a remembrance of the sacrifice and assurance of the salvation which Christ has given us.

That God desires to give us all things in his name, whence it follows that outside of this life we need no [intercession of the saints or any] mediator except himself.

That no Christian is bound to do those things which God has not decreed, therefore one may eat at all times all food, where from one learns that the decree about cheese and butter is a Roman swindle.

That no special person can impose the ban upon anyone, but the Church, that is, the congregation of those among whom the one to be banned dwells, together with their watchman, i.e., the pastor.

All that the spiritual so-called state [i.e., the papal church] claims to have of power and protection belongs to the lay [i.e., the secular magistracy], if they wish to be Christians.

Greater offence I know not than that one does not allow priests to have wives, but permits them to hire prostitutes.

Christ has borne all our pains and labor. Hence whoever assigns to works of penance what belongs to Christ errs and slanders God.

The true divine Scriptures know naught about purgatory after this life.

The Scriptures know no priests except those who proclaim the word of God.

Ulrich Zwingli (1484–1531), *Selected Works*, ed. by Samuel M. Jackson (Philadelphia: University of Pennsylvania Press, 1972), pp. 111–117.

Conrad Grebel and the Swiss Brethren Conrad Grebel (1498–1526), with whom Anabaptism originated, performed the first adult rebaptism in Zurich in January 1525. Initially a coworker of Zwingli's and an even greater biblical literalist, Grebel broke openly with him. In a religious disputation in October 1523, Zwingli supported the city government's plea for a peaceful, gradual removal of resented traditional religious practices—not the rush to perfection the Anabaptists demand.

The alternative of the Swiss Brethren, as Grebel's group came to be called, was embodied in the *Schleitheim Confession* of 1527. This document distinguished Anabaptists not only by their practice of adult baptism, but also by their pacifism, refusal to swear oaths, and nonparticipation in the offices of secular government. By both choice and coercion, Anabaptists physically separated from established society to form a more perfect communion modeled on the first Christians. Because of the close connection between religious and civic life in the sixteenth century, the political authorities also viewed such separatism as a threat to basic social bonds, even as a form of sedition.

The Anabaptist Reign in Münster At first, Anabaptism drew adherents from all social classes. As Lutherans and Zwinglians joined with Catholics in opposition and persecuted them within the cities, however, a more rural, agrarian class came to make up the great majority of Anabaptists. In 1529, rebaptism became a capital offense within the Holy Roman Empire. At least 1,000 and perhaps as many as 5,000 men and women were executed for rebaptizing themselves as adults between 1525 and 1618.

Anabaptists are burned at the stake in Muenster. Foto Marburg/Art Resource, NY

radicals. The skeletons of their leaders long hung in public view as a warning to all who would so offend traditional Christian sensitivities. After this episode, moderate, pacifistic Anabaptism became the norm among most nonconformists. Menno Simons (1496–1561), the founder of the Mennonites, set an example of nonprovocative separatist Anabaptism, which became the historical form in which Anabaptist sects survived down to the present.

Spiritualists   Another diverse and highly individualistic group of Protestant dissenters was the Spiritualists. These were mostly isolated individuals distinguished by their disdain for external, institutional religion. They believed the only religious authority was the Spirit of God, which spoke not in some past revelation, but here and now in the heart and mind of every listening individual. Among them were several renegade Lutherans. Thomas Müntzer (d. 1525), who had close contacts with Anabaptist leaders in Germany and Switzerland, died as a leader of a peasants' revolt in Frankenhausen, Germany. Sebastian Franck (d. 1541), a critic of all dogmatic religion, proclaimed the religious autonomy and freedom of every individual soul. Caspar Schwenckfeld (d. 1561) was a prolific writer and wanderer after whom the Schwenckfeldian Church is named.

Antitrinitarians   A final group of persecuted radical Protestants also destined for prominence in the modern world was the Antitrinitarians. These were exponents of a commonsense, rational, and ethical religion. Prominent among them were the Spaniard Michael Servetus (1511–1553), executed in 1553 in Geneva at the encouragement of John Calvin for "blasphemies against the Holy Trinity." The Italians, Lelio (d. 1562) and Faustus (d. 1604) Sozzini, the founders of Socinianism, also stand out. These thinkers were the strongest opponents of Calvinism, especially its belief in original sin and **predestination**, and have a deserved reputation as defenders of religious toleration.

John Calvin and the Genevan Reformation

In the second half of the sixteenth century, Calvinism replaced Lutheranism as the dominant Protestant force in Europe. Calvinism was the religious ideology that inspired or accompanied massive political resistance in France, the Netherlands, and Scotland. During the

Brutal measures were universally applied against nonconformists after Anabaptist extremists came to power in the German city of Münster in 1534–1535. Led by two Dutch emigrants—a baker, Jan Matthys of Haarlem, and a tailor, Jan Beukelsz of Leiden—the Anabaptists in Münster forced Lutherans and Catholics in the city either to convert or to emigrate. After their departure, the city was blockaded by besieging armies. Under such pressures, Münster was transformed into an Old Testament theocracy, replete with charismatic leaders and the practice of polygamy. The latter was implemented as a measure of social control to deal with the many recently widowed and deserted women left behind in the city. Women opposed to the practice were allowed to leave polygymous marriages.

These developments shocked the outside world, and Protestant and Catholic armies united to crush the reign of Elector Frederick III (r. 1559–1576), Calvinism established itself within the geographical region of the Palatinate, the German state in the Rhineland in which the Thirty Years' War, the worst of the wars of religion, would break out in 1618. Calvinists believed strongly in both divine predestination and the individual's responsibility to reorder society according to God's plan. They were determined to transform society so men and women lived their lives externally as they professed to believe internally and were presumably destined to live eternally.

The namesake of Calvinism and its perfect embodiment, John Calvin (1509–1564), was born into a well-to-do French family, the son of the secretary to the bishop of Noyon. At age twelve, he received church benefices that financed the best possible education at Parisian colleges and a law degree. In the 1520s, he identified with the French reform party. Although he would finally reject this group as ineffectual compromisers, its members contributed much to his intellectual preparation as a religious reformer.

It was probably in the spring of 1534 that Calvin experienced that conversion to Protestantism by which he said his "long stubborn heart" was "made teachable" by God. His own hard experience became a personal model of reform by which he would measure the recalcitrant citizenry of Geneva. His mature theology stressed the sovereignty of God's will over all creation and the necessity of humankind's conformity to it. In May 1534, he

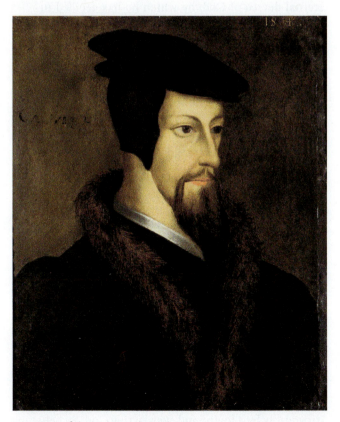

A portrait of the young John Calvin. Erich Lessing/Art Resource, NY

dramatically surrendered the benefices that had educated him and joined the budding Reformation in Geneva.

Political Revolt and Religious Reform in Geneva

Whereas in Saxony religious reform paved the way for a political revolution against the emperor, in Geneva a political revolution against the local prince-bishop laid the foundation for the religious change. Genevans revolted against their resident prince-bishop in the late 1520s, and the city council assumed his legal and political powers in 1527.

In late 1533, the Protestant city of Bern dispatched two reformers to Geneva: Guillaume Farel (1489–1565) and Antoine Froment (1508–1581). In the summer of 1535, after much internal turmoil, the Protestants triumphed, and the traditional Mass and other religious practices were removed. On May 21, 1536, Geneva voted officially to adopt the Reformation: "by living according to the Gospel and the Word of God . . . without any more Masses, statues, idols, or other papal abuses." Calvin arrived in Geneva in July 1536 after these events. He was actually en route to a scholarly refuge in Strasbourg, in flight from the persecution of French Protestants. Warring between France and Spain at this time forced him to turn sharply south to Geneva. The Protestant leader there was William Farel, who persuaded him to stay in the city and assist the expansion of the French Reformation, threatening him with divine vengeance if he turned away from the task.

Calvin seized the opportunity and drew up the articles for the governance of the new church, as well as a catechism to guide and discipline the citizens. Both were presented for approval before the city councils in early 1537. Because of the strong measures they proposed to govern Geneva's moral life, many suspected the reformers were intent on creating a "new papacy." Opponents soon feared Calvin and Farel were going too far too fast. Geneva's powerful Protestant ally, Bern, which had adopted a more moderate Protestant reform, pressured Geneva's magistrates to restore traditional religious ceremonies and holidays that Calvin and Farel had abolished. When the reformers opposed their actions, they were exiled from the city.

Read the Document
"John Calvin, 'Ecclesiastical Ordinances' (Geneva, Switzerland), 1533" on **MyHistoryLab.com**

Calvin went to Strasbourg, a model Protestant city, where he became pastor to French exiles and wrote biblical commentaries. He also produced a second edition of his masterful *Institutes of the Christian Religion*, which many consider to be the definitive theological statement of the Protestant faith. Most importantly for Calvin he had learned from the Strasbourg reformer Martin Bucer how to achieve his goals.

Calvin's Geneva In 1540, Geneva elected officials both favorable to Calvin and determined to establish full Genevan political and religious independence from Bern.

CALVIN ON PREDESTINATION

John Calvin taught the most stringent doctrine of "supra-lapsarian" predestination: that God foreordained all of his creatures either to heaven or to hell before He created them and let them live out their lives. In Calvin's mind, this teaching was God's assurance that none of his creatures could in any way earn their salvation by their own good works. However, they were still expected to do good works for their neighbors and behave as if they were the true children of God, serving others without any thought of self whatsoever, and leaving their eternal fate solely in God's hands, whether their final destiny was heaven or hell.

Explain Calvin's doctrines of predestination and foreknowledge: are they one and the same? How appealing is this doctrine to you? Does it make one want to love God? How does this doctrine compare with Martin Luther's doctrine of salvation by faith alone? Are they saying the same thing? How does Calvin's predestination compare with Roman Catholic faith and good works?

No one who wishes to be thought religious dares outright to deny predestination, by which God chooses some for the hope of life, and condemns others to eternal death. But men entangle it with captious quibbles; and especially those who make foreknowledge the ground of it. We indeed attribute to God both predestination and foreknowledge; but we call it absurd to subordinate one to the other. When we attribute foreknowledge to God we mean that all things have always been and eternally remain before God's eyes so that to his knowledge nothing is future or past, but all things are present; and present not in the sense that they are reproduced in imagination (as we are aware of past events which are retained in our memory), but present in the sense that he really sees and observes them placed, as it were, before his eyes. And this foreknowledge extends over the whole universe and over every creature. By predestination we mean the eternal decree of God, by which <u>he has decided in his own mind</u> what he wishes to happen in the case of each individual. For all men are not created on an equal footing, but for some eternal life is preordained, for others, eternal damnation . . .

From *Documents of the Christian Church*, ed. Henry Bettenson (New York: Oxford University Press 1947), p. 30.

They knew Calvin would be a valuable ally in that undertaking and invited him to return. This he did in September 1540, never to leave the city again. Within months of his return, the city implemented new ecclesiastical ordinances that provided for cooperation between the magistrates and the clergy in matters of internal discipline.

Following the Strasbourg model, the Genevan Church established four offices: (1) pastors, of whom there were five; (2) teachers, or doctors, to instruct the populace and defend true doctrine; (3) elders, twelve laypeople chosen by and from the Genevan councils and empowered to "oversee the life of everybody"; and last (4) deacons to dispense church goods and services to the poor and the sick.

The controversial doctrine of predestination was at the center of Calvin's theology as justification by faith was at Luther's. Both doctrines have been criticized, Luther's for seeming to deny the believer's need to do good works and Calvin's for seeming to deny the existence of human free will. Luther believed works were a mark of a true Christian, even though they did not make him such or save him. Calvin did not discuss predestination until the end of his great theological work, the *Institutes of the Christian Religion*. Explaining why he delayed its discussion, he described predestination as a doctrine only for mature Christians. Whereas it offended nonbelievers, true Christians might take consolation from it. For true believers, predestination recognized that the world and all who dwell in it are in God's hands from eternity to eternity, regardless of all else. When the world seems utterly godless and the devil to be its only lord, the true Christian takes consolation from the knowledge that his present life and future destiny are determined irrevocably by a loving and ever-lasting God. By believing that, and living as the Bible instructed them to do, Calvinists found consoling, presumptive evidence that they were among God's elect.

Possessed of such assurance, Calvinists turned their energies to transforming society spiritually and morally. Faith, Calvin taught, did not sit idly in the mind but conformed one's every action to God's law. The "elect" should at least live in a manifestly God-pleasing way if they are truly God's "elect." In the attempted realization of that goal, Calvin spared no effort. The consistory, or Geneva's regulatory court, became his instrument of power. Composed of the elders and the pastors and presided over by one of the city's chief magistrates, this body implemented the strictest moral discipline.

Among the personal conflicts in Geneva that gave Calvin the reputation of a stern moralist, none proved more damaging than his role in the capture and execution in 1553 of the Spanish physician and amateur theologian Michael Servetus, who had already been condemned by the Inquisition for heresy. Servetus died at the stake in Protestant Geneva for denying the doctrine of the Holy Trinity, a subject on which he had written a book scandalous to the church authorities.

After 1555, Geneva soon became home to thousands of exiled Protestants who had been driven out of France, England, and Scotland. Refugees numbering more than 5,000, most of them utterly loyal to Calvin, made up more than one-third of Geneva's population. All of Geneva's magistrates were now devout Calvinists, greatly strengthening Calvin's position in the city.

To the thousands of persecuted Protestants who flocked to Geneva in midcentury, the city was a beacon and a refuge, Europe's only free city. During Calvin's lifetime, Geneva also gained the reputation of being a "woman's paradise" because its laws severely punished men who beat their wives, behavior deemed unbefitting a true Calvinist Christian.

▼ Political Consolidation of the Lutheran Reformation

By 1530, the Reformation was in Europe to stay. It would, however, take several decades and major attempts to eradicate it, before all would recognize this fact. With the political triumph of Lutheranism in the empire by the 1550s, Protestant movements elsewhere gained a new lease on life.

The Diet of Augsburg

Emperor Charles V devoted most of his first decade to the pursuit of politics and military campaigns outside the empire, particularly in Spain and Italy. In 1530, he returned to the empire to direct the Diet of Augsburg. This assembly of Protestant and Catholic representatives had been called to address the growing religious division within the empire in the wake of the Reformation's success. With its terms dictated by the Catholic emperor, the diet adjourned with a blunt and unrealistic order to all Lutherans to revert to Catholicism.

The Reformation was by this time too firmly established for that to occur. In February 1531, the Lutherans responded with the formation of their own defensive alliance, the Schmalkaldic League. The league took as its banner the **Augsburg Confession**, a moderate statement of Protestant beliefs that had been spurned by the emperor at the Diet of Augsburg. In 1538, Luther drew up a more strongly worded Protestant confession known as the *Schmalkaldic Articles*. Under the leadership of Landgrave Philip of Hesse and Elector John Frederick of Saxony, the league achieved a stalemate with the emperor, who was again distracted by renewed war with France and the ever-resilient Turks.

The Expansion of the Reformation

In the 1530s, German Lutherans formed regional consistories, judicial bodies composed of theologians and lawyers, which oversaw and administered the new Protestant churches and replaced the old Catholic episcopates. Educational reforms provided for compulsory primary education, schools for girls, a humanist revision of the traditional curriculum, and instruction of the laity in the new religion.

The Reformation also entrenched itself elsewhere. Introduced into Denmark by King Christian II (r. 1513–1523), Lutheranism thrived there under Frederick I (r. 1523–1533), who joined the Schmalkaldic League. Under Christian III (r. 1536–1559), Lutheranism became the official state religion.

In Sweden, King Gustavus Vasa (r. 1523–1560), supported by a Swedish nobility greedy for church lands, embraced Lutheranism, confiscated church property, and subjected the clergy to royal authority at the Diet of Vesteras (1527).

In politically splintered Poland, Lutherans, Anabaptists, Calvinists, and even Antitrinitarians found room to practice their beliefs. Primarily because of the absence of a central political authority, Poland became a model of religious pluralism and toleration in the second half of the sixteenth century.

Reaction Against Protestants

Charles V made abortive efforts in 1540–1541 to enforce a compromise between Protestants and Catholics. As these and other conciliar efforts failed, he turned to a military solution. In 1547, imperial armies crushed the Protestant Schmalkaldic League, defeating and capturing John Frederick of Saxony and Philip of Hesse.

The emperor established puppet rulers in Saxony and Hesse and issued an imperial law mandating that Protestants everywhere readopt old Catholic beliefs and practices. Protestants were granted a few cosmetic concessions, for example, clerical marriage (with papal approval of individual cases) and communion in both bread and wine. Many Protestant leaders went into exile. In Germany, the city of Magdeburg became a refuge for persecuted Protestants and the center of Lutheran resistance.

The Peace of Augsburg

The Reformation was too entrenched by 1547 to be ended even by brute force. Maurice of Saxony, handpicked by Charles V to rule Saxony, had recognized the inevitable and shifted his allegiance to the Lutherans. Confronted by fierce resistance and weary from three decades of war, the emperor was forced to relent. After a defeat by Protestant armies in 1552, Charles reinstated the Protestant leaders and guaranteed Lutherans religious freedoms in the Peace of Passau (August 1552). With this declaration, he effectively surrendered his lifelong quest for European religious unity.

The Peace of Augsburg in September 1555 made the division of Christendom permanent. This agreement recognized in law what had already been well established in practice: *Cuius regio, eius religio*, meaning the ruler of a land would determine its religion. Lutherans were permitted to retain all church lands forcibly seized before 1552. An "ecclesiastical reservation" was added, however, that was intended to prevent high Catholic prelates who converted to Protestantism from taking their lands, titles, and privileges with them. People discontented with the religion of their region were permitted to migrate to another.

The Peace of Augsburg did not extend official recognition to Calvinism and Anabaptism as legal forms of Christian belief and practice. Anabaptists had long adjusted to such exclusion by forming their own separatist communities. Calvinists, however, were not separatists. They remained determined to secure the right to worship publicly as they pleased, and to shape society according to their own religious convictions. While Anabaptists retreated and Lutherans enjoyed the security of an established religion, Calvinists organized to lead national revolutions throughout northern Europe in the second half of the sixteenth century.

▼ The English Reformation to 1553

Late medieval England had a well-earned reputation for maintaining the rights of the crown against the pope. Edward I (r. 1272–1307) had rejected efforts by Pope Boniface VIII to prevent secular taxation of the clergy.

Statutes of Provisors and Praemunire passed in the mid-fourteenth century laid a foundation for curtailing payments and judicial appeals to Rome and rejecting papal appointments in England. Lollardy, a derisive description of the lower and middle working classes, joined with humanism and widespread anticlerical sentiment in preparing the way for Protestant ideas, which entered England in the early sixteenth century.

The Preconditions of Reform

In the early 1520s, future English reformers met in Cambridge to discuss Lutheran writings smuggled into England by merchants and scholars. One of these future reformers was William Tyndale (ca. 1492–1536), who translated the New Testament into English in 1524–1525 while in Germany. Printed in Cologne and Worms, Tyndale's New Testament began to circulate in England in 1526.

Cardinal Thomas Wolsey (ca. 1475–1530), the chief minister of King Henry VIII (r. 1509–1547), and Sir Thomas More (1478–1535), Wolsey's successor, guided royal opposition to incipient English Protestantism. The king himself defended the seven sacraments against Luther, receiving as a reward the title "Defender of the Faith" from Pope Leo X. Following Luther's intemperate reply to Henry's amateur theological attack, More wrote a lengthy *Response to Luther* in 1523.

The King's Affair

Lollardy and humanism may have provided some native seeds for religious reform, but it was Henry's unhappy marriage to Catherine of Aragon (d. 1536) and obsession to get a male heir that broke the soil and allowed the seeds to take root. In 1509, Henry had married Catherine, the daughter of Ferdinand and Isabella of Spain and the aunt of Emperor Charles V. By 1527, the union had produced only one surviving child, a daughter, Mary. Although women could inherit the throne, Henry fretted over the political consequences of leaving only a female heir. In this period, people believed it unnatural for women to rule over men. At best a woman ruler foreshadowed a contested reign, at worst turmoil and revolution. By the end of the century, Elizabeth's strong rule would expose such fears as greatly exaggerated.

Henry came even to believe that God had cursed his union with Catherine, who had many miscarriages and stillbirths. The reason lay in Catherine's previous marriage to Henry's brother Arthur. After Arthur's premature death, Henry's father, Henry VII, betrothed her to Henry to keep the English alliance with Spain intact. The two were wed in 1509, a few days before Henry VIII received his crown. Because marriage to the wife of one's brother was prohibited by both canon and biblical law

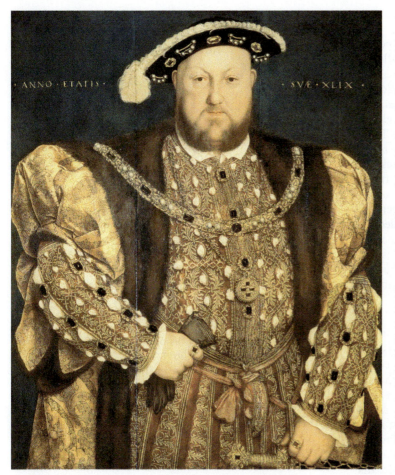

Hans Holbein the Younger (1497–1543) was the most famous portrait painter of the Reformation. Here he portrays a seemingly almighty Henry VIII.
© Scala/Art Resource

of much popular resentment. When he failed to secure the annulment through no fault of his own, he was dismissed in disgrace in 1529. Thomas Cranmer (1489–1556) and Thomas Cromwell (1485–1540), both of whom harbored Lutheran sympathies, thereafter became the king's closest advisers. Finding the way to a papal annulment closed, Henry's new advisers struck a different course: Why not simply declare the king supreme in English spiritual affairs as he was in English temporal affairs? Then the king could settle the king's affair himself.

The "Reformation Parliament"

In 1529, Parliament convened for what would be a seven-year session that earned it the title of the "Reformation Parliament." During this period, it passed a flood of legislation that harassed, and finally placed royal reins on, the clergy. In so doing, it established a precedent that would remain a feature of English government: Whenever fundamental changes are made in religion, the monarch must consult with and work through Parliament. In January 1531, the Convocation (a legislative assembly representing the English clergy) publicly recognized Henry as head of the church in England "as far as the law of Christ allows." In 1532, Parliament published official grievances against the church, ranging from alleged indifference to the needs of the laity to an excessive number of religious holidays. In the same year, Parliament passed the Submission of the Clergy, which effectively placed canon law under royal control and thereby the clergy under royal jurisdiction.

In January 1533, Henry wed the pregnant Anne Boleyn, with Thomas Cranmer officiating. In February 1533, Parliament made the king the highest court of appeal for all English subjects. In March 1533, Cranmer became archbishop of Canterbury and led the Convocation in invalidating the king's marriage to Catherine. In 1534, Parliament ended all payments by the English clergy and laity to Rome and gave Henry sole jurisdiction over high ecclesiastical appointments. The Act of Succession in the same year made Anne Boleyn's children legitimate heirs to the throne, and the **Act of Supremacy** declared Henry "the only supreme head in earth of the Church of England."

Read the **Document**
"The Act of Supremacy (England), 1534" on
MyHistoryLab.com

When Thomas More and John Fisher, bishop of Rochester, refused to recognize the Act of Succession and the Act of Supremacy, Henry had them executed, making clear his determination to have his way regardless of the cost. In 1536 and 1538, Parliament dissolved England's monasteries and nunneries.

(see Leviticus 18:16, 20:21), the marriage had required a special dispensation from Pope Julius II.

By 1527, Henry was also thoroughly enamored of Anne Boleyn, one of Catherine's ladies-in-waiting. He determined to put Catherine aside and take Anne as his wife. This he could not do in Catholic England, however, without a papal annulment of the marriage to Catherine. Therein lay a special problem. The year 1527 was also when imperial soldiers fighting in Italy mutinied and sacked Rome. Pope Clement VII was then a prisoner of Emperor Charles V, who also happened to be Catherine's nephew, and he was not about to encourage the pope to annul the royal marriage. Even if such coercion had not existed, it would have been virtually impossible for the pope to grant an annulment of a marriage that not only had survived for eighteen years but had also been made possible in the first place by a special papal dispensation.

Cardinal Wolsey, who aspired to become pope, was placed in charge of securing the royal annulment. Lord Chancellor since 1515 and papal legate-at-large since 1518, Wolsey had long been Henry's heavy and the object

Wives of Henry VIII

Henry's domestic life lacked the consistency of his political life. In 1536, Anne Boleyn was executed for alleged treason and adultery, and her daughter Elizabeth, like Elizabeth's half-sister Mary before her, was declared illegitimate by her father. Henry had four more marriages. His third wife, Jane Seymour, died in 1537 shortly after giving birth to the future Edward VI. Henry wed Anne of Cleves sight unseen on the advice of Cromwell, the purpose being to create by the marriage an alliance with the Protestant princes of Germany. Neither the alliance nor the marriage proved worth the trouble; the marriage was annulled by Parliament, and Cromwell was dismissed and executed. Catherine Howard, Henry's fifth wife, was beheaded for adultery in 1542. His last wife, Catherine Parr, a patron of humanists and reformers, for whom Henry was the third husband, survived him to marry still a fourth time—obviously she was a match for the English king.

The King's Religious Conservatism

Henry's boldness in politics and domestic affairs did not extend to religion. True, because of Henry's actions, the pope had ceased to be head of the English church and English Bibles were placed in English churches, but despite the break with Rome, Henry remained decidedly conservative in his religious beliefs. With the Ten Articles of 1536, he made only mild concessions to Protestant tenets. Otherwise Catholic doctrine was maintained in a country filled with Protestant sentiment. Despite his many wives and amorous adventures, Henry forbade the English clergy to marry and threatened to execute clergy who were caught twice in concubinage.

Angered by the growing popularity of Protestant views, even among his chief advisers, Henry struck directly at them in the Six Articles of 1539. These reaffirmed transubstantiation, denied the Eucharistic cup to the laity, declared celibate vows inviolable, provided for private Masses, and ordered the continuation of oral confession. Protestants referred to the articles as the "whip with six stings," a clear warning from the king that religious reform would not race ahead in England during his reign. Although William Tyndale's English New Testament grew into the Coverdale Bible (1535) and the Great Bible (1539), and the latter was mandated for every English parish, England had to await Henry's death before it could become a genuinely Protestant country.

The Protestant Reformation under Edward VI

When Henry died in 1547, his son and successor, Edward VI (d. 1553), was only ten years old. Edward reigned under the successive regencies of Edward Seymour, who became the duke of Somerset (1547–1550), and the earl of

---

MAIN EVENTS OF THE ENGLISH REFORMATION

1529	Reformation Parliament convenes
1532	Parliament passes the Submission of the Clergy
1533	Henry VIII weds Anne Boleyn; Convocation invalidates marriage to Catherine of Aragon
1534	Act of Succession makes Anne Boleyn's children legitimate heirs to the English throne
1534	Act of Supremacy declares Henry VIII "the only supreme head of the Church of England"
1535	Thomas More executed for opposition to Acts of Succession and Supremacy
1535	Publication of Coverdale Bible
1539	Henry VIII imposes the Six Articles
1547	Edward VI succeeds to the throne under protectorships of Somerset and Northumberland
1549	First Act of Uniformity imposes Book of Common Prayer on English churches
1553–1558	Mary Tudor restores Catholic doctrine
1558–1603	Elizabeth I fashions an Anglican religious settlement

---

Warwick, who became known as the duke of Northumberland (1550–1553). During this time, England enacted Protestant Reformation. The new king and Somerset corresponded directly with John Calvin. During Somerset's regency, Henry's Six Articles and laws against Protestant heresy were repealed, and clerical marriage and communion with cup were sanctioned.

In 1547, the chantries, places where endowed Masses had traditionally been said for the dead, were dissolved. In 1549, the Act of Uniformity imposed Thomas Cranmer's *Book of Common Prayer* on all English churches. Images and altars were removed from the churches in 1550. After Charles V's victory over the German princes in 1547, German Protestant leaders had fled to England for refuge. Several of these refugees, with Martin Bucer prominent among them, now directly assisted the completion of the English Reformation.

The Second Act of Uniformity, passed in 1552, imposed a revised *Book of Common Prayer* on all English churches. A forty-two-article confession of faith, also written by Thomas Cranmer, set forth a moderate Protestant doctrine. It taught justification by faith and the supremacy of Holy Scripture, denied transubstantiation (although not the real presence), and recognized only two sacraments.

All these changes were short-lived, however. In 1553, Catherine of Aragon's daughter succeeded Edward (who had died in his teens) to the throne as Mary I

(d. 1558) and restored Catholic doctrine and practice with a single-mindedness rivaling that of her father. It was not until the reign of Anne Boleyn's daughter, Elizabeth I (r. 1558–1603), that England worked out a lasting religious settlement.

▼ Catholic Reform and Counter-Reformation

The Protestant Reformation did not take the medieval church completely by surprise. There were many internal criticisms and efforts at reform before there was a Counter-Reformation in reaction to Protestant successes.

View the **Closer Look** "Martin Luther as Satan Tempting Jesus" on **MyHistoryLab.com**

Sources of Catholic Reform

Before the Reformation began, ambitious proposals had been made for church reform. But sixteenth-century popes, ever mindful of how the councils of Constance and Basel had stripped the pope of his traditional powers, squelched such efforts to change the laws and institutions of the church.

Despite such papal foot-dragging, the old church was not without its reformers. Many new religious orders also sprang up in the sixteenth century to lead a broad revival of piety within the church. The first of these orders was the Theatines, founded in 1524 to groom devout and reform-minded leaders at the higher levels of the church hierarchy. One of the co-founders was Bishop Gian Pietro Carafa, who would be Pope Paul IV (r. 1555–1559). Another new order, whose mission pointed in the opposite direction, was the Capuchins. Recognized by the pope in 1528, they sought to return to the original ideals of Saint Francis and became popular among the ordinary people to whom they directed their ministry. The Somaschi, who became active in the mid-1520s, and the Barnabites, founded in 1530, worked to repair the moral, spiritual, and physical damage done to people in war-torn Italy.

For women, there was the influential new order of Ursulines. Founded in 1535, it established convents in Italy and France for the religious education of girls from all social classes. Another new order, the Oratorians, officially recognized in 1575, was an elite group of clerics devoted to the promotion of religious literature and church music. Among their members was the great hymnist and musician Giovanni Perluigi da Palestrina (1526–1594).

In addition to these lay and clerical movements, the mystical piety of medieval monasticism was revived and popularized by two Spanish mystics, Saint Teresa of Avila (1515–1582) and Saint John of the Cross (1542–1591).

Ignatius of Loyola and the Jesuits

Of the various reform groups, none was more instrumental in the success of the Counter-Reformation than the Society of Jesus, the new order of Jesuits. Organized by Ignatius of Loyola in the 1530s, the church recognized it in 1540. The society grew within a century from its original ten members to more than 15,000 members scattered throughout the world, with thriving missions in India, Japan, and the Americas.

Watch the **Video** "The Global Mission of the Jesuits (Thomas Taylor)" on **MyHistoryLab.com**

The founder of the Jesuits, Ignatius of Loyola (1491–1556), was a heroic figure. A dashing courtier and *soldiero* in his youth, he began his spiritual pilgrimage in 1521 after he had been seriously wounded during a battle with the French. During a lengthy and painful convalescence, he passed the time by reading Christian classics. So impressed was he with the heroic self-sacrifice of the church's saints and their methods of overcoming mental anguish and pain that he underwent a profound religious conversion. Henceforth, he, too, would serve the church as a soldier of Christ.

After recuperating, Ignatius applied the lessons he had learned during his convalescence to a program of religious and moral self-discipline that came to be embodied in the *Spiritual Exercises*. This psychologically perceptive devotional guide contained mental and emotional exercises designed to teach one absolute spiritual self-mastery over one's feelings. It taught that a person could shape his or her own behavior—even create a new religious self—through disciplined study and regular practice.

Read the **Document** "Ignatius Loyola, *Rules for Thinking with the Church* (1535)" on **MyHistoryLab.com**

Whereas in Jesuit eyes Protestants had distinguished themselves by disobedience and religious innovation, the exercises of Ignatius were intended to teach good Catholics to deny themselves and submit without question to higher church authority and spiritual direction. Perfect discipline and self-control were the essential conditions of such obedience. To these were added the enthusiasm of traditional spirituality and mysticism and uncompromising loyalty to the church's cause. This potent combination helped counter the Reformation and win many Protestants back to the Catholic fold, especially in Austria and parts of Germany. (See Map 11–3, p. 342.)

The Council of Trent (1545–1563)

The broad success of the Reformation and the insistence of the Emperor Charles V forced Pope Paul III (r. 1534–1549) to call a general council of the church to reassert church doctrine. In anticipation, the pope appointed a reform commission, chaired by Caspar Contarini (1483–1542), a leading liberal theologian. His report, presented to the pope in February 1537, was so critical of the fiscal practices and

Map 11–3 THE RELIGIOUS SITUATION ABOUT **1560** By 1560, Luther, Zwingli, and Loyola were dead, Calvin was near the end of his life, the English break from Rome was complete, and the last session of the Council of Trent was about to assemble. This map shows "religious geography" of western Europe at the time.

simony of the papal Curia that Paul attempted unsuccessfully to suppress its publication, while Protestants circulated it as justification of their criticism.

The long-delayed council of the church met in 1545 in the imperial city of Trent in northern Italy. There were three sessions, spread over eighteen years, with long interruptions due to war, plague, and imperial and papal politics. The council met from 1545 to 1547, from 1551 to 1552, and from 1562 to 1563, a period that spanned the reigns of four different popes.

Unlike the general councils of the fifteenth century, Trent was strictly under the pope's control, with high Italian prelates prominent in the proceedings. At its final session in 1562, more than three-quarters of the council fathers were Italians. Voting was limited to the high levels of the clergy; university theologians, the lower clergy, and the laity did not share in the council's decisions.

The council's most important reforms concerned internal church discipline. Steps were taken to curtail the selling of church offices and other religious goods. Many bishops who resided in Rome were forced to move to their dioceses. Trent strengthened the authority of local bishops so they could effectively discipline popular religious practices. The bishops were also subjected to new rules that required them to be highly visible by preaching regularly and conducting annual visitations of their diocesan parishes. Parish priests were required to be neatly dressed, better educated, strictly celibate, and active among their parishioners. To train priests, Trent also called for a seminary in every diocese.

Document

THE OBEDIENCE AND POWER OF THE JESUITS

No religious body has been more obedient to and self-sacrificing for the Roman Church than the Society of Jesus, founded by Ignatius of Loyola: Consider the pledge of the Society, printed below.

Is there any room for individual belief, or opinion, in the Jesuit creed? Has that creed served the Church well? How does "suppression of self" and blind obedience "like a corpse" differ from the creeds of the Protestants? Is this Jesuitical discipline—being "a stick in the hand of one's superiors"—the secret of Jesuit success? Among the Protestants is John Calvin the closest to this stark discipline? Is Luther's creed the most lenient?

Let us with the utmost pains strain every nerve of our strength to exhibit this virtue of obedience, firstly to the Highest Pontiff, then to the Superiors of the Society; so that in all things, to which obedience can be extended with charity, we may be most ready to obey his voice, just as if it issued from Christ our Lord . . . directing to this goal all our strength and intention in the Lord, that holy obedience may be enjoined on us with great readiness, with spiritual joy and perseverance; by persuading ourselves that all things [commanded] are just; by rejecting with a kind of blind obedience all opposing opinion or judgment of our own. . . . And let each one persuade himself that they ought live under obedience to allow themselves to be one and ruled by divine providence working through their Superiors exactly as if they were a corpse which suffers itself to be borne and handled in any way whatsoever; or just as an old man's stick which serves him who holds it in his hand wherever and for whatever purpose he wishes to use it . . .

From *Documents of the Christian Church*, ed. Henry Bettenson (New York: Oxford University Press, 1947), p. 366.

Not a single doctrinal concession was made to the Protestants, however. Instead, the Council of Trent reaffirmed the traditional Scholastic education of the clergy; the role of good works in salvation; the authority of tradition; the seven sacraments; transubstantiation; the withholding of the Eucharistic cup from the laity; clerical celibacy; purgatory; the veneration of saints, relics, and sacred images; and indulgences. The council resolved medieval Scholastic quarrels in favor of the theology of Saint Thomas Aquinas, further enhancing his authority within the church. Thereafter, the church offered its strongest resistance to groups like the Jansenists, who endorsed the medieval Augustinian tradition, a source of alternative Catholic, as well as many Protestant, doctrines.

▶ Read the Document
"The Council of Trent (Italian states), 1545–1563" on
MyHistoryLab.com

Rulers initially resisted Trent's reform decrees, fearing a revival of papal political power and new confessional conflicts within their lands. Over time, however, and with the pope's assurances that religious reforms were his sole intent, the new legislation took hold, and parish life revived under a devout and better-trained clergy.

▼ The Social Significance of the Reformation in Western Europe

The Lutheran, Zwinglian, and Calvinist reformers all sought to work within the framework of reigning political power. Luther, Zwingli, and Calvin saw themselves and their followers as subject to definite civic responsibilities and obligations. Their political conservatism has led scholars to characterize them as "magisterial reformers," meaning not only that they were the leaders of the major Protestant movements, but also that they succeeded by the force of the magistrate's sword. Some have argued that this willingness to resort to coercion led the reformers to compromise their principles. They themselves, however, never contemplated reform outside or against the societies of which they were members.

They wanted reform to take shape within reigning laws and institutions. They thus remained highly sensitive to what was politically and socially possible in their age. Some scholars believe the reformers were so cautious that they changed late medieval society very little and actually encouraged acceptance of the sociopolitical status quo.

The Revolution in Religious Practices and Institutions

The Reformation may have been politically conservative, but by the end of the sixteenth century, it had brought about radical changes in traditional religious practices and institutions in those lands where it succeeded.

Religion in Fifteenth-Century Life In the fifteenth century, on the streets of the great cities of Europe that later turned Protestant (for example, Zurich, Strasbourg,

PROTESTANT REFORMATION AND CATHOLIC REFORM ON THE CONTINENT	
1517	Luther posts ninety-five theses against indulgences
1519	Charles I of Spain elected Holy Roman Emperor (as Charles V)
1519	Luther challenges authority of pope and inerrancy of church councils at Leipzig Debate
1521	Papal bull excommunicates Luther for heresy
1521	Diet of Worms condemns Luther
1521–1522	Luther translates the New Testament into German
1524–1525	Peasants' revolt in Germany
1527	The *Schleitheim Confession* of the Anabaptists
1529	Marburg Colloquy between Luther and Zwingli
1530	Diet of Augsburg fails to settle religious differences
1531	Formation of Protestant Schmalkaldic League
1534–1535	Anabaptists assume political power in Münster
1536	Calvin arrives in Geneva
1540	Jesuits, founded by Ignatius of Loyola, recognized as order by pope
1546	Luther dies
1547	Armies of Charles V crush Schmalkaldic League
1555	Peace of Augsburg recognizes rights of Lutherans to worship as they please
1545–1563	Council of Trent institutes reforms and responds to the Reformation

Nuremberg, and Geneva), the clergy and the religious were everywhere. They made up 6–8 percent of the urban population, and they exercised considerable political as well as spiritual power. They legislated and taxed, they tried cases in special church courts, and they enforced their laws with threats of excommunication.

The church calendar regulated daily life. About one-third of the year was given over to some kind of religious observance or celebration. There were frequent periods of fasting. On almost a hundred days out of the year, a pious Christian could not, without special dispensation, eat eggs, butter, animal fat, or meat.

Monasteries, and especially nunneries, were prominent and influential institutions. The children of society's most powerful citizens resided there. Local aristocrats identified with particular churches and chapels, whose walls recorded their lineage and proclaimed their generosity. On the streets, friars begged alms from passersby. In the churches, the Mass and liturgy were read entirely in Latin. Images of saints were regularly displayed, and on certain holidays their relics were paraded about and venerated.

Local religious shrines enjoyed a booming business. Pilgrims gathered there by the hundreds—even thousands—many sick and dying, all in search of a cure or a miracle, but also for diversion and entertainment. Several times during the year, special preachers arrived in the city to sell letters of indulgence.

Many clergy walked the streets with concubines and children, although they were sworn to celibacy and forbidden to marry. The church tolerated such relationships upon payment of penitential fines.

People everywhere complained about the clergy's exemption from taxation and also often from the civil criminal code. People also grumbled about having to support church offices whose occupants actually lived and worked elsewhere, turning the cure of souls over to poorly trained and paid substitutes. Townspeople expressed concern that the church had too much influence over education and culture.

Religion in Sixteenth-Century Life In these same cities, after the Reformation had firmly established itself, few changes in politics and society were evident. The same aristocratic families governed as before, and the rich generally got richer and the poor poorer. Overall numbers of clergy fell by two-thirds, and religious holidays shrank by one-third. Cloisters were nearly gone, and many that remained were transformed into hospices for the sick and poor or into educational institutions, their endowments turned over to these new purposes. A few cloisters remained for devout old monks and nuns who could not be pensioned off or lacked families and friends to care for them. These remaining cloisters died out with their present inhabitants, since no new religious were allowed to enter.

The churches were reduced in number by at least one-third, and worship was conducted almost completely in the vernacular. In some, particularly those in Zwinglian cities, the walls were stripped bare and whitewashed to make sure the congregation meditated only on God's word. The laity observed no obligatory fasts. Indulgence preachers no longer appeared. Local shrines were closed down, and anyone found openly venerating saints, relics, and images was subject to fine and punishment.

Copies of Luther's translation of the New Testament (1522) or, more often, excerpts from it could be found in private homes, and the new clergy encouraged meditation on the Bible. The clergy could marry, and most did. They paid taxes and were punished for their crimes in civil courts. Committees composed of roughly equal numbers of laity and clergy, over whose decisions secular magistrates had the last word, regulated domestic moral life.

Not all Protestant clergy remained enthusiastic about this new lay authority in religion. And the laity was also ambivalent about certain aspects of the Reformation. Over half of the original converts returned to the Catholic fold before the end of the sixteenth century. Whereas one-half of Europe could be counted in the Protestant camp in the mid-sixteenth century, only one-fifth would be there by the mid-seventeenth century.[2]

The Reformation and Education

Another major cultural achievement of the Reformation was its implementation of many of the educational reforms of humanism in new Protestant schools and universities. Many Protestant reformers in Germany, France, and England were humanists. And even when their views on church doctrine and human nature separated them from the humanist movement, the Protestant reformers continued to share a common opposition to Scholasticism and a belief in the unity of wisdom, eloquence, and action. The humanist program of studies, providing the language skills to deal authoritatively with original sources, proved to be a more appropriate tool for the elaboration of Protestant doctrine than it did for Scholastic dialectic, which remained ascendant in the Counter-Reformation.

The Catholic counter-reformers recognized the close connections between humanism and the Reformation. Ignatius of Loyola observed how the new learning had been embraced by and served the Protestant cause. In his *Spiritual Exercises*, he insisted that when the Bible and the Church Fathers were read directly, they be read under the guidance of the authoritative Scholastic theologians: Peter Lombard, Bonaventure, and Thomas Aquinas. Aquinas especially, Ignatius argued, being "of more recent date," had the clearest understanding of what Scripture and the Fathers meant and, therefore, he should guide the study of the past.

When, in August 1518, Philip Melanchthon (1497–1560), "the praeceptor of Germany," a young humanist and professor of Greek, arrived at the University of Wittenberg, his first act was to reform the curriculum on the humanist model. In his inaugural address, entitled *On Improving the Studies of the Young*, Melanchthon presented himself as a defender of good letters and classical studies against "barbarians who practice barbarous arts." By the latter, he meant the Scholastic theologians of the later Middle Ages, whose methods of seeking to reconcile the views of conflicting authorities by disputation had, he believed, undermined both good letters and sound biblical doctrine. Melanchthon saw Scholastic dominance breeding contempt for the Greek language and classical learning, and so urged the careful study of history, poetry, and other humanist disciplines.

Together, Luther and Melanchthon restructured Wittenberg's curriculum. Commentaries on Lombard's *Sentences* were dropped, as was canon law. Straightforward historical study replaced Scholastic lectures on Aristotle. Students read primary sources directly, rather than by way of accepted Scholastic commentators. Candidates for theological degrees defended the new doctrine on the basis of their own study of the Bible. New chairs of Greek and Hebrew were created.

In Geneva, John Calvin and his successor, Theodore Beza, founded the Genevan Academy, which later evolved into the University of Geneva. Calvinist refugees who studied there later carried Protestant educational reforms to France, Scotland, England, and the New World.

Some famous contemporaries decried what they saw as a narrowing of the original humanist program as Protestants took it over. Erasmus, for example, came to fear the Reformation as a threat to the liberal arts and good learning. Sebastian Franck pointed to parallels between Luther's and Zwingli's debates over Christ's presence in the Eucharist and such old Scholastic disputations as that over the Immaculate Conception of the Virgin.

Humanist culture and learning nonetheless remained indebted to the Reformation. The Protestant endorsement of the humanist program of studies remained as significant for the humanist movement as the latter had been for the Reformation. Protestant schools and universities consolidated and preserved for the modern world many of the basic pedagogical achievements of humanism. There, the *studia humanitatis*, although often as little more than a handmaiden to theological doctrine, found a permanent home, one that remained hospitable even in the heyday of conservative Protestantism.

The Reformation and the Changing Role of Women

The Protestant reformers favored clerical marriage and opposed monasticism and the celibate life. From this position, they challenged the medieval tendency alternately

[2]Geoffrey Parker, *Europe in Crisis, 1598–1648* (Ithaca, NY: Cornell University Press, 1979), p. 50.

to degrade women as temptresses (following the model of Eve) and to exalt them as virgins (following the model of Mary). Protestants opposed the popular antiwoman and antimarriage literature of the Middle Ages. They praised woman in her own right, but especially in her biblical vocation as mother and housewife. Although wives remained subject to their husbands, new laws gave them greater security and protection.

Read the Document
"Catherine Zell, 'Letter to Ludwig Rabus,' 1556–1558" on
MyHistoryLab.com

Relief of sexual frustration and a remedy for fornication were prominent in Protestant arguments for universal marriage. But the reformers also viewed their wives as indispensable companions in their work, and this not solely because they took domestic cares off their husbands' minds. Luther, who married in 1525 at the age of forty-two, wrote the following of women:

Imagine what it would be like without women. The home, cities, economic life, and government would virtually disappear. Men cannot do without women. Even if it were possible for men to beget and bear children, they still could not do without women.[3]

John Calvin wrote this upon the death of his wife:

I have been bereaved of the best companion of my life, of one who, had it been so ordered, would not only have been the willing sharer of my indigence, but even of my death. During her life she was the faithful helper of my ministry.[4]

Such tributes were intended to counter Catholic criticism of clerical marriage as a distraction of the clergy from their ministry. They were an expression of the high value Protestants placed on marriage and family life. In opposition to the celibate ideal of the Middle Ages, Protestants stressed, as no religious movement before them had ever done, the sacredness of home and family.

The ideal of the companionate marriage—that is, of husband and wife as coworkers in a special God-ordained community of the family, sharing authority equally within the household—led to an expansion of the grounds for divorce in Protestant lands as early as the 1520s. Women gained an equal right with men to divorce and remarry in good conscience—unlike the situation in Catholicism, where only a separation from bed and table, not divorce and remarriage, was permitted a couple in a failed marriage. The reformers were more willing to permit divorce and remarriage on grounds of adultery and abandonment than were secular magistrates, who feared liberal divorce laws would lead to social upheaval.

Typical of reforms and revolutions in their early stages, Protestant doctrines emboldened women as well as men. Renegade nuns wrote exposés of the nunnery in the name of Christian freedom and justification by faith, declaring the nunnery was no special woman's place at all and that supervisory male clergy (who alone could hear the nuns' confessions and administer sacraments to them) made their lives as unpleasant and burdensome as any abusive husband. Women in the higher classes, who enjoyed new social and political freedoms during the Renaissance, found in Protestant theology a religious complement to their greater independence in other walks of life. Some cloistered noblewomen, however, protested the closing of nunneries, arguing that the cloister provided them a more interesting and independent way of life than they would have known in the secular world.

Because Protestants wanted women to become pious housewives, they encouraged the education of girls to literacy in the vernacular, with the expectation that they would thereafter model their lives on the Bible. However, women also found biblical passages that made clear their equality to men in the presence of God. Education also gave some women roles as independent authors on behalf of the Reformation. Although small advances from a modern perspective, these were also steps toward the emancipation of women.

▼ Family Life in Early Modern Europe

Changes in the timing and duration of marriage, family size, and infant and child care suggest that family life was under a variety of social and economic pressures in the sixteenth and seventeenth centuries.

Later Marriages

Between 1500 and 1800, men and women in Western Europe married at later ages than they had in previous centuries: men in their mid- to late twenties, and women in their early to mid-twenties. The canonical, or church-sanctioned, age for marriage remained fourteen for men and twelve for women. The church also recognized as valid free, private exchanges of vows between a man and a woman for whom no impediment to marriage existed. After the Reformation, which condemned such clandestine unions, both Protestants and Catholics required parental consent and public vows in church before a marriage could be deemed fully licit.

Late marriage in the West reflected the difficulty couples had supporting themselves independently. It simply took the average couple a longer time than before to prepare themselves materially for marriage. In

---

[3]*Luther's Works*, Vol. 54: *Table Talk*, ed. and trans. by Theodore G. Tappert (Philadelphia: Fortress Press, 1967), p. 161.

[4]*Letters of John Calvin*, Vol. 2, trans. by J. Bonnet (Edinburgh, UK: T. Constable, 1858), p. 216; E. G. Schwiebert, *Luther and His Times* (St. Louis, MO: Concordia, 1950), pp. 226–227, 266–268, 581–602; Steven Ozment, *Protestants: The Birth of a Revolution* (New York: Doubleday, 1992), pp. 17, 154, 159–162.

the sixteenth century, one in five women never married, and these, combined with the estimated 15 percent who were unmarried widows, constituted a large unmarried female population. A later marriage was also a shorter marriage; in an age when few people lived into their sixties, couples who married in their thirties spent less time together than couples who married in their twenties. Also, because women who bore children for the first time at advanced ages had higher mortality rates, late marriage meant more frequent remarriage for men. As the rapid growth of orphanages and foundling homes between 1600 and 1800 makes clear, delayed marriage increased premarital sex and the number of illegitimate children.

Arranged Marriages

Marriage tended to be "arranged" in the sense that the parents met and discussed the terms of the marriage before the prospective bride and bridegroom became directly party to the preparations. The wealth and social standing of the bride and the bridegroom, however, were not the only things considered when youth married. By the fifteenth century, it was usual for the future bride and bridegroom to have known each other and to have had some prior relationship. Also, parents respected the couple's emotional feeling for one another. Parents did not force total strangers to live together, and children had a legal right to resist a coerced marriage, which was by definition invalid. The best marriage was one desired by both the bride and groom and their families.

Family Size

The Western European family was conjugal, or nuclear, consisting of a father and a mother and two to four children who survived into adulthood. This nuclear family lived within a larger household, including in-laws, servants, laborers, and boarders. The average husband and wife had six to seven children, a new birth about every two years. Of these, an estimated one-third died by age five, and one-half by their teens. Rare was the family, at any social level, that did not experience child death.

Birth Control

Artificial birth control (sponges, acidic ointments) has existed since antiquity. The church's condemnation of *coitus interruptus* (male withdrawal before ejaculation) during the thirteenth and fourteenth centuries suggests the existence of a contraceptive mentality, that is, a conscious, regular effort at birth control. Early birth control measures, when applied, were not very effective, and for both historical and moral reasons, the church opposed them. According to Saint Thomas Aquinas, a moral act

must aid and abet, never frustrate, nature's goal, and the natural end of sex was the birth of children and their godly rearing within the bounds of holy matrimony and the community of the church.

Wet Nursing

The church allied with the physicians of early modern Europe on another intimate family matter. Both condemned women who hired wet nurses to suckle their newborn children. The practice was popular among upper-class women and reflected their social standing. It appears to have increased the risk of infant mortality by exposing infants to a strange and shared milk supply from women who were often not as healthy as the infants' own mothers and lived under less sanitary conditions. Nursing was distasteful to some upper-class women, whose husbands also preferred that they not do it. Among women, vanity and convenience appear to have been motives for hiring a wet nurse, while for husbands, even more was at stake. Because the church forbade lactating women from indulging in sexual intercourse, a nursing wife could become a reluctant lover. Nursing also had a contraceptive effect (about 75 percent effective). Some women prolonged nursing their children to delay a new pregnancy, and some husbands cooperated in this form of family planning. For other husbands, however, especially noblemen and royalty who desired an abundance of male heirs, nursing seemed to rob them of offspring and jeopardize their patrimony—hence their support of hired wet nurses.

Loving Families?

The traditional Western European family had features that seem cold and distant. Children between the ages of eight and thirteen were routinely sent from their homes into apprenticeships, school, or employment in the homes and businesses of relatives, friends, and occasionally strangers. The emotional ties between spouses also seem to have been as tenuous as those between parents and children. Widowers and widows often married again within a few months of their spouses' deaths, and marriages with extreme difference in age between partners suggest limited affection.

In response to modern-day criticism, an early modern parent might well have asked: "What greater love can parents have for their children than to equip them well for a worldly vocation?" A well-apprenticed child was a self-supporting child, and hence a child with a future. In light of the comparatively primitive living conditions, contemporaries also appreciated the purely utilitarian and humane side of marriage and understood when widowers and widows quickly remarried. Marriages with extreme disparity in age, however, were no more the norm in early modern Europe than the practice of wet

TABLE MANNERS

PLEASURE AT TABLE in the sixteenth century was considered a matter of self-control. The well-dressed table taught the lessons of life as well as offered its bread. Neatness and order showed respect, respect ensured attentiveness, and attentiveness made for learning. The union of pleasure and discipline at mealtime was believed to inculcate in the young the traits that would keep them free and safe in an unforgiving world. Here is how Hans Sachs, a sixteenth-century father, expected children to behave:

Listen you children who are going to table.
Wash your hands and cut your nails.
Do not sit at the head of the table;
This is reserved for the father of the house.
Do not commence eating until a blessing has
    been said.
Dine in God's name
And permit the eldest to begin first.
Proceed in a disciplined manner.
Do not snort or smack like a pig.
Do not reach violently for bread,
Lest you may knock over a glass.
Do not cut bread on your chest,
Or conceal pieces of bread or pastry under
    your hands.
Do not tear pieces for your plate with your teeth.
Do not stir food around on your plate
Or linger over it.
Do not fill your spoon too full.
Rushing through your meal is bad manners.

Do not reach for more food
While your mouth is still full,
Nor talk with your mouth full.
Be moderate; do not fall upon your plate like
    an animal.
Be the last to cut your meat and break your fish.
Chew your food with your mouth closed.
Do not lick the corners of your mouth like a dog.
Do not hover greedily over your food.
Wipe your mouth before you drink,
So that you do not grease up your wine.
Drink politely and avoid coughing into your cup.
Do not belch or cry out.
With drink be most prudent.
Sit smartly, undisturbed, humble . . .
Do not stare at a person
As if you were watching him eat.
Do not elbow the person sitting next to you.
Sit up straight; be a model of gracefulness.
Do not rock back and forth on the bench,
Lest you let loose a stink.
Do not kick your feet under the table.
Guard yourself against all shameful
Words, gossip, ridicule, and laughter . . .
If sexual play occurs at table,
Pretend you do not see it.
Never start a quarrel,
Quarreling at table is most despicable.
Say nothing that might offend another.
Do not blow your nose
Or do other shocking things.
Do not pick your nose.
If you must pick your teeth, be discreet about it.
Never scratch your head
(This goes for girls and women too);
Or fish out lice.
Let no one wipe his mouth on the table cloth,
Or lay his head in his hands.
Do not lean back against the wall
Until the meal is finished.
Silently praise and thank God
For the food he has graciously provided. . . .

From S. Ozment, *When Fathers Ruled: Family Life in Reformation Europe* (Cambridge, MA: Harvard University Press, 1983), pp. 142–43.

A family meal.   bpk, Berlin/Kupferstichkabinett, Staatliche Museen, Berlin, Germany/Joerg P. Anders/Art Resource, NY

How do table manners prepare a child for life?

Has table etiquette changed since the sixteenth century?

nursing, and they received just as much criticism and ridicule.

▼ Literary Imagination in Transition

Alongside the political and cultural changes brought about by the new religious systems of the Reformation (Lutheranism, Calvinism, and Puritanism) and Catholic Reform, medieval outlooks and religious values continued to be debated, embraced, and rejected into the seventeenth century. Major literary figures of the post-Reformation period had elements of both the old and the new in their own new transitional works. Two who stand out are Miguel de Cervantes Saavedra (1547–1616), writing in still deeply Catholic Spain, and William Shakespeare (1564–1616), who wrote in newly Anglican England.

Miguel de Cervantes Saavedra: Rejection of Idealism

Spanish literature of the sixteenth and seventeenth centuries reflects the peculiar religious and political history of Spain in this period. Traditional Catholic teaching was a major influence on Spanish life. Since the joint reign of Ferdinand and Isabella (1479–1504), the church had received the unqualified support of the reigning political power. Although there was religious reform in Spain, and genuine Protestant groups were persecuted for "Lutheranism," a Protestant Reformation never occurred there, thanks largely to the entrenched power of the church and the Inquisition.

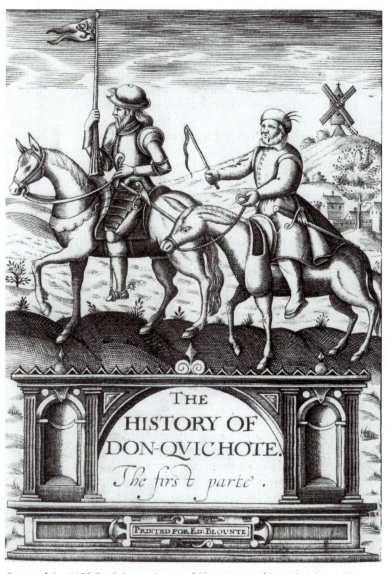

Cover of the 1620 English translation of *The History of Don-Quichote, The Firste Parte.* HIP/Art Resource, NY

A second influence on Spanish literature was the aggressive piety of Spanish rulers. Their intertwining of Catholic piety and political power underlay a third influence: preoccupation with medieval chivalric virtues, in particular, questions of honor and loyalty. The novels and plays of the period almost invariably focus on a special test of character, bordering on the heroic, that threatens honor and reputation. In this regard, Spanish literature remained more Catholic and medieval than that of England and France, where major Protestant movements had occurred. Two of the most important Spanish writers of this period became priests (the dramatists Lope de Vega and Pedro Calderón de la Barca). The writer generally acknowledged to be Spain's greatest, Cervantes, was preoccupied in his work with the strengths and weaknesses of traditional religious idealism.

Cervantes (1547–1616) had only a smattering of formal education. He educated himself by wide reading in popular literature and immersion in the "school of life." As a young man, he worked in Rome for a Spanish cardinal. As a soldier, he was decorated for gallantry in the Battle of Lepanto against the Turks (1571). He also spent five years as a slave in Algiers after his ship was pirated in 1575. Later, while working as a tax collector, he was imprisoned several times for padding his accounts, and it was in prison that he began, in 1603, to write his most famous work, *Don Quixote.*

Read the **Document**
"Miguel de Cervantes, *Don Quixote*" on **MyHistoryLab.com**

The first part of *Don Quixote* appeared in 1605. The intent of this work seems to have been to satirize the chivalric romances then popular in Spain. But Cervantes could not conceal his deep affection for the character he created as an object of ridicule. The work is satire only on the surface and appeals as much to philosophers and theologians as to students of Spanish literature. Cervantes presented Don Quixote as a none-too-stable middle-aged man. Driven mad by reading too many chivalric romances, he had come to believe he was an aspiring knight who had to prove his worthiness by brave deeds. To this end, he donned a rusty suit of armor and chose for his inspiration an unworthy peasant girl (Dulcinea), whom he fancied to be a noble lady to whom he could, with honor, dedicate his life.

Don Quixote's foil—Sancho Panza, a clever, worldly wise peasant who serves as Quixote's squire—watches with bemused skepticism as his lord does battle with a windmill (which he has mistaken for a dragon) and repeatedly makes a fool of himself as he gallops across the countryside. The story ends tragically with Don Quixote's humiliating defeat at the hand of a well-meaning friend who, disguised as a knight, bested Quixote in combat and forced him to renounce his quest for knighthood. Don Quixote did not, however, come to his senses but rather returned to his village to die a brokenhearted old man.

Throughout the novel, Cervantes juxtaposes the down-to-earth realism of Sancho Panza with the old-fashioned religious idealism of Don Quixote. The reader perceives that Cervantes admired the one as much as the other and meant to portray both as representing attitudes necessary for a happy life.

William Shakespeare: Dramatist of the Age

There is much less factual knowledge about Shakespeare (1564–1616) than we would expect of the greatest playwright in the English language. He married at the early age of eighteen, in 1582, and he and his wife, Anne Hathaway, were the parents of three children (including twins) by 1585. He apparently worked as a schoolteacher for a time and in this capacity gained his broad knowledge of Renaissance literature. His own reading and enthusiasm for the learning of his day are manifest in the many literary allusions that appear in his plays.

Shakespeare lived the life of a country gentleman. There is none of the Puritan distress over worldliness in his work. He took the new commercialism and the bawdy pleasures of the Elizabethan Age in stride and with amusement. He was a radical neither in politics nor religion. The few allusions in his works to the Puritans seem more critical than complimentary.

That Shakespeare was interested in politics is apparent from his historical plays and the references to contemporary political events that fill all his work. He viewed government through the character of the individual ruler, whether Richard III or Elizabeth Tudor, rather than in terms of ideal systems or social goals. By modern standards, he was a political conservative, accepting the social rankings and the power structure of his day and demonstrating unquestioned patriotism.

Shakespeare knew the theater as one who participated in every phase of its life—as a playwright, an actor, and part owner of a theater. He was a member and principal writer of a famous company of actors known as the King's Men. Between 1590 and 1610, many of his plays were performed at court, where he moved with comfort and received enthusiastic royal patronage.

Elizabethan drama was already a distinctive form when Shakespeare began writing. Unlike French drama of the seventeenth century, which was dominated by classical models, English drama developed in the sixteenth and seventeenth centuries as a blending of many forms: classical comedies and tragedies, medieval morality plays, and contemporary Italian short stories.

Two contemporaries, Thomas Kyd and Christopher Marlowe, influenced Shakespeare's tragedies. Kyd (1558–1594) wrote the first dramatic version of *Hamlet*. The tragedies of Marlowe (1564–1593) set a model for character, poetry, and style that only Shakespeare among the English playwrights of the period surpassed. Shakespeare synthesized the best past and current achievements. A keen student of human motivation and passion, he had a unique talent for getting into people's minds.

Shakespeare wrote histories, comedies, and tragedies. *Richard III* (1593), an early play, stands out among the histories, although some scholars view the picture it presents of Richard as an unprincipled villain as "Tudor propaganda." Shakespeare's comedies, although not attaining the heights of his tragedies, surpass his history plays in originality.

Shakespeare's tragedies are considered his unique achievement. Four of these were written within a three-year period: *Hamlet* (1603), *Othello* (1604), *King Lear* (1605), and *Macbeth* (1606). The most original of the tragedies, *Romeo and Juliet* (1597), transformed an old popular story into a moving drama of "star-cross'd lovers." Both Romeo and Juliet, denied a marriage by their warring families, die tragic deaths. Romeo, believing Juliet to be dead when she has merely taken a sleeping potion, poisons himself. When Juliet awakes to find Romeo dead, she kills herself with his dagger.

Shakespeare's works struck universal human themes, many of which were deeply rooted in contemporary religious traditions. His plays were immensely popular with both the playgoers and the play readers of Elizabethan England. Still today, the works of no other dramatist from his age are performed in theaters or on film more regularly than his.

In Perspective

During the early Middle Ages, Christendom had been divided into Western and Eastern churches with irreconcilable theological differences. When, in 1517, Martin Luther posted ninety-five theses questioning the selling of indulgences and the traditional sacrament of penance that lay behind them, he created a division within Western Christendom itself—an internal division between Protestants and Catholics.

The Lutheran protest came at a time of political and social discontent with the church. Not only princes and magistrates but many ordinary people as well resented traditional clerical rights and privileges. The clergy were exempted from many secular laws and taxes while remaining powerful landowners whose personal lifestyles were not all that different from those of the laity. Spiritual and secular protest combined to make the Protestant Reformation a successful assault on the old church. In town after town and region after region within Protestant lands, the major institutions and practices of traditional piety were transformed.

It soon became clear, however, that the division would not stop with the Lutherans. Making Scripture the only arbiter in religion had opened a Pandora's box.

People proved to have different ideas about what Scripture taught. Indeed, there seemed to be as many points of view as there were readers. Rapidly, the Reformation created Lutheran, Zwinglian, Anabaptist, Spiritualist, Calvinist, and Anglican versions of biblical religion—a splintering of Protestantism that has endured and increased until today.

Catholics had been pursuing reform before the Reformation broke out in Germany, although without papal enthusiasm and certainly not along clear Protestant lines. When major reforms finally came in the Catholic Church around the mid-sixteenth century, they were doctrinally reactionary, but administratively and spiritually flexible. The church enforced strict obedience and conformity to its teaching, but it also provided the laity with a better educated and disciplined clergy. For laity who wanted a deeper and more individual piety, experimentation with proven spiritual practices was now permitted. By century's end, such measures had countered, and in some areas even spectacularly reversed, Protestant gains.

After the Reformation, pluralism steadily became a fact of Western religious life. It did so at first only by sheer force, since no one religious body was then prepared to concede the validity of alternative Christian beliefs and practices. During the sixteenth and seventeenth centuries, only those groups that fought doggedly for their faith gained the right to practice it freely. Despite these struggles, religious pluralism endured. Never again would there be only a Catholic Christian Church in Europe.

KEY TERMS

Act of Supremacy (p. 339)
Anabaptists (p. 332)

Augsburg Confession (p. 337)

electors (p. 325)
indulgence (p. 324)

predestination (p. 334)
Reformation (p. 321)

REVIEW QUESTIONS

1. What problems in the church contributed to the Protestant Reformation? Why was the church unable to suppress dissent as it had earlier?

2. What were the basic similarities and differences between the ideas of Luther and Zwingli? Between Luther and Calvin? How did the differences tend to affect the success of the Protestant movement?

3. Why did the Reformation begin in Germany? What political factors contributed to its success there as opposed to in France, Spain, or Italy?

4. What was the Catholic Counter-Reformation? What reforms did the Council of Trent introduce? Was the

Protestant Reformation healthy for the Catholic Church?

5. Why did Henry VIII break with Rome? Was the "new" church he established really Protestant? How did the English church change under his successors?

6. How did the Reformation affect women in the sixteenth and seventeenth centuries? How did relations between men and women, family size, and child care change during this period?

SUGGESTED READINGS

H. Bloom, *Shakespeare: The Invention of the Human* (1998). An analysis of the greatest writer in the English language.

T. A. Brady, Jr. ed., *Handbook of European History: Late Middle Ages, Renaissance, Reformation* (1995). Essays summarizing recent Reformation research.

P. Collinson, *The Reformation* (2004). Portrays the Reformation as creating religious pluralism and civil liberties.

E. Duffy, *The Stripping of the Altars: Traditional Religion in England, 1400–1580* (1992). Argues that popular Catholic piety survived the Reformation in England.

M. Duran, *Cervantes* (1974). Detailed biography.

B. S. Gregory, *Salvation at Stake: Christian Martyrdom in Early Modern Europe* (1999). Massive, enthralling study of religion.

R. Houlbrooke, *English Family Life, 1450–1716: An Anthology from Diaries* (1988). A rich collection of documents illustrating family relationships.

J. C. Hutchison, *Albrecht Dürer: A Biography* (1990). An art historian chronicles both the life and work of the artist.

H. Jedin, *A History of the Council of Trent*, Vols. 1 and 2 (1957–1961). Still the gold standard.

P. Johnston and R. W. Scribner, *The Reformation in Germany and Switzerland* (1993). Reformation from the bottom up.

B. J. Kaplan, *Divided by Faith* (2007), The birth of toleration in Early Modern Europe.

D. MacCulloch, *The Reformation* (2004). Finds old Catholics and non-Protestant Evangelicals to be the forerunners of modern religion.

H. A. Oberman, *Luther: Man between God and the Devil* (1989). The best account of Luther's life, written by a Dutch master.

J. O'Malley, *The First Jesuits* (1993). Detailed account of the creation of the Society of Jesus and its original purposes.

S. Ozment, *The Age of Reform, 1250–1550: An Intellectual and Religious History of Late Medieval and Reformation Europe* (1980). Broad survey of major religious ideas and beliefs.

B. Roberts, *Through the Keyhole: Dutch Child-Rearing Practices in the 17th and 18th Centuries* (1998). A study of three elite families.

Q. Skinner, *The Foundations of Modern Political Thought II: The Age of Reformation* (1978). A comprehensive survey that treats every political thinker and tract.

D. Starkey, *Elizabeth: The Struggle for the Throne* (2000). Complex, riveting account by a sympathetic historian.

L. Stone, *The Family, Sex, and Marriage in England 1500–1800* (1977). A controversial oldie, but enduring in many respects.

G. Strauss, ed. and trans., *Manifestations of Discontent in Germany on the Eve of the Reformation* (1971). Rich collection of both rural and urban grievances.

F. Wendel, *Calvin: The Origins and Development of His Religious Thought*, trans. by P. Mairet (1963). Arguably the best treatment of Calvin's theology.

H. Wunder, *He Is the Sun, She Is the Moon: A History of Women in Early Modern Germany* (1998). A model of gender history.

MyHistoryLab™ MEDIA ASSIGNMENTS

Find these resources in the Media Assignments folder for Chapter 11 on **MyHistoryLab**.

QUESTIONS FOR ANALYSIS

1. How do you think these engravings, produced on a large scale, influenced the direction of Christian belief in this period?

   Section: **Society and Religion**
   View the **Closer Look** A Saint At Peace in the Grasp of Temptation, p. 322

2. Which of Luther's propositions do you think the Catholic Church would have found most alarming?

   Section: **Martin Luther and the German Reformation to 1525**
   Read the **Document** Martin Luther, "Ninety-Five Theses" (Holy Roman Empire), 1517, p. 325

3. How did the work of the Jesuits differ from the work of earlier orders, such as the Benedictines or Franciscans?

   Section: **Catholic Reform and Counter-Reformation**
   Watch the **Video** The Global Mission of the Jesuits (Thomas Taylor), p. 341

4. Was this act a political or religious decision?

   Section: **The English Reformation to 1553**
   Read the **Document** The Act of Supremacy (England), 1534, p. 339

5. How did such widely distributed images influence the religious debates of the Reformation?

   Section: **Martin Luther and the German Reformation to 1525**
   View the **Image** Johann Tetzel Selling Indulgences, p. 325

OTHER RESOURCES FROM THIS CHAPTER

Society and Religion
View the **Map** Map Discovery: The Spread of Printing, p. 323

Martin Luther and the German Reformation to 1525
View the **Map** The Hapsburgs in Europe After the Peace of Augsburg, 1555, p. 326

Read the **Document** Martin Luther, *Against the Murderous, Thieving Hordes of Peasants* (1525), p. 328

The massacre of worshipping Protestants at Vassy, France (March 1, 1562), which began the French wars of religion. An engraving by an unidentified seventeenth-century artist.   The Granger Collection

((•⊏ **Listen** to the **Chapter Audio** on **MyHistoryLab.com**

12

The Age of Religious Wars

▼ **Renewed Religious Struggle**

▼ **The French Wars of Religion (1562–1598)**
Appeal of Calvinism • Catherine de Médicis and the Guises • The Rise to Power of Henry of Navarre • The Edict of Nantes

▼ **Imperial Spain and Philip II (r. 1556–1598)**
Pillars of Spanish Power • The Revolt in the Netherlands

▼ **England and Spain (1553–1603)**
Mary I (r. 1553–1558) • Elizabeth I (r. 1558–1603)

▼ **The Thirty Years' War (1618–1648)**
Preconditions for War • Four Periods of War • The Treaty of Westphalia

▼ **In Perspective**

LEARNING OBJECTIVES

How did religious conflict in Europe evolve over the course of the second half of the sixteenth century?

What caused the civil war between the Huguenots and the Catholics in France and what was the outcome?

How was Philip II able to dominate international politics for much of the latter half of the sixteenth century?

What role did Catholic and Protestant extremism play in the struggle for supremacy between England and Spain?

What toll did the Thirty Years' War take on Germany?

THE LATE SIXTEENTH and seventeenth centuries saw combined religious and political conflicts fired by religion and state-building across Europe. New confessional and dynastic rivalries born of the Reformation continued to fuel bloody wars for much of the century, giving it the accursed name "The Age of Religious Wars." Both genuine religious belief and uncompromising dynastic expansion fueled the wars. In France, the Netherlands, England, and Scotland, Calvinists fought Catholic rulers for the right to govern and maintain their own territories, while practicing their religious confession openly without fear. In the first half of the seventeenth century, Lutherans, Calvinists, and Catholics marched against one another in central and northern Europe in what is today remembered as "The

Thirty Years' War." By the mid-seventeenth century, English Puritans successfully revolted against both the Stuart monarchy and the Anglican Church. (See Chapter 13.)

▼ Renewed Religious Struggle

In the first half of the sixteenth century, religious conflict had been confined to central Europe and was primarily a struggle by Lutherans and Zwinglians to secure rights and freedoms for themselves. In the second half of the century, the focus shifted to Western Europe—to France, the Netherlands, England, and Scotland—and became a struggle by Calvinists for recognition. After the Peace of Augsburg (1555) and acceptance of the political principle that a region's ruler determined its religion (*cuius regio, eius religio*), Lutheranism became a fully legal confession in the Holy Roman Empire. The Peace of Augsburg did not, however, extend recognition to non-Lutheran Protestants. Anabaptists and other sectarian separatists continued to be scorned as heretics and anarchists, while Calvinists were not strong enough to seize legal standing.

Outside the empire, the struggle for political and religious freedom had intensified in most lands. After the Council of Trent adjourned in 1563, Catholics organized a Jesuit-led international counteroffensive against Protestants. At the time of John Calvin's death (1564), Geneva had become both a refuge for Europe's persecuted Protestants and an international school for Protestant resistance, producing leaders equal to the new Catholic challenge.

Genevan Calvinism and Roman Catholicism, as revived by the Council of Trent, were two equally dogmatic, aggressive, and irreconcilable forces. Calvinists may have looked like "new papists" to their critics when they dominated cities like Geneva. But when, as minorities, they found their civil and religious rights denied, they became firebrands and revolutionaries. Calvinists adopted a political organization that magnified regional and local authority. Boards of **presbyters**, or elders, represented and instructed the individual congregations that were directly shaping policies both sacred and secular.

By contrast, the **Counter-Reformation** sponsored a centralized episcopal church system hierarchically arranged from pope to parish priest, stressing obedience without question to the person at the top. The high clergy—the pope and his bishops—not the synods of local churches, were supreme. Calvinism proved attractive to proponents of political decentralization who opposed hierarchical rule, whereas the Roman Catholic Church, an institution also devoted to one head and one law, found absolute monarchy congenial.

The opposition between the two religions may be seen in their respective art and architecture. The Catholic Counter-Reformation found the baroque style congenial. A successor to mannerism, **baroque** art presented life in a grandiose, three-dimensional display of raw energy. The great baroque artists Peter Paul Rubens (1571–1640) and Gianlorenzo Bernini (1598–1680) were Catholics. By contrast, the works of prominent Protestant artists were restrained, as can be seen in the gentle, searching portraits of the Dutch Mennonite, Rembrandt van Rijn (1606–1669). (See the juxtaposition of Bavarian Catholic and Palatine Calvinist churches in "A Closer Look: Baroque and Plain Church: Architectural Reflections of Belief," page 357.)

As the religious wars engulfed Europe, the intellectuals perceived the wisdom of religious pluralism and toleration more quickly than did the politicians. A new skepticism, relativism, and individualism became respectable in the sixteenth and seventeenth centuries. (See Chapter 14.) Bold humanist Sebastian Castellio (1515–1563) had a pithy censure for John Calvin after his role in the execution of Anti-Trinitarian physician Michael Servetus. "To kill a man is not to defend a doctrine, but to kill a man."[1] French essayist Michel de Montaigne (1533–1592) also asked in scorn of the dogmatic mind, "What do I know?" Lutheran Valentin Weigel (1533–1588), surveying a half-century of religious strife in Germany, advised people to look within themselves for religious truth, and no longer to the hardened churches and their creeds.

Such skeptical views gained currency in larger political circles only at the cost of painful sacrifice. Religious strife and civil war were best held in check where rulers acted to subordinate theological doctrine to political unity, urging tolerance, moderation, and compromise—even indifference—in religious matters. Rulers of this kind came to be known as ***politiques***, and the most successful among them was Elizabeth I of England. By contrast, Mary I of England, Philip II of Spain, and Oliver Cromwell—all of whom took their religion with the utmost seriousness and refused any compromise—did not, in the end, achieve their political goals.

The wars of religion were both internal national conflicts and truly international wars. Catholic and Protestant subjects struggled against one another for control of the crown of France, the Netherlands, and England. The Catholic governments of France and Spain conspired and finally sent armies against Protestant regimes in England and the Netherlands. The outbreak of the Thirty Years' War in 1618 made the international dimension of the religious conflict especially clear: before it ended in 1648, the war drew every major European nation directly or indirectly into its deadly net.

---

[1]*Contra libellum Calvini* (N.P., 1562), p. E2a.

▼ The French Wars of Religion (1562–1598)

French Protestants are known as **Huguenots**, a term derived from Besançon Hugues, the leader of Geneva's political revolt against the House of Savoy in the 1520s, which had been a prelude to the city's Calvinist Reformation. Huguenots were already under surveillance in France in the early 1520s when Lutheran writings and doctrines began to circulate in Paris. The capture of French king Francis I by the forces of Emperor Charles V at the Battle of Pavia (1525) provided a motive for the first wave of Protestant persecution in France. The French government hoped thereby to pacify the Habsburg victor, a fierce opponent of German Protestants, and to win their king's swift release.

A second major crackdown came a decade later. When Protestants plastered Paris and other cities with anti-Catholic placards on October 18, 1534, mass arrests of suspected Protestants followed. The government retaliation drove John Calvin and other members of the French reform party into exile. In 1540, the Edict of Fontainebleau subjected French Protestants to the Inquisition. Henry II (r. 1547–1559) established new measures against Protestants in the Edict of Chateaubriand in 1551. Save for a few brief interludes, the French monarchy remained a staunch foe of the Protestants until the ascension to the throne of Henry IV of Navarre in 1589.

The Habsburg-Valois wars (see Chapter 11) had ended with the Treaty of Cateau-Cambrésis in 1559, after which Europe experienced a moment of peace. The same year, however, marked the beginning of internal French conflict and a shift of the European balance of power away from France to Spain. The shift began with an accident. During a tournament held to celebrate the marriage of his thirteen-year-old daughter to Philip II, the son of Charles V and heir to the Spanish Habsburg lands, the French king, Henry II, was mortally wounded when a lance pierced his visor. This unforeseen event brought to the throne his sickly fifteen-year-old son, Francis II, who died after reigning only a year (1559–1560). With the monarchy weakened, three powerful families saw their chance to control France and began to compete for the young king's ear: the Bourbons, whose power lay in the south and west; the Montmorency-Chatillons, who controlled the center of France; and the strongest among them, the Guises, who were dominant in eastern France.

The Guises had little trouble establishing firm control over the young king. Francis, duke of Guise, had been Henry II's general and his brothers, Charles and Louis, were cardinals of the church. Mary Stuart, Queen of Scots, the eighteen-year-old widow of Francis II, was their niece. Throughout the latter half of the sixteenth century, the name "Guise" was interchangeable with militant, reactionary Catholicism.

The Bourbon and Montmorency-Chatillon families, in contrast, developed strong Huguenot sympathies, largely for political reasons. The Bourbon Louis I, prince of Condé (d. 1569), and the Montmorency-Chatillon admiral Gaspard de Coligny (1519–1572) became the political leaders of the French Protestant resistance. They collaborated early in an abortive plot to kidnap Francis II from his Guise advisers in the Conspiracy of Amboise in 1560. Calvin, who considered such tactics a disgrace to the Reformation, condemned this conspiracy.

Appeal of Calvinism

Often for different reasons, ambitious aristocrats and discontented townspeople joined the Calvinist churches in opposing the Guise-dominated French monarchy. In 1561, more than 2,000 Huguenot congregations existed throughout France. Yet Huguenots were a majority of the population in only two regions: Dauphiné and Languedoc. Although they made up only about one-fifteenth of the population, Huguenots held important geographic areas and were heavily represented among the more powerful segments of French society. A good two-fifths of the French aristocracy became Huguenots. Many apparently hoped to establish within France a principle of territorial sovereignty akin to what the Peace of Augsburg had secured within the Holy Roman Empire. Calvinism thus served the forces of political decentralization.

John Calvin and Theodore Beza sought to advance their cause by currying favor with powerful aristocrats. Beza converted Jeanne d'Albert, the mother of the future Henry IV. The prince of Condé was apparently converted in 1558 under the influence of his Calvinist wife. For many aristocrats—Condé probably among them—Calvinist religious convictions proved useful to their political goals.

The military organization of Condé and Coligny progressively merged with the religious organization of the French Huguenot churches, creating a potent combination that benefited both political and religious dissidents. Calvinism justified and inspired political resistance, while the resistance made Calvinism a viable religion in Catholic France. Each side had much to gain from the other. The confluence of secular and religious motives cast suspicion on the religious appeal of Calvinism. Clearly, religious conviction was neither the only, nor the main, reason for becoming a Calvinist in France in the second half of the sixteenth century.

Catherine de Médicis and the Guises

Following Francis II's death in 1560, the queen mother, Catherine de Médicis (1519–1589) became regent for her minor son, Charles IX (r. 1560–1574). At a meeting in Poissy, she tried unsuccessfully to reconcile the

A Closer LOOK

View the Closer Look on MyHistoryLab.com

BAROQUE AND PLAIN CHURCH: ARCHITECTURAL REFLECTIONS OF BELIEF

CONTRAST AN eighteenth-century Catholic baroque church in Ottobeuren, Bavaria, and a seventeenth-century Calvinist plain church in the Palatinate. The Catholic church pops with sculptures, paintings, and ornamentation, while the Calvinist church has been stripped of every possible decoration.

Decorated altars dominate the interior of the Catholic church and make the sacrifice of the Eucharist in the Mass the center of worship. Here, the intent is to inspire worshippers to self-transcendence.

Vanni/Art Resource, NY

The open Bible and raised pulpit dominate the Protestant church. Here, the intent is to keep worshippers' attention on God's word and their own mortal souls to prevent any form of decoration from distracting them.

What were the prominent features of a Catholic Church?

Of a Calvinist Church?

What might explain or account for the differences in the two churches?

German National Museum, Nuremberg, Germany

Catherine de Médicis (1519–1589) exercised power in France during the reigns of her three sons, Francis II (r. 1559–1560), Charles IX (r. 1560–1574), and Henry III (r. 1574–1589). North Wind Picture Archives/Alamy

Protestant and Catholic factions. Fearing the power and guile of the Guises, Catherine, whose first concern was always to preserve the monarchy, sought allies among the Protestants. In 1562, after conversations with Beza and Coligny, she issued the January Edict, which granted Protestants freedom to worship publicly outside towns—although only privately within them—and to hold synods. In March 1562, this royal toleration came to an abrupt end when the duke of Guise surprised a Protestant congregation at Vassy in Champagne and massacred many worshippers. That event marked the beginning of the French wars of religion.

◗ View the Map "Map Discovery: Religious Divisions in France During the Wars of Religion" on MyHistoryLab.com

Had Condé and the Huguenot armies rushed immediately to the queen's side after this attack, Protestants might well have secured an alliance with the crown. But the queen mother's fear of Guise power was great. Condé's hesitation, however, placed the young king and the queen mother, against their deepest wishes, under firm Guise control. Cooperation with the Guises became the only alternative to capitulation to the Protestants.

The Peace of Saint-Germain-en-Laye   During the first French war of religion, fought between April 1562 and March 1563, the duke of Guise was assassinated. It was a measure of the international character of the struggle in France that troops from Hesse and the Palatinate fought alongside the Huguenots. A brief resumption of hostilities in 1567–1568 was followed by the bloodiest of all the conflicts, between September 1568 and August 1570. Condé was killed, and Huguenot leadership passed to Coligny. This was actually a blessing in disguise for the Protestants because Coligny was far the better military strategist. In the peace of Saint-Germain-en-Laye (1570), which ended the third war, the crown, acknowledging the power of the Protestant nobility, granted the Huguenots religious freedoms within their territories and the right to fortify their cities.

Perpetually caught between fanatical Huguenot and Guise extremes, Queen Catherine always sought to balance one side against the other. Like the Guises, she wanted a Catholic France, but feared a Guise-dominated monarchy. After the Peace of Saint-Germain-en-Laye, the crown tilted manifestly toward the Bourbon faction and the Huguenots, and Coligny became Charles IX's most trusted adviser. Unknown to the king, Catherine began to plot with the Guises against the ascendant Protestants. As she had earlier sought Protestant support when Guise power threatened to subdue the monarchy, she now sought Guise support as Protestant influence grew.

There was reason for Catherine to fear Coligny's hold on the king. Louis of Nassau, the leader of Protestant resistance in the Netherlands, had gained Coligny's ear. Coligny used his influence to win the king of France over to a French invasion of the Netherlands in support of the Dutch Protestants. This would have placed France squarely on a collision course with mighty Spain. Catherine recognized far better than her son that France stood little chance in such a contest. News of the stunning Spanish victory over the Turks at Lepanto in October 1571 had sobered Catherine and her advisors.

The Saint Bartholomew's Day Massacre   When Catherine lent her support to the infamous Saint Bartholomew's Day Massacre of Protestants, she did so out of a far less reasoned judgment. Her decision appears to have been made in near panic. On August 22, 1572, four days after the Huguenot Henry of Navarre had married the king's sister, still another sign of growing Protestant power, Coligny was struck down, although not killed, by an assassin's bullet. Catherine had apparently been party to the Guise plot to eliminate Coligny. After its failure, she feared both the king's reaction to her complicity with the Guises and Coligny's response. Catherine convinced Charles that a Huguenot coup was afoot, inspired by Coligny, and that only the swift execution of Protestant leaders could save the crown from a Protestant attack on Paris.

On Saint Bartholomew's Day, August 24, 1572, Coligny and 3,000 fellow Huguenots were butchered in Paris. Within three days coordinated attacks across France killed an estimated 20,000 Huguenots. It is a date that has ever since lived in infamy for Protestants.

Pope Gregory XIII and Philip II of Spain reportedly greeted the news of the Protestant massacre with special religious celebrations. Philip had good reason to rejoice. By throwing France into civil war, the massacre ended any planned French opposition to his efforts to subdue his rebellious subjects in the Netherlands. But the massacre of thousands of Protestants also gave the discerning Catholic world cause for new alarm. The event changed the nature of the struggle between Protestants and Catholics both within and beyond the borders of France. It was thereafter no longer an internal contest between Guise and Bourbon factions for French political influence, nor was it simply a Huguenot campaign to win basic religious freedoms. Henceforth, in Protestant eyes, it became an international struggle for sheer survival against an adversary whose cruelty justified any means of resistance.

▶ Read the Document
"Massacre of St. Bartholomew (1572)" on
MyHistoryLab.com

Protestant Resistance Theory   Only as Protestants faced suppression and sure defeat did they begin to sanction active political resistance. At first, they tried to practice the biblical precept of obedient subjection to worldly authority (Romans 13:1). Luther had only grudgingly approved resistance to the emperor after the Diet of Augsburg in 1530. In 1550, Lutherans in Magdeburg published an influential defense of the right of lower authorities to oppose the emperor's order that all Lutherans return to the Catholic fold.

Calvin, who never faced a total political defeat after his return to Geneva in September 1540, had always condemned willful disobedience and rebellion against lawfully constituted governments as un-Christian. Yet he also taught that lower magistrates, as part of the lawfully constituted government, had the right and duty to oppose tyrannical higher authority.

The exiled Scots reformer John Knox (1513–1572), who had seen Mary of Guise, the Regent of Scotland, and Mary I of England crush his cause, laid the groundwork for later Calvinist resistance. In his *First Blast of the Trumpet against the Terrible Regiment of Women* (1558), he declared that the removal of a heathen tyrant was not only permissible, but also a Christian duty. He had the Catholic queen of England in mind.

After the great massacre of French Protestants on Saint Bartholomew's Day 1572, Calvinists everywhere came to appreciate the need for an active defense of their religious rights. Classical Huguenot theories of resistance appeared in three major works of the 1570s. The first was the *Franco-Gallia* of François Hotman (1573), a humanist argument that the representative Estates General of France historically held higher authority than the French king. The second was Theodore Beza's *On the Right of Magistrates over Their Subjects* (1574), which justified the correction and even the overthrow of tyrannical rulers by lower authorities. (See the Document "Theodore Beza Defends the Right to Resist Tyranny," page 360.) Finally, Philippe du Plessis Mornay's *Defense of Liberty against Tyrants* (1579) admonished princes, nobles, and magistrates beneath the king, as guardians of the rights of the body politic, to take up arms against tyranny in other lands.

The Rise to Power of Henry of Navarre

Henry III (r. 1574–1589) was the last of Henry II's sons to wear the French crown. He found the monarchy wedged between a radical Catholic League, formed in 1576 by Henry of Guise, and vengeful Huguenots. Neither group would have been reluctant to assassinate a ruler they considered heretical and a tyrant. Like the queen mother, Henry sought to steer a middle course. In this effort, he received support from a growing body of neutral Catholics and Huguenots, who put the political survival of France above its religious unity. Such *politiques* were prepared to compromise religious creeds to save the nation.

The Peace of Beaulieu in May 1576 granted the Huguenots almost complete religious and civil freedom. France, however, was not ready then for such sweeping toleration. Within seven months of the Peace, the Catholic League forced Henry to return to the illusory quest for absolute religious unity in France. In October 1577, the king truncated the Peace of Beaulieu and once again limited areas of permitted Huguenot worship. Thereafter, Huguenot and Catholic factions returned to their accustomed anarchical military solutions. The Protestants were led by Henry of Navarre, a legal heir to the French throne by virtue of his descent in a direct male line from St. Louis IX (d. 1270).

In the mid-1580s, the Catholic League, with Spanish support, became dominant in Paris. In what came to be known as the Day of the Barricades, Henry III attempted to rout the league with a surprise attack in 1588. The effort failed, and the king had to flee Paris. Forced by his weakened position into unkingly guerrilla tactics, and also emboldened by news of the English victory over the Spanish Armada in 1588, Henry had both the duke and the cardinal of Guise assassinated. These murders sent France reeling once again. Led by still another Guise brother, the Catholic League reacted with a fury that matched the earlier Huguenot response to the Massacre of Saint Bartholomew's Day. The king was now forced to strike an alliance with the Protestant Henry of Navarre in April 1589.

As the two Henrys prepared to attack the Guise stronghold of Paris, however, an enraged Dominican friar killed Henry III. Thereupon, the Bourbon Huguenot Henry of Navarre succeeded the childless Valois king to the French throne as Henry IV (r. 1589–1610). Pope Sixtus V and King Philip II were aghast at the sudden prospect of a Protestant France. They had always wanted France to be religiously Catholic and politically weak, and they now acted to achieve that end. Spain rushed troops to support the besieged Catholic League. Philip II apparently even hoped to place his eldest daughter, Isabella, the granddaughter of Henry II and Catherine de Médicis, on the French throne.

Direct Spanish intervention in the affairs of France seemed only to strengthen Henry IV's grasp on the crown.

Document

THEODORE BEZA DEFENDS THE RIGHT TO RESIST TYRANNY

One of the oldest problems in political and social theory has been that of knowing when resistance to repression in matters of conscience is justified. Since Luther's day, Protestant reformers, although accused by their Catholic critics of fomenting social division and revolution, had urged their followers to strict obedience to established political authority. After the 1572 massacre of Saint Bartholomew's Day, however, Protestant pampheteers urged Protestants to resist tyrants and persecutors with armed force. Here, in 1574, Theodore Beza points out the obligation of rulers to their subjects and the latter's right to resist rulers who fail to meet the conditions of their office.

Who has the obligation to act against a tyrannical king or a ruler? What are the circumstances that empower the lower officers of a kingdom to take charge? In what sense, and when, are the people "prior to the sovereign and all magistrates"? Where in earlier centuries have the rights of the people been declared to be "prior to all the magistrates"?

It is apparent that there is a mutual obligation between the king and the officers of a kingdom; that the government of the kingdom is not in the hands of the king in its entirety, but only the sovereign degree; that each of the officers has a share in accord with his degree; and that there are definite conditions on either side. If these conditions are not observed by the inferior officers, it is the part of the sovereign to dismiss and punish them. . . . If the king, hereditary or elective, clearly goes back on the conditions without which he would not have been recognized and acknowledged, can there be any doubt that the lesser magistrates of the kingdom, of the cities, and of the provinces, the administration of which they have received from the sovereignty itself, are free of their oath, at least to the extent that they are entitled to resist flagrant oppression of the realm which they swore to defend and protect according to their office and their particular jurisdiction? . . .

We must now speak of the third class of subjects, which though admittedly subject to the sovereign in a certain respect, is, in another respect, and in cases of necessity the protector of the rights of the sovereignty itself, and is established to hold the sovereign to his duty, and even, if need be, to constrain and punish him. . . . The people is prior to all the magistrates, and does not exist for them, but they for it. . . . Whenever law and equity prevailed, nations neither created nor accepted kings except upon definite conditions. From this it follows that when kings flagrantly violate these terms, these who have the power to give them their authority have no less power to deprive them of it.

From Julian H. Franklin, trans. and ed., *Constitutionalism and Resistance in the Sixteenth Century: Three Treatises* (New York: Pegasus, 1969), pp. 111–114.

The French people viewed his right to hereditary succession more seriously than his Protestantism. Henry was also widely liked. Notoriously informal in dress and manner—which made him especially popular with the soldiers—Henry also had the wit and charm to neutralize the strongest enemy in a face-to-face confrontation. He came to the throne as a *politique*, long weary with religious strife and fully prepared to place political peace above absolute religious unity. He believed a royal policy of tolerant Catholicism would be the best way to achieve such peace. On July 25, 1593, he publicly abandoned the Protestant faith and embraced the traditional and majority religion of his country. "Paris is worth a Mass," he is reported to have said.

It was, in fact, a decision he had made only after a long period of personal agonizing. The Huguenots were horrified, and Pope Clement VIII was skeptical of Henry's sincerity, but most of the French church and people, having known internal strife too long, rallied to his side. By 1596, the Catholic League was dispersed, its ties with Spain were broken, and the wars of religion in France, to all intents, had ground to a close.

The Edict of Nantes

On April 13, 1598, Henry IV's Edict of Nantes proclaimed a formal religious settlement. The following month, on May 2, 1598, the Treaty of Vervins ended hostilities between France and Spain.

Read the **Document**
"The Edict of Nantes (France), 1598" on **MyHistoryLab.com**

In 1591, Henry IV had already assured the Huguenots of at least qualified religious freedoms. The Edict of Nantes made good that promise. It recognized minority religious rights within what was to remain an officially

Henry IV of France (r. 1589–1610) on horseback, painted in 1594.   Réunion des Musées Nationaux/Art Resource, NY

Catholic country. This religious truce—and it was never more than that—granted the Huguenots, who by this time numbered well over a million, freedom of public worship, the right of assembly, admission to public offices and universities, and permission to maintain fortified towns. They were to exercise most of the new freedoms, however, within their own towns and territories. Concession of the right to fortify their towns revealed the continuing distrust between French Protestants and Catholics. As significant as it was, the edict only transformed a long hot war between irreconcilable enemies into a long cold one. To its critics, it had created a state within a state.

A Catholic fanatic assassinated Henry IV in May 1610. Although he is best remembered for the Edict of Nantes, Henry IV's political and economic policies were equally important. They laid the foundations for the transformation of France into the absolute state it would become under Cardinal Richelieu and Louis XIV. (See Chapter 13.) Ironically, in pursuit of the political and religious unity that had escaped Henry IV, Louis XIV, calling for "one king, one law, one faith," would revoke the Edict of Nantes in 1685, an action that forced France and the rest of Europe to learn again by bitter experience the hard lessons of the wars of religion.

▼ Imperial Spain and Philip II (r. 1556–1598)

Pillars of Spanish Power

Until the English defeated the mighty Spanish Armada in 1588, no one person stood larger in the second half of the sixteenth century than Philip II of Spain. Philip was heir to the intensely Catholic and militarily supreme western Habsburg kingdom. His father, Charles V, had given the eastern Habsburg lands of Austria, Bohemia, and Hungary to Philip's uncle, the emperor Ferdinand I (r. 1558–1564). These lands, together with the imperial title, remained in the possession of the Austrian branch of the family until 1918.

View the Image
"Hispania Slaying
Leviathan" on
MyHistoryLab.com

New World Riches Populous and wealthy Castile gave Philip a solid home base. The regular arrival in Seville of bullion from the Spanish colonies in the New World provided additional wealth. In the 1540s, great silver mines had been opened in Potosí in present-day Bolivia and in Zacatecas in Mexico. These provided the great sums needed to pay the king's bankers and mercenaries. He nonetheless never managed to erase the debts his father left or to finance his own foreign adventures fully. He later contributed to the bankruptcy of the Fuggers when, at the end of his life, he defaulted on his enormous debts.

Increased Population The new American wealth brought dramatic social change to the peoples of Europe during the second half of the sixteenth century. As Europe became richer, it was also becoming more populous. In the economically and politically active towns of France, England, and the Netherlands, populations had tripled and quadrupled by the early seventeenth century. Europe's population exceeded 70 million by 1600.

The combination of increased wealth and population triggered inflation. A steady 2-percent-a-year rise in prices in much of Europe had serious cumulative effects by the mid-sixteenth century. There were more people and more coinage in circulation than before, but less food and fewer jobs; wages stagnated while prices doubled and tripled in much of Europe.

This was especially the case in Spain. Because the new wealth was concentrated in the hands of a few, the traditional gap between the haves—the propertied, privileged, and educated classes—and the have-nots widened. Nowhere did the unprivileged suffer more than in Spain, where the Castilian peasantry, the backbone of Philip II's great empire, became the most heavily taxed people of Europe. Those whose labor contributed most to making possible Spanish hegemony in Europe in the second half of the sixteenth century prospered least from it.

Efficient Bureaucracy and Military A subjugated peasantry and wealth from the New World were not the only pillars of Spanish strength. Philip II shrewdly organized the lesser nobility into a loyal and efficient national bureaucracy. A reclusive man, he managed his kingdom by pen and paper rather than by personal presence. He was also a learned and pious Catholic, although some popes suspected he used religion as much for political as for devotional purposes. That he was a generous patron of the arts and culture can be seen in his unique retreat outside Madrid, the Escorial, a combination palace, church, tomb, and monastery. Philip also knew personal sorrows: His mad and treacherous son, Don Carlos, died under suspicious circumstances in 1568—some contemporaries suspected that Philip had him quietly executed—only three months before the death of his queen.

Supremacy in the Mediterranean During the first half of Philip's reign, attention focused almost exclusively on the Mediterranean and the Turkish threat. By history, geography, and choice, Spain had traditionally been Catholic Europe's champion against Islam. During the 1560s, the Turks advanced deep into Austria, and their fleets dominated the Mediterranean. Between 1568 and 1570, armies under Philip's half-brother, Don John of Austria (1547–1578), the illegitimate son of Charles V, suppressed and dispersed the Moors in Granada.

Read the Document
"Venetian Observations
on the Ottoman Empire
(late 16th c.)" on
MyHistoryLab.com

In May 1571, a Holy League of Spain, Venice, Genoa, and the pope, again under Don John's command, formed to check Turkish belligerence in the Mediterranean. In the largest naval battle of the sixteenth century, Don John's fleet engaged the Ottoman navy under Ali Pasha off Lepanto in the Gulf of Corinth on October 7, 1571. Before the engagement ended, over a third of the Turkish fleet had been sunk or captured, and 30,000 Turks had died. However, the resilient Ottomans still maintained their base in Cyprus and would soon rebuild their fleet and regain control of the eastern Mediterranean. For the moment, however, the Mediterranean belonged to Spain, and the Europeans were left to fight each other. Philip's armies also suppressed resistance in neighboring Portugal, when Philip inherited the throne of that kingdom in 1580. The union with Portugal not only enhanced Spanish sea power, but it also brought Portugal's overseas empire in Africa, India, and Brazil into the Spanish orbit.

The Revolt in the Netherlands

The spectacular Spanish military success in southern Europe was not repeated in northern Europe. When Philip attempted to impose his will within the Netherlands and on England and France, he learned the lessons of defeat. The resistance of the Netherlands especially proved the undoing of Spanish dreams of world empire. (See Map 12–1, p. 364.)

Cardinal Granvelle The Netherlands was the richest area not only of Philip's Hapsburg kingdom, but of Europe as well. In 1559, Philip departed the Netherlands for Spain, never again to return. His half-sister, Margaret of Parma, assisted by a special council of state, became regent in his place. The council was headed by the extremely able Antoine Perrenot (1517–1586), known after 1561 as Cardinal Granvelle, who hoped to check Protestant gains by internal church reforms. He planned to break down the traditional local autonomy of the seventeen Netherlands provinces by stages and establish in its place a centralized royal government directed from Madrid. A politically docile and religiously uniform country was the goal.

The merchant towns of the Netherlands were, however, Europe's most independent; many, like magnificent Antwerp, were also Calvinist strongholds. By tradition and habit, the people of the Netherlands were far more disposed to variety and toleration than to obedient conformity and hierarchical order. Two members of the council of state led a stubborn opposition to the Spanish overlords, who now attempted to reimpose their traditional rule with a vengeance. They were the Count of Egmont (1522–1568) and William of Nassau, the Prince of Orange (1533–1584), known as "the Silent" because of his small circle of confidants.

Like other successful rulers in this period, William of Orange placed the political autonomy and well-being of the Netherlands above religious creeds. He personally was successively a confessed Catholic, Lutheran, and Calvinist. In 1561, he married Anne of Saxony, the daughter of the Lutheran elector Maurice and the granddaughter of the late landgrave Philip of Hesse. He maintained his Catholic practices until 1567, the year he turned Lutheran. After the Saint Bartholomew's Day Massacre (1572), Orange (as he was called) became an avowed Calvinist.

In 1561, Cardinal Granvelle proceeded with his planned ecclesiastical reorganization of the Netherlands. It was intended to tighten the control of the Catholic hierarchy over the country and to accelerate its consolidation as a Spanish ward. Organizing the Dutch nobility in opposition, Orange and Egmont succeeded in gaining Granvelle's removal from office in 1564. Aristocratic control of the country after Granvelle's departure, however, proved woefully inefficient. Popular unrest grew, especially among urban artisans, who joined the congregations of radical Calvinist preachers in large numbers.

The Compromise The year 1564 also saw the first fusion of political and religious opposition to Regent Margaret's government. This opposition resulted from Philip II's unwise insistence on trying to enforce the decrees of the Council of Trent throughout the Netherlands. William of Orange's younger brother, Louis of Nassau, who had been raised a Lutheran, led the opposition with support from the Calvinist-inclined lesser nobility and townspeople. A national covenant called the *Compromise* was

Map 12–1 **The Netherlands during the Reformation** The northern and southern provinces of the Netherlands. The former, the United Provinces, were mostly Protestant in the second half of the sixteenth century; the southern Spanish Netherlands made peace with Spain and remained largely Catholic.

drawn up, a solemn pledge to resist the decrees of Trent and the Inquisition. Grievances were loudly and persistently voiced. When Regent Margaret's government spurned the protesters as "beggars" in 1566, Calvinists rioted throughout the country. Louis called for aid from French Huguenots and German Lutherans, and a full-scale rebellion against the Spanish regency appeared imminent.

The Duke of Alba The rebellion failed to materialize, however, because the higher nobility of the Netherlands would not support it. Their shock at Calvinist iconoclasm and anarchy was as great as their resentment of Granvelle's more subtle repression. Philip, determined to

make an example of the Protestant rebels, dispatched the duke of Alba to suppress the revolt. His army of 10,000 journeyed northward from Milan in 1567 in a show of combined Spanish and papal might. A special tribunal, known to the Spanish as the Council of Troubles and among the Netherlanders as the Council of Blood, reigned over the land. Before Alba's reign of terror ended, the counts of Egmont and Horn and several thousand suspected heretics were publicly executed.

The Spanish levied new taxes, forcing the Netherlands to pay for the suppression of its own revolt. One, the "tenth penny," a 10 percent sales tax, met such resistance from merchants and artisans that it could not be collected in some areas even after reduction to 3 percent. Combined persecution and taxation sent tens of thousands fleeing from the Netherlands during Alba's six-year rule, a man more hated than Granvelle or the radical Calvinists had ever been.

Resistance and Unification   William of Orange was an exile in Germany during these turbulent years. He now emerged as the leader of a broad movement for the independence of the Netherlands from Spain. The northern, Calvinist-inclined provinces of Holland, Zeeland, and Utrecht, of which Orange was the *Stadholder*, or governor, became his base. As in France, political resistance in the Netherlands gained both organization and inspiration by merging with Calvinism.

The early victories of the resistance attest to the popular character of the revolt. A case in point is the capture of the port city of Brill by the "Sea Beggars," an international group of anti-Spanish exiles and criminals, among them many Englishmen. William of Orange did not hesitate to enlist their services. Their brazen piracy, however, had forced Queen Elizabeth to disassociate herself from them and to bar their ships from English ports. In 1572, the Beggars captured Brill and other seaports in Zeeland and Holland. Mixing with the native population, they quickly sparked rebellions against Alba in town after town and spread the resistance southward. In 1574, the people of Leiden heroically resisted a long Spanish siege. The Dutch opened the dikes and flooded their country to repulse the hated Spanish. The faltering Alba had by that time ceded power to Don Luis de Requesens, who replaced him as commander of the Spanish forces in the Netherlands in November 1573.

The Pacification of Ghent   The greatest atrocity of the war came after Requesens's death in 1576. Spanish mercenaries, leaderless and unpaid, ran amok in Antwerp on November 4, 1576, leaving 7,000 people dead in the streets. The event came to be known as the Spanish Fury.

These atrocities accomplished in just four days what neither religion nor patriotism had previously been able to do. The ten largely Catholic southern provinces (what is roughly modern Belgium) now came together with the seven largely Protestant northern provinces (what is roughly the modern Netherlands) in unified opposition to Spain. This union, known as the Pacification of Ghent, was accomplished on November 8, 1576. It declared internal regional sovereignty in matters of religion, a key clause that permitted political cooperation among the signatories, who were not agreed over religion. It was a Netherlands version of the territorial settlement of religious differences brought about in the Holy Roman Empire in 1555 by the Peace of Augsburg. Four

provinces initially held out, but they soon made the resistance unanimous by joining the all-embracing Union of Brussels in January 1577. For the next two years, the Spanish faced a unified and determined Netherlands.

View the **Map** "The Netherlands During the Dutch Revolt, ca. 1580" on **MyHistoryLab.com**

Don John, the victor over the Turks at Lepanto in 1571, had taken command of Spanish land forces in November 1576. He now experienced his first defeat. Confronted by unified Netherlands' resistance, he signed the humiliating Perpetual Edict in February 1577, which provided for the removal of all Spanish troops from the Netherlands within twenty days. The withdrawal gave the country to William of Orange and effectively ended, for the time being, whatever plans Philip may have had for using the Netherlands as a staging area for an invasion of England.

The Union of Arras and the Union of Utrecht   The Spanish, however, were nothing if not persistent. Don John and Alexander Farnese of Parma, the Regent Margaret's son, revived Spanish power in the southern provinces, where fear of Calvinist extremism had moved the leaders to break the Union of Brussels. In January 1579, the southern provinces formed the Union of Arras and soon made peace with Spain. These provinces later served the cause of the Counter-Reformation. The northern provinces responded by forming the Union of Utrecht.

Netherlands Independence   Seizing what now appeared to be a last opportunity to break the back of Netherlands' resistance, Philip II declared William of Orange an outlaw and placed a bounty of 25,000 crowns on his head. The act predictably stiffened the resistance of the northern provinces. In a defiant speech to the Estates General of Holland in December 1580 known as "the Apology," Orange publicly denounced Philip as a heathen tyrant whom the Netherlands need no longer obey.

On July 22, 1581, the member provinces of the Union of Utrecht met in The Hague and formally declared Philip no longer their ruler. They turned instead to the French duke of Alençon, the youngest son of Catherine de Médicis. The southern provinces had also earlier looked to him as a possible middle way between Spanish and Calvinist overlordship. All the northern provinces save Holland and Zeeland (which distrusted him almost as much as they did Philip II) accepted Alençon as their "sovereign" but with the clear understanding that he would be only a titular ruler. Yet Alençon, an ambitious failure, saw this as his one chance at greatness. When he rashly attempted to take actual control of the provinces in 1583, he was deposed and returned to France.

Spanish efforts to reconquer the Netherlands continued into the 1580s. William of Orange, assassinated in July

NOT LONGE TIME SINCE I SAWE A COWE. DID FLAVNDERS REPRESENTE VPON WHOSE BACKE KINGE PHILIP RODE AS BEING MALECONTNT.

THE QVEENE OF ENGLAND GIVING HAY WHEARE ON THE COW DID FEEDE. AS ONE THAT WAS HER GREATEST HELPE. IN HER DISTRESSE AND NEEDE.

THE PRINCE OF ORANGE MILKT THE CO AND MADE HIS PVRSE THE PAYLE THE COW DID SHYT IN MONSIEVRS HAND WHILE HE DID HOLD HER TAYLE.

The Milch Cow, a sixteenth-century satirical painting depicting the Netherlands as a cow in whom all the great powers of Europe have an interest. Elizabeth of England is feeding her (England had long-standing commercial ties with Flanders); Philip II of Spain is attempting to ride her (Spain was trying to reassert its control over the entire area); William of Orange is trying to milk her (he was the leader of the anti-Spanish rebellion); and the king of France holds her tail (France hoped to profit from the rebellion at Spain's expense). Rijksmuseum, Amsterdam

1584, was succeeded by his seventeen-year-old son, Maurice (1567–1625), who, with the assistance of England and France, continued the Dutch resistance. Fortunately for the Netherlands, Philip II began now to meddle directly in French and English affairs. He signed a secret treaty with the Guises (the Treaty of Joinville in December 1584) and sent armies under Alexander Farnese into France in 1590. Hostilities with the English also increased. Gradually, they built to a climax in 1588, when Philip's great Armada was defeated in the English Channel.

These new fronts overextended Spain's resources, thus strengthening the Netherlands. Spanish preoccupation with France and England now permitted the northern provinces to drive out all Spanish soldiers by 1593. In 1596, France and England formally recognized their independence. Peace was not, however, concluded with Spain until 1609, when the Twelve Years' Truce gave the northern provinces virtual independence. Full recognition came with the Peace of Westphalia in 1648.

▼ England and Spain (1553–1603)

Before Edward VI died in 1553, he agreed to a plan to make Lady Jane Grey his successor in place of the Catholic Mary Tudor (r. 1553–1558). Jane was the teenage daughter of a powerful Protestant nobleman and the granddaughter of Henry VIII's younger sister Mary. Unfortunately for poor Jane, popular support for the principle of hereditary monarchy was too strong to deprive Mary of her rightful rule. Uprisings in London and elsewhere led to Jane Grey's removal from the throne within days of her crowning, and she was eventually beheaded.

Mary I (r. 1553–1558)

Once enthroned, Mary proceeded to act even beyond the worst fears of the Protestants. In 1554, she entered a highly unpopular political marriage with Philip (later Philip II) of Spain, a symbol of militant Catholicism to English Protestants. At his direction, she pursued a foreign policy that in 1558 cost England its last enclave on the Continent, Calais.

Mary's domestic measures were equally shocking to the English people and even more divisive. During

Portrait of Mary I (r. 1553–1558), Queen of England. Queen Mary I, 1554 (oil on panel) by Sir Anthonis Mor (Antonio Moro) (1517/20-76/7). Prado, Madrid, Spain/ Bridgeman Art Library

her reign, Parliament repealed the Protestant statutes of Edward and reverted to the Catholic religious practice of her father, Henry VIII. The great Protestant leaders of the Edwardian Age—John Hooper, Hugh Latimer, and Thomas Cranmer—were executed for heresy. Hundreds of Protestants either joined them in martyrdom (287 were burned at the stake during Mary's reign) or fled to the Continent. These "Marian exiles" settled in Germany and Switzerland. John Knox, the future leader of the Reformation in Scotland, was prominent among them. There, they waited for the time when a Protestant counteroffensive could be launched in their homelands. Many of these exiles later held positions in the Church of England under Elizabeth I's reign.

Elizabeth I (r. 1558–1603)

Mary's successor was her half-sister, Elizabeth I, the daughter of Henry VIII and Anne Boleyn. Elizabeth had remarkable and enduring successes in both domestic and foreign policy. Assisted by a shrewd adviser, Sir William Cecil (1520–1598), she built a true kingdom on the ruins of Mary's reign. Between 1559 and 1603, she and Cecil guided a religious settlement through Parliament that prevented religious differences from tearing England apart in the sixteenth century. A ruler who subordinated religious to political unity, Elizabeth merged a centralized episcopal system that she firmly controlled with broadly defined Protestant doctrine and traditional Catholic ritual. The resulting Anglican Church contained inflexible religious extremes for decades.

In 1559, the Act of Supremacy passed Parliament. It repealed all of the anti-Protestant legislation of Mary Tudor's reign and asserted Elizabeth's right as "supreme governor" over both spiritual and temporal affairs. In the same year, the Act of Uniformity mandated a revised version of the second *Book of Common Prayer* (1552) for every English parish. A decade later, the **Thirty-Nine Articles**, a revision of Thomas Cranmer's original forty-two, made a moderate Protestantism the official religion within the Church of England.

Read the **Document** "Acts of Uniformity, 1559" on **MyHistoryLab.com**

Catholic and Protestant Extremists Elizabeth hoped to avoid both Catholic and Protestant extremism by pursuing a middle way. Her first archbishop of Canterbury, Matthew Parker (d. 1575), represented this ideal. Elizabeth could not prevent the emergence of subversive Catholic and Protestant zealots, however. When she ascended the throne, Catholics were in the majority in England. The extremists among them, encouraged by

The Great Debate Over Religious Tolerance

📖 Read the **Compare and Connect** on **MyHistoryLab.com**

ON OCTOBER 27, 1553, Spanish physician and amateur theologian Michael Servetus died at the stake in Geneva for alleged "blasphemies against the Holy Trinity." A bold and confident man, he had also incurred the wrath of Rome before badgering John Calvin in Geneva on theological issues. In the wake of Servetus's execution, Calvin was much criticized for fighting heresy with capital punishment. In 1544, he came to his own defense in a tract entitled *Defense of the Orthodox Faith in the Holy Trinity Against the Monstrous Errors of Michael Servetus of Spain*. Thereafter, Sebastian Castellio, an accomplished humanist and former rector of the college in Geneva, whom Calvin had driven out of the city years earlier, began a series of writings against Calvin. One of his titles, *Whether Heretics Should Be Punished By the Sword of the Magistrates*, was an anonymous anthology on religious toleration that included a supporting excerpt from John Calvin himself! Writing over the years under several pseudonyms, Castellio excerpted statements from Calvin's works and put them in a sustained "debate" with his own liberal point of view.

QUESTIONS

1. Why does Calvin believe that heresy deserves capital punishment?

2. What are Castellio's best rebuttal arguments?

3. Why does Castellio write under pseudonyms?

CALVIN: Kings are duty bound to defend the doctrine of piety.

CASTELLIO: [Yes, but] to kill a man is not to defend doctrine, but rather to kill a man . . .

CALVIN: What of today? The majority of people have lost all sense of shame and openly mock God. They burst as boldly into God's awesome mysteries as pigs poke their snouts into costly storehouses.

CASTELLIO: Calvin appears to be criticizing himself. For truly the awesome mysteries of God are the Trinity, predestination, and election. But this man [Calvin] speaks so assuredly about these matters that one would think he was in Paradise. So thorny is his own teaching about the Trinity . . . that by his own curiosity he weakens and makes doubtful the consciences of the simple. He has taught so crudely about predestination that innumerable men have been seduced into a security as great as that which existed before the Flood . . .

Tell me, in brief, what you think about predestination.

CALVIN: I have been taught the following about predestination: All men are not created in an equal state. Rather in eternity, God, by inevitable decree, determined in advance those whom he would save and those whom he would damn to destruction. Those whom he has deemed worthy of salvation have been chosen by his mercy without consideration of their worthiness. And those given damnation, he shuts off from life by a just and irreprehensible, albeit incomprehensible, judgment.

CASTELLIO: So you maintain that certain men are created by God already marked for damnation so that they cannot be saved?

CALVIN: Precisely.

CASTELLIO: But what if they *should* obey God? Would they not then be saved?

CALVIN: They would then be saved. However, they are not able to obey God, because God excludes them from the knowledge of his name and the spirit of his justification so that they can and will do only evil and are inclined only to every kind of sin.

CASTELLIO: Hence, they have that inclination [to sin] from God's creation and predestination?

CALVIN: They have it so, just as surely as God has created the wolf with the inclination to eat sheep!

CASTELLIO: Therefore they have been damned and rejected by God even before they existed?

CALVIN: Exactly.

CASTELLIO: But are they not damned for their sins?

CALVIN: Indeed so. Those who were destined to that [damned] lot are completely worthy of it.

CASTELLIO: When were they worthy of it?

Queen Elizabeth I of England (r. 1558–1603) served as an example of religious tolerance during her reign. Despite her Protestant sympathies, she steered clear of both Catholic and Protestant extremism and, despite proven cases of Catholic treason and even attempted regicide, she executed fewer Catholics during her forty-five years on the throne than Mary Tudor had executed Protestants during her brief five-year reign.   Courtesy of the Library of Congress, Rare Book and Special Collections Division

CALVIN: When they were destined to it?

CASTELLIO: Then they have 'been' before they 'are.' Do you see what you are saying?!

CALVIN: I don't understand.

CASTELLIO: If they were worthy, then they 'were.' For to be worthy is to be. And if you concede that they have been damned before they are, then they have 'been' before they were.

CALVIN: God elects the foolish things of the world to confound the wise.

CASTELLIO: Calvin and his kind reject the foolish things of the world so that they may exalt the wise [themselves]. Hence, they admit hardly any-one into . . . their circle who is not accomplished in sciences and languages. . . . If Christ himself came to them, he would certainly be turned away if he spoke no Latin . . .

[But] Christ wishes to be judged by common sense and refers the matters of the gospel to human judgment. . . . He would never have employed such analogies had he wished to deprive us of our common sense. And who would have believed him had he taught things repugnant to nature and contradictory to human experience . . . ? What kind of master would he have been, had he said to the woman who cried out to him and washed his feet with her hair: "O woman, whatever your sin, it was done by God's decree!" ∎

From Steven Ozment, *Mysticism and Dissent: Religious Ideology and Social Protest in the Sixteenth Century* (New Haven, CT: Yale University Press), pp. 171–179.

GOING TO THE THEATER

THE MODERN ENGLISH stage play originated in the religious dramas that educated and entertained medieval Europeans for centuries before Shakespeare's birth in 1564. Teaching a lesson as well as telling a suspenseful story, these dramas were known as *morality plays* and typically were presented in the countryside by roving bands of players under church supervision. The medieval theater usually consisted of a small circular field for the actors, ringed by earthen mounds for the spectators. The circular stage was divided into four quadrants, each with its own tent at the four points of the compass: heaven at the east, evil at the north, worldly rulers at the west, and good characters at the south.

Each player emerged from his tent in turn to speak his lines, then went back in to await his next appearance. This format was a way of shifting scenes and a forerunner of the custom in modern theaters of ending a scene by lowering a curtain.

In England in the fifteenth century, as the urban population grew, ambitious promoters moved their productions into the courtyards of inns. London, the seat of the royal court, became the center of English theatrical life.

This sheltered, urban setting gave theater companies several advantages. Audiences were larger, and the inns could be easily renovated to provide permanent stages and more complex sets. The enclosed courtyards also made it easier to keep out nonpaying crashers, the greatest enemies of the new showmen—capitalists who produced and often wrote the plays and had to make a living from them.

Several of London's more scrupulous clergymen decried another advantage of the combined inn and theater—the opportunity it gave for sexual license. By the sixteenth century, the allegorical moralizing of the medieval country theater had evolved into the ribald, worldly entertainment of the London stage. Going to the theater was now more like being part of a festival than listening to a sermon. The workmen and young women who comprised much of the audience found it convenient to hire rooms in which they might romance one another during or after the performance.

London's theater world reached full maturity in the late sixteenth and early seventeenth centuries. The Rose and The Globe theaters, where many of Shakespeare's plays were presented, were built in the 1590s on the south bank of the River Thames, reachable only by water taxis. During Shakespeare's heyday, some 40,000 waterboys were said to ferry customers to these theaters. Performances by troupes of adult males or boys (women were banned from the stage) were often rowdy affairs, the crowds egged on both by the witty repartee on stage and the food and beer sold in the pit.

Sources: E. K. Chambers, *The Elizabethan Stage*, Vols. I–IV (Oxford, UK: Oxford University Press, 1923); Lawrence M. Clopper, *Drama, Play, and Game: English Festive Culture in the Medieval and Early Modern Period* (Chicago: University of Chicago Press, 2001); F. E. Halliday, *Shakespeare in His Age* (New York: Duckworth, 1956).

What were the basic elements and purpose of the medieval stage?

What was carried over from it to the Elizabethan theater?

A seventeenth-century sketch of the Swan Theater, which stood near Shakespeare's Globe Theater on the south bank of the Thames. The Bridgeman Art Library the Jesuits, plotted against her. The Spanish, piqued both by Elizabeth's Protestant sympathies and by her refusal to take Philip II's hand in marriage, encouraged and later directly assisted Catholic radicals. Elizabeth deliberately remained unmarried throughout her reign, using the possibility of a royal marriage to her diplomatic advantage.

Catholic extremists hoped eventually to replace Elizabeth with Mary Stuart, Queen of Scots. Unlike Elizabeth, who had been declared illegitimate during the reign of her father, Mary Stuart had an unblemished claim to the throne by way of her grandmother Margaret, the sister of Henry VIII. Elizabeth acted swiftly against Catholic assassination plots, rarely letting her emotions override her political instincts. Despite proven cases of Catholic treason and even attempted regicide, she executed fewer Catholics during her forty-five years on the throne than Mary Tudor had executed Protestants during her brief five-year reign.

Read the Document
"Anonymous Government Agent: 'Arrest of Edmund Campion and His Associates,' 1581" on **MyHistoryLab.com**

Elizabeth showed little mercy, however, to any who threatened the unity of her rule. She dealt cautiously with the Puritans, who were Protestants working within the national church to "purify" it of every vestige of "popery" and to make its Protestant doctrine more precise. The Puritans had two special grievances against her reign:

1. The retention of Catholic ceremony and vestments within the Church of England, which made it appear to the casual observer that no Reformation had occurred.

2. The continuation of the episcopal system of church governance, which conceived the English church to be theologically the true successor to Rome, while placing it politically under the firm hand of the queen and her compliant archbishop.

Sixteenth-century Puritans were not true separatists. They enjoyed popular support and were led by widely respected men like Thomas Cartwright (d. 1603). They worked through Parliament to create an alternative national church of semiautonomous congregations governed by representative presbyteries (hence, **Presbyterians**), following the model of Calvin and Geneva. Elizabeth dealt firmly, but subtly, with them, conceding nothing that lessened the hierarchical unity of the Church of England and her control over it.

The more extreme Puritans wanted every congregation to be autonomous, a law unto itself, with neither higher episcopal nor presbyterian control. They came to be known as **Congregationalists**. Elizabeth and her

An idealized likeness of Elizabeth Tudor when she was a princess, attributed to Flemish court painter L. B. Teerling, ca. 1551. The painting shows her blazing red hair and alludes to her learning by the addition of books.   UNKNOWN, formerly attributed to William Scrots. Elizabeth I, when Princess (1533–1603). Royal Collection Trust/© HM Queen Elizabeth II 2012

second archbishop of Canterbury, John Whitgift (d. 1604), refused to tolerate this group, whose views on independence they found patently subversive. The Conventicle Act of 1593 gave such separatists the option either to conform to the practices of the Church of England or face exile or death.

Deterioration of Relations with Spain   A series of events led inexorably to war between England and Spain, despite the sincere desires of both Philip II and Elizabeth to avoid a confrontation. In 1567, the Spanish duke of Alba marched his mighty army into the Netherlands, which was, from the English point of view, simply a convenient staging area for a Spanish invasion of England. Pope Pius V (r. 1566–1572), who favored a military conquest of Protestant England, "excommunicated" Elizabeth for heresy in 1570. This mischievous act encouraged both internal resistance and international intrigue against the queen. Two years later, as noted earlier, the piratical sea beggars, many of whom were Englishmen, occupied the port of Brill in the Netherlands and aroused the surrounding countryside against the Spanish.

Following Don John's demonstration of Spain's awesome sea power at Lepanto in 1571, England signed a mutual defense pact with France. Also in the 1570s, Elizabeth's famous seamen John Hawkins (1532–1595) and Sir Francis Drake (1545?–1596) began to prey regularly on Spanish shipping in the Americas. Drake's circumnavigation of the globe between 1577 and 1580 was one in a series of dramatic demonstrations of English ascendancy on the high seas.

After the Saint Bartholomew's Day Massacre, Elizabeth was the only protector of Protestants in France and the Netherlands. In 1585, she signed the Treaty of Nonsuch, which provided English soldiers and cavalry to the Netherlands. Funds that had previously been funneled covertly to support Henry of Navarre's army in France now flowed openly.

Mary, Queen of Scots

These events made a tinderbox of English–Spanish relations. The spark that finally touched it off was Elizabeth's execution of Mary, Queen of Scots (1542–1587).

Mary Stuart was the daughter of King James V of Scotland and Mary of Guise and had resided in France from the time she was six years old. This thoroughly French and Catholic queen had returned to Scotland after the death of her husband, the French king Francis II, in 1561. There she found a successful, fervent Protestant Reformation legally sanctioned the year before by the Treaty of Edinburgh (1560). As hereditary heir to the throne of Scotland, Mary remained queen by divine and human right and the Protestants who controlled her realm did not intimidate her. She established an international French court culture, the gaiety and sophistication of which impressed many Protestant nobles whose religion often made their lives exceedingly dour.

The ever-vigilant Scottish reformer John Knox watched Mary closely. He fumed publicly and always with effect against the queen's private Mass and other Catholic practices, which Scottish law made a capital offense for everyone else. Knox won support in his role of watchdog from Elizabeth and Cecil. Elizabeth personally despised Knox and never forgave him for writing the *First Blast of the Trumpet against the Terrible Regiment of Women*, a work aimed at provoking a revolt against Mary Tudor but, unfortunately for Knox, published in the year of Elizabeth's ascent to the throne. Elizabeth and Cecil tolerated Knox because they knew he would never permit Scotland to succumb to young Mary's French and Catholic ways.

In 1568, a public scandal forced Mary's abdication and flight to her cousin Elizabeth in England. Mary's reputed lover, the earl of Bothwell, was, with cause, suspected of having killed her legal husband, Lord Darnley. When a packed court acquitted Bothwell, he subsequently married Mary. The outraged reaction from Protestant nobles forced Mary to surrender the throne to her one-year-old son, the future James VI of Scotland and, later, Elizabeth's successor as King James I of England. Because of Mary's clear claim to the English throne, she was an international symbol of a possible Catholic England and consumed by the desire to be England's queen. For this reason, her presence in England, where she resided under house arrest for nineteen years, was a constant discomfort to Elizabeth.

In 1583, Elizabeth's vigilant secretary, Sir Francis Walsingham, uncovered a plot against Elizabeth involving the Spanish ambassador Bernardino de Mendoza. After Mendoza's deportation in January 1584, popular antipathy toward Spain and support for Protestant resistance in France and the Netherlands became massive throughout England.

In 1586, Walsingham uncovered still another plot against Elizabeth, the so-called Babington plot, after Anthony Babington, who was caught seeking Spanish support for an attempt on the queen's life. This time he had uncontestable proof of Mary's complicity. Elizabeth believed the execution of a sovereign, even a dethroned sovereign, weakened royalty everywhere. She was also aware of the outcry that Mary's execution would create throughout the Catholic world, and she sincerely wanted peace with English Catholics. Yet she really had no choice in the matter and consented to Mary's execution, which took place on February 18, 1587. This event dashed all Catholic hopes for a bloodless reconversion of Protestant England. After the execution of the Catholic queen of Scotland, Pope Sixtus V (r. 1585–1590), who feared Spanish domination almost as much as he abhorred English Protestantism, could no longer withhold public support for a Spanish invasion of England. Philip II ordered his Armada to make ready.

The Armada

In the spring of 1587, Sir Francis Drake shelled the port of Cádiz, inflicting heavy damages on Spanish ships and stores and interrupting Spain's war preparations. After "singeing the beard of Spain's king," as he put it, Drake raided the coast of Portugal, further incapacitating the Spanish. These strikes forced the Spanish to postpone their invasion of England until 1588.

Read the **Document**
"John Hawkins Reports on the Spanish Armada" on
MyHistoryLab.com

On May 30 of that year, 130 ships bearing 25,000 sailors and soldiers under the command of the duke of Medina-Sidonia set sail for England. In the end,

Engraving showing the destruction of the Spanish Armada by Captain Morgan. © Lebrecht Music and Arts Photo Library/Alamy

however, the English won a stunning victory. The invasion barges that were to transport Spanish soldiers from the galleons onto English shores were prevented from leaving Calais and Dunkirk. The swifter English and Netherlands' ships, helped by what came to be known as an "English wind," dispersed the waiting Spanish fleet, over one-third of which never returned to Spain.

The news of the Armada's defeat gave heart to Protestant resistance everywhere. Although Spain continued to win impressive victories in the 1590s, it never fully recovered. Spanish soldiers faced unified and inspired French, English, and Dutch armies. By the time of Philip's death on September 13, 1598, his forces had been rebuffed on all fronts. His seventeenth-century successors were all inferior leaders who never knew responsibilities equal to his, nor did Spain ever again know such imperial grandeur. The French soon dominated the Continent, and in the New World the Dutch and the English whittled away at Spain's overseas empire.

Elizabeth died on March 23, 1603, leaving behind her a strong nation poised to expand into a global empire.

▼ The Thirty Years' War (1618–1648)

The Thirty Years' War in the Holy Roman Empire was the last and most destructive of the wars of religion. Religious and political differences had long set Catholics against Protestants and Calvinists against Lutherans. What made the Thirty Years' War so devastating was the entrenched hatred of the various sides and their seeming determination to sacrifice all for their religious beliefs. When the hostilities ended in 1648, the peace terms shaped the map of northern Europe much as we know it today.

Read the **Document**
"Thirty Years' War (1618) Rushworth" on **MyHistoryLab.com**

Preconditions for War

Fragmented Germany In the second half of the sixteenth century, Germany was an almost ungovernable land of about 360 autonomous political entities.

(See Map 12–2.) There were independent secular principalities (duchies, landgraviates, and marches), ecclesiastical principalities (archbishoprics, bishoprics, and abbeys), numerous free cities, and knights ruling small areas from castles. The Peace of Augsburg (1555) had given each of them significant sovereignty within its own borders. Each levied its own tolls and tariffs and coined its own money, which made land travel and trade between the various regions difficult to impossible. Many of these little lands also had great power pretensions. As the seventeenth century opened, Germany was decentralized and fragmented; it was not a unified nation like Spain, England, or even strife-filled France.

Because of its central location, Germany had always been Europe's highway for merchants and traders going north, south, east, and west. Europe's rulers pressed in on Germany both because of trade and because some held lands or legal privileges within certain German principalities. German princes, in their turn, looked to import and export markets beyond German borders and opposed efforts to consolidate the Holy Roman Empire, lest their territorial rights, confirmed by the Peace of Augsburg, be overturned. German princes were

Map 12–2 GERMANY IN 1547 Mid-sixteenth-century Germany was an almost ungovernable land of about 360 autonomous political entities. Originally "Map of Germany Showing Its Great Division/Fragmentation in the 16th Century" from Hajo Holborn, *A History of Germany: The Reformation.* Copyright © 1982 by Princeton University Press. Reprinted by permission of Princeton University Press.

not loath to turn to Catholic France or to the kings of Denmark and Sweden for allies against the Habsburg emperor.

After the Council of Trent, Protestants in the empire suspected the existence of an imperial and papal conspiracy to re-create the Catholic Europe of pre-Reformation times. The imperial diet, which the German princes controlled, demanded strict observance of the constitutional rights of Germans, as set forth in agreements with the emperor since the mid-fourteenth century. In the late sixteenth century, the emperor ruled only to the degree to which he was prepared to use force of arms against his subjects.

Religious Division Religious conflict accentuated the international and internal political divisions. (See Map 12–3.) During this period, the population within the

Holy Roman Empire was about equally divided between Catholics and Protestants, the latter having perhaps a slight numerical edge by 1600. The terms of the Peace of Augsburg had attempted to freeze the territorial holdings of the Lutherans and the Catholics (the so-called *ecclesiastical reservation*). In the intervening years, however, the Lutherans had gained and kept political control in some Catholic areas, as had the Catholics in a few previously Lutheran areas. Such territorial reversals, or the threat of them, only increased the suspicion and antipathy between the two sides.

The Lutherans had been far more successful in securing their rights to worship in Catholic lands than the Catholics had been in securing such rights in Lutheran lands. The Catholic rulers, who were in a weakened position after the Reformation, had made, but resented, concessions to Protestant communities within their

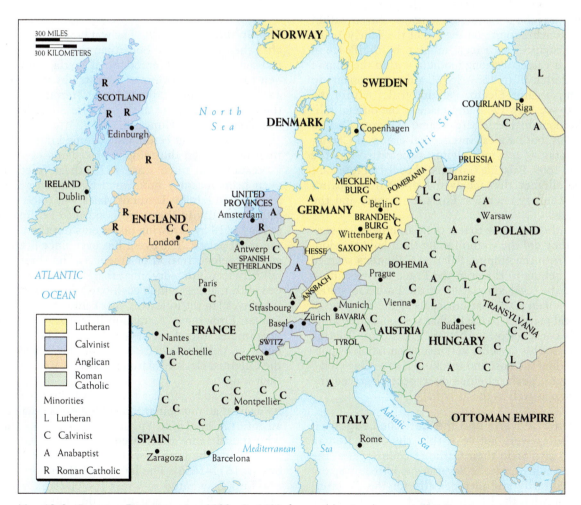

Map 12–3 **RELIGIOUS DIVISIONS ABOUT 1600** By 1600, few could seriously expect Christians to return to a uniform religious allegiance. In Spain and southern Italy, Catholicism remained relatively unchallenged, but note the existence elsewhere of large religious minorities, both Catholic and Protestant.

territories. With the passage of time, they demanded that all ecclesiastical princes, electors, archbishops, bishops, and abbots who had deserted the Catholic for the Protestant side be immediately deprived of their religious offices and that their ecclesiastical holdings be promptly returned to Catholic control in accordance with the ecclesiastical reservation. However, the Lutherans and, even more so, the Calvinists in the Palatinate ignored this stipulation at every opportunity.

There was also religious strife in the empire between liberal and conservative Lutherans and between Lutherans and the growing numbers of Calvinists. The last half of the sixteenth century was a time of warring Protestant factions within German universities. And in addition to the heightened religious strife, a new scientific and material culture was becoming ascendant in intellectual and political circles, increasing the anxiety of religious people of all persuasions.

Calvinism and the Palatinate

As elsewhere in Europe, Calvinism was the political and religious leaven within the Holy Roman Empire on the eve of the Thirty Years' War. Unrecognized as a legal religion by the Peace of Augsburg, it gained a strong foothold within the empire when Frederick III (r. 1559–1576), a devout convert to Calvinism, became Elector Palatine (ruler within the Palatinate; see Map 12–3) and made it the official religion of his domain. Heidelberg became a German Geneva in the 1560s: both a great intellectual center of Calvinism and a staging area for Calvinist penetration into the empire. By 1609, Palatine Calvinists headed a Protestant defensive alliance that received support from Spain's sixteenth-century enemies: England, France, and the Netherlands.

The Lutherans came to fear the Calvinists almost as much as they did the Catholics. By their bold missionary forays into the empire, Palatine Calvinists seemed to the Lutherans to threaten the Peace of Augsburg—and hence the legal foundation of the Lutheran states. Also, outspoken Calvinist criticism of the doctrine of Christ's real presence in the Eucharist shocked the more religiously conservative Lutherans. The Elector Palatine once expressed his disbelief in transubstantiation by publicly shredding the host and mocking it as a "fine God." To Lutherans, such religious disrespect disgraced the Reformation as well as the elector.

Maximilian of Bavaria and the Catholic League

If the Calvinists were active within the Holy Roman Empire, so also were their Catholic counterparts, the Jesuits. Staunchly Catholic Bavaria, supported by Spain, became militarily and ideologically for the Counter-Reformation what the Palatinate was for Protestantism. From Bavaria, the Jesuits launched successful missions throughout the empire, winning such major cities as Strasbourg and Osnabrück back to the Catholic fold by 1600. In 1609, Maximilian I, duke of Bavaria (r. 1597–1651), organized a Catholic league to counter a new Protestant alliance that had been formed in the same year under the leadership of Calvinist Elector Palatine, Frederick IV (r. 1583–1610). When the league fielded a great army under the command of Count Johann von Tilly, the stage was set, both internally and internationally, for the worst of the religious wars, the Thirty Years' War. (See Map 12–4.)

Four Periods of War

The war went through four distinguishable periods. During its course, it drew in every major Western European nation—at least diplomatically and financially if not by direct military intervention. The four periods were the Bohemian (1618–1625), the Danish (1625–1629), the Swedish (1630–1635), and the Swedish-French (1635–1648).

The Bohemian Period

The war broke out in Bohemia after the ascent to the Bohemian throne in 1618 of the Habsburg Ferdinand, archduke of Styria, who was also heir to the imperial throne. Educated by the Jesuits and a fervent Catholic, Ferdinand was determined to restore the traditional faith to the eastern Habsburg lands (Austria, Bohemia, and Hungary).

No sooner had Ferdinand become king of Bohemia than he revoked the religious freedoms of Bohemian Protestants. In force since 1575, these freedoms had even been recently broadened by Emperor Rudolf II (r. 1576–1612) in his Letter of Majesty in 1609. The Protestant nobility in Prague responded to Ferdinand's act in May 1618 by throwing his regents out the window of the royal palace. The event has ever since been known as the "defenestration of Prague." (The three officials fell fifty feet into a dry moat that, fortunately, was padded with manure, which cushioned their fall and spared their lives.) In the following year Ferdinand became Holy Roman Emperor as Ferdinand II (r. 1619–1637) by the unanimous vote of the seven electors. The Bohemians, however, defiantly deposed him in Prague and declared the Calvinist elector Palatine, Frederick V (r. 1616–1623), their king.

What had begun as a revolt of the Protestant nobility against an unpopular king of Bohemia escalated into an international war. Spain sent troops to Ferdinand, who found more motivated allies in Maximilian of Bavaria and the Lutheran elector John George I of Saxony (r. 1611–1656). The latter had their own agendas. Maximilian wanted to wrest the electoral title from his distant Palatine cousin, while John George saw a sure route to territorial gain by joining in an easy victory over the weaker elector Palatine. This was not the only time politics and greed would overshadow

Map 12–4 THE HOLY ROMAN EMPIRE ABOUT 1618 On the eve of the Thirty Years' War, the Holy Roman Empire was politically and religiously fragmented, as revealed by this somewhat simplified map. Lutherans dominated the north and Catholics the south; Calvinists controlled the United Provinces and the Palatinate and were important in Switzerland and Brandenburg.

religion during the long conflict, although Lutheran-Calvinist religious animosity also overrode a common Protestantism.

Ferdinand's army under Tilly routed Frederick V's troops at the Battle of White Mountain in 1620. By 1622, Ferdinand had not only subdued and re-Catholicized Bohemia but conquered the Palatinate as well. Meanwhile, Maximilian of Bavaria pressed the conflict into northwestern Germany, laying claim to land as he went.

The Danish Period These events raised new fears that a reconquest and re-Catholicization of the empire now

loomed, which was precisely Ferdinand II's design. The Lutheran king Christian IV (r. 1588–1648) of Denmark, who already held territory within the empire as the duke of Holstein, was eager to extend Danish influence over the coastal towns of the North Sea. With English, French, and Dutch encouragement, he picked up the Protestant banner of resistance, opening the Danish period of the conflict (1625–1629). Entering Germany with his army in 1626, he was, however, quickly humiliated by Maximilian and forced to retreat into Denmark.

As military success made Maximilian stronger and an untrustworthy ally, Emperor Ferdinand sought a more

Bohemian protesters throw three of Emperor Ferdinand II's agents out of windows at Hradschin Castle in Prague to protest his revocation of Protestant freedoms.   Bildarchiv Preussischer Kulturbesitz/Art Resource, NY

pliant tool for his policies in Albrecht of Wallenstein (1583–1634), a powerful mercenary. Another opportunistic Protestant, Wallenstein had gained a great deal of territory by joining Ferdinand during the conquest of Bohemia. A brilliant and ruthless military strategist, Wallenstein carried Ferdinand's campaign into Denmark. By 1628, he commanded a crack army of more than 100,000 men and also became a law unto himself, completely outside of the emperor's control.

Wallenstein, however, had so broken Protestant resistance that Ferdinand could issue the Edict of Restitution in 1629, reasserting the Catholic safeguards of the Peace of Augsburg (1555). It reaffirmed the illegality of Calvinism—a completely unrealistic move by 1629—and it ordered the return of all church lands the Lutherans had acquired since 1552, an equally unrealistic goal despite its legal basis. Compliance would have involved the return of no fewer than sixteen bishoprics and twenty-eight cities and towns to Catholic allegiance. The new edict struck panic in the hearts of Protestants and Habsburg opponents everywhere.

The Swedish Period   Gustavus Adolphus II of Sweden (r. 1611–1632), a deeply pious king of a unified Lutheran nation, became the new leader of Protestant forces within the empire, opening the Swedish period of the war (1630–1635). He was controlled by two interested bystanders: (1) the French minister Cardinal Richelieu (1585–1642), whose foreign policy was to protect French interests by keeping the Habsburg armies tied down in Germany, and (2) the Dutch, who had not forgotten Spanish Habsburg rule in the sixteenth century. In alliance with the electors of Brandenburg and Saxony, the Swedish king won a smashing victory at Breitenfeld in 1630—one that reversed the course of the war so dramatically that it has been regarded as the most decisive engagement of the long conflict.

🔍 **View the Map**
"Map Discovery: The Rise of Sweden" on
MyHistoryLab.com

One of the reasons for the overwhelming Swedish victory at Breitenfeld was the military genius of Gustavus Adolphus. The Swedish king brought a new mobility to warfare by having both his infantry and his cavalry employ fire-and-charge tactics. At six deep, his infantry squares were smaller than the traditional ones, yet he filled them with equal numbers of musketeers and pikemen. His cavalry also alternated pistol shots with charges with the sword. His artillery was lighter and more mobile in battle. Each unit of his army—infantry, cavalry, and artillery—had both defensive and offensive capability and could quickly change from one to the other.

Gustavus Adolphus died at the hands of Wallenstein's forces during the Battle of Lützen (November 1632)—a costly engagement for both sides that created a brief standstill. Ferdinand had long resented Wallenstein's independence, although he was the major factor in imperial success. In 1634, Ferdinand had Wallenstein assassinated. By that time, not only had the great

general served his purpose for the emperor, but, ever opportunistic, he was openly trying to strike bargains with the Protestants for his services. The episode is a telling commentary on this war without honor. Despite the deep religious motivations, greed and political gain were the real forces at work in the Thirty Years' War. Even allies that owed one another their success were not above treating each other as mortal enemies.

In the Peace of Prague in 1635, the German Protestant states, led by Saxony, reached a compromise with Ferdinand. France and the Netherlands, however, continued to support Sweden. Desiring to maximize their investment in the war, they refused to join the agreement. Their resistance to settlement plunged the war into its fourth and most devastating phase.

Document

THE DESTRUCTION OF MAGDEBURG, MAY 1631

During the Swedish phase of the Thirty Years' War, an imperial army totally destroyed the Lutheran city of Magdeburg. The following description of the occupation of the city communicates the suffering inflicted on ordinary citizens on both sides, as largely foreign armies destroyed their land.

Is religion the driving force behind this destruction? Who, or what, could have stopped the carnage? Who in the end gained the most, if anything?

Thus it came about that the ecclesiastical city and all its inhabitants fell into the hands of the enemy, whose violence and cruelty were due in part to their common hatred of the adherents of the [Protestant] Augsburg Confession, and in part to their being embittered by the chain shot which had been fired at them and by the derision and insults that the Magdeburgers had heaped upon them from the ramparts.

Then was there naught but beating and burning, plundering, torture, and murder. Everyone of the enemy was bent on securing much booty. When a marauding party entered a house, if its master had anything to give, he might thereby purchase respite and protection for himself and his family till the next man, who also wanted something, came along. It was only when everything had been brought forth and there was nothing left to give that the real trouble commenced. Then, what with blows and threats

of shooting, stabbing, and hanging, the poor people were so terrified that if they had had anything left they would have brought it forth.

In this frenzied rage, the great and splendid city that had stood like a fair princess in the land was now, in its hour of direst need . . . given over to the flames. Thousands of innocent men, women, and children, in the midst of heartrending shrieks were tortured and put to death in so cruel and shameful a manner that no words would suffice to describe, nor no tears to bewail it . . .

Thus in a single day this noble and famous city, the pride of the whole country, went up in fire and smoke, and the remnant of its citizens with their wives and children were taken as prisoners and driven away by the enemy with weeping and wailing that could be heard from afar, while the cinders and ashes from the town were carried by the winds to neighboring towns.

From J. H. Robinson, *Readings in European History*, Vol. II (Boston: Athenaeum, 1906), pp. 211–212.

The Swedish–French Period The French openly entered the war in 1635, sending men and munitions as well as financial subsidies. Thereafter, the war dragged on for thirteen years, with French, Swedish, and Spanish soldiers looting the length and breadth of Germany—warring, it seemed, simply for the sake of warfare itself. The Germans, long weary of the devastation, were too disunited to repulse the foreign armies; they simply suffered. By the time peace talks began at Münster and Osnabrück in Westphalia in 1644, the war had killed an estimated one-third of the German population. It has been called the worst European catastrophe since the Black Death of the fourteenth century.

🔍 View the Map "Map Discovery: Population Loss in Germany During the Thirty Years War" on **MyHistoryLab.com**

The Treaty of Westphalia

The Treaty of Westphalia in 1648 ended all hostilities within the Holy Roman Empire. It was the first general peace in Europe after a war unprecedented for its number of warring parties. (See Map 12–5.) Written not in Latin, but in French, henceforth to become the international diplomatic language, the treaty rescinded Ferdinand's Edict of Restitution and reasserted the major feature of the religious settlement of the Peace of Augsburg ninety-three years earlier: The ruler of a land determines the official religion of that land. The treaty also gave the Calvinists their long-sought legal recognition. The independence of the Swiss Confederacy and the United Provinces of the Netherlands, long recognized in fact, was now proclaimed in law. Bavaria became an elector state, Brandenburg-Prussia emerged as the most powerful northern German state, and the other German princes became supreme over their principalities. Yet, as guarantors of the treaty, Sweden and France found many opportunities to meddle in German affairs until the century's end—France for reasons of considerable territorial gain. Because the treaty broadened the legal status of Protestantism, the pope opposed it altogether, but he had no power to prevent it.

France and Spain remained at war outside the empire until 1659, when French victories forced the humiliating Treaty of the Pyrenees on the Spanish. Thereafter France became Europe's dominant power, and Habsburg Spain never recovered. (See Chapter 13.)

By confirming the territorial sovereignty of Germany's many political entities, the Treaty of Westphalia perpetuated German division and political weakness into the modern period. Only two German states attained any international significance during the seventeenth century: Austria and Brandenburg-Prussia. The petty regionalism within the empire also reflected on a small scale the drift of larger European politics. In

The Dutch celebrate the Treaty of Westphalia, ending the Thirty Years' War. © North Wind Picture Archives/Alamy

Map 12–5 **EUROPE IN 1648** At the end of the Thirty Years' War, Spain still had extensive possessions. Austria and Brandenburg-Prussia were rising powers, the independence of the United Provinces and Switzerland was recognized, and Sweden had footholds in northern Germany.

the seventeenth century, distinctive nation-states, each with their own political, cultural, and religious identity, reached maturity and firmly established the competitive nationalism of the modern world.

Read the **Document**
"The Peace of Westphalia, 1648" on **MyHistoryLab.com**

In Perspective

Religion and politics played major roles in each of the great conflicts of the Age of Religious Wars—the internal struggle in France, Spain's unsuccessful effort to subdue the Netherlands, England's successful resistance to Spain, and the intervention of virtually every major European power in the hapless Holy Roman Empire during the first half of the seventeenth century. Each conflict involved parties and armies of different religious persuasions in a life-or-death political struggle.

The wars ended with the recognition of minority religious rights and a guarantee of the traditional boundaries of political sovereignty. In France, the Edict of Nantes (1598) brought peace by granting Huguenots basic religious and civil freedoms and by recognizing their towns and territories. With the departure of the Spanish, peace and sovereignty also came to the Netherlands, guaranteed initially by the Twelve Years' Truce (1609) and secured fully by the Peace of Westphalia (1648). The conflict between England and Spain ended with the removal of the Spanish threat to English sovereignty in politics and religion, which resulted from the execution of Mary, Queen of Scots (1587) and the English victory over the Armada (1588). In the Holy Roman Empire, peace came with the reaffirmation of the political principle of the Peace of Augsburg (1555), as the Peace of Westphalia brought the Thirty Years' War to an end by again recognizing the sovereignty of rulers within their lands and their right to determine the religious beliefs of their subjects. Europe at midcentury had real, if brief, peace.

KEY TERMS

baroque (p. 355)
Congregationalists (p. 371)
Counter-Reformation (p. 355)
Huguenots (p. 356)
politiques (p. 355)
Presbyterians (p. 371)
presbyters (p. 355)
Thirty-Nine Articles (p. 367)

REVIEW QUESTIONS

1. How did politics shape the religious positions of the French leaders? What led to the Saint Bartholomew's Day Massacre, and what did it achieve?
2. How did Spain gain a position of dominance in the sixteenth century? What were Philip II's successes and failures?
3. Henry of Navarre (Henry IV of France), Elizabeth I, and William of Orange were all *politiques*. What does that term mean and why does it apply to these three rulers?
4. What led to the establishment of the Anglican Church in England? Why did Mary I fail? What was Elizabeth I's settlement, and why was it difficult to impose on England? Who were her detractors and what were their criticisms?
5. Why was the Thirty Years' War fought? Was politics or religion more important in determining the outcome of the war? What were the main terms of the Treaty of Westphalia in 1648?
6. Why has the Thirty Years' War been called the outstanding example in European history of meaningless conflict? Was it really such? Were the results worth the cost of the war?

SUGGESTED READINGS

R. G. Ash, *The Thirty Years War, the Holy Roman Empire, and Europe* (1997). Big picture, small picture.

F. Braudel, *The Mediterranean and the Mediterranean World in the Age of Philip the Second*, Vols. 1 and 2 (1976). Widely acclaimed "big picture" by a master historian.

N. Z. Davis, *Society and Culture in Early Modern France* (1975). Essays on popular culture.

R. Dunn, *The Age of Religious Wars, 1559–1689* (1979). Excellent brief survey of every major conflict.

L. Febvre, "The Origins of the French Reformation: A Badly-Put Question," in Peter Burke, ed., *A New Kind of History* (1973), pp. 44–88. Trail-blazing analysis of the motives behind religious and political change.

J. H. Franklin, ed. and trans., *Constitutionalism and Resistance in the Sixteenth Century: Three Treatises by Hotman, Beza, and Mornay* (1969). Three defenders of the right to resist tyranny.

J. Guy, *Tudor England* (1990). The standard history and a good synthesis of recent scholarship.

T. Helfferich, ed., *The Thirty Years War: A Documented History* (2009). A sweeping history based on new documents from the participating lands.

D. Loades, *Mary Tudor* (1989). Authoritative and good storytelling.

G. Mattingly, *The Armada* (1959). A masterpiece resembling a novel in style.

J. E. Neale, *The Age of Catherine de Médicis* (1962). Short, concise summary.

S. Ozment, *A Mighty Fortress: A New History of the German People* (2004). Succinct summary.

A. Soman, ed., *The Massacre of St. Bartholomew's Day: Reappraisals and Documents* (1974). Essays from an international symposium on the anniversary of the massacre.

C. Wedgwood, *William the Silent* (1944). Eloquent political biography of William of Orange.

A. B. Weir, *The Life of Elizabeth I* (1998). Detailed portrayal of a successful ruler.

P. H. Wilson, *Europe's Tragedy: A History of the Thirty Years War* (2009). Very readable and up-to-date.

J. Wormald, *Mary, Queen of Scots: A Study in Failure* (1991). Mary portrayed as out of touch with her country and her times.

MyHistoryLab™ MEDIA ASSIGNMENTS

Find these resources in the Media Assignments folder for Chapter 12 on **MyHistoryLab**.

QUESTIONS FOR ANALYSIS

1. How does the design of this Calvinist church reflect the main religious goals of Protestantism?

   Section: **The French Wars of Religion (1562–1598)**
   View the **Closer Look** Baroque and Plain Church: Architectural Reflections of Belief, p. 357

2. What do you consider the primary goal of this act?

   Section: **England and Spain (1553–1603)**
   Read the **Document** Acts of Uniformity, 1559, p. 367

3. Why was population loss from the Thirty Years' War so high in Germany?

   Section: **The Thirty Years' War (1618–1648)**
   View the **Map** Map Discovery: Population Loss in Germany During the Thirty Years War, p. 380

4. Who gained the most territorially under the Peace of Westphalia?

   Section: **The Thirty Years' War (1618–1648)**
   Read the **Document** The Peace of Westphalia, 1648, p. 382

5. Why did this author cast the Spanish conquests as a religious conflict?

   Section: **Imperial Spain and Philip II (r. 1556–1598)**
   View the **Image** Hispania Slaying Leviathan, p. 362

OTHER RESOURCES FROM THIS CHAPTER

The French Wars of Religion (1562–1598)
View the **Map** Map Discovery: Religious Divisions in France During the Wars of Religion, p. 358

Read the **Document** Massacre of St. Bartholomew (1572), p. 359

Read the **Document** The Edict of Nantes (France), 1598, p. 361

Imperial Spain and Philip II (r. 1556–1598)
Read the **Document** Venetian Observations on the Ottoman Empire (late 16th c.), p. 362

View the **Map** The Netherlands During the Dutch Revolt, ca. 1580, p. 365

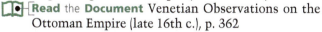

Peter the Great (r. 1682–1725), seeking to make Russia a military power after West European models reorganized the country's political, social, and economic structures. He also radically changed the relationship of the Russian Church to the Russian state. His reign saw Russia enter fully into European power politics. *The Apotheosis of Tsar Peter the Great 1672–1725 by unknown artist, 1710.* bpk, Berlin/Museum of History, Moscow, Russia/ Alfredo Dagli Orti/Art Resource, NY

((•—[**Listen** to the **Chapter Audio** on **MyHistoryLab.com**

13

European State Consolidation in the Seventeenth and Eighteenth Centuries

LEARNING OBJECTIVES

What was the Dutch Golden Age and what led to its decline?

What factors led to the different political paths taken by England and France in the seventeenth century?

How did conflicts over taxation and religion lead to civil war in Stuart England?

Why were efforts to establish absolute monarchy successful in France but unsuccessful in England?

What were the main characteristics that defined the Polish, Austrian, and Prussian states in the seventeenth and eighteenth centuries?

How did Peter the Great transform Russia into a powerful, centralized nation?

BETWEEN THE EARLY seventeenth and the mid-twentieth centuries, no region so dominated other parts of the world politically, militarily, and economically as Europe. Such had not been the case before that date and would not be the case after World War II. However, for approximately three and a half centuries, Europe became the chief driving force in one world historical development after another. This era of European dominance, which appears quite temporary in the larger scope of history, also coincided with a shift in power within Europe itself from the Mediterranean, where Spain and Portugal had taken the lead in the conquest and early exploitation of the Americas, to the states of northwest and later north-central Europe.

During the seventeenth and early eighteenth centuries, certain states in northern Europe organized themselves politically so as to be able to dominate Europe and later to influence and even govern other large areas of the world through military might and economic strength. Even within the region of northern Europe, there occurred a sorting out of influence among political states with some successfully establishing long-term positions of dominance and others passing from the scene after relatively brief periods of either military or economic strength.

By the mid-eighteenth century, five major states had come to dominate European politics and would continue to do so until at least World War I. They were Great Britain, France, Austria, Prussia, and Russia. Through their military strength, economic development, and, in some cases, colonial empires, they would affect virtually every other world civilization. Within Europe, these states established their dominance at the expense of Spain, Portugal, the United Provinces of the Netherlands, Poland, Sweden, and the Ottoman Empire. Equally essential to their rise was the weakness of the Holy Roman Empire after the Peace of Westphalia (1648).

In western Europe, Britain and France emerged as the dominant powers. This development represented a shift of influence away from Spain and the United Netherlands. Both of the latter countries had been powerful and important during the sixteenth and seventeenth centuries, but they became politically and militarily marginal during the eighteenth century. Neither, however, disappeared from the map, and both retained considerable economic vitality and influence. Spanish power declined after the War of the Spanish Succession. The case of the Netherlands was more complicated.

▼ The Netherlands: Golden Age to Decline

The seven provinces that became the United Provinces of the Netherlands emerged as a nation after revolting against Spain in 1572. During the seventeenth century, the Dutch engaged in a series of naval wars with England. Then, in 1672, the armies of Louis XIV invaded the Netherlands. Prince William III of Orange (1650–1702), the grandson of William the Silent (1533–1584) and the hereditary chief executive, or *stadtholder*, of Holland, the most important of the provinces, rallied the Dutch and eventually led the entire European coalition against France. As a part of that strategy, he answered the invitation of Protestant English aristocrats in 1688 to assume, along with his wife Mary, the English throne.

During both the seventeenth and eighteenth centuries, the political and economic life of the Netherlands differed from that of the rest of Europe. The other major nations pursued paths toward strong central government, generally under monarchies, as with France, or in the case of England, under a strong parliamentary system. By contrast, the Netherlands was formally a republic. Each of the provinces retained considerable authority, and the central government, embodied in the States General that met in the Hague, exercised its authority through a kind of ongoing negotiation with the provinces. Prosperous and populous Holland dominated the States General. The Dutch deeply distrusted monarchy and the ambitions of the House of Orange. Nonetheless, when confronted with major military challenges, the Dutch would permit the House of Orange and, most notably, William III to assume dominant leadership. These political arrangements proved highly resilient and allowed the republic to establish itself permanently in the European state system during the seventeenth century. When William died in 1702 and the wars with France ended in 1714, the Dutch reverted to their republican structures.

Although the provinces making up the Netherlands were traditionally identified with the Protestant cause in Europe, toleration marked Dutch religious life. The Calvinist Reformed Church was the official church of the nation, but it was not an established church. There was always a significant number of Roman Catholics and Protestants who did not belong to the Reformed Church. The country also became a haven for Jews. Consequently, while governments in other European states attempted to impose a single religion on their people or tore themselves apart in religious conflict, in the Netherlands peoples of differing religious faiths lived together peacefully.

Urban Prosperity

Beyond the climate of religious toleration, what most amazed seventeenth-century contemporaries about the Dutch Republic was its economic prosperity. Its remarkable economic achievement was built on the foundations of high urban consolidation, transformed agriculture, extensive trade and finance, and an overseas commercial empire.

In the Netherlands, more people lived in cities than in any other area of Europe. Key transformations in

Dutch farming that served as the model for the rest of Europe made this urban transformation possible. During the seventeenth century, the Dutch drained and reclaimed land from the sea, which they used for highly profitable farming. Because Dutch shipping provided a steady supply of cheap grain, Dutch farmers themselves could produce more profitable dairy products and beef and cultivate cash products such as tulip bulbs.

Dutch fishermen dominated the market for herring and supplied much of the continent's dried fish. The Dutch also supplied textiles to many parts of Europe. Dutch ships appeared in harbors all over the continent, with their captains purchasing goods that they then transported and resold at a profit to other nations. The overseas trades also supported a vast shipbuilding and ship supply industry. The most advanced financial system of the day supported all of this trade, commerce, and manufacturing.

View the **Closer Look**
"Cape Town: A Dutch Refueling Station" on **MyHistoryLab.com**

The final foundation of Dutch prosperity was a seaborne empire. Dutch traders established a major presence in East Asia, particularly in spice-producing areas of Java, the Moluccas, and Sri Lanka. The vehicle for this penetration was the Dutch East India Company (chartered in 1602). The company eventually displaced Portuguese dominance in the spice trade of East Asia and for many years prevented English traders from establishing a major presence there. Initially, the Dutch had only wanted commercial dominance of the spice trade, but in time, they moved toward producing the spices themselves, which required them to control many of the islands that now constitute Indonesia. The Netherlands remained the colonial master of this region until after World War II.

Read the **Document**
"Jan van Linschoten on Dutch Business in the Indian Ocean" on **MyHistoryLab.com**

Economic Decline

The decline in political influence of the United Provinces of the Netherlands occurred in the eighteenth century. After the death of William III of Britain in 1702, the provinces prevented the emergence of another strong *stadtholder*. Unified political leadership therefore vanished. Naval supremacy slowly but steadily passed to the British. The fishing industry declined, and the Dutch lost their technological superiority in shipbuilding. Countries between which Dutch ships had once carried goods now traded directly with each other.

Similar stagnation overtook the Dutch domestic industries. The disunity of the provinces hastened this economic decline and prevented action that might have halted it.

What saved the United Provinces from becoming completely insignificant in European affairs was their continued financial dominance. Well past the middle of the eighteenth century, Dutch banks continued to finance European trade, and the Amsterdam stock exchange remained an important financial institution.

The technologically advanced fleet of the Dutch East India Company, shown here at anchor in Amsterdam, linked the Netherlands' economy with that of southeast Asia. Andries van Eertvelt (1590–1652), *The Return to Amsterdam of the Fleet of the Dutch East India Company in 1599.* Oil on copper. Johnny van Haeften Gallery, London. The Bridgeman Art Library

▼ Two Models of European Political Development

The United Netherlands, like Venice and the Swiss cantons, was a republic governed without a monarch. Elsewhere in Europe monarchy of two fundamentally different patterns predominated in response to the military challenges of international conflict.

The two models became known as **parliamentary monarchy** and **political absolutism**. England embodied the first, and France, the second. Neither model was inevitable for either country, but each resulted from the historical developments and political personalities that molded each nation during the seventeenth century.

The political forces that led to the creation of these two models had arisen from military concerns. During the second half of the sixteenth century, changes in military organization, weapons, and tactics sharply increased the cost of warfare. Because their traditional sources of income could not finance these growing expenses, in addition to the other costs of government, monarchs sought new revenues. Only monarchies that succeeded in building a secure financial base that was not deeply dependent on the support of noble estates, diets, or assemblies achieved absolute rule. The French monarchy succeeded in this effort, whereas the English monarchy failed. That success and failure led to the two models

Read the **Document**
"Jacques-Benigne Bossuet, Politics Drawn from the Very Words of the Holy Scripture" on **MyHistoryLab.com**

of government—political absolutism in France and parliamentary monarchy in England—that shaped subsequent political development in Europe.

The divergent developments of England and France in the seventeenth century would have surprised most people in 1600. It was not inevitable that the English monarchy would have to govern through Parliament or that the French monarchy would avoid dealing with national political institutions that could significantly limit its authority. The Stuart kings of England aspired to the autocracy Louis XIV achieved, and some English political philosophers eloquently defended the **divine right of kings** and absolute rule. At the beginning of the seventeenth century, the English monarchy was strong. Queen Elizabeth, after a reign of almost forty-five years (1558–1603), was much revered. Parliament met only when the monarch summoned it to provide financial support. France, however, was emerging from the turmoil of its religious wars. The strife of that conflict had torn French society apart. The monarchy was relatively weak. Henry IV, who had become king in 1589, pursued a policy of religious toleration. The French nobles had significant military forces at their disposal and in the middle of the seventeenth century rebelled against the king. These conditions would change dramatically in both nations by the late seventeenth century.

▼ Constitutional Crisis and Settlement in Stuart England

James I

In 1603 James VI, the son of Mary Stuart, Queen of Scots, who had been King of Scotland since 1567, succeeded without opposition or incident the childless Elizabeth I as James I of England. He also inherited a large royal debt and a fiercely divided church. A strong believer in the divine right of kings, he expected to rule with a minimum of consultation beyond his own royal court.

Read the **Document**
"James I on the Divine Right of Kings (1598)" on **MyHistoryLab.com**

Parliament met only when the monarch summoned it, which James hoped to do rarely. In place of parliamentarily approved revenues, James developed other sources of income, largely by levying new custom duties known as *impositions*. Members of Parliament regarded this as an affront to their authority over the royal purse, but they did not seek a serious confrontation. Rather, throughout James's reign they wrangled and negotiated.

The religious problem also festered under James. Since the days of Elizabeth, **Puritans** within the Church of England had sought to eliminate elaborate religious ceremonies and replace the hierarchical episcopal system of church governance under bishops appointed by the king with a more representative Presbyterian form like that of the Calvinist churches in Scotland and on the Continent. At the Hampton Court Conference of January 1604, James rebuffed the Puritans and firmly declared his intention to maintain and even enhance the Anglican episcopacy. Thereafter, both sides had deep suspicions of the other. (See "King James I Defends Popular Recreation against the Puritans," page 389.)

Religious dissenters began to leave England. In 1620, Puritan separatists founded Plymouth Colony on Cape Cod Bay in North America, preferring flight from England to Anglican conformity. Later in the 1620s, a larger, better financed group of Puritans left England to found the Massachusetts Bay Colony. In each case, the colonists believed that reformation would or could not go far enough in England and that only in America could they worship freely and organize a truly reformed church.

James's court became a center of scandal and corruption. He governed by favorites, of whom the most influential was the duke of Buckingham, whom rumor made the king's homosexual lover. Buckingham controlled royal patronage and openly sold peerages and titles to the highest bidders—a practice that angered the nobility because it cheapened their rank. There had always been court favorites, but seldom before had a single person so controlled access to the monarch.

James's foreign policy roused further opposition and doubt about his Protestant loyalty. In 1604, he concluded a much-needed peace with Spain, England's longtime

Document

KING JAMES I DEFENDS POPULAR RECREATION AGAINST THE PURITANS

The English Puritans believed in strict observance of the Sabbath, disapproving any sports, games, or general social conviviality on Sunday. James I thought these strictures prevented many Roman Catholics from joining the Church of England. In 1618, he ordered the clergy of the Church of England to read the Book of Sports from their pulpits. In this declaration, he permitted people to engage in certain sports and games after church services. His hope was to allow innocent recreations on Sunday while encouraging people to attend the Church of England. Despite the king's good intentions, the order offended the Puritans. The clergy resisted his order and he had to withdraw it.

What motives of state might have led James I to issue this declaration? How does he attempt to make it favorable to the Church of England? Why might so many clergy have refused to read this statement to their congregations?

With our own ears we heard the general complaint of our people, that they were barred from all lawful recreation and exercise upon the Sunday's afternoon, after the ending of all divine service, which cannot but produce two evils: the one the hindering of the conversion of many [Roman Catholic subjects], whom their priests will take occasion hereby to vex, persuading them that no honest mirth or recreation is lawful or tolerable in our religion, which cannot but breed a great discontentment in our people's hearts, especially as such as are peradventure upon the point of turning [to the Church of England]: the other inconvenience is, that this prohibition barreth the common and meaner sort of people from using such exercises as may make their bodies more able for war, when we or our successors shall have occasion to use them; and in place thereof sets up filthy tipplings and drunkenness, and breeds a number of idle and discontented speeches in their ale-houses. For when shall the common people have leave to exercise, if not upon the Sundays and holy days, seeing they must apply their labor and win their living in all working days? . . .

[A]s for our good people's lawful recreation, our pleasure likewise is, that after the end of divine service our good people be not disturbed, . . . or discouraged from any lawful recreation, such as dancing, either men or women; archery for men, leaping, vaulting, or any other such harmless recreation, or from having of Hay-games, Whitsun-ales, and Morris-dances; and the setting up of May-poles and other sports therewith used; . . . but withal we do here account still as prohibited all unlawful games to be used upon Sundays only, as bear and bull-baitings . . . and at all times in the meaner sort of people by law prohibited, bowling.

And likewise we bar from this benefit and liberty all such known as recusants [Roman Catholics], either men or women, as will abstain from coming to church or divine service, being therefore unworthy of any lawful recreation after the said service, that will not first come to the church and serve God; prohibiting in like sort the said recreations to any that, though [they] conform in religion [i.e., members of the Church of England], are not present in the church at the service of God, before their going to the said recreations.

From Henry Bettenson, ed., *Documents of the Christian Church*, 2nd ed. (London: Oxford University Press, 1963), pp. 400–403. By permission of Oxford University Press.

adversary. The war had been ruinously expensive, but his subjects considered the peace a sign of pro-Catholic sentiment. James's unsuccessful attempt to relax penal laws against Catholics further increased suspicions, as did his wise hesitancy in 1618 to rush English troops to the aid of German Protestants at the outbreak of the Thirty Years'

War. His failed efforts to arrange a marriage between his son Charles and a Spanish princess, and then Charles's marriage in 1625 to Henrietta Marie, the Catholic daughter of Henry IV of France, further increased religious concern. In 1624, shortly before James's death, England again went to war against Spain, largely in response to parliamentary pressures.

EARLY CONTROVERSY OVER TOBACCO AND SMOKING

SMOKING TODAY IS widely condemned throughout the West, but the controversy over tobacco goes back to the earliest European encounter with the plant, which was native to the Americas.

On his first voyage in 1492 Christopher Columbus saw Native Americans smoking tobacco. Later, the first Spanish missionaries associated smoking with pagan religious practices and tried to stop Native Americans from using tobacco. Once tobacco reached Europe in the late sixteenth century, more opposition to smoking arose (although—ironically—some physicians thought it might cure diseases of the lungs and internal organs). As early as 1610, Sir Francis Bacon (1561–1626) noted that smokers found it difficult to stop smoking. The Christian clergy throughout Europe denounced smoking as immoral, and Muslim clerics condemned the practice as contrary to Islam when it spread to the Ottoman Empire. Nonetheless, smoking tobacco in pipes became popular.

The chief British critic of the new practice was none other than King James I (r. 1603–1625). While he defended Sunday sports against Puritan critics who believed any amusements on the Sabbath were sinful, he detested smoking. In 1604, he published his *Counterblaste to Tobacco* in which he declared, "Have you not reason then to be ashamed, and to forbear this filthy novelty . . . ? In your abuse thereof sinning against God, harming yourselves in person . . . and taking thereby the marks . . . of vanity upon you. . . . A custom loathsome to the eye, hateful to the nose, harmful to the brain, dangerous to the lungs, and the black stinking fume thereof, nearest resembling the horrible Stygian smoke of the pit that is bottomless."[1]

To discourage smoking, James's government put a high tax on tobacco. Yet when a brisk trade in smuggled tobacco developed, the government decided to lower the tax to a level where people would not seek to evade it. In 1614, James created a royal monopoly to import tobacco into England, which created a steady government revenue that the increasingly unpopular king badly needed. James, like governments to the present day, may also have regarded this policy as a tax on sin. By 1619, James approved the incorporation of a company of clay pipe makers in London, and 40,000 pounds of tobacco arrived from Virginia the next year. Other European governments would also find tobacco a significant source of tax revenue. Often they would tax tobacco and at the same time attempt to regulate its use, especially among the young.

Which groups in Europe in the sixteenth and seventeenth centuries opposed the habit of smoking tobacco?

Why did the English government under King James I modify its opposition to tobacco?

[1] *A Counterblaste to Tobacco* (1604), reprinted by the Rodale Press, London, 1954, p. 36.

Practically from the moment of its introduction into Europe tobacco smoking was controversial. Here a court jester is portrayed as exhaling rabbits from a pipe as three pipe-smoking gentlemen look on.
Christel Gerstenberg/Fine Art Value/Corbis

Charles I

Parliament had favored the war with Spain but would not adequately finance it because its members distrusted the monarchy. Unable to gain adequate funds from Parliament, Charles I (r. 1625–1649), like his father, resorted to extra-parliamentary measures. These included levying new tariffs and duties, attempting to collect discontinued taxes, and subjecting English property owners to a so-called forced loan (a tax theoretically to be repaid) and then imprisoning those who refused to pay. All these actions, as well as quartering troops in private homes, challenged local political influence of nobles and landowners.

When Parliament met in 1628, its members would grant new funds only if Charles recognized the Petition of Right. This document required that henceforth there should be no forced loans or taxation without the consent of Parliament, that no freeman should be imprisoned without due cause, and that troops should not be billeted in private homes. Charles agreed to the petition,

King CHARLES the FIRST in the HOUSE of COMMONS, demanding the FIVE impeached MEMBERS to be delivered up to his AUTHORITY.

One of the key moments in the conflict between Charles I and Parliament occurred in January 1642 when Charles personally arrived at the House of Commons intent on arresting five members who had been responsible for opposing him. They had already escaped. Thereafter Charles departed London to raise his army. The event was subsequently often portrayed in English art. The present illustration is from an eighteenth-century engraving. The Granger Collection, New York

but whether he would keep his word was doubtful. The next year after further disputes, Charles dissolved Parliament and did not recall it until 1640.

Years of Personal Rule To conserve his limited resources, Charles made peace with France in 1629 and Spain in 1630, again rousing fears that he was too friendly to Roman Catholic powers. To allow Charles to rule without renegotiating financial arrangements with Parliament, his chief adviser, Thomas Wentworth (1593–1641; after 1640, earl of Strafford), imposed strict efficiency and administrative centralization in the government and exploited every legal fundraising device, enforcing previously neglected laws and extending existing taxes into new areas.

Charles might have ruled indefinitely without Parliament had not his religious policies provoked war with Scotland. James I had allowed a wide variety of religious observances in England, Scotland, and Ireland; by contrast, Charles hoped to impose religious conformity at least within England and Scotland. In 1637, Charles and his high-church Archbishop William Laud (1573–1645), against the opposition of both the English Puritans and the Presbyterian Scots, tried to impose on Scotland the English episcopal system and a prayer book almost identical to the Anglican Book of Common Prayer.

The Scots rebelled, and Charles, with insufficient resources for war, was forced in 1640 to call Parliament. It refused even to consider funds for war until the king agreed to redress a long list of political and religious grievances. The king, in response, immediately dissolved that Parliament—hence its name, the Short Parliament (April–May 1640). When the Scots defeated an English army at the Battle of Newburn in the summer of 1640, Charles reconvened Parliament—this time on its terms—for a long and fateful duration.

The Long Parliament and Civil War

The landowners and the merchant classes represented in Parliament had long resented the king's financial measures and paternalistic rule. The Puritans in Parliament resented his religious policies and distrusted the influence of his Roman Catholic wife. What became known as the Long Parliament (1640–1660) thus acted with widespread support and general unanimity when it convened in November 1640.

The House of Commons impeached both Strafford and Laud. Both were executed—Strafford in 1641, Laud in 1645. Parliament abolished the courts that had enforced royal policy and prohibited the levying of new taxes without its consent. Finally, Parliament resolved that no more than three years should elapse between its meetings and that the king could not dissolve it without its own consent.

Parliament, however, was sharply divided over religion. Both moderate Puritans (the Presbyterians) and more extreme Puritans (the Independents) wanted to abolish bishops and the Book of Common Prayer. Yet religious conservatives in both houses of Parliament were determined to preserve the Church of England in its current form.

These divisions intensified in October 1641, when Parliament was asked to raise funds for an army to suppress the rebellion in Scotland. Charles's opponents argued that he could not be trusted with an army and that Parliament should become the commander-in-chief of English armed forces. In January 1642, Charles invaded Parliament, intending to arrest certain of his opponents, but they escaped. The king then left London and began to raise an army. Shocked, a majority of the House of Commons passed the Militia Ordinance, which gave Parliament authority to raise an army of its own. The die was now cast. For the next four years (1642–1646), civil war engulfed England with the king's supporters known as Cavaliers and the parliamentary opposition as Roundheads.

🔍 **View** the **Map**
"Map Discovery: English Civil War" on **MyHistoryLab.com**

Oliver Cromwell and the Puritan Republic

Two factors led finally to Parliament's victory. The first was an alliance with Scotland in 1643 that committed Parliament to a Presbyterian system of church government. The second was the reorganization of the parliamentary army under Oliver Cromwell (1599–1658), a country squire of iron discipline and strong, independent religious sentiment. Cromwell and his "godly men" were willing to tolerate an established majority church, but only if it permitted Protestant dissenters to worship outside it.

Defeated militarily by June 1645, for the next several years Charles tried to take advantage of divisions within Parliament, but Cromwell and his army foiled him. Members who might have been sympathetic to the monarch were expelled from Parliament in December 1648. After a trial by a special court, Charles was executed on January 30, 1649, as a public criminal. Parliament then abolished the monarchy, the House of Lords, and the Anglican Church.

From 1649 to 1660, England became officially a Puritan republic, although Cromwell dominated it. His army brutally conquered Scotland and Ireland, where his radically Protestant army carried out numerous atrocities against Irish Catholics. As a national leader, however, Cromwell proved to be no politician. When in 1653 the House of Commons wanted to disband his expensive army of 50,000 men, Cromwell instead disbanded Parliament. He ruled thereafter as Lord Protector.

🔍 **View** the **Image**
"Allegorical View of Cromwell as Savior of England" on **MyHistoryLab.com**

Cromwell's military dictatorship, however, proved no more effective than Charles's rule and became just as harsh and hated. People deeply resented his Puritan prohibitions of drunkenness, theatergoing, and dancing. Political liberty vanished in the name of religious conformity. When

Oliver Cromwell's New Model Army defeated the royalists in the English Civil War. After the execution of Charles I in 1649, Cromwell dominated the short-lived English republic, conquered Ireland and Scotland, and ruled as Lord Protector from 1653 until his death in 1658. Anthony Van Dyck/Beryl Peters Collection/Alamy

Cromwell died in 1658, the English were ready by 1660 to restore both the Anglican Church and the monarchy.

Charles II and the Restoration of the Monarchy

After negotiations with the army, Charles II (r. 1660–1685) returned to England amid great rejoicing. A man of considerable charm and political skill, Charles set a refreshing new tone after eleven years of somber Puritanism. England returned to the status quo of 1642, with a hereditary monarch, a Parliament of Lords and Commons that met only when the king summoned it, and the Anglican Church, with its bishops and prayer book, supreme in religion.

The king, however, had secret Catholic sympathies and favored religious toleration. He wanted to allow loyal Catholics and Puritans to worship freely. Yet ultraroyalists in Parliament between 1661 and 1665, through a series of laws known as the Clarendon Code, excluded Roman Catholics, Presbyterians, and Independents from the official religious and political life of the nation.

In 1670 by the Treaty of Dover, England and France formally allied against the Dutch, their chief commercial competitor. In a secret portion of this treaty, Charles pledged to announce his conversion to Catholicism as soon as conditions in England permitted this to happen. In return for this announcement (which Charles never

AN ACCOUNT OF THE EXECUTION OF CHARLES I

Convicted of "high treason and other high crimes," Charles I was beheaded on January 30, 1649. In his last minutes he conversed calmly with the attending bishop and executioner, anxious only that the executioner not strike before he gave the signal.

Why was it so dangerous to end a king's rule by executing him? What made this king stand so brave and strong to the very end? Might the king's strong belief in God and himself give the masses a reason to second guess his execution—or was the execution a happy event for all? Did the king's execution threaten law and order and invite anarchy?

To the executioner he said, "I shall say but very short prayers, and when I thrust out my hands—"

Then he called to the bishop for his cap, and having put it on, asked the executioner, "Does your hair trouble you?" and the executioner desired him to put it under his cap, which as he was doing by help of the bishop and the executioner, he turned to the bishop and said, "I have a good cause, and a gracious God on my side."

The bishop said, "There is but one stage more, which, though turbulent and troublesome, yet is a very short one. . . . It will carry you from earth to heaven . . . to a crown of glory. . . ."

Then the king asked the executioner, "Is my hair well?"

And taking off his cloak and George [the Order of the Garter, bearing a figure of Saint George], he delivered his George to the bishop.

Then putting off his doublet and being in his waistcoat, he put on his cloak again, and looking upon the block, said to the executioner, "You must set it fast."

The executioner. "It is fast, sir."

King. "It might have been a little higher."

Executioner. "It can be no higher, sir."

King. "When I put out my hands this way, then—"

Then having said a few words to himself, as he stood with hands and eyes lifted up, immediately stopping down he laid his neck upon the block; and the executioner, again putting his hair under his cap, his Majesty, thinking he had been going to strike, bade him, "Stay for the sign."

Executioner. "Yes, I will, as it please your Majesty."

After a very short pause, his Majesty stretching forth his hands, the executioner at one blow severed his head from his body; which being held up and showed to the people, was with his body put into a coffin covered with black velvet and carried into his lodging.

His blood was taken up by divers persons for different ends; by some as trophies of the villainy; by others as relics of a martyr.

From J. H. Robinson, ed., *Readings in European History*, Vol. 2 (Boston: Atheneum, 1906), pp. 244–245.

---

made), Louis XIV promised to pay Charles a substantial subsidy. In an attempt to unite the English people behind the war with Holland, and as a sign of good faith to Louis XIV, Charles issued a Declaration of Indulgence in 1672, suspending all laws against Roman Catholics and non-Anglican Protestants. Parliament refused to fund the war, however, until Charles rescinded the measure. After he did so, Parliament passed the Test Act requiring all civil and military officials of the crown to swear an oath against the doctrine of transubstantiation—which no loyal Roman Catholic could honestly do. Parliament had aimed the Test Act largely at the king's brother, James, duke of York, heir to the throne and a recent, devout convert to Catholicism.

In 1678, a notorious liar named Titus Oates swore before a magistrate that Charles's Catholic wife, through her physician, was plotting with Jesuits and Irishmen to kill the king so James could assume the throne. Parliament believed Oates. In the ensuing hysteria, known as the Popish Plot, several innocent people were tried and executed. Riding the crest of anti-Catholic sentiment and led by the earl of Shaftesbury (1621–1683), opposition members of Parliament, called Whigs, made an unsuccessful effort to exclude James from succession to the throne.

More suspicious than ever of Parliament, Charles II turned again to increased customs duties and the assistance of Louis XIV for extra income. By these means, he was able to rule from 1681 to 1685 without recalling Parliament. In

ENGLAND IN THE SEVENTEENTH CENTURY

1603	James VI of Scotland becomes James I of England
1604	Hampton Court conference
1611	Publication of the authorized, or King James, version of the English Bible
1625	Charles I becomes English monarch
1628	Petition of Right
1629	Charles I dissolves Parliament and embarks on eleven years of personal rule
1640	April–May, Short Parliament; November, Long Parliament convenes
1642	Outbreak of the Civil War
1645	Charles I defeated at Naseby
1648	Pride's Purge
1649	Charles I executed
1649–1660	Various attempts at a Puritan Commonwealth
1660	Charles II restored to the English throne
1670	Secret Treaty of Dover between France and England
1672	Parliament passes the Test Act
1678	Popish Plot
1685	James II becomes king of England
1688	"Glorious Revolution"
1689	William and Mary proclaimed English monarchs
1701	Acts of Settlement provides for Hanoverian succession
1702–1714	Reign of Queen Anne, the last of the Stuarts
1707	Act of Union between England and Scotland
1713	Treaty of Utrecht ends the War of the Spanish Succession
1714	George I becomes king of Great Britain and establishes the Hanoverian dynasty
1721–1742	Robert Walpole dominates British politics
1727	George II becomes king of Great Britain

those years, Charles drove Shaftesbury into exile, executed several Whig leaders for treason, and bullied local corporations into electing members of Parliament submissive to the royal will. When Charles died in 1685 (after a deathbed conversion to Catholicism), he left James the prospect of a Parliament filled with royal friends.

The "Glorious Revolution"

When James II (r. 1685–1688) became king, he immediately demanded the repeal of the Test Act. When Parliament balked, he dissolved it and proceeded to appoint Catholics to high positions in both his court and the army. In 1687, he issued another Declaration of Indulgence suspending all religious tests and permitting free worship. In June 1688, James imprisoned seven Anglican bishops who had refused to publicize his suspension of laws against the Catholics. Each of these actions represented a direct royal attack on the local authority of nobles, landowners, the church, and other corporate bodies whose members believed they possessed particular legal privileges. James not only sought to aid his fellow Roman Catholics but also to pursue absolutist policies similar to those of Louis XIV whom he deeply admired.

The English had hoped that James would be succeeded by Mary (r. 1689–1694), his Protestant eldest daughter. She was the wife of William III of Orange, the leader of European opposition to Louis XIV. But on June 20, James II's Catholic second wife gave birth to a son. There was now a Catholic male heir to the throne. The Parliamentary opposition invited William to invade England to preserve its "traditional liberties," that is, the Anglican Church and parliamentary government.

William of Orange arrived with his army in November 1688 and was received with considerable popular support. James fled to France, and Parliament, in 1689, proclaimed William III and Mary II the new monarchs, thus completing the "**Glorious Revolution**." William and Mary, in turn, recognized a Bill of Rights that limited the powers of the monarchy and guaranteed the civil liberties of the English privileged classes. Henceforth, England's monarchs would be subject to law and would rule by the consent of Parliament, which was to be called into session every three years. The Bill of Rights also prohibited Roman Catholics from occupying the English throne. The Toleration Act of 1689 permitted worship by all Protestants and outlawed only Roman Catholics and those who denied the Christian doctrine of the Trinity. It did not, however, extend full political rights to persons outside the Church of England.

As will be seen more fully in the next chapter, in 1690 John Locke published his *Second Treatise of Civil Government*, which defended the idea that government resided in the consent of the governed. This view directly opposed Tory support for absolutism as well as absolutist political thought on the continent. (See "Compare and Connect: The Debate over the Origin and Character of Political Authority," pages 400–401.)

The Revolution of 1688 has traditionally been seen as a relatively peaceful event. Recent scholarship, however, has disclosed considerable resistance in both Scotland and Ireland, which resulted in significant loss of life. Conversely events in England itself now appear driven not only by the long-recognized actions of the political elite, but also by a genuinely popular resistance to James II. Furthermore, the political results of the revolution went well beyond the assertion of parliamentary authority. In one area of government policy after another the reign of William and Mary marked important new departures for Britain. These included not only the aforementioned embrace of moderate religious toleration, but also a turn to policies favoring more modern economic activity resembling that of the Netherlands and a redirection of foreign policy toward direct opposition to France whereas both Charles II and James II had sought to imitate French absolutism and to pursue close relationships with Louis XIV.

The parliamentary measure closing this century of strife was the Act of Settlement (1701), which provided for the English crown to go to the Protestant House of Hanover in Germany if Queen Anne (r. 1702–1714), the second daughter of James II and the heir to the childless William III, died without issue. Thus, at Anne's death in 1714, the Elector of Hanover became King George I of Great Britain (r. 1714–1727) since England and Scotland had been combined in an Act of Union in 1707.

The Age of Walpole

George I almost immediately confronted a challenge to his title. James Edward Stuart (1688–1766), the Catholic son of James II, landed in Scotland in December 1715, but met defeat less than two months later.

Despite the victory over the Stuart pretender, the political situation after 1715 remained in flux until Sir Robert Walpole (1676–1745) took over the helm of

Sir Robert Walpole (1676–1745), far left, is shown talking with the Speaker of the House of Commons. Walpole, who dominated British political life from 1721 to 1742, is considered the first prime minister of Britain. Mansell/ TimePix/Getty Images, Inc.

government. Walpole's ascendancy from 1721 to 1742 was based on royal support, his ability to handle the House of Commons, and his control of government patronage. Walpole maintained peace abroad and promoted the status quo at home. Britain's foreign trade spread from New England to India. Because the central government refrained from interfering with the local political influence of nobles and other landowners, they were willing to serve as local government administrators, judges, and military commanders, and to collect and pay the taxes to support a powerful military force, particularly a strong navy. As a result, Great Britain became not only a European power of the first order but eventually a world power as well.

The power of the British monarchs and their ministers had real limits. Parliament could not wholly ignore popular pressure. Even with the extensive use of patronage, many members of Parliament maintained independent views. Newspapers and public debate flourished. Free speech could be exercised, as could freedom of association. There was no large standing army. There existed significant religious toleration. Walpole's enemies could and did openly oppose his policies, which would not have been possible on the Continent. Consequently, the English state combined considerable military power with both religious and political liberty. British political life became the model for all progressive Europeans who questioned the absolutist political developments of the Continent. Furthermore, many of the political values that had emerged in the British Isles during the seventeenth century also took deep root among their North American colonies.

▼ Rise of Absolute Monarchy in France: The World of Louis XIV

Historians once portrayed Louis XIV's reign (r. 1643–1715) as a time when the French monarchy exerted far-reaching, direct control of the nation at all levels. A somewhat different picture has now emerged.

View the **Map** "Map Discovery: France Under Louis XIV" on **MyHistoryLab.com**

The French monarchy, which had faced numerous challenges from strong, well-armed nobles and discontented Protestants during the first half of the seventeenth century, only gradually achieved the firm authority for which it became renowned later in the century. The groundwork for Louis XIV's absolutism had been laid by two powerful chief ministers, Cardinal Richelieu (1585–1642) under Louis XIII (r. 1610–1643), and then by Cardinal Mazarin (1602–1661). Both Richelieu and Mazarin attempted to impose direct royal administration on France. Richelieu had also circumscribed many of the political privileges Henry IV had extended to French

Protestants in the Edict of Nantes (1598). The centralizing policies of Richelieu and then of Mazarin, however, finally provoked a series of widespread rebellions among French nobles between 1649 and 1652 known as the *Fronde* (after the slingshots used by street boys).

Though unsuccessful, these rebellions convinced Louis XIV and his advisors that heavy-handed policies could endanger the throne. Thereafter Louis would concentrate unprecedented authority in the monarchy, but he would be more subtle than his predecessors. His genius was to make the monarchy the most important and powerful political institution in France while also assuring the nobles and other wealthy groups of their social standing and influence on the local level. Rather than destroying existing local social and political institutions, Louis largely worked through them. Nevertheless, the king was clearly the senior partner in the relationship.

Years of Personal Rule

On the death of Mazarin in 1661, Louis XIV assumed personal control of the government at the age of twenty-three. He appointed no single chief minister. Rebellious nobles would now be challenging the king directly; they could not claim to be resisting only a bad minister.

Louis XIV of France came to symbolize absolute monarchy though such government was not as absolute as the term implied. This state portrait was intended to convey the grandeur of the king and of his authority. The portrait was brought into royal council meetings when the king himself was absent. Hyacinthe Rigaud (1659–1743), *Portrait of Louis XIV*. Louvre, Paris, France. Dorling Kindersley Media Library/Max Alexander. © Dorling Kindersley, courtesy of l'Etablissement public du musée et du domaine national de Versailles

Louis devoted enormous personal energy to his political tasks. He ruled through councils that controlled foreign affairs, the army, domestic administration, and economic regulations. Each day he spent hours with the ministers of these councils, whom he chose from families long in royal service or from among people just beginning to rise in the social structure. Unlike the more ancient noble families, the latter had no real or potential power bases in the provinces and depended solely on the king for their standing in both government and society.

Louis made sure, however, that the nobility and other major social groups would benefit from the growth of his own authority. Although he controlled foreign affairs and limited the influence of noble institutions on the monarchy, he never tried to abolish those institutions or limit their local authority. The crown, for example, usually conferred informally with regional judicial bodies, called *parlements*, before making rulings that would affect them. Likewise, the crown would rarely enact economic regulations without consulting local opinion. Louis did, however, clash with the Parlement of Paris, which had the right to register royal laws. In 1673, he curtailed its power by requiring it to register laws before raising any questions about them. Many regional parlements and other authorities, however, had long resented the power of that Parisian body and thus supported the monarch.

Versailles

Louis and his advisors became masters of propaganda and political image creation. Louis never missed an opportunity to impress the grandeur of his crown on the French people but most especially on the French nobility. He did so by the manipulation of symbols. For example, when the *dauphin* (the heir to the French throne) was born in 1662, Louis appeared for the celebration dressed as a Roman emperor. He also dominated the nobility by demonstrating that he could outspend them and create a greater social display than the strongest nobles in the land.

The central element of the image of the monarchy was the palace of Versailles, which, when completed, was the largest secular structure in Europe. More than any other monarch of the day, Louis XIV used the physical setting of his court to exert political control. Versailles, built between 1676 and 1708 on the outskirts of Paris, became Louis's permanent residence after 1682. It was a temple to royalty, designed and decorated to proclaim the glory of the Sun King, as Louis was known. A spectacular estate with magnificent fountains and gardens, it housed thousands of the more important nobles, royal officials, and servants. The stables alone could hold 12,000 horses. Some nobles paid for their own residence at the palace, thus depleting their resources; others required royal patronage to remain in residence. In either

A Closer LOOK

⟟ View the **Closer Look** on **MyHistoryLab.com**

VERSAILLES

LOUIS XIV CONSTRUCTED his great palace at Versailles, as painted here in 1668 by Pierre Patel the Elder (1605–1676), to demonstrate the new centralized power he sought to embody in the French monarchy.

The outer wings, extending from the front of the central structure, housed governmental offices.

The central building is the hunting lodge his father Louis XIII built earlier in the century. Its interior and added wings were decorated with themes from mythology, presenting Louis XIV as the "Sun King" around whom his kingdom revolved.

The gardens and ponds behind the main structure were sites of elaborative entertainment, concerts, and fireworks. Given the extravagant scale of the palace and gardens, it took armies of servants with shears to keep the green forest lawn and vegetation (*tapis vert*) "royal."

Pierre Patel, *Perspective View of Versailles*. Chateaux de Versailles et de Trianon, Versailles, France. Musée du Château de Versailles/Gianni Dagli Orti/The Art Archive at Art Resource, NY

How might the size alone of Versailles, as experienced by visitors and by viewers of paintings and prints of the structure, have served to overawe Louis's subjects? What other buildings of the day might have approached Versailles in size? In particular, how might French nobility have reacted to the setting?

Do you think some people who saw Versailles or images of it might have wondered how this extraordinary royal community was financed and might have drawn critical conclusions about the structure of French taxes?

By the end of his life Louis rarely ventured outside Versailles and neither did his eighteenth-century royal successors. How might the limitation of so much royal experience to the region of Versailles have distorted the monarchs' view of their kingdom?

How might the images of Louis in mythological scenes created a sense that he and his power were vaster than those of ordinary mortals?

case they became dependent on the monarch. Although it consumed over half of Louis's annual revenues, Versailles paid significant political dividends.

Because Louis ruled personally, he was himself the chief source of favors and patronage in France. To emphasize his prominence, he organized life at court around every aspect of his own daily routine. Elaborate etiquette governed every detail of life at Versailles. Moments near the king were important to most court nobles because they were effectively excluded from the real business of government. The king's rising and dressing were times of rare intimacy, when nobles could whisper their special requests in his ear. Fortunate nobles held his night candle when he went to his bed.

Some nobles, of course, avoided Versailles. They managed their estates and cultivated their local influence. Many others were simply too poor to cut a figure at court. All the nobility understood, however, that Louis, unlike Richelieu and Mazarin, would not threaten their local social standing. Louis supported France's traditional social structure and the social privileges of the nobility. Yet even the most powerful nobles knew they could strike only a modest figure when compared to the Sun King.

King by Divine Right

An important source for Louis's concept of royal authority was his devout tutor, political theorist Bishop Jacques-Bénigne Bossuet (1627–1704). Bossuet defended what he called the "divine right of kings" and cited examples of Old Testament rulers divinely appointed by and answerable only to God. Medieval popes had insisted that only God could judge a pope, so Bossuet argued that only God could judge the king. Although kings might be duty bound to reflect God's will in their rule, yet as God's regents on earth they could not be bound to the dictates of mere nobles and parliaments. Such assumptions lay behind Louis XIV's alleged declaration: *L'état, c'est moi* ("I am the state"). (See "Compare and Connect: The Debate over the Origin and Character of Political Authority," pages 400–401.)

Despite these claims, Louis's rule did not exert the oppressive control over the daily lives of his subjects that police states would do in the nineteenth and twentieth centuries. His absolutism functioned primarily in the classic areas of European state action—the making of war and peace, the regulation of religion, and the oversight of economic activity. Even at the height of his power, local institutions, some controlled by townspeople and others by nobles, retained their administrative authority. The king and his ministers supported the social and financial privileges of these local elites. In contrast to the Stuart kings of England, however, Louis firmly prevented them from interfering with his authority on the national level. This system would endure until a financial crisis demoralized the French monarchy in the 1780s.

Louis's Early Wars

By the late 1660s, France was superior to any other European nation in population, administrative bureaucracy, army, and national unity. Because of the economic policies of Jean-Baptiste Colbert (1619–1683), his most brilliant minister, Louis could afford to raise and maintain a large and powerful army. His enemies and some later historians claimed that Louis wished to dominate all of Europe, but it would appear that his chief military and foreign policy goal was to achieve secure international boundaries for France. He was particularly concerned to secure its northern borders along the Spanish Netherlands, the Franche-Comté, Alsace, and Lorraine from which foreign armies had invaded France and could easily do so again. Louis was also determined to frustrate Habsburg ambitions that endangered France and, as part of that goal, sought to secure his southern borders toward Spain. Whether reacting to external events or pursuing his own ambitions, Louis's pursuit of French interests threatened and terrified neighboring states and led them to form coalitions against France.

The early wars of Louis XIV included conflicts with Spain and the United Netherlands. The first was the War of the Devolution in which Louis supported the alleged

FRANCE FROM LOUIS XIV TO CARDINAL FLEURY

1643	Louis ascends the French throne at the age of five
1643–1661	Cardinal Mazarin directs the French government
1648	Peace of Westphalia
1649–1652	The *Fronde* revolt
1653	The pope declares Jansenism a heresy
1660	Papal ban on Jansenists enforced in France
1661	Louis commences personal rule
1667–1668	War of Devolution
1670	Secret Treaty of Dover between France and Great Britain
1672–1679	French war against the Netherlands
1685	Louis revokes the Edict of Nantes
1688–1697	War of the League of Augsburg
1701	Outbreak of the War of the Spanish Succession
1713	Treaty of Utrecht between France and Great Britain
1714	Treaty of Rastatt between France and the Empire and Holland
1715	Death of Louis XIV
1715–1720	Regency of the duke of Orléans in France
1720	Mississippi Bubble bursts in France
1726–1743	Cardinal Fleury serves as Louis XV's chief minister

right of his first wife, Marie Thérèse, to inherit the Spanish Netherlands. He contended that through complex legal arrangements they should have "devolved" upon her, hence the name of the war. In 1667, Louis's armies invaded Flanders and the Franche-Comté. He was repulsed by the Triple Alliance of England, Sweden, and the United Provinces. By the Treaty of Aix-la-Chapelle (1668), he gained control of certain towns bordering the Spanish Netherlands. (See Map 13–1.)

In 1670, with the secret Treaty of Dover, England and France became allies against the Dutch. Louis invaded the Netherlands again in 1672. The Prince of Orange, the future William III of England, forged an alliance with the Holy Roman Emperor, Spain, Lorraine, and Brandenburg against Louis, now regarded as a menace to the whole of western Europe, Catholic and Protestant alike. The war ended inconclusively with the Peace of Nijmwegen, signed with different parties in successive years (1678, 1679). France gained more territory, including the Franche-Comté.

Louis's Repressive Religious Policies

Like Richelieu before him, Louis believed that political unity and stability required religious conformity. To that end he carried out repressive actions against both Roman Catholics and Protestants.

Suppression of the Jansenists The French crown and the French Roman Catholic church had long jealously guarded their ecclesiastical independence or "**Gallican Liberties**" from papal authority in Rome. However,

Map 13–1 THE FIRST THREE WARS OF LOUIS XIV This map shows the territorial changes resulting from Louis XIV's first three major wars (1667–1697).

The Debate over the Origin and Character of Political Authority

📖 Read the **Compare and Connect** on **MyHistoryLab.com**

DURING THE SECOND half of the seventeenth century a profound dispute occurred among European political phi-losophers over the origin and character of political authority. Some political philosophers, here illustrated by the French bishop Jacques-Bénigne Bossuet, contended that monarchs governed absolutely by virtue of authority derived from God. Other philosophers, here illustrated by the English writer John Locke, contended that political authority originated in the consent of the governed and that such authority was inherently limited in its scope.

QUESTIONS

1. Why might Bossuet have wished to make such extravagant claims for absolute royal power?

2. How might these claims be transferred to any form of government?

3. How does Bossuet's argument for absolute royal authority lead also to the need for a single uniform religion in France?

4. Why does Locke find an absolute monarch in con-flict with his subjects and they with him?

5. How do Locke's views serve to provide a foundation for parliamentary government?

6. How might subjects governed according to Bossuet's and Locke's principles relate differently to their monarchs and to the officials of monarchs administering their local communities?

I. Bishop Bossuet Defends the Divine Right of Kings

The revolutions of the seventeenth century caused many to fear anarchy far more than tyranny, among them the influential French bishop Jacques-Bénigne Bossuet (1627–1704), the leader of French Catholicism in the second half of the seventeenth century. Louis XIV made him court preacher and tutor to his son, for whom Bossuet wrote a celebrated universal history. In the following excerpt, Bossuet defends the divine right and absolute power of kings. He depicts kings as embracing in their person the whole body of the state and the will of the people they govern and, as such, as being immune from judgment by any mere mortal.

The royal power is absolute. . . . The prince need render account of his acts to no one. "I counsel thee to keep the king's commandment, and that in regard of the oath of God. Be not hasty to go out of his sight; stand not on an evil thing for he doeth whatsoever pleaseth him. Where the word of a king is, there is power; and who may say unto him, What doest thou? Whoso keepeth the commandment shall feel no evil thing" [Eccles. 8:2–5]. Without this absolute author-ity the king could neither do good nor repress evil. It is necessary that his power be such that no one can

hope to escape him, and finally, the only protection of individuals against the public authority should be their innocence. This confirms the teaching of St. Paul: "Wilt thou then not be afraid of the power? Do that which is good" [Rom. 13:3].

God is infinite, God is all. The prince, as prince, is not regarded as a private person: he is a public person-age, all the state is in him; the will of all the people is included in his. As all perfection and all strength are united in God, so all the power of individuals is united in the person of the prince. What grandeur that a single man should embody so much! . . .

Behold an immense people united in a single per-son; behold this holy power, paternal and absolute; behold the secret cause which governs the whole body of the state, contained in a single head: you see the image of God in the king, and you have the idea of royal majesty. God is holiness itself, goodness itself, and power itself. In these things lies the majesty of God. In the image of these things lies the majesty of the prince. ■

From *Politics Drawn from the Very Words of Holy Scripture*, as quoted in James Harvey Robinson, ed., *Readings in European History*, Vol. 2 (Boston: Athenaeum, 1906), pp. 275–276.

II. John Locke Denounces the Idea of Absolute Monarchy

John Locke (1632–1704) was the most important English philosopher of the late seventeenth century. As will be seen in Chapter 14 he wrote on a wide variety of subjects including both political philosophy and religious toleration. In 1690 he published his second Treatise of Civil Government. *In this work he defended limitations on government and rooted political authority in the consent of the governed. He drafted the treatise in the late 1670s in response to Tory assertions of absolute monarchy set forth by supporters of Charles II. The treatise was published in the wake of the Revolution of 1688 and was read at the time as a justification of that event. Locke's thought would almost a century later influence the American Declaration of Independence. In the passages below Locke explains that under absolute monarchy citizens must submit to an authority from which they can make no appeal. Consequently, there is a necessary conflict between citizens and the absolute monarchy. It was to escape such conflict and to secure property and liberty that human beings had left the state of nature to found civil society.*

Man being born . . . with a title to perfect freedom, and an uncontrolled enjoyment of all the rights and privileges of the law of nature, equally with any other man, or number of men in the world, hath by nature a power, not only to preserve his property, that is, his life, liberty and estate, against the injuries and attempts of other men; but to judge of, and punish the breaches of that law in others, as he is persuaded the offence deserve. . . . [T]here and there only is political society, where every one of the members hath quitted this natural power, resigned it up into the hands of the community in all cases that excludes him not from appealing for protection to the law established by it. And thus all private judgment of every particular member being excluded, the community comes to be umpire, by settled standing rules, indifferent, and the same to all parties; and by men having authority from the community, for the execution of those rules, decides all the differences that may happen between any members of that society concerning any matter of right . . .

Whenever therefore any number of men are so united into one society, as to quit every one his executive power of the law of nature, and to resign it to the public, there and there only is a political, or civil society. . . .

Hence it is evident, that absolute monarchy, which by some men is counted the only government in the world, is indeed inconsistent with civil society, and so can be no form of civil government at all; for the end of civil society, being to avoid, and remedy those inconveniencies of the state of nature, which necessarily follow from every man's being judge in his own case, by setting up a known authority, to which every one of that society may appeal upon any injury received, or controversy that may arise, and which every one of the society ought to obey; where-ever any persons are, who have not such an authority to appeal to, for the decision of any difference between them, there those persons are still in the state of nature; and so is every absolute prince, in respect of those who are under his dominion.

For he being supposed to have all, both legislative and executive power in himself alone, there is no judge to be found, no appeal lies open to any one, who may fairly, and indifferently, and with authority decide, and from whose decision relief and redress may be expected of any injury or inconveniency, that may be suffered from the prince, or by his order: so that such a man, however intitled, czar, or grand seignior, or how you please, is as much in the state of nature, with all under his dominion, as he is with the rest of mankind: for where-ever any two men are, who have no standing rule, and common judge to appeal to on earth, for the determination of controversies of right betwixt them, there they are still in the state of nature, and under all the inconveniencies of it . . . ■

Title page from *Two Treatises of Government* by John Locke, London, 1690. Courtesy of the Library of Congress, Rosenwald Collection, Rare Book and Special Collections Division

From John Locke, *Of Civil Government*, paragraphs 87, 89, 90, 91 in *Two Treatises of Government*, a new ed. (London: 1824), pp. 179–183.

after the conversion to Roman Catholicism of Henry IV in 1593, the Jesuits, fiercely loyal to the authority of the Pope, had monopolized the education of French upper-class men, and their devout students promoted the religious reforms and doctrines of the Council of Trent. As a measure of their success, Jesuits served as confessors to Henry IV, Louis XIII, and Louis XIV.

A Roman Catholic religious movement known as **Jansenism** arose in the 1630s in opposition to the theology and the political influence of the Jesuits. Jansenists adhered to the teachings of St. Augustine (354–430) that had also influenced many Protestant doctrines. Serious and uncompromising, they particularly opposed Jesuit teachings about free will. They believed with Augustine that original sin had so corrupted humankind that individuals could by their own effort do nothing good nor contribute anything to their own salvation. The namesake of the movement, Cornelius Jansen (d. 1638), was a Flemish theologian and the bishop of Ypres. His posthumously published *Augustinus* (1640) assailed Jesuit teaching on grace and salvation as morally lax.

Jansenism made considerable progress among prominent families in Paris. They were opposed to the Jesuits and supported Jansenist religious communities such as the convent at Port-Royal outside Paris. Jansenists, whose Augustinian theology resembled Calvinism, were known to live extremely pious and morally austere lives. In these respects, though firm Roman Catholics, they resembled English Puritans. Also, like the Puritans, the Jansenists became associated with opposition to royal authority, and families of Jansenist sympathies had been involved in the *Fronde*.

On May 31, 1653, Pope Innocent X declared heretical five Jansenist theological propositions on grace and salvation. In 1656, the pope banned Jansen's *Augustinus*. In 1660, Louis permitted the papal bull banning Jansenism to be enforced in France. He also eventually closed down the Port-Royal community. Thereafter, Jansenists either retracted their views or went underground. In 1713, Pope Clement XI issued the bull *Unigenitus*, which again extensively condemned Jansenist teaching. The now aged Louis XIV ordered the French church to accept the bull despite internal ecclesiastical opposition.

The theological issues surrounding Jansenism were complex. By persecuting the Jansenists, however, Louis XIV turned his back on the long tradition of protecting the Gallican Liberties of the French Church and fostered within the French Church a core of opposition to royal authority. This had long-term political significance. During the eighteenth century after the death of Louis XIV, the Parlement of Paris and other French judicial bodies would reassert their authority in opposition to the monarchy. These courts were sympathetic to the Jansenists because of their common resistance to royal authority. Jansenism, because of its austere morality, then also came to embody a set of religious and moral values that contrasted with

Françoise d'Aubigne, Madame de Maintenon (1635–1719), a mistress to Louis XIV, secretly married him after his first wife's death. The deeply pious Maintenon influenced Louis's policy to make Roman Catholicism France's only religion. Pierre Mignard (1612–1695), *Portrait of Francoise d'Aubigne, Marquise de Maintenon (1635–1719), mistress and second wife of Louis XIV*, c. 1694. Oil on canvas, 128 × 97 cm. Inv.: MV 3637. Chateaux de Versailles et de Trianon, Versailles, France/RMN-Grand Palais/Gérard Blot/Art Resource, NY

what eighteenth-century public opinion saw as the corruption of the mid-eighteenth-century French royal court.

Revocation of the Edict of Nantes

After the Edict of Nantes in 1598, relations between the Catholic majority (nine-tenths of the French population) and the Protestant minority had remained hostile. There were about 1.75 million Huguenots in France in the 1660s (out of an overall population of around 18 million), but their numbers were declining. The French Catholic church had long supported their persecution as both pious and patriotic.

After the Peace of Nijmwegen, Louis launched a methodical campaign against the Huguenots in an effort to unify France religiously. He was also influenced in this policy by his mistress who became his second wife, Madame de Maintenon (1635–1719), a deeply pious Catholic who drew Louis toward a much more devout religious observance. Louis hounded Huguenots out of public life, banning them from government office and excluding them from such professions as printing and medicine. He used financial incentives to encourage them to convert to Catholicism. In 1681, he bullied them by quartering troops in their towns. Finally, in October 1685, Louis revoked the Edict of Nantes, and extensive religious repression followed. Protestant churches and schools were closed, Protestant ministers exiled, nonconverting laity were condemned to be galley slaves, and Protestant children were baptized by Catholic priests. (See the Document "Louis XIV Revokes the Edict of Nantes," page 404.)

The revocation was a major blunder. Henceforth, Protestants across Europe considered Louis a fanatic who must be resisted at all costs. More than a quarter million people, many of whom were highly skilled, left France. They formed new communities abroad and joined the resistance to Louis in England, Germany, Holland, and the New World. As a result of the revocation of the Edict of Nantes and the ongoing persecution of Jansenists, France became a symbol of religious repression in contrast to England's reputation for moderate, if not complete, religious toleration.

Louis's Later Wars

The League of Augsburg and the Nine Years' War

After the Treaty of Nijmwegen in 1678–1679, Louis maintained his army at full strength and restlessly probed beyond his borders. In 1681 his forces occupied the free city of Strasbourg on the Rhine River, prompting new defensive coalitions to form against him. One of these, the League of Augsburg, grew to include England, Spain, Sweden, the United Provinces, and the major German states. It also had the support of the Habsburg emperor Leopold I (r. 1658–1705). Between 1689 and 1697, the League and France battled each other in the Nine Years' War, while England and France struggled to control North America.

The Peace of Ryswick, signed in September 1697, which ended the war, secured Holland's borders and thwarted Louis's expansion into Germany.

War of the Spanish Succession

On November 1, 1700, the last Habsburg king of Spain, Charles II (r. 1665–1700), died without direct heirs. Before his death, negotiations had begun among the nations involved to partition his inheritance in a way that would preserve the existing balance of power. Charles II, however, left his entire inheritance to Louis's grandson Philip of Anjou, who became Philip V of Spain (r. 1700–1746).

Spain and the vast trade with its American empire appeared to have fallen to France. In September 1701, England, Holland, and the Holy Roman Empire formed the Grand Alliance to preserve the balance of power by once and for all securing Flanders as a neutral barrier between Holland and France and by gaining for the emperor, who was also a Habsburg, his fair share of the Spanish inheritance. Louis soon increased the political stakes by recognizing the Stuart claim to the English throne.

In 1701 the War of the Spanish Succession (1701–1714) began, and it soon enveloped western Europe. For the first time in Louis's reign France went to war with inadequate finances, a poorly equipped army, and mediocre generals.

The English, in contrast, had advanced weaponry (flintlock rifles, paper cartridges, and ring bayonets) and superior tactics (thin, maneuverable troop columns rather than the traditional deep ones). John Churchill, the Duke of Marlborough (1650–1722), bested Louis's soldiers in every major engagement, although French arms triumphed in Spain. After 1709 the war became a bloody stalemate.

France finally made peace with England at Utrecht in July 1713, and with Holland and the emperor at Rastatt in March 1714. Philip V remained king of Spain, but England got Gibraltar and the island of Minorca, making it a Mediterranean power. (See Map 13–2, p. 405.) Louis also recognized the right of the House of Hanover to the English throne.

France After Louis XIV

Despite its military reverses in the War of the Spanish Succession, France remained a great power. It was less strong in 1715 than in 1680, but it still possessed the largest European population, an advanced, if troubled, economy, and the administrative structure bequeathed it by Louis XIV. Moreover, even if France and its resources had been drained by the last of Louis's wars, the other major states of Europe were similarly debilitated.

Louis XIV was succeeded by his five-year-old great-grandson Louis XV (r. 1715–1774). The young boy's uncle, the duke of Orléans, became regent and remained so until his death in 1720. The regency, marked by financial and moral scandals, further undermined the faltering prestige of the monarchy.

John Law and the Mississippi Bubble

The duke of Orléans was a gambler, and for a time he turned over the financial management of the kingdom to John Law (1671–1729), a Scottish mathematician and fellow gambler. Law believed an increase in the paper-money supply would stimulate France's economic recovery. With the permission of the regent, he established a bank in Paris that issued paper money. Law then organized a monopoly, called the Mississippi Company, on trading privileges with the French colony of Louisiana in North America.

The Mississippi Company also took over the management of the French national debt. The company issued shares of its own stock in exchange for government bonds, which had fallen sharply in value. To redeem large quantities of bonds, Law encouraged speculation in the Mississippi Company stock. In 1719, the price of the stock rose handsomely. Smart investors, however, took their profits by selling their stock in exchange for paper money from Law's bank, which they then sought to exchange for gold. The bank, however, lacked enough gold to redeem all the paper money brought to it.

Document

LOUIS XIV REVOKES THE EDICT OF NANTES

Believing a country could not be governed by one king and one law unless it was also under one religious system, Louis XIV stunned much of Europe in October 1685 by revoking the Edict of Nantes, which had protected the religious freedoms and civil rights of French Protestants since 1598. Years of serious, often violent, persecution of French Protestants followed this revocation. Consequently, after 1685 in the minds of many Europeans political absolutism was associated with intolerance and religious persecution. Paradoxically, Pope Innocent XI (1676–1689) opposed Louis XIV's revocation of the Edict of Nantes because he understood that this act and other aspects of Louis's ecclesiastical policy were intended as political measures to allow his government to dominate the Roman Catholic Church in France.

Compare this document to the one on page 410 in which the elector of Brandenburg welcomes displaced French Protestants into his domains.

What specific actions does this declaration order against Protestants? Does it offer any incentives for Protestants to convert to Catholicism? How does this declaration compare with the English Test Act?

Art. 1. Know that we ... with our certain knowledge, full power and royal authority, have by this present, perpetual and irrevocable edict, suppressed and revoked the edict of the aforesaid king our grandfather, given at Nantes in the month of April, 1598, in all its extent ... together with all the concessions made by [this] and other edicts, declarations, and decrees, to the people of the so-called Reformed religion, of whatever nature they be ... and in consequence we desire ... that all the temples of the people of the aforesaid so-called Reformed religion situated in our kingdom ... should be demolished forthwith.

Art. 2. We forbid our subjects of the so-called Reformed religion to assemble any more for public worship of the above-mentioned religion. ...

Art. 3. We likewise forbid all lords, of whatever rank they may be, to carry out heretical services in houses and fiefs ... the penalty for ... the said worship being confiscation of their body and possessions.

Art. 4. We order all ministers of the aforesaid so-called Reformed religion who do not wish to be converted and to embrace the Catholic, Apostolic, and Roman religion, to depart from our kingdom and the lands subject to us within fifteen days from the publication of our present edict ... on pain of the galleys.

Art. 5. We desire that those among the said [Reformed] ministers who shall be converted [to the Catholic religion] shall continue to enjoy during their life, and their wives shall enjoy after their death as long as they remain widows, the same exemptions from taxation and billeting of soldiers, which they enjoyed while they fulfilled the function of ministers. ...

Art. 8. With regard to children who shall be born to those of the aforesaid so-called Reformed religion, we desire that they be baptized by their parish priests. We command the fathers and mothers to send them to the churches for that purpose, on penalty of a fine of 500 livres or more if they fail to do so; and afterwards, the children shall be brought up in the Catholic, Apostolic, and Roman religion. ...

Art. 10. All our subjects of the so-called Reformed religion, with their wives and children, are to be strongly and repeatedly prohibited from leaving our aforesaid kingdom ... or of taking out ... their possessions and effects. ...

The members of the so-called Reformed religion, while awaiting God's pleasure to enlighten them like the others, can live in the towns and districts of our kingdom ... and continue their occupation there, and enjoy their possessions ... on condition ... that they do not make public profession of [their religion].

From S. Z. Ehler and John B. Morrall, eds. and trans., *Church and State Through the Centuries: A Collection of Historic Documents* (New York: Biblo & Tannen, 1967), pp. 209–213. Reprinted by permission of Biblo and Tannen Booksellers and Publishers.

Map 13–2 **EUROPE IN 1714** The War of the Spanish Succession ended a year before the death of Louis XIV. The Bourbons had secured the Spanish throne, but Spain had forfeited its possessions in Flanders and Italy.

In February 1720, all gold payments were halted in France. Soon thereafter, Law himself fled the country. The Mississippi Bubble, as the affair was called, had burst. The fiasco brought disgrace on the government that had sponsored Law. The Mississippi Company was later reorganized and functioned profitably, but fear of paper money and speculation marked French economic life for decades.

Renewed Authority of the Parlements

The duke of Orléans made a second decision that also lessened the power of the monarchy. He attempted to draw the French nobility once again into the decision-making processes of the government. He set up a system of councils on which nobles were to serve along with bureaucrats. The years of idle noble domestication at Versailles, however, had worked too well, and the nobility seemed to lack both the talent and the desire to govern. The experiment failed.

Despite this failure, the great French nobles did not surrender their ancient ambition to assert their rights, privileges, and local influence over those of the monarchy. The chief feature of eighteenth-century French political life was the attempt of the nobility to use its authority to limit the power of the monarchy. The most effective instrument in this process was the previously mentioned parlements, or courts dominated by the nobility.

The duke of Orléans reversed the previously noted policy of Louis XIV and formally approved the reinstitution of the full power of the Parlement of Paris to allow or disallow laws. Moreover, throughout the eighteenth century that and other local parlements also succeeded in identifying their authority and resistance to the monarchy with wider public opinion. This situation meant that until the revolution in 1789, the parlements became natural centers not only for aristocratic, but also for popular, resistance to

La Rue Quincampoix.

The impending collapse of John Law's bank triggered a financial panic throughout France. Desperate investors sought to exchange their paper currency for gold and silver before the banks' supply of precious metals was exhausted. *La Rue Quincampoix*, The Law Affair, c. 1797 (coloured engraving), French School (18th century). Musee de la Ville de Paris, Musee Carnavalet, Paris, France/Archives Charmet/The Bridgeman Art Library International

royal authority. In a vast transformation from the days of Louis XIV, the parlements rather than the monarchy would come to be seen as more nearly representing the nation.

By 1726, the general political direction of the nation had come under the authority of Cardinal Fleury (1653–1743). He worked to maintain the authority of the monarchy, including ongoing repression of the Jansenists, while continuing to preserve the local interests of the French nobility. Like Walpole in Britain, he pursued economic prosperity at home and peace abroad. Again like Walpole, after 1740, Fleury could not prevent France from entering a worldwide colonial conflict. (See Chapter 17.)

▼ Central and Eastern Europe

Central and eastern Europe were economically much less advanced than western Europe. Except for the Baltic ports, the economy was agrarian. There were fewer cities and many more large estates worked by serfs. The states in this region did not possess overseas empires; nor did they engage in extensive overseas trade of any kind,

View the **Map** "Eastern Europe, ca. 1550" on **MyHistoryLab.com**

Under Louis XV (r. 1715–1774) France suffered major defeats in Europe and around the world and lost most of its North American empire. Louis himself was an ineffective ruler, and during his reign, the monarchy encountered numerous challenges from the French aristocracy. CORBIS/Bettmann

except for supplying grain to western Europe—grain, more often than not, carried on western European ships.

During the sixteenth and early seventeenth centuries, the political authorities in this region, which lay largely east of the Elbe River, were weak. The almost constant warfare of the seventeenth century had led to a habit of temporary and shifting political loyalties with princes and aristocracies of small states refusing to subordinate themselves to central monarchical authorities.

During the last half of the seventeenth century, however, three strong dynasties, whose rulers aspired to the absolutism then being constructed in France, emerged in central and eastern Europe. After the Peace of Westphalia in 1648, the Austrian Habsburgs recognized the basic weakness of the position of the Holy Roman Emperor and started to consolidate their power outside Germany. At the same time, Prussia under the Hohenzollern dynasty emerged as a factor in north German politics and as a major challenger to the Habsburg domination of Germany. Most important, Russia under the Romanov dynasty at the opening of the eighteenth century became a military and naval power of the first order. These three monarchies would dominate central and eastern Europe until the close of World War I in 1918. By contrast, during the eighteenth century Poland became the single most conspicuous example in Europe of a land that failed to establish a viable centralized government.

Poland: Absence of Strong Central Authority

In no other part of Europe was the failure to maintain a competitive political position as complete as in Poland. In 1683 King John III Sobieski (r. 1674–1696) had led a Polish army to rescue Vienna from a Turkish siege. Following that spectacular effort, however, Poland became a byword for the dangers of aristocratic independence.

The Polish monarchy was elective, but the deep distrust and divisions among the nobility usually prevented their electing a king from among themselves. Sobieski was a notable exception. Most of the Polish monarchs were foreigners and the tools of foreign powers. The Polish nobles did have a central legislative body called the **Sejm**, or diet. It included only nobles and specifically excluded representatives from corporate bodies, such as the towns. The diet, however, had a practice known as the *liberum veto*, whereby the staunch opposition of any single member, who might have been bribed by a foreign power, could require the body to disband. Such opposition, termed "exploding the diet," was most often the work of a group of dissatisfied nobles rather than of one person. Nonetheless, the requirement of unanimity was a major stumbling block to effective government. The price of this noble liberty would eventually be the disappearance of Poland from the map of Europe in the late eighteenth century.

The Habsburg Empire and the Pragmatic Sanction

The close of the Thirty Years' War marked a fundamental turning point in the history of the Austrian Habsburgs. Previously, in alliance with their Spanish cousins, they had hoped to bring all of Germany under their control and back to the Catholic fold. In this they had failed, and the decline of Spanish power meant that the Austrian Habsburgs were on their own. (See Map 13–3, p. 408.)

After 1648, the Habsburg family retained a firm hold on the title of Holy Roman Emperor, but the power of the emperor depended less on the force of arms than on the cooperation he could elicit from the various political bodies in the empire. These included large German units (such as Saxony, Hanover, Bavaria, and Brandenburg) and

In 1683 the Ottomans laid siege to Vienna. Only the arrival of Polish forces under King John III Sobieski (r. 1674–1696) saved the Habsburg capital. Erich Lessing/Art Resource, NY

scores of small German cities, bishoprics, principalities, and territories of independent knights. While establishing their new dominance among the German states, the Habsburgs also began to consolidate their power and influence within their hereditary possessions outside the Holy Roman Empire, which included the Crown of Saint Wenceslas, encompassing the kingdom of Bohemia (in the modern Czech Republic) and the duchies of Moravia and Silesia; and the Crown of Saint Stephen, which ruled Hungary, Croatia, and Transylvania. Much of Hungary was only liberated from the Turks at the end of the seventeenth century (1699).

Through the Treaty of Rastatt in 1714, the Habsburgs further extended their domains, receiving the former Spanish (thereafter Austrian) Netherlands and Lombardy in northern Italy. Thereafter, the Habsburgs' power and influence would be based primarily on their territories outside of Germany.

In each of their many territories the Habsburgs ruled by virtue of a different title—king, archduke, duke—and they needed the cooperation of the local nobility, which was not always forthcoming. They repeatedly had to bargain with nobles in one part of Europe to maintain their position in another. Their domains were so geographically diverse and the people who lived in them of so many different languages and customs that almost no grounds existed on which to unify them politically. Even Roman Catholicism proved ineffective as a common bond, particularly in Hungary, where many Magyar nobles were Calvinist and seemed ever ready to rebel. Over the years the Habsburg rulers established various central councils to chart common policies for their far-flung domains.

Map 13–3 THE AUSTRIAN HABSBURG EMPIRE, 1521–1772 The empire had three main units—Austria, Bohemia, and Hungary. Expansion was mainly eastward: eastern Hungary from the Ottomans (seventeenth century) and Galicia from Poland (1772). Meantime, Silesia was lost after 1740, but the Habsburgs remained Holy Roman Emperors.

Virtually all of these bodies, however, dealt with only a portion of the Habsburg holdings.

Despite these internal difficulties, Leopold I (r. 1658–1705) managed to resist the advances of the Ottoman Empire into central Europe, which included a siege of Vienna in 1683, and to thwart the aggression of Louis XIV. He achieved Ottoman recognition of his sovereignty over Hungary in 1699 and extended his territorial holdings over much of the Balkan Peninsula and western Romania. These conquests allowed the Habsburgs to hope to develop Mediterranean trade through the port of Trieste on the northern coast of the Adriatic Sea and helped compensate for their loss of effective power over the Holy Roman Empire. Strength in the East gave them greater political leverage in Germany. Joseph I (r. 1705–1711) continued Leopold's policies.

When Charles VI (r. 1711–1740) succeeded Joseph, a new problem was added to the chronic one of territorial diversity. He had no male heir, and there was only the weakest of precedents for a female ruler of the Habsburg domains. Charles feared that on his death the Austrian Habsburg lands might fall prey to the surrounding powers, as had those of the Spanish Habsburgs in 1700. He was determined to prevent that disaster and to provide his domains with the semblance of legal unity. To those ends, he devoted most of his reign to seeking the approval of his family, the estates of his realms, and the major foreign powers for a document called the ***Pragmatic Sanction.***

This instrument provided the legal basis for a single line of inheritance within the Habsburg dynasty through Charles VI's daughter Maria Theresa (r. 1740–1780). Other members of the Habsburg family recognized her as the rightful heir. After extracting various concessions from Charles, the nobles of the various Habsburg domains and the other European rulers also

---

AUSTRIA AND PRUSSIA IN THE LATE SEVENTEENTH AND EARLY EIGHTEENTH CENTURIES

1640–1688	Reign of Frederick William, the Great Elector
1658–1705	Leopold I rules Austria and resists the Turkish invasions
1683	Turkish siege of Vienna
1688–1713	Reign of Frederick I of Prussia
1699	Peace treaty between Turks and Habsburgs
1711–1740	Charles VI rules Austria and secures agreement to the Pragmatic Sanction
1713–1740	Frederick William I builds up the military power of Prussia
1740	Maria Theresa succeeds to the Habsburg throne
1740	Frederick II violates the Pragmatic Sanction by invading Silesia

recognized her. Consequently, when Charles VI died in October 1740, he believed that he had secured legal unity for the Habsburg Empire and a safe succession for his daughter. He had indeed established a permanent line of succession and the basis for future legal bonds within the Habsburg holdings. Despite the Pragmatic Sanction, however, his failure to provide his daughter with a strong army or a full treasury left her inheritance open to foreign aggression. Less than two months after his death, the fragility of the foreign agreements became apparent. In December 1740, Frederick II of Prussia invaded the Habsburg province of Silesia in eastern Germany. Maria Theresa had to fight for her inheritance.

Prussia and the Hohenzollerns

The rise of Prussia occurred within the German power vacuum created by the Peace of Westphalia. It is the story of the extraordinary Hohenzollern family, which had ruled Brandenburg since 1417. Through inheritance the family had acquired the duchy of Cleves, and the counties of Mark and Ravensburg in 1614, East Prussia in 1618, and Pomerania in 1648. (See Map 13–4.) Except for Pomerania, none of these lands shared a border with Brandenburg. East Prussia lay inside Poland and outside the authority of the Holy Roman Emperor. All of the territories lacked good natural resources, and many of them were devastated during the Thirty Years' War. Still, by the late seventeenth century, the geographically scattered Hohenzollern holdings represented a block of territory within the Holy Roman Empire, second in size only to that of the Habsburgs.

View the **Map** "Rise of Prussia, 1440–1795" on **MyHistoryLab.com**

The person who began to forge these areas into a modern state was Frederick William (r. 1640–1688), who became known as the Great Elector. He established himself and his successors as the central uniting power by breaking the local noble estates, organizing a royal bureaucracy, and building a strong army. (See the Document "The Great Elector Welcomes Protestant Refugees from France," page 410.)

Between 1655 and 1660, Sweden and Poland fought each other across the Great Elector's holdings in Pomerania and East Prussia. Frederick William had neither an adequate army nor the tax revenues to confront this threat. In 1655, the Brandenburg estates refused to grant him new taxes; however, he proceeded to collect them by military force. In 1659, a different grant of taxes, originally made in 1653, elapsed; Frederick William continued to collect them as well as those he had imposed by his own authority. He used the money to build an army, which allowed him to continue to enforce his will without the approval of the nobility. Similar coercion took place against the nobles in his other territories.

Map 13–4 **EXPANSION OF BRANDENBURG-PRUSSIA** In the seventeenth century Brandenburg-Prussia expanded mainly by acquiring dynastic titles in geographically separated lands. In the eighteenth century it expanded through aggression to the east, seizing Silesia in 1740 and various parts of Poland in 1772, 1793, and 1795.

There was, however, a political and social trade-off between the Elector and his various nobles. In exchange for their obedience to the Hohenzollerns, the **Junkers**, or German noble landlords, received the right to demand obedience from their serfs. Frederick William also tended to choose as the local administrators of the tax structure men who would normally have been members of the noble branch of the old parliament. He thus co-opted potential opponents into his service.

The taxes fell most heavily on the backs of the peasants and the urban classes. As the years passed, Junkers increasingly dominated the army officer corps, and this situation became even more pronounced during the eighteenth century. All officials and army officers took an oath of loyalty directly to the Elector. The army and the Elector thus came to embody the otherwise absent unity of the state. The army made Prussia a valuable potential ally.

Document

THE GREAT ELECTOR WELCOMES PROTESTANT REFUGEES FROM FRANCE

The Hohenzollern dynasty of Brandenburg–Prussia pursued a policy of religious toleration. The family itself was Calvinist, whereas most of its subjects were Lutherans. When Louis XIV of France revoked the Edict of Nantes in 1685, Frederick William, the Great Elector, seized the opportunity to invite French Protestants into his realms. As his proclamation indicates, he wanted to attract persons with productive skills who could aid the economic development of his domains.

In reading this document, do you believe religious or economic concerns more nearly led the elector of Brandenburg to welcome the French Protestants? What specific privileges did the elector extend to them? To what extent were these privileges a welcoming measure, and to what extent were they inducements to emigrate to Brandenburg? In what kind of economic activity does the elector expect the French refugees to engage?

We, Friedrich Wilhelm, by Grace of God Margrave of Brandenburg. . . . Do hereby proclaim and make known to all and sundry that since the cruel persecutions and rigorous ill-treatment in which Our co-religionists of the Evangelical-Reformed faith have for some time past been subjected in the Kingdom of France, have caused many families to remove themselves and to betake themselves out of the said Kingdom into other lands, We now . . . have been moved graciously to offer them through this Edict . . . a secure and free refuge in all Our Lands and Provinces. . . .

Since Our Lands are not only well and amply endowed with all things necessary to support life, but also very well-suited to the reestablishment of all kinds of manufactures and trade and traffic by land and water, We permit, indeed, to those settling therein free choice to establish themselves where it is most convenient for their profession and way of living. . . .

The personal property which they bring with them, including merchandise and other wares, is to be totally exempt from any taxes, customs dues, licenses, or other imposts of any description, and not detained in any way. . . .

As soon as these Our French co-religionists of the Evangelical-Reformed faith have settled in any town or village, they shall be admitted to the domiciliary rights and craft freedoms customary there, gratis and without payments of any fee; and shall be entitled to the benefits, rights, and privileges enjoyed by Our other, native, subjects, residing there. . . .

Not only are those who wish to establish manufacture of cloth, stuffs, hats, or other objects in which they are skilled to enjoy all necessary freedoms, privileges and facilities, but also provision is to be made for them to be assisted and helped as far as possible with money and anything else which they need to realize their intention. . . .

Those who settle in the country and wish to maintain themselves by agriculture are to be given a certain plot of land to bring under cultivation and provided with whatever they need to establish themselves initially. . . .

From C. A. Macartney, ed., *The Habsburg and Hohenzollern Dynasties in the Seventeenth and Eighteenth Centuries* (New York: Walker, 1970), pp. 270–273.

Yet even with the considerable accomplishments of the Great Elector, the house of Hohenzollern did not possess a crown. The achievement of a royal title was one of the few state-building accomplishments of Frederick I (r. 1688–1713). This son of the Great Elector was the least "Prussian" of his family during these crucial years. He built palaces, founded Halle University (1694), patronized the arts, and lived luxuriously. In the War of the Spanish Succession, he put his army at the disposal of the Habsburg Holy Roman Emperor Leopold I. In exchange, the emperor permitted Frederick to assume the title of "King in Prussia" in 1701.

His successor, Frederick William I (r. 1713–1740), was both the most eccentric monarch to rule the Hohenzollern domains and one of the most effective. He organized the bureaucracy along military lines. The discipline that he applied to the army was fanatical. The Prussian military grew from about 39,000 in 1713 to over 80,000 in 1740, making it the third or fourth largest army in Europe. Prussia's population, in contrast, ranked thirteenth in size. Separate laws applied to the army and to civilians. Laws, customs, and royal attention made the officer corps the highest social class of the state. Military service thus attracted the sons of Junkers. In this fashion the army, the Junker nobility, and the monarchy became forged into a single political entity. Military priorities and values dominated Prussian government, society, and daily life as in no other state in Europe. It has often been said that whereas other states possessed armies, the Prussian army possessed its state.

Although Frederick William I built the best army in Europe, he avoided conflict. His army was a symbol of Prussian power and unity, not an instrument for foreign adventures or aggression. At his death in 1740, he passed to his son Frederick II, later known as Frederick the Great (r. 1740–1786), this superb military machine, but not the wisdom to refrain from using it. Almost immediately on coming to the throne, Frederick II upset the Pragmatic Sanction and invaded Silesia. He thus crystallized the Austrian–Prussian rivalry for the control of Germany that would dominate central European affairs for over a century.

▼ Russia Enters the European Political Arena

The emergence of Russia in the late seventeenth century as an active European power was a wholly new factor in European politics. Previously, Russia had been considered part of Europe only by courtesy. Before 1673, it did not send permanent ambassadors to western Europe, though it had sent various diplomatic missions since the fifteenth century. Geographically and politically, it lay on the periphery. Hemmed in by Sweden on the

View the Map
"Map Discovery: The Rise of Russia" on
MyHistoryLab.com

Baltic and by the Ottoman Empire on the Black Sea, Russia had no warm-water ports. Its chief outlet for trade to the West was Archangel on the White Sea, which was ice free for only part of the year.

The Romanov Dynasty

The reign of Ivan IV (r. 1533–1584), later known as Ivan the Terrible, had commenced well but ended badly. About midway in his reign he underwent a personality change that led him to move from a program of sensible reform of law, government, and the army toward violent personal tyranny. A period known as the "Time of Troubles" followed upon his death. In 1613, hoping to end the uncertainty, an assembly of nobles elected as tsar a seventeen-year-old boy named Michael Romanov (r. 1613–1645). Thus began the dynasty that ruled Russia until 1917.

Michael Romanov and his two successors, Aleksei (r. 1654–1676) and Theodore II (r. 1676–1682), brought stability and modest bureaucratic centralization to Russia. The country remained, however, weak and impoverished. After years of turmoil, the *boyars*, the old nobility, still largely controlled the bureaucracy. Furthermore, the government and the tsars faced the danger of mutiny from the *streltsy*, or guards of the Moscow garrison.

Peter the Great

In 1682, another boy—ten years old at the time—ascended the fragile Russian throne as co-ruler with his half-brother. His name was Peter (r. 1682–1725), and Russia would never be the same after him. He and the sickly Ivan V had come to power on the shoulders of the *streltsy*, who expected to be rewarded for their support. Violence and bloodshed had surrounded the disputed succession. Matters became even more confused when the boys' sister, Sophia, was named regent. Peter's followers overthrew her in 1689. From that date onward, Peter ruled personally, although in theory he shared the crown until Ivan died in 1696. The dangers and turmoil of his youth convinced Peter of two things: First, the power of the tsar must be made secure from the jealousy of the *boyars* and the greed of the *streltsy*; second, Russian military power must be increased. In both respects, he self-consciously resembled Louis XIV of France, who had experienced the turmoil of the *Fronde* during his youth and resolved to establish a strong monarchy safe from the nobility and defended by a powerful army.

View the Image
"Peter the Great" on
MyHistoryLab.com

Northwestern Europe, particularly the military resources of the maritime powers, fascinated Peter I, who eventually became known as Peter the Great. In 1697, he made a famous visit in transparent disguise to western Europe. There he dined and talked with the great and the powerful, who considered this almost seven-foot-tall ruler crude. He spent his happiest moments on the trip inspecting shipyards, docks, and the manufacture of military hardware in England and the Netherlands. An imitator of the first order, Peter returned to Moscow determined to copy what he had seen abroad, for he knew warfare would be necessary to make Russia a great power. Yet he understood his goal would require him to confront the long-standing power and traditions of the Russian nobles.

Taming the *Streltsy* and *Boyars* In 1698, while Peter was abroad, the *streltsy* had rebelled. Upon his return, Peter brutally suppressed the revolt with private tortures and public executions, in which Peter's own ministers took part. Approximately a thousand of the rebels were put to death, and their corpses remained on public display to discourage disloyalty.

The new military establishment that Peter built would serve the tsar and not itself. He introduced effective and ruthless policies of conscription, drafting an unprecedented 130,000 soldiers during the first decade of the eighteenth century and almost 300,000 troops by the end of his reign. He had adopted policies for the officer corps and general military discipline patterned on those of West European armies.

Peter also made a sustained attack on the *boyars* and their attachment to traditional Russian culture. After his European journey, he personally shaved the long beards of the court *boyars* and sheared off the customary long hand-covering sleeves of their shirts and coats, which had made them the butt of jokes among other European courts. Peter became highly skilled at balancing one group off against another while never completely excluding any as he set about to organize Russian government and military forces along the lines of the more powerful European states.

Developing a Navy In the mid-1690s, Peter oversaw the construction of ships to protect his interests in the Black Sea against the Ottoman Empire. In 1695, he began a war with the Ottomans and captured Azov on the Black Sea in 1696.[1] Part of the reason for Peter's trip to western Europe in 1697 was to learn how to build still better warships, this time for combat on the Baltic. The construction of a Baltic fleet was essential in Peter's struggles with Sweden that over the years accounted for many of his major steps toward westernizing his realm.

Russian Expansion in the Baltic: The Great Northern War

Following the end of the Thirty Years' War in 1648, Sweden had consolidated its control of the Baltic, thus preventing Russian possession of a port on that sea and permitting Polish and German access to the sea only on Swedish

terms. The Swedes also had one of the better armies in Europe. Sweden's economy, however, based primarily on the export of iron, was not strong enough to ensure continued political success.

View the **Map** "Map Discovery: Russia Under Peter the Great" on **MyHistoryLab.com**

In 1697, Charles XII (r. 1697–1718) came to the Swedish throne. He was headstrong, to say the least, and perhaps insane. In 1700, Peter the Great began a drive to the west against Swedish territory to gain a foothold on the Baltic. In the resulting Great Northern War (1700–1721), Charles XII led a vigorous and often brilliant campaign, defeating the Russians at the Battle of Narva (1700). As the conflict dragged on, however, Peter was able to strengthen his forces. By 1709, he decisively defeated the Swedes at the Battle of Poltava in Ukraine. Thereafter, the Swedes could maintain only a holding action against their enemies. Charles himself sought refuge in Turkey and did not return to Sweden until 1714. He was killed under uncertain circumstances four years later while fighting the Danes in Norway. When the Great Northern War came to a close in 1721, the Peace of Nystad confirmed the Russian conquest of Estonia, Livonia, and part of Finland. Henceforth, Russia possessed ice-free ports and a permanent influence on European affairs.

Founding St. Petersburg At one point, the domestic and foreign policies of Peter the Great intersected. This was at the site on the Gulf of Finland where he founded his new capital city of St. Petersburg in 1703. There he built government structures and compelled the *boyars* to construct town houses. He thus imitated those European monarchs who had copied Louis XIV by constructing

Vie des bords de la Neva en descendant la rivière entre le Palais d'hyver de Sa Majesté Imperiale & les batimens de l'Academie des Sciences

Peter the Great built St. Petersburg on the Gulf of Finland to provide Russia with better contact with western Europe. He moved Russia's capital there from Moscow in 1712. This is an eighteenth-century view of the city. The Granger Collection

---

[1] Although Peter had to return Azov to the Ottomans in 1711, its recapture became a goal of Russian foreign policy. See Chapter 18.

smaller versions of Versailles. The founding of St. Petersburg went beyond establishing a central imperial court, however; it symbolized a new Western orientation of Russia and Peter's determination to hold his position on the Baltic coast. Moreover, he and his successors employed architects from western Europe for many of the most prominent buildings in and around the city. Consequently, St. Petersburg looked different from the old capital Moscow and other Russian cities.

View the **Image**
"View of St. Petersburg from the first Russian newspaper, *Vedomosti*" on **MyHistoryLab.com**

The Case of Peter's Son Aleksei   Peter's son Aleksei had been born to his first wife whom he had divorced in 1698. Peter was jealous of the young man, who had never demonstrated strong intelligence or ambition. (See "Peter the Great Tells His Son to Acquire Military Skills," page 414.) By 1716, Peter was becoming convinced that his opponents looked to Aleksei as a focus for their possible sedition while Russia remained at war with Sweden. There was some truth to these concerns because the next year Aleksei went to Vienna where he attempted to enter into a vague conspiracy with the Habsburg emperor Charles VI. Compromised by this trip, Aleksei then returned to Russia surrounded by rumors and suspicions.

Peter, who was investigating official corruption, realized his son might become a rallying point for those he accused. Early in 1718, when Aleksei reappeared in St. Petersburg, the tsar began to look into his son's relationships with Charles VI. Peter discovered that had Aleksei and Charles VI succeeded in organizing a conspiracy, many Russian nobles, officials, and churchmen might have joined them. During this six-month investigation, Peter personally interrogated Aleksei, who was eventually condemned to death and died under mysterious circumstances on June 26, 1718.

Reforms of Peter the Great's Final Years   The interrogations surrounding Aleksei had revealed greater degrees of court opposition than Peter had suspected. Recognizing he could not eliminate his opponents the way he had attacked the *streltsy* in 1698, Peter undertook radical administrative reforms designed to bring the nobility and the Russian Orthodox Church more closely under the authority of persons loyal to the tsar.

Administrative Colleges   In December 1717, while his son was returning to Russia, Peter reorganized his domestic administration to sustain his own personal authority and to fight rampant corruption. To achieve this goal, Peter looked to Swedish institutions called *colleges*—bureaus of several persons operating according to written instructions rather than departments headed by a single minister. He created eight of these colleges to oversee matters such as the collection of taxes, foreign relations, war, and economic affairs. Each college

RISE OF RUSSIAN POWER

1533–1584	Reign of Ivan the Terrible
1584–1613	"Time of Troubles"
1613	Michael Romanov becomes tsar
1682	Peter the Great, age ten, becomes tsar
1689	Peter assumes personal rule
1696	Russia captures Azov on the Black Sea from the Turks
1697	European tour of Peter the Great
1698	Peter returns to Russia to put down the revolt of the streltsy
1700	The Great Northern War opens between Russia and Sweden; Russia defeated at Narva by Swedish army of Charles XII
1703	St. Petersburg founded
1709	Russia defeats Sweden at the Battle of Poltava
1718	Charles XII of Sweden dies
1718	Aleksei, son of Peter the Great, dies in prison under mysterious circumstances
1721	Peace of Nystad ends the Great Northern War
1721	Peter establishes a synod for the Russian church
1722	Peter issues the Table of Ranks
1725	Peter dies, leaving an uncertain succession

was to receive advice from a foreigner. Peter divided the members of these colleges between nobles and persons he was certain would be personally loyal to himself.

Table of Ranks   Peter made another major administrative reform with important consequences when in 1722 he published a **Table of Ranks**, which was intended to draw the nobility into state service. That table equated a person's social position and privileges with his rank in the bureaucracy or the military, rather than with his lineage among the traditional landed nobility, many of whom continued to resent the changes Peter had introduced into Russia. Peter thus made the social standing of individual *boyars* a function of their willingness to serve the central state.

Achieving Secular Control of the Church   Peter also moved to suppress the independence of the Russian Orthodox Church where some bishops and clergy had displayed sympathy for the tsar's son. In 1721, Peter simply abolished the position of *patriarch*, the bishop who had been head of the church. In its place he established a government department called the *Holy Synod*, which consisted of several bishops headed by a layman, called the *procurator general*. This body would govern the church in accordance with the tsar's secular

PETER THE GREAT TELLS HIS SON TO ACQUIRE MILITARY SKILLS

Enormous hostility existed between Peter the Great and his son Aleksei. Peter believed his son was not prepared to inherit the throne. In October 1715, he composed a long letter to Aleksei in which he berated him for refusing to take military matters seriously. The letter indicates how an early eighteenth-century ruler saw the conduct of warfare as a fundamental part of the role of a monarch. Peter also points to Louis XIV of France as a role model. Peter and Aleksei did not reach an agreement. Aleksei died under mysterious circumstances in 1718, with Peter possibly responsible for his death.

How did Peter use the recent war with Sweden to argue for the necessity of his son acquiring military skills? What concept of leadership does Peter attempt to communicate to his son? Why did Peter see military prowess as the most important ability in a ruler?

You cannot be ignorant of what is known to all the world, to what degree our people groaned under the oppression of the Swede before the beginning of the present war. . . . You know what it has cost us in the beginning of this war . . . to make ourselves experienced in the art of war, and to put a stop to those advantages which our implacable enemies obtained over us. . . .

But you even will not so much as hear warlike exercises mentioned: though it was by them that we broke through that obscurity in which we were involved, and that we make ourselves known to nations, whose esteem we share at present.

I do not exhort you to make war without lawful reasons: I only desire you to apply yourself to learn the art of it: for it is impossible to govern well without knowing the rules and discipline of it, was it for no other end than for the defense of the country. . . .

You mistake, if you think it is enough for a prince to have good generals to act under his order. Everyone looks upon the head; they study its inclinations and conform themselves to them: all the world own this. . . .

You have no inclination to learn war. You do not apply yourself to it, and consequently you will never learn it: And how then can you command others, and judge of the reward which those deserve who do their duty, or punish others who fail of it? You will do nothing, nor judge of anything but by the assent and help of others, like a young bird that holds up his bill to be fed. . . .

If you think there are some, whose affairs do not fail of success, though they do not go to war themselves; it is true: But they do not go themselves, yet they have an inclination for it, and understand it.

For instance, the late King of France did not always take the field in person; but it is known to what degree he loved war, and what glorious exploits he performed in it, which make his campaigns to be called the theatre and school of the world. His inclinations were not confined solely to military affairs, he also loved mechanics, manufacture and other establishment, which rendered his kingdom more flourishing than any other whatsoever.

From Friedrich C. Weber, *The Present State of Russia* (London, 1722), 2, pp. 97–100; P. F. Riley, *The Global Experience*, 3rd ed., Vol. 2, © 1998. Reprinted by permission of Prentice Hall, Inc., Upper Saddle River, NJ.

requirements. This ecclesiastical reorganization was the most radical transformation of a traditional institution in Peter's reign.

For all the numerous decisive actions Peter had taken since 1718, he still had not settled on a successor. Consequently, when he died in 1725, there was no clear line of succession to the throne. For more than thirty years, soldiers and nobles again determined who ruled Russia.

Peter had laid the foundations of a modern Russia, but not the foundations of a stable state.

In Perspective

By the second quarter of the eighteenth century, the major European powers were not yet nation-states in which the citizens felt themselves united by a shared sense of community, culture, language, and history. Rather, they were monarchies in which the personality of the ruler and the personal relationships of the great noble families continued to exercise considerable influence over public affairs. The monarchs, except in Great Britain, had generally succeeded in making their power greater than that of the nobility. The power of the aristocracy and its capacity to resist or obstruct the policies of the monarch were not destroyed, however.

In Britain, of course, the nobility had tamed the monarchy, but even there tension between nobles and monarchs would continue throughout the rest of the century.

In foreign affairs, the new arrangement of military and diplomatic power established early in the century prepared the way for two long conflicts. The first was a commercial rivalry for trade and the overseas empire between France and Great Britain. During the reign of Louis XIV, these two nations had collided over the French bid for dominance in Europe. During the eighteenth century, they would duel for control of commerce on other continents. The second arena of warfare would arise in central Europe, where Austria and Prussia fought for the leadership of the German states.

Behind these international conflicts and the domestic rivalry of monarchs and nobles, however, the society of eighteenth-century Europe began to change. The character and the structures of the societies over which the monarchs ruled were beginning to take on some features associated with the modern age. These economic and social developments would eventually transform the life of Europe to a degree beside which the state-building of the early eighteenth-century monarchs paled. Parallel to that economic advance, Europeans came to have new knowledge and understanding of nature.

KEY TERMS

divine right of kings (p. 388)
Fronde (p. 396)
Gallican Liberties (p. 399)
Glorious Revolution (p. 394)
Jansenism (p. 402)
Junkers (p. 410)
parlements (p. 396)
parliamentary monarchy (p. 388)
political absolutism (p. 388)
Pragmatic Sanction (p. 408)
Puritans (p. 388)
Sejm (p. 407)
Table of Ranks (p. 413)

REVIEW QUESTIONS

1. What were the sources of Dutch prosperity and why did the Netherlands decline in the eighteenth century? Why did England and France develop different systems of government and religious policies?
2. Why did the English king and Parliament quarrel in the 1640s? What were the most important issues behind the war between them, and who bears more responsibility for it? What was the Glorious Revolution, and why did it take place? What role did religion play in seventeenth-century English politics? Do you think the victory of Parliament over the monarchy in England was inevitable?
3. Why did France become an absolute monarchy? How did Louis XIV consolidate his monarchy? What limits were there on his authority? What was Louis's religious policy? What were the goals of his foreign policy? How did he use ceremony and his royal court to strengthen his authority? What features of French government might Europeans outside of France have feared?
4. How were the Hohenzollerns able to forge their diverse landholdings into the state of Prussia? Who were the major personalities involved in this process and what were their individual contributions? Why was the military so important in Prussia? What major problems did the Habsburgs face and how did they seek to resolve them? Which family, the Hohenzollerns or the Habsburgs, was more successful and why?
5. How and why did Russia emerge as a great power but Poland did not? How were Peter the Great's domestic reforms related to his military ambitions? What were his methods of reform? How did family conflict influence his later policies? Was Peter a successful ruler? In what respects might one regard Peter as an imitator of Louis XIV?

SUGGESTED READINGS

W. Beik, *Louis XIV and Absolutism: A Brief Study with Documents* (2000). An excellent collection by a major scholar of absolutism.
T. Blanning, *The Pursuit of Glory: Europe 1648–1815* (2007). The best recent synthesis of the emergence of the modern European state system.
J. Brewer, *The Sinews of Power: War, Money and the English State, 1688–1783* (1989). An important study of the financial basis of English power.
P. Burke, *The Fabrication of Louis XIV* (1992). Examines how Louis XIV used art to forge his public image.

C. Clark, *The Rise and Downfall of Prussia 1600–1947* (2006). A stunning survey.

P. Collinson, *The Religion of Protestants: The Church in English Society, 1559–1625* (1982). Remains the best introduction to Puritanism.

R. Cust, *Charles I* (2007). The definitive biography.

N. Davis, *God's Playground: A History of Poland: The Origins to 1795* (2005). The recent revision of a classic survey.

J. De Vries and A. van der Woude, *The First Modern Economy* (1997). Compares Holland to other European nations.

P. G. Dwyer, *The Rise of Prussia 1700–1830* (2002). An excellent collection of essays.

T. Harris, *Restoration: Charles II and His Kingdom, 1660–1685* (2006). A major exploration of the tumultuous years of the restoration of the English monarchy after the civil war.

L. Hughes, *Russia in the Age of Peter the Great* (2000). A major overview of the history and society of Peter's time.

C. J. Ingrao, *The Habsburg Monarchy, 1618–1815* (2000). The best recent survey.

J. I. Israel, *The Dutch Republic: Its Rise, Greatness, and Fall, 1477–1806* (1995). The major work of the subject.

M. Kishlansky, *A Monarchy Transformed: Britain, 1603–1714* (1996). An important overview.

J. Lukowski and H. Zawadzki, *A Concise History of Poland* (2006). A straightforward survey.

D. McKay, *The Great Elector: Frederick William of Brandenburg–Prussia* (2001). An account of the origins of Prussian power.

S. Pincus, *England's Glorious Revolution 1688–1689: A Brief History with Documents* (2005). A useful collection by an outstanding historian of the subject.

G. Treasure, *Louis XIV* (2001). The best, most accessible recent study.

MyHistoryLab™ Media Assignments

Find these resources in the Media Assignments folder for Chapter 13 on **MyHistoryLab**.

QUESTIONS FOR ANALYSIS

1. How does Versailles, as a seat of government, support Louis's ideas on political authority?

   Section: **Rise of Absolute Monarchy in France: The World of Louis XIV**
   View the **Closer Look** Versailles, p. 397

2. According to this monarch, what are the duties and privileges of the king?

   Section: **Constitutional Crisis and Settlement in Stuart England**
   Read the **Document** James I on the Divine Right of Kings (1598), p. 388

3. Prior to the time of Peter the Great, what had been the main direction of Russian expansion?

   Section: **Russia Enters the European Political Arena**
   View the **Map** Map Discovery: The Rise of Russia, p. 411

4. What factors made possible the growth of Prussia as a new European power?

   Section: **Central and Eastern Europe**
   View the **Map** Rise of Prussia, 1440–1795, p. 409

5. Why does Bossuet found his arguments on the Bible?

   Section: **Two Models of European Political Development**
   Read the **Document** Jacques-Benigne Bossuet, *Politics Drawn from the Very Words of the Holy Scripture*, p. 388

OTHER RESOURCES FROM THIS CHAPTER

The Netherlands: Golden Age to Decline

View the **Closer Look** Cape Town: A Dutch Refueling Station, p. 387

Read the **Document** Jan van Linschoten on Dutch Business in the Indian Ocean, p. 387

Constitutional Crisis and Settlement in Stuart England

View the **Map** Map Discovery: English Civil War, p. 392

View the **Image** Allegorical View of Cromwell as Savior of England, p. 392

Rise of Absolute Monarchy in France: The World of Louis XIV

View the **Map** Map Discovery: France Under Louis XIV, p. 395

Read the **Document** Louis de Rouvroy, duc de Saint-Simon, Memoires, p. 396

Read the **Compare and Connect** The Debate over the Origin and Character of Political Authority, p. 400

Central and Eastern Europe

View the **Map** Eastern Europe, ca. 1550, p. 406

Russia Enters the European Political Arena

View the **Image** Peter the Great, p. 411

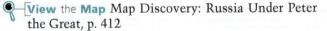
View the **Map** Map Discovery: Russia Under Peter the Great, p. 412

View the **Image** View of St. Petersburg from the first Russian newspaper, *Vedomosti*, p. 413

The great Dutch artist Rembrandt van Rijn (1606–1669) recorded the contemporary life of the United Provinces of the Netherlands during its golden age. The new sciences, including medicine, made much progress in the Netherlands, which was a center for publishing and instrument making and known for its religious toleration. *The Anatomy Lesson of Dr. Tulp* (1632) presents the dissection of a cadaver of an executed criminal by noted Dutch physician Dr. Nicolass Tulp, who stands on the right surrounded by other members of the Amsterdam guild of surgeons. Such dissections were a controversial part of new emerging medical education, with only one a year permitted in Amsterdam. The dramatic use of light and darkness is characteristic of the painting of the baroque style.   Rembrandt van Rijn (1606–1669). *The Anatomy Lesson of Dr. Tulp.* Mauritshuis, The Hague, The Netherlands. SCALA/Art Resource, NY

((•─[**Listen** to the **Chapter Audio** on **MyHistoryLab.com**

14

New Directions in Thought and Culture in the Sixteenth and Seventeenth Centuries

LEARNING OBJECTIVES

What was the scientific revolution?

What impact did the new science have on philosophy?

What was the social and political context for scientific inquiry in the seventeenth century?

What role did women play in the scientific revolution?

What efforts were made to reconcile the new science and religion?

What explains the witch hunts and panics of the sixteenth and seventeenth centuries?

How did baroque art serve both religious and secular ends?

THE SIXTEENTH AND seventeenth centuries witnessed a sweeping change in the scientific view of the universe. An earth-centered picture gave way to one in which the earth was only another planet orbiting about the sun. The sun itself became one of millions of stars. This transformation of humankind's perception of its place in the larger scheme of things led to a profound rethinking of moral and religious matters, as well as of scientific theory. Faith and reason needed new modes of reconciliation, as did faith and science. The new ideas and methods of science, usually termed *natural philosophy* at the time, challenged those modes of thought associated with late medieval times: Scholasticism and Aristotelian philosophy.

The impact of the new science that explored the realm of the stars through the newly invented telescope and the world of microorganisms through the newly invented microscope must be viewed in the context of two other factors that simultaneously challenged traditional modes of European thought and culture in the sixteenth and seventeenth centuries. The first of these was the Reformation, which permanently divided the religious unity of central and western Europe and fostered decades of warfare and theological dispute. Although by no means a complete break with medieval thought, the theology of the Reformation did question many ideas associated with medieval Christianity and society. The second factor was the cultural impact of Europe's encounter with the New World of the Americas. The interaction with the Americas meant that Europeans directly or indirectly acquired knowledge of new peoples, plants, and animals wholly different from their own and about which Europeans in neither ancient nor medieval times had any information. Consequently, new uncertainties and unfamiliar vistas confronted many Europeans as they considered their souls, geographical knowledge, and physical nature.

Side by side with this new knowledge and science, however, came a new wave of superstition and persecution. The changing world of religion, politics, and knowledge also created profound fear and anxiety among both the simple and the learned, resulting in the worst witch hunts in European history.

▼ The Scientific Revolution

The process that established the new view of the universe is normally termed the **scientific revolution**. The revolution-in-science metaphor must be used carefully, however. Not everything associated with the "new" science was necessarily new. Sixteenth- and seventeenth-century natural philosophers were often reexamining and rethinking theories and data from the ancient world and the late Middle Ages. Moreover, the word *revolution* normally denotes rapid, collective political change involving many people. The scientific revolution was not rapid. It was a complex movement with many false starts and brilliant people suggesting wrong as well as useful ideas. Nor did it involve more than a few hundred people who labored in widely separated studies and crude laboratories located in Poland, Italy, Denmark, Bohemia, France, and Great Britain. Furthermore, the achievements of the new science were not simply the function of isolated brilliant scientific minds. The leading figures of the scientific revolution often drew on the aid of artisans and craftspeople to help them construct new instruments for experimentation and to carry out those experiments. Thus, the scientific revolution involved older knowledge as well as new discoveries. Additionally, because the practice of science involves social activity as well as knowledge, the revolution also saw the establishment of new social institutions to support the emerging scientific enterprise.

Natural knowledge was only in the process of becoming science as we know it today during the era of the scientific revolution. In fact the word *scientist*, which was only coined in the 1830s, did not yet exist in the seventeenth century, nor did anything resembling the modern scientific career. Individuals devoted to natural philosophy might work in universities or in the court of a prince or even in their own homes and workshops. Only in the second half of the seventeenth century did formal societies and academies devoted to the pursuit of natural philosophy come into existence. Even then the entire process of the pursuit of natural knowledge was a largely informal one.

Yet by the close of the seventeenth century, the new scientific concepts and the methods of their construction were so impressive that they set the standard for assessing the validity of knowledge in the Western world. From the early seventeenth century through the end of the twentieth century, science achieved greater cultural authority in the Western world than any other form of intellectual activity, and the authority and application of scientific knowledge became one of the defining characteristics of modern Western civilization.

Although new knowledge emerged in many areas during the sixteenth and seventeenth centuries, including medicine, chemistry, and natural history, the scientific achievements that most captured the learned imagination and persuaded people of the cultural power of natural knowledge were those that occurred in astronomy.

Nicolaus Copernicus Rejects an Earth-Centered Universe

Nicolaus Copernicus (1473–1543) was a Polish priest and an astronomer who enjoyed a high reputation during his life, but was not known for strikingly original or unorthodox thought. He had been educated first at the University of Kraków in Poland and later in Italy. In 1543, the year of his death, Copernicus published *On the Revolutions of the Heavenly Spheres*, which has been described as "a revolution-making rather than a revolutionary text."[1] What Copernicus did was to provide an intellectual springboard for a complete criticism of the then-dominant view of the position of the earth in the universe. He had undertaken this task to help the papacy reform the calendar, so that it could correctly calculate the date for Easter based on a more accurate understanding of astronomy.

Read the **Document**
"Nicolaus Copernicus: *On the Revolution of the Heavenly Spheres* (1500s)" on **MyHistoryLab.com**

The Ptolemaic System In Copernicus' time, the standard explanation of the place of the earth in the heavens combined the mathematical astronomy of Ptolemy, contained in his work entitled the *Almagest* (150 C.E.), with the physical cosmology of Aristotle. Over the centuries, commentators on Ptolemy's work had developed several alternative **Ptolemaic systems**, on the basis of which they made mathematical calculations relating to astronomy. Most of these writers assumed the earth was the center of the universe, an outlook known as *geocentrism*. Drawing on Aristotle, these commentators assumed that above the earth lay a series of concentric spheres, probably fluid in character, one of which contained the moon, another the sun, and still others the planets and the stars. At the outer regions of these spheres lay the realm of God and the angels. The earth had to be the center because of its heaviness. The stars and the other heavenly bodies had to be enclosed in the spheres so they could move, since nothing could move unless something was actually moving it. The state of rest was presumed to be natural; motion required explanation. This was the astronomy found in such works as Dante's *Divine Comedy*.

The Ptolemaic model gave rise to many problems, which had long been recognized. The most important was the observed motions of the planets. At certain times the planets appeared to be going backward. The Ptolemaic model accounted for these motions primarily through epicycles. The planet moved uniformly about a small circle (an *epicycle*), and the center of the epicycle moved uniformly about a larger circle (called a *deferent*), with the earth at or near its center. The combination of these two motions, as viewed from the earth, was meant to replicate the changing planetary positions among the fixed stars—and did so to a high degree of accuracy. The circles employed in Ptolemaic systems were not meant to represent the actual paths of anything; that is, they were not orbits. Rather, they were the components of purely mathematical models meant to predict planetary positions. Other intellectual, but nonobservational, difficulties related to the immense speed at which the spheres had to move around the earth. To say the least, the Ptolemaic systems were cluttered. They were effective, however, as long as one assumed Aristotelian physics to be correct.

Copernicus' Universe Copernicus' *On the Revolutions of the Heavenly Spheres* challenged the Ptolemaic picture in the most conservative manner possible. He adopted many elements of the Ptolemaic model, but transferred them to a *heliocentric* (sun-centered) model, which assumed the earth moved about the sun in a circle. Copernicus' model, which retained epicycles, was actually no more accurate than Ptolemy's. However, Copernicus could claim certain advantages over the ancient model. In particular, the epicycles were smaller. The retrograde motion of the planets was now explained as a result of an optical illusion that arose because people were observing them from earth, which was itself moving. Furthermore, Copernicus argued that the farther planets were from the sun, the longer they took to revolve around it. The length of these individual revolutions made it easier to determine the order of the planets, how they ranked in terms of distance from the sun.

View the **Image**
"Illustrations for *The Emperor's Astronomy*" on **MyHistoryLab.com**

The repositioning of the earth had not been Copernicus' goal. Rather, he appears to have set out to achieve new intelligibility and mathematical elegance in astronomy by rejecting Aristotle's cosmology and by removing the earth from the center of the universe. His system was no more accurate than the existing ones for predicting the location of the planets. He had used no new evidence. The major impact of his work was to provide another way of confronting some of the difficulties inherent in Ptolemaic astronomy. The Copernican system did not immediately replace the old astronomy, but it allowed other people who were also discontented with the Ptolemaic view to think in new directions. Indeed, for at least a century, only a minority of natural philosophers and astronomers embraced the Copernican system.

View the **Closer Look** "The Copernican Universe" on **MyHistoryLab.com**

Tycho Brahe and Johannes Kepler Make New Scientific Observations

Danish astronomer Tycho Brahe (1546–1601) took the next major step toward the conception of a sun-centered system. He did not embrace Copernicus' view of

[1]Thomas S. Kuhn, *The Copernican Revolution: Planetary Astronomy in the Development of Western Thought* (New York: Vintage, 1959), p. 135.

This 1543 map of the heavens based on the writings of Nicholas Copernicus shows the earth and the other planets moving about the sun. Until well into the 1600s, however, astronomers continued to debate whether the sun revolved around the earth. British Library, London, UK/British Library Board. All Rights Reserved/The Bridgeman Art Library

the universe and actually spent most of his life advocating an earth-centered system. He suggested that Mercury and Venus revolved around the sun, but that the moon, the sun, and the other planets revolved around the earth. In pursuit of his own theory, Brahe constructed scientific instruments with which he made more extensive naked-eye observations of the planets than anyone else had ever done. His labors produced a vast body of astronomical data from which his successors could work.

When Brahe died, his assistant, Johannes Kepler (1571–1630), a German astronomer, took possession of

these tables. Kepler was a convinced Copernican and a more consistently rigorous advocate of a heliocentric model than Copernicus himself had been. Like Copernicus, Kepler was deeply influenced by Renaissance Neoplatonism, which held the sun in special honor. In keeping with this outlook, Kepler was determined to find in Brahe's numbers mathematical harmonies that would support a sun-centered universe. After much work, Kepler discovered that to keep the sun at the center of things, he must abandon the circular components of Copernicus' model, particularly the epicycles. Based on the mathematical relationships that emerged from his study of Brahe's observations, Kepler set forth the first astronomical model that actually portrayed motion—that is, the path of the planets—and those orbits were elliptical, not circular. Kepler published his findings in his 1609 book entitled *The New Astronomy*. He had used Copernicus' sun-centered universe and Brahe's empirical data to solve the problem of planetary motion.

Kepler had also defined a new problem. None of the available theories could explain why the planetary orbits were elliptical or, for that matter, why planetary motion was orbital at all rather than simply moving off along a tangent. That solution awaited the work of Sir Isaac Newton.

Galileo Galilei Argues for a Universe of Mathematical Laws

From Copernicus to Brahe to Kepler, there had been little new information about the heavens that might not have been known to Ptolemy. In 1609, however, the same year that Kepler published *The New Astronomy*, an Italian mathematician and natural philosopher named Galileo Galilei (1564–1642) first turned a telescope on the heavens. Using that recently invented Dutch instrument, he saw stars where none had been known to exist, mountains on the moon, spots moving across the sun, and moons orbiting Jupiter. The heavens were far more complex than anyone had suspected. These discoveries, with some work, could have been accommodated into the Ptolemaic model. Such accommodation would, however, have required a highly technical understanding of Ptolemaic astronomy. Galileo knew that few people who controlled patronage possessed such complex knowledge. Consequently, in the *Starry Messenger* (1610) and *Letters on Sunspots* (1613), he used his considerable rhetorical skills to argue that his newly observed physical evidence, particularly the phases of Venus, required a Copernican interpretation of the heavens.

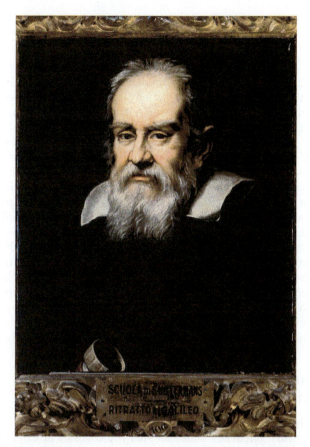

Galileo Galilei achieved a Europeanwide reputation as a mathematician, instrument maker, and astronomer. His use of the telescope revealed sights of objects in the heavens never previously viewed by human beings. His writings in defense of the Copernican system became increasingly controversial and eventually led to his condemnation by Roman Catholic authorities. Justus Sustermans (1597–1681), "Portrait of Galileo Galilei." Galleria Palatina, Palazzo Pitti, Florence, Italy. Nimatallah/Art Resource, NY

📖 **Read** the **Document**
"Galileo, 'Third Letter on Sunspots' (Italian States), 1612" on **MyHistoryLab.com**

Galileo's career illustrates that the forging of the new science involved more than just presenting arguments and evidence. In 1610, he had left the University of Padua for Florence, where he became the philosopher and mathematician to the Grand Duke of Tuscany, who was a Medici. Galileo was now pursuing natural philosophy in a princely court and had become dependent on princely patronage. To win such support both for his continued work and for his theories, he named the moons of Jupiter after the Medicis. As a natural philosopher working with the new telescope,

he had literally presented recently discovered heavenly bodies to his patron. By his political skills and his excellent prose, he had transformed himself into a high-profile advocate of Copernicanism. Galileo's problems with the Roman Catholic Church (see page 434) arose from both his ideas and his flair for self-advertisement.

Galileo not only popularized the Copernican system, but he also articulated the concept of a universe subject to mathematical laws. More than any other writer of the century, he argued that nature displayed mathematical regularity in its most minute details:

Philosophy is written in that great book which ever lies before our eyes—I mean the universe—but we cannot understand it if we do not first learn the language and grasp the symbols in which it is written. This book is written in the mathematical language, and the symbols are triangles, circles, and other geometrical figures, without whose help it is impossible to comprehend a single word of it; without which one wanders through a dark labyrinth.[2]

The universe was rational; however, its rationality was not that of medieval scholastic logic, but of mathematics. Copernicus had thought that the heavens conformed to mathematical regularity; Galileo saw this regularity throughout physical nature.

A world of quantities was replacing one of qualities. All aspects of the world—including color, beauty, and taste—would increasingly be described in terms of the mathematical relationships among quantities. Mathematical models would eventually be applied even to social relations. The new natural philosophy portrayed nature as cold, rational, mathematical, and mechanistic. What was real and lasting was what was mathematically measurable. For many people, the power of the mathematical arguments that appeared irrefutable proved more persuasive than the new information from physical observation that produced so much controversy. Few intellectual shifts have wrought such momentous changes for Western civilization.

Isaac Newton Discovers the Laws of Gravitation

The question that continued to perplex seventeenth-century scientists who accepted the theories of Copernicus, Kepler, and Galileo was how the planets and other heavenly bodies moved in an orderly fashion. The Ptolemaic and Aristotelian answer had been the spheres and a universe arranged in the order of the heaviness of its parts. Many unsatisfactory theories had been set forth to deal with the question. It was this issue of planetary motion that Englishman Isaac Newton (1642–1727) addressed and, in so doing, established a basis for physics that endured for more than two centuries.

In 1687, Newton published *The Mathematical Principles of Natural Philosophy*, better known by its Latin title of *Principia Mathematica*. Much of the research and thinking for this great work had taken place more than fifteen years earlier. Galileo's mathematical bias permeated Newton's thought, as did his view that inertia applied to bodies both at rest and in motion. Newton reasoned that the planets and all other physical objects in the universe moved through mutual attraction, or gravity. Every object in the universe affected every other object through gravity. The attraction of gravity explained why the planets moved in an orderly, rather than a chaotic, manner. Newton had found that "the

Sir Isaac Newton's experiments dealing with light passing through a prism became a model for writers praising the experimental method. CORBIS/Bettmann

force of gravity towards the whole planet did arise from and was compounded of the forces of gravity towards all its parts, and towards every one part was in the inverse proportion of the squares of the distances from the part."[3] Newton demonstrated this relationship mathematically; he made no attempt to explain the nature of gravity itself.

Read the **Document** "Isaac Newton, from *Opticks*" on **MyHistoryLab.com**

Newton was a mathematical genius, but he also upheld the importance of empirical data and observation. Like Francis Bacon, he believed in empiricism—that one must observe phenomena before attempting to explain them. The final test of any theory or hypothesis for him was whether it described what was actually observed. Newton was a great opponent of the rationalism of French philosopher René Descartes (see page 425), which he believed included insufficient guards against error. Consequently, as Newton's own theory of universal

[2]Quoted in E. A. Burtt, *The Metaphysical Foundations of Modern Physical Science* (Garden City, NY: Anchor-Doubleday, 1954), p. 75.

[3]Quoted in A. Rupert Hall, *From Galileo to Newton, 1630–1720* (London: Fontana, 1970), p. 300.

gravitation became increasingly accepted, so, too, was Baconian empiricism.

▼ Philosophy Responds to Changing Science

The revolution in scientific thought contributed directly to a major reexamination of Western philosophy. Several of the most important figures in the scientific revolution, such as Bacon and Descartes, were also philosophers discontented with the scholastic heritage. Bacon stressed the importance of empirical research. Descartes attempted to find certainty through the exploration of his own thinking processes. Newton's interests likewise extended to philosophy; he wrote broadly on many topics, including scientific method and theology.

Nature as Mechanism

If a single idea informed all of these philosophers, though in different ways, it was the idea of *mechanism*. The proponents of the new science sought to explain the world in terms of mechanical metaphors, or the language of machinery. The image to which many of them turned was that of the clock. Johannes Kepler once wrote, "I am much occupied with the investigation of the physical causes. My aim in this is to show that the machine of the universe is not similar to a divine animated being, but similar to a clock."[4] Nature conceived as machinery removed much of the mystery of the world and the previous assumption of the presence of divine purpose in nature. The qualities that seemed to inhere in matter came to be understood as the result of mechanical arrangement. Some writers came to understand God as a kind of divine watchmaker or mechanic who had arranged the world as a machine that would thereafter function automatically. The drive to a mechanical understanding of nature also meant that the language of science and of natural philosophy would become largely that of mathematics. The emphasis that Galileo had placed on mathematics spread to other areas of thought.

This new mode of thinking transformed physical nature from a realm in which Europeans looked for symbolic or sacramental meaning related to the divine into a realm where they looked for utility or usefulness. Previously, philosophers had often believed a correct understanding of the natural order would reveal divine mysteries or knowledge relating to sacred history. Henceforth, they would tend to see knowledge of nature as revealing nothing beyond itself—nothing about divine purposes for the

life of humankind on earth. Natural knowledge became the path toward the physical improvement of human beings through their ability to command and manipulate the processes of nature. Many people associated with the new science also believed such knowledge would strengthen the power of their monarchs.

Francis Bacon: The Empirical Method

Bacon (1561–1626) was an Englishman of almost universal accomplishment. He was a lawyer, a high royal official, and the author of histories, moral essays, and philosophical discourses. Traditionally, he has been regarded as the father of **empiricism** and of experimentation in science. Much of this reputation was actually unearned. Bacon was not a natural philosopher, except in the most amateur fashion. His real accomplishment was setting an intellectual tone and helping create a climate conducive to scientific work.

In books such as *The Advancement of Learning* (1605), the *Novum Organum* (1620), and *The New Atlantis* (1627), Bacon attacked the scholastic belief that most truth had already been discovered and only required explanation, as well as the scholastic reverence for authority in intellectual life. He believed scholastic thinkers paid too much attention to tradition and to the knowledge of the ancients. He urged contemporaries to strike out on their own in search of a new understanding of nature. He wanted seventeenth-century Europeans to have confidence in themselves and their own abilities rather than in the people and methods of the past. Bacon was one of the first major European writers to champion innovation and change.

Read the Document *"The Novum Organum (1620)"* on **MyHistoryLab.com**

Bacon believed that human knowledge should produce useful results—deeds rather than words. In particular, knowledge of nature should be enlisted to improve the human condition. These goals required modifying or abandoning scholastic modes of learning and thinking. Bacon contended, "The [scholastic] logic now in use serves more to fix and give stability to the errors which have their foundation in commonly received notions than to help the search after truth."[5] Scholastic philosophers could not escape from their syllogisms to examine the foundations of their thought and intellectual presuppositions. Bacon urged that philosophers and investigators of nature examine the evidence of their senses before constructing logical speculations. In a famous passage, he divided all philosophers into "men of experiment and men of dogmas" and then observed,

[4]Quoted in Steven Shapin, *The Scientific Revolution* (Chicago: University of Chicago Press, 1996), p. 33.

[5]Quoted in Franklin Baumer, *Main Currents of Western Thought*, 4th ed. (New Haven, CT: Yale University Press, 1978), p. 281.

Published in 1620, *Novum Organum* ("new organ or instrument") by Francis Bacon is one of the most important works of the scientific revolution. In this and other works Bacon attacked the long-held belief that most truth had already been discovered. This allegorical image, from the frontispiece of *Novum Organum*, shows a ship striking out for unknown territories, seeking, as did Bacon, for a new understanding of the natural world. The ship is flanked by the mythical pillars of Hercules that stand at the point where the Mediterranean meets the Atlantic— the realm of the unknown and unexplored. Courtesy of the Library of Congress

The men of experiment are like the ant, they only collect and use; the reasoners resemble spiders, who make cobwebs out of their own substance. But the bee takes a middle course: it gathers its material from the flowers of the garden and of the field,

but transforms and digests it by a power of its own. Not unlike this is the true business of philosophy.[6]

By directing natural philosophy toward an examination of empirical evidence, Bacon hoped it would achieve new knowledge and thus new capabilities for humankind.

Bacon boldly compared himself with Columbus, plotting a new route to intellectual discovery. The comparison is significant because it displays the consciousness of a changing world that appears so often in writers of the late sixteenth and early seventeenth centuries. They were rejecting the past not from simple contempt or arrogance, but rather from a firm understanding that the world was much more complicated than their medieval forebearers had thought. Neither Europe nor European thought could remain self-contained. Like the new worlds on the globe, new worlds of the mind were also emerging.

Most of the people in Bacon's day, including the intellectuals influenced by humanism, thought that the best era of human history lay in antiquity. Bacon dissented vigorously from that view. He looked to a future of material improvement achieved through the empirical examination of nature. His own theory of induction from empirical evidence was unsystematic, but his insistence on appealing to experience influenced others whose methods were more productive. He and others of his outlook received almost daily support from the reports not only of European explorers, but also of ordinary seamen who now sailed all over the world and could describe wondrous cultures, as well as plants and animals, unknown to the European ancients.

Bacon believed that expanding natural knowledge had a practical purpose and its goal was human improvement. Some scientific investigation does have this character. Much pure research does not. Bacon, however, linked science and material progress in the public mind. This was a powerful idea that still influences Western civilization. It has made science and those who can appeal to the authority of science major forces for change and innovation. Thus, although not

[6]Quoted in Baumer, *Main Currents of Western Thought*, p. 288.

making any major scientific contribution himself, Bacon directed investigators of nature to a new method and a new purpose. As a person actively associated with politics, Bacon also believed the pursuit of new knowledge would increase the power of governments and monarchies. Again, his thought in this area opened the way for the eventual strong links between governments and the scientific enterprise.

René Descartes: The Method of Rational Deduction

Descartes (1596–1650) was a gifted mathematician who invented analytic geometry. His most important contribution, however, was to develop a scientific method that relied more on deduction—reasoning from general principle to arrive at specific facts—than empirical observation and induction.

In 1637, he published his *Discourse on Method*, in which he rejected scholastic philosophy and education and advocated thought founded on a mathematical model. (See "Compare and Connect: Descartes and Swift Debate the Scientific Enterprise," pages 436–437.) The work appeared in French rather than in Latin because Descartes wanted it to have wide circulation and application. In the *Discourse*, he began by saying he would doubt everything except those propositions about which he could have clear and distinct ideas. This approach rejected all forms of intellectual authority, except the conviction of his own reason. Descartes concluded that he could not doubt his own act of thinking and his own existence. From this base, he proceeded to deduce the existence of God. The presence of God was important to Descartes because God guaranteed the correctness of clear and distinct ideas. Since God was not a deceiver, the ideas of God-given reason could not be false.

On the basis of such an analysis, Descartes concluded that human reason could fully comprehend the world. He divided existing things into two basic categories: thinking things and things occupying space—mind and body, respectively. Thinking was the defining quality of the mind, and extension (the property by which things occupy space) was the defining quality of material bodies. Human reason could grasp

Queen Christina of Sweden (r. 1632–1654), shown here with French philosopher and scientist René Descartes, was one of many women from the elite classes interested in the new science. In 1649 she invited Descartes to live at her court in Stockholm, but he died a few months after moving to Sweden. Pierre-Louis the Younger Dumesnil (1698–1781), *Christina of Sweden (1626–89) and her Court: Detail of the Queen and René Descartes (1596–1650) at the Table*. Oil on canvas. Chateau de Versailles, France/Bridgeman Art Library

and understand the world of extension, which became the realm of the natural philosopher. That world had no place for spirits, divinity, or anything nonmaterial. Descartes separated mind from body to banish nonmaterial matters from the realm of scientific speculation and analysis. Reason was to be applied only

Read the **Document**
"Rene Descartes, *The Discourse on Method*" on **MyHistoryLab.com**

to the mechanical realm of matter or to the exploration of itself.

Descartes' emphasis on deduction, rational speculation, and internal reflection by the mind, all of which he explored more fully in his *Meditations* of 1641, have influenced philosophers from his time to the present. His deductive methodology, however, eventually lost favor to **scientific induction**, whereby scientists draw generalizations derived from and test hypotheses against empirical observations.

Thomas Hobbes: Apologist for Absolute Government

Nowhere did the impact of the methods of the new science so deeply affect political thought as in the thought of Thomas Hobbes (1588–1679), the most original political philosopher of the seventeenth century.

An urbane and much-traveled man, Hobbes enthusiastically supported the new scientific movement. During the 1630s, he visited Paris, where he came to know Descartes, and Italy, where he spent time with Galileo. He took special interest in the works of William Harvey (1578–1657), who was famous for his discovery of the circulation of blood through the body. Hobbes was also a superb classicist. His earliest published work was the first English translation of Thucydides' *History of the Peloponnesian War* and is still being reprinted today. Part of Hobbes's dark view of human nature would appear to derive from Thucydides' historical analysis.

Hobbes had written works of political philosophy before the English Civil War, but the turmoil of that struggle led him in 1651 to publish his influential work *Leviathan*. His aim was to provide a rigorous philosophical justification for a strong central political authority. Hobbes portrayed human beings and society in a thoroughly materialistic and mechanical way. He traced all psychological processes to bare sensation and regarded all human motivations as egoistical, intended to increase pleasure and minimize pain. According to his analysis, human reasoning penetrated to no deeper reality or wisdom than those physical sensations. Consequently, for Hobbes, unlike both previous Christian and ancient philosophers, human beings exist only to meet the needs of daily life, not for higher

The famous title page illustration for Hobbes's *Leviathan*. The ruler is pictured as absolute lord of his lands, but note that the ruler incorporates the mass of individuals whose self-interests are best served by their willing consent to accept him and cooperate with him.   Courtesy of the Library of Congress

spiritual ends or for any larger moral purpose. Only a sovereign commonwealth established by a contract between the ruler and the ruled could enable human beings to meet those needs by limiting the free exercise

■ Read the **Document** "Thomas Hobbes, *The Leviathan*" on **MyHistoryLab.com** of the natural human pursuit of self-interest with all its potential for conflict.

According to Hobbes, human beings in their natural state are inclined to a "perpetual and restless desire" for power. Because all people want and, in their natural state, possess a natural right to everything, their equality breeds enmity, competition, diffidence, and perpetual quarreling—"a war of every man against every man," as Hobbes put it in a famous summary:

In such condition there is no place for industry, because the fruit thereof is uncertain; and consequently no culture of the Earth; no navigation nor use of the commodities that may be imported by sea; no commodious building; no instruments of moving and removing such things as require much force; no knowledge of the face of the Earth; no account of time; no arts; no letters; no society; and, which is worst of all, continual fear and danger of violent death; and the life of man solitary, poor, nasty, brutish, and short.[7]

As seen in this passage, Hobbes, contrary to Aristotle and Christian thinkers like Thomas Aquinas (1225–1274), rejected the view that human beings are naturally sociable. Rather, they are self-centered creatures who lack a master. Thus, whereas earlier and later philosophers saw the original human state as a paradise from which humankind had fallen, Hobbes saw it as a state of natural, inevitable conflict in which neither safety, security, nor any final authority existed. Human beings in this state of nature were constantly haunted by fear of destruction and death.

Human beings escaped this terrible state of nature, according to Hobbes, only by entering into a particular kind of political contract according to which they agreed to live in a commonwealth tightly ruled by a recognized sovereign. This contract obliged every person, for the sake of peace and self-defense, to agree to set aside personal rights to all things and to be content with as much liberty against others as he or she would allow others against him- or herself. All agreed to live according to a secularized version of the golden rule, "Do not that to another which you would not have done to yourself."[8]

Because, however, words and promises are insufficient to guarantee this agreement, the contract also established the coercive use of force by the sovereign to compel compliance. Believing the dangers of anarchy to be always greater than those of tyranny, Hobbes thought that rulers should be absolute and unlimited in their power, once established as authority. Hobbes's political philosophy has no room for protest in the name of individual conscience or for individual appeal to some other legitimate authority beyond the sovereign. In a reply to

critics of his position on sovereign authority, Hobbes pointed out the alternative:

The greatest [unhappiness] that in any form of government can possibly happen to the people in general is scarce sensible in respect of the miseries and horrible calamities that accompany a civil war or that dissolute condition of masterless men, without subjection to laws and a coercive power to tie their hands from rapine and revenge.[9]

The specific structure of this absolute government was not of enormous concern to Hobbes. He believed absolute authority might be lodged in either a monarch or a legislative body, but once that person or body had been granted authority, there existed no argument for appeal. For all practical purposes, obedience to the Hobbesian sovereign was absolute.

Hobbes's argument for an absolute political authority that could assure order aroused sharp opposition. Monarchists objected to his willingness to assign sovereign authority to a legislature. Republicans rejected his willingness to accept a monarchical authority. Many Christian writers, including those who supported the divine right of kings, furiously criticized his materialist arguments for an absolute political authority. Other Christian writers attacked his refusal to recognize the authority of either God or the church as standing beside or above his secular sovereign. The religious critique of Hobbes meant that his thought had little immediate practical impact, but his ideas influenced philosophical literature from the late seventeenth century onward.

John Locke: Defender of Moderate Liberty and Toleration

Locke (1632–1704) proved to be the most influential philosophical and political thinker of the seventeenth century. Although he was less original than Hobbes, his political writings became a major source of criticism of absolutism and provided a foundation for later liberal political philosophy in both Europe and America. His philosophical works dealing with human knowledge became the most important work of psychology for the eighteenth century.

Locke's family had Puritan sympathies, and during the English Civil War his father had fought for the parliamentary forces against the Stuart monarchy. Although a highly intellectual person who was well read in all the major seventeenth-century natural philosophers, Locke became deeply involved with the tumultuous politics of the English Restoration period. He was a close associate of Anthony Ashley Cooper, the earl of Shaftesbury (1621–1683), considered by his contemporaries to be a

---

[7]Thomas Hobbes, *Leviathan*, Parts I and II, ed. by H. W. Schneider (Indianapolis, IN: Bobbs-Merrill, 1958), pp. 86, 106–107.

[8]Hobbes, *Leviathan*, Parts I and II, p. 130.

[9]Hobbes, *Leviathan*, Parts I and II, p. 152.

John Locke (1632–1704), defender of the rights of the people against rulers who think their power absolute. Everett Collection Inc/Alamy

radical in both religion and politics. Shaftesbury organized an unsuccessful rebellion against Charles II in 1682, after which both he and Locke, who lived with him, were forced to flee to Holland.

During his years of association with Shaftesbury and the opposition to Charles II, Locke wrote two treatises on government that were eventually published in 1690. In the first of these, he rejected arguments for absolute government that based political authority on the patriarchal model of fathers ruling over a family. After the publication of this treatise, no major political philosopher again appealed to the patriarchal model. In that regard, though not widely read today, Locke's *First Treatise of Government* proved enormously important by clearing the philosophical decks, so to speak, of a long-standing traditional argument that could not stand up to rigorous analysis.

In his *Second Treatise of Government*, Locke presented an extended argument for a government that must necessarily be both responsible for and responsive to the concerns of the governed. Locke portrayed the natural human state as one of perfect freedom and equality in which everyone enjoyed, in an unregulated fashion, the natural rights of life, liberty, and property. Locke, contrary to Hobbes, regarded human beings in their natural state as creatures of reason and basic goodwill rather than of uncontrolled passion and selfishness. For Locke, human beings possess a strong capacity for dwelling more or less peacefully in society before they enter a political contract. What they experience in the state of nature is not a state of war, but a condition of competition and modest conflict that requires a political authority to sort out problems rather than to impose sovereign authority. They enter into the contract to form political society to secure and preserve the rights, liberty, and property that they already possess prior to the existence of political authority. In this respect, government exists to protect the best achievements and liberty of the state of nature, not to overcome them. Thus, by its very foundation, Locke's government is one of limited authority. (See "John Locke Denounces the Idea of Absolute Monarchy" in the previous chapter, page 401.)

The conflict that Hobbes believed characterized the state of nature emerged for Locke only when rulers failed to preserve people's natural freedom and attempted to enslave them by absolute rule. The relationship between rulers and the governed is that of trust, and if the rulers betray that trust, the governed have the right to replace them. In this regard, Locke's position resembled that of Thomas Aquinas, who also permitted rebellion when government violated laws of nature.

In his *Letter Concerning Toleration* (1689), Locke used the premises of the as yet unpublished *Second Treatise* to defend extensive religious toleration among Christians, which he saw as an answer to the destructive religious conflict of the past two centuries. To make his case for toleration, Locke claimed that each individual was required to work out his or her own religious salvation and these efforts might lead various people to join different religious groups. For its part, government existed by its very nature to preserve property, not to make religious decisions for its citizens. Governments that attempted to impose religious uniformity thus misunderstood their real purpose. Moreover, government-imposed religious uniformity could not achieve real religious ends because assent to religious truth must be freely given by the individual's conscience rather than by force. Consequently, Locke urged a wide degree of religious toleration among differing voluntary Christian groups. He did not, however, extend toleration to Roman Catholics, whom he believed to have given allegiance to a foreign prince (i.e., the pope), to non-Christians, or to atheists, whom he believed could not be trusted to keep their word. Despite these limitations, Locke's *Letter Concerning Toleration* established a powerful foundation for the future extension of toleration, religious liberty, and the separation of church and state. His vision of such expansive toleration was partially realized in England after 1688 and most fully in the United States after the American Revolution.

Finally, just as Newton had set forth laws of astronomy and gravitation, Locke hoped to elucidate the basic structures of human thought. He did so in the most immediately influential of his books, his *Essay Concerning Human Understanding* (1690), which became the major work of European psychology during the eighteenth century. There, Locke portrayed a person's mind at birth as a blank tablet whose content would be determined by sense experience. His vision of the mind has been aptly compared to an early version of behaviorism. It was a

▶️ **Read** the **Document**
"John Locke, Essay Concerning Human Understanding" on **MyHistoryLab.com**

reformer's psychology, which contended that the human condition could be improved by changing the environment.

Locke's view of psychology rejected the Christian understanding of original sin, yet he believed his psychology had preserved religious knowledge. He thought such knowledge came through divine revelation in Scripture and also from the conclusions that human reason could draw from observing nature. He hoped this interpretation of religious knowledge would prevent human beings from falling into what he regarded as fanaticism

arising from the claims of alleged private revelations and irrationality arising from superstition. For Locke, reason and revelation were compatible and together could sustain a moderate religious faith that would avoid religious conflict.

▼ The New Institutions of Expanding Natural Knowledge

One of the most fundamental features of the expansion of science was the emerging idea that *genuinely new knowledge* about nature and humankind could be discovered. In the late Middle Ages, the recovery of Aristotle and the rise of humanistic learning looked back to the ancients to rediscover the kind of knowledge that later Europeans needed. Luther and other Reformers had seen themselves as recovering a better understanding of the original Christian message. By contrast, the proponents of the new natural knowledge and the new philosophy sought to pursue what Bacon called the advancement of learning. New knowledge would be continuously created. This outlook required new institutions.

The expansion of natural knowledge had powerful social implications. Both the new science and the philosophical outlook associated with it opposed Scholasticism and Aristotelianism. These were not simply disembodied philosophical outlooks, but ways of approaching the world of knowledge most scholars in the universities of the day still believed in. Such scholars had a clear, vested interest in preserving those traditional outlooks. As they saw it, they were defending the ancients against the moderns. Not surprisingly, the advanced thinkers of the seventeenth century often criticized the universities. For example, in his *Discourse on Method*, Descartes was highly critical of the education he had received. Hobbes filled the *Leviathan* with caustic remarks about the kind of learning then dominating schools and universities, and Locke advocated educational reform.

Some of the criticism of universities was exaggerated. Medical faculties, on the whole, welcomed the advancement of learning in their fields of study. Most of the natural philosophers had themselves received their education at universities. Moreover, however slowly new ideas might penetrate universities, the expanding world of natural knowledge would be taught to future generations. With that diffusion of science into the universities came new supporters of scientific knowledge beyond the small group of natural philosophers themselves. Universities also provided much of the physical and financial support for teaching and investigating natural philosophy and employed many scientists, the most important of

---

MAJOR WORKS OF THE SCIENTIFIC REVOLUTION

1543	*On the Revolutions of the Heavenly Spheres* (Copernicus)
1605	*The Advancement of Learning* (Bacon)
1609	*The New Astronomy* (Kepler)
1610	*The Starry Messenger* (Galileo)
1620	*Novum Organum* (Bacon)
1632	*Dialogue on the Two Chief World Systems* (Galileo)
1637	*Discourse on Method* (Descartes)
1651	*Leviathan* (Hobbes)
1687	*Principia Mathematica* (Newton)
1689	*Letter Concerning Toleration* (Locke)
1690	*An Essay Concerning Human Understanding* (Locke)
1690	*Treatises of Government* (Locke)

Colbert was Louis XIV's most influential minister. He sought to expand the economic life of France and to associate the monarchy with the emerging new science from which he hoped might flow new inventions and productive technology. Here he is portrayed presenting members of the French Academy of Science to the monarch. *On the founding of the French Academy.* Henri Testelin (1616–1695) (after Le Brun). Minister of Finance Colbert presenting the members of the Royal Academy of Science (founded in 1667) to Louis XIV. Study for a tapestry. Photo: Gerard Blot. Chateaux de Versailles et de Trianon, Versailles, France. Reunion des Musées Nationaux/Art Resource, NY

whom was Newton himself. University support of science did, however, vary according to country, with the Italian universities being far more supportive than the French.

Yet because of the reluctance of universities to rapidly assimilate the new science, its pioneers quickly understood that they required a framework for cooperating and sharing of information that went beyond existing intellectual institutions. Consequently, they and their supporters established what have been termed "institutions of sharing" that allowed information and ideas associated with the new science to be gathered, exchanged, and debated.[10] The most famous of these institutions was the Royal Society of London, founded in 1660, whose members consciously saw themselves as following the path Bacon had laid out almost a half-century earlier. The Royal Society had been preceded by the Academy of Experiments in Florence in 1657 and was

followed by the French Academy of Science in 1666. Germany only slowly overcame the destruction of the Thirty Years' War, and the Berlin Academy of Science was not founded until 1700. In addition to these major institutions, the new science was discussed and experiments were carried out in many local societies and academies.

These societies met regularly to hear papers and observe experiments. One of the reasons many early experiments achieved credibility was that they had been observed by persons of social respectability who belonged to one or more of the societies and who, because of their social standing, were presumed to be truthful witnesses of what they had observed. These groups also published information relating to natural philosophy and often organized libraries for their members. Perhaps most important, they attempted to separate the discussion and exploration of natural philosophy from the religious and political conflicts of the day. They intended science to exemplify an arena for the polite exchange of ideas and for civil disagreement and debate. This particular function of

---

[10]Lewis Pyenson and Susan Sheets-Pyenson, *Servants of Nature: A History of Scientific Institutions, Enterprises, and Sensibilities* (New York: W. W. Norton, 1999), p. 75.

A Closer LOOK

View the **Closer Look** on **MyHistoryLab.com**

THE SCIENCES AND THE ARTS

PAINTERS DURING the seventeenth century were keenly aware that they lived in an age of expanding knowledge of nature and of the world. Adriaen van Stalbemt (1580–1662) portrayed this close interrelationship of *The Sciences and the Arts*. Across Europe various societies were founded to study the expanding realm of natural knowledge. As in this painting, women only were rarely admitted to the meetings of these societies or to the rooms where the new natural knowledge was pursued or discussed.

The paintings on the wall illustrate the great masters of the day, some of whom drew on ancient mythological themes, others biblical scenes, and still others contemporary landscapes. Sophisticated viewers would have been able to identify each painting and its artist. The themes from the Bible and ancient mythology here are intended to contrast with the symbols of modern knowledge displayed elsewhere in the room.

On the red, covered table stands an astronomical instrument that natural philosophers used to illustrate the theories of Copernicus, Kepler, and Galileo.

On the table on the right stands a globe and volumes of maps that allow observers to trace the explorations of the Americas and other parts of the non-European world.

Adriaen van Stalbemt (1580–1662), *The Sciences and the Arts*. Wood, 93 × 114 cm. Inv. 1405. Museo del Prado, Madrid, Spain. Photograph © Erich Lessing, Art Resource, NY

What does this painting reflect about mid seventeenth-century Europe?

What are some of the political, religious, and cultural issues of the day?

What commentary might the painter be making with regard to the state of art and science at the time?

science as fostering civility became one of its major attractions.

The activities of the societies also constituted a kind of crossroads between their own members always drawn from the literate classes, and people outside the elite classes, whose skills and practical knowledge might be important for advancing the new science. The latter included craftspeople who could manufacture scientific instruments, sailors whose travels had taken them to foreign parts and who might report on the plants and animals they had seen there, and workers who had practical knowledge of problems in the countryside. In this respect, the expansion of the European economy and the drive toward empires contributed to the growth of the scientific endeavor by bringing back to Europe specimens and experiences that required classification, analysis, and observation.

In good Baconian fashion, the members of the societies presented science as an enterprise that could aid the goals of government and the growth of the economy. For example, mathematicians portrayed themselves as being useful for solving surveying and other engineering problems and for improving armaments. Furthermore, people who had ideas for improving production, navigation, or military artillery might seek the support of the associated societies. In the English context, these people became known as *projectors* and were often regarded as people simply eager to sell their often improbable ideas to the highest bidder. Nonetheless, their activities brought the new science and technology before a wider public. (See "Compare and Connect: Descartes and Swift Debate the Scientific Enterprise," pages 436–437.)

The work, publications, and interaction of the scientific societies with both the government and private business established a distinct role and presence for scientific knowledge in European social life. By 1700, that presence was relatively modest, but it would grow steadily during the coming decades. The groups associated with the new science saw themselves as championing modern practical achievements of applied knowledge and urging religious toleration, mutual forbearance, and political liberty. Such people would form the social base for the eighteenth-century movement known as the **Enlightenment**.

▼ Women in the World of the Scientific Revolution

The absence of women in the emergence of the new science of the seventeenth century has been a matter of much historical speculation. What characteristics of early modern European intellectual and cultural life worked against extensive contributions by women? Why have we heard so little of the activity by women that did actually occur in regard to the new science?

The same factors that had long excluded women from participating in most intellectual life continued to exclude them from working in the emerging natural philosophy. Traditionally, the institutions of European intellectual life had all but excluded women. Both monasteries and universities had been institutions associated with celibate male clerical culture. Other than a few exceptions in Italy, women had not been admitted to either medieval or early modern European universities; they would continue to be excluded from them until the end of the nineteenth century. Women could and did exercise influence over princely courts where natural philosophers, such as Galileo, sought patronage, but they usually did not determine those patronage decisions or benefit from them. Queen Christina of Sweden (r. 1632–1654), who brought René Descartes to Stockholm to provide the regulations for a new science academy, was an exception. When various scientific societies were founded, women were not admitted to membership. In that regard, there were virtually no social spaces that might have permitted women to pursue science easily.

Yet a few isolated women from two different social settings did manage to engage in the new scientific activity: noblewomen and women from the artisan class. In both cases, they could do so only through their husbands or male relatives.

The social standing of certain noblewomen allowed them to command the attention of ambitious natural philosophers who were part of their husbands' social circle. Margaret Cavendish (1623–1673) actually made significant contributions to the scientific literature of the day. As a girl she had been privately tutored and become widely read. Her marriage to the duke of Newcastle introduced her into a circle of natural philosophers. She understood the new science, quarreled with the ideas of Descartes and Hobbes, and criticized the Royal Society for being more interested in novel scientific instruments than in solving practical problems. Her most important works were *Observations Upon Experimental Philosophy* (1666) and *Grounds of Natural Philosophy* (1668). She was the only woman in the seventeenth century to be allowed to visit a meeting of the Royal Society of London. (See "Margaret Cavendish Questions the Fascination with Scientific Instruments," page 434.)

Women associated with artisan crafts actually achieved greater freedom to pursue the new sciences than did noblewomen. Traditionally, women had worked in artisan workshops, often with their husbands, and might take over the business when their spouse died. In Germany, much study of astronomy occurred in these settings, with women assisting their fathers or husbands. One German female astronomer, Maria Cunitz, published

Margaret Cavendish, who wrote widely on scientific subjects, was the most accomplished woman associated with the new science in seventeenth-century England.   ImageWorks/Mary Evans Picture Library Ltd.

the completion of observations required to create an accurate calendar. After much debate, the academy formally rejected her application on the grounds of her gender, although its members knew of her ability and previous accomplishments. Years later, she returned to the Berlin Academy as an assistant to her son, who had been appointed astronomer. Again, the academy insisted that she leave, forcing her to abandon astronomy. She died in 1720.

Such policies of exclusion, however, did not altogether prevent women from acquiring knowledge about scientific endeavors. Margaret Cavendish had composed a *Description of a New World, Called the Blazing World* (1666) to introduce women to the new science. Other examples of scientific writings for a female audience were Bernard de Fontenelle's *Conversations on the Plurality of Worlds* and Francesco Algarotti's *Newtonianism for Ladies* (1737). During the 1730s, Emilie du Châtelet (1706–1749) aided Voltaire in his composition of an important French popularization of Newton's science. Her knowledge of mathematics was more extensive than his and crucial to his completing his book. She also translated Newton's *Principia* into French, an accomplishment made possible only by her exceptional understanding of advanced mathematics.

Still, with few exceptions, women were barred from science and medicine until the late nineteenth century, and not until the twentieth century did they enter these fields in significant numbers. Not only did the institutions of science exclude them, but also, the ideas associated with medical practice, philosophy, and biology suggested that women and their minds were essentially different from, and inferior to, men. By the early eighteenth century, despite isolated precedents of women pursuing natural knowledge, reading scientific literature, and engaging socially with natural philosophers, it had become a fundamental assumption of European intellectual life that the pursuit of knowledge about nature was a male vocation.

a book on astronomy that many people thought her husband had written until he added a preface supporting her sole authorship. Elisabetha and Johannes Hevelius constituted a wife-and-husband astronomical team, as did Maria Winkelmann and her husband Gottfried Kirch. In each case, the wife served as the assistant to an artisan astronomer. Although Winkelmann discovered a comet in 1702, it was not until 1930 that the discovery was ascribed to her rather than to her husband. Nonetheless, contemporary philosophers did recognize her abilities and understanding of astronomy. Winkelmann had worked jointly with her husband who was the official astronomer of the Berlin Academy of Sciences and was responsible for an official calendar the academy published. When her husband died in 1710, Winkelmann applied for permission to continue the work, basing her application for the post on the guild's tradition of allowing women to continue their husbands' work, in this case

▼ The New Science and Religious Faith

For many contemporaries, the new science posed a potential challenge to religion. Three major issues were at stake. First, certain theories and discoveries did not agree

MARGARET CAVENDISH QUESTIONS THE FASCINATION WITH SCIENTIFIC INSTRUMENTS

Margaret Cavendish, duchess of Newcastle, was the most scientifically informed woman of seventeenth-century England. She read widely in natural philosophy and had many acquaintances who were involved in the new science. Although she was enthusiastic about the promise of science, she also frequently criticized some of its leading proponents, including Descartes and Hobbes. She was skeptical of the activities of the newly established Royal Society of London, where she was once permitted to visit. She believed some of its members had become overly enthusiastic about experimentation and new scientific instruments for their own sakes and had begun to ignore the practical questions that she thought science should address. In this respect, her criticism of the Royal Society and its experiments is a Baconian one. She thought the society had replaced scholastic speculation with experimental speculation and that both kinds of speculation ignored important problems of immediate utility.

Why might Margaret Cavendish think that the experiments that were reported about new optical instruments dealt with superficial wonders? Why does she contrast experimental philosophy with the beneficial arts? Do you find a feminist perspective in her comparison of the men of the Royal Society with boys playing with bubbles?

Art has intoxicated so many men's brains, and wholly imployed their thoughts and bodily actions about phaenomena, or the exterior figure of objects, as all better Arts and Studies are laid aside. . . . But though there be numerous Books written of the wonder of these [experimental optical] Glasses, yet I cannot perceive any such; at best, they are but superficial wonders, as I may call them. But could Experimental Philosophers find out more beneficial Arts then our Fore-fathers have done, either for the better increase of Vegetables and brute Animals to nourish our bodies, or better and commodious contrivances in the Art of Architecture to build us houses, or for the advancing of trade and traffick . . . it would not only be worth their labour, but of as much praise as could be given to them: But, as Boys that play with watry Bubbles . . . are worthy of reproof rather than praise, for wasting their time with useless sports; so those that addict themselves to unprofitable Arts, spend more time than they reap benefit thereby.

From Margaret Cavendish, *Observations Upon Experimental Philosophy*, to which is added, *The Description of a New Blazing World* (London, 1666), pp. 10–11, as quoted in Anna Battigelli, *Margaret Cavendish and the Exiles of the Mind* (Lexington: University of Kentucky Press, 1998), p. 94.

with biblical statements about the heavens. Second, who would decide conflicts between religion and science—church authorities or the natural philosophers? Finally, for many religious thinkers, the new science seemed to replace a universe of spiritual meaning and significance with a purely materialistic one. Yet most of the natural philosophers genuinely saw their work as supporting religious belief by contributing to a deeper knowledge of the divine. Their efforts and those of their supporters to reconcile faith and the new science constituted a fundamental factor in the spread of science and its widespread acceptance in educated European circles. The process was not an easy one.

The Case of Galileo

The condemnation of Galileo by Roman Catholic authorities in 1633 is the single most famous incident of conflict between modern science and religious institutions. For centuries it was interpreted as exemplifying the forces of religion smothering scientific knowledge. More recent research has modified that picture.

The condemnation of Copernicanism and of Galileo occurred at a particularly difficult moment in the history of the Roman Catholic Church. In response to Protestant emphasis on private interpretation of Scripture, the Council of Trent (1545–1563) had stated that only the church itself possessed the authority to interpret the Bible. Furthermore, after the Council, the Roman Catholic Church had adopted a more literalist mode of reading the Bible in response to the Protestant emphasis on the authority of Scripture. Galileo's championing of Copernicanism took place in this particular climate of opinion and practice when the Roman Catholic Church, on the one hand, could not surrender the interpretation of the Bible to a layman and, on the other, had difficulty moving beyond a literal reading of the Bible, lest the Protestants accuse it of abandoning Scripture.

In a *Letter to the Grand Duchess Christina* (1615), Galileo, as a layman, had published his own views about how scripture should be interpreted to accommodate the new science. (See "Galileo Discusses the Relationship of Science to the Bible," page 438.) To certain Roman Catholic authorities, his actions resembled those of a Protestant who looked to himself rather than the church to understand the Bible. In 1615 and 1616, he visited Rome and discussed his views openly and aggressively. In early 1616, however, the Roman Catholic Inquisition formally censured Copernicus' views, placing *On the Revolutions of the Heavenly Spheres* in the Index of Prohibited Books. The ground for the condemnation was Copernicus' disagreement with the literal word of the Bible and the biblical interpretations of the Church Fathers. It should be recalled that at the time fully satisfactory empirical evidence to support Copernicus did not yet exist, even in Galileo's mind.

Read the Document
"Galileo Galilei, Letter to the Grand Duchess Christina (1630s)" on **MyHistoryLab.com**

Galileo, who was not on trial in 1616, was formally informed of the condemnation of Copernicanism. Exactly what agreement he and the Roman Catholic authorities reached as to what he would be permitted to write about Copernicanism remains unclear. It appears that he agreed not to advocate that Copernican astronomy was actually physically true, but only to suggest that it could be true in theory.

In 1623, however, a Florentine acquaintance of Galileo's was elected as Pope Urban VIII. He gave Galileo permission to resume discussing the Copernican system, which he did in *Dialogue on the Two Chief World Systems* (1632). The book clearly was designed to defend the physical truthfulness of Copernicanism. Moreover, the voices in the dialogue favoring the older system appeared slow-witted—and those voices presented the views of Pope Urban. Feeling humiliated and betrayed, the pope ordered an investigation of Galileo's book. The actual issue in Galileo's trial of 1633 was whether he had disobeyed the mandate of 1616, and he was held to have done so even though the exact nature of that mandate was less than certain. Galileo was condemned, required to renounce his views, and placed under the equivalent of house arrest in his home near Florence for the last nine years of his life.

Although much more complicated than a simple case of a conflict between science and religion, the condemnation of Galileo cast a long and troubled shadow over the relationship of the emerging new science and the authority of the Roman Catholic Church. The controversy continued into the late twentieth century, when Pope John Paul II formally ordered the reassessment of the Galileo case. In 1992, the Roman Catholic Church admitted that errors had occurred, particularly in the biblical interpretation of Pope Urban VIII's advisers.

Blaise Pascal: Reason and Faith

Blaise Pascal (1623–1662), a French mathematician and a physical scientist who surrendered his wealth to pursue an austere, self-disciplined life, made one of the most influential efforts to reconcile faith and the new science. He aspired to write a work that would refute both dogmatism (which he saw epitomized by the Jesuits) and skepticism. Pascal considered the Jesuits' casuistry (i.e., arguments designed to minimize and excuse sinful acts) a distortion of Christian teaching. He rejected the skeptics of his age because they either denied religion altogether (atheists) or accepted it only as it conformed to reason (deists). He never produced a definitive refutation of the two sides. Rather, he formulated his views on these matters in piecemeal fashion in a provocative collection of reflections on humankind and religion published posthumously under the title *Pensées* (*Thoughts*).

Pascal allied himself with the Jansenists, seventeenth-century Catholic opponents of the Jesuits. (See Chapter 13.) His sister was a member of the Jansenist convent of Port-Royal, near Paris. The Jansenists shared with the Calvinists Saint Augustine's belief in human beings' total sinfulness, their eternal predestination to heaven or hell by God, and their complete dependence on faith and grace for knowledge of God and salvation.

Pascal believed that in religious matters, only the reasons of the heart and a "leap of faith" could prevail. For him, religion was not the domain of reason and science. He saw two essential truths in the Christian religion: A loving God exists, and human beings, because they are corrupt by nature, are utterly unworthy of God. He believed the atheists and the deists of his age had overestimated reason. To Pascal, reason itself was too weak to resolve the problems of human nature and destiny. Ultimately, reason should drive those who truly heeded it to faith in God and reliance on divine grace.

Pascal made a famous wager with the skeptics. It is a better bet, he argued, to believe God exists and to stake everything on his promised mercy than not to do so. This is because, if God does exist, the believer will gain everything, whereas, should God prove not to exist, comparatively little will have been lost by having believed in him.

Convinced that belief in God improved life psychologically and disciplined it morally (regardless of whether God proved in the end to exist), Pascal worked

Descartes and Swift Debate the Scientific Enterprise

Read the **Compare and Connect** on **MyHistoryLab.com**

THROUGHOUT THE SEVENTEENTH and eighteenth centuries various writers asserted that the growth of natural knowledge held the promise of improving the human situation. Others, who did not dispute the truth or correctness of the new natural knowledge, nonetheless questioned whether it could actually improve the human situation. In these two documents the French philosopher René Descartes upholds the former position while many decades later the English satirist Jonathan Swift questions the usefulness of the new natural knowledge pursued by the Royal Society of London and by implication by other European scientific academies.

QUESTIONS

1. How does Descartes compare the usefulness of science with previous speculative philosophy?

2. What, if any, limits does he place on the extension of scientific knowledge?

3. Why might Swift have so emphasized what he saw as the impracticality of science?

4. How might Swift's presentation be seen as manifesting jealousy of a literary figure toward the growing influence of science?

5. How does Swift's passage serve as an effort to refute the promise of science championed by Bacon and Descartes?

I. Descartes Explores the Promise of Expanding Natural Knowledge

In 1637, Descartes published his Discourse on Method. *He wrote against what he believed to be the useless speculations of scholastic philosophy. He championed the careful investigation of physical nature on the grounds that it would expand the scope of human knowledge beyond anything previously achieved and, in doing so, make human beings the masters of nature. This passage contains much of the broad intellectual and cultural argument that led to the ever-growing influence and authority of science from the seventeenth century onward.*

My speculations were indeed truly pleasing to me; but I recognize that other men have theirs, which perhaps please them even more. As soon, however, as I had acquired some general notions regarding physics, and on beginning to make trial of them in various special difficulties had observed how far they can carry us and how much they differ from the principles hitherto employed, I believed that I could not keep them hidden without grievously sinning against the law which lays us under obligation to promote, as far as in us lies, the general good of all mankind. For they led me to see that it is possible to obtain knowledge highly useful in life, and that in place of the speculative philosophy taught in the Schools we can have a practical philosophy, by means of which, knowing the force and the actions of fire, water, air, and of the stars, of the heavens, and of all the bodies that surround us—knowing them as distinctly as

An illustration from *Discourse on Method* by René Descartes (1637). Courtesy of the Library of Congress

we know the various crafts of the artisans—we may in the same fashion employ them in all the uses for which they are suited, thus rendering ourselves the masters and possessors of nature. This is to be desired, not only with a view to the invention of an infinity of arts by which we would be enabled to enjoy without heavy labor the fruits of the earth and all its conveniences, but above all for the preservation of health, which is, without doubt, of all blessings in this life, the first of all goods and the foundation on which the others rest. For the mind is so dependent on the temper and disposition of the bodily organisms that if any means can ever be found to render men wiser and more capable than they have hitherto been, I believe that it is in the science of medicine that the means must be sought. . . . With no wish to depreciate it, I am yet sure there is no one, even of those engaged in the profession, who does not admit that all we know is almost nothing in comparison with what remains to be discovered; and that we could be freed from innumerable maladies, both of body and of mind, and even perhaps from the infirmities of age, if we had sufficient knowledge of their causes and of the remedies provided by nature. ■

From René Descartes, *Discourse on Method*, in Norman Kemp Smith, ed., *Descartes's Philosophical Writings* (New York: The Modern Library, 1958), pp. 130–131. Reprinted by permission of Macmillan Press Ltd.

II. Jonathan Swift Satirizes Scientific Societies

Swift, the greatest author of English satire in the eighteenth century, was a deeply pessimistic person who thought much of the promise held forth for scientific enterprise would never be realized. In the Third Voyage of Gulliver's Travels, *published in 1726, Swift portrays Gulliver as visiting the land of Lagardo where he encounters a learned academy filled with scholars pursuing outlandish projects. Swift lists the efforts of a whole series of Projectors, each of which is more impractical than the next. This passage in which Swift pillories the various people who hoped to receive patronage for projects from persons associated with the Royal Society of London remains one of the most famous satires of science in the English language. That Swift wrote it is a testimony to the cultural authority that science had achieved by the early eighteenth century.*

Gulliver reports a conversation he encountered while visiting Lagardo:

"The Sum of his Discourse was to this Effect. That about Forty Years ago, certain Persons went up to *Laputa*, either upon Business or Diversion; and after five Months Continuance, came back with a very little Smattering in Mathematics, but full of Volatile Spirits acquired in that Airy Region. That these Persons upon their Return, began to dislike the Management of every Thing below; and fell into Schemes of putting all Arts, Sciences, Languages, and Mechanics upon a new Foot. To this End they procured a Royal Patent for erecting an Academy of *Projectors* in *Lagado*; And the Humour prevailed so strongly among the People, that there is not a Town of any Consequence in the Kingdom without such an Academy. In these Colleges, the Professors contrive new Rules and Methods of Agriculture and Building, and new Instruments and Tools for all Trades and Manufactures, whereby, as they undertake, one Man shall do the Work of Ten; a Palace may be built in a Week, of Materials so durable as to last for ever without repairing.

All the Fruits of the Earth shall come to Maturity at whatever Season we think fit to chuse; and increase an Hundred Fold more than they do at present; with innumerable other happy Proposals. The only Inconvenience is, that none of these Projects are yet brought to Perfection; and in the mean time, the whole Country lies miserably waste, the Houses in Ruins, and the People without Food or Cloaths. By all which, instead of being discouraged they are Fifty Times more violently bent upon prosecuting their Schemes, driven equally on by Hope and Depair. . . ."

Gulliver then reports what he found occurring in the rooms of an academy in Lagardo:

"The first Man I saw . . . had been Eight Years upon a Project for extracting Sun-Beams out of Cucumbers, which were to be put into Vials hermetically sealed, and let out to warm the Air in raw inclement Summers. . . .

"I saw another at work to calcine ice into Gunpowder . . .

"There was another most ingenius Architect who had contrived a new Method for building Houses, by beginning at the Roof, and working downwards to the Foundation. . . .

In another Apartment I was highly pleased with a Projector, who had found a Device of plowing the Ground with Hogs, to save the Charges of Plows, Cattle, and Labour. The Method is this: In an Acre of Ground you bury at six Inches Distance, and eight deep, a quantity of Acorns, Dates, Chesnuts, and other Masts or Vegetables whereof these Animals are fondest; then you drive six Hundred or more of them into the Field, where in a few Days they will root up the whole Ground in search of their Food, and make it fit for sowing, at the same time manuring it with their Dung. It is true, upon Experiment they found the Charge and Trouble very great, and they had little or no Crop. However, it is not doubted that this Invention may be capable of great Improvement." ■

From Jonathan Swift, *Gulliver's Travels*, Part III, chaps. iv and v (New York: The Heritage Press, 1960), pp. 193–194, 197–199.

Document

GALILEO DISCUSSES THE RELATIONSHIP OF SCIENCE TO THE BIBLE

The religious authorities were often critical of the discoveries and theories of sixteenth- and seventeenth-century science. For years before his condemnation by the Roman Catholic Church in 1633, Galileo had contended that scientific theory and religious piety were compatible. In his Letter to the Grand Duchess Christina *(of Tuscany), written in 1615, he argued that God had revealed truth in both the Bible and physical nature and that the truth of physical nature did not contradict the Bible if the latter were properly understood. Galileo encountered difficulties regarding this letter because it represented a layman telling church authorities how to read the Bible.*

Is Galileo's argument based on science or theology? Did the church believe that nature was as much a revelation of God as the Bible was? As Galileo describes them, which is the surer revelation of God, Nature, or the Bible? Why might the pope reject Galileo's argument?

The reason produced for condemning the opinion that the Earth moves and the sun stands still is that in many places in the Bible one may read that the sun moves and the Earth stands still. . . .

With regard to this argument, I think in the first place that it is very pious to say and prudent to affirm that the holy Bible can never speak untruth—whenever its true meaning is understood. But I believe nobody will deny that it is often very abstruse, and may say things which are quite different from what its bare words signify. . . .

This being granted, I think that in discussions of physical problems we ought to begin not from the authority of scriptural passages, but from sense experiences and necessary demonstrations; for the holy Bible and the phenomena of nature proceed alike from the divine Word, the former as the dictate of the Holy Ghost and the latter as the observant executrix of God's commands. It is necessary for the Bible, in order to be accommodated to the understanding of every man, to speak many things which appear to differ from the absolute truth so far as the bare meaning of the words is concerned. But Nature, on the other hand, is inexorable and immutable; she never transgresses the laws imposed upon her, or cares a whit whether her abstruse reasons and methods of operation are understandable to men. For that reason it appears that nothing physical which sense-experience sets before our eyes, or which necessary demonstrations prove to us, ought to be called in question (much less condemned) upon the testimony of biblical passages which may have some different meaning beneath their words. For the Bible is not chained in every expression to conditions as strict as those which govern all physical effects; nor is God any less excellently revealed in Nature's actions than in the sacred statements of the Bible. . . .

From this I do not mean to infer that we need not have an extraordinary esteem for the passages of holy Scripture. On the contrary, having arrived at any certainties in physics, we ought to utilize these as the most appropriate aids in the true exposition of the Bible and in the investigation of those meanings which are necessarily contained therein for these must be concordant with demonstrated truths. I should judge the authority of the Bible was designed to persuade men of those articles and propositions which, surpassing all human reasoning, could not be made credible by science, or by any other means than through the very mouth of the Holy Spirit. . . .

But I do not feel obliged to believe that the same God who has endowed us with senses, reason, and intellect has intended to forgo their use and by some other means to give us knowledge which we can attain by them.

to strengthen traditional religious belief. He urged his contemporaries to seek self-understanding by "learned ignorance" and to discover humankind's greatness by recognizing its misery. He hoped thereby to counter what he believed to be the false optimism of the new rationalism and science.

The English Approach to Science and Religion

Francis Bacon established a key framework for reconciling science and religion that long influenced the English-speaking world. He argued there were two books of divine revelation: the Bible and nature. In studying nature, the natural philosopher could achieve a deeper knowledge of things divine, just as could the theologian studying the Bible. Because both books of revelation shared the same author, they must be compatible. Whatever discord

might first appear between science and religion must eventually be reconciled. Natural theology based on a scientific understanding of the natural order would thus support theology derived from Scripture.

Later in the seventeenth century, with the work of Newton, the natural universe became a realm of law and regularity. Most natural philosophers were devout people who saw in the new picture of physical nature a new picture of God. The Creator of this rational, lawful nature must also be rational. To study nature was to come to a better understanding of that Creator. Science and religious faith were not only compatible, but also mutually supportive. As Newton wrote, "The main Business of Natural Philosophy is to argue from Phaenomena without feigning Hypothesis, and to deduce Causes from Effects, till we come to the very first Cause, which certainly is not mechanical."[11]

[11]Quoted in Baumer, *Main Currents of Western Thought*, p. 323.

Document

MAN: A MEAN BETWEEN NOTHING AND EVERYTHING

Pascal wrote against what he considered to be the presumption of the "modern" thinkers of his day, among them, Montaigne and Descartes. He believed that they failed to appreciate the limitations of mankind, as it perched precariously between God and nothing.

According to Pascal, what is the essence of man? Was Pascal a deeply religious man who embraced the Christian church? Why did he join the Jansenists rather than the Jesuits? How would you describe his personal religious beliefs? Can he be compared with modern spiritual and scientific writers?

72 . . . . For in fact what is man in nature? A Nothing in comparison with the infinite, an All in comparison with the Nothing, a mean between nothing and everything. Since he is infinitely removed from comprehending the extremes, the end of things and their beginning are hopelessly hidden from him in impenetrable secret: he is equally incapable of seeing the Nothing from which he was made, and the Infinite in which he is swallowed up.

What will he do then, but perceive the appearance of the middle of things in an eternal despair of knowing either their beginning or their end. All things proceed from the Nothing, and are borne towards the Infinite. Who will follow these marvelous processes? The Author of these wonders understands them. None other can do so . . .

This is our true state; this is what makes us incapable of certain knowledge and of absolute ignorance. We sail within a vast sphere, ever drifting in uncertainty, driven from end to end. When we think to attach ourselves to any point and to fasten to it, it wavers and leaves us; and if we follow it, it eludes our grasp, slips past us, and vanishes forever. Nothing stays for us. This is our natural condition, and yet most contrary to our inclination. We burn with desire to find solid ground and an ultimate sure foundation whereon to build a tower reaching to the Infinite. But our whole groundwork cracks, and the earth opens to abysses.

Let us therefore not look for certainty and stability. Our reason is always deceived by fickle shadows; nothing can fix the finite between the two Infinites, which both enclose and fly from it.

From *Pascal's Pensées* (New York: E. P. Dutton & Co., 1958), pp. 17–18.

The religious thought associated with such deducing of religious conclusions from nature became known as *physico-theology*. This reconciliation of faith and science allowed the new physics and astronomy to spread rapidly. At the very time when Europeans were finally tiring of the wars of religion, the new science provided the basis for a view of God that might lead away from irrational disputes and wars over religious doctrine. Faith in a rational God encouraged faith in the rationality of human beings and in their capacity to improve their lot once liberated from the traditions of the past. The scientific revolution provided the great model for the desirability of change and of criticism of inherited views.

Finally, the new science and the technological and economic innovations associated with its culture came again, especially among English thinkers, to be interpreted as part of a divine plan. By the late seventeenth century, natural philosophy and its practical achievements had become associated in the public mind with consumption and the market economy. Writers such as the Englishman John Ray in *The Wisdom of God Manifested in His Works of Creation* (1690) argued it was evident that God had placed human beings in the world to understand it and then, having understood it, to turn it to productive, practical use through rationality. Scientific advance and economic enterprise came to be interpreted in the public mind as the fulfillment of God's plan: Human beings were meant to improve the world. This outlook provided a religious justification for the processes of economic improvement that would characterize much of eighteenth-century Western Europe.

▼ Continuing Superstition

Despite great optimism among certain European thinkers associated with the new ideas in science and philosophy, traditional beliefs and fears long retained their hold on Western popular culture. During the sixteenth and seventeenth centuries, Europeans remained preoccupied with sin, death, and the devil. Religious people, including many among the learned and many who were sympathetic to the emerging scientific ideas, continued to believe in the power of magic and the occult. Until the end of the seventeenth century, almost all Europeans in one way or another believed in the devil and the power of demons.

Witch Hunts and Panic

Nowhere is the dark side of early modern thought and culture more strikingly visible than in the witch hunts and panics that erupted in almost every Western land. Between 1400 and 1700, courts sentenced an estimated 70,000 to 100,000 people to death for harmful magic (*maleficium*) and diabolical witchcraft. In addition to inflicting harm on their neighbors, witches were said to attend mass meetings known as *sabbats*, to which they were also believed to fly. They were also believed to indulge in sexual orgies with the devil, who appeared in animal form, most often as a he-goat. Other imagined charges against them were cannibalism—particularly the devouring of small Christian children—and a variety of ritual acts and practices, often sexual in nature, that denied or perverted Christian beliefs.

Why did witch panics occur in the sixteenth and early seventeenth centuries? The disruptions created by religious division and warfare were major factors. The peak years of the religious wars were also those of the witch hunts. Some blame the Reformation for the panics by taking away the traditional defenses against the devil and demons, thereby compelling gullible believers to protect themselves by searching out and executing witches.

● Watch the Video
"Video Lectures: Witch Hunts" on
MyHistoryLab.com

Village Origins

The roots of belief in witches are found in both popular and elite culture. In village societies, respected "cunning folk" helped the simple folk cope with natural disasters and disabilities incurred by magical powers. For settled people, these were important services that kept village life moving forward in times of calamity. The alleged possession of magical powers, for good or ill, made one an important person within village society. Those who were most in need of security and influence, particularly old, impoverished single or widowed women, often made claims to possessing such authority. Occult, village beliefs may also have been a way to defy urban Christian society's attempts to impose its orthodox beliefs, laws, and institutions on the countryside. Under church persecution local fertility cults, whose semipagan practices were intended to ensure good harvests, acquired the features of diabolical witchcraft.

Influence of the Clergy

Popular belief in magical power was the essential foundation of the witch hunts. Had ordinary people not believed that "gifted persons" could help or harm by magical means, and had they not been willing to accuse them, the hunts would never have occurred; however, the contribution of Christian theologians was equally great. When the church expanded into areas where its power and influence were small, it encountered semipagan cultures rich in folkloric beliefs and practices that predated Christianity. There, it clashed with so-called cunning men and women, who were respected spiritual authorities in local communities, the folk equivalents of Christian priests. In the eyes of the simple folk, Christian clergy also practiced a kind of high magic. They could transform bread and wine into the body and blood of Christ (the sacrament of the Eucharist) and eternal penalties for sin into temporal ones (the sacrament of Penance or Confession). They also claimed the power to cast out demons who possess the faithful.

In the late thirteenth century, the church declared its so-called magic to be not that of the occult, but the true powers invested in them by the Christian God. Since occult powers were not innate to humans, the theologians reasoned, they must come either from God or from the devil. Those from God were properly exercised within and by the church. Any who practiced magic outside and against the church did so on behalf of the devil. From such reasoning grew allegations of "pacts" between nonpriestly magicians and Satan.

In working its will, the church had an important ally in the princes of the age, who were attempting to extend and consolidate their authority over villages and towns within their lands. As the church sought to supplant folk magic with the true power of church ritual, the princes sought to supplant customary laws with Roman law. Here the stage was set for a one-sided conflict. Witch

trials became one of the ways church and state realized their overlapping goals. To identify, try, and execute witches became a demonstration of absolute spiritual and political authority over a village or a town.

Who Were the Witches?

Roughly 80 percent of the victims of witch hunts were women, most single and aged over forty. This has suggested to some that misogyny fueled the witch hunts. Inspired by male hatred and sexual fear of strong women, and occurring at a time when not a few women were breaking out from under male control, witch hunts were a conspiracy of males against females.

A perhaps better argument holds that women were targeted in higher numbers for more commonsensical reasons. (See "Why More Women Than Men Are Witches," p. 442.) Three groups of women appear especially to have drawn the clerical witch-hunters' attention. The first was widows, who, living alone in the world after the deaths of their husbands, were now often

An engraving showing three women and a child being burned at the stake during the great witch trial of Schongau, 1589–1592.
INTERFOTO/Alamy

dependent on others, unhappy, and known to strike out. A second group was midwives, whose work made them unpopular when mothers and/or newborns died in childbirth. (See "Encountering the Past: Midwives," page 443.) Surviving family members remembered those deaths.

Finally, there were women healers and herbalists, who were targeted because their work gave them a moral and spiritual authority over people which the church wished to reserve for its priests. These women found themselves on the front lines in disproportionate numbers when the

---

Document

WHY MORE WOMEN THAN MEN ARE WITCHES

A classic of misogyny, The Hammer of Witches *(1486), written by two Dominican monks, Heinrich Krämer and Jacob Sprenger, was sanctioned by Pope Innocent VIII as an official guide to the church's detection and punishment of witches. Here, Krämer and Sprenger explain why they believe most witches are women rather than men.*

Why would two Dominican monks say such things about women? What are the biblical passages that they believe justify them? Do their descriptions have any basis in the actual behavior of women in that age? What is the rivalry between married and unmarried people that they refer to?

Why are there more superstitious women than men? The first [reason] is that they are more credulous; and since the chief aim of the devil is to corrupt faith, therefore he rather attacks them. . . . The second reason is that women are naturally more impressionable and ready to receive the influence of a disembodied spirit. . . . The third reason is that they have slippery tongues and are unable to conceal from their fellow-women those things which by evil arts they know; and since they are weak, they find an easy and secret manner of vindicating themselves by witchcraft. . . . [Therefore] since women are feebler both in mind and body, it is not surprising that they should come more under the spell of witchcraft. For as regards intellect, or the understanding of spiritual things, they seem to be of a different nature from men, a fact which is vouched for by the logic of the authorities, backed by various examples from the Scriptures. . . . .

But the natural reason [for woman's proclivity to witchcraft] is that she is more carnal than a man, as is clear from her many carnal abominations. And it should be noted that there was a defect in the formation of the first woman, since she was formed from a bent rib, that is, a rib of the breast, which is bent as it were in a contrary direction to a man.

And since through this defect she is an imperfect animal, she always deceives. . . . .

As to her other mental quality, her natural will, when she hates someone whom she formerly loved, then she seethes with anger and impatience in her whole soul, just as the tides of the sea are always heaving and boiling. . . . .

Truly the most powerful cause which contributes to the increase of witches is the woeful rivalry between married folk and unmarried women and men. This [jealousy or rivalry exists] even among holy women, so what must it be among the others . . . ?

Just as through the first defect in their intelligence women are more prone [than men] to abjure the faith, so through their second defect of inordinate affections and passions they search for, brood over, and inflict various vengeances, either by witchcraft or by some other means. Wherefore it is no wonder that so great a number of witches exist in this sex. . . . [Indeed, witchcraft] is better called the heresy of witches than of wizards, since the name is taken from the more powerful party [that is, the greater number, who are women]. Blessed be the Highest who has so far preserved the male sex from so great a crime.

From *Malleus Maleficarum*, trans. by Montague Summers (Bungay, Suffolk, UK: John Rodker, 1928), pp. 41–47. Reprinted by permission.

MIDWIVES

ALTHOUGH WOMEN IN early modern Europe generally found themselves excluded from the world of the new science, midwives across Europe oversaw the delivery of children until well into the eighteenth century. Often known as *wise women* because of their knowledge and medical skills, midwives were among the few women who carried out independent economic and public roles.

Midwifery was a trade, often pursued by elderly or widowed women of the lower social classes, for which women apprenticed for several years. In the 1630s, the Hôtel Dieu, a public hospital near Paris, set up a basic course for training midwives. Unlike other skilled workers and tradesmen, however, midwives were not allowed to organize guilds or associations to protect their trade, pass on their skills, and stabilize their incomes. Instead, civil or church authorities, who were invariably men, licensed midwives and often appointed upper-class women, known as honorable women, to supervise them.

Personal respectability and respect for the privacy of the women they attended were essential qualities for successful midwives. They were present at some of the most private moments in the lives of women and their families and were expected not to gossip about family secrets. Furthermore, women from all social classes feared that if their attending midwives were not of good character their own babies might be stillborn or imperfectly formed. Careless or incompetent midwives who injured mother or child could lose their license.

Midwives also performed important religious and civic functions at births. In emergencies they could baptize a frail newborn. They also often registered births and were officially required both to discourage abortion and infanticide and to report those activities when they occurred to the authorities. The respectability of midwives also gave them legal standing to testify to a child's legitimacy or illegitimacy.

Midwifery was one of numerous skills and occupations associated with women in early modern Europe that men took over during the eighteenth century. (See Chapter 16.) Male medical practitioners claimed to possess better training, which was available to them in medical schools, and more professional knowledge about delivering children. Over time, civil and medical authorities began to demand that people who delivered children be trained as doctors in medical schools, which women were not allowed to attend until well into the nineteenth century. In particular, the use of forceps by male surgeons to deliver a child involved a level of training unavailable to women. Yet even as medical professionalization became entrenched, midwives continued to provide their services to the poor and rural populations of Europe.

Sources: Linda Schiebinger, *The Mind Has No Sex?: Women in the Origins of Modern Science* (Cambridge, MA: Harvard University Press, 1989); Hilary Marland, ed., *The Art of Midwifery: Early Modern Midwives in Europe* (London: Routledge, 1993).

What types of women became midwives in early modern Europe?

How did the authorities regulate the practice of midwifery?

Why did male professionals gradually replace midwives in delivering babies?

Until well into the eighteenth century, midwives oversaw the delivery of most children in Europe. CORBIS church declared war on those who practiced magic without its special blessing. Social position, vocation, and influence, not gender per se, put old, single women in harm's way. Nowhere do we find women being randomly rounded up for burning. The witch hunts targeted specific women.

View the Closer Look "Women and Witchcraft" on MyHistoryLab.com

End of the Witch Hunts

Several factors helped end the witch hunts. One was the emergence of a more scientific point of view. In the seventeenth century, mind and matter came to be viewed as two independent realities, making it harder to believe that thoughts in the mind or words on the lips could alter physical things. A witch's curse was mere words. With advances in medicine, the rise of insurance companies, and the availability of lawyers, people gained greater physical security against the physical afflictions and natural calamities that drove the witch panics. Also, the witch hunts began to get too far out of hand. Tortured witches, when asked whom they saw at witches' sabbats, sometimes alleged having seen leading townspeople there, and even the judges themselves! At this point the witch trials simply could no longer serve the interests of those conducting them. In the minds of skeptical lawyers, politicians, and clergy the witch hunts had become dysfunctional and only threatened anarchy in villages and towns.

▼ Baroque Art

Art historians use the term *baroque* to denote the style associated with seventeenth-century painting, sculpture, and architecture. As with other terms used in art history, the word *baroque* covers a variety of related styles that developed during the century and moved in different directions in different countries. Baroque painters depicted their subjects in a thoroughly naturalistic, rather than an idealized, manner. This faithfulness to nature paralleled the interest in natural knowledge associated with the rise of the new science and the deeper understanding of human anatomy that was achieved during this period. These painters, the most famous of whom was Michelangelo Caravaggio (1573–1610), also were

devoted to picturing sharp contrasts between light and darkness, which created dramatic scenes in their painting. Consequently both baroque painting and sculpture have been seen as theatrical and intending to draw the observer into an emotional involvement with the subject that is being portrayed.

View the Closer Look "Rembrandt, *The Anatomy Lesson of Dr. Tulp*" on MyHistoryLab.com

The work of Baroque artists served both religious and secular ends. Baroque painters, especially in Roman Catholic countries, often portrayed scenes from the Bible and from the lives of saints intended to instruct the observer in religious truths. Artists used the same style of painting, however, to present objects and scenes of everyday life in new realistic detail. Such was the case with Dutch painters of still lifes who portrayed all

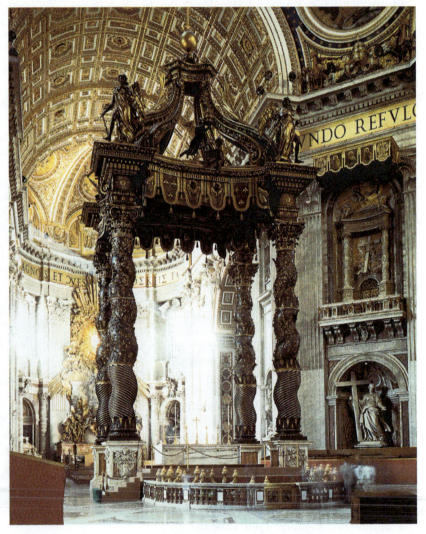

Bernini designed the elaborate Baldacchino that stands under the dome of St. Peter's Basilica. It is one of the major examples of baroque interior decoration. Scala/Art Resource, NY

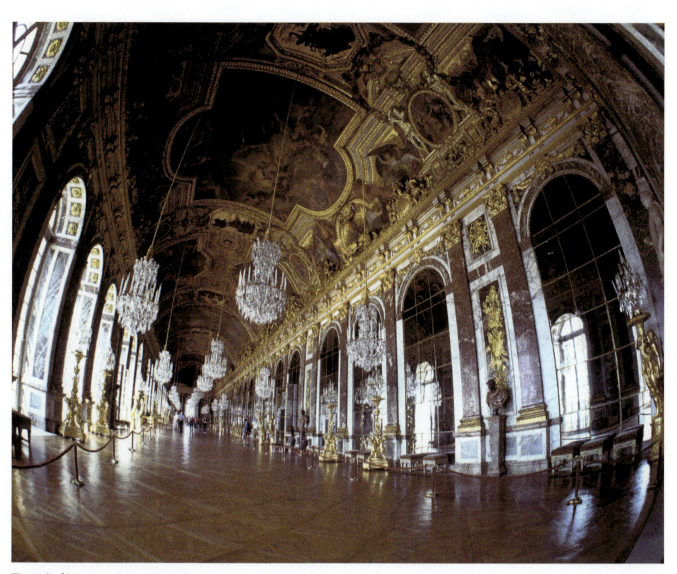

The Hall of Mirrors, palace at Versailles. © Russell Kord/Alamy

manner of elaborate foodstuffs as well as with artists such as Louis Le Nain (1593–1648) who painted scenes of French peasant life (see Chapter 15, page 456).

Baroque art became associated, rightly or wrongly, with both Roman Catholicism and absolutist politics. Baroque art first emerged in papal Rome. Gian Lorenzo Bernini's work (1598–1680) in St. Peter's Basilica was the most famous example of baroque decoration. At the direction of Pope Urban VIII (r. 1623–1644), during whose reign Galileo was condemned, Bernini designed and oversaw the construction of the great tabernacle that stands beneath the church's towering dome and directly over the space where St. Peter is said to be buried. Behind the tabernacle, Bernini also designed a monument to papal authority with the chair of St. Peter resting on the shoulders of four of the church fathers. In front of the

cathedral, he designed the two vast colonnades that he said symbolized the arms of the church reaching out to the world. In the church of Santa Maria de la Vittoria in Rome, Bernini created the dramatic sculpture of the Spanish mystic St. Teresa of Avila (1515–1582), depicting her in religious ecstasy.

The association of baroque art with Roman Catholicism had its counterpart in the secular world. Charles I (r. 1625–1649) of England, during the 1630s when he ruled as an all-but-absolute monarch without calling Parliament, employed Roman Catholic Flemish artist Peter Paul Rubens (1577–1640) to decorate the ceiling of the Banqueting Hall at his palace in London with paintings commemorating his father James I (r. 1603–1625). Rubens was the leading religious painter of the Catholic Reformation. Charles's employment of him fed Puritan suspicions that the king harbored Roman Catholic sympathies. Consequently, it was not by coincidence that Charles I was led to his execution in 1649 through the Rubens-decorated Banqueting Hall to his death on the scaffold erected outside.

The most elaborate baroque monument to political absolutism was Louis XIV's palace at Versailles. (See Chapter 13.) The exterior of the palace was classical in its restrained design. Room after room in the interior, however, was decorated with vast, dramatic paintings and murals presenting Louis as the Sun King. The Hall of Mirrors, which runs across the entire rear of the palace, allowed for a glittering and elaborate play of light the purpose of which was to reflect the power of the monarch. In the gardens of Versailles fountains depicted mythical gods as if they had come to pay court or to amuse the Sun King. Monarchs across Europe, Protestant as well as Catholic, who hoped to imitate Louis's absolutism in their own domains, erected similar, if smaller, palaces filled with elaborate decoration. Baroque architecture dominated the capitals of the rulers of the smaller German states as well as the imperial court of the Habsburgs in Vienna.

View the **Architectural Panorama** "Blenheim Palace" on **MyHistoryLab.com**

In Perspective

The scientific revolution and the thought of writers whose work was contemporaneous with it mark a major turning point in the history of Western culture and eventually had a worldwide impact. The scientific and political ideas of the late sixteenth and seventeenth centuries gradually overturned many of the most fundamental premises of the medieval worldview. The sun replaced the earth as the center of the solar system. The solar system itself came to be viewed as one of many possible systems in the universe. The new knowledge of the physical universe gave rise to challenges to the authority of the church and Scripture. Mathematics began to replace theology and metaphysics as the tool for understanding nature.

Parallel to these developments and sometimes related to them, political thought became much less concerned with religious issues. Hobbes's theory of political obligation made virtually no reference to God. Locke's theories about politics recognized God, but paid little attention to Scripture. He also championed greater freedom of religious and political expression. Locke's ideas about psychology emphasized the influence of environment on human character and action. All of these new ideas gradually displaced or reshaped theological and religious modes of thought and placed humankind and life on earth at the center of Western thinking. Intellectuals in the West consequently developed greater self-confidence in their own capacity to shape the world and their own lives.

None of this change came easily, however. The new science and enlightenment were accompanied by new anxieties that were reflected in a growing preoccupation with sin, death, and the devil. The worst expression of this preoccupation was a succession of witch hunts and trials that took the lives of as many as 100,000 people between 1400 and 1700.

KEY TERMS

baroque (p. 444)
empiricism (p. 423)

Enlightenment (p. 432)
Ptolemaic systems (p. 419)

scientific revolution (p. 418)

REVIEW QUESTIONS

1. What did Copernicus, Brahe, Kepler, Galileo, and Newton each contribute to the scientific revolution? Which do you think made the most important contributions and why? What did Francis Bacon contribute to the foundation of scientific thought?

2. How would you define the term *scientific revolution*? In what ways was it truly revolutionary? Which is more enduring, a political revolution or an intellectual one?

3. What were the differences between the political philosophies of Thomas Hobbes and John Locke? How did each view human nature? Would you rather live under a government designed by Hobbes or by Locke? Why?
4. Why were women unable to participate fully in the new science? How did family relationships help some women become involved in the advance of natural philosophy?

5. Why did the Catholic Church condemn Galileo? How did Pascal seek to reconcile faith and reason? How did English natural theology support economic expansion?
6. How do you explain the phenomena of witchcraft and witch hunts in an age of scientific enlightenment? Why did the witch panics occur in the late sixteenth and early seventeenth centuries? How might the Reformation have contributed to them?

SUGGESTED READINGS

J. Barry, M. Hester, and G. Roberts, eds., *Witchcraft in Early Modern Europe: Studies in Culture and Belief* (1998). A collection of recent essays.

M. Biagioli, *Galileo Courtier: The Practice of Science in the Culture of Absolutism* (1993). A major revisionist work.

J. A. Conner, *Kepler's Witch: An Astronomer's Discovery of Cosmic Order Amid Religious War, Political Intrigue, and the Heresy Trial of His Mother* (2005). Fascinating account of Kepler's effort to vindicate his mother against charges of witchcraft.

P. Dear, *Revolutionizing the Sciences: European Knowledge and Its Ambitions, 1500–1700* (2001). A broad-ranging study of both the ideas and institutions of the new science.

M. Feingold, *The Newtonian Moment: Isaac Newton and the Making of Modern Culture* (2004). A superb, well-illustrated volume.

S. Gaukroger, *The Emergence of a Scientific Culture: Science and the Shaping of Modernity* (2007). A challenging book exploring the differing understanding of natural knowledge in early modern European culture.

J. Gleik, *Isaac Newton* (2003). Highly accessible to the general reader.

I. Harris, *The Mind of John Locke: A Study of Political Theory in Its Intellectual Setting* (1994). The most comprehensive recent treatment.

J. L. Heilbron, *The Sun in the Church: Cathedrals as Solar Observatories* (2000). Explores uses made of Roman Catholic cathedrals to make astronomical observations.

K. J. Howell, *God's Two Books: Copernican Cosmology and Biblical Interpretation in Early Modern Science* (2002). The clearest discussion of this important subject.

L. Jardine, *Ingenious Pursuits: Building the Scientific Revolution* (1999). A lively exploration of the interface of personalities, new knowledge, and English society.

A. C. Kors and E. Peters, eds., *European Witchcraft, 1100–1700* (1972). The classics of witch belief, a massive anthology.

P. Machamer, ed., *The Cambridge Companion to Galileo* (1998). Essays that aid the understanding of the entire spectrum of the new science.

J. Marshall, *John Locke, Toleration and Early Enlightenment Culture* (2006). A magisterial and challenging survey of the background of seventeenth-century arguments for and against toleration.

J. R. Martin, *Baroque* (1977). A classic introduction to Baroque art.

M. Osler, *Rethinking the Scientific Revolution* (2000). A collection of revisionist essays particularly exploring issues of the interrelationship of the new science and religion.

R. Popkin, *The History of Scepticism: From Savonarola to Bayle* (2003). A classic study of the fear of loss of intellectual certainty.

J. Repcheck, *Copernicus' Secret: How the Scientific Revolution Began* (2007). A highly accessible biography of Copernicus.

L. Schiebinger, *The Mind Has No Sex?: Women in the Origins of Modern Science* (1989). A major study of the subject.

W. R. Shea and M. Artigas, *Galileo in Rome: The Rise and Fall of a Troublesome Genius* (2003). Argues that Galileo in part brought about his own condemnation.

MyHistoryLab™ MEDIA ASSIGNMENTS

Find these resources in the Media Assignments folder for Chapter 14 on **MyHistoryLab**.

QUESTIONS FOR ANALYSIS

1. What is the artist's main purpose in painting this scene?

Section: **The New Institutions of Expanding Natural Knowledge**
View the Closer Look The Sciences and the Arts, p. 431

2. What was Copernicus' main criticism of the Ptolemaic system?

Section: **The Scientific Revolution**
Read the Document Nicolaus Copernicus: *On the Revolution of the Heavenly Spheres* (1500), p. 419

3. What conditions gave rise to an increase in accusations of witchcraft in the Early Modern period?

Section: **Continuing Superstition**
Watch the Video Video Lectures: Witch Hunts, p. 440

4. Why has Galileo written to this ruler?

Section: **The New Science and Religious Faith**

📖 **Read** the **Document** Galileo Galilei, Letter to the Grand Duchess Christina (1630s), p. 435

5. For Hobbes, how does the nature of human society influence the shape government should take?

Section: **Philosophy Responds to Changing Science**

📖 **Read** the **Document** Thomas Hobbes, *The Leviathan*, p. 426

OTHER RESOURCES FROM THIS CHAPTER

The Scientific Revolution

🔍 **View** the **Image** Illustrations for *The Emperor's Astronomy*, p. 419

🔍 **View** the **Closer Look** The Copernican Universe, p. 419

📖 **Read** the **Document** Galileo, "Third Letter on Sunspots" (Italian States), 1612, p. 421

📖 **Read** the **Document** Isaac Newton, from *Opticks*, p. 422

Philosophy Responds to Changing Science

📖 **Read** the **Document** *The Novum Organum* (1620), p. 423

📖 **Read** the **Document** Rene Descartes, *The Discourse on Method*, p. 425

📖 **Read** the **Document** John Locke, *Essay Concerning Human Understanding*, p. 429

The New Science and Religious Faith

📖 **Read** the **Compare and Connect** Descartes and Swift Debate the Scientific Enterprise, p. 436

Continuing Superstition

🔍 **View** the **Closer Look** Women and Witchcraft, p. 444

Baroque Art

🔍 **View** the **Closer Look** Rembrandt, *The Anatomy Lesson of Dr. Tulp*, p. 444

🔍 **View** the **Architectural Panorama** Blenheim Palace, p. 446

During the eighteenth century farm women normally worked in the home and performed such tasks as churning butter as well as caring for children. As time passed tasks such as making butter were mechanized and women were displaced from such work.   Francis Wheatley (RA) (1747–1801) *Morning*, signed and dated 1799, oil on canvas, 17½ × 21½ in. (44.5 × 54.5 cm). Yale Center for British Art, Paul Mellon Collection, USA/ Bridgeman Art Library (B1977.14.120)

((•—[**Listen** to the **Chapter Audio** on **MyHistoryLab.com**

15

Society and Economy Under the Old Regime in the Eighteenth Century

LEARNING OBJECTIVES

How did tradition, hierarchy, and privilege shape life in the Old Regime?

What was the foundation of the wealth and power for the eighteenth-century aristocracy?

How were peasants and serfs tied to the land in eighteenth-century Europe?

What role did the family play in the economy of preindustrial Europe?

What led to the agricultural revolution of the eighteenth century?

Why did the Industrial Revolution begin in Britain?

What problems arose as a result of the growth of cities?

How did the suppression of Jews in European cities lead to the formation of ghettos?

DURING THE FRENCH Revolution and the turmoil that upheaval spawned, it became customary to refer to the patterns of social, political, and economic relationships that had existed in France before 1789 as the *ancien régime*, or the **Old Regime**. The term has come to be applied generally to the life and institutions of pre-revolutionary Europe. Politically, on the continent, though not in Great Britain, it meant the rule of theoretically absolute monarchies with growing bureaucracies and aristocratically led armies. Economically, a scarcity of food, the predominance of agriculture, slow transport, a low level of iron production, comparatively unsophisticated financial institutions, and, in some cases, competitive commercial overseas empires characterized the Old Regime. Socially, men and women living during the period saw themselves less as individuals than as members of distinct corporate bodies that possessed certain privileges or rights as a group.

Tradition, hierarchy, a corporate feeling, and privilege were the chief social characteristics of the Old Regime. Yet it was by no means a static society. Change and innovation were fermenting in its midst. Farming became more commercialized, and both food production and the size of the population increased. The early stages of the Industrial Revolution made more consumer goods available, and domestic consumption expanded throughout the century. The colonies in the Americas provided strong demand for European goods and manufactures. Merchants in seaports and other cities were expanding their businesses. By preparing their states for war, European governments put new demands on the resources and the economic organizations of their nations. The spirit of rationality that had been so important to the scientific revolution of the seventeenth century continued to manifest itself in the economic life of the eighteenth century. The Old Regime itself fostered the changes that eventually transformed it into a different kind of society.

▼ Major Features of Life in the Old Regime

Socially, pre-revolutionary Europe was based on (1) aristocratic elites possessing a wide variety of inherited legal privileges; (2) established churches intimately related to the state and the aristocracy; (3) an urban labor force usually organized into guilds; and (4) a rural peasantry subject to high taxes and feudal dues. Of course, the men and women living during this period did not know it was the Old Regime. Most of them earned their livelihoods and passed their lives as their forebearers had done for generations before them and as they expected their children to do after them.

 Read the **Document**
"De Staël on the Ancien Regime (1789)" on **MyHistoryLab.com**

Maintenance of Tradition

During the eighteenth century, the past weighed more heavily on people's minds than did the future. Few persons outside the government bureaucracies, the expanding merchant groups, and the movement for reform called the Enlightenment (see Chapter 17) considered change or innovation desirable. This was especially true of social relationships. Both nobles and peasants, for different reasons, repeatedly called for the restoration of traditional, or customary, rights. The nobles asserted what they considered their ancient rights against the intrusion of the expanding monarchical bureaucracies. The peasants, through petitions and revolts, called for the revival or the maintenance of the customary manorial rights that allowed them access to particular lands, courts, or grievance procedures.

Except for the early industrial development in Britain and the accompanying expansion of personal consumption, the eighteenth-century economy was also predominantly traditional. The quality and quantity of the grain harvest remained the most important fact of life for most of the population and the gravest concern for governments.

Hierarchy and Privilege

Closely related to this traditional social and economic outlook was the hierarchical structure of the society. The medieval sense of rank and degree not only persisted, but also became more rigid during the century. In several continental cities, sumptuary laws regulating the dress of the different classes remained on the books. These laws forbade persons in one class or occupation from wearing clothes like those worn by their social superiors. The laws, which sought to make the social hierarchy easily visible, were largely ineffective by this time. What really enforced the hierarchy was the corporate nature of social relationships.

Each state or society was considered a community composed of numerous smaller communities. Eighteenth-century Europeans did not enjoy what Americans regard as "individual rights." Instead, a person enjoyed such rights and privileges as were guaranteed to the particular communities or groups of which he or she was a part. The "community" might include the village, the municipality, the nobility, the church, the guild, a university, or the parish. In turn, each of these bodies enjoyed certain privileges, some great and some small. The privileges might involve exemption from taxation or from some especially humiliating punishment, the right to practice a trade or craft, the right of one's children to pursue a particular occupation, or, for the church, the right to collect the tithe.

▼ The Aristocracy

The eighteenth century was the great age of the aristocracy. The nobility constituted approximately 1–5 percent of the population of any given country. Yet in every country, it was the single wealthiest sector of the population; had the widest degree of social, political, and economic power; and set the tone of polite society. In most countries, the nobility had their own separate house in the parliament, estates, or diet. Only nobles had any kind of representation in Hungary and Poland. Land continued to provide the aristocracy with its largest source of income, but aristocrats did not merely own estates: Their influence was felt throughout social and economic life. In much of Europe, however, manual labor was regarded as beneath a noble. In Spain, it was assumed that even the poorer nobles would lead lives of idleness. In other nations, however, the nobility often fostered economic innovation and embraced the commercial spirit. Such willingness to change helped protect the nobility's wealth and, in both Great Britain and France, gave them common interest with the commercial classes who were also eager to see the economy grow and protect their property.

Varieties of Aristocratic Privilege

To be an aristocrat was a matter of birth and legal privilege. This much the aristocracy had in common across the Continent. In almost every other respect, they differed markedly from country to country.

British Nobility   The smallest, wealthiest, best defined, and most socially responsible aristocracy resided in Great Britain. It consisted of about four hundred families, and the eldest male members of each family sat in the House of Lords. Through the corruptions of the electoral system, these families also controlled many seats in the House of Commons. The estates of the British nobility ranged from a few thousand to 50,000 acres, from which they received rents. The nobles owned about one-fourth of all the arable land in the country. Increasingly, the British aristocracy invested its wealth in commerce, canals, urban real estate, mines, and even industrial ventures. Because only the eldest son inherited the title (called a "peerage"), the right to sit in the House of Lords, and the land, younger sons moved into commerce, the army, the professions, and the church. British landowners in both houses of Parliament levied taxes and also paid them. They had few significant legal privileges, but their direct or indirect control of local government gave them immense political power and social influence. The aristocracy dominated the society and politics of the English counties. Their country houses, many of which were built in the eighteenth century, were the centers of local society.

French Nobility   The situation of the continental nobilities was less clear-cut. In France, the approximately 400,000 nobles were divided between nobles "of the sword," or those whose nobility was derived from military service, and those "of the robe," who had acquired their titles either by serving in the bureaucracy or by having purchased them. The two groups had quarreled in the past but often cooperated during the eighteenth century to defend their common privileges.

The French nobles were also divided between those who held office or favor with the royal court at Versailles and those who did not. The court nobility reaped the immense wealth that could be gained from holding high office. The nobles' hold on such offices intensified during the century. By the late 1780s, appointments to the church, the army, and the bureaucracy, as well as other profitable positions, tended to go to the nobles already established in court circles. Whereas these well-connected aristocrats were rich, the provincial nobility, called *hobereaux*, were often little better off than wealthy peasants.

Despite differences in rank, origin, and wealth, certain hereditary privileges set all French aristocrats apart from the rest of society. They were exempt from many taxes. For example, most French nobles did not pay the *taille*, or land tax, the basic tax of the Old Regime. The nobles were technically liable for payment of the *vingtième*, or the "twentieth," which resembled an income tax, but they rarely had to pay it in full. The nobles were not liable for the royal *corvées*, or forced labor on public works, which fell on the peasants. In addition to these exemptions, French nobles could collect feudal dues from their tenants and enjoyed exclusive hunting and fishing privileges.

Eastern European Nobilities   East of the Elbe River, the character of the nobility became even more complicated and repressive. Throughout the area, the military traditions of the aristocracy remained important. In Poland, there were thousands of nobles, or *szlachta*, who were entirely exempt from taxes after 1741. Until 1768, these Polish aristocrats possessed the right of life and death over their serfs. Most of the Polish nobility were relatively poor. A few rich nobles who had immense estates exercised political power in the fragile Polish state.

In Austria and Hungary, the nobility continued to possess broad judicial powers over the peasantry through their manorial courts. They also enjoyed various degrees of exemption from taxation. The wealthiest of them, Prince Esterhazy of Hungary, owned 10 million acres of land.

In Prussia, after the accession of Frederick the Great in 1740, the position of the Junker nobles became much stronger. Frederick's various wars required their full support. He drew his officers almost wholly from

A Closer ▶ LOOK

⌕ View the Closer Look on MyHistoryLab.com

AN ARISTOCRATIC COUPLE

PORTRAITS, SUCH AS this one of the English landowner, *Robert Andrews and His Wife*, by Thomas Gainsborough (1728–1788), contain many clues to the aristocratic dominance of landed society.

Andrew's gun and dog indicate his exclusive right to hunt on his land.

His wife's sitting against the expanse of his landed estate suggests the character of their legal relationship, whereby he could have controlled her property, which would have thus become an extension of his.

National Gallery, London/Art Resource, NY

The market price of the wheat raised on his estate, known in England as corn (right foreground) would have been protected by various import laws enacted by the English Parliament, whose membership was dominated by landowners such as Andrews himself.

With his dog, rifle, and wife at his sides Andrew stands over his estate as if he owned the whole world. What cares and dangers would a man of his high standing have?

Do the darkening clouds in the background suggest that all may not be well?

Might the great space the painter has left in Mrs. Andrews' very thin lap point to an expectant child?

the Junker class. Nobles also increasingly made up the bureaucracy. As in other parts of eastern Europe, the Prussian nobles had extensive judicial authority over the serfs.

In Russia, the eighteenth century saw what amounted to the creation of the nobility. Peter the Great's (r. 1682–1725) linking of state service and noble social status through the Table of Ranks (1722) established among Russian nobles a self-conscious class identity that had not previously existed. Thereafter, they were determined to resist compulsory state service. In 1736, Empress Anna (r. 1730–1740) reduced such service to twenty-five years. In 1762, Peter III (r. 1762) exempted the greatest nobles entirely from compulsory service. In 1785, in the Charter of the Nobility, Catherine the Great (r. 1762–1796) legally defined the rights and privileges of noble men and women in exchange for the assurance that the nobility would serve the state voluntarily. Noble privileges included the right of transmitting noble status to a nobleman's wife and children, the judicial protection of noble rights and property, considerable power over the serfs, and exemption from personal taxes.

Aristocratic Resurgence

The Russian Charter of the Nobility constituted one aspect of the broader European-wide development termed the *aristocratic resurgence*. This was the nobility's reaction to the threat to their social position and privileges that they felt from the expanding power of the monarchies. This resurgence took several forms in the eighteenth century.

First, all nobilities tried to preserve their exclusiveness by making it more difficult to become a noble. Second, they pushed to reserve appointments to the officer corps of the armies, the senior posts in the bureaucracies and government ministries, and the upper ranks of the church exclusively for nobles. By doing this, they hoped to resist the encroaching power of the monarchies.

Third, the nobles attempted to use the authority of existing aristocratically controlled institutions against the power of the monarchies. These institutions included the British Parliament, the French courts, or *parlements*, and the local aristocratic estates and provincial diets in Germany and the Habsburg Empire.

Fourth, the nobility sought to improve its financial position by gaining further exemptions from taxation or by collecting higher rents or long-forgotten feudal dues from the peasantry. The nobility tried to shore up its position by various appeals to traditional and often ancient privileges that had lapsed over time. This aristocratic challenge to the monarchies was a fundamental political fact of the day and a potentially disruptive one.

■ **Read** the **Document**
"Voltaire, on Social Conditions in Eighteenth-Century France" on
MyHistoryLab.com

▼ The Land and Its Tillers

Land was the economic basis of eighteenth-century life and the foundation of the status and power of the nobility. Well over three-fourths of all Europeans lived in the country, and few of them ever traveled more than a few miles from their birthplace. Except for the nobility and the wealthier nonaristocratic landowners, most people who dwelled on the land were poor, and in many regions, desperately poor. They lived in various states of economic and social dependency, exploitation, and vulnerability. (See "Compare and Connect: Two Eighteenth-Century Writers Contemplate the Effects of Different Economic Structures," pages 462–463.)

Peasants and Serfs

Rural social dependency related directly to the land. The nature of the dependency differed sharply for free peasants, such as English tenants and most French cultivators, and for the serfs of Germany, Austria, and Russia, who were legally bound to a particular plot of land and a particular lord. Yet everywhere, the class that owned most of the land also controlled the local government and the courts. For example, in Great Britain, all farmers and smaller tenants had the legal rights of English citizens. The justices of the peace, however, who presided over the county courts and who could call out the local militia, were always substantial landowners, as were the members of Parliament, who made the laws. In eastern Europe, the landowners presided over the manorial courts. On the Continent, the burden of taxation fell on the tillers of the soil.

■ **Read** the **Document**
"The Marquis de Mirabeau, *The Friend of Men, or Treatise on Population*, 1756" on
MyHistoryLab.com

Obligations of Peasants The power of the landlord increased as one moved across Europe from west to east. Most French peasants owned some land, but there were a few serfs in eastern France. Nearly all French peasants were subject to certain feudal dues, called *banalités*. These included the required use-for-payment of the lord's, or *seigneur's*, mill to grind grain and his oven to bake bread. The seigneur could also require a certain number of days each year of the peasant's labor. This practice of forced labor was termed the *corvée*. Because French peasants rarely possessed enough land to support their families, they had to rent more land from the seigneur and were also subject to feudal dues attached to those plots. In Prussia and Austria, despite attempts by the monarchies late in the century to improve the lot of the serfs, the landlords continued to exercise almost complete control over them. In many of the Habsburg lands, law and custom required the serfs to provide service, or *robot*, to the lords.

Serfs were worst off in Russia. There, nobles reckoned their wealth by the number of "souls," or male serfs, they owned rather than the size of their acreage. Russian landlords, in effect, regarded serfs merely as economic commodities. They could demand as many as six days a week of labor, known as *barshchina*, from the serfs. Like Prussian and Austrian landlords, they enjoyed the right to punish their serfs. On their own authority,

Eighteenth-century France had some of the best roads in the world, but they were often built with forced labor. French peasants were required to work part of each year on such projects. This system, called the *corvée*, was not abolished until the French Revolution in 1789. *Louvre, Paris, France/Erich Lessing/Art Resource, NY*

Russian landlords could even exile a serf to Siberia. Serfs had no legal recourse against the orders and whims of their lords. There was little difference between Russian serfdom and slavery.

View the **Map**
"Russian Serfs" on
MyHistoryLab.com

In southeastern Europe, where the Ottoman Empire held sway, peasants were free, though landlords tried to exert authority in every way. The domain of the landlords was termed a *çift*. The landlord was often an absentee who managed the estate through an overseer. During the seventeenth and eighteenth centuries, these landlords, like those elsewhere in Europe, often became more commercially oriented and turned to the production of crops—such as cotton, vegetables, potatoes, and maize—that they could sell in the market.

A scarcity of labor rather than the recognition of their legal rights supported the independence of the southeastern European peasants. A peasant might migrate from one landlord to another. Because the second landlord needed the peasant's labor, he had no reason to return him to the original landlord. During the seventeenth and eighteenth centuries, however, disorder originating in Constantinople (now Istanbul), the capital, spilled over into the Balkan Peninsula. In this climate, landlords increased their authority by offering their peasants protection from bandits or rebels who might destroy peasant villages. As in medieval times, the manor house or armed enclosure of a local landlord became the peasants' refuge. These landlords also owned all the housing and tools the peasants needed to work the land and also furnished their seed grain. Consequently, despite legal independence, Balkan peasants under the Ottoman Empire became largely dependent on the landlords, though never to the extent of serfs in eastern Europe or Russia.

Peasant Rebellions The Russian monarchy itself contributed to the further degradation of the serfs. Peter the Great gave whole villages to favored nobles. Later in the century, Catherine the Great confirmed the authority of the nobles over their serfs in exchange for the landowners' political cooperation. Russia experienced vast peasant unrest, with well over fifty peasant revolts between 1762 and 1769. These culminated in Pugachev's Rebellion between 1773 and 1775, when Emelyan Pugachev (1726–1775) promised the serfs land of their own and freedom from their lords. All of southern Russia was in turmoil until the government brutally suppressed the rebellion. Thereafter, any thought of improving the condition of the serfs was set aside for a generation.

Emelyan Pugachev (1726–1775) led the largest peasant revolt in Russian history. In this contemporary propaganda picture he is shown in chains. An inscription in Russian and German was printed below the picture decrying the evils of revolution and insurrection. *Bildarchiv Preussischer Kulturbesitz*

Pugachev's was the largest peasant uprising of the eighteenth century, but smaller peasant revolts or disturbances took place in Bohemia in 1775, in Transylvania in 1784, in Moravia in 1786, and in Austria in 1789. There were almost no revolts in Western Europe, but England experienced many rural riots. Rural rebellions were violent, but the peasants and serfs normally directed their wrath against property rather than persons. The rebels usually sought to reassert traditional or customary rights against practices that they perceived as innovations. Their targets were carefully chosen and included unfair pricing, onerous new or increased feudal dues, changes in methods of payment or land use, unjust officials, or extraordinarily brutal overseers and landlords. Peasant revolts were thus conservative in nature.

Aristocratic Domination of the Countryside: The English Game Laws

One of the clearest examples of aristocratic domination of the countryside and of aristocratic manipulation of the law to its own advantage was the English legislation on hunting.

Between 1671 and 1831, English landowners had the exclusive legal right to hunt game animals, including, in particular, hares, partridges, pheasants, and moor fowl. Similar legislation covered other animals such as deer, the killing of which by an unauthorized person became a capital offense in the eighteenth century. By law, only persons owning a particular amount of landed property could hunt these animals. Excluded from the right to hunt were all persons renting land, wealthy city merchants who did not own land, and poor people in cities, villages, and the countryside. The poor were excluded because the elite believed that allowing them to enjoy the sport of hunting would undermine their work habits. The city merchants were excluded because the landed gentry in Parliament wanted to demonstrate visibly and legally the superiority of landed wealth over commercial wealth. Thus, the various game laws upheld the superior status of the aristocracy and the landed gentry.

The game laws were a prime example of legislation related directly to economic and social status. The gentry who benefited from the laws and whose parliamentary representatives had passed them also served as the local justices of the peace who enforced the laws and punished their violation. The justices of the peace could levy fines and even have poachers impressed into the army. Gentry could also take civil legal action against wealthier poachers, such as rich farmers who rented land, and thus saddle them with immense legal fees. The gentry also employed gamekeepers to protect game from poachers. The gamekeepers were known to kill the dogs belonging to people suspected of poaching. By the middle of the century, gamekeepers had devised guns to shoot poachers who tripped their hidden levers.

A small industry arose to circumvent the game laws, however. Many poor people living either on an estate or in a nearby village would kill game for food. They believed the game actually belonged to the community, and this poaching increased during hard times. Poaching was thus one way for the poor to find food.

Even more important was the black market in game animals that the demand in the cities for this kind of luxury meat sustained. This created the possibility of poaching for profit, and, indeed, poaching technically meant stealing or killing game for sale. Local people from both the countryside and the villages would steal the game and then sell it to intermediaries called *higglers*. Later, coachmen took over this function. The higglers and the coachmen would smuggle the game into the cities, where poulterers would sell it at a premium price. Everyone involved made a bit of money along the way. During the second half of the century, English aristocrats began to construct large game preserves. The rural poor, who had lost their rights to communal land as a result of its enclosure by the large landowners, resented these preserves, which soon became hunting grounds to organized gangs of poachers.

Penalties against poaching increased in the 1790s after the outbreak of the French Revolution, but so did the amount of poaching as the economic hardships increased. Britain's participation in the wars of the era put a greater burden on poor people as the demand for food in English cities grew along with their population. By the 1820s, both landowners and reformers called for a change in the law. In 1831, Parliament rewrote the game laws, retaining the landowners' possession of the game, but permitting them to allow other people to hunt it. Poaching continued, but the exclusive right of the landed classes to hunt game had ended.

▼ Family Structures and the Family Economy

In preindustrial Europe, the household was the basic unit of production and consumption. Few productive establishments employed more than a handful of people not belonging to the family of the owner, and those rare exceptions were in cities. Most Europeans, however, lived in rural areas. There, as well as in small towns and cities, the household mode of organization predominated on farms, in artisans' workshops, and in small merchants' shops. With that mode of economic organization, there developed what is known as the **family economy**. Its structure, as described here, had prevailed over most of Europe for centuries.

During the seventeenth century the French Le Nain brothers painted scenes of French peasant life. Although the images softened many of the harsh realities of peasant existence, the clothing and the interiors were based on actual models and convey the character of the life of better-off French peasants whose lives would have continued very much the same into the eighteenth century. Erich Lessing/Art Resource, NY

Households

What was a household in the preindustrial Europe of the Old Regime? There were two basic models, one characterizing northwestern Europe and the other eastern Europe.

Northwestern Europe In northwestern Europe, the household almost invariably consisted of a married couple, their children through their early teenage years, and their servants. Except for the few wealthy people, households usually consisted of not more than five or six members. Furthermore, in these households, more than two generations of a family rarely lived under the same roof. High mortality and late marriage prevented a formation of families of three generations or more. In other words, grandparents rarely lived in the same household as their grandchildren, and families consisted of parents and children. The family structure of northwestern Europe was thus nuclear rather than extended.

Historians used to assume that before industrialization Europeans lived in extended familial settings, with several generations living together in a household.

Demographic investigation has now sharply reversed this picture. Children lived with their parents only until their early teens. Then they normally left home, usually to enter the workforce of young servants who lived and worked in another household. A child of a skilled artisan might remain with his or her parents to learn a valuable skill; but only rarely would more than one child do so, because children earned more working outside the home.

Those young men and women who had left home would eventually marry and form their own independent households. This practice of moving away from home is known as *neolocalism*. These young people married relatively late. Men were usually over twenty-six, and women over twenty-three. The new couple usually had children as soon after marriage as possible. Frequently, the woman was already pregnant at marriage. Family and community pressure often compelled the man to marry her. In any case, premarital sexual relations were common. The new couple would soon employ a servant, who, together with their growing children, would undertake whatever form of livelihood the household used to support itself.

The word *servant* in this context does not refer to someone looking after the needs of wealthy people. Rather, in preindustrial Europe, a servant was a person—either male or female—who was hired, often under a clear contract, to work for the head of the household in exchange for room, board, and wages. The servant was usually young and by no means always socially inferior to his or her employer. Normally, the servant was an integral part of the household and ate with the family.

Young men and women became servants when their labor was no longer needed in their parents' household or when they could earn more money for their family outside the parental household. Being a servant for several years—often as many as eight or ten years—allowed young people to acquire the productive skills and the monetary savings necessary to begin their own household. These years spent as servants largely account for the late age of marriage in northwestern Europe.

Eastern Europe As one moved eastward across the Continent, the structure of the household and the pattern of marriage changed. In eastern Europe, both men and women usually married before the age of twenty. Consequently, children were born to much younger parents. Often—especially among Russian serfs—wives were older than their husbands. Eastern European households were generally larger than those in the West. Frequently a rural Russian household consisted of more than nine, and possibly more than twenty, members, with three or perhaps even four generations of the same family living together. Early marriage made this situation more likely. In Russia, marrying involved not starting a new household, but remaining in and expanding one already established.

The landholding structure in eastern Europe accounts, at least in part, for these patterns of marriage and the family. The lords of the manor who owned land wanted to ensure that it would be cultivated, so they could receive their rents. Thus, in Poland, for example, landlords might forbid marriage between their own serfs and those from another estate. They might also require widows and widowers to remarry to ensure adequate labor for a particular plot of land. Polish landlords also frowned on the hiring of free laborers—the equivalent of servants in the West—to help cultivate land. The landlords preferred to use other serfs. This practice inhibited the formation of independent households. In Russia, landlords ordered the families of young people in their villages to arrange marriages within a short set time. These lords discouraged single-generation family households because the death or serious illness of one person in such a household might mean the land assigned to it would go out of cultivation.

The Family Economy

Throughout Europe, most people worked within the family economy. That is to say, the household was the basic unit of production and consumption. Almost everyone lived within a household of some kind because it was virtually impossible for ordinary people to support themselves independently. Indeed, except for members of religious orders, people living outside a household were viewed with great suspicion. They were considered potentially criminal, disruptive, or at least dependent on the charity of others. Everywhere beggars met deep hostility.

Depending on their ages and skills, everyone in the household worked. The need to survive poor harvests or economic slumps meant that no one could be idle. Within this family economy, all goods and income produced went to the benefit of the household rather than to the individual family member. On a farm, much of the effort went directly into raising food or producing other agricultural goods that could be exchanged for food. Few Western Europeans, however, had enough land to support their household from farming alone. Thus, one or more family members might work elsewhere and send wages home; for example, the father and older children might work as harvesters, fishermen, or engage in other labor either in the neighborhood or farther from home. If the father was such a migrant worker, his wife and their younger children would have to work the family farm. This was not an uncommon pattern.

The family economy also dominated the life of skilled urban artisans. The father was usually the chief artisan. He normally employed one or more servants but would expect his children to work in the enterprise also. He usually trained his eldest child in the trade. His wife often sold his wares or opened a small shop of her own. Wives of merchants also frequently ran their husbands' businesses, especially when the husband traveled to purchase new goods. In any case, everyone in the family was involved. If business was poor, family members would look for employment elsewhere—not to support themselves as individuals, but to ensure the survival of the family unit.

In Western Europe, the death of a father often brought disaster to the household. The continuing economic life of the family usually depended on his land or skills. The widow might take on the farm or the business, or his children might do so. The widow usually sought to remarry quickly to restore the labor and skills of a male to the household and to prevent herself from becoming dependent on relatives or charity.

The high mortality rate of the time meant that many households were reconstituted second-family groups that included stepchildren. Because of the advanced age of the widow or economic hard times, however, some households might simply dissolve. The widow became dependent on charity or relatives. The children became similarly dependent or entered the workforce as servants earlier than they would have otherwise. In other cases, the situation could be so desperate that they would resort to crime or to begging. The personal, emotional, and economic vulnerability of the family cannot be overemphasized.

In Eastern Europe, the family economy functioned in the context of serfdom and landlord domination. Peasants clearly thought in terms of their families and expanding the land available for cultivation. The village structure may have mitigated the pressures of the family economy, as did the multigenerational family. Dependence on the available land was the chief fact of life. There were many fewer artisan and merchant households, and there was far less geographical mobility than in Western Europe.

Women and the Family Economy

The family economy established many of the chief constraints on the lives and personal experiences of women in preindustrial society. Most of the historical research that has been undertaken on this subject relates to Western Europe. There, a woman's life experience was largely the function of her capacity to establish and maintain a household. For women, marriage was an economic necessity, as well as an institution that fulfilled sexual and psychological needs. Outside a household, a woman's life was vulnerable and precarious. Some women became economically independent, but they were the exception. Normally, unless she were an aristocrat or a member of a religious order, a woman probably could not support herself solely by her own efforts. Consequently, a woman devoted much of her life first to maintaining her parents' household and then to devising some means of getting her own household to live in as an adult. Bearing and rearing children were usually subordinate to these goals.

By the age of seven, a girl would have begun to help with the household work. On a farm, this might mean looking after chickens, watering the animals, or carrying food to the adults working the land. In an urban artisan's household, she would do light work, perhaps cleaning or carrying, and later sewing or weaving. The girl would remain in her parents' home as long as she made a real contribution to the family enterprise or as long as her labor elsewhere was not more remunerative to the family.

An artisan's daughter might not leave home until marriage, because at home she could learn increasingly valuable skills associated with the trade. The situation was different for the much larger number of girls growing up on farms. Their parents and brothers could often do all the necessary farm work, and a girl's labor at home quickly became of little value to her family. She would then leave home, usually between the age of twelve and fourteen years. She might take up residence on another farm, but more likely she would migrate to a nearby town or city. She would rarely travel more than thirty miles from her parents' household. She would then normally become a servant, once again living in a household, but this time in the household of an employer. Having left home, the young woman's chief goal was to accumulate enough capital for a dowry. Her savings would make her eligible for marriage because they would allow her to make the necessary contribution to form a household with her husband. Marriage within the family economy was a joint economic undertaking, and the wife was expected to make an immediate contribution of capital to establish the household. A young woman might well work for ten years or more to accumulate a dowry. This practice meant that marriage was usually postponed until her mid- to late twenties.

Within marriage, earning enough money or producing enough farm goods to ensure an adequate food supply dominated women's concerns. Domestic duties, childbearing, and childrearing were subordinate to economic pressures. Consequently, couples tried to limit the number of children they had, usually through the practice of *coitus interruptus*, the withdrawal of the male before ejaculation.

The work of married women differed markedly between city and country and was in many ways a function of their husbands' occupations. If the peasant household had enough land to support itself, the wife spent much of her time literally carrying things for her husband—water, food, seed, harvested grain, and the like. Such landholdings, however, were few. If the husband had to do work besides farming, such as fishing or migrant labor, the wife might actually be in charge of the farm and do the plowing, planting, and harvesting. In the city, the wife of an artisan or a merchant might be in charge of the household finances and help manage the business. When her husband died, she might take over the business and perhaps hire an artisan. Finally, if economic disaster struck the family, it was usually the wife who organized what Olwen Hufton has called the "economy of expedients,"[1] within which family members might be sent off to find work elsewhere or even to beg in the streets.

Despite all this economic activity, women found many occupations and professions closed to them because they were female. They labored with less education than men because in such a society women at all levels of life consistently found fewer opportunities for education than did men. They often received lower wages than men for the same work. The mechanization of agriculture and the textile industries, which is discussed later in this chapter, made these disabilities worse.

Children and the World of the Family Economy

For women of all social ranks, childbirth meant fear and vulnerability. Contagious diseases endangered both mother and child. Puerperal fever was frequent, as were other infections from unsterilized medical instruments. Not all midwives were skillful practitioners. Furthermore, most mothers gave birth in conditions of immense poverty and wretched housing. Assuming both mother and child survived, the mother might nurse the infant, but often the child would be sent to a wet nurse. The wealthy may have done this for convenience, but economic necessity dictated it for the poor. The structures and customs of the family economy did not permit a

[1]Olwen Hufton, "Women and the Family Economy in Eighteenth-Century France," *French Historical Studies* 9 (1976), p. 19.

woman to devote herself entirely to rearing a child. The wet-nursing industry was well organized, with urban children being frequently transported to wet nurses in the country, where they would remain for months or even years.

The birth of a child was not always welcome. The child might represent another economic burden on an already hard-pressed household, or it might be illegitimate. The number of illegitimate births seems to have increased during the eighteenth century, possibly because increased migration of the population led to fleeting romances.

Through at least the end of the seventeenth century, unwanted or illegitimate births could lead to infanticide, especially among the poor. The parents might smother the infant or expose it to the elements. These practices were one result of both the ignorance and the prejudice surrounding contraception.

The late seventeenth and the early eighteenth centuries saw a new interest in preserving the lives of abandoned children. Although foundling hospitals established to care for abandoned children had existed before, their size and number expanded during these years. Two of the most famous were the Paris Foundling Hospital (1670) and the London Foundling Hospital (1739). Such hospitals cared for thousands of children, and the demand for their services increased during the eighteenth century. For example, early in the century, an average of 1,700 children a year were admitted to the Paris Foundling Hospital. In the peak year of 1772, however, that number rose to 7,676 children. Not all of those children came from Paris. Many had been brought to the city from the provinces, where local foundling homes and hospitals were overburdened. The London Foundling Hospital lacked the income to deal with all the children brought to it. In the middle of the eighteenth century, the hospital found itself compelled to choose children for admission by a lottery system.

Sadness and tragedy surrounded abandoned children. Most of them were illegitimate infants from across the social spectrum. Many, however, were left with the foundling hospitals because their parents could not support them. There was a close relationship between rising food prices and increasing numbers of abandoned children in Paris. Parents would sometimes leave personal tokens or saints' medals on the abandoned baby in the vain hope they might one day be able to reclaim the child. Few children were reclaimed. Leaving a child at a foundling hospital did not guarantee its survival. In Paris, only about 10 percent of all abandoned children lived to the age of ten.

Despite all of these perils of early childhood, children did grow up and come of age across Europe. The world of the child may not have received the kind of attention it does today, but during the eighteenth century, the seeds of that modern sensibility were sown.

Particularly among the upper classes, new interest arose in educating children. In most areas, education remained firmly in the hands of the churches. As economic skills became more demanding, literacy became more valuable, and literacy rates rose during the century. Yet most Europeans remained illiterate. Not until the late nineteenth century was the world of childhood inextricably linked to the process of education. Then children would be reared to become members of a national citizenry. In the Old Regime, they were reared to make their contribution to the economy of their parents' family and then to set up their own households.

▼ The Revolution in Agriculture

Thus far, this chapter has examined those groups that sought stability and that, except for certain members of the nobility, resisted change. Other groups, however, wished to pursue significant new directions in social and economic life. The remainder of the chapter considers those forces and developments that would transform European life during the next century. These developments first appeared in agriculture.

The main goal of traditional peasant society was a stability that would ensure the local food supply. Despite differences in rural customs across Europe, the tillers resisted changes that might endanger the sure supply of food, which they generally believed traditional methods of cultivation would provide. The food supply was never certain, and the farther east one traveled, the more uncertain it became. Failure of the harvest meant not only hardship, but also death from either outright starvation or malnutrition. People living in the countryside often had more difficulty finding food than did city dwellers, whose local government usually stored reserve supplies of grain.

Poor harvests also played havoc with prices. Smaller supplies or larger demand raised grain prices. Even small increases in the cost of food could exert heavy pressure on peasant or artisan families. If prices increased sharply, many of those families fell back on poor relief from their local government or the church.

Historians now believe that during the eighteenth century bread prices slowly but steadily rose, spurred largely by population growth. Since bread was their main food, this inflation put pressure on the poor. Prices rose faster than urban wages and brought no appreciable advantage to the small peasant producer. However, the rise in grain prices benefited landowners and those wealthier peasants who had surplus grain to sell.

The rising grain prices gave landlords an opportunity to improve their incomes and lifestyle. To achieve those ends, landlords in Western Europe began a series

The English agricultural improver Jethro Tull devised this seed drill, which increased wheat crops by planting seed deep in the soil rather than just casting it randomly on the surface. Image Works/Mary Evans Picture Library Ltd.

of innovations in farm production that became known as the **Agricultural Revolution.** Landlords commercialized agriculture and thereby challenged the traditional peasant ways of production. Peasant revolts and disturbances often resulted. The governments of Europe, hungry for new taxes and dependent on the goodwill of the nobility, used their armies and militias to smash peasants who defended traditional practices.

New Crops and New Methods

The drive to improve agricultural production began during the sixteenth and seventeenth centuries in the Low Countries, where the pressures of the growing population and the shortage of land required changes in cultivation. Dutch landlords and farmers devised better ways to build dikes and to drain land so they could farm more land. They also experimented with new crops, such as clover and turnips, that would increase the supply of animal fodder and restore the soil. These improvements became so famous that early in the seventeenth century English landlords hired Cornelius Vermuyden, a Dutch engineer, to drain thousands of acres of land around Cambridge.

⊙ **View** the **Image**
"Diderot's Encyclopedia—
Plate Illustrating
Agricultural Techniques"
on **MyHistoryLab.com**

English landlords provided the most striking examples of eighteenth-century agricultural improvement. They originated almost no genuinely new farming methods, but they popularized ideas developed in the previous century either in the Low Countries or in England. Some of these landlords and agricultural innovators became famous. For example, Jethro Tull (1674–1741) was willing to conduct experiments himself and to finance the experiments of others. Many of his ideas, such as the

rejection of manure as fertilizer, were wrong. Others, however, such as using iron plows to turn the earth more deeply and planting wheat by a drill rather than by just casting seeds, were excellent. His methods permitted land to be cultivated for longer periods without having to leave it fallow.

Charles "Turnip" Townsend (1674–1738) encouraged other important innovations. He learned from the Dutch how to cultivate sandy soil with fertilizers. He also instituted crop rotation, using wheat, turnips, barley, and clover. This new system of rotation replaced the fallow field with one sown with a crop that both restored nutrients to the soil and supplied animal fodder. The additional fodder meant that more livestock could be raised. These fodders allowed animals to be fed during the winter and assured a year-round supply of meat. The larger number of animals increased the quantity of manure available as fertilizer for the grain crops. Consequently, in the long run, both animals and human beings had more food.

A third British agricultural improver was Robert Bakewell (1725–1795), who pioneered new methods of animal breeding that produced more and better animals and more milk and meat. These and other innovations received widespread discussion in the works of Arthur Young (1741–1820), who edited the *Annals of Agriculture*. In 1793, he became secretary of the British Board of Agriculture. Young traveled widely across Europe, and his books are among the most important documents of life during the late eighteenth century.

Enclosure Replaces Open-Field Method Many of the agricultural innovations, which were adopted only slowly, were incompatible with the existing organization of land in England. Small cultivators who lived in village communities still farmed most of the soil. Each farmer tilled an assortment of unconnected strips. The two- or three-field systems of rotation left large portions of land fallow and unproductive each year. Animals grazed on the common land in the summer and on the stubble of the harvest in the winter. Until at least the mid-eighteenth century, the whole community decided what crops to plant. The entire system discouraged improvement and favored the poorer farmers, who needed the common land and stubble fields for their animals. The village method precluded expanding pastureland to raise more animals that would, in turn, produce more manure for fertilizer. Thus, the methods of traditional production aimed at a steady, but not a growing, supply of food.

In 1700, approximately half the arable land in England was farmed by this open-field method. By the second half of the century, the rising price of wheat encouraged landlords to consolidate or enclose their lands to increase production. The **enclosures** were intended to use land more rationally and to achieve greater commercial profits. The process involved the fencing of common lands, the reclamation of previously untilled waste, and the transformation of strips into block fields. These procedures brought turmoil to the economic and social life of the countryside. Riots often ensued.

View the **Map** "Map Discovery: English Common Lands Enclosed by Acts of Parliament, 1700–1850" on **MyHistoryLab.com**

Because many English farmers either owned their strips or rented them in a manner that amounted to ownership, the larger landlords usually resorted to parliamentary acts to legalize the enclosure of the land, which they owned but rented to the farmers. Because the large landowners controlled Parliament, such measures passed easily. Between 1761 and 1792, almost 500,000 acres were enclosed through acts of Parliament, compared with 75,000 acres between 1727 and 1760. In 1801, a general enclosure act streamlined the process.

The enclosures were controversial at the time and have remained so among historians. They permitted the extension of both farming and innovation and thus increased food production on larger agricultural units. They also disrupted small traditional communities; they forced off the land independent farmers, who had needed the common pasturage, and poor cottage dwellers, who had lived on the reclaimed wasteland. The enclosures, however, did not depopulate the countryside. In some counties where the enclosures took place, the population increased. New soil had come into production, and services that supported farming also expanded.

The enclosures did not create the labor force for the British Industrial Revolution. What the enclosures most conspicuously displayed was the introduction of the entrepreneurial or capitalistic attitude of the urban merchant into the countryside. This commercialization of agriculture, which spread from Britain slowly across the Continent during the next century, strained the paternal relationship between the governing and governed classes. Previously, landlords had often looked after the welfare of the lower orders through price controls or waivers of rent during hard times. As the landlords became increasingly concerned about profits, they began to leave the peasants to the mercy of the marketplace.

Limited Improvements in Eastern Europe Improving agriculture tended to characterize farm production west of the Elbe River. Dutch farming was efficient. In France, despite the efforts of the government to improve agriculture, enclosures were restricted. Yet many people in France wanted to improve agricultural methods. These new procedures benefited the ruling classes because better agriculture increased their incomes and assured a larger food supply, which discouraged social unrest. (See "Compare and Connect: Two Eighteenth-Century Writers Contemplate the Effects of Different Economic Structures," pages 462–463.)

In Prussia, Austria, Poland, and Russia, agricultural improvement was limited. Nothing in the relationship of the serfs to their lords encouraged innovation. In eastern Europe, the chief method of increasing production was to bring previously untilled lands under the plow. The landlords or their agents, and not the villages, normally directed farm management. By extending tillage, the great landlords sought to squeeze more labor from their serfs, rather than greater productivity from the soil. Eastern European landlords, like their western counterparts, sought to increase their profits, but they were less ambitious and successful. The only significant nutritional gain they achieved was the introduction of maize and the potato. Livestock production did not increase significantly.

Expansion of the Population

The population explosion with which the entire world must contend today had its origins in the eighteenth century. Before that time, Europe's population had experienced dramatic increases, but plagues, wars, or famine had redressed the balance. Beginning in the second quarter of the eighteenth century, the population began to increase steadily. The need to feed this population caused food prices to rise, which spurred agricultural innovation. The need to provide everyday consumer goods for the expanding numbers of people fueled the demand side of the Industrial Revolution.

In 1700, Europe's population, excluding the European provinces of the Ottoman Empire, was probably between 100 million and 120 million people. By 1800, the figures had risen to almost 190 million and by 1850, to 260 million. The population of England and Wales rose from 6 million in 1750 to more than 10 million in 1800. France grew from 18 million in 1715 to about 26 million in 1789. Russia's population increased from 19 million in 1722 to 29 million in 1766. Such extraordinary sustained growth put new demands on all resources and considerable pressure on the existing social organization.

View the **Map** "Map Discovery: Population Growth in Europe, 1800–1850" on **MyHistoryLab.com**

The population expansion occurred across the Continent in both the country and the cities. Only a limited consensus exists among scholars about the causes of this growth. The death rate clearly declined. There were fewer wars and epidemics in the eighteenth century. Hygiene and sanitation also improved. Better medical knowledge and techniques, however, did not contribute much to the decline in deaths. The more important medical advances came after the initial population explosion and would not have affected it directly.

Instead, changes in the food supply itself may have allowed population growth to be sustained. Improved and expanding grain production made one contribution.

Two Eighteenth-Century Writers Contemplate the Effects of Different Economic Structures

📖 Read the **Compare and Connect** on **MyHistoryLab.com**

AMONG EIGHTEENTH-CENTURY public officials and commentators there existed a broad agreement that European economic life needed to be reorganized and stimulated to achieve greater productivity and wealth. These writers also understood that different modes of productive activity resulted in very different kinds of society. In these two documents a French writer bemoans problems of French agriculture and landholding while a Scottish writer praises the wealth and good society that flow from growing commerce and refinement of both mechanical and liberal arts.

QUESTIONS

1. Why does Turgot favor those farmers who can make investments in the land they rent from a proprietor?

2. What are the structures of the métayer system? Why did it lead to poor investments and lower harvests?

3. Why does Hume link industry and the arts?

4. How does he see a commercial, improving economy producing important intellectual outlooks and social skills?

5. What benefits to agriculture might Hume have assigned to prosperous cities, and what benefits might Turgot have seen agriculture contributing to urban life?

I. Turgot Decries French Landholding

During the eighteenth century, many observers became keenly aware that different kinds of landholding led to different attitudes toward work and to different levels of production and wealth. Robert Jacques Turgot (1727–1781), who later became finance minister of France, analyzed these differences in an effort to reform French agriculture. He was especially concerned with arrangements that encouraged long-term investment. The métayer system Turgot discusses was an arrangement whereby landowners had land farmed by peasants who received part of the harvest as payment for working the land, but the peasant had no long-term interest in improving the land. Virtually all observers regarded the system as inefficient.

The real and fundamental distinction between the areas of large-scale cultivation and those where farming is done only on a small scale is that in the former, the landowners make deals with *fermiers* or tenant farmers who promise them a fixed payment for their land in exchange for the right to cultivate it during a certain number of years. These tenant farmers are responsible for all the expenses of cultivation, ploughing, seeds, and for stocking the farm with cattle, other animals, and tools. These tenant farmers are true agricultural entrepreneurs; like all other entrepreneurs, they have their own capital, which they use to make a profit by cultivating land . . .

[The demand for land that makes it valuable is a result of] this indispensable kind of men who have not only their own labor, but capital to consecrate to agriculture, and who have no other occupation except to work the land, not to earn their living by the sweat of their brow as workers do, but to use their capital in a profitable way, like the shipowners of Nantes and Bordeaux who use theirs in overseas commerce. . . .

[The sharecropping system]: The regions of small-scale agriculture, which is to say at least four-sevenths of the land in the kingdom, are areas where there are no agricultural entrepreneurs, where a landowner who wants to profit from his land can only find unfortunate peasants who have no resources except their own labor, where he has to use his own money for all the expenses of growing crops, livestock, tools, seeds, and even to lend his *métayer* (sharecropper) enough to feed himself until the first harvest. In this situation, a landowner who has no resources other than his land, would have to leave it unplanted . . .

After having deducted the cost of seed and of any interest payments due on the land, the landowner and the sharecropper divide what is left of the profits, according to the agreement they have made. The landowner, who has advanced all the money, runs all the risks of loss due to harvest failures and the loss of animals; he is the only real agricultural entrepreneur. The sharecropper is just a workman, a farmhand whom he pays with a share of the profits instead of wages. But this kind of landowner doesn't have the same advantages as the entrepreneurial farmer, who directs everything himself with attention and intelligence. The landowner has to trust all the money he advances to a man who may be negligent or dishonest, and who can't be held responsible for anything.

This kind of sharecropper, accustomed to most meager existence and without any hope or even any desire of improving his condition, farms badly and doesn't even try to use the land for products that can be sold for the best profit. He prefers to grow things that take less work and that he can consume himself, such as buckwheat and especially chestnuts, which only have to be collected. He doesn't even worry about not having enough to eat; he knows that, if the harvest fails, his master will have to feed him to avoid having to abandon his land. ■

From *Œuvres, et documents les concernant*, by Robert Jacques Turgot, ed. by F, Schelle, 5 vols. (Paris, 1914), Vol. II, pp. 448–450. Translated by Jeremy D. Popkin.

This is the detail of a 1739 map by Louis Bretez, a member of the Academy of Painting and Sculpture, showing an aerial view of the city of Paris. The primary function of the map was to reestablish Paris as the universal model of a capital city.   Library of Congress

II. David Hume Praises Luxury and the Refinement of the Arts

David Hume (1711–1776) was a Scottish philosopher, historian, and economic commentator. He was deeply committed to the modernization of the Scottish and wider European economy through the growth of commerce and the fostering of improved means of mechanical production. In this essay published in 1752 he outlined the beneficial social consequence he saw resulting from commercial wealth and new mechanical inventions. He believed such economic activity not only increased riches but also produced a population capable of providing a national defense. He was quite concerned to demonstrate that luxury and the economy that fostered it would not lead to moral decay.

In times when industry and the arts flourish, men are kept in perpetual occupation, and enjoy, as their reward, the occupation itself, as well as those pleasures which are the fruit of their labour. The mind acquires new vigour; enlarges its powers and faculties; and by an assiduity in honest industry, both satisfies its natural appetites, and prevents the growth of unnatural ones, which commonly spring up, when nourished by ease and idleness. . . .

Another advantage of industry and of refinements in the mechanical arts, is, that they commonly produce some refinements in the liberal; nor can one be carried to perfection, without being accompanied, in some degree, with the other. . . .

The more these refined arts advance, the more sociable men become. . . . They flock into cities; love to receive and communicate knowledge; to show their wit or their breeding; their taste in conversation or living, in clothes or furniture. Curiosity allures the wise; vanity the foolish, and pleasure both. Particular clubs and societies are everywhere formed: Both sexes meet in an easy and sociable manner: and the tempers of men, as well as their behaviour, refine apace. So that, beside the improvements which they receive from knowledge and the liberal arts, it is impossible but they must feel an encrease of humanity, from the very habit of conversing together, and contributing to each other's pleasure and entertainment. Thus *industry*, *knowledge*, and *humanity*, are linked together by an indissoluble chain, and are found, from experience as well as reason, to be peculiar to the more polished, and, what are commonly denominated, the more luxurious ages. . . .

But industry, knowledge, and humanity are not advantageous in private life alone: They diffuse their beneficial influence on the *public*, and render the government as great and flourishing as they make individuals happy and prosperous. The encrease and consumption of all the commodities . . . are advantageous to society; because . . . they are a kind of *storehouse* of labour, which, in the exigencies of state, may be turned to the public service. In a nation, where there is no demand for such superfluities, men sink into indolence, lose all enjoyment of life, and are useless to the public, which cannot maintain or support its fleets and armies, from the industry of such slothful members. ■

From David Hume, "Of Refinement in the Arts (1752)," in *Essays: Moral, Political and Literary* (Indianapolis, IN: Liberty Classics, 1985), pp. 270–272.

Another and even more important change was the cultivation of the potato. This tuber was a product of the New World and came into widespread European production during the eighteenth century. (See "The West & The World," page 509.) On a single acre, a peasant family could grow enough potatoes to feed itself for an entire year. This more certain food supply enabled more children to survive to adulthood and rear children of their own.

The impact of the population explosion can hardly be overestimated. It created new demands for food, goods, jobs, and services. It provided a new pool of labor. Traditional modes of production and living had to be revised. More people lived in the countryside than could find employment there. Migration increased. There were also more people who might become socially and politically discontented. Because the population growth fed on itself, these pressures and demands continued to increase. The society and the social practices of the Old Regime literally outgrew their traditional bounds.

▼ The Industrial Revolution of the Eighteenth Century

The second half of the eighteenth century witnessed the beginning of the industrialization of the European economy. That achievement of sustained economic growth is termed the **Industrial Revolution**. Previously, the economy of a province or a country might grow, but growth soon reached a plateau. Since the late eighteenth century, however, the economy of Europe has managed to expand at an almost uninterrupted pace. Depressions and recessions have been temporary, and even during such economic downturns, the Western economy has continued to grow.

At considerable social cost, industrialization made possible the production of more goods and services than ever before in human history. Industrialization in Europe eventually overcame the economy of scarcity. The new means of production demanded new kinds of skills, new discipline in work, and a large labor force. The goods produced met immediate consumer demand and also created new demands. In the long run, industrialization raised the standard of living and overcame the poverty that most Europeans, who lived during the eighteenth century and earlier, had taken for granted. It gave human beings greater control over nature than they had

ever known before; yet by the mid-nineteenth century, industrialism would also cause new and unanticipated problems with the environment.

During the eighteenth century, people did not call these economic developments a *revolution*. That term came to be applied to the British economic phenomena only after the French Revolution. Then continental writers observed that what had taken place in Britain was the economic equivalent of the political events in France, hence an Industrial Revolution. It was revolutionary less in its speed, which was on the whole rather slow, than in its implications for the future of European society.

A Revolution in Consumption

The most familiar side of the Industrial Revolution was the invention of new machinery, the establishment of factories, and the creation of a new kind of workforce. Recent studies, however, have emphasized the demand side of the process and the vast increase in both the desire and the possibility of consuming goods and services that arose in the early eighteenth century.

The inventions of the Industrial Revolution increased the supply of consumer goods as never before in history. The supply of goods was only one side of the economic equation, however. An unprecedented demand for the humble goods of everyday life created the supply. Those

Consumption of all forms of consumer goods increased greatly in the eighteenth century. This engraving illustrates a shop, probably in Paris. Here women, working apparently for a woman manager, are making dresses and hats to meet the demands of the fashion trade. As the document on page 471 demonstrates, some women writers urged more such employment opportunities for women. Bildarchiv Preussischer Kulturbesitz goods included clothing, buttons, toys, china, furniture, rugs, kitchen utensils, candlesticks, brassware, silverware, pewterware, glassware, watches, jewelry, soap, beer, wines, and foodstuffs. It was the ever-increasing demand for these goods that sparked the ingenuity of designers and inventors. Furthermore, consumer demand seemed unlimited. (See the "Compare and Connect: Two Eighteenth-Century Writers Contemplate the Effects of Different Economic Structures," pages 462–463.)

Many social factors helped establish the markets for these consumer goods. During the seventeenth century, the Dutch had enjoyed enormous prosperity and had led the way in new forms of consumption. For reasons that are still not clear, during the eighteenth century, first the English and then the people on the Continent came to have more disposable income. This wealth may have resulted from the improvements in agriculture. Those incomes allowed people to buy consumer goods that previous generations had inherited or did not possess. What is key to this change in consumption is that it depended primarily on expanding the various domestic markets in Europe.

This revolution, if that is not too strong a term, in consumption was not automatic. People became persuaded that they needed or wanted new consumer goods. Often, entrepreneurs caused it to happen by developing new methods of marketing. For example, English porcelain manufacturer Josiah Wedgwood (1730–1795) first attempted to find customers among the royal family and the aristocracy. Once he had gained their business with luxury goods, he then produced a less expensive version of the chinaware for middle-class customers. He also used advertising, opened showrooms in London, and sent salespeople all over Britain with samples and catalogs of his wares. On the Continent, his salespeople used bilingual catalogs. There seemed to be no limit to the markets for consumer goods that social emulation on the one hand and advertising on the other could stimulate.

Furthermore, the process of change in style itself became institutionalized. New fashions and inventions were always better than old ones. If new kinds of goods could be produced, there usually was a market for them. If one product did not find a market, its failure provided a lesson for how to develop a different new product.

This expansion of consumption quietly, but steadily, challenged the social assumptions of the day. Fashion publications made all levels of society aware of new styles. Clothing fashions could be copied. Servants could begin to dress well if not luxuriously. Changes in the consumption of food and drink demanded new kinds of dishware for the home. Tea and coffee became staples. The brewing industry became fully commercialized. Those developments entailed the need for new kinds of cups and mugs and many more of them.

There would always be critics of this consumer economy. The vision of luxury and comfort it offered contrasted with the asceticism of ancient Sparta and contemporary Christian ethics. Yet, the ever-increasing consumption and production of the goods of everyday life became hallmarks of modern Western society from the eighteenth century to our own day. It would be difficult to overestimate the importance of the desire for consumer goods and the higher standard of living that they made possible in Western history after the eighteenth century. The presence and accessibility of such goods became the hallmark of a nation's prosperity. It was the absence of such consumer goods, as well as of civil liberties, that during the 1980s led to such deep discontent with the communist regimes in Eastern Europe and the former Soviet Union.

Industrial Leadership of Great Britain

Great Britain was the home of the Industrial Revolution and, until the middle of the nineteenth century, remained the industrial leader of Europe. Several factors contributed to the early start in Britain.

View the **Map** "Map Discovery: Concentrations of Industry in Great Britain, 1750–1820" on **MyHistoryLab.com**

Great Britain took the lead in the **consumer revolution** that expanded the demand for goods that could be efficiently supplied. London was the largest city in Europe. It was the center of a world of fashion and taste to which hundreds of thousands, if not millions, of British citizens were exposed each year. In London, these people learned to want the consumer goods they saw on visits for business and pleasure. Newspapers thrived in Britain during the eighteenth century, and the advertising they printed increased consumer wants. The social structure of Britain encouraged people to imitate the lifestyles of their social superiors. It seems to have been in Britain that a world of fashion first developed that led people to want to accumulate goods. In addition to the domestic consumer demand, the British economy benefited from demand from the colonies in North America.

Britain was also the single largest free-trade area in Europe. The British had good roads and waterways without internal tolls or other trade barriers. The country had rich deposits of coal and iron ore. Its political structure was stable, and property was absolutely secure. The sound systems of banking and public credit established a stable climate for investment. Taxation in Britain was heavy, but it was efficiently and fairly collected, largely from indirect taxes. Furthermore, British taxes received legal approval through Parliament, with all social classes and all regions of the nation paying the same taxes. In contrast to the Continent, there was no pattern of privileged tax exemptions.

Finally, British society was mobile by the standards of the time. Persons who had money or could earn it could rise socially. The British aristocracy would receive into its ranks people who had amassed large fortunes. Even persons of wealth who did not join the aristocracy could enjoy their riches, receive social recognition, and exert political influence. No one of these factors preordained the British advance toward industrialism. Together, however, when added to the progressive state of British agriculture, they provided the nation with the marginal advantage to create a new mode of economic production.

New Methods of Textile Production

The industry that pioneered the Industrial Revolution and met the growing consumer demand was the production of textiles for clothing. Textile production is the key example of industrialism emerging to supply the demands of an ever-growing market for everyday goods. Furthermore, it illustrates the surprising fact that much of the earliest industrial change took place not in cities, but in the countryside.

Although the eighteenth-century economy was primarily agricultural, manufacturing also permeated rural areas. The peasant family living in a one- or two-room cottage, rather than the factory, was the basic unit of production. The same peasants who tilled the land in spring and summer often spun thread or wove textiles in the winter.

Under what is termed the ***domestic system of textile production***, or putting-out system of textile production, agents of urban textile merchants took wool or other unfinished fibers to the homes of peasants, who spun it into thread. The agent then transported the thread to other peasants, who wove it into the finished product. The merchant sold the wares. In thousands of peasant cottages from Ireland to Austria, there stood a spinning wheel or a hand loom. Sometimes the spinners or weavers owned their own equipment, but more often than not by the middle of the century, the merchant capitalist owned the machinery as well as the raw material.

The domestic system of textile production was a basic feature of this family economy and would continue to be so in Britain and on the Continent well into the nineteenth century. By the mid-eighteenth century, however, production bottlenecks had developed within the domestic system. The demand for cotton textiles was growing more rapidly than production, especially in Britain, which had a large domestic and North American market for these goods. Inventors devised some of the most famous machines of the early Industrial Revolution to meet consumer demand for cotton textiles.

The Spinning Jenny Cotton textile weavers had the technical capacity to produce the quantity of fabric demanded. The spinners, however, did not have the

James Hargreaves's spinning jenny permitted the spinning of numerous spindles of thread on a single machine. akg-images

equipment to produce as much thread as the weavers needed. John Kay's invention of the flying shuttle, which increased the productivity of the weavers, had created this imbalance during the 1730s. Thereafter, manufacturers and merchants offered prizes for the invention of a machine to eliminate this bottleneck.

About 1765, James Hargreaves (d. 1778) invented the **spinning jenny**. Initially, this machine allowed 16 spindles of thread to be spun, but by the close of the century, it could operate 120 spindles.

The Water Frame The spinning jenny broke the bottleneck between the productive capacity of the spinners and the weavers, but it was still a piece of machinery used in the cottage. The invention that took cotton textile manufacture out of the home and put it into the factory was Richard Arkwright's (1732–1792) **water frame**, patented in 1769. This was a water-powered device designed to permit the production of a purely cotton fabric, rather than a cotton fabric containing linen fiber for durability. Eventually Arkwright lost his patent rights, and other manufacturers used his invention freely. As a result, many factories sprang up in the countryside near streams that provided the necessary water power. From the 1780s onward, the cotton industry could meet an ever-expanding demand. Cotton output increased by 800 percent between 1780 and 1800. By 1815, cotton composed 40 percent of the value of British domestic exports and by 1830, just over 50 percent.

Document

MANCHESTER'S CALICO PRINTERS PROTEST THE USE OF NEW MACHINERY

The introduction of the new machines associated with the Industrial Revolution stirred much protest. With machines able to duplicate the skills of laborers, workers feared the loss of jobs and the resulting loss of status when their chief means of livelihood lay in their possession of those displaced and now mechanized skills. The following letter was sent anonymously to a Manchester manufacturer by English workers. It shows the outrage of those workers, the intimidation they were willing to use as threats, and their own economic fears.

How might new machines adversely affect the livelihood of workers? Did the workers have other complaints against Mr. Taylor in addition to the introduction of new machinery? How have these workers reached an agreement to protect the interests of James Hobson? How do the workers combine the threat of violent actions with claims that other actions they have taken are legal?

Mr. Taylor, If you don't discharge James Hobson from the House of Correction we will burn your House about your Ears for we have sworn to stand by one another and you must immediately give over any more Mashen Work for we are determined there shall be no more of them made use of in the Trade and it will be madness for you to contend with the Trade as we are combined by Oath to fix Prices we can afford to pay him a Guinea Week and not hurt the fund if you was to keep him there till Dumsday therefore mind you comply with the above or by God we will keep our Words with you we will make some rare Bunfires in this Countey and at your Peril to call any more Meetings mind that we will make the Mosney Pepel shake in their Shoes we are determined to destroy all Sorts of Masheens for Printing in the Kingdom for there is more hands then is work for so no more from the ingerd Gurnemen Rember we are a great number sworn nor you must not advertise the Men that you say run away from you when your il Usage was the Cause of their going we will punish you for that our Meetings are legal for we want nothing but what is honest and to work for selvs and familers and you want to starve us but it is better for you and a few more which we have marked to die then such a Number of Pore Men and their famerles to be starved.

From *London Gazette*, 1786, p. 36, as reprinted in Douglas Hay, ed., *Albion's Fatal Tree* (New York: Pantheon Books, 1975), p. 318.

The Industrial Revolution had commenced in earnest by the 1780s, but the full economic and social ramifications of this unleashing of human productive capacity were not really felt until the early nineteenth century. The expansion of industry and the incorporation of new inventions often occurred slowly. For example, Edmund Cartwright (1743–1822) invented the power loom for machine weaving in the late 1780s. Yet not until the 1830s were there more power-loom weavers than hand-loom weavers in Britain. Nor did all the social ramifications of industrialism appear immediately. The first cotton mills used water power, were located in the country, and rarely employed more than two dozen workers.

Not until the late-century application of the steam engine, perfected by James Watt (1736–1819) in 1769, to run textile machinery could factories easily be located in or near urban centers. The steam engine not only vastly increased and regularized the available energy, but also made possible the combination of urbanization and industrialization.

The Steam Engine

More than any other invention, the steam engine permitted industrialization to grow on itself and to expand into one area of production after another. This machine provided for the first time in human history a steady and essentially unlimited source of inanimate power. Unlike engines powered by water or wind, the steam engine, driven by burning coal, provided a portable source of industrial power that did not fail or falter as the seasons of the year changed. Unlike human or animal power, the steam engine depended on mineral energy that never tired. Finally, the steam engine could be applied to many industrial and, eventually, transportation uses.

■ **Read** the **Document**
"James Watt on Steam Engines (mid to late 1700s)" on **MyHistoryLab.com**

Thomas Newcomen (1663–1729) in the early eighteenth century had invented the first practical engine to use steam power. When the steam that had been induced into the cylinder condensed, it caused the piston of this device to fall. The Newcomen machine was large and inefficient in its use of energy because both the condenser and the cylinder were heated, and practically untransportable. Despite these problems, English mine operators used the Newcomen machines to pump water out of coal and tin mines. By the third quarter of the eighteenth century, almost a hundred Newcomen machines were operating in the mining districts of England.

During the 1760s, James Watt, a Scottish engineer and machine maker, began to experiment with a model of a Newcomen machine at the University of Glasgow. He gradually understood that separating the condenser from the piston and the cylinder would achieve much greater efficiency. In 1769, he patented his new invention, but transforming his idea into a practical application presented difficulties. His design required precise metalwork. Watt soon found a partner in Matthew Boulton (1728–1809), a successful toy and button manufacturer in Birmingham, the city with the most skilled metalworkers in Britain. Watt and Boulton, in turn, consulted with John Wilkinson (1728–1808), a cannon manufacturer, to drill the precise metal cylinders Watt's design required. In 1776, the Watt steam engine found its first commercial application pumping water from mines in Cornwall.

The use of the steam engine spread slowly because until 1800 Watt retained the exclusive patent rights. He was also reluctant to make further changes to permit the engine to operate more rapidly. Boulton eventually persuaded him to make modifications and improvements that allowed the engines to be used not only for pumping, but also for running cotton mills. By the early nineteenth century, the steam engine had become the prime mover for all industry. With its application to ships and then to wagons on iron rails, the steam engine also revolutionized transportation.

■ **Read** the **Document**
"Richard Guest, *The Creation of the Steam Loom*" on **MyHistoryLab.com**

Newcomen's steam engine had a major impact on the growth of industrialization. 1747© The Print Collector/Alamy

Iron Production

The manufacture of high-quality iron has been basic to modern industrial development. Iron is the chief element of all heavy industry and of land or sea transport. Most productive machinery itself is also manufactured from iron. During the early eighteenth century, British ironmakers produced somewhat less than 25,000 tons of iron annually. Three factors held back the production. First, charcoal rather than coke was used to smelt the ore. Charcoal, derived from wood, was becoming scarce as forests in Britain diminished, and it does not burn at as high a temperature as coke, derived from coal. Second, until the perfection of the steam engine, furnaces could not achieve high enough blasts. Finally, the demand for iron was limited. The elimination of the first two problems also eliminated the third.

Eventually, British ironmakers began to use coke, and the steam engine provided new power for the blast furnaces. Coke was an abundant fuel because of Britain's large coal deposits. The steam engine both improved iron production and increased the demand for iron.

In 1784, Henry Cort (1740–1800) introduced a new puddling process, that is, a new method for melting and stirring molten ore. Cort's process allowed the removal

MAJOR INVENTIONS IN THE TEXTILE-MANUFACTURING REVOLUTION	
1733	John Kay's flying shuttle
1765	James Hargreaves's spinning jenny (patented 1770)
1769	James Watt's steam engine patent
1769	Richard Arkwright's water frame patent
1787	Edmund Cartwright's power loom

of more slag (the impurities that bubbled to the top of the molten metal) and thus the production of purer iron. Cort also developed a rolling mill that continuously shaped the still-molten metal into bars, rails, or other forms. Previously, the metal had to be pounded into these forms.

All these innovations achieved a better, more versatile, cheaper product. The demand for iron consequently grew. By the early nineteenth century, the British produced over a million tons annually. The lower cost of iron, in turn, lowered the cost of steam engines and allowed them to be used more widely.

View the **Architectural Simulation** "Cast Iron Construction" on **MyHistoryLab.com**

During the eighteenth century, most goods were produced in small workshops, such as this iron forge painted by Joseph Wright of Derby (1734–1797), or in the homes of artisans. Not until very late in the century, with the early stages of industrialization, did a few factories appear. In the small early workshops, it would not have been uncommon for the family of the owner to visit, as portrayed in this painting. *The Iron Forge*, 1772 (oil on canvas) by Joseph Wright of Derby (1734–1797). Broadlands Trust, Hampshire, UK/Bridgeman Art Library, London

The Impact of the Agricultural and Industrial Revolutions on Working Women

The transformation of agriculture and industry led to a series of seemingly modest changes that, taken collectively, diminished the importance and the role of those women already in the workforce.

Women had been an important part of traditional European agriculture. They worked in and often were permitted to glean the grain left over after the general harvest. Women also managed industries like milking and cheese production. However, primarily in Western Europe, increasing commercialization and mechanization eroded these traditional roles. Machinery operated by men displaced the work of women in the field and their skills in dairying and home industry, particularly in Britain. Even nonmechanized labor came to favor men. For example, during the late eighteenth century, heavy scythes wielded by men replaced the lighter sickles that women had used to harvest grain. Moreover, the drive to maximize profits led landlords to enclose lands and curtail customary rights like gleaning.

This transformation of farming constricted women's ability to earn their living from the land. Women came to be viewed as opponents of agricultural improvement because these improvements hurt them economically. As a result, proponents of the new agriculture often demeaned the role of women in farming and their related work. Indeed, the vast literature on agricultural improvement specifically advocated removing women from the agricultural workforce.

A similar process took place in textile manufacturing, where mechanization deprived many women of one of their most traditional means of earning income. Before mechanization thousands of women worked at spinning wheels to produce thread that hand-loom weavers, who were often their husbands, then wove. The earlier, small spinning jennies did not immediately disrupt this situation because women could use them in the loft of a home, but the larger ones required a factory setting where men often ran the machinery. As a result, most women spinners were put out of work, and those women who did move into the factory labor force performed less skilled work than men. In the long run, however, the mechanization of spinning left many other women without one of their most traditional means of earning income.

Many working women, displaced from spinning thread or from farming, slowly turned to cottage industries—such as knitting, button making, straw plaiting, bonnet making, or glove stitching—that invariably earned them less than their former occupations had. In later generations, women who earlier would have been spinners or farm workers moved directly into cottage industries. The work and skills these occupations involved were considered inferior; and because it paid so poorly, women who did this work might become prostitutes or engage in other criminal activity. Consequently, the reputations and social standing of many working women suffered.

Among women who did not work in the cottage industries, thousands became domestic servants in the homes of landed or commercial families. During the nineteenth century, such domestic service became the largest area of female employment. It was far more respectable than the cottage industries but was isolated from the technologically advanced world of factory manufacture or transport.

By the end of the eighteenth century, the work and workplaces of men and women were becoming increasingly separate and distinct. In this respect, many people, such as English writer Priscilla Wakefield (1750–1832), believed the kinds of employment open to women had narrowed. Wakefield called for new occupations for women. (See the Document "Priscilla Wakefield Demands More Occupations for Women," on page 463.)

This shift in female employment, or what one historian has termed "this defamation of women workers,"[2] produced several long-term results. First, women's work, whether in cottage industries or domestic service, became associated with the home rather than with places where men worked. Second, the laboring life of most women was removed from the new technologies in farming, transportation, and manufacturing. Woman's work thus appeared traditional, and people assumed women could do only such work. Third, during the nineteenth and early twentieth centuries, Europeans also assumed most women worked only to supplement their husbands' income. Finally, because the work women did was considered marginal and only as supplementing a male income, men were paid much more than women. Most people associate the Industrial Revolution with factories, but for many working women, these revolutions led to a life located more in homes than ever before. Indeed, in the nineteenth century, one, though only one, motive behind efforts to restrict the hours and improve the conditions of women in factories was the belief that it was bad for them to be there in the first place. The larger picture of the relationship of the new industrial workplace to family life is addressed in Chapter 21.

▼ The Growth of Cities

Remarkable changes occurred in the pattern of city growth between 1500 and 1800. In 1500, within Europe (excluding Hungary and Russia) 156 cities had a population greater than 10,000. Only four of those cities—Paris, Milan, Venice, and Naples—had populations larger than 100,000. By 1800, 363 cities had 10,000 or more inhabitants, and 17 of them had populations larger than 100,000. The percentage of the European population living in urban areas had risen from just over 5 percent to just over 9 percent. A major shift in urban concentration from southern, Mediterranean Europe to the north had also occurred.

Patterns of Preindustrial Urbanization

The eighteenth century witnessed a considerable growth of towns, closely related to the tumult of the day and the revolutions with which the century closed. London

[2]Deborah Valenze, *The First Industrial Woman* (New York: Oxford University Press, 1995), p. 183.

Document

PRISCILLA WAKEFIELD DEMANDS MORE OCCUPATIONS FOR WOMEN

At the end of the eighteenth century, Priscilla Wakefield was one of several English women writers who began to demand a wider life for women. She was concerned that women found themselves able to pursue only occupations that paid poorly. They were often excluded from work because of their alleged physical weakness. She also believed women should receive equal wages for equal work. These issues reflected a narrowing of opportunities for women that had occurred in England during the second half of the eighteenth century. As a result of the mechanization of both agriculture and the textile industry, many found traditional occupations were closing to women. Wakefield is thus addressing a general question of opportunities available to women and more recent developments. Many of the issues she raised have yet to be adequately addressed.

What arguments were used at the end of the eighteenth century to limit the kinds of employment that women might enter? Why did women receive less pay than men for similar or the same work? What occupations traditionally filled by men does Wakefield believe women might also pursue?

Another heavy discouragement to the industry of women, is the inequality of the reward of their labor, compared with that of men; an injustice which pervades every species of employment performed by both sexes.

In employments which depend on bodily strength, the distinction is just; for it cannot be pretended that the generality of women can earn as much as men, when the produce of their labor is the result of corporeal exertion; but it is a subject of great regret, that this inequality should prevail even where an equal share of skill and application is exerted. Male stay-makers, mantua-makers, and hair-dressers, are better paid than female artists of the same professions; but surely it will never be urged as an apology for this disproportion, that women are not as capable of making stays, gowns, dressing hair, and similar arts, as men; if they are not superior to them, it can only be accounted for upon this principle, that the prices they receive for their labor are not sufficient to repay them for the expense of qualifying themselves for their business; and that they sink under the mortification of being regarded as artisans of inferior estimation. . . .

Besides these employments which are commonly performed by women, and those already shown to be suitable for such persons as are above the condition of hard labor, there are some professions and trades customarily in the hands of men, which might be conveniently exercised by either sex. Watchmaking requiring more ingenuity than strength, seems peculiarly adapted to women; as do many parts of the business of stationer, particularly, ruling account books or making pens. The compounding of medicines in an apothecary's shop, requires no other talents than care and exactness; and if opening a vein occasionally be an indispensable requisite, a woman may acquire the capacity of doing it, for those of her own sex at least, without any reasonable objection. . . . Pastry and confectionery appear particularly consonant to the habits of women, though generally performed by men; perhaps the heat of the ovens, and the strength requisite to fill and empty them, may render male assistants necessary; but certain women are most eligible to mix up the ingredients, and prepare the various kinds of cakes for baking. Light turnery and toy-making depend more upon dexterity and invention than force, and are therefore suitable work for women and children. . . .

Farming, as far as respects the theory, is commensurate with the powers of the female mind: nor is the practice of inspecting agricultural processes incompatible with the delicacy of their frames if their constitution be good.

From Priscilla Wakefield, *Reflections on the Present Condition of the Female Sex* (1798) (London, 1817), pp. 125–127, as quoted in Bridget Hill, ed., *Eighteenth-Century Women: An Anthology* (London: George Allen & Unwin, 1984), pp. 227–228.

grew from about 700,000 inhabitants in 1700 to almost 1 million in 1800. By the time of the French Revolution, Paris had more than 500,000 inhabitants. Berlin's population tripled during the century, reaching 170,000 in 1800. Warsaw had 30,000 inhabitants in 1730, but almost 120,000 in 1794. St. Petersburg, founded in 1703, numbered more than 250,000 inhabitants a century later. The number of smaller cities with 20,000 to 50,000 people also increased considerably. This urban growth must, however, be kept in perspective. Even in France and Great Britain, probably somewhat less than 20 percent of the population lived in cities. And the town of 10,000 inhabitants was much more common than the giant urban center.

These raw figures conceal significant changes that took place in how cities grew and how the population redistributed itself. The major urban development of the sixteenth century had been followed by a leveling off, and even a decline, in the seventeenth. New growth began in the early eighteenth century and accelerated during the late eighteenth and the early nineteenth centuries.

Between 1500 and 1750, major urban expansion took place within already established and generally already large cities. After 1750, the pattern changed with the birth of new cities and the rapid growth of older, smaller cities.

Growth of Capitals and Ports In particular, between 1600 and 1750, the cities that grew most vigorously were capitals and ports. This situation reflects the success of monarchical state-building during those years and the consequent burgeoning of bureaucracies, armies, courts, and other groups who lived in the capitals. The growth of port cities, in turn, reflects the expansion of European overseas trade—especially that of the Atlantic routes. Except for Manchester in England and Lyons in France, the new urban conglomerates were nonindustrial cities.

Furthermore, between 1600 and 1750, cities with populations of fewer than 40,000 inhabitants declined. These included older landlocked trading centers, medieval industrial cities, and ecclesiastical centers. They contributed less to the new political regimes, and the expansion of the putting-out system transferred production from medieval cities to the countryside because rural labor was cheaper than urban labor.

The Emergence of New Cities and the Growth of Small Towns In the mid-eighteenth century, a new pattern emerged. The rate of growth of existing large cities declined, new cities emerged, and existing smaller cities grew. Several factors were at work in the process, which Jan De Vries has termed "an urban growth from below."[3] First was the general overall population increase. Second, the early stages of the Industrial Revolution, particularly in Britain, occurred in the countryside and fostered the growth of smaller towns and cities located near factories. Factory organization itself led to new concentrations of population.

Cities also grew as a result of the new prosperity of European agriculture, even where there was little industrialization. Improved agricultural production promoted the growth of nearby market towns and other urban centers that served agriculture or allowed more prosperous farmers to have access to consumer goods and recreation. This new pattern of urban growth—new cities and the expansion of smaller existing ones—would continue into the nineteenth century.

Urban Classes

Social divisions were as marked in eighteenth-century cities as they were in nineteenth-century industrial centers. The urban rich were often visibly segregated from the urban poor. Aristocrats and the upper middle class lived in fashionable town houses, often constructed around newly laid-out green squares. The poorest town dwellers usually congregated along the rivers. Small merchants and artisans lived above their shops. Whole families might live in a single room. Modern sanitary facilities were unknown. Pure water was rare. Cattle, pigs, goats, and other animals roamed the streets. All reports on the cities of Europe during this period emphasize both the striking grace and beauty of the dwellings of the wealthy and the dirt, filth, and stench that filled the streets. (See "Encountering the Past: Water, Washing, and Bathing," page 474.)

Poverty was not just an urban problem; it was usually worse in the countryside. In the city, however, poverty was more visible in the form of crime, prostitution, vagrancy, begging, and alcoholism. Many a young man or woman from the countryside migrated to the nearest city to seek a better life, only to discover poor housing, little food, disease, degradation, and finally death. It did not require the Industrial Revolution and the urban factories to make the cities into hellholes for the poor and the dispossessed. The full darkness of London life during the midcentury "gin age," when consumption of that liquor blinded and killed many poor people, is evident in the engravings of William Hogarth (1697–1764).

View the **Image** "Gin Lane, William Hogarth" on **MyHistoryLab.com**

Also contrasting with the serenity of the aristocratic and upper-commercial-class lifestyle were the public

---

[3]Jan De Vries, "Patterns of Urbanization in Pre-Industrial Europe, 1500–1800," in H. Schmal, ed., *Patterns of Urbanization since 1500* (London: Croom Helm, 1981), p. 103.

executions that took place all over Europe, the breaking of men and women on instruments of torture in Paris, and the public floggings in Russia. Brutality condoned and carried out by the ruling classes was a fact of everyday life.

The Upper Classes   At the top of the urban social structure stood a generally small group of nobles, large merchants, bankers, financiers, clergy, and government officials. These upper-class men controlled the political and economic affairs of the town. Normally, they constituted a self-appointed and self-electing oligarchy that governed the city through its corporation or city council. Some form of royal charter usually gave the city corporation its authority and the power to select its own members. In a few cities on the Continent, artisan guilds controlled the corporations, but generally, the local nobility and the wealthiest commercial people dominated the councils.

The Middle Class   Another group in the city was the prosperous, but not always immensely wealthy, merchants, trades people, bankers, and professional people. They were the most dynamic element of the urban population and made up the middle class, or bourgeoisie. The concept of the middle class was much less clear-cut than that of the nobility. The middle class itself was and would remain diverse and divided, with persons employed in the professions often resentful of those who drew their incomes from commerce. Less wealthy members of the middle class of whatever occupation resented wealthier members who might be connected to the nobility through social or business relationships.

The middle class had less wealth than most nobles, but more than urban artisans. Middle-class people lived in the cities and towns, and their sources of income had little or nothing to do with the land. In one way or another, they all benefited from expanding trade and commerce, whether as merchants, lawyers, or small-factory owners. Theirs was a world in which earning and saving of money enabled rapid social mobility and change in lifestyle. They saw themselves as willing to put their capital and energy to work, whereas they portrayed the nobility as idle. The members of the middle class tended to be economically aggressive and socially ambitious. People often made fun of them for these characteristics and were jealous of their success. The middle class normally supported reform, change, and economic growth. They also wanted more rational regulations for trade and commerce, as did some progressive aristocrats.

The middle class was made up of people whose lives fostered the revolution in consumption. On one hand, as owners of factories and of wholesale and retail businesses, they produced and sold goods for the expanding consumer market; on the other hand, members of the middle class were among the chief consumers. It was to

their homes that the vast array of new consumer goods made their way. They were also the people whose social values most fully embraced the commercial spirit. They might not enjoy the titles or privileges of the nobility, but they could enjoy material comfort and prosperity. It was this style of life that less well-off people could emulate as they sought to acquire consumer goods for themselves.

During the eighteenth century, the relationship between the middle class and the aristocracy was complicated. On one hand, the nobles, especially in England and France, increasingly embraced the commercial spirit associated with the middle class by improving their estates and investing in cities. On the other hand, wealthy members of the middle class often tried to imitate the lifestyle of the nobility by purchasing landed estates. The aspirations of the middle class for social mobility, however, conflicted with the determination of the nobles to maintain and reassert their own privileges and to protect their own wealth. Middle-class commercial figures—traders, bankers, manufacturers, and lawyers—often found their pursuit of profit and prestige blocked by the privileges of the nobility and its social exclusiveness, by the inefficiency of monarchical bureaucracies dominated by the nobility, or by aristocrats who controlled patronage and government contracts.

The bourgeoisie was not rising to challenge the nobility; rather, both were seeking to increase their existing political power and social prestige. The tensions that arose between the nobles and the middle class during the eighteenth century normally involved issues of power-sharing or access to political influence, rather than clashes over values or goals associated with class.

The middle class in the cities also feared the lower urban classes as much as they envied the nobility. The lower orders were a potentially violent element in society, a threat to property, and, in their poverty, a drain on national resources. The lower classes, however, were much more varied than either the city aristocracy or the middle class cared to admit.

Artisans   Shopkeepers, artisans, and wage earners were the single largest group in any city. They were grocers, butchers, fishmongers, carpenters, cabinetmakers, smiths, printers, hand-loom weavers, and tailors, to give a few examples. They had their own culture, values, and institutions. Like the peasants, they were, in many respects, conservative. Their economic position was vulnerable. If a poor harvest raised the price of food, their own businesses suffered. These urban classes also contributed to the revolution in consumption, however. They could buy more goods than ever before, and, to the extent their incomes permitted, many of them sought to copy the domestic consumption of the middle class.

Read the Document
"Jacques-Louis Menetra, *Journal of My Life*" on **MyHistoryLab.com**

WATER, WASHING, AND BATHING

BEFORE THE LATE nineteenth century, clean water was scarce in Europe. Except for the few households and institutions that had their own wells, water had to be carried from a public fountain or public well. Drought in summer and freezing in winter could lead to shortages.

Governments made little effort to provide water. Everyone assumed that people required little water for their personal use—less than 7.5 liters per day, according to one eighteenth-century commentator. (The average American uses 210 liters per day.) Commerce and agriculture used much more water than individuals: to power mills in the cloth and dye trades, and to quench the thirst of work animals and irrigate fields.

Attitudes toward personal appearance also determined the use of water. In the Middle Ages, public bathhouses were not uncommon. The appearance of the body—cleanliness—was believed to reflect the state of the soul, and townspeople and aristocrats bathed fairly often. However, during the Renaissance and the Reformation, the quality and condition of clothing, not bodily cleanliness, were thought to mirror the soul. Clean clothes also revealed a person's social status—clothes made the man and the woman.

Moreover, from the late Middle Ages through the end of the eighteenth century, etiquette and

In the eighteenth century washing linen clothing by hand was a major task of women servants. Chardin, Jean-Baptise Simeon (1699–1779)/Hermitage, St. Petersburg, Russia/Scala/Art Resource, NY

medical manuals advised people to wash only those parts of their bodies that could be seen in public—the hands, the face, the neck, and the feet. All forms of public bathing were associated with immoral behavior—public bathing meant public nudity, and prostitutes frequented bathhouses.

The switch from woolen to linen clothing accompanied the decline in bathing. By the sixteenth century, easily washable linen clothing had begun to replace woolen garments in much of Western Europe. Clean linen shirts or blouses allowed persons who had not bathed to appear clean. Possession of large quantities of freshly laundered linens was a sign of high social status.

Appearance thus became more important than bodily hygiene. Medical opinion supported these practices. Physicians believed odors or *miasma* (bad air), such as might be found in soiled linens—along with lice, fleas, and other vermin—caused disease. One should therefore change one's shirt every few days but avoid baths, which might let the bad air enter the body through the open pores. Consequently, in an age in which there were practically no personal bathtubs, thousands of shirts were washed each week, almost always by female laundresses, in every city.

Attitudes toward bathing only began to change toward the middle of the eighteenth century when writers argued that frequent bathing might lead to greater health. Large public baths, such as had been known in the ancient world and were a fixture of the Ottoman Empire, revived during the nineteenth century, and the germ theory of disease led health authorities to urge people to bathe often to rid their bodies of germs. The great water projects of the nineteenth century (see Chapter 23) would assure vast quantities of water for personal hygiene.

Sources: Daniel Roche, *The Culture of Clothing: Dress and Fashion in the "Ancien Regime"* (Cambridge, UK: Cambridge University Press, 1994); Georges Vigarello, *Concepts of Cleanliness: Changing Attitudes in France since the Middle Ages* (Cambridge, UK: Cambridge University Press, 1988); Alain Corbin, *The Foul and the Fragrant: Odor and the French Social Imagination* (Cambridge, MA: Harvard University Press, 1988).

Why did bathing become less frequent after the late Middle Ages?

How did the use of linen clothing contribute to this change?

This engraving illustrates a metalworking shop such as might have been found in almost any town of significance in Europe. Most of the people employed in the shop probably belonged to the same family. Note that two women are also working. The wife may very well have been the person in charge of keeping the accounts of the business. The two younger boys might be children of the owner or apprentices in the trade, or both. The Granger Collection, New York

they felt that what was economically "just" had been offended, artisans frequently manifested their displeasure by rioting. The most sensitive area was the price of bread, the staple food of the poor. If a baker or a grain merchant announced a price that was considered unjustly high, a riot might well ensue. Artisan leaders would confiscate the bread or grain and sell it for what the urban crowd considered a "just price." They would then give the money paid for the grain or bread to the baker or merchant.

The danger of bread riots restrained the greed of merchants. Such disturbances represented a collective method of imposing the "just price" in place of the price the commercial marketplace set. Thus, bread and food riots, which occurred throughout Europe, were not irrational acts of screaming, hungry people, but highly ritualized social phenomena of the Old Regime and its economy of scarcity.

Other kinds of riots also characterized eighteenth-century society and politics. The riot was a way in which people who were excluded in every other way from the political processes could make their will known. Sometimes religious bigotry led to urban riots. For example, in 1753, London Protestant mobs compelled the government to withdraw an act to legalize Jewish naturalization. In 1780, the same rabidly Protestant spirit manifested itself in the Gordon riots. Lord George Gordon (1751–1793) had raised the specter of an imaginary Catholic plot after the government relieved military recruits from having to take specifically anti-Catholic oaths.

In these riots and in food riots, violence was normally directed against property rather than people. The rioters themselves were not disreputable people but usually small shopkeepers, freeholders, artisans, and wage earners. They usually wanted only to restore a traditional right or practice that seemed endangered. Nevertheless, their actions could cause considerable turmoil and destruction.

During the last half of the century, urban riots increasingly involved political ends. Though often simultaneous with economic disturbances, the political riot always had nonartisan leadership or instigators. In fact, an eighteenth-century "crowd" was often the tool of the upper classes. In Paris, the aristocratic *parlement* often urged crowd action in its disputes with the monarchy. In Geneva, middle-class citizens supported artisan riots

The lives of these artisans and shopkeepers centered on their work and their neighborhoods. They usually lived near or at their place of employment. Most of them worked in shops with fewer than a half dozen other artisans. Their primary institution had historically been the guild, but by the eighteenth century, the guilds rarely exercised the influence their predecessors had in medieval or early modern Europe.

Nevertheless, the guilds were not to be ignored. They played a conservative role. Rather than seeking economic growth or innovation, they tried to preserve the jobs and skills of their members. In many countries, the guilds still determined who could pursue a craft. To lessen competition, they attempted to prevent too many people from learning a particular skill.

The guilds also provided a framework for social and economic advancement. At an early age, a boy might become an apprentice to learn a craft or trade. After several years, he would be made a journeyman. Still later, if successful and competent, he might become a master. The artisan could also receive social benefits from the guilds, including aid for his family during sickness or the promise of admission for his son. The guilds were the chief protection for artisans against the workings of the commercial market. They were particularly strong in central Europe.

The Urban Riot

The artisan class, with its generally conservative outlook, maintained a rather fine sense of social and economic justice based largely on traditional practices. If against the local oligarchy. In Great Britain in 1792, the government incited mobs to attack English sympathizers of the French Revolution. Such outbursts indicate that the crowd or mob had entered the European political and social arena well before the revolution in France.

▼ The Jewish Population: The Age of the Ghetto

Although the small Jewish communities of Amsterdam and other Western European cities became famous for their intellectual life and financial institutions, most European Jews lived in Eastern Europe. In the eighteenth century and thereafter, the Jewish population of Europe was concentrated in Poland, Lithuania, and Ukraine, where no fewer than 3 million Jews dwelled. Perhaps 150,000 Jews lived in the Habsburg lands, primarily Bohemia, around 1760. Fewer than 100,000 Jews lived in Germany. France had approximately 40,000 Jews. England and Holland each had a Jewish population of fewer than 10,000. There were even smaller groups of Jews elsewhere.

In 1762, Catherine the Great of Russia specifically excluded Jews from a manifesto that welcomed foreigners to settle in Russia. She relaxed the exclusion a few years later, but Jews during her reign often felt they needed assurances of imperial protection for their livelihoods and religious practices against the ordinances of local officials. (See the Document "Belorussian Jews Petition Catherine the Great," page 477.) After the first partition of Poland of 1772, discussed in Chapter 17, the Russian Empire included a large Jewish population, and the number of Jews in Prussia and under Austrian rule also increased.

Jews dwelled in most nations without enjoying the rights and privileges that other subjects had unless monarchs specifically granted them to Jews. Jews were regarded as a kind of resident alien whose residence might well be temporary or changed at the whim of rulers.

No matter where they dwelled, Old Regime Jews lived apart in separate communities from non-Jewish Europeans. These communities might be distinct districts of cities, known as **ghettos**, or in primarily Jewish villages in the countryside. Jews were also treated as a distinct people religiously and legally. In Poland for much of the century, they were virtually self-governing. In other areas, they lived under the burden of discriminatory legislation. Except in England, Jews could not and did not mix in the mainstream of the societies in which they dwelled. This period, which may be said to have begun with the expulsion of the Jews from Spain at the end of the fifteenth century, is known as the age of the ghetto, or separate community.

During the seventeenth century, a few Jews had helped finance the wars of major rulers. These financiers often became close to the rulers and were known as "court Jews." Perhaps the most famous was Samuel Oppenheimer (1630–1703), who helped the Habsburgs finance their struggle against the Turks and the defense of Vienna. However, these loans were often not repaid. The court Jews and their financial abilities became famous. They tended to marry among themselves.

Most European Jews, however, lived in poverty. They occupied the most undesirable sections of cities or poor villages. Some were small-time moneylenders, but most worked at the lowest occupations. Their religious beliefs, rituals, and community set them apart. Virtually all laws and social institutions kept them socially inferior to and apart from their Christian neighbors.

During the Old Regime, European Jews were separated from non-Jews, typically in districts known as ghettos. Relegated to the least desirable section of a city or to rural villages, most lived in poverty. This watercolor painting depicts a street in Kazimlesz, the Jewish quarter of Kraków, Poland. Judaica Collection, Max Berger, Vienna, Austria. Photograph © Erich Lessing/ Art Resource, NY

BELORUSSIAN JEWS PETITION CATHERINE THE GREAT

In the 1780s, through military expansion, Empress Catherine the Great of Russia (see Chapter 17) annexed Belorussia, bringing a new Jewish minority under her imperial government. In response to her decree, governing many aspects of the region's law and economy, Belorussian Jews petitioned the empress to protect certain of their traditional rights regarding the distillation and sale of spirits. They also petitioned for protection in court and for the right to retain their own traditional practices and courts for matters relating to their own community. The petition indicates how in Russia, as elsewhere in Europe, Jews were treated as a people apart. It also illustrates how Jews, like other minorities in Old Regime Europe, sought both to receive the protection of monarchies against arbitrary local officials and to maintain long-standing social practices. The document reveals the Jews' dependence on the goodwill of the non-Jewish community.

How do the petitioners attempt to appeal to long-standing custom to defend their interests? How does the petition suggest that Jewish law and practice, distinct from the rest of the society, governed Jewish social life? In the context of this petition, which non-Jewish authorities may actually or potentially influence Jewish life?

According to an ancient custom, when the squires built a new village, they summoned the Jews to reside there and gave them certain privileges for several years and then permanent liberty to distill spirits, brew beer and mead, and sell these drinks. On this basis, the Jews built houses and distillation plants at considerable expense. . . . A new decree of Her Imperial Majesty . . . reserved [this right] to the squires. . . . But a decree of the governor-general of Belorussia has now forbidden the squires to farm out distillation in their villages to Jews, even if the squires want to do this. As a result, the poor Jews who built houses in small villages and promoted both this trade and distillation have been deprived of these and left completely impoverished. But until all the Jewish people are totally ruined, the Jewish merchants suffer restraints equally with the poor rural Jews, since their law obliges them to assist all who share their religious faith. They therefore request an imperial decree authorizing the squire, if he wishes, to farm out distillation to Jews in rural areas.

Although, with Her Imperial Majesty's permission, Jews may be elected as officials . . . , Jews are allotted fewer votes than other people and hence no Jew can ever attain office. Consequently, Jews have no one to defend them in courts and find themselves in a desperate situation—given their fear and ignorance of Russian—in case of misfortune, even if innocent. To consummate all the good already bestowed, Jews dare to petition that an equal number of electors be required from Jews as from others (or, at least, that in matters involving Jews and non-Jews, a representative from the Jewish community hold equal rights with non-Jews, be present to accompany Jews in court, and attend the interrogation of Jews). But cases involving only Jews (except for promissory notes and debts) should be handled solely in Jewish courts, because Jews assume obligations among themselves, make agreements and conclude all kinds of deals in the Jewish language and in accordance with Jewish rites and laws (which are not known to others). Moreover, those who transgress their laws and order should be judged in Jewish courts. [Similarly, preserve intact all their customs and holidays in the spirit of their faith, as is mercifully assured in the imperial manifesto.]

From *From Supplication to Revolution: A Documentary Social History of Imperial Russia* by Gregory L. Freeze. Copyright © 1988 by Oxford University Press, Inc. Used by permission of Oxford University Press, Inc.

Under the Old Regime, it is important to emphasize that this discrimination was based on religious separateness. Jews who converted to Christianity were welcomed, even if not always warmly, into the major political and social institutions of Gentile European society. Until the last two decades of the eighteenth century, in every part of Europe, however, those Jews who remained loyal to their faith were subject to various religious, civil, and social disabilities. They could not pursue the professions freely, they often could not change residence without official permission, and they were excluded from the political structures of the nations in which they lived. Jews could be expelled from their homes, and their property could be confiscated. They could be required to listen to sermons that insulted their religion. Their children could be taken away from them and given Christian instruction. They knew their non-Jewish neighbors might suddenly turn against them and kill them.

In subsequent chapters, it will be shown how the end of the Old Regime brought major changes in the lives of European Jews and in their relationship to the larger culture.

In Perspective

Near the close of the eighteenth century, European society was on the brink of a new era. That society had remained traditional and corporate largely because of an economy of scarcity. Beginning in the eighteenth century, however, the commercial spirit and the values of the marketplace, although not new, were permitted fuller play than ever before in European history. The newly unleashed commercial spirit led increasingly to a conception of human beings as individuals rather than as members of communities. In particular, that spirit manifested itself in the Agricultural and Industrial Revolutions, as well as in the drive toward greater consumption. Together, those two vast changes in production overcame most of the scarcity that had haunted Europe and the West generally. The accompanying changes in landholding and production would transform the European social structure.

The expansion of the population further stimulated change. More people meant more labor, more energy, and more minds contributing to the creation and solution of social difficulties. Cities had to accommodate expanding populations. Corporate groups, such as the guilds, had to confront the existence of a larger labor force. New wealth meant that birth would eventually become less and less a determining factor in social relationships, except for the social roles assigned to the two sexes. Class structure and social hierarchy remained, but the boundaries became more blurred.

Finally, the conflicting ambitions of monarchs, the nobility, and the middle class generated innovation. In the pursuit of new revenues, the monarchs interfered with the privileges of the nobles. In the name of ancient rights, the nobles attempted to secure and expand their existing social privileges. The middle class, in all of its diversity, was growing wealthier from trade, commerce, and the practice of the professions. Its members wanted social prestige and influence equal to their wealth. They resented privileges, frowned on hierarchy, and rejected tradition.

All these factors meant the society of the eighteenth century stood at the close of one era in European history and at the opening of another.

KEY TERMS

Agricultural Revolution (p. 460)
aristocratic resurgence (p. 453)
consumer revolution (p. 465)
domestic system of textile production (p. 466)
enclosures (p. 460)
family economy (p. 455)
ghettos (p. 476)
Industrial Revolution (p. 464)
Old Regime (p. 450)
spinning jenny (p. 466)
water frame (p. 466)

REVIEW QUESTIONS

1. What kinds of privileges separated European aristocrats from other social groups? How did their privileges and influence affect other people living in the countryside? What was the condition of serfs in central and eastern Europe?
2. How would you define the term *family economy?* How did the family economy constrain the lives of women in preindustrial Europe?
3. What caused the Agricultural Revolution? How did the English aristocracy contribute to the Agricultural Revolution? Why did peasants revolt in the eighteenth century?
4. Why did Europe's population increase in the eighteenth century? How did population growth affect consumption?
5. What was the Industrial Revolution and what caused it? Why did Great Britain take the lead in the

Industrial Revolution? How did consumers contribute to the Industrial Revolution?

6. How did the distribution of population in cities and towns change? How did the lifestyle of the upper class compare to that of the middle and lower classes? What were some of the causes of urban riots?

7. Where were the largest Jewish populations in eighteenth-century Europe? What was their social and legal position? What were the sources of prejudices against Jews?

SUGGESTED READINGS

J. Blum, *Lord and Peasant in Russia from the Ninth to the Nineteenth Century* (1961). Remains a classic discussion.

J. Burnet, *Gender, Work and Wages in Industrial Revolution Britain* (2008). A major revisionist study of the wage structure for work by men and women.

P. M. Deane, *The First Industrial Revolution* (1999). A well-balanced and systematic treatment.

P. Earle, *The Making of the English Middle Class: Business, Community, and Family Life in London, 1660–1730* (1989). The most careful study of the subject.

M. W. Flinn, *The European Demographic System, 1500–1820* (1981). Remains a major summary.

E. Hobsbawm, *Industry and Empire: The Birth of the Industrial Revolution* (1999). A survey by a major historian of the subject.

K. Honeyman, *Women, Gender and Industrialization in England, 1700–1850* (2000). Emphasizes how certain work or economic roles became associated with either men or women.

O. H. Hufton, *The Poor of Eighteenth-Century France, 1750–1789* (1975). A brilliant study of poverty and the family economy.

A. Kahan, *The Plow, the Hammer, and the Knout: An Economic History of Eighteenth-Century Russia* (1985). An extensive and detailed treatment.

S. King and G. Timmons, *Making Sense of the Industrial Revolution: English Economy and Society, 1700–1850* (2001). Examines the Industrial Revolution through the social institutions that brought it about and were changed by it.

K. Morgan, *The Birth of Industrial Britain: Social Change, 1750–1850* (2004). A useful brief overview.

M. Overton, *Agricultural Revolution in England: The Transformation of the Agrarian Economy, 1500–1850* (1996). A highly accessible treatment.

J. R. Ruff, *Violence in Early Modern Europe 1500–1800* (2001). An excellent survey of an important and disturbing topic.

P. Stearns, *The Industrial Revolution in World History* (2007). A broad interpretive account.

D. Valenze, *The First Industrial Woman* (1995). An elegant, penetrating volume.

E. A. Wrigley, *Continuity, Chance and Change: The Character of the Industrial Revolution in England* (1994). A major conceptual reassessment.

MyHistoryLab™ MEDIA ASSIGNMENTS

Find these resources in the Media Assignments folder for Chapter 15 on **MyHistoryLab**.

QUESTIONS FOR ANALYSIS

1. What are some of the privileges of aristocracy in Europe illustrated by this painting?

   Section: **The Aristrocracy**
   View the **Closer Look** An Aristocratic Couple, p. 452

2. What explains the patterns of greater and lesser concentrations of serfs in Russia in this period?

   Section: **The Land and Its Tillers**
   View the **Map** Russian Serfs, p. 454

3. What areas seem to have been more immune to enclosure?

   Section: **The Revolution in Agriculture**
   View the **Map** Map Discovery: English Common Lands Enclosed by Acts of Parliament, 1700–1850, p. 461

4. What were some of the problems James Watt had to overcome to make a useful steam engine?

   Section: **The Industrial Revolution in the Eighteenth Century**
   Read the **Document** James Watt on Steam Engines (mid to late 1700s), p. 468

5. What was the role of the church in Menetra's life?

   Section: **The Growth of Cities**
   Read the **Document** Jacques-Louis Menetra, *Journal of My Life*, p. 473

OTHER RESOURCES FROM THIS CHAPTER

Major Features of Life in the Old Regime
Read the **Document** De Staël on the Ancien Regime (1789), p. 450

The Aristocracy
Read the **Document** Voltaire, on Social Conditions in Eighteenth-Century France, p. 453

General James Wolfe was mortally wounded during his victory over the French at Quebec in 1759. This painting by American artist Benjamin West (1738–1820) became famous for portraying the dying Wolfe and the officers around him in poses modeled after classical statues.   Quebec House, Westerham, Kent, Great Britain/National Trust Photo Library/John Hammond/Art Resource, NY

((•—[**Listen** to the **Chapter Audio**
on **MyHistoryLab.com**

16

The Transatlantic Economy, Trade Wars, and Colonial Rebellion

LEARNING OBJECTIVES

How did European contact with the rest of the world evolve in the centuries since the Renaissance?

What were the characteristics of European mercantile empires?

How did Spanish colonial organization reflect its imperial goals?

What were the origins of slavery in the Americas?

Why did mid-eighteenth-century European wars often involve both continental and global conflicts?

What were the causes of the American Revolution?

THE MID-EIGHTEENTH century witnessed a renewal of European warfare on a worldwide scale. The conflict involved two separate, but interrelated, rivalries. Austria and Prussia fought for dominance in central Europe while Great Britain and France dueled for commercial and colonial supremacy in Europe, North America, and Asia. The wars were long, extensive, and costly in both effort and money. They resulted in a new balance of power on the Continent and on the high seas. Prussia emerged as a great power, and Great Britain gained a world empire.

The expense of these wars led every major European government to reconstruct its policies of taxation and finance after the Peace of Paris of 1763. Among the results of these policies were the American Revolution, state-led reform in central Europe, a continuing financial crisis for the French monarchy, and a reform of the Spanish Empire in South America.

▼ Periods of European Overseas Empires

Since the Renaissance, European contacts with the rest of the world have gone through four distinct stages. The first was that of the European discovery, exploration, initial conquest, and settlement of the New World. This phase also witnessed the penetration of Southeast Asian markets by Portugal and the Netherlands, which established major imperial outposts and influence in the region. This period closed by the end of the seventeenth century. (See Chapter 10.)

The second era—that of the mercantile empires, which are largely the concern of this chapter—was one of colonial trade rivalry among Spain, France, and Great Britain. Although during the sixteenth and seventeenth centuries differing motives had led to the establishment of overseas European empires, by the eighteenth century they generally existed to foster trade and commerce. These commercial goals required continuing warfare against indigenous peoples in an attempt to acquire their land. They also, however, led to intense rivalry and conflicts between the European powers themselves. As a result, the various imperial ventures led to the creation of large navies and a series of major naval wars at midcentury—wars that in turn became linked to warfare on the European continent. The Anglo-French side of the contest has often been compared to a second Hundred Years' War, with theaters of conflict in Europe, the Americas, West Africa, and India.

A fundamental element in these first two periods of European imperial ventures in the Americas was

◉ Watch the Video
"The Origins of Modern Imperialism and Colonialism" on **MyHistoryLab.com**

During the seventeenth and eighteenth centuries, European maritime nations established overseas empires and set up trading monopolies within them in an effort to magnify their economic strength. As this painting of the Old Custom House Quay in London suggests, trade from these empires and the tariffs imposed on it were expected to generate revenue for the home country. But behind many of the goods carried in the great sailing ships in the harbor and landed on these docks lay the labor of African slaves working on the plantations of North and South America.   Samuel Scott "Old Custom House Quay" Collection. V & A Images, The Victoria and Albert Museum, London

the presence of slavery. By the eighteenth century, the slave population of the New World consisted almost entirely of a black population that had either recently been forcibly imported from Africa or born to slaves whose forebears had been forcibly imported from Africa. Both the forced migration of so many people from one continent to another and the mid-Atlantic plantation economies that such slave labor supported were unprecedented in history. The creation in the Americas of this slave-based plantation economy led directly to over three centuries of extensive involvement by Europeans and white Americans in the slave trade with Africa—particularly, with the societies of West Africa. In turn, on the American continent the slave trade created extensive communities of Africans from the Chesapeake region of Maryland and Virginia south to Brazil. The Africans brought to the American experience not only their labor, but also their languages, customs, and ethnic associations. The Atlantic economy and the societies that arose in the Americas were, consequently, the creation of both Europeans and Africans while, as a result of European incursions into their territory, Native Americans were pressed toward the margins of those societies. In this respect from the sixteenth century onward Africans became a significant factor in the forging of European prosperity and industrialization. They were not only commodities in the slave trade that enriched western European economies and laborers in the New World plantation economy, the wealth and products of which enriched the daily life of peoples in Europe and European settlers and their descendants in the Americas, but also contributors to distinctive American cultures.

Finally, during the second period, both the British colonies of the North American seaboard and the Spanish colonies of Mexico and Central and South America emancipated themselves from European control. This era of independence, part of which is discussed in this chapter and part in Chapter 20, may be said to have closed during the 1820s. This same revolutionary era witnessed the beginning of the antislavery movement that extended through the third quarter of the nineteenth century. (See "The West and the World: The Abolition of Slavery in the Transatlantic Economy,." p. 679.)

The third stage of European contact with the non-European world occurred in the nineteenth century. During that period, European governments largely turned from their involvement in the Americas and carved out new formal empires involving the direct European administration of indigenous peoples in Africa and Asia. Those nineteenth-century empires also included new areas of European settlement, such as Australia, New Zealand, South Africa, and Algeria. The bases of these empires were trade, national honor, Christian missionary enterprise, and military strategy. Unlike the previous two eras, the nineteenth-century empires were based on formally free labor forces, although they still involved much harsh treatment of nonwhite indigenous populations. (See Chapter 25.)

The last period of European empire began in the mid-twentieth century, with the decolonization of peoples who had previously lived under European colonial rule. (See Chapter 29.)

During the four-and-one-half centuries before decolonization, Europeans exerted political, military, and economic dominance over much of the rest of the world that was far disproportional to the geographic size or population of Europe. Europeans frequently treated other peoples as social, intellectual, economic, and racial inferiors. Europeans ravaged existing cultures because of greed, religious zeal, or political ambition. These actions are major facts of both European and world history and remain significant factors in the contemporary relationships between Europe and its former colonies, as well as between the United States and those former colonies. What allowed the Europeans to exert such influence and domination over so much of the world for such a long period of time was not any innate cultural superiority, but a combination of epidemiological advantage and technological supremacy related to naval power and gunpowder. European diseases weakened indigenous populations in the New World; ships and guns allowed the Europeans to exercise their will almost wherever they chose.

▼ Mercantile Empires

Navies and merchant shipping were the keystones of the mercantile empires that were meant to bring profit to a nation rather than to provide areas for settlement. The Treaty of Utrecht (1713) established the boundaries of empire during the first half of the eighteenth century.

Except for Brazil, which Portugal governed, and Dutch Guiana, Spain controlled all of mainland South America. In North America, Spain ruled vast territories including Florida, Mexico, California, and the Southwest. The Spanish also governed Central America and the islands of Cuba, Puerto Rico, Trinidad, and the eastern part of Hispaniola that is today the Dominican Republic.

The British Empire consisted of the colonies along the North Atlantic seaboard, Nova Scotia, Newfoundland, Bermuda, Jamaica, and Barbados. Britain also possessed a few trading stations on the Indian subcontinent.

The French domains covered the Saint Lawrence River valley and the Ohio and Mississippi River valleys. They included the West Indian islands of Guadeloupe and Martinique as well as the western half of Hispaniola, then called Saint Domingue and today known as Haiti. France also maintained stations in India and on the West Coast of Africa. To the French and British merchant communities, India appeared as a vast potential market for European goods, as well as the source of calico cloth and spices that were in great demand in Europe.

The Dutch controlled Surinam, or Dutch Guiana, in South America, Cape Colony in what is today South Africa, and trading stations in West Africa, Sri Lanka, and Bengal in India. Most importantly, they also controlled the trade with Java in what is now Indonesia. The Dutch had opened these markets largely in the seventeenth century and had created a vast trading empire far larger in extent, wealth, and importance than the geographical size of the United Netherlands would have led one to expect. The Dutch had been daring sailors and they made important technological innovations in sailing.

All of these powers, as well as Denmark, also possessed numerous smaller islands in the Caribbean. In the eighteenth century, the major rivalries existed among the Spanish, the French, and the British. Together, they were able to prevent other European powers, such as Austria, from securing substantial colonies outside of Europe.

Mercantilist Goals

If any formal economic theory lay behind the conduct of eighteenth-century empires, it was **mercantilism**, whereby governments heavily regulated trade and commerce in hope of increasing national wealth. The terms *mercantilism* and *mercantile system* were invented by later opponents and critics of the system, but its defenders believed mercantilism was the best way for a nation to gain a favorable trade balance of gold and silver bullion.

▶ Read the **Document**
"Jean Baptiste Colbert, 'Mercantilism: Dissertation on Alliances' " on
MyHistoryLab.com

They regarded bullion as the measure of a country's wealth, and believed a nation was truly wealthy only if it amassed more bullion than its rivals. The mercantilist statesmen and traders regarded the world as an arena of scarce resources and economic limitations. Mercantilist thinking assumed that only modest levels of economic growth were possible. Such thinking predated the expansion of agricultural and later industrial productivity, discussed in the previous chapter. Before such sustained economic growth began, the wealth of one nation was assumed to grow or increase largely at the direct expense of another nation. That is to say, the wealth of one state might expand only if its armies or navies conquered the domestic or colonial territory of another state and thus gained the productive capacity of that area, or if a state expanded its trading monopoly over new territory, or if, by smuggling, it could intrude on the trading monopoly of another state.

From beginning to end, the economic well-being of the home country was the primary concern of mercantilist writers. Colonies existed to provide markets and natural resources for the industries of the home country, as well as an outlet for surplus capital. In turn, the home country was to protect and administer the colonies. Both sides assumed the colonies were the subordinate partner in the relationship. To encourage the home country and its colonies to trade exclusively with each other, governments used navigation laws, tariffs, bounties to encourage production, and prohibitions against trading with the subjects of other monarchs. National monopoly was the ruling principle.

Although they made sense on paper, by the early eighteenth century, mercantilist assumptions were far removed from the economic realities of the colonies. The colonial and home markets simply did not mesh. Spain could not produce enough goods for South America.

Economic production in the British North American colonies challenged English manufacturing and led to British attempts to limit certain colonial industries, such as iron and hat making.

Colonists of different countries wished to trade with each other. English colonists could buy sugar more cheaply from the French West Indies than from English suppliers. The traders and merchants of one nation always hoped to break the monopoly of another. For all these reasons, the eighteenth century became what one historian many years ago termed the "golden age of smugglers."[1] Governments could not effectively control their subjects' activities. Clashes among colonists and, in North America, between settlers and indigenous peoples, led to conflicts between European governments.

French–British Rivalry

Major flash points existed between France and Britain in North America. Their colonists quarreled endlessly with each other over the coveted regions of the lower Saint Lawrence River valley, upper New England, and, later, the Ohio River valley. Other rivalries arose over fishing rights, the fur trade, and alliances with Native Americans. Native Americans, in turn, used imperial rivalries to serve their own purposes.

The heart of the eighteenth-century colonial rivalry in the Americas, however, lay in the West Indies. These tropical islands, close to the American continents, were the jewels of empire. The West Indies plantations raised tobacco, cotton, indigo, coffee, and, most importantly, sugar. European demand for these commodities rose tremendously as they increasingly became part of daily life. Sugar in particular had become a staple rather than a luxury. It was used in coffee, tea, and cocoa, for making candy and preserving fruits, and in the brewing industry. There seemed no limit to its uses, no limit to consumer demand for it, and, for a time, almost no limit to the riches it might bring to plantation owners. The profitable cultivation of these products during the seventeenth and eighteenth centuries relied upon the exploitation of African slave labor. (See "Encountering the Past: Sugar Enters the Western Diet,." page 491.)

India was another area of French–British rivalry. In India, both France and Britain granted legal monopolies on trade to privileged chartered companies (the *Compagnie des Indes* and the East India Company). Although the trade of India and Asia figured only marginally in the economics of early eighteenth-century empire, some Europeans hoped to develop profitable commerce with India. Others regarded India as a springboard into the even larger potential market of China. The original

---

[1]Walter Dorn, *Competition for Empire, 1740–1763* (New York: Harper, 1940), p. 266.

European footholds in India were trading posts called *factories*. They existed through privileges granted by various Indian governments that in theory were themselves subject to the decaying Mughal Empire, which exercised little effective authority.

Two circumstances in the mid-eighteenth century changed this situation in India. First, the administration and government of several Indian states had weakened. Second, Joseph Dupleix (1697–1763) for the French and Robert Clive (1725–1774) for the British saw the developing power vacuum as an opportunity to increase the control of their respective companies. To maintain their own security and to expand their privileges, each of the two companies began in effect to take over the government of some of the regions. Each group of Europeans hoped to checkmate the other.

The Dutch maintained their extensive commercial empire further to the east in what today is Indonesia. By the eighteenth century, the other European powers more or less acknowledged Dutch predominance in that region.

▼ The Spanish Colonial System

Spanish control of its American Empire involved two aspects: government and monopolistic trade regulation. Both were more rigid in appearance than in practice. Actual government was often informal, and the trade monopoly was frequently breached. Until the mid-eighteenth century, the primary purpose of the Spanish Empire was to supply Spain with the precious metals mined in the New World.

View the **Map**
"European Global Empires, 1600–1800" on **MyHistoryLab.com**

Colonial Government

Because Queen Isabella of Castile (r. 1474–1504) had commissioned Columbus, the technical legal link between the New World and Spain was the crown of Castile. Its powers both at home and in America were subject to few limitations. The Castilian monarch assigned the government of America to the Council of the Indies, which, with the monarch, nominated the viceroys of New Spain (Mexico) and Peru. These viceroys served as the chief executives in the New World and carried out the laws issued by the Council of the Indies.

Each of the viceroyalties was divided into several subordinate judicial councils, known as *audiencias*. A variety of local officers, the most important of which were the *corregidores*, presided over municipal councils. All of these officers represented a vast array of patronage, which the monarchy usually bestowed on persons born in Spain. Virtually all power flowed from the top of this political structure downward; in effect, local initiative or self-government scarcely existed.

Trade Regulation

The colonial political structures functioned largely to support Spanish commercial self-interests. The *Casa de Contratación* (House of Trade) in Seville regulated all trade with the New World. The *Casa* was the most influential institution of the Spanish Empire. Its members worked closely with the *Consulado* (Merchant Guild) of Seville and other groups involved with American commerce in Cádiz, the only port authorized for use in the American trade.

A complicated system of trade and bullion fleets administered from Seville maintained Spain's trade monopoly. Each year, a fleet of commercial vessels (the *flota*), controlled by Seville merchants and escorted by warships, carried merchandise from Spain to a few specified ports in America, including Portobello, Veracruz, and Cartagena on the Atlantic coast. There were no authorized ports on the Pacific Coast. Areas far to the south, such as Buenos Aires on the Río de la Plata, received goods only after the shipments had been unloaded at one of the authorized ports. After selling their wares, the ships were loaded with silver and gold bullion; they usually spent the winter in heavily fortified Caribbean ports and then sailed back to Spain. The *flota* system always worked imperfectly, but trade outside it was illegal. Regulations prohibited the Spanish colonists within the American Empire from establishing direct trade with each other and from building their own shipping and commercial industry. Foreign merchants were also forbidden to breach the Spanish monopoly. Spanish ships continued to transport precious metals and coins from the Americas to Spain through the early nineteenth century. Modern-day treasure hunters still occasionally discover troves of precious metal from shipwrecked vessels of the colonial Spanish Empire.

Colonial Reform under the Spanish Bourbon Monarchs

A crucial change occurred in the Spanish colonial system in the early eighteenth century. The War of the Spanish Succession (1701–1714) and the Treaty of Utrecht (1713) led to a change in the dynasty holding the Spanish throne: the Spanish Habsburgs were replaced by the Bourbons of France. The Bourbon king Philip V (r. 1700–1746) and his successors tried to use French administrative skills to reinvigorate the imperial trade monopoly, which had lapsed under the last Spanish Habsburgs, and thus to improve Spain's economic and political power in Europe.

Under Philip V, Spanish coastal patrol vessels tried to suppress smuggling in American waters. (See the Document "Buccaneers Prowl the High Seas,." page 488.) An incident arising from this policy led to war with England in 1739, the year in which Philip established the viceroyalty of New Granada in the area that today includes Venezuela, Colombia, and Ecuador. His goal was to strengthen the royal government there, but the ensuing wars exposed the vulnerability of the Spanish empire to naval attack and economic penetration. Government circles then became convinced that the colonial system had to be reformed.

Charles III (r. 1759–1788), the most important of the imperial reformers, attempted to reassert Spain's control of the empire. Like his Bourbon predecessors, Charles emphasized royal ministers rather than councils. Thus, the role of both the Council of the Indies and the *Casa de Contratación* diminished. After 1765, Charles abolished the monopolies of Seville and Cádiz and permitted other Spanish cities to trade with America. He also opened more South American and Caribbean ports to trade and authorized commerce between Spanish ports in America. In 1776, he organized a fourth viceroyalty in the region of Río de la Plata, which included much of present-day Argentina, Uruguay, Paraguay, and Bolivia. (See Map 16–1.)

To increase the efficiency of tax collection and end bureaucratic corruption, Charles III introduced the institution of the *intendant* into the Spanish Empire. These royal bureaucrats were patterned on the famously effective agents of French royal administration during the absolutist reign of Louis XIV.

The late-eighteenth-century Bourbon reforms stimulated the imperial Spanish economy. Trade expanded and became more varied. These reforms, however, also brought the empire more fully under direct Spanish control. Many *peninsulares* (persons born in Spain) entered the New World to fill new posts, which were often the most profitable jobs in the region. Expanding trade brought more Spanish merchants to Latin America. The economy remained export oriented, and the colonies' economic life was still organized to benefit Spain. As a result of these policies, the **creoles** (persons of European descent born in the Spanish colonies) came to feel they were second-class subjects. In time, their resentment would provide a major source of the discontent leading to the wars of independence in the early nineteenth century. The imperial reforms of Charles III were the Spanish analog to the new colonial measures the British government undertook after 1763, which, as will be seen later in this chapter, led to the American Revolution.

▼ Black African Slavery, the Plantation System, and the Atlantic Economy

Slavery had existed in various parts of Europe since ancient times. Before the eighteenth century, little or no moral or religious stigma was attached to slave owning or slave trading. It had a continuous existence in the Mediterranean world, where the sources of slaves changed over the centuries. After the conquest of Constantinople in 1453, the Ottoman Empire forbade the exportation of white slaves from regions under its control, but continued to enslave young Christian boys

The Silver Mines of Potosí. The Spanish had discovered precious metals in their South American Empire early in the sixteenth century; the mines provided Spain with a vast treasure in silver until the eighteenth century. The silver mines of Potosí were worked by conscripted Indian laborers under extremely harsh conditions (note the head impaled on a stake in the foreground). © INTERFOTO/Alamy

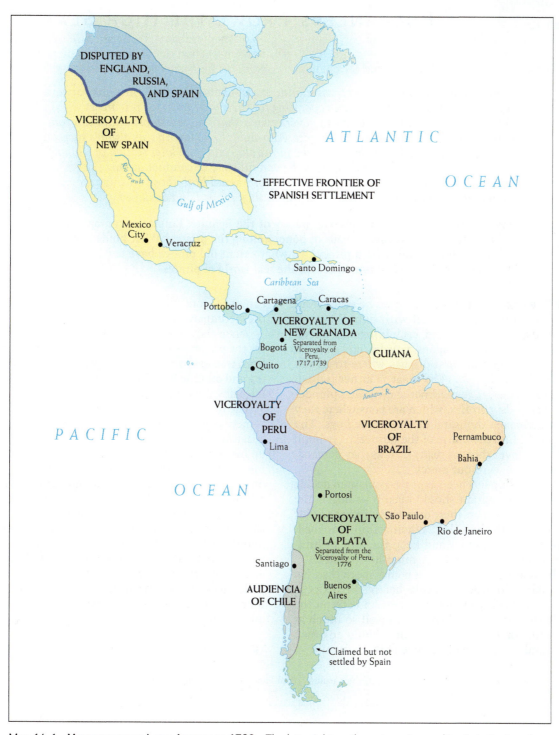

Map 16–1 **VICEROYALTIES IN LATIN AMERICA IN 1780**   The late eighteenth-century viceroyalties in Latin America display the effort of the Spanish Bourbon monarchy to establish more direct control of the colonies. They sought this control through the introduction of more royal officials and by establishing more governmental districts.

Document

BUCCANEERS PROWL THE HIGH SEAS

Piracy was a major problem for transatlantic trade. There was often a fine line between freewheeling buccaneering pirates operating for their own gain and privateers who in effect worked for various European governments that wanted to penetrate the commercial monopoly of the Spanish Empire. Alexander Exquemelin was a ship's surgeon who for a time plied his trade on board a pirate ship and then later settled in Holland. His account of those days emphasizes the careful code of conduct among the pirates themselves and the harshness of their behavior toward both those on ships they captured and poor farmers and fishermen whom they robbed and enslaved.

How did the restrictive commercial policy of the Spanish Empire encourage piracy and privateering? Was there a code of honor among the pirates? What kinds of people may have suffered most from piracy? To what extent did pirates have any respect for individual freedom? How romantic was the real world of pirates?

When a buccaneer is going to sea he sends word to all who wish to sail with him. When all are ready, they go on board, each bringing what he needs in the way of weapons, powder, and shot.

On the ship, they first discuss where to go and get food supplies. . . . The meat is either [salted] pork or turtle. . . . Sometimes they go and plunder the Spaniards' *corrales*, which are pens where they keep perhaps a thousand head of tame hogs. The rovers . . . find the house of the farmer . . . [whom] unless he gives them as many hogs as they demand, they hang . . . without mercy. . . .

When a ship has been captured, the men decide whether the captain should keep it or not: if the prize is better than their own vessel, they take it and set fire to the other. When a ship is robbed, nobody must plunder and keep the loot to himself. Everything taken . . . must be shared . . . , without any man enjoying a penny more than his fair share. To prevent deceit, before the booty is distributed everyone has to swear an oath on the Bible that he has not kept for himself so much as the value of a sixpence. . . . And should any man be found to have made a false oath, he would be banished from the rovers, and never be allowed in their company. . . .

When they have captured a ship, the buccaneers set the prisoners on shore as soon as possible, apart from two or three whom they keep to do the cooking and other work they themselves do not care for, releasing these men after two or three years.

The rovers frequently put in for fresh supplies at some island or other, often . . . lying off the south coast of Cuba. . . . Everyone goes ashore and sets up his tent, and they take turns to go on marauding expeditions in their canoes. They take prisoner . . . poor men who catch and set turtles for a living, to provide for their wives and children. Once captured, these men have to catch turtle for the rovers as long as they remain on the island. Should the rovers intend to cruise along a coast where turtle abound, they take the fishermen along with them. The poor fellows may be compelled to stay away from their wives and families four or five years, with no news whether they are alive or dead.

👁 —Watch the Video "Piracy" on MyHistoryLab.com

From Alexander O. Exquemelin, *The Buccaneers of America*, trans. by Alexis Brown (Baltimore: Penguin, 1969), pp. 70–72.

from Southeastern Europe and convert them to Islam under the *devşirme* system. The Portuguese imported African slaves into the Iberian Peninsula from the Canary Islands and West Africa. Black slaves from Africa were also not uncommon in other parts of the Mediterranean, and a few found their way into northern Europe. There they were favored as personal servants in royal courts or in wealthy homes because of the novelty of their color.

Yet, from the sixteenth century onward, first within the West Indies and the Spanish and Portuguese settlements in South America and then in the British colonies on the South Atlantic seaboard of North America, slave labor became a fundamental social and economic factor. The development of those plantation economies based on slave labor led to unprecedented interaction between the peoples of Europe and Africa and between the European settlers in the Americas and Africa. From that point onward, Africa and Africans were drawn into the Western experience as never before in history.

Watch the **Video**
"Author Video Podcast: From Triangular Trade to an Atlantic System: Rethinking the Links That Created the Atlantic World" on **MyHistoryLab.com**

The African Presence in the Americas

Once they had encountered and begun to settle the New World, the Spanish and Portuguese faced a severe shortage of labor. They and most of the French and English settlers who came later had no intention of undertaking manual work themselves. At first, they used Native Americans as laborers, but during the sixteenth century as well as afterward, disease killed hundreds of thousands of indigenous people. As a result, labor soon became scarce. The Spanish and Portuguese then turned to the labor of imported African slaves. Settlers in the English colonies of North America during the seventeenth century turned more slowly to slavery, with the largest number coming to the Chesapeake Bay region of Virginia and Maryland and later into the low country of the Carolinas. Until the end of the transatlantic slave trade in the nineteenth century, which African peoples became sold into slavery during any given decade largely depended on internal African warfare and state-building.

The major sources for slaves were slave markets on the West African Coast from Senegambia to Angola. Slavery and an extensive slave trade had existed in West Africa for centuries. Just as particular social and economic conditions in Europe had led to the voyages of exploration and settlement, political and military conditions in Africa and warfare among various African nations similarly created a supply of slaves that certain African societies were willing to sell to Europeans. European slave traders did not confront a passive situation in West Africa over which they exercised their will by force and commerce. Rather, they encountered dynamic African societies working out their own internal historic power relationships and rivalries in which Africans sold and acquired other Africans from different regions and nations as slaves.

The West Indies, Brazil, and Sugar To grasp the full impact of the forced immigration of Africans to the Americas, we must take into account the entire picture of the transatlantic economy. Far more slaves were imported into the West Indies and Brazil than into North America. Although citizens of the United States mark the beginning of slavery in 1619 with the arrival of African slaves on a Dutch ship in Jamestown, Virginia, over a century of slave trading in the West Indies and South America had preceded that event. Indeed, by the late sixteenth century, Africans had become a major social presence in the West Indies and in the major cities of both Spanish and Portuguese South America. Their presence and influence in these regions would grow over the centuries. The sugar plantations on which many Caribbean economies depended were so deadly and slave mortality rates were so high that plantation owners had to import enslaved Africans continually; the constant influx of new African slaves sustained the African cultural presence in the West Indies. African labor and African immigrant slave communities were the most prominent social features of these regions, making the development of their economies and cultures what one historian has described as "a Euro-African phenomenon."[2] In these places, African slaves equaled or more generally surpassed the numbers of white European settlers in what soon constituted multiracial societies. Someone passing through the marketplace of these towns and cities would have heard a vast number of African, as well as European, languages. Although Native American labor continued to be exploited on the South American continent, it was increasingly a

This eighteenth-century print shows bound African captives being forced to a slaving port. It was largely African middlemen who captured slaves in the interior and marched them to the coast. North Wind Picture Archives

[2]John Thornton, *Africa and the Africans in the Making of the Atlantic World, 1400–1800*, 2nd ed. (Cambridge, UK: Cambridge University Press, 1998), p. 140.

marginal presence in the ever-expanding African slave-based plantation economy of the Atlantic seaboard, the Caribbean, and offshore islands.

Within much of Spanish South America, the numbers of slaves declined during the late seventeenth century, and slavery became somewhat less fundamental there than elsewhere. Slavery continued to expand its influence, however, in Brazil and in the Caribbean through the spreading cultivation of sugar to meet the demand of the European market. By the close of the seventeenth century, the Caribbean islands were the world center for the production of sugar. The opening of new areas of cultivation and other economic enterprises required additional slaves during the eighteenth century. The growing prosperity of sugar islands that had begun to be exploited in the late seventeenth century, as well as the new sugar, coffee, and tobacco regions of Brazil, where gold mining also required additional slaves, encouraged slave commerce and drove up prices to be paid for slaves. In Brazil, the West Indies, and the southern British colonies, European prosperity and African slavery went hand in hand.

View the **Image** "Sugar Plantation, Brazil" on **MyHistoryLab.com**

A vast increase in the number of Africans brought as slaves to the Americas occurred during the eighteenth century, with most arriving in the Caribbean or Brazil. Early in the century, as many as 20,000 new Africans a year arrived in the West Indies as slaves. By 1725, it has been estimated that almost 90 percent of the population of Jamaica consisted of black slaves. After the midcentury, the numbers were even larger. The influx of new Africans in most areas—even in the British colonies—meant the numbers of new forced immigrants outnumbered the slaves of African descent already present.

Sugar was extremely profitable for European plantation owners and British merchants, and palatable among European consumers, but it was catastrophic for the slaves who grew it in the West Indies and Brazil. One historian has recently called it a "murderous commodity."[3] Newly imported African slaves succumbed to new diseases against which they had no immunity. They were overworked in the fields and the mills on plantations that combined the dangers of agricultural and industrial work in an intense and never-ending labor cycle. Even slaves who survived the initial exposure to new pathogens remained particularly vulnerable to disease because they were malnourished. For all these reasons, the mortality rate among slaves was high, and the birth rate was low. Slave populations were replenished not through births but through the continuing slave trade from Africa. Consequently, one of the key factors in the social life of many of the areas of American slavery during the eighteenth century was the presence of persons newly arrived from Africa, carrying with them African languages, religion, culture, and local African ethnic identities that they would infuse into the already existing slave communities. Thus, the eighteenth century witnessed an enormous new African presence throughout the Americas.

Slavery and the Transatlantic Economy

Different nations dominated the slave trade in different periods. During the sixteenth century, the Portuguese and the Spanish were most involved. The Dutch supplanted them during most of the seventeenth century. Thereafter, during the late seventeenth and eighteenth centuries, the English were the chief slave traders. French traders also participated in the trade.

View the **Map** "Map Discovery: Atlantic Slave Trade, ca. 1600–1650" on **MyHistoryLab.com**

Slavery touched most of the economy of the transatlantic world. (See Map 16–2, p. 493.) Colonial trade followed roughly a geographic triangle. European goods—often guns—were carried to Africa to be exchanged for slaves, who were then taken to the West Indies, where they were traded for sugar and other tropical products, which were then shipped to Europe. Not all ships covered all three legs of the triangle. Another major trade pattern existed between New England and the West Indies with New England fish, rum, or lumber being traded for sugar. At various times, the prosperity of such cities as Amsterdam, Liverpool, England, and Nantes, France, rested largely on the slave trade. Cities in the British North American colonies, such as Newport, Rhode Island, profited from slavery sometimes by trading in slaves, but more often by supplying other goods to the West Indian market. All the shippers who handled cotton, tobacco, and sugar depended on slavery, though they might not have had direct contact with the institution, as did all the manufacturers and merchants who produced finished products for the consumer market and even shipbuilders who constructed the vessels used to carry people and goods across the Atlantic.

As had been the case during previous centuries, eighteenth-century political turmoil in Africa, such as the civil wars in the Kingdom of Kongo (modern Angola and Republic of Congo), increased the supply of slaves during that period. These Kongo wars had originated in a dispute over succession to the throne in the late seventeenth century and continued into the eighteenth. Some captives were simply sold to European slave traders calling at ports along the West African coast. Other African leaders conducted slave raids and sold their captives to finance the purchase of more weapons. Similar political unrest and turmoil in the Gold

---

[3]Vincent Brown, "Eating the Dead: Consumption and Regeneration in the History of Sugar," *Food and Foodways* 16 (2008): 117.

SUGAR ENTERS THE WESTERN DIET

BEFORE THE EUROPEAN discovery of the Americas, sugar was a luxury product that only the wealthy could afford. Because it requires subtropical temperatures and heavy rainfall, sugarcane could not be grown in Europe. Sugar had to be imported, at great expense, from the Arab world or from the Spanish and Portuguese islands off the coast of Africa, which were too arid for the plant to flourish.

The Caribbean, however, is ideal for sugarcane. Columbus carried it to the New World in 1493, and within about a decade sugar was being cultivated—by slaves—on Santo Domingo.

Yet, sugar production did not begin to soar until Britain and France established themselves in the Caribbean in the seventeenth century and the demand for sugar began to grow in Europe, first slowly and then insatiably. By the eighteenth century, the small British and French islands in the Caribbean where sugar was produced by African slave labor had become some of the most valuable real estate on earth.

Whereas the North American colonies imported Caribbean molasses to make rum, Europeans desired sugar to sweeten other foods. Sugar, the largest colonial import into Britain, embodied the mercantile policy of a closed economic system. It was raised in British colonies, paid for by British exports, shipped on British ships, insured by British firms, refined in British cities, and consumed on British tables.

The voracious demand for sugar as a sweetener was tied up with three other tropical products—coffee, tea, and chocolate—that European consumers began to drink in enormous quantities in the seventeenth and eighteenth centuries. Each of these beverages is a stimulant, which helps explain their popularity, but by themselves they taste bitter. Sugar made them palatable to European consumers. The demand for sugar and these drinks became mutually reinforcing: English markets for coffee, chocolate, tea, and sugar grew together.

As the production of sugar rose, its price fell. The cheaper sugar became, the more of it Europeans consumed. By the end of the eighteenth century, tea with sugar was cheaper than beer or milk, and it had become the most popular drink among the British poor (while remaining an elegant drink for the wealthy). Workers in English factories could feel energized by a short break and a cup of sweetened tea, even though the tea provided less nutrition than the food and beverages it replaced. Tea was easier to prepare than warm porridge, and more stimulating than nutrient-rich beer.

During the nineteenth century, sugar consumption continued to expand, and sugar became even cheaper when free-trade policies reduced protective import duties and when the French began to manufacture it from sugar beets, which could easily be grown in Europe. Nineteenth-century Westerners developed the custom of ending a meal with dessert, food usually sweetened with sugar.

From Sidney Mintz, *Sweetness and Power: The Place of Sugar in Modern History* (New York: Penguin Books, 1985).

How did the colonization of the Americas affect the European demand for sugar?

Why did sugar consumption increase so rapidly in Europe during the eighteenth and nineteenth centuries?

Sugar was both raised and processed on plantations such as this one in Brazil. Library of Congress

A Closer ▶ LOOK

🔍 View the **Closer Look** on **MyHistoryLab.com**

A SUGAR PLANTATION IN THE WEST INDIES

WEST INDIES SUGAR plantations, owned by Europeans who often stayed only long enough to make their fortunes, were located on the fertile islands of the Caribbean. Employing slave laborers imported from Africa, the sugar plantations combined agricultural production of sugarcane and the industrial processing of it into sugar for export to Europe. Both stages were potentially deadly; the latter involved slaves working with dangerous machinery often near fires and hot metal equipment used in the distillation process.

The production of sugar from the cane occurred in structures near the sugarcane fields themselves. Note the aqueducts carrying water to power some machinery.

Plantation owners generally lived in a "Great House" on high wind-swept areas of their estates while slaves dwelled in humble housing close to the areas where sugarcane was cultivated and animals used for food and sugar production were grazed.

The Granger Collection, New York

What do the locations of buildings on the image of the plantation tell you about the expected roles of different people in maintaining sugar plantation life?

What is the impression of sugar plantation work that these images are trying to create?

From the perspective of a sugar plantation owner, what makes a plantation successful?

Raw sugarcane from the nearby fields was placed between the vertical crushers to extract juice to be distilled into sugar crystals elsewhere on the plantation in cauldrons over fires.

Animal power was used to move the crushers until the late eighteenth century when some wealthy plantation owners replaced horses or mules with steam engines.

Denis Diderot, *Encyclopedie, ou, Dictionnaire Raisonné des Sciences, des Arts et des Métiers.* Recueil de Planches, sur les Sciences. (Paris, 1762), vol. 1. Special Collections, University of Virginia Library

Map 16–2 **THE SLAVE TRADE, 1400–1860** Slavery is an ancient institution and complex slave-trading routes were in existence in Africa, the Middle East, and Asia for centuries, but it was the need to supply labor for the plantations of the Americas that led to the greatest movement of peoples across the face of the earth.

Coast area (modern Ghana) during the eighteenth century increased the supply of African captives to be sold into American slavery. Consequently, warfare in West Africa, often far into the interior, and the economic development of the American Atlantic seaboard were closely related.

The Experience of Slavery

The Portuguese, Spanish, Dutch, French, and English slave traders forcibly transported nearly 12 million (perhaps more; the exact numbers are disputed) Africans to the New World—the largest forced intercontinental migration in human history. During the first four centuries of settlement, far more black slaves came involuntarily to the New World than did free European settlers

or European indentured servants. The conditions of slaves' passage across the Atlantic were wretched. Quarters were unspeakably cramped, food was bad, disease was rampant. Many Africans died in the "First Passage" that took them from their native villages to the African coast; many more perished during the crossing, or "Middle Passage." (See "Compare and Connect: The Atlantic Passage,." pages 494–495.) There were always more African men than women transported, so it was difficult to preserve traditional African extended family structures. During the passage and later, many Africans attempted to re-create such structures among themselves, even if they were not actually related by direct family ties.

In the Americas, the slave population was divided among new Africans recently arrived, old Africans who had lived there for some years, and creoles who were the descendants of earlier generations of African slaves.

The Atlantic Passage

📖 Read the **Compare and Connect** on **MyHistoryLab.com**

SLAVERY LAY AT the core of the eighteenth-century transatlantic economy. At the heart of slavery lay the forced transportation in slave ships across the Atlantic of millions of Africans to the Americas. The frightening and horrific character of the Atlantic, or "Middle," Passage became widely known through the memoirs of sailors and slave trade captains. Groups who, beginning in the mid-eighteenth century, sought the abolition of slavery publicized the inhumanity of the passage in published attacks on the slave trade. They also provided and widely distributed illustrations of slave ships, such as the *Brookes*.

QUESTIONS

1. Who are the various people described in this document who in one way or another were involved in or profited from the slave trade?

2. What dangers did the Africans face on the voyage?

3. What contemporary attitudes could have led this captain to treat and think of his human cargo simply as goods to be transported?

4. How might the publication of the interior compartments of a slave ship have served the cause of antislavery? How and why might this illustration of a slave ship have proved more persuasive in rousing antislavery sentiment than a prose description?

5. How would this illustration and the description of the Atlantic Passage have contrasted with contemporary illustrations and memoirs of victorious naval battles on the high seas?

I. A Slave Trader Describes the Atlantic Passage

During 1693 and 1694, Captain Thomas Phillips carried slaves from Africa to Barbados on the ship Hannibal. *The financial backer of the voyage was the Royal African Company of London, which held an English crown monopoly on slave trading. Phillips sailed to the west coast of Africa, where he purchased Africans who had been sold into slavery by an African king. Then he set sail westward.*

Having bought my complement of 700 slaves, 480 men and 220 women, and finish'd all my business at Whidaw [on the Gold Coast of Africa], I took my leave of the old king and his *cappasheirs* [attendants], and parted, with many affectionate expressions on both sides, being forced to promise him that I would return again the next year, with several things he desired me to bring from England. . . . I set sail the 27th of July in the morning, accompany'd with the East-India Merchant, who had bought 650 slaves, for the Island of St. Thomas . . . from which we took our departure on August 25th and set sail for Barbadoes.

We spent in our passage from St. Thomas to Barbadoes two months eleven days, from the 25th of August to the 4th of November following: in which time there happened such sickness and mortality among my poor men and Negroes. Of the first we buried 14, and of the last 320, which was a great detriment to our voyage, the Royal African Company losing ten pounds by every slave that died, and the owners of the ship ten pounds ten shillings, being the freight agreed on to be paid by the charter-party for every Negro delivered alive ashore to the African Company's agents at Barbadoes. . . . The loss in all amounted to near 6500 pounds sterling.

The distemper which my men as well as the blacks mostly died of was the white flux, which was so violent and inveterate that no medicine would in the least check it, so that when any of our men were seized with it, we esteemed him a dead man, as he generally proved. . . .

The Negroes are so incident to [subject to] the smallpox that few ships that carry them escape without it, and sometimes it makes vast havoc and destruction among them. But tho' we had 100 at a time sick of it, and that it went thro' the ship, yet we lost not above a dozen by it. All the assistance we gave the diseased was only as much water as they desir'd to drink, and some palm-oil to annoint their sores, and they would generally recover without any other helps but what kind nature gave them. . . .

But what the smallpox spar'd, the flux swept off, to our great regret, after all our pains and care to give them their messes in due order and season, keeping their lodgings as clean and sweet as possible, and enduring so much misery and stench so long among a parcel of creatures nastier than swine, and after all our expectations to be defeated by their mortality. . . .

No gold-finders can endure so much noisome slavery as they do who carry Negroes; for those have some respite and satisfaction, but we endure twice the misery; and yet by their mortality our voyages are ruin'd, and we pine and fret ourselves to death, and take so much pains to so little purpose. ■

From Thomas Phillips, "Journal," *A Collection of Voyages and Travels*, Vol. 6, ed. by Awnsham and John Churchill (London, 1746), as quoted in Thomas Howard, ed., *Black Voyage: Eyewitness Accounts of the Atlantic Slave Trade* (Boston: Little, Brown & Company, 1971), pp. 85–87.

II. The Slave Ship *Brookes*

This print records the main decks of the 320-ton slave ship *Brookes*. It was first published in 1789 by abolitionists hoping to influence a new regulation of the slave trade. The original image contained seven different views of a slave ship, including the two reproduced here. The popularization of this image is considered to be one of the major breakthroughs in the nineteenth-century movement against slavery. ■

The average space for each African destined for slavery in the Americas was 78 inches by 16 inches, smaller than an adult coffin. The Africans were normally shackled to assure discipline, to prevent rebellions that might injure the crew or lead to the slaves' escape, and to break down normal social relations between the captives. Iron shackles also prevented Africans from committing suicide on the voyage.

The ship measured 25 feet wide and 100 feet long. Men and women were separated by barriers dividing sections of the ship.

Library of Congress

Through the most inhumane commercial use of space, between 609 and 740 slaves were crammed on board the Brookes for the nightmarish passage to America. A Parliamentary inquiry in 1788 found that the ship had been designed to carry no more than approximately 450 persons. There are only 420 persons depicted in this image, so the conditions on board the Brookes in the 1780s would have been even more crowded.

495

Plantation owners preferred the two latter groups, who were already accustomed to the life of slavery. They sold for higher prices. The newly arrived Africans were subjected to a process known as *seasoning*, during which they were prepared for the laborious discipline of slavery and made to understand that they were no longer free. The process of forcible reeducation might involve receiving new names, acquiring new work skills, and learning, to some extent, the local European language, in addition to physical intimidation. Some newly arrived Africans worked in a kind of apprentice relationship to older African slaves of similar ethnic backgrounds. Other slaves were broken into slave labor through work on field gangs. Occasionally, plantation owners preferred to buy younger Africans, whom they thought might be more easily acculturated to the labor conditions of the Americas. Generally, North American plantation owners were willing to purchase only recently arrived Africans who had already been seasoned in the West Indies.

Language and Culture The plantation to which the slaves eventually arrived always lay in a more or less isolated rural setting, but its inhabitants could sometimes visit their counterparts on other plantations or in nearby towns on market days. Within the sharply restricted confines of slavery, the recently arrived Africans were able, at least for a time, to sustain elements of their own culture and social structures. From the West Indies southward throughout the eighteenth century, there were more people whose first language was African rather than European. For example, Coromantee was the predominant language on Jamaica. In South Carolina and on St. Domingue, most African slaves spoke Kikongo to each other. It would take more than two generations for the colonial language to dominate, and even then the result was often a dialect combining an African and a European language.

Through these languages, Africans on plantation estates could organize themselves into nations with similar, though not necessarily identical, ethnic ties to regions of West Africa. The loyalty achieved through a shared African language in the American setting created a solidarity among African slaves that was wider than what in Africa had probably been a primary loyalty to a village. These nations that the plantation experience organized and sustained also became the basis for a wide variety of religious communities among African slaves that had roots in their African experience. In this manner, some Africans maintained a loyalty to the Islamic faith of their homeland. Nevertheless, as reminders of the pain of the Middle Passage, some newly arrived Africans were ostracized by established slave communities in the Americas.

Many of the African nations on plantations, such as those of Brazil, organized lay religious brotherhoods that carried out various kinds of charitable work within the slave communities. In the Americas, the various African nations would elect their own kings and queens, who might preside over gatherings of the members of the nation drawn from various plantations.

The shared language of a particular African nation in the Americas enabled the slaves to communicate among themselves during revolts such as that in South Carolina in 1739, in Jamaica in the early 1760s, and, most successfully, during the Haitian Revolution of the 1790s. In the South Carolina revolt, the slave owners believed their slaves had communicated among themselves by playing African drums. In the aftermath of the revolt, the owners attempted to suppress such drum playing in the slave community.

Daily Life The living conditions of plantation slaves differed from colony to colony. Black slaves living in Portuguese areas had the fewest legal protections. In the Spanish colonies, the church attempted to provide some protection for black slaves, but devoted more effort toward the welfare of Native Americans. Spanish law, however, allowed for self-purchase and manumission, leading to substantial communities of free blacks. Slave codes were developed in the British and the French colonies during the seventeenth century, but they provided only the most limited protection to slaves while assuring dominance to their owners. Slave owners always feared a revolt, and legislation and other regulations were intended to prevent one. All slave laws favored the master rather than the slave. Slave masters were permitted to whip slaves and inflict other harsh corporal punishment. Furthermore, slaves were often forbidden to gather in large groups lest they plan a revolt. In most of these slave societies, the law did not recognize slave marriages. Legally, the children of slaves were slaves, and the owner of their parents owned them too.

The daily life of most slaves during these centuries involved hard agricultural labor, poor diet, and inadequate housing. Owners could separate slave families, or their members could be sold separately after owners died. The slaves' welfare and their lives were sacrificed to the continuing expansion of the sugar, rice, and tobacco plantations that made their owners wealthy and that produced goods for European consumers. While climate, occupation, labor regime, possibility of emancipation, and the character of their masters could lead to variations in the quality of life of slaves, all slaves lived at another human being's mercy, in conditions dependent on his or her whim or fortune. The commonality of their exposed and difficult lives makes it impossible to call any form of slavery "mild."

Conversion to Christianity Most African slaves transported to the Americas were, like the Native Americans, eventually converted to Christianity. In the Spanish, French, and Portuguese domains, they became Roman Catholics. In the English colonies, most became Protestants of one denomination or another. Both forms of

Slaves on the plantations of the American South were the chattel property of their masters, and their lives were grim. Some artists sought to disguise this harsh reality by depicting the lighter moments of slave society as in this scene of slaves dancing. MPI/Stringer/Archive Photos/Getty Images

Christianity preached to slaves to accept both their slavery and a natural social hierarchy with their masters at the top. The abolitionists' later insistence that Christianity and slavery were incompatible was not a widespread belief before the mid-seventeenth century.

Although organized African religion eventually disappeared in the Americas, especially in the British colonies, some African religious practices survived in muted forms, gradually separated from African religious belief. These included an African understanding of nature and the cosmos, and the belief in people with special spiritual powers, such as conjurers and healers. Although many slaves found tremendous comfort in their Christianity, the original conversion of Africans to Christianity was nonetheless another example, like that of the Native Americans, of the forcible replacement of a set of non-European cultural values in the context of New World economies and social structures.

European Racial Attitudes Slavery had not always been racial: Christians and Muslims had been enslaving one another for centuries in the Mediterranean before Atlantic plantation slavery was established. While scholars disagree about whether slavery or racism came first, the slave trade was key in transforming religious understandings of difference into racial ones. In the Atlantic system of slavery, that slaves were black and masters were white was as fundamental as that slaves were chattel property. The European settlers in the Americas and the slave traders carried with them prejudices against black Africans. Many Europeans considered Africans to be uncivilized savages. Still others

 Read the Document
" 'A Defense of the Slave Trade,' July 1740" on
MyHistoryLab.com

looked down on them simply because they were slaves. Furthermore, many European languages and cultures attached negative connotations to the idea and image of blackness. In virtually all these plantation societies, race was an important element in keeping black slaves in subservience. Racial thinking about slavery became especially important in the nineteenth century.

The plantations that stretched from the Middle Atlantic colonies of North America through the West Indies and into Brazil constituted a vast corridor of slave societies in which social and economic subordination was based on both involuntary servitude and race. These societies had not existed before the European discovery and exploitation of the Americas. In its complete dependence on slave labor and racial differences, this kind of society was unique in both European and world history. Its social and economic influence transformed not only the plantation societies themselves, but West Africa, Western Europe, and New England as well. It existed from the sixteenth century through the late nineteenth century, when the emancipation of slaves had been completed through the slave revolt of Saint Domingue, which became Haiti (1794), the British outlawing of the slave trade (1807), the United States outlawing of the slave trade (1808), the Latin American wars of independence, the Emancipation Proclamation of 1863 and the Civil War in the United States, and the Brazilian emancipation of 1888. To the present day, every society in which plantation slavery once existed still contends with the long-term effects of that institution. Many scholars of Africa see the depopulation caused by the slave trade as a key factor in Africa's vulnerability to colonization in the nineteenth century and a root cause of economic and political instability in that continent today.

▼ Mid-Eighteenth-Century Wars

The chattel slavery that characterized the plantation economies of the New World conflicts with early-twentieth century European views about human rights, but before the Enlightenment and the abolitionist movement of the late eighteenth century, such views were irrelevant to the way people thought about labor. Similarly, in the mid-eighteenth century, statesmen had no principled commitment to peace as superior to war. The statesmen of the period generally assumed that warfare could further national interests. No forces or powers saw it in their interest to prevent war or maintain peace. Since all eighteenth-century wars (before the French Revolution) were fought by professional armies and navies, the conflicts rarely affected civilian populations deeply. Wars did not lead to domestic political or social upheaval, and peace did not bring international stability. Consequently, European nations often viewed periods of peace at the conclusion of a war simply as opportunities to recoup their strength so that they could start fighting again to seize another nation's territory or disrupt another empire's trading monopoly.

The two fundamental areas of great power rivalry were the overseas empires and central and eastern Europe. Conflict in one of these regions repeatedly overlapped with conflict in the other, and this interaction influenced strategy and the pattern of alliances among the great powers.

The War of Jenkins's Ear

By the mid-eighteenth century, the West Indies had become a hotbed of trade rivalry and illegal smuggling. Much to British chagrin, the Spanish government took its own alleged trading monopoly seriously and maintained coastal patrols, which boarded and searched English vessels to look for contraband.

In 1731, during one such boarding operation, there was a fight, and the Spaniards cut off the ear of an English captain named Robert Jenkins. Thereafter he carried about his severed ear preserved in a jar of brandy. This incident was of little importance until 1738, when Jenkins appeared before the British Parliament, reportedly brandishing his ear as an example of Spanish atrocities to British merchants in the West Indies. British merchants and West Indian planters lobbied Parliament to prevent Spanish intervention in their trade. Sir Robert Walpole (1676–1745), the British prime minister, could not resist these pressures. In late 1739, Britain went to war with Spain. This war might have been a relatively minor event, but because of developments in continental European politics, it became the opening encounter to a series of European wars fought across the world until 1815.

The War of the Austrian Succession (1740–1748)

In December 1740, only seven months after becoming king of Prussia, Frederick II (r. 1740–1786) opportunistically seized the Austrian province of Silesia in eastern Germany. The new Habsburg ruler, Maria Theresa (r. 1740–1780), had only occupied the throne herself for two months, was only twenty-three, and was a woman whose

control of the dynasty's holdings had yet to be established. The invasion shattered the provisions of the Pragmatic Sanction (see Chapter 13) and upset the continental balance of power. The young king of Prussia had treated the House of Habsburg simply as another German state rather than as the leading power in the region. Silesia was a valuable possession, and Frederick was determined to keep his ill-gotten prize.

Maria Theresa Preserves the Habsburg Empire The Prussian seizure of Silesia could have marked the opening of a general hunting season on Habsburg holdings and the beginning of revolts by Habsburg subjects. Instead, it led to new political allegiances. Although Maria Theresa was unable to regain Silesia, her preservation of the Habsburg Empire as a major political power was itself a great achievement.

Maria Theresa won loyalty and support from her various subjects by granting new privileges to the nobility. Most significantly, the empress recognized Hungary as the most important of her crowns and promised the

Maria Theresa of Austria provided the leadership that saved the Habsburg Empire from possible disintegration after the Prussian invasion of Silesia in 1740. Martin van Meytens: *Kaiserin Maria Theresia mit ihrer Familie auf der Schloßterasse von Schönbrunn.* Kunsthistorisches Museum, Vienna, Austria

Hungarian nobility local autonomy. Following in her father's footsteps, she preserved the Habsburg state, but at considerable cost to the power of the central monarchy.

Hungary would continue to be, as it had been in the past, a particularly troublesome area in the Habsburg Empire. When the monarchy was strong and secure, it could ignore guarantees made to Hungary. When the monarchy was threatened, or when the Hungarians could stir up enough opposition, the Habsburgs promised new concessions.

France Draws Great Britain into the War The war over the Austrian succession and the British–Spanish commercial conflict could have remained separate disputes. What united them was the role of France. Just as British merchant interests had pushed Sir Robert Walpole into war, aggressive court aristocrats compelled the elderly Cardinal Fleury (1653–1743), first minister of Louis XV (r. 1715–1774), to abandon France's planned naval attack on British trade and instead to support the Prussian aggression against Austria, the traditional enemy of France. This was among the more fateful decisions in French history.

In the first place, aid to Prussia consolidated a new and powerful state in central Europe. That new power could, and indeed later did, endanger France. Second, the French move against Austria brought Great Britain into the continental war, as Britain sought to make sure the Low Countries remained in the friendly hands of Austria, not France. In 1744, the British–French conflict expanded into the New World where France supported Spain against Britain. As a result, French military and economic resources were badly divided. France could not bring sufficient strength to the colonial struggle. Having chosen to continue the old continental struggle with Austria, France lost the colonial struggle for the future against Great Britain. The war ended in a stalemate in 1748 with the Treaty of Aix-la-Chapelle. Prussia retained Silesia, and Spain renewed the privilege granted Britain in the Treaty of Utrecht (1713) to import slaves into the Spanish colonies.

The "Diplomatic Revolution" of 1756

Although the Treaty of Aix-la-Chapelle had brought peace in Europe, France and Great Britain continued to struggle unofficially in the Ohio River valley and in upper New England. These clashes were the prelude to what is known in American history as the French and Indian War, which formally erupted in the summer of 1755.

Before war commenced again in Europe, however, a dramatic shift of alliances took place, in part the result of events in North America. The British king, George II (r. 1727–1760), who was also the Elector of Hanover, thought the French might attack Hanover in response to the conflict in America. Frederick II feared an alliance of

Russia and Austria. In January 1756, Britain and Prussia signed the Convention of Westminster, a defensive alliance aimed at preventing the entry of foreign troops into the German states. The convention meant that Great Britain, the ally of Austria since the wars of Louis XIV, had now joined forces with Austria's major eighteenth-century enemy.

The new alliance deeply troubled Maria Theresa, but it delighted her foreign minister, Prince Wenzel Anton Kaunitz (1711–1794). He had long thought an alliance with France was Austria's best chance of defeating Prussia. The Convention of Westminster made possible this alliance, which would have been unthinkable a few years earlier. France was agreeable because Frederick had not consulted with French ministers before coming to his understanding with Britain. So, in May 1756, France and Austria signed a defensive alliance. Kaunitz had succeeded in completely reversing the direction that French foreign policy had followed since the sixteenth century. France would now fight to restore Austrian supremacy in central Europe.

The Seven Years' War (1756–1763)

Britain and France had already been engaged in protracted conflict in North America. Now Frederick II precipitated a European war that extended that colonial rivalry.

View the **Map** "Map Discovery: The Seven Years War" on **MyHistoryLab.com**

Frederick the Great Opens Hostilities In August 1756, Frederick II opened what would become the Seven Years' War by invading the neighboring German state of Saxony. Frederick considered this to be a preemptive strike against a conspiracy by Saxony, Austria, and France to destroy Prussian power. He regarded the invasion as a continuation of the defensive strategy of the Convention of Westminster. The invasion itself, however, created the very destructive alliance that Frederick feared. In the spring of 1757, France and Austria made a new alliance dedicated to the destruction of Prussia. Sweden, Russia, and many of the smaller German states joined them.

Two factors in addition to Frederick's skilled leadership saved Prussia. First, Britain furnished considerable financial aid. Second, in 1762, Empress Elizabeth of Russia (r. 1741–1762) died. Her successor, Tsar Peter III, greatly admired Frederick. Although Peter II was murdered the same year, he reigned long enough to make immediate peace with Prussia, thus relieving Frederick of one enemy and allowing him to hold off Austria and France. The Treaty of Hubertusburg of 1763 ended the continental conflict with no significant changes in prewar borders. The prewar balance of power, however, continued to tilt in Prussia's favor. After this war, Frederick II came to be called Frederick the Great. Prussia, formerly a small German state overshadowed by the

Habsburgs, now firmly stood among the ranks of the great powers.

William Pitt's Strategy for Winning North America

The survival of Prussia was less impressive to the rest of Europe than were the victories of Great Britain in every theater of conflict. The architect of these victories was William Pitt the Elder (1708–1778), a person of colossal ego and administrative genius. Although he had previously criticized British involvement in Continental disputes, once he became secretary of state in charge of the war in 1757, he pumped huge sums into the coffers of Frederick the Great. He regarded the German conflict as a way to divert French resources and attention from the colonial struggle. He later boasted of having won America on the plains of Germany.

North America was the center of Pitt's real concern. Put simply, he wanted all of North America east of the Mississippi for Great Britain, and he came very close to getting it all. He sent more than 40,000 regular English and colonial troops against the French in Canada. Never had so many soldiers been devoted to colonial warfare. He achieved unprecedented cooperation with the American colonies, whose leaders realized they might finally defeat their French neighbors. Native Americans tried to exploit the dispute between the European powers to gain advantages against their own rivals, although their priorities were rarely allowed to direct military strategy.

The French government was unwilling and unable to direct similar resources against the English in America. Their military administration was corrupt, the military and political commands in Canada were divided, and France could not adequately supply its North American forces. In September 1759, on the Plains of Abraham, overlooking the valley of the Saint Lawrence River at Quebec City, the British army under James Wolfe defeated the French under Louis Joseph de Montcalm. The French Empire in Canada was ending.

Pitt's colonial vision, however, extended beyond the Saint Lawrence valley and the Great Lakes basin. The major islands of the French West Indies fell to British fleets. Income from the sale of captured sugar helped finance the British war effort. British slave interests secured the bulk of the French slave trade for themselves. Between 1755 and 1760, the value of the French colonial trade fell by more than 80 percent. In India, the British forces under the command of Robert Clive defeated France's Indian allies in 1757 at the Battle of Plassey. This victory opened the way for the eventual conquest of Bengal in northeast India and later of the entire subcontinent by the British East India Company. (See Chapter 25.) Never had Great Britain or any other European power experienced such a complete worldwide military victory.

The Treaty of Paris of 1763

The Treaty of Paris of 1763 reflected somewhat less of a victory than Britain had won on the battlefield. Pitt was no longer in office.

This scene, painted by artist Edward Penny, shows Robert Clive receiving a sum of money from Siraj-ud-daulah, the Mughal Nawab of Bengal, for injured officers and soldiers at Plassey. Clive's victory in 1757 at the Battle of Plassey led to English domination of the Indian subcontinent for almost two centuries. Clive had won the battle largely through bribing many of the Nawab's troops and potential allies. Erich Lessing/British Library, London, Great Britain/Art Resource, NY

CONFLICTS OF THE MID-EIGHTEENTH CENTURY	
1713	Treaty of Utrecht
1739	Outbreak of War of Jenkins's Ear between England and Spain
1740	Outbreak of War of the Austrian Succession
1748	Treaty of Aix-la-Chapelle ends War of Austrian Succession
1756	Convention of Westminster between England and Prussia
1756	Outbreak of Seven Years' War
1757	Battle of Plassey
1759	British forces capture Quebec
1763	Treaty of Hubertusburg
1763	Treaty of Paris ends Seven Years' War

The new king, George III (r. 1760–1820), and Pitt had quarreled over policy, and the minister had resigned. His replacement was the Earl of Bute (1713–1792), a favorite of the young monarch. Bute was responsible for the peace settlement. Britain received all of Canada, the Ohio River valley, and the eastern half of the Mississippi River valley. To Pitt's consternation, Britain returned Pondicherry and Chandernagore in India and the West Indian sugar islands of Guadeloupe and Martinique to the French. Nevertheless, with the British East India Company imposing its authority on weakened indigenous governments in India and large territorial holdings in North America, from this time until World War II, Great Britain was a world power, not just a European one.

View the Map "Map Discovery: British Possessions in North America and the Caribbean After the Treaty of Paris" on **MyHistoryLab.com**

The Seven Years' War had been a vast worldwide conflict. Tens of thousands of soldiers and sailors had been killed or wounded around the globe. At great internal sacrifice, Prussia had permanently wrested Silesia from Austria and had fundamentally undermined the integrity of the Holy Roman Empire. Habsburg power now depended largely on the dynasty's own domains—especially Hungary. France found its colonial dominions and influence substantially reduced. The Spanish Empire remained largely intact, but the British were more confident than ever that they could penetrate its markets.

The quarter century of warfare also caused a long series of domestic crises among the European powers. Defeat convinced many in France of the necessity for political and administrative reform. The financial burdens of the wars had astounded all participants. Every power had to increase its revenues to pay its war debt and finance its preparation for the next conflict. Nowhere did this search for revenue lead to more far-ranging consequences than in the British colonies in North America.

▼ The American Revolution and Europe

The revolt of the British colonies in North America was an event in both transatlantic and European history. It marked the beginning of the end of European colonial domination of the American continents. The colonial American revolt that led eventually to revolution erupted from problems of revenue collection common to all the major powers after the Seven Years' War. The War of the American Revolution also continued the conflict between France and Great Britain. French support of the colonists deepened the existing financial and administrative difficulties of the French monarchy.

Resistance to the Imperial Search for Revenue

After the Treaty of Paris of 1763, the British government faced two imperial problems. The first was the sheer cost of maintaining their empire, which the British felt they could no longer carry alone. The national debt had risen considerably, as had domestic taxation. Since the American colonies had been the chief beneficiaries of the conflict, the British felt it was rational for the colonies henceforth to bear part of the cost of their protection and administration. The second problem was the vast expanse of new territory in North America that the British had to organize. This included all the land from the mouth of the Saint Lawrence River to the Mississippi River, with its French settlers and, more importantly, its Native Americans. (See Map 16–3, p. 502.) Even after the end of the French and Indian War, as the North American theater of the Seven Years' War was known, the British continued to spend a lot of money to maintain what was in some ways a military occupation of their new territories in the interior of North America.

The British drive for revenue began in 1764 with the passage of the Sugar Act under the ministry of George Grenville (1712–1770). The measure attempted to produce more revenue from imports into the colonies by the rigorous collection of what was actually a lower tax. Smugglers who violated the law were to be tried in admiralty courts without juries. The next year, Parliament passed the Stamp Act, which put a tax on legal documents and other items such as newspapers. The British considered these taxes legal, because Parliament had approved the decision to collect them, and fair, because the money was to be spent in the colonies.

The Americans responded that they alone, through their colonial assemblies, had the right to tax themselves and that they were not represented in Parliament. They feared that if their colonial government was financed from outside, they would lose control over it. In October 1765, the Stamp Act Congress met in America and drew up a protest to the crown. Groups known as the Sons of Liberty roused up disorder in the colonies, particularly in Massachusetts. The colonists agreed to refuse to import British goods. In 1766, Parliament repealed the Stamp Act, but through the Declaratory Act insisted it had the power to legislate for the colonies.

View the Image "1765 Stamp Act Protest" on **MyHistoryLab.com**

The Stamp Act crisis set the pattern for the next ten years. Parliament, under the leadership of a royal minister, would approve revenue or administrative legislation. The Americans would then resist by reasoned argument, economic pressure, and violence. Then the British would repeal the legislation, and the process would begin again. Each time, tempers on both sides became more frayed and positions more irreconcilable. With each clash, the

Map 16–3 **NORTH AMERICA IN 1763** In the year of the victory over France, the English colonies lay along the Atlantic seaboard. The difficulties of organizing authority over the previous French territory in Canada and west of the Appalachian Mountains would contribute to the coming of the American Revolution.

colonists more fully developed their own thinking about political liberty.

The Crisis and Independence

In 1767, Charles Townshend (1725–1767), as Chancellor of the Exchequer, the British finance minister, led Parliament to pass a series of revenue acts relating to colonial imports. The colonists again resisted. The ministry sent over its own customs agents to administer the laws. To protect these new officers, the British sent troops to Boston in 1768. Predictable tensions resulted. In March 1770, British troops killed five citizens in an incident that came to be known in the colonies as the Boston Massacre. That same year, Parliament repealed all of the Townshend duties except the one on tea.

In May 1773, Parliament passed a new law relating to the sale of tea by the East India Company. The measure permitted the direct importation of tea into the American colonies. It actually lowered the price of tea while retaining the tax imposed without the colonists' consent. In some cities, the colonists refused to permit the unloading of the tea; in Boston, a shipload of tea was thrown into the harbor.

View the Image "Boston Harbor" on MyHistoryLab.com

The British ministry of Lord North (1732–1792) was determined to assert the authority of Parliament over the colonies. During 1774, Parliament passed a series of laws known in American history as the **Intolerable Acts**. These measures closed the port of Boston, reorganized the government of Massachusetts, allowed troops to be quartered in private homes, and removed the trials of royal customs officials to England. The same year, the Quebec Act extended the boundaries of Quebec to include the Ohio River valley. The Americans regarded the Quebec Act as an attempt to prevent their mode of self-government from spreading beyond the Appalachian Mountains.

During these years, citizens critical of British policy had established committees of correspondence throughout the colonies. They made the various sections of the eastern seaboard aware of common problems and encouraged united action. In September 1774, these committees organized the First Continental Congress in Philadelphia. This body hoped to persuade Parliament to restore self-government in the colonies and abandon its direct supervision of colonial affairs. Conciliation, however, was not forthcoming. In April and June 1775, colonists and British regular troops clashed in the Battles of Lexington and Concord and the Battle of Bunker Hill. The colonial assemblies began to meet under their own authority rather than under that of the king.

The Second Continental Congress gathered in May 1775. While it still sought conciliation with Britain, it also began to conduct the government of the colonies. By August 1775, George III had declared the colonies in rebellion. During the winter, Thomas Paine's (1737–1809) pamphlet *Common Sense* galvanized public opinion in favor of separation from Great Britain. (See the Document "Thomas Paine's *Common Sense*," page 503.) A colonial army and navy were organized. In April 1776, the Continental Congress opened American ports to the trade of all nations. On July 4, 1776, the Continental Congress adopted the Declaration of Independence. Early in 1778, Benjamin Franklin (1706–1790) persuaded the French government to support the rebellion, which thus widened into a European conflict. In 1779, the Spanish also joined the war against Britain. The War of the American Revolution continued until 1781, when the forces of George Washington defeated those of Lord Cornwallis at Yorktown. The 1783 Treaty of Paris concluded the conflict, and the thirteen American colonies established their independence.

Document

THOMAS PAINE'S "COMMON SENSE"

�֎

Thomas Paine moved from England to Philadelphia in the fall of 1774. In January 1776, he published a pamphlet, Common Sense, *that would become one of the most influential political documents in American history. Paine's simple, direct style made his argument accessible to even illiterate colonists; the pamphlet was widely reproduced and read aloud in taverns and other public venues. For the first time, Americans were confronted with a convincing argument that only independence would serve their interests.*

According to Paine, what concrete harm does an association with Great Britain do to the colonies? What lessons does he draw from the wars of the 1750s and 1760s? Could his concerns be addressed by a reform of the relationship between the Crown and the Colonies?

The Sun never shined on a cause of greater worth. 'Tis not the affair of a City, a County, a Province, or a Kingdom; but of a Continent—of at least one-eighth part of the habitable Globe. 'Tis not the concern of a day, a year, or an age; posterity are virtually involved in the contest, and will be more or less affected even to the end of time, by the proceedings now. Now is the seed-time of Continental union, faith and honour.

. . .

I have heard it asserted by some, that as America has flourished under her former connection with Great Britain, the same connection is necessary towards her future happiness, and will always have the same effect. Nothing can be more fallacious than this kind of argument. We may as well assert that because a child has thrived upon milk, that it is never to have meat . . .

America would have flourished as much, and probably much more, had no European power taken any notice of her. The commerce by which she hath enriched herself are the necessaries of life, and will always have a market while eating is the custom of Europe. . . . Our corn will fetch its price in any market in Europe.

. . .

But the injuries and disadvantages which we sustain by that connection, are without number; and our duty to mankind at large, as well as to ourselves, instruct us to renounce the alliance: because, any submission to, or dependence on, Great Britain, tends directly to involve this Continent in European wars and quarrels, and set us at variance with nations who would otherwise seek our friendship, and against whom we have neither anger nor complaint. As Europe is our market for trade, we ought to form no partial connection with any part of it. It is the true interest of America to steer clear of European contentions, which she never can do, while, by her dependence on Britain, she is made the makeweight in the scale of British politics.

Europe is too thickly planted with Kingdoms to be long at peace, and whenever a war breaks out between England and any foreign power, the trade of America goes to ruin, BECAUSE OF HER CONNECTION WITH BRITAIN.

. . .

There is something very absurd, in supposing a continent to be perpetually governed by an island.

From Thomas Paine, *Common Sense; addressed to the Inhabitants of America* (Philadelphia: Bell, 1776).

American Political Ideas

The political ideas of the American colonists had largely arisen out of the struggle of the seventeenth-century English aristocrats and gentry against the absolutism of the Stuart monarchs. The American colonists looked to the English Revolution of 1688 as having established many of their own fundamental political liberties. The colonists claimed that, through the measures imposed from 1763 to 1776, George III and the British Parliament were attacking those liberties and dissolving the bonds of moral and political allegiance that had formerly

⬛◖ Read the Document
"The Declaration of Independence (1776)" on **MyHistoryLab.com**

united the two peoples. Consequently, the colonists employed a theory that had developed to justify an aristocratic rebellion to support their own popular revolution.

These Whig political ideas, largely derived from the writings of John Locke, were, however, only a part of the English ideological heritage that affected the Americans. Throughout the eighteenth century, they had become familiar with a series of British political writers called the **Commonwealthmen**, who held republican political ideas that had their intellectual roots in the most radical thought of the Puritan revolution. During the early eighteenth century, these writers, the most influential of whom were John Trenchard (1662–1723) and Thomas Gordon (d. 1750) in *Cato's Letters* (1720–1723), had relentlessly criticized the government patronage and parliamentary management of Sir Robert Walpole

Many Americans fiercely objected to the British Parliament's attempts to tax the colonies. This print of a British tax collector being tarred and feathered warned officials of what could happen to them if they tried to collect these taxes. Philip Dawe (c. 1750–c. 1785), *The Bostonians Paying the Excise-Man or Tarring & Feathering*. London, 1774. Colored Engraving. The Gilder Lehman Collection on deposit at the Pierpont Morgan Library. GL 4961.01. Private Collection/Art Resource, NY

and his successors. They argued that such government was corrupt and undermined liberty, that parliamentary taxation was simply a means of financing political corruption, and that standing armies were instruments of tyranny. In Great Britain, this republican political tradition had only a marginal impact because most British subjects regarded themselves as the freest people in the world. Colonists, however, often accepted the radical books and pamphlets at face value. The policy of Great Britain toward America following the Treaty of Paris of 1763 had made many colonists believe the worst fears of the Commonwealthmen were coming true. Political events coinciding with the accession of George III to the throne appeared to confirm these fears.

Events in Great Britain

George III also believed the king should choose his own ministers and that Parliament should function under royal, rather than aristocratic, management. When William Pitt resigned in 1761, George ignored the great Whig families that had run the country since 1715 and appointed the Earl of Bute as his first minister.

Between 1761 and 1770, George tried one minister after another, but each, in turn, failed to gain enough support from the various factions in the House of Commons. Finally, in 1770, he turned to Lord North, who remained the king's first minister until 1782. Powerful Whig families and other political spokespersons claimed that George III was attempting to impose a tyranny. What they meant was that the king was attempting to curb the power of a particular group of the aristocracy. George III certainly was seeking to restore more royal influence to the government of Great Britain, but he was not trying to make himself a tyrant.

The Challenge of John Wilkes John Wilkes (1725-1797), a London political radical and member of Parliament, published a newspaper called *The North Briton*. In issue number 45 (April 1763), Wilkes strongly criticized Earl Bute's handling of peace negotiations with France. Wilkes was arrested under the authority of a general warrant issued by the secretary of state. He pleaded the privileges of a member of Parliament and was released. Despite widespread popular support of Wilkes, and although they concluded that the general warrant had been illegal, the House of Commons ruled that issue number 45 of *The North Briton* constituted seditious libel, and it expelled Wilkes. He soon fled the country and was outlawed.

In 1768, Wilkes returned to England and was reelected to Parliament, but the House of Commons, under the influence of George III's friends, refused to seat him even after he was elected three more times. Large, unruly demonstrations of shopkeepers, artisans, and small-property owners supported Wilkes as

"Wilkes and Liberty" was a popular slogan among political radicals in England long after Wilkes' 1763 arrest for seditious libel. In this 1771 mezzotint, "The City Chanters," women sell ballads in front of the Fleet prison; one of the sheets is labeled "An Irregular Ode to Wilkes & Liberty." Wilkes' widespread popularity among the "middling and inferior set of people, who stand most in need of protection," as he referred to his constituency, contributed to the ruling elites' anxieties. © Timewatch Images/Alamy

did aristocratic politicians who wished to humiliate George III. "Wilkes and Liberty" became the slogan of political radicals and many noble opponents of the monarch. Wilkes was finally seated in 1774, after having become the lord mayor of London.

The American colonists followed these developments closely. Events in Britain confirmed their fears about a monarchical and parliamentary conspiracy against liberty. The Wilkes affair displayed the arbitrary power of the monarch, the corruption of the House of Commons, and the contempt of both for popular electors. That same monarch and Parliament were attempting to overturn the traditional relationship of Great Britain to its colonies by imposing parliamentary taxes. The same government had then landed troops in Boston, changed the government of Massachusetts, and undermined the traditional right of jury trial. All of these events confirmed the portrait of political tyranny that had developed over the years in the minds of politically engaged colonists.

Movement for Parliamentary Reform

The political influences between America and Britain operated both ways. The colonial demand for no taxation without representation and the criticism of the adequacy of the British system of representation struck at the core of the eighteenth-century British political structure. British subjects at home who were no more directly represented in the House of Commons than were the American

colonists could adopt the colonial arguments. The colonial questioning of the tax-levying authority of the House of Commons was related to the protest of John Wilkes. Both the colonists and Wilkes challenged the power of the monarch and the authority of Parliament. Moreover, both the colonial leaders and Wilkes appealed over the head of legally constituted political authorities to popular opinion and popular demonstrations. Both protested the power of a largely self-selected aristocratic political body.

The American colonists also demonstrated to Europe how a politically restive people in the Old Regime could fight tyranny and protect political liberty. They established revolutionary, but orderly, political bodies that could function outside the existing political framework: the congress and the convention. These began with the Stamp Act Congress of 1765 and culminated in the Constitutional Convention of 1787. The legitimacy of these congresses and conventions lay not in existing law, but in the alleged consent of the governed. This approach represented a new way to found a government.

Toward the end of the War of the American Revolution, calls for parliamentary reform arose in Britain itself. The method proposed for changing the system was the extralegal Association Movement.

The Yorkshire Association Movement

By the close of the 1770s, many in Britain resented the mismanagement of the American war, the high taxes, and Lord North's ministry. In northern England in 1778, Christopher Wyvil (1740–1822), a landowner and retired clergyman, organized the Yorkshire Association Movement. Property owners, or freeholders, of Yorkshire met in a mass meeting to demand moderate changes in the corrupt system of parliamentary elections. They organized corresponding societies elsewhere. The Association Movement was a popular attempt to establish an extralegal institution to reform the government.

Parliament was not insensitive to the demands of the Association Movement. In April 1780, the Commons passed a resolution that called for lessening the power of the crown. In 1782, Parliament adopted a measure that abolished some patronage at the disposal of the monarch. These actions, however, did not prevent George III from appointing a minister of his own choice. In 1783, shifts in Parliament obliged Lord North to form a ministry with Charles James Fox (1749–1806), a longtime critic of George III, to the king's distress.

In 1783, the king approached William Pitt the Younger (1759–1806), son of the victorious war minister, to manage the House of Commons. During the election of 1784, Pitt received immense patronage support from the crown and constructed a House of Commons favorable to the monarch. Thereafter, Pitt sought to formulate trade policies that would give his ministry broad popularity. In 1785, he attempted one measure of modest parliamentary reform. When it failed, the young prime minister, who had been only twenty-four at the time of his appointment, abandoned the cause of reform.

By the mid-1780s, George III had achieved part of what he had sought since 1761. Economically, British trade with America after independence had actually increased. Domestically, George III had reasserted the influence of the monarchy in political affairs. The cost of his years of dominance had been high, however. His own mental illness, which would eventually require a regency, weakened royal power. On both sides of the Atlantic, the issue of popular sovereignty had been widely discussed. The American colonies had been lost.

Broader Impact of the American Revolution

The Americans—through their state constitutions, the Articles of Confederation, and the federal Constitution adopted in 1788—had demonstrated to Europe the

---

EVENTS IN BRITAIN AND AMERICA RELATING TO THE AMERICAN REVOLUTION

1760	George III becomes king
1763	Treaty of Paris concludes the Seven Years' War
1763	John Wilkes publishes issue number 45 of *The North Briton*
1764	Sugar Act
1765	Stamp Act
1766	Stamp Act repealed and Declaratory Act passed
1767	Townshend Acts
1768	Parliament refuses to seat John Wilkes after his election
1770	Lord North becomes George III's chief minister
1770	Boston Massacre
1773	Boston Tea Party
1774	Intolerable Acts
1774	First Continental Congress
1775	Second Continental Congress
1776	Declaration of Independence
1778	France enters the war on the side of America
1778	Yorkshire Association Movement founded
1781	British forces surrender at Yorktown
1783	Treaty of Paris concludes War of the American Revolution

---

possibility of government without kings and hereditary nobilities. They had established the example of a nation in which written documents based on popular consent and popular sovereignty—rather than on divine law, natural law, tradition, or the will of kings—were the highest political and legal authority. The political novelty of these assertions should not be ignored.

As the crisis with Britain unfolded during the 1760s and 1770s, the American colonists had come to see themselves first as preserving traditional English liberties against the tyrannical crown and corrupt Parliament and then as developing a whole new sense of liberty. By the mid-1770s, the colonists had rejected monarchical government and embraced republican political ideals. Once a constitution was adopted, they would insist on a Bill of Rights specifically protecting a whole series of civil liberties. The Americans would reject the aristocratic social hierarchy that had existed in the colonies and embrace democratic ideals—even if the franchise remained limited. They would assert the equality of white male citizens not only before the law, but also in ordinary social relations. When it came to white men, they would reject social status based on birth and inheritance and assert the necessity of the liberty for all citizens to improve their social standing and economic lot by engaging in free commercial activity. They did not free their slaves, nor did they address issues of the rights of women or of Native Americans. Yet in making their revolution, the American colonists of the eighteenth century produced a society that would eventually expand the circle of political and social liberty. In all these respects, the American Revolution was a genuinely radical movement, whose influence would widen as Americans moved across the continent and as other peoples began to question traditional modes of European government.

◉ Watch the **Video** "Revolutions in the Atlantic World" on **MyHistoryLab.com**

In Perspective

During the sixteenth and seventeenth centuries, the West European maritime powers established extensive commercial, mercantile empires in North and South America. The point of these empires was to extract wealth and to establish commercial advantage for the colonial power. Spain had the largest of these empires, but by the end of the seventeenth century, Britain and France had also each established a major American presence. As a vast plantation economy emerged, significant portions of these American empires became economically dependent on slave labor, drawn from the forced importation of Africans. Through this large slave labor force, African linguistic, social, and religious influences became major cultural factors in these regions.

During the eighteenth century, the great European powers engaged in warfare over their American empires and over their power in India. These colonial wars became entangled in dynastic wars in central and eastern Europe and resulted in worldwide midcentury European conflict.

In the New World, Britain, France, and Spain battled for commercial dominance. France and Britain also clashed in India. By the third quarter of the century, Britain had ousted France from its major holdings in North America and from any significant presence in India. Spain, though no longer a military power of the first order, had managed to maintain its vast colonial empire in Latin America and much of its monopoly over the region's trade.

On the Continent, France, Austria, and Prussia collided over conflicting territorial and dynastic ambitions. Britain used the continental wars to divert France from the colonial arena. With British aid, Prussia had emerged in 1763 as a major continental power. Austria had lost territory to Prussia, while France had accumulated a vast debt.

The midcentury conflicts, in turn, led to major changes in all the European states. Each of the monarchies needed more money and tried to govern itself more efficiently. This problem led Britain to attempt to tax the North American colonies, which led to a revolution and the colonies' independence. Already deeply in debt, the French monarchy aided the Americans, fell into a deeper financial crisis, and soon clashed sharply with the nobility as royal ministers tried to find new revenues. That clash eventually unleashed the French Revolution. Spain moved to administer its Latin American empire more efficiently, which increased revolutionary discontent in the early nineteenth century. In preparation for future wars, the rulers of Prussia, Austria, and Russia pursued a mode of activist government known as Enlightened Absolutism (see Chapter 17). In that regard, the mid-eighteenth-century wars set in motion most of the major political developments of the next half-century.

KEY TERMS

Commonwealthmen (p. 504)

creoles (p. 486)

Intolerable Acts (p. 502)

mercantilism (p. 484)

peninsulares (p. 486)

REVIEW QUESTIONS

1. What were the fundamental ideas associated with mercantile theory? Did they work? Which European country was most successful in establishing a mercantile empire? Least successful? Why?

2. What were the main points of conflict between Britain and France in North America, the West Indies, and India? How did the triangles of trade function among the Americas, Europe, and Africa?

3. How was the Spanish colonial empire in the Americas organized and managed? What changes did the Bourbon monarchs institute in the Spanish Empire?

4. What was the nature of slavery in the Americas? How was it linked to the economies of the Americas,

Europe, and Africa? Why was the plantation system unprecedented? How did the plantation system contribute to the inhumane treatment of slaves?

5. What were the results of the Seven Years' War? Which countries emerged in a stronger position and why?

6. How did European ideas and political developments influence the American colonists? How did their actions, in turn, influence Europe? What was the relationship between American colonial radicals and contemporary political radicals in Great Britain?

SUGGESTED READINGS

F. Anderson, *Crucible of War: The Seven Years' War and the Fate of Empire in British North America, 1754–1766* (2001). A splendid narrative account.

B. Bailyn, *The Ideological Origins of the American Revolution* (1992). An important work illustrating the role of English radical thought in the perceptions of the colonists.

C. A. Bayly, *Imperial Meridian: The British Empire and the World, 1780–1830* (1989). A major study of the empire after the loss of America.

I. Berlin, *Many Thousands Gone: The First Two Centuries of Slavery in North America* (1998). The most extensive recent

treatment emphasizing the differences in the slave economy during different decades.

R. Blackburn, *The Making of New World Slavery from the Baroque to the Modern, 1492–1800* (1997). An extraordinary work.

M. A. Burkholder and L. L. Johnson, *Colonial Latin America* (2004). A standard synthesis.

L. Colley, *Britons: Forging the Nation, 1707–1837* (1992). Important discussions of the recovery from the loss of America.

D. B. Davis, *Inhuman Bondage: The Rise and Fall of Slavery in the New World* (2006). A splendid overview by a leading scholar.

D. B. Davis, *The Problem of Slavery in the Age of Revolution, 1770–1823* (1975). A major work on both European and American history.

J. Elliott, *Empires of the Atlantic: Britain and Spain in America 1492–1830* (2006). A brilliant and accessible comparative history.

J. J. Ellis, *His Excellency: George Washington* (2004). A biography that explores the entire era of the American Revolution.

R. Harms, *The Diligent: A Voyage through the Worlds of the Slave Trade* (2002). A powerful narrative of the voyage of a French slave trader.

H. S. Klein, *The Atlantic Slave Trade* (1999). A succinct synthesis based on recent literature.

P. Langford, *A Polite and Commercial People: England, 1717–1783* (1989). An excellent survey covering social history, politics, the overseas wars, and the American Revolution.

P. Maier, *American Scripture: Making the Declaration of Independence* (1997). Replaces previous works on the subject.

A. Pagden, *Lords of All the World: Ideologies of Empire in Spain, Britain, and France, 1492–1830* (1995). One of the few comparative studies of the empires during this period.

M. Rediker, *Villains of All Nations: Atlantic Pirates in the Golden Age* (2008). A serious historical treatment of the subject.

S. Smallwood, *Saltwater Slavery: A Middle Passage from Africa to American Diaspora* (2007). An exploration of the harrowing experience of slave transportation across the Atlantic.

J. Thornton, *Africa and the Africans in the Making of the Atlantic World, 1400–1800*, 2nd ed. (1998). A discussion of the role of Africans in the emergence of the transatlantic economy.

J. Winik, *The Great Upheaval: America and the Birth of the Modern World, 1788–1800* (2007). Sets the founding of the American republic in a transatlantic political context.

G. S. Wood, *The American Revolution: A History* (2002). A major interpretation.

MyHistoryLab™ MEDIA ASSIGNMENTS

Find these resources in the Media Assignments folder for Chapter 16 on **MyHistoryLab**.

QUESTIONS FOR ANALYSIS

1. Why were plantations organized in this way, with the sugar refining, fields, and dwellings at the same site?

   Section: **Black African Slavery, the Plantation System, and the Atlantic Economy**

   View the **Closer Look** A Sugar Plantation in the West Indies, p. 492

2. What are the principles on which this author defends the slave trade?

   Section: **Black African Slavery, the Plantation System, and the Atlantic Economy**

   Read the **Document** "A Defense of the Slave Trade," July 1740, p. 497

3. After watching this video, what do you think was most important in the spread of revolutions from one side of the Atlantic to the other?

   Section: **The American Revolution and Europe**

   Watch the **Video** Revolutions in the Atlantic World, p. 506

4. How did ideas enunciated in the English Civil War influence American political rhetoric?

   Section: **The American Revolution and Europe**

   Read the **Document** The Declaration of Independence (1776), p. 503

5. For Colbert, what was the relationship between mercantilism and colonization?

   Section: **Mercantile Empires**

   Read the **Document** Jean Baptiste Colbert, "Mercantilism: Dissertation on Alliances," p. 484

OTHER RESOURCES FROM THIS CHAPTER

Periods of European Overseas Empires

Watch the **Video** The Origins of Modern Imperialism and Colonialism, p. 482

The Spanish Colonial System

View the **Map** European Global Empires, 1600–1800, p. 485

Black African Slavery, the Plantation System, and the Atlantic Economy

Watch the **Video** Piracy, p. 488

Watch the **Video** Author Video Podcast: From Triangular Trade to an Atlantic System: Rethinking the Links That Created the Atlantic World, p. 489

View the **Image** Sugar Plantation, Brazil, p. 490

View the **Map** Map Discovery: Atlantic Slave Trade, ca. 1600–1650, p. 490

Read the **Compare and Connect** The Atlantic Passage, p. 494

Mid-Eighteenth-Century Wars

View the **Map** Map Discovery: The Seven Years War, p. 499

View the **Map** Map Discovery: British Possessions in North America and the Caribbean After the Treaty of Paris, p. 501

The American Revolution and Europe

View the **Image** 1765 Stamp Act Protest, p. 501

View the **Image** Boston Harbor, p. 502

THE WEST & THE WORLD

The Columbian Exchange: Disease, Animals, and Agriculture

THE EUROPEAN ENCOUNTER with the Americas produced remarkable ecological transformations that have shaped the world to the present moment. The same ships that carried Europeans and Africans to the New World also transported animals, plants, and germs that had never before appeared in the Americas. There was a similar transport back to Europe and Africa. Alfred Crosby, the leading historian of this process, has named this cross-continental flow "the Columbian exchange." Many tragedies arose from the encounter between the people of the Americas and those of Europe, as well as from the forging of new nations and civilizations in the Americas.

Diseases Enter the Americas

With the exception of a few ships that had gone astray or, in the case of the Vikings, that had gone in search of new lands, the American continents had been biologically separated from Europe, Africa, and Asia for tens of thousands of years. In the Americas no native animals could serve as major beasts of burden, except for the llama, which could not transport more than about a hundred pounds. Nor did animals constitute a major source of protein for Native Americans, whose diets consisted largely of maize, beans, peppers, yams, and potatoes. Moreover, it also appears that native peoples had lived on the long-isolated American continents without experiencing major epidemics.

By the second voyage of Columbus (1493), that picture began to change in remarkable ways. On his return voyage to Hispaniola and other islands of the Caribbean, Columbus brought a number of animals and plants that were previously unknown to the New World. The men on all his voyages and those on subsequent European voyages also carried diseases novel to the Americas.

Diseases transported by Europeans ultimately accounted for the conquest of the people of the Americas as much as advanced European weaponry. Much controversy surrounds the question of the actual size of the populations of Native Americans in the Caribbean islands, Mexico, Peru, and the North Atlantic coast. All accounts present those populations as quite significant, with those of Mexico in particular numbering many millions. Yet in the first two centuries after the encounter, wherever Europeans went either as settlers or as conquerors, extremely large numbers of Native Americans died

Nothing so destroyed the life of the Native Americans whom the Spanish encountered as the introduction of smallpox. With no immune defenses to this new disease, millions of Native Americans died of smallpox during the sixteenth and seventeenth centuries. The Granger Collection

509

from diseases they had never before encountered. The most deadly such disease was smallpox, which killed millions of people. Beyond the devastation wrought by that disease, bubonic plague, typhoid, typhus, influenza, measles, chicken pox, whooping cough, malaria, and diphtheria produced deadly results in more localized epidemics. For example, an unknown disease, but quite possibly typhus, caused major losses among the Native Americans of New England between approximately 1616 and 1619.

Native Americans appear to have been highly susceptible to these diseases because, with no earlier exposure, they lacked immunity. Wherever such outbreaks are recorded, Europeans either contracted or died from them at a much lower rate than the Native Americans. These diseases would continue to victimize Native Americans at a higher rate than Americans of European descent through the end of the nineteenth century, when smallpox and measles still killed large numbers of the Plains Indian peoples of North America.

Although many historical and medical questions still surround the subject, it appears likely that syphilis, which became a rampant venereal disease in Europe at the close of the fifteenth century and eventually spread around the globe, was first transmitted to Europe by the returning crew on Columbus' ships. It seems to have been an entirely new disease, spawned through a mutation when the causal agent for yaws migrated from the Americas to new climatic settings in Europe. Until the discovery of penicillin in the 1940s, syphilis remained a major concern of public health throughout the world.

Animals and Agriculture

The introduction of European livestock to the Americas quite simply revolutionized the agriculture of two continents. The most important new animals were pigs, cattle, horses, goats, and sheep. Once transported to the New World, these animals multiplied at unprecedented rates. The place where this first occurred was in the islands of the Caribbean, during the first forty years of Spanish settlement and exploitation. This situation established the foundation for the later Spanish conquest of both Mexico and Peru by providing the Spanish with strong breeds of animals, especially horses, acclimated to the Americas when they set out to conquer the mainland of South America.

The horse became first the animal of conquest and then the animal of colonial Latin American culture. Native Americans had no experience with such large animals that would obey the will of a human rider. Mounted Spanish horsemen struck fear into these people, and for good reason. After the conquest, however, the Americas

from Mexico southward became the largest horse-breeding region of the world, with ranches raising thousands of animals. Horses became relatively cheap, and even Native Americans could acquire them. By the nineteenth century, the possession of horses would allow the Plains Indians of North America to resist the advance of their white attackers.

The flourishing of pigs, cattle, and sheep allowed a vast economic exploitation of the Americas. These animals produced enormous quantities of hides and wool. Their presence in such large numbers also meant the Americas from the sixteenth century through the present would support a diet more plentiful in animal protein than anywhere else in the world.

Europeans also brought their own plants to the New World, including peaches, oranges, grapes, melons, bananas, rice, onions, radishes, and various green

Within one year of Columbus's encounter with the Americas, the event had been captured in this woodcut (c. 1493). Columbus's several voyages, and those of later Europeans as well, introduced not only European warfare but also began a vast ecological exchange of plants, animals, and diseases between the Old and New Worlds. Courtesy of the Library of Congress

510

vegetables. Socially, for three centuries the most significant of these was sugarcane, whose cultivation created the major demand for slavery throughout the transatlantic plantation economy. Nutritionally, European wheat would, over the course of time, allow the Americas not only to feed themselves, but also to export large amounts of grain throughout the world. This American production of wheat on the vast plains of the two continents contrasted sharply with the difficulty Europeans faced raising grain in the northern and northeastern parts of the Continent, particularly in Russia.

No significant animals from the Americas, except the turkey, actually came to be raised in Europe. The Americas did send to Europe, however, a series of plants that eventually changed the European diet: maize, potatoes, sweet potatoes, peppers, beans, manioc (tapioca), peanuts, squash, pumpkin, pineapple, cocoa, and tomatoes. All of these, to a greater or lesser degree, eventually entered the diet of Europeans and of European settlers and their descendants in the Americas. Maize and the potato, however, had the most transforming impact. Each of these two crops became a major staple in European farming, as well as in the European diet. Both crops grow rapidly, supplying food quickly and steadily if not attacked by disease. Tobacco, we should note, originated in the Americas, too.

Maize was established as a crop in Spain within thirty years of the country's encounter with the New World. A century and a half later it was commonplace in the Spanish diet, and its cultivation had spread to Italy and France. Maize produced more grain for the seed and farming effort than wheat did. Throughout Europe, maize was associated primarily with fodder for animals. As early as the eighteenth century, travelers noted the presence of polenta in the peasant diet, and other forms of maize dishes spread.

The Spanish encountered the potato only when Pizarro conquered Peru, where it was a major part of the Native American food supply. It was adopted slowly by Europeans because it needed to be raised in climates more temperate than those of Spain and the Mediterranean. It appears to have become a major peasant food in Scotland, Ireland, and parts of Germany during the eighteenth century. It became more widely cultivated elsewhere in Europe only after new strains of the plant were imported from Chile in the late nineteenth century. In the middle of the seventeenth century, Irish peasants were urged to cultivate the potato as a major source of cheap nutrition that could grow in quantity on a small plot. The food shortages arising from the wars of Louis XIV and then during the eighteenth century led farmers in northern Europe to adopt the potato for similar reasons. It was nutrient insurance against failure of the grain harvest. There is good reason to believe the cultivation of the potato was one of the major causes of the population increase in eighteenth- and nineteenth-century Europe. It was the quintessential food of the poor. By the mid-nineteenth century, Irish peasants had become almost wholly dependent on the potato as a source of food. In the middle of the 1840s, an American parasite infected the Irish potato crop. The result of the failure of the crop and misguided policy-making was the death of hundreds of thousands of Irish peasants and the migration of still more hundreds of thousands to the Americas and elsewhere in the world.

Define the Columbian exchange. What was the impact of European diseases on the Americas? Why was the impact so profound? Why could so many European crops grow well in the Americas? What was the cultural impact of animals taken from Europe to the Americas? How did food from the Americas change the diet of Europe and then later, as Europeans immigrated, the diet of the entire world?

View the Image Columbus's Encounter with the Indians on **MyHistoryLab.com**

Watch the Video What Is Columbus' Legacy? on **MyHistoryLab.com**

View the Image Columbian Exchange on **MyHistoryLab.com**

Read the Document Smallpox epidemic in Mexico, 1520, from Bernardino de Sahagún, *Florentine Codex: General History of the Things of New Spain*, 1585 on **MyHistoryLab.com**

The salon of Madame Marie Thérèse Geoffrin (1699–1777) was one of the most important Parisian gathering spots for Enlightenment writers during the middle of the eighteenth century. Well-connected women such as Madame Geoffrin were instrumental in helping the philosophes they patronized to bring their ideas to the attention of influential people in French society and politics.   Chateaux de Malmaison et Bois-Preau, Rueil-Malmaison/© RMN-Grand Palais/Art Resource, NY

((•─|**Listen** to the **Chapter Audio** on **MyHistoryLab.com**

17

The Age of Enlightenment: Eighteenth-Century Thought

LEARNING OBJECTIVES

What was the intellectual and social background of the Enlightenment?

Who were the *philosophes?*

How did the *philosophes* challenge traditional religious ideas and institutions?

How did the *philosophes* apply Enlightenment ideas to social and economic problems?

How did the *philosophes* apply Enlightenment ideas to political issues?

What role did women play in the Enlightenment?

How did Rococo and Neoclassicism styles reflect and contribute to the prevailing trends of the age?

What was enlightened absolutism?

OVER THE COURSE of the eighteenth century, the expanding literate sectors of European society became increasingly convinced that the human condition could be improved through science, education, philosophy, economic growth, and political reform. This attitude is now commonplace, but it came into its own only after 1700. It represents one of the primary continuing intellectual inheritances from the age of Enlightenment.

The Enlightenment was inspired by the scientific revolution (see Chapter 14), but it was a self-conscious movement in its own right. Unlike the scientific revolution, which came to be called by that name only in the twentieth century, the Enlightenment was named by its own participants, who discussed vigorously what sorts of improvement were most enlightening. While it had its roots in the seventeenth century, the Enlightenment did not reach its height until the second half of the eighteenth century. By 1784, when the German philosopher Immanuel Kant defined Enlightenment as "man's emergence from his self-imposed immaturity," the term was well known across the continent. From 1740 to the French Revolution, Enlightened thinkers and writers challenged traditional intellectual and ecclesiastical authority in the name of reason. They believed that human beings could comprehend the operation of physical nature and mold it to achieve material and moral improvement, economic growth, and administrative reform. They advocated agricultural improvement, increased commerce and consumption, and the application of innovative rational methods to traditional social and economic practices. The rationality of the physical universe became a standard against which they measured and criticized the customs and traditions of society. In religious matters they generally advocated a policy of toleration that opposed the claims to exclusive religious privilege made by state-supported established churches whether Roman Catholic or Protestant. As the criticisms of Enlightenment writers penetrated every corner of contemporary society, politics, and religious opinion, the spirit of innovation and improvement came to characterize modern European society.

Although many participants in the Enlightenment looked to France and Britain as models, the movement found adherents in cities and towns across the continent. Their common interest in reason and reform transcended national boundaries as well as the divide between republican and monarchist political systems. Some of the ideas and outlooks of the Enlightenment had a direct impact on rulers in central and eastern Europe. These rulers, whose policies came to be called *enlightened absolutism*, sought to centralize their authority so as to reform their countries. They often attempted to restructure religious institutions and to sponsor economic growth. The confidence with which enlightened thinkers, or *philosophes*, believed they could describe the entire universe made it possible for one German writer to publish a book in 1719 with the typically ambitious title "Rational Thoughts On God, the World, the Human Soul and All Things in General."

The Enlightenment had its limits. Enlightened absolutists pursued some military and foreign policies that were in direct opposition to enlightened ideals. Enlightened thinkers throughout Europe continued to believe strongly in social hierarchies that left little room for the equality of women or people from outside of Europe. Nonetheless, both the Enlightenment writers and the absolutist monarchs inspired by them were forces for modernization in European life.

▼ Formative Influences on the Enlightenment

The Newtonian worldview, the political stability and commercial prosperity of Great Britain after 1688, the need for administrative and economic reform in France after the wars of Louis XIV, the consolidation of what is known as a *print culture*, and the increased opportunities for classification and comparison created by interactions with peoples on other continents were the chief factors that fostered the ideas of the Enlightenment and the call for reform throughout Europe.

Read the **Document**
"Immanuel Kant Defines the Enlightenment, 1784" on **MyHistoryLab.com**

Isaac Newton (1642–1727) and John Locke (1632–1704) (see Chapter 14) were the major intellectual forerunners of the Enlightenment. As both literacy and publishing increased, their ideas became known to more and more people. Emilie Du Châtelet (1706–1749) translated Newton's *Principia Mathematica* into French and provided explanatory annotation, helping to spread his influence. The achievements of the Scientific Revolution from Copernicus to Newton had persuaded natural philosophers and then many other writers that traditions of thought inherited from both the ancient and medieval Christian worlds were incorrect or confused and needed to be challenged. Newton's formulation of the law of universal gravitation exemplified the newly perceived power of the human mind. Newtonian physics had portrayed a pattern of mechanical and mathematical rationality in the physical world. During the eighteenth century, thinkers from a variety of backgrounds began to apply this insight to society. If nature was rational, they reasoned, society, too, should be organized rationally. Furthermore, Newton had encouraged natural philosophers to approach the study of nature directly and to avoid metaphysics and supernaturalism. He had insisted on the use of empirical experience to check rational speculation. This emphasis on concrete experience became a key feature of Enlightenment thought.

Newton's physics and Locke's psychology provided the theoretical basis for a reformist approach to society. The domestic stability of Great Britain after the Revolution of 1688 furnished a living example of a society in which, to many contemporaries, enlightened reforms appeared to benefit everyone. England permitted religious toleration to all except Unitarians and Roman Catholics, and even they were not actively persecuted. Relative freedom of the press and free speech prevailed.

The authority of the monarchy was limited, and political sovereignty resided in Parliament. The courts protected citizens from arbitrary government action. The army was small. Furthermore, the domestic economic life of Great Britain displayed far less regulation than that of France or other continental nations, and English commerce flourished. As reformist observers on the Continent noted, these liberal policies had produced neither disorder nor instability, but rather economic prosperity, political stability, and a loyal citizenry.

This view may have been idealized, but England was nonetheless significantly freer than any other European monarchy at the time. Many writers of the continental Enlightenment contrasted what they regarded as the wise, progressive features of English life with the absence of religious toleration, the extensive literary censorship, the possibility of arbitrary arrest, the overregulation of the economy, and the influence of aristocratic military values in their own nations and most particularly in France.

The Emergence of a Print Culture

The Enlightenment flourished in a *print culture*, that is, a culture in which books, journals, newspapers, and pamphlets had achieved a status of their own. In the past, print culture had deeply influenced the intellectual and religious movements associated with Renaissance humanism, the Reformation, and the Counter-Reformation. During the seventeenth century, a lively world of publication had arisen, which many governments sought to censor. During the eighteenth century, the volume of printed material—books, journals, magazines, and daily newspapers—increased sharply throughout Europe. Prose came to be valued as highly as poetry, and the novel emerged as a distinct literary genre.

Read the Document
"Denis Diderot, Preliminary Discourse from *The Encyclopedia* (France), 1751" on **MyHistoryLab.com**

One of the driving forces behind this expansion of printed materials was the increase in literacy that occurred across Europe. Significantly more people, especially in the urban centers of Western and central Europe, could read. As a result, the printed word became the chief vehicle for communicating information and ideas and would remain so until the electronic revolution of our own day.

A growing concern with everyday life and material concerns—with secular as opposed to religious issues—accompanied this expansion of printed forms. Toward the end of the seventeenth century, half the books published in Paris were religious; by the 1780s, only about 10 percent were. An English journal observed unhappily in 1790: "Novels spring into existence like insects on the banks of the Nile; and, if we may be indulged in another comparison, cover the shelves of circulating libraries, as locusts crowd the fields of Asia. Their great and growing number is a serious evil; for, in general, they exhibit delusive views of human life; and while they amuse, frequently they poison the mind."[1] While people criticized the moral influence of the novel, they did not deny its influence.

Books were not inexpensive in the eighteenth century, but they, and the ideas they conveyed, circulated in a variety of ways to reach a broad public. Private and public libraries, as the previous quotation noted, grew in number, allowing single copies to reach many readers. Authors might also publish the same material in

The frontispiece to Voltaire's 1738 work, *Elements of the Philosophy of Newton* shows Voltaire writing by a light deflected from the celestial Newton by a woman, his muse and lover, Emilie Du Châtelet. Du Châtelet helped Voltaire work through and come to understand Newton's *Principia Mathematica* during the course of her own translations.   © Lebrecht Music and Arts Photo Library/Alamy

[1] T. C. W. Blanning, *The Culture of Power and the Power of Culture: Old Regime Europe 1660–1789* (Oxford, UK: Oxford University Press, 2002), p. 151.

different formats—first in serial form in newspapers or journals, and later collected together in a book.

Within both aristocratic and middle-class society, people were increasingly expected to be familiar with books and secular ideas. Popular publications, such as *The Spectator*, begun in 1711 by Joseph Addison (1672–1719) and Richard Steele (1672–1729), fostered the value of polite conversation and the reading of books. Coffeehouses became centers for discussing writing and ideas. (See "Encountering the Past: Coffeehouses and Enlightenment," page 517.) The lodges of Freemasons provided another site for discussing secular ideas and secular books.

The expanding market for printed matter allowed writers to earn a living from their work for the first time, making authorship an occupation. Parisian ladies who hosted fashionable salons sought out popular writers. Some writers, notably Alexander Pope (1688–1744) in England and Voltaire in France, grew wealthy, providing an example for their young colleagues. In a challenge to older aristocratic values, status for authors in this new print culture was based on merit and commercial competition, not heredity and patronage.

A division, however, soon emerged between high and low literary culture. Successful authors of the Enlightenment addressed themselves to monarchs, nobles, the upper middle classes, and professional groups, and they were read and accepted in these upper levels of society. Other aspiring authors found social and economic disappointment. They lived marginally, writing professionally for whatever newspaper or journal would pay for their work. Many of these lesser writers grew resentful, blaming a corrupt society for their lack of success. They often espoused radical ideas or took moderate Enlightenment ideas to radical extremes, transmitting them in this embittered form to their audience.

An expanding, literate public and the growing influence of secular printed materials created a new and increasingly influential social force called *public opinion*. This force—the collective effect on political and social life of views circulated in print and discussed in the home, the workplace, and centers of leisure—seems not to have existed before the middle of the eighteenth century. Books and newspapers could have thousands of readers, who in effect supported the writers whose works they bought, as they discussed their ideas and circulated them widely. The writers, in turn, had to answer only to their readers. The result changed the cultural and political climate in Europe. In 1775, a new member of the French Academy declared:

A tribunal has arisen independent of all powers and that all powers respect, that appreciates all talents, that pronounces on all people of merit. And in an enlightened century, in a century in which each citizen can speak to the entire nation by way of print, those who have a talent for instructing men and a gift for moving them—in a word, men of letters—are, amid the public

dispersed, what the orators of Rome and Athens were in the middle of the public assembled.[2]

Governments could no longer operate wholly in secret or with disregard to the larger public sphere. They, as well as their critics, had to explain and discuss their views and policies openly.

Continental European governments sensed the political power of the new print culture. They initially regulated the book trade, censored books and newspapers, confiscated offending titles, and imprisoned offending authors. The eventual expansion of freedom of the press represented also an expansion of print culture—with its independent readers, authors, and publishers—and the challenge it posed to traditional intellectual, social, and political authorities.

▼ The Philosophes

The writers and critics who flourished in the expanding print culture and who championed reform and toleration were known as the **philosophes**. Not usually philosophers in a formal sense, but more frequently literary figures, economists, or historians, these figures sought to apply the rules of reason, criticism, and common sense to nearly all the major institutions, economic practices, and exclusivist religious policies of the day. The most famous philosophes included Voltaire, Montesquieu, Diderot, d'Alembert, Rousseau, Hume, Gibbon, Smith, Lessing, and Kant.

Read the **Document**
"Voltaire, on Social Conditions in Eighteenth-Century France" on **MyHistoryLab.com**

A few of these philosophes, particularly those in Germany, were university professors. Most, however, were free agents who might be found in London coffeehouses, Edinburgh drinking spots, the salons of fashionable Parisian ladies, the country houses of reform-minded nobles, or the courts of the most powerful monarchs on the Continent. In eastern Europe, they were often royal bureaucrats. They were not an organized group; they disagreed on many issues and did not necessarily like or respect each other. Their relationship to one another and to lesser figures of the same turn of mind has been compared with that of a family, which, despite quarrels and tensions, preserves a basic unity. Another historian has portrayed the participants in the Enlightenment across many different local cultures as "members of a wider intellectual movement, dedicated to understanding and publicizing the cause of human betterment on this earth."[3]

[2]Chrétien-Guillaume Malesherbes, as quoted in Roger Chartier, *The Cultural Origins of the French Revolution*, trans. by Lydia G. Cochran (Durham, NC: Duke University Press, 1991), pp. 30–31.

[3]John Robertson, *The Case for the Enlightenment: Scotland and Napes 1680–1760* (Cambridge: 2005), p. 377.

The philosophes drew the bulk of their readership from the prosperous commercial and professional urban classes who had enough income to buy and the leisure to read the philosophes' works. Along with forward-looking aristocrats, these readers discussed the reformers' writings and ideas in local philosophical societies, Freemason lodges, and clubs. The writers of the Enlightenment provided an intellectual ferment and a major source of ideas that could be used to undermine existing social practices and political structures based on aristocratic privilege. They taught their contemporaries, including reform-minded aristocrats, how to pose pointed, critical questions. Moreover, the philosophes generally supported the expansion of trade, the improvement of agriculture and transport, and the invention of new manufacturing machinery that were transforming the society and the economy of the eighteenth century and enlarging the business and commercial classes.

The chief bond among the philosophes was their common desire to advocate reason and reform religion, political thought, society, government, and the economy for the sake of human liberty. As historian Peter Gay once suggested, this goal included "freedom from arbitrary power, freedom of speech, freedom of trade, freedom to realize one's talents, freedom of aesthetic response, freedom, in a word, of moral man to make his way in the world."[4] In order to bring meaningful improvement to the lives of more than men in Europe's chattering classes, these ideas had to be pushed further than Enlightened thinkers would allow. They have also been challenged over the last three centuries. Nevertheless, no other single set of ideas has done so much to shape and define the modern Western world.

Philosophes and Patrons

The successful philosophe required not only bold ideas and a sharp wit, but also the patronage of wealthy and powerful supporters. While rulers and aristocrats were often eager to promote and profit from philosophes and their reformist ideas, on more than one occasion, Enlightenment writers and thinkers came up against the limits of what their patrons would support. By far the most influential of the philosophes was François-Marie Arouet, known to posterity by his pen name Voltaire (1694–1778). Voltaire's career was full of disruptions caused by his offenses against the rulers of France. During the 1720s, Voltaire had offended first the French monarch and then certain nobles by his politically and socially irreverent poetry and plays. He was arrested and twice briefly imprisoned, in comfortable conditions, in the Bastille, the royal prison-fortress in Paris. In 1726, to escape the wrath of a powerful aristocrat whom he had offended, Voltaire went into exile in England. There he visited its best literary circles, observed its tolerant intellectual and religious climate, relished the freedom he felt in its moderate political atmosphere, and admired its science and economic prosperity. In 1728 he returned to France and, in 1733, published *Letters on the English*. The book praised the virtues of the English, especially their religious liberty, and implicitly criticized the abuses of French society. The Parlement of Paris condemned the book, and the authorities harassed Voltaire. He moved to Cirey from which, if necessary, he could easily escape France into what was then the nearby independent duchy of Lorraine. There he lived with Countess Emilie Du Châtelet (1706–1749), a brilliant mathematician, discussed in Chapter 14, who became his mistress and muse. In 1738, with her considerable help, he published *Elements of the Philosophy of Newton*, which more than any other single book popularized the thought of Isaac Newton across the continent. In 1749, Du Châtelet died.

Shortly thereafter, Voltaire took up residence for three years in Berlin at the court of Frederick the Great of Prussia with whom he had corresponded for several years. The residency ended unhappily. Voltaire briefly settled in Switzerland near Geneva but clashed with local conservative Calvinist clergy. Thereafter he acquired the estate of Ferney, just across the French border, but close enough to flee to Geneva should the French authorities bother him. His extremely popular plays, essays, histories, and stories along with his far-flung correspondence made him the literary dictator of Europe. For the rest of his long life, he turned the venom of his satire and sarcasm against one evil after another in French and European life.

In 1755 a huge earthquake struck Lisbon, Portugal, killing at least 60,000 people. Voltaire wrote a deeply pessimistic poem commemorating the event. Other contemporary writers questioned his pessimism, arguing for a more optimistic view of life and nature. In 1759, Voltaire replied in the novel *Candide*, his still widely read satire attacking war, religious persecution, and what he considered unwarranted optimism about the human condition. Like most of the philosophes, Voltaire believed human society could and should be improved, but he was never certain that reform, if achieved, would be permanent. In that respect his thought reflected the broader pessimistic undercurrent of the Enlightenment. As his fellow philosophe Jean d'Alembert wrote, "Barbarism lasts for centuries; it seems that it is our natural element; reason and good taste are only passing."[5]

Voltaire died in 1778 in Paris after a triumphal return to that city, which he had not seen for decades.

Read the Document
"Voltaire, *Letters on England*" on
MyHistoryLab.com

---

[4]Gay, *The Enlightenment*, p. 3.

[5]Jean Le Rond d'Alembert, *Preliminary Discourse to the Encyclopedia of Diderot*, trans. by Richard N. Schwab (Indianapolis, IN: Bobbs-Merrill, 1985), p. 103.

COFFEEHOUSES AND ENLIGHTENMENT

THE IDEAS OF the Enlightenment spread through not only books and journals, but also public conversation. They took on a life of their own in public discussions in a new popular institution of European social life—the coffeehouse.

Coffee, originally imported into Europe from the Ottoman Empire, is the chief Turkish contribution to the Western diet. Coffeehouses had long existed in the Muslim world, encouraged by the Islamic prohibition on alcoholic drink. The first European coffeehouse appeared in Venice in the 1640s, and the first coffeehouse in Vienna opened its doors in 1683 with coffee left behind when the Turks abandoned their siege of the city.

By the middle of the eighteenth century, thousands of coffeehouses dotted European cities and towns. They varied tremendously in atmosphere and clientele, from coffeehouses like Tom and Moll King's that offered "late-night rakish carousing and prostitution" to others more like libraries with "twenty or thirty men sitting around in deep silence, reading newspapers, and drinking port."[1]

Throughout Europe, the coffeehouse provided a social arena for the open, spontaneous discussion of events, politics, literature, and ideas—but only for men (respectable women did not enter coffeehouses). By furnishing copies of newspapers and other journals, the proprietors of coffeehouses linked their customers to the growing print culture. In London coffeehouses, members of the Royal Society and other men associated with the new science mixed with merchants and bankers. Some London coffeehouse proprietors invited learned persons to lecture, usually for a fee, on Newtonian physics, the mechanical philosophy, ethics, and the relationship of science and religion.

Lloyd's of London, which would become one of the most important insurance markets in the world in the nineteenth century, flourished in the eighteenth century as a coffeehouse where ships' captains and insurers could exchange news and conduct business.

In France the philosophes, such as Voltaire, Rousseau, and Diderot, looked to the café as a place to meet other writers. By 1743, a German commented, "A coffeehouse is like a political stock exchange, where the most gallant and wittiest heads of every estate come together. They engage in wide-ranging and edifying talk, issue well-founded judgments on matters concerning the political and the scholarly world, converse sagaciously about the most secret news from all courts and states, and unveil the most hidden truths."[2]

One irony, however, should be noted about the eighteenth-century European coffeehouses. Although they provided one of the chief locations for the public discussion of the ideas of the Enlightenment, which fostered greater liberty of thought in Europe, the coffee and sugar consumed in these establishments were cultivated by slave labor on plantations in the Caribbean and Brazil. The coffeehouse was one of many institutions of European life that was intimately connected to the transatlantic plantation slave economy.

How did coffeehouses help spread the ideas of the Enlightenment?

How was the consumption of coffee related to the transatlantic slave trade?

[1]Brian Cowan, *The Social Life of Coffee: The Emergence of the British Coffeehouse* (New Haven, CT: Yale University Press, 2005), 166 and 86.

[2]Quoted in James Van Horn Melton, *The Rise of the Public in Enlightenment Europe* (Cambridge, UK: Cambridge University Press, 2001), p. 243.

W. Dickinson, "The Coffeehouse Patriots; or news, from St. Eustatia" (London, 15 October 1781). Satirical attacks on coffeehouse patrons, who in this cartoon are accused of putting their own business interests ahead of political allegiance to the crown, were common by the late eighteenth century. The men of commerce gathered in the center of the room, sharing a newspaper, are upset by the news that St. Eustatius, a Dutch Caribbean port used by British merchants for illegal trade with the American colonies, had been captured by the British. The furnishings and animals were all typical of the London coffeehouse of the late eighteenth century.   Library of Congress

Like Voltaire, Immanuel Kant (1724–1804) admired Frederick the Great. Unlike Voltaire, Kant's relationship with authority did not require years of restless travel. Born in the capital of Prussia, Königsberg, Kant spent his entire life in the city. In 1784, he published an essay answering the question "What is Enlightenment?" in which he defined enlightenment as "man's emergence from his self-incurred immaturity." Through the application of reason, men could earn the right to be considered fully autonomous adults, no longer dependent on the guidance of church or state authorities to determine what is right. According to Kant, this condition of full autonomy had not yet been achieved, and his age was therefore "an age of Enlightenment" but not "an Enlightened age." At the same time, Kant credited Frederick the Great for recognizing his subjects' right to freedom of thought, and most especially freedom of religious ideas. When Kant's views on religious freedom were criticized by one of Frederick the Great's successors, Kant decided that his loyalty to his monarch required he cease publishing on the topic, but only until the accession of the next king. "Repudiation and denial of one's inner conviction are evil, but silence in a case like the present one is the duty of a subject; and while all that one says must be true, this does not mean that it is one's duty to speak out the whole truth in public."[6]

▼ The Enlightenment and Religion

For many, but not all, philosophes of the eighteenth century, ecclesiastical institutions, especially in their frequently privileged position as official parts of the state, were the chief impediment to human improvement and happiness. Voltaire's cry, "Crush the Infamous Thing," summed up the attitude of a number of philosophes toward the intolerance that they believed characterized some parts of organized Christianity. Almost all varieties of Christianity, especially Roman Catholicism, as well as Judaism and Islam, were the targets of their criticism.

The philosophes complained that Christian churches hindered the pursuit of a rational life and the scientific study of humanity and nature. Both Roman Catholic and Protestant clergy taught that humans were basically depraved, becoming worthy only through divine grace. According to the doctrine of original sin, improvement in human nature on earth was impossible. Religion thus turned attention away from this world to the world to come. For example, the philosophes argued that the Calvinist doctrine of predestination denied that virtuous behavior in this life could affect the fate of a person's soul after death. Mired in conflicts over obscure doctrines, the churches promoted intolerance and bigotry, inciting torture, war, and other forms of human suffering.

[6]Immanuel Kant, *Political Writings*, ed. by H. Reiss (Cambridge, UK: Cambridge University Press, 1991), p. 2.

With this attack, the philosophes challenged not only a set of ideas, but also some of Europe's most powerful institutions. The churches were deeply enmeshed in the power structure of the Old Regime. They owned large amounts of land and collected tithes from peasants before any secular authority collected its taxes. Most clergy were legally exempt from taxes and made only annual voluntary grants to the government. The upper clergy in most countries were relatives or clients of aristocrats. High clerics were actively involved in politics. Bishops served in the British House of Lords and on the Continent, cardinals and bishops advised rulers or were sovereign princes themselves. In Protestant countries, the leading local landowner usually appointed the parish clergyman. Membership in the state church conferred political and social advantages. Those who did not belong to it were often excluded from political life, the universities, and the professions. Clergy frequently provided intellectual justification for the social and political status quo, and they were active agents of religious and literary censorship.

Deism

The philosophes, although critical of many religious institutions and frequently anticlerical, did not oppose all religion. In Scotland, for example, the enlightened historian William Robertson (1721–1793) was the head of the Scottish Presbyterian Kirk. In England, Anglican clergymen did much to popularize the thought of Newton. In France, several of the leading philosophes were Catholic priests. What the philosophes sought, however, was religion without fanaticism and intolerance, a religious life that would largely substitute human reason for the authority of churches. The Newtonian worldview had convinced many writers that nature was rational. Therefore, the God who had created nature must also be rational, and the religion through which that God was worshipped should be rational. Most of them believed the life of religion and of reason could be combined, giving rise to a broad set of ideas known as **deism**.

The title of one of the earliest deist works, *Christianity Not Mysterious* (1696) by John Toland (1670–1722), indicates the general tenor of this religious outlook. Toland and later deist writers promoted religion as a natural and rational, rather than a supernatural and mystical, phenomenon. In this respect they differed from Newton and Locke, both of whom regarded themselves as Christians (though not necessarily theologically orthodox ones). Deists regarded God as a kind of divine watchmaker who had created the mechanism of nature, set it in motion, and then departed.

The deists' informal creed had two major points. The first was a belief in the existence of God, which they thought the contemplation of nature could empirically justify, and in this respect many Protestant and Roman Catholic writers fully agreed with them. Because nature provided evidence of a rational God, that deity must also favor rational morality. So the second point in the deists' creed was a belief in life after death, when rewards and punishments would be meted out according to the virtue of the lives people led on this earth.

Deism, Enlightenment writers urged, was empirical, tolerant, reasonable, and capable of encouraging virtuous living. Voltaire once wrote,

The only gospel one ought to read is the great book of Nature, written by the hand of God and sealed with his seal. The only religion that ought to be professed is the religion of worshiping God and being a good man.[7]

Deists hoped that wide acceptance of their faith would end rivalry among the various Christian sects and with it religious fanaticism, conflict, and persecution. They also felt deism would remove the need for priests and ministers, who, in their view, were often responsible for fomenting religious differences and denominational hatred. Deistic thought led some contemporaries to believe God had revealed himself in different ways and that many religions might embody divine truth.

There was never a formal or extensive deist movement, but deist ideas spread informally throughout the culture and provided for some people a framework for a nondogmatic religious outlook. Most deist writers were strongly anticlerical and were for that reason regarded as politically radical, an association that was strengthened by the links between Unitarians and political radicalism. Christian writers often attacked the deists and thus actually spread their ideas. In this respect, religious controversy arising from orthodox writers placed new religious ideas into the public sphere as much or more than the actual publications of unorthodox authors.

Toleration

The philosophes presented religious toleration as a primary social condition for the virtuous life. Again Voltaire took the polemical lead in championing this cause. In 1762, the Roman Catholic political authorities in the city of Toulouse ordered the execution of a Huguenot named Jean Calas, who had been accused of murdering his son to prevent him from converting to Roman Catholicism. Calas was viciously tortured and publicly strangled without ever confessing his guilt.

Voltaire learned of the case only after Calas's death. In 1763, he published his *Treatise on Tolerance* and hounded the authorities for a new investigation. Finally, in 1765, the judicial decision against the unfortunate man was reversed. For Voltaire, the case illustrated the fruits of religious fanaticism and the need for rational reform of judicial processes.

Read the Document
"Voltaire, 'On Universal Toleration'" on **MyHistoryLab.com**

[7]J. H. Randall, *The Making of the Modern Mind*, rev. ed. (New York: Houghton Mifflin, 1940), p. 292.

In 1779, German playwright and critic Gotthold Lessing (1729–1781) wrote *Nathan the Wise*, a plea for toleration not only of different Christian groups, but also of religious faiths other than Christianity. The premise behind all of these calls for toleration was, in effect, that life on earth and human relationships should not be subordinated to religious zeal that permitted one group of people to persecute, harm, or repress other groups.

Some Enlightenment writers also spoke favorably of the Islamic faith. Deist John Toland, who opposed prejudice against both Jews and Muslims, contended that Islam derived from early Christian writings and was thus a form of Christianity. These views so offended most of his contemporaries that Toland became known as a "Mohametan" Christian. Edward Gibbon, who blamed Christianity for contributing to the fall of the Roman Empire, wrote respectfully of Muhammad's leadership and Islam's success in conquering so vast a territory in the first century of its existence. Other commentators approved of Islam's tolerance and the charitable work of Muslims.

One of the most positive commentators on eighteenth-century Islam was a woman. Between 1716 and 1718, Lady Mary Wortley Montagu (1689–1762) lived in Istanbul with her husband, the British ambassador to Turkey. She wrote a series of letters about her experiences there that were published the year after her death. In these *Turkish Embassy Letters*, she praised much about Ottoman society and urged the English to copy the Turkish practice of vaccination against smallpox. Unlike European males, Montagu had access to the private quarters of women in Istanbul. In contrast to the constraints under which English women found themselves, she thought upper-class Turkish women were remarkably free and well treated by their husbands despite having to wear clothing that completely covered them in public. In fact, Montagu thought the anonymity these coverings bestowed allowed Turkish women to move freely about Istanbul. She also considered the magnificent Ottoman architecture better than anything in Western Europe. Montagu repeatedly criticized the misinformation that prevailed in Europe about the Ottoman Empire and declared that many of the hostile comments about Islam and Islamic morality were simply wrong.

Read the Document
"Lady Mary Wortley Montagu, Letters: (a) on Constantinople; (b) on Smallpox; (c) on Vaccination in Turkey" on **MyHistoryLab.com**

Radical Enlightenment Criticism of Christianity

Some philosophes went beyond the formulation of a rational religious alternative to Christianity and the advocacy of toleration to attack the churches and the clergy with vehemence. Scottish philosopher David Hume (1711–1776) argued in "Of Miracles," a chapter in his *Inquiry into Human Nature* (1748), that no empirical evidence supported the belief in divine miracles central to much of Christianity. Voltaire repeatedly questioned the truthfulness of priests and the morality of the Bible. In his *Philosophical Dictionary* (1764), he humorously pointed out inconsistencies in biblical narratives and immoral acts of the biblical heroes. Many of these ideas had existed before the Enlightenment in the anti–Roman Catholic polemics of Protestant writers and were brought back into circulation by the philosophes.

A few, but actually very few, philosophes went further than criticism. Baron d'Holbach (1723–1789) and Julien Offray de La Mettrie (1709–1751) embraced positions close to atheism and materialism. Theirs was distinctly a minority position, however. Most of the philosophes sought not the abolition of religion, but its transformation into a humane force that would encourage virtuous living. In the words of the title of a work by Kant, they sought to pursue *Religion within the Limits of Reason Alone* (1793).

The Limits of Toleration

Despite their emphasis on toleration, the philosophes' criticisms of traditional religion often reflected an implicit contempt not only for Christianity but also, and sometimes more vehemently, for Judaism and, as we see later, for Islam as well. Their attack on the veracity of biblical miracles and biblical history undermined the authority of the Hebrew scriptures as well as the Christian. Some philosophes characterized Judaism as a more primitive faith than Christianity and one from which philosophical rationalism provided a path of escape. The Enlightenment view of religion thus served in some ways to further stigmatize Jews and Judaism in the eyes of non-Jewish Europeans.

Unlike Judaism, Islam had few adherents in eighteenth-century Europe, with the notable exception of the Balkan Peninsula. Although European merchants traded with the Ottoman Empire or with those parts of South Asia where Islam prevailed, most Europeans came to know what little they did know about the Islamic world and Islam as a religion through books—the religious commentaries of Christian missionaries, histories, and the reports of travelers—that, with rare exceptions, were hostile to Islam and deeply misleading.

European universities did endow professorships to study Arabic during the seventeenth century, but these university scholars generally agreed with theological critics that Islam too often embodied religious fanaticism. Even relatively well-informed works based on knowledge of Arabic and Islamic sources—such as Barthélemy d'Herbelot's *Bibliothèque orientale* (*Oriental Library*), a reference book published in 1697; Simon Ockley's *History of the Saracens* (1718); and George Sale's introduction to the first full English translation of the Qur'an (1734)—were largely hostile to their subject. All of these books continued to be reprinted and remained influential well into the nineteenth century, demonstrating how little information disinterested Europeans had about Islam.

Enlightenment philosophes spoke with two voices regarding Islam. Voltaire indicated his opinion along with that of many of his contemporaries in the title of his 1742 tragedy *Fanaticism, or Mohammed the Prophet*. Although he sometimes spoke well of the Qur'an, Voltaire declared in a later historical work, "We must suppose that Muhammed, like all enthusiasts, violently impressed by his own ideas, retailed them in good faith, fortified them with fancies, deceived himself in deceiving others, and

Few Europeans visited the Ottoman Empire. What little they knew about it came from reports of travelers and from illustrations such as this 1710 view of Constantinople, the empire's capital. © Historical Picture Archive/CORBIS

Document

DU CHÂTELET EXPLAINS HAPPINESS SCIENTIFICALLY

Contemplating the sources and benefits of happiness was a popular pursuit among Enlightenment thinkers. Most of them were written by men, but accomplished mathematician Emilie Du Châtelet also addressed this theme. She wrote her essay, "Discourse on Happiness," over the course of nearly twenty years, in between other projects. When she began, she lived with Voltaire on her estate at Cirey; by the time she was finished, she was nearing the end of a pregnancy and feared (correctly) that she would not survive the birth of her child.

How does Du Châtelet's emphasis on attaining happiness in this life contradict the teachings of the Catholic Church? How does she define moral behavior? What sets Du Châtelet's readers apart from the rest of society? How does this assist in their pursuit of happiness? Why is scholarship particularly important to women, according to Du Châtelet, and how does her opinion differ from her fellow *philosophes*?

One must begin by saying to oneself, and by convincing oneself, that we have nothing to do in the world but to obtain for ourselves some agreeable sensations and feelings. The moralists who say to men, curb your passions and master your desires if you want to be happy, do not know the route to happiness. One is only happy because of satisfied tastes and passions . . .

My goal is not to write for all sorts of social orders and all sorts of people; all ranks are not susceptible to the same kind of happiness. I write only for those who are called people of quality, that is to say, for those who are born with a fortune already made, more or less distinguished, more or less opulent, but such that they can maintain their station without being ashamed, and they are perhaps not the easiest to make happy. . . .

I say that one cannot be happy and immoral, and the demonstration of this axiom lies in the depths of the hearts of all men. I put it to them, even to the most villainous, that there is not one of them to whom the reproaches of his conscience—that is

to say, of his innermost feeling, the scorn that he feels he deserves and that he experiences, as soon as he is aware of it—there is not one to whom these are not a kind of torture. By villains I do not mean thieves, assassins, poisoners; they do not belong in the category of those for whom I write. Villains are the false and perfidious, the slanderers, the informers, the ungrateful. In a word, all those who have vices the laws do not curb, but against which custom and society have brought formal judgments. These formal judgments are all the more terrible, as they are always carried out.

Undeniably, the love of study is much less necessary to the happiness of men than it is to that of women. Men have infinite resources for their happiness that women lack. They have many means to attain glory. . . . But women are excluded, by definition, from every kind of glory, and when, by chance, one is born with a rather superior soul, only study remains to console her for all the exclusions and dependencies to which she finds herself condemned by her place in society.

From Emilie Du Châtelet, *Selected Philosophical and Scientific Writings*, edited by Judith Zinsser, translated by Isabelle Bour and Judith Zinsser (Chicago: University of Chicago Press, 2009), pp. 349–351, 357.

finally sustained with deceit a doctrine he believed to be good."[8] Thus, for Voltaire, Muhammad and Islam in general represented simply one more example of the religious fanaticism he had so often criticized among Christians.

[8]Theodore Besterman, *Voltaire* (New York: Harcourt, Brace, & World, 1969), p. 409.

Some philosophes criticized Islam on cultural and political grounds. In *The Persian Letters* (1721), supposedly written by two Muslim Persians visiting Europe, the young philosophe Charles de Montesquieu used Islamic culture as a foil to criticize European society. Yet, by the time he wrote his more influential *Spirit of the Laws*

(1748), discussed more fully later in this chapter, Montesquieu associated Islamic society with the passivity that he ascribed to people subject to political despotism. Like other Europeans, Montesquieu believed the excessive influence of Islamic religious leaders prevented the Ottoman Empire from adapting itself to new advances in technology.

European voices demanding fairness and expressing empathy for Islam were rare throughout the eighteenth century. As one historian has commented, "The basic Christian attitude was still what it had been for a millennium: a rejection of the claim of Muslims that Muhammad was a prophet and the Qur'an the word of God, mingled with a memory of periods of fear and conflict, and also, a few thinkers and scholars apart, with legends, usually hostile and often contemptuous."[9]

The Jewish Enlightenment

Like Catholics and Protestants engaged in the Enlightenment, Jewish thinkers of the eighteenth century embraced the new emphasis on reason as well as new discoveries in science and philosophy as a way of reinvigorating their faith. According to one historian, "the Enlightenment posed a set of questions to which all of the religions in [Europe] found it necessary to provide answers," and Jews were no exception.[10] The Jewish Enlightenment, sometimes known by the Hebrew word *Haskalah*, involved both an engagement with the secular world and also a vibrant study of Jewish religious books. Two major Jewish writers—one a few decades before the opening of the Enlightenment and one toward the close—entered the larger debate over religion and the place of Jews in European life. These were Baruch Spinoza (1632–1677), who lived in the Netherlands, and the German Moses Mendelssohn (1729–1786), who lived in Berlin, the center of the Jewish Enlightenment. Spinoza set the example for a secularized version of Judaism, and Mendelsohn established the main outlines of an assimilationist position. Although their approaches displayed certain similarities, there were also important differences.

The new science of the mid-seventeenth century deeply influenced Spinoza, the son of a Jewish merchant of Amsterdam. Like his contemporaries, Hobbes and Descartes, he looked to the power of human reason to reconceptualize traditional thought. In that regard his thinking reflected the age of scientific revolution and looked toward the later Enlightenment. His stance of championing toleration while condemning Judaism itself would later characterize the outlook of many non-Jewish Europeans regarding the assimilation of Jews into European civic life. It was, however, an outlook that Jewish communities themselves could not welcome without considerable modification.

Moses Mendelssohn, the leading Jewish philosopher of the eighteenth century, was known as the "Jewish Socrates." Writing almost a century after Spinoza, he also advocated the entry of Jews into modern European life. In contrast to Spinoza, however, Mendelssohn argued that Jews could combine loyalty to Judaism with adherence to rational, Enlightenment values. Mendelssohn could hold this position in part because of the influence of Lessing's arguments for toleration. Indeed, Mendelssohn had been the chief model for Lessing's character *Nathan the Wise*.

Mendelssohn's most influential work was *Jerusalem; or, On Ecclesiastical Power and Judaism* (1783) in which he argued both for extensive religious toleration and for maintaining the religious distinction of Jewish communities. Mendelssohn urged that religious diversity within a nation did not harm loyalty to the government; therefore, governments should be religiously neutral and Jews should enjoy the same civil rights as other subjects. Then, in the spirit of the deists, he presented Judaism as one of many religious paths revealed by God. Jewish law and practice were intended for the moral benefit of Jewish communities; other religions similarly served other people. Consequently,

Moses Mendelssohn, the leading philosopher of the Jewish enlightenment, was often called the "Jewish Socrates." bpk, Berlin/Staatsbibliothek zu Berlin, Stiftung Preussischer Kulturbesitz, Berlin, Germany/Ruth Schacht. Mendelssohn Archive/Art Resource, NY

[9]A. Hourani, *Islam in European Thought* (Cambridge, UK: Cambridge University Press, 1991), p. 136.

[10]David Sorkin, *The Berlin Haskalah and German Religious Thought: Orphans of Knowledge* (London: Vallentine Mitchell, 2000), p. 4.

various communities should be permitted to practice their religious faith alongside other religious groups.

Unlike Spinoza, Mendelssohn wished to advocate religious toleration while genuinely sustaining the traditional religious practices and faith of Judaism. Nevertheless, Mendelssohn believed Jewish communities should not have the right to excommunicate their members over differences in theological opinions or if their members embraced modern secular ideas. He thus sought both toleration of Jews within European society and toleration by Jews of a wider spectrum of opinion within their own communities. His hope was that the rationalism of the Enlightenment would provide the foundation for both types of toleration. Mendelssohn thus set forth a far more extensive vision of religious toleration than had John Locke almost a century earlier.

▼ The Enlightenment and Society

The *Encyclopedia:* Freedom and Economic Improvement

The midcentury witnessed the publication of the *Encyclopedia*, one of the greatest monuments of the Enlightenment and its most monumental undertaking in the realm of print culture. Under the leadership of Denis Diderot (1713–1784) and Jean Le Rond d'Alembert (1717–1783), the first volume appeared in 1751. Eventually, numbering seventeen volumes of text and eleven of plates (illustrations), the project was completed in 1772. No other work of the Enlightenment so illustrated the movement's determination to probe life on earth rather than in the religious realm. As one writer in the *Encyclopedia* observed, "Man is the unique point to which we must refer everything, if we wish to interest and please amongst considerations the most arid and details the most dry."[11] The use of the word *man* in this passage was not simply an accident of language. Most philosophes, as we shall see later in the chapter, were thinking primarily of men, not women, when they framed their reformist ideas.

The *Encyclopedia*, in part a collective plea for freedom of expression, reached fruition only after many attempts to censor it and halt its publication. It was the product of the collective effort of more than a hundred authors, and its editors had at one time or another solicited articles from all the major French philosophes. It included the most advanced critical ideas of the time on religion, government, and philosophy. To avoid official censure, these ideas often had to be hidden in obscure articles or under the cover of irony. The *Encyclopedia* also included numerous important articles and illustrations on manufacturing, canal-building, ship construction, and improved

"Anatomy," one of the many illustrations included in Diderot's *Encyclopedia*, provided labels for each of the bones in an articulated skeleton that were then identified and named in the text.   bpk, Berlin/Engraving by A.J. Defehrt (1723–1774). From "Encyclopédie" by Denis Diderot and Jean le Rond d'Alembert/Art Resource, NY

agriculture, making it an important source of knowledge about eighteenth-century social and economic life.

Between 14,000 and 16,000 copies of various editions of the *Encyclopedia* were sold before 1789. The project had been designed to secularize learning and to undermine intellectual assumptions that lingered from the Middle Ages and the Reformation. The articles on politics, ethics, and society ignored divine law and concentrated on humanity and its immediate well-being. The Encyclopedists looked to antiquity rather than to the Christian centuries for their intellectual and ethical models. For them, the future welfare of humankind lay not in pleasing God or following divine commandments, but rather in harnessing the power and resources of the earth and in living at peace with one's fellow human beings. The publication of the *Encyclopedia* was greeted by enthusiasts of Enlightenment thought all over the Continent, and was read in German and Russian intellectual and political circles.

Beccaria and Reform of Criminal Law

Although the term did not appear until later, the idea of *social science* originated with the Enlightenment. Philosophes hoped to end human cruelty by discovering

[11]F. L. Baumer, *Main Currents of Western Thought*, 4th ed. (New Haven, CT: Yale University Press, 1978), p. 374.

social laws and making people aware of them. These concerns are most evident in the philosophes' work on law and prisons.

In 1764, Marquis Cesare Beccaria (1738–1794), an Italian aristocrat and philosophe, published *On Crimes and Punishments*, in which he applied critical analysis to the problem of making punishments both effective and just. He wanted the laws of monarchs and legislatures—that is, positive law—to conform with the rational laws of nature. He rigorously and eloquently attacked both torture and capital punishment. He thought the criminal justice system should ensure a speedy trial and certain punishment and the intent of punishment should be to deter further crime. The purpose of laws was not to impose the will of God or some other ideal of perfection, but to secure the greatest good or happiness for the greatest number of human beings. This utilitarian philosophy based on happiness in this life permeated most Enlightenment writing on practical reforms and profoundly influenced rulers in central and eastern Europe.

📖 **Read the Document**
"Cesare Beccaria, On Crimes and Punishments" on **MyHistoryLab.com**

The Physiocrats and Economic Freedom

Economic policy was another area in which the philosophes saw existing legislation and administration preventing the operation of natural social laws. They believed mercantilist legislation (designed to protect a country's trade from external competition) and the regulation of labor by governments and guilds actually hampered the expansion of trade, manufacture, and agriculture. In France, these economic reformers were called the **physiocrats**. Their leading spokesmen were François Quesnay (1694–1774) and Pierre Dupont de Nemours (1739–1817).

The physiocrats believed the primary role of government was to protect property and to permit its owners to use it freely. They argued that agriculture was the basis on which all economic production depended. They favored the consolidation of small peasant holdings into larger, more efficient farms. Here, as elsewhere, the rationalism of the Enlightenment was closely connected to the spirit of improvement that influenced so much of eighteenth-century European economic life.

Adam Smith on Economic Growth and Social Progress

The most important economic work of the Enlightenment was Adam Smith's (1723–1790) *Inquiry into the Nature and Causes of the Wealth of Nations* (1776). Smith, who was for a time a professor at Glasgow University in Scotland, believed economic liberty was the foundation of a natural economic system. As a result, he urged that the mercantile system of England—including the navigation acts governing colonial trade, the bounties the government gave to favored merchants and industries, most tariffs, trading monopolies, and the domestic regulation of labor and manufacture—be abolished. These regulations were intended to preserve the wealth of the nation, to capture wealth from other nations, and to maximize the work available for the nation's laborers. Smith argued, however, that they hindered the expansion of wealth and production. The best way to encourage economic growth, he maintained, was to allow individuals to pursue their own selfish economic interests. As self-interested individuals sought to enrich themselves by meeting the needs of others in the marketplace, the economy would expand. Consumers would find their wants met as manufacturers and merchants competed for their business.

Mercantilism assumed that the earth's resources were limited and scarce, so one nation could acquire wealth only at the expense of others. Smith's book challenged this assumption. He saw the resources of nature—water, air, soil, and minerals—as boundless. To him, they demanded exploitation for the enrichment and comfort of humankind.

Smith is usually regarded as the founder of *laissez-faire* economic thought and policy, which favors a limited role for the government in economic life. *The Wealth of Nations* was, however, a complex book and Smith was no simple dogmatist. For example, he did not oppose all government activity in the economy. The government, he argued, should provide schools, armies, navies, and roads. It should also undertake certain commercial ventures, such as opening dangerous new trade routes that were economically desirable, but too expensive or risky for private enterprise. The public should in particular support education of those people who occupied the humbler occupations of life. (See "Adam Smith Calls for Government Action to Support the Education of the Poor," page 525.)

Within *The Wealth of Nations*, Smith, like other Scottish thinkers of the day, embraced an important theory of human social and economic development, known as the *four-stage theory*. According to this theory, human societies can be classified as hunting and gathering, pastoral or herding, agricultural, or commercial. The hunters and gatherers have little or no settled life. Pastoral societies are nomadic like the herds they tend, but develop some private property. Agricultural or farming societies are settled and have clear-cut property arrangements. Finally, the commercial state includes advanced cities, the manufacture of numerous items for wide consumption, extensive trade between cities and the countryside, and elaborate forms of property and financial arrangements. Smith and other writers described the passage of human society through these stages as a movement from barbarism to civilization.

ADAM SMITH CALLS FOR GOVERNMENT ACTION TO SUPPORT THE EDUCATION OF THE POOR

Adam Smith in The Wealth of Nations *had argued that the division of labor increased the productive capacity of human beings and hence economic growth and the accumulation of wealth. Smith, however, also recognized that the division of labor might over the course of time take a very heavy toll on the lives of workers involved in repetitive activities of production. In this passage he describes that human toll and then calls for government action to provide education for the poor. He also believed that workers should pay for part of their education, making the schoolmaster accountable to paying students.*

What does Smith portray as the results of repetitive work caused by the division of labor? Why does he place so much emphasis on mental and emotional costs? How does he see this situation as undermining civic interest? What solutions does he propose?

In the progress of the division of labour, the employment of the far greater part of those who live by labour, that is, of the great body of the people, comes to be confined to a few very simple operations, frequently to one or two. But the understandings of the greater part of men are necessarily formed by their ordinary employments. The man whose whole life is spent in performing a few simple operations, of which the effects too are, perhaps, always the same, or very nearly the same, has no occasion to exert his understanding, or to exercise his invention in finding out expedients for removing difficulties which never occur. He naturally loses, therefore, the habit of such exertion, and generally becomes as stupid and ignorant as it is possible for a human creature to become. The torpor of his mind renders him not only incapable of relishing or bearing a part in any rational conversation, but of conceiving any generous, noble, or tender sentiment, and consequently of forming any just judgment concerning many even of the ordinary duties of private life. Of the great and extensive interest of his country he is altogether incapable of judging; and unless very particular pains have been taken to render him otherwise, he is equally incapable of defending his country in war. The uniformity of his stationary life naturally corrupts the courage of his mind, and makes him regard with abhorrence the irregular, uncertain, and adventurous life of a soldier. It corrupts even the activity of his body, and renders him incapable of exerting his strength with vigour and perseverance, in any other employment than that to which he has been bred. His dexterity at his own particular trade seems, in this manner, to be acquired at the expence of his intellectual, social, and martial virtues. But in every improved and civilized society this is the state into which the labouring poor, that is, the great body of the people, must necessarily fall, unless government takes some pains to prevent it. . . .

The common people . . . have little time to spare for education. Their parents can scarce afford to maintain them even in infancy. As soon as they are able to work, they must apply to some trade by which they can earn their subsistence. . . . But though the common people cannot . . . be so well instructed as people of some rank and fortune, the most essential parts of education, however, to read, write, and account, can be acquired at so early a period of life, that the greater part even of those who are to be bred to the lowest occupations, have time to acquire them before they can be employed in those occupations. For a very small expence the public can facilitate, can encourage, and can even impose upon almost the whole body of the people, the necessity of acquiring those most essential parts of education.

From Adam Smith, *An Inquiry into the Nature and Causes of the Wealth of Nations* (London: T. Nelson & Sons, 1852), pp. 327–328.

The four-stage theory implicitly evaluated the later stages of economic development and the people dwelling in them as higher, more progressive, and more civilized than the earlier ones. A social theorist using this theory could thus quickly look at a society and, on the basis of the state of its economic development and organizations, rank it in terms of the stage it had achieved. The commercial stage described society as it appeared in northwestern Europe. Thus, Smith's theory allowed Europeans to look about the world and always find themselves at the highest level of human achievement. This outlook helped Europeans justify their economic and imperial domination of the world during the following century. They repeatedly portrayed themselves as bringing a higher level of civilization to people elsewhere who, according to the four-stage theory, lived in lower stages of human social and economic development. Europeans thus imbued with the spirit of the Enlightenment presented themselves as carrying out a civilizing mission to the rest of the world. (See Chapter 25.)

▼ Political Thought of the Philosophes

Nowhere was the philosophes' reformist agenda, as well as tensions among themselves, so apparent as in their political thought. Most philosophes were discontented with certain political features of their countries, but French philosophes were especially discontented. There, the corruption around the royal court, the blundering of the bureaucracy, the less-than-glorious midcentury wars, and the power of the church seemed to make all problems worse. Consequently, the most important political thought of the Enlightenment occurred in France. The French philosophes, however, were divided over how to solve their country's problems. Their proposed solutions spanned a wide political spectrum, from aristocratic reform to democracy to absolute monarchy.

Montesquieu and *Spirit of the Laws*

Charles Louis de Secondat, baron de Montesquieu (1689–1755), was a lawyer, a noble of the robe, and a member of a provincial *parlement*. He also belonged to the Bordeaux Academy of Science, before which he presented papers on scientific topics.

Although living comfortably within the bosom of French society, he saw the need for reform. In 1721, as already noted, he published *The Persian Letters* to satirize contemporary institutions. Behind the humor lay an exposition of the cruelty and irrationality of European life.

Montesquieu held up the example of the British constitution as the wisest model for regulating the power of government. Montesquieu's *Spirit of the Laws* (1748), one of the most influential books of the century, exhibits the internal tensions of the Enlightenment. In it, Montesquieu pursued an empirical method, taking illustrative examples from the political experience of both ancient and modern polities. From these, he concluded that no single set of political laws could apply to all peoples at all times and in all places. The good political life depended rather on the relationship among many variables. Whether the best form of government for a country was a monarchy or a republic, for example, depended on that country's size, population, social and religious customs, economic structure, traditions, and climate. Only a careful examination and evaluation of these elements could reveal what mode of government would most benefit a particular people.

Read the **Document**
"Baron de Montesquieu, Excerpt from *The Spirit of the Laws*" on **MyHistoryLab.com**

For France, Montesquieu favored a monarchical government tempered and limited by various intermediary institutions, including the aristocracy, the towns, and the other corporate bodies that enjoyed liberties the monarch had to respect. These corporate bodies might be said to represent segments of the general population and thus of public opinion. In France, he regarded the aristocratic courts, or *parlements*, as a major example of an intermediary association. Their role was to limit the power of the monarchy and thus to preserve the liberty of its subjects.

In championing these aristocratic bodies and the general oppositional role of the aristocracy, Montesquieu was a political conservative. He adopted this conservatism in the hope of achieving reform, however, for he believed the oppressive and inefficient absolutism of the monarchy accounted for the degradation of French life.

One of Montesquieu's most influential ideas was that of the division of power in government. In Great Britain, he believed, executive power resided in the king, legislative power in the Parliament, and judicial power in the courts. He thought any two branches could check and balance the power of the other. His perception of the eighteenth-century British constitution was incorrect because he failed to see how patronage and electoral corruption allowed a handful of powerful aristocrats to dominate the government. Moreover, he was also unaware of the emerging cabinet system, which was slowly making the executive power a creature of the Parliament.

Nevertheless, Montesquieu's analysis illustrated his strong belief that monarchs should be subject to constitutional limits on their power and that a separate legislature, not the monarch, should formulate laws. For this reason, although he set out to defend the political privileges of the French aristocracy, Montesquieu's ideas have had a profound effect on the constitutional form of liberal democracies for more than two centuries.

Rousseau: A Radical Critique of Modern Society

Jean-Jacques Rousseau (1712–1778) was a strange, isolated genius who never felt particularly comfortable with the other philosophes. His own life was troubled. He could form few close friendships. He sired numerous children, whom he abandoned to foundling hospitals. Yet perhaps more than any other writer of the mid-eighteenth century, he transcended the political thought and values of his own time. Rousseau hated the world and the society in which he lived. It seemed to him impossible for human beings living according to the commercial values of his time to achieve moral, virtuous, or sincere lives. In 1750, in *Discourse on the Moral Effects of the Arts and Sciences*, Rousseau contended that the process of civilization and the Enlightenment had corrupted human nature. In 1755, in *Discourse on the Origin of Inequality*, he blamed much of the evil in the world on the uneven distribution of property. He argued that human beings in a primeval state of nature had been good, but that as they eventually formed social relations and then social institutions, they had lost that goodness. Society itself was the source of human evil for Rousseau, and one manifestation of that unnatural evil was unequal distribution of property.

In both discourses, Rousseau brilliantly and directly challenged the social fabric of the day. He questioned the concepts of material and intellectual progress and the morality of a society in which commerce, industry, and the preservation of property rights were regarded as among the most important human activities. The other philosophes generally believed life would improve if people could enjoy more of the fruits of the earth or could produce more goods. Rousseau raised the more fundamental questions of what constitutes the good life and how human society can be reshaped to achieve that life. This question has haunted European social thought ever since the eighteenth century.

Rousseau carried these same concerns into his political thought. His most extensive discussion of politics appeared in *The Social Contract* (1762). Although the book attracted little immediate attention, by the end of the century it was widely read in France. Compared with Montesquieu's *Spirit of the Laws*, *The Social Contract* is an abstract book. It does not propose specific reforms but outlines the kind of political structure that Rousseau believed would overcome the evils of contemporary politics and society.

In the tradition of John Locke, most eighteenth-century political thinkers regarded human beings as individuals and society as a collection of individuals pursuing personal, selfish goals. These writers wished to liberate individuals from the undue bonds of government. Rousseau picked up the stick from the other end. His book opens with the declaration, "All men are born free, but everywhere they are in

In this image of Rousseau sitting at his desk in Neufchâtel, Switzerland, the writer wears his favorite Armenian hat, which became notorious during his 1766 visit to England. Rousseau was often depicted admiring the Swiss landscape. © Mary Evans Picture Library/Alamy

chains."[12] The rest of the volume is a defense of the chains of a properly organized society over its members.

Rousseau suggested that society is more important than its individual members because they are what they are only by virtue of their relationship to the larger community. Independent human beings living alone can achieve little. Through their relationship to the larger political community, they become moral creatures capable of significant action. The question then becomes: What kind of community allows people to behave morally? In his two previous discourses, Rousseau had explained that the contemporaneous European society was not such a community; it was merely an aggregate of competing individuals whose chief social goal was to preserve selfish independence despite all potential social bonds and obligations.

Rousseau envisioned a society in which each person could maintain personal freedom while behaving as a loyal member of the larger community. Drawing on the traditions of Plato and Calvin, he defined freedom as obedience to law. In his case, the law to be obeyed was

[12]Jean-Jacques Rousseau, *The Social Contract and Discourses*, trans. by G. D. H. Cole (New York: Dutton, 1950), p. 3.

that created by the general will. In a society with virtuous customs and morals in which citizens have adequate information on important issues, the concept of the general will is normally equivalent to the will of a majority of voting citizens. Democratic participation in decision making would bind the individual citizen to the community. Rousseau believed the general will, thus understood, must always be right and that to obey the general will is to be free. This argument led him to the notorious conclusion that under certain circumstances some people must be forced to be free. Rousseau's politics thus constituted a justification for radical direct democracy and for collective action against individual citizens.

Rousseau had, in effect, attacked the eighteenth-century cult of the individual and the fruits of selfishness. He stood at odds with the commercial spirit that was transforming the society in which he lived. Rousseau would have disapproved of the main thrust of Adam Smith's *Wealth of Nations*, which he may or may not have read, and would no doubt have preferred a study on the virtue of nations. Smith wanted people to be prosperous; Rousseau wanted them to be good even if being good meant they might remain poor. He saw human beings not as independent individuals, but as creatures enmeshed in necessary social relationships. He believed loyalty to the community should be encouraged. As one device to that end, he suggested a properly governed society should decree a civic religion based on the creed of deism. Such a shared religion could, he argued, help unify a society even if it had to be enforced by repressive legislation.

Rousseau had only a marginal impact on his own time. The other philosophes questioned his critique of material improvement. Aristocrats and royal ministers could hardly be expected to welcome his proposal for radical democracy. Too many people were either making or hoping to make money to appreciate his criticism of commercial values. With the exception of *The Social Contract*, all of Rousseau's works, including portions of the banned *Emile*, were published in Russia in the 1760s and 1770s, but Catherine the Great did not take his ideas seriously. He proved, however, to be a figure to whom later generations returned. Leading figures in the French Revolution were familiar with his writing, and he influenced writers in the nineteenth and twentieth centuries who were critical of the general tenor and direction of Western culture. Rousseau exemplified for later generations the critic who dared to question the very foundations of social thought and action.

Enlightened Critics of European Empires

Most European thinkers associated with the Enlightenment favored the extension of European empires across the world. Like the Scottish writers who embraced the

The caption of this image is taken from Voltaire's play, *Mahomet*, and reads "All mortals are equal; it is not birth but virtue that makes the difference." "All Mortals are Equal, it is not Birth but Virtue that Makes the Difference," 1793 (coloured engraving), French School, (18th century)/Bibliotheque Nationale, Paris, France/ The Bridgeman Art Library four-stage theory, they believed that the extension of the political structures and economies of northwestern Europe amounted to the spread of progress and civilization. The Scottish commentators and their followers were not without their criticisms of European civilization and of excessive economic regulation in contemporary empires, but on the whole, they believed European civilization superior to that of other cultures.

A few Enlightenment voices, however, did criticize the European empires on moral grounds, especially the European conquest of the Americas, the treatment of Native Americans, and the enslavement of Africans on the two American continents. The most important of these critics were Denis Diderot, Nicolas de Condorcet, and two German philosophers, Immanuel Kant and Johann Gottlieb Herder (1744–1803). (See the Document "Denis Diderot Condemns European Empires," page 530.)

What ideas allowed these figures from the Enlightenment to criticize their empires? As Sankar Muthu has recently written, "The first and most basic idea is that human beings deserve some modicum of moral and political respect simply because of the fact that they are human."[13] In other words, the Enlightenment critics of their empires argued for a form of shared humanity that the sixteenth-century European conquerors and their successors in the Americas and in other areas of imperial conquest had ignored. Immanuel Kant wrote, "When America, the Negro countries, the Spice Islands, the Cape, and so forth were discovered, they were to them [the Europeans], countries belonging to no one, since they counted the inhabitants as *nothing*."[14] Kant, Diderot, and Herder rejected this dismissive outlook and the harsh policies that had flowed from it. They believed no single definition of human nature could be made the standard throughout the world and then used to dehumanize people whose appearance or culture differed from it.

A second of these critical ideas was the conviction that the people whom Europeans had encountered in the Americas had possessed cultures that should have been respected and understood rather than destroyed. Some Europeans in the early years of the encounter with America had argued that while the native peoples were human, their way of life was too degraded to treat them as the human equals of Europeans. In the late eighteenth century, Herder rejected such a view, "'European culture' is a mere abstraction, an empty concept. Where does or did it actually exist in its entirety? In which nation? In which period? . . . Only a misanthrope could regard European culture as the universal condition of our species. The culture of *man* is not the culture of the *European*; it manifests itself according to time and place in every people."[15] For Herder, human beings living in different societies

possessed the capacity as human beings to develop in culturally different fashions. He thus embraced an outlook later known as *cultural relativism*.

A third idea, closely related to the second, was that human beings may develop distinct cultures possessing intrinsic values that cannot be compared, one to the detriment of another, because each culture possesses deep inner social and linguistic complexities that make any simple comparison impossible. Indeed, Diderot, Kant, and Herder argued that being a human includes the ability to develop a variety of distinctly different cultures.

These arguments critical of empire often involved criticism of New World slavery and were part of the antislavery movement to be discussed in Chapter 20. Whereas the antislavery arguments took strong hold in both Europe and America from the late eighteenth century onward, the arguments critical of empires did not. They remained isolated from the rest of Enlightenment political thought and would not be strongly revived until new anticolonial voices were raised in Europe and the non-European world at the close of the nineteenth century.

▼ Women in the Thought and Practice of the Enlightenment

Women, especially in France, helped significantly to promote the careers of the philosophes. In Paris, the salons of women such as Marie-Thérèse Geoffrin (1699–1777), Julie de Lespinasse (1733–1776), and Claudine de Tencin (1689–1749) gave the philosophes access to useful social and political contacts and a receptive environment in which to circulate their ideas. Association with a fashionable salon brought philosophes increased social status and added luster and respectability to their ideas. Philosophes clearly enjoyed the opportunity to be the center of attention that a salon provided, and their presence at them could boost the sales of their works. The women who organized the salons were well connected to political figures who could help protect the philosophes and secure royal pensions for them. The marquise de Pompadour (1721–1764), the mistress of King Louis XV, played a key role in overcoming efforts to censor the *Encyclopedia*. She also hindered the publication of works attacking the philosophes. Other salon hostesses distributed the writings of the philosophes among their friends. Madame de Tencin promoted Montesquieu's *Spirit of the Laws* in this way.

Despite this help and support from the learned women of Paris and other urban centers, the philosophes were on the whole not committed to advocating equality for women. Many urged better and broader education for women. They criticized the education women did receive as overly religious, and they tended to reject ascetic views of sexual relations. In general, however, they displayed traditional views toward women and advocated no radical changes in their social condition.

[13]Sankar Muthu, *Enlightenment Against Empire* (Princeton, NJ: Princeton University Press, 2003), p. 268. This section draws primarily from this excellent recent book.
[14]Muthu, *Enlightenment Against Empire*, p. 267.
[15]F. M. Barnard, *Self-Direction and Political Legitimacy: Rousseau and Herder* (Oxford, UK: Clarendon Press, 1988), p. 227.

Document

DENIS DIDEROT CONDEMNS
EUROPEAN EMPIRES

Denis Diderot was one of the most prolific writers of the Enlightenment. He is most famous as the editor of the Encyclopedia. *Some of his writings were published without being directly attributed to him. Among these were his contributions to Abbé G. T. Raynal's* History of the Two Indies, *published in various editions after 1772. Diderot's contributions appear to have been made in 1780. Raynal's entire* History *was critical of the European colonial empires that had arisen since the Spanish encounter with the New World. Diderot particularly condemned the inhumane treatment of the native populations of the Americas, the greed all Europeans displayed, and the various forms of forced labor.*

What is the basis for Diderot's view that Europeans have behaved tyrannically? How does he portray the behavior of Europeans in foreign areas? What specific social results does he associate with European greed?

Let the European nations make their own judgment and give themselves the name they deserve. . . . Their explorers arrive in a region of the New World unoccupied by anyone from the Old World, and immediately bury a small strip of metal on which they have engraved these words: *This country belongs to us.* Any why does it belong to you?

. . . You have no right to the natural products of the country where you land, and you claim a right over your fellow-men. Instead of recognizing this man as a brother you only see him as a slave, a beast of burden. Oh my fellow citizens! You think like that and you behave like that; and you have ideas of justice, a morality, a holy religion . . . in common with whose whom you treat so tyrannically.

* * *

Beyond the Equator a man is neither English, Dutch, French, Spanish, nor Portuguese. He retains only those principles and prejudices of his native country which justify or excuse his conduct. He crawls when he is weak; he is violent when strong; he is in a hurry to acquire, in a hurry to enjoy, and

capable of every crime which will lead him most quickly to his goals. He is a domestic tiger returning to the forest; the thirst for blood takes hold of him once more. This is how all the Europeans, every one of them, indistinctly, have appeared in the countries of the New World. There they have assumed a common frenzy—the thirst for gold.

* * *

The Spaniard, the first to be thrown up by the waves onto the shores of the New World, thought he had no duty to people who did not share his color, customs, or religion. He saw in them only tools for his greed, and he clapped them in irons. These weak men, not used to work, soon died in the foul air of the mines, or in other occupations which were virtually as lethal. Then people called for slaves from Africa. Their number has gone up as more land has been cultivated. The Portuguese, Dutch, English, French, Danes, all the nations, free or subjected, have without remorse sought to increase their fortune in the sweat, blood and despair of these unfortunates. What a horrible system!

From "Extracts from the Histoire des Deux Indes," "6 Principles of Colonisation" (Book 8, Chap. I; IV, 105–108), pp. 176–177; "7 National Character at Home and Overseas" (Book 9, Chap. I; IV, 233–235), p. 178; "14 Slavery and Liberty" (Book 11, Chap. 24, V, 275–278), p. 178 in *Political Writings* by Denis Diderot, trans. by John Hope Mason and Robert Wokler. © Cambridge University Press 1992. Reprinted with the permission of Cambridge University Press.

Montesquieu, for example, maintained that the status of women in a society was the result of climate, the political regime, culture, and women's physiology. He believed women were not naturally inferior to men and should have a wider role in society. He showed himself well aware of the kinds of personal, emotional, and sexual repression European women endured in his day. He

sympathetically observed the value placed on women's appearance and the prejudice women met as they aged. In *The Persian Letters*, he included a long exchange about the repression of women in a Persian harem, condemning by implication the restrictions on women in European society. Yet Montesquieu's willingness to consider social change for women in European life had limits. Although

MAJOR WORKS OF THE ENLIGHTENMENT AND THEIR PUBLICATION DATES

1687	Newton's *Principia Mathematica*
1690	Locke's *Essay Concerning Human Understanding*
1696	Toland's *Christianity Not Mysterious*
1719	Wolff's *Rational Thoughts On God, the World, the Human Soul and All Things in General*
1721	Montesquieu's *Persian Letters*
1733	Voltaire's *Letters on the English*
1738	Voltaire's *Elements of the Philosophy of Newton*
1748	Montesquieu's *Spirit of the Laws*
1748	Hume's *Inquiry into Human Nature*, with the chapter "Of Miracles"
1750	Rousseau's *Discourse on the Moral Effects of the Arts and Sciences*
1751	First volume of the *Encyclopedia*, edited by Diderot
1755	Rousseau's *Discourse on the Origin of Inequality*
1759	Voltaire's *Candide*
1762	Rousseau's *Social Contract* and *Émile*
1763	Voltaire's *Treatise on Tolerance*
1764	Voltaire's *Philosophical Dictionary*
1764	Beccaria's *On Crimes and Punishments*
1776	Gibbon's *Decline and Fall of the Roman Empire*
1776	Smith's *Wealth of Nations*
1779	Lessing's *Nathan the Wise*
1783	Mendelssohn's *Jerusalem; or, On Ecclesiastical Power and Judaism*
1784	Kant's *"What is Enlightenment?"*
1792	Wollstonecraft's *Vindication of the Rights of Woman*
1793	Kant's *Religion within the Limits of Reason Alone*

women were reared to be frivolous and unconcerned with important issues. The Encyclopedists discussed women primarily within a family context—as daughters, wives, and mothers—and presented motherhood as a woman's most important occupation. On sexual behavior, the Encyclopedists upheld an unquestioned double standard.

In contrast to the articles, however, illustrations in the *Encyclopedia* showed women deeply involved in the economic activities of the day. The illustrations also portrayed the activities of lower-class and working-class women, about whom the articles had little to say.

One of the most influential analyses of the position of women came from Jean-Jacques Rousseau. This most radical of all Enlightenment political theorists when it came to relations between men urged a traditional and conservative role for women. In his novel *Émile* (1762) (discussed again in Chapter 19), he set forth a radical version of the view that men and women occupy separate spheres. He declared that women should be educated for a position subordinate to men, emphasizing especially women's function in bearing and rearing children. In his vision, there was little else for women to do but make themselves pleasing to men. He portrayed them as weaker and inferior to men in virtually all respects, except perhaps for their capacity for feeling and giving love. He excluded them from political life. Only men were to populate the world of citizenship, political action, and civic virtue. Women were relegated to the domestic sphere. (See the Document "Rousseau Argues for Separate Spheres for Men and Women," page 533.) Many of these attitudes were not new—some have roots as ancient as Roman law—but Rousseau's powerful presentation and the influence of his other writings gave them new life in the late eighteenth century. Rousseau deeply influenced many leaders of the French Revolution, who, as shall be seen in the next chapter, often incorporated his view on gender roles in their policies.

Despite these views and despite his own ill treatment of the women who bore his many children, Rousseau achieved a vast following among women in the eighteenth century. He is credited with persuading thousands of upper-class women to breast-feed their own children rather than putting them out to wet nurses. One explanation for this influence is that his writings, although they did not advocate liberating women or expanding their social or economic roles, did stress the importance of their emotions. He portrayed the domestic life and the role of wife and mother as a noble and fulfilling vocation, giving middle- and upper-class women a sense that their daily occupations had a purpose. He assigned them a degree of influence in the domestic sphere that they could not have competing with men outside it.

In 1792, in *A Vindication of the Rights of Woman*, Mary Wollstonecraft (1759–1797) brought Rousseau before the judgment of the rational Enlightenment ideal of progressive knowledge. The immediate incentive for this essay was her opposition to certain policies of the

in the *Spirit of the Laws* he indicated a belief in the equality of the sexes, he still retained a traditional view of marriage and family and expected men to dominate those institutions. Furthermore, although he supported the right of women to divorce and opposed laws that oppressed them, he upheld the ideal of female chastity.

The views about women expressed in the *Encyclopedia* were even less generous than those of Montesquieu. The *Encyclopedia* suggested ways to improve women's lives, but it did not emphasize that the condition of women needed reform. Almost all the contributors were men, and the editors, Diderot and d'Alembert, saw no need to include many articles by women. Most of the articles that dealt with women specifically or in connection with other subjects often emphasized their physical weakness and inferiority, usually attributed to menstruation or childbearing. Some contributors favored the social equality of women, others opposed it, and still others were indifferent. The articles conveyed a general sense that

French Revolution, unfavorable to women, that Rousseau had inspired. Wollstonecraft (who, like so many women of her day, died of puerperal fever, a form of blood poisoning caused by unsanitary conditions during childbirth) accused Rousseau and others after him who upheld traditional roles for women of attempting to narrow women's vision and limit their experience. She argued that to relegate women to the separate domestic sphere because of supposed limitations of their physiology was to make them the sensual slaves of men. Confined in this separate sphere, they were the victims of male tyranny, their obedience was blind, and they could never achieve their own moral or intellectual identity. Denying good education to women would impede the progress of all humanity. Wollstonecraft demanded for women the kind of liberty that male writers of the Enlightenment had been championing for men for more than a century. In doing so, she placed herself among the philosophes and broadened the agenda of the Enlightenment to include the rights of women as well as those of men. (See the Document "Mary Wollstonecraft Criticizes Rousseau's View of Women," page 534.)

Read the **Document**
"Mary Wollstonecraft, Introduction to *A Vindication of the Rights of Woman*" on **MyHistoryLab.com**

Mary Wollstonecraft in her *A Vindication of the Rights of Woman* defended equality of women with men on the grounds of men and women sharing the capacity of human reason. CORBIS/ Bettmann

▼ Rococo and Neoclassical Styles in Eighteenth-Century Art

Two contrasting styles dominated eighteenth-century European art and architecture. The **Rococo** style embraced lavish, often lighthearted decoration with an emphasis on pastel colors and the play of light. **Neoclassicism** embodied a return to figurative and architectural models drawn from the Renaissance and the ancient world. The Rococo became associated with the aristocracies of the Old Regime while Neoclassicism recalled ancient republican values that implicitly criticized the Old Regime and, toward the end of the century, was embraced by the French Revolution and Napoleon.

Rococo architecture and decoration originated in early eighteenth-century France. After Louis XIV's death in 1715, the Regent Philippe d'Orleans (1674–1723) and the French aristocracy spent less time at Versailles and began to enjoy the diversions of Paris. There, wealthy French aristocrats built houses known as *hôtels*. Their designers compensated for the relatively small scale and nondescript exteriors of these mansions with interiors that were elaborately decorated and painted in light colors to make the rooms seem brighter and more spacious. It was in such aristocratic urban settings that fashionable Parisian hostesses held the salons the philosophes attended. Louis XV also liked Rococo art, and he had both Madame de Pompadour and other mistresses painted, sometimes in compromising poses, by Rococo artists, especially Francois Boucher (1700–1770). Consequently, Rococo also became known as the Style of Louis XV, suggesting a social and political world more accommodating to the French aristocracy and less religiously austere than that of Louis XIV.

Beyond such domestic and personally intimate settings in France, the Rococo style spread across Europe and was adapted to many public buildings and churches. One of the most spectacular Rococo spaces was the Imperial Hall (*Kaisarsaal*) built in Würzburg, Bavaria, to the design of Balthasar Neumann (1687–1753) with ceilings painted with scenes from Greek mythology by the Venetian Gian Battista Tiepolo (1696–1770).

The paintings associated with Rococo art often portrayed the aristocracy, and particularly the French aristocracy, at play. Artists depicted what were known as *fêtes galantes* or scenes of elegant parties in lush gardens. The paintings showed not reality, but an idealized landscape with carefree men and women pursuing a life of leisure, romance, and seduction. Among the most prominent of such artists was Jean-Antoine Watteau (1684–1721) in whose *Pilgrimage to Isle of Cithera* young lovers embark to pay homage to the goddess Venus. Other artists such as Boucher and Jean-Honoré Fragonard (1732–1806) produced works filled with female nudes and with men and women in sexually suggestive poses.

View the **Closer Look** "Watteau's *The Signboard of Gersaint*" on **MyHistoryLab.com**

Document

ROUSSEAU ARGUES FOR SEPARATE SPHERES FOR MEN AND WOMEN

Rousseau published Émile, *a novel about education, in 1762. In it, he made one of the most influential arguments of the eighteenth century for distinct social roles for men and women. Furthermore, he portrayed women as fundamentally subordinate to men. In the next document, Mary Wollstonecraft, a contemporary, presents a rebuttal.*

How does Rousseau move from the physical differences between men and women to an argument for distinct social roles and social spheres? What would be the proper kinds of social activities for women in Rousseau's vision? What kind of education would he think appropriate for women? What kind of evidence of his assertions does Rousseau present?

There is no parity between the two sexes in regard to the consequences of sex. The male is male only at certain moments. The female is female her whole life or at least during her whole youth. Everything constantly recalls her sex to her; and, to fulfill its functions well, she needs a constitution which corresponds to it. She needs care during her pregnancy; she needs rest at the time of childbirth; she needs a soft and sedentary life to suckle her children; she needs patience and gentleness, a zeal and an affection that nothing can rebuff in order to raise her children. She serves as the link between them and their father; she alone makes him love them and gives him the confidence to call them his own. How much tenderness and care is required to maintain the union of the whole family! And, finally, all this must come not from virtues but from tastes, or else the human species would soon be extinguished.

The strictness of the relative duties of the two sexes is not and cannot be the same. When woman complains on this score about unjust man-made inequality, she is wrong. This inequality is not a human institution—or, at least, it is the work not of prejudice but of reason. It is up to the sex that nature has charged with the bearing of children to be responsible for them to the other sex. Doubtless it is not permitted to anyone to violate his faith, and every unfaithful husband who deprives his wife of the only reward of the austere duties of her sex is an unjust and barbarous man. But the unfaithful woman does more; she dissolves the family and breaks all the bonds of nature. . . .

Once it is demonstrated that man and woman are not and ought not be constituted in the same way in either character or temperament, it follows that they ought not to have the same education. In following nature's directions, man and woman ought to act in concert, but they ought not to do the same things. The goal of their labors is common, but their labors themselves are different, and consequently so are the tastes directing them. . . .

The good constitution of children initially depends on that of their mothers. The first education of men depends on the care of women. Men's morals, their passions, their tastes, their pleasures, their very happiness also depend on women. Thus the whole education of women ought to relate to men. To please men, to be useful to them, to make herself loved and honored by them, to raise them when young, to care for them when grown, to counsel them, to console them, to make their lives agreeable and sweet— these are the duties of women at all times, and they ought to be taught from childhood. So long as one does not return to this principle, one will deviate from the goal, and all the precepts taught to women will be of no use for their happiness or for ours.

MARY WOLLSTONECRAFT CRITICIZES ROUSSEAU'S VIEW OF WOMEN

Mary Wollstonecraft published A Vindication of the Rights of Woman *in 1792, thirty years after Rousseau's* Émile *had appeared. In this pioneering feminist work, she criticizes and rejects Rousseau's argument for distinct and separate spheres for men and women. She portrays that argument as defending the continued bondage of women to men and as hindering the wider education of the entire human race.*

What criticisms does Wollstonecraft direct against Rousseau's views? Why does Wollstonecraft emphasize a new kind of education for women?

[T]he most perfect education . . . is such an exercise of the understanding as is best calculated to strengthen the body and form the heart. Or, in other words, to enable the individual to attain such habits of virtue as will render it independent. In fact, it is a farce to call any being virtuous whose virtues do not result from the exercise of its own reason. This was Rousseau's opinion respecting men: I extend it to women. . . .

I may be accused of arrogance; still I must declare what I firmly believe, that all the writers who have written on the subject of female education and manners from Rousseau to Dr. Gregory [a Scottish physician], have contributed to render women more artificial, weak characters, than they would otherwise have been; and, consequently, more useless members of society. . . .

Strengthen the female mind by enlarging it, and there will be an end to blind obedience; but, as blind obedience is ever fought for by power, tyrants and sensualists are in the right when they endeavour to keep women in the dark, because the former only wants slaves, and the latter a plaything. The sensualist, indeed, has been the most dangerous of tyrants, and women have been duped by their lovers, as princes by their ministers, whilst dreaming that they reigned over them.

Rousseau declares that a woman should never, for a moment, feel herself independent, that she should be governed by fear to exercise her *natural* cunning, and made a coquettish slave in order to render her a more alluring object of desire, a *sweeter* companion to man, whenever he chooses to relax himself. He carries the arguments, which he pretends to draw from the indications of nature, still further, and insinuates that truth and fortitude, the cornerstones of all human virtue, should be cultivated with certain restrictions, because, with respect to the female character, obedience is the grand lesson which ought to be impressed with unrelenting rigour.

What nonsense! When will a great man arise with sufficient strength of mind to puff away the fumes which pride and sensuality have thus spread over the subject! If women are by nature inferior to men, their virtues must be the same in quality, if not in degree, or virtue is a relative idea; consequently, their conduct should be founded on the same principles, and have the same aim.

Connected with man as daughters, wives, and mothers, their moral character may be estimated by their manner of fulfilling those simple duties; but the end, the grand end of their exertions should be to unfold their own faculties and acquire the dignity of conscious virtue. . . .

But avoiding . . . any direct comparison of the two sexes collectively, or frankly acknowledging the inferiority of women according to the present appearance of things, I shall only insist that men have increased that inferiority till women are almost sunk below the standard of rational creatures. Let their faculties have room to unfold, and their virtues to gain strength, and then determine where the whole sex must stand in the intellectual scale. . . .

I . . . will venture to assert, that till women are more rationally educated, the progress of human virtue and improvement in knowledge must receive continual checks. . . .

The mother, who wishes to give true dignity of character to her daughter, must, regardless of the sneers of ignorance, proceed on a plan diametrically opposite to that which Rousseau has recommended with all the deluding charms of eloquence and philosophical sophistry: for his eloquence renders absurdities plausible, and his dogmatic conclusions puzzle, without convincing, those who have not ability to refute them.

From Mary Wollstonecraft, *A Vindication of the Rights of Woman* (1792).

In this 1756 portrait of Madame de Pompadour, painted by the French artist François Boucher, the opulence of her lifestyle is as prominent as the features of her face.   bpk, Berlin/Alte Pinakothek, Bayerische Staatsgemaeldesammlungen, Munich, Germany/Art Resource, NY

As the eighteenth century wore on, the way of life illustrated in Rococo paintings and of more popular prints produced from them convinced many people in France that the monarchy, the court, and the aristocracy were frivolous and decadent. In reality, as seen in Chapter 15, many French and European aristocrats were hardworking and disciplined, and Louis XVI, who succeeded Louis XV in 1774, was a well-intentioned, pious, and highly moral monarch. Nonetheless, the lighthearted carelessness of Rococo art increased hostility toward the political and social elites of the Old Regime.

Contemporaries, moreover, did not have to wait for the tumult of the French Revolution to view art that directly criticized the society Rococo art portrayed. The mid-eighteenth century witnessed a new admiration for the art of the ancient world. In 1755, Johann Joachim Winckelmann (1717–1768), a German archaeologist, published *Thoughts on the Imitation of Greek Works in Painting and Sculpture,* followed in 1764 by *The History of Ancient Art.* In both works he either directly or indirectly contrasted the superficiality of the Rococo with the seriousness of ancient art and architecture. His books and the simultaneous rediscovery and partial excavation of the ancient Roman cities of Pompeii and Herculaneum in southern Italy fostered the rise of *Neoclassicism* in art and architecture. This movement constituted a return to themes, topics, and styles drawn from antiquity itself and from the Renaissance appeal to antiquity.

The popularity of the city of Rome as a destination for artists and aristocratic tourists contributed to the rise of Neoclassicism. European aristocrats who came to Italy in the mid-eighteenth century on what was called "the

Jean-Antoine Watteau, *The Music Party* (1718). This oil painting portrays young French aristocrats enjoying a leisurely musical serenade. Men, women, children, and pets repose to the left, while an African servant—another sign of the party's high status—cools champagne behind the musician's back.   © Peter Barritt/Alamy

The color, the light, and the elaborate decorative details associated with Rococo style are splendidly exemplified in the Imperial Hall (Kaisarsaal) built in Würzburg, Bavaria, according to the design of Balthasar Neumann (1687–1753). Art Resource, NY

Grand Tour" increasingly admired both the ancient and Renaissance art that was on view there and the Neoclassical works that contemporary artists were producing there. Not only did these wealthy and influential travelers purchase paintings and statues to bring home with them, but they also commissioned architects to rebuild their own houses and public buildings in Neoclassical style.

Figures in Neoclassical paintings rarely suggest movement and often seem to stand still in a kind of tableau illustrating a moral theme. These paintings were didactic rather than emotional or playful. Their subject matter was usually concerned with public life or public morals, rather than depicting intimate family life, daily routine, or the leisure activity favored by Rococo painters.

Many Neoclassical painters used scenes of heroism and self-sacrifice from ancient history to draw

contemporary moral and political lessons. Such scenes provided a sharp moral contrast to the works of Watteau or Boucher in which lovers seek only pleasure and escape from care.

Other Neoclassical artists intended their paintings to be a form of direct political criticism. Jacques-Louis David (1748–1825), the foremost French Neoclassical painter, used ancient republican themes in the 1780s to emphasize the corruption of French monarchical government. His *Oath of the Horatii* in 1784 (see "A Closer Look: An Eighteenth-Century Artist Appeals to the Ancient World," p. 537) illustrates a scene, derived from the ancient Roman historian Livy, of soldiers taking an oath to die for the Roman Republic. The painting also portrays the concept of separate spheres for men and women. While the brothers take the oath to defend

The passion for neoclassical architecture stretched from France to the eastern reaches of Europe. This palace in Warsaw was designed in 1764 to 1795 by Domenico Merlini for the King of Poland, Stanisław August Poniatowski (1732–1798). © LOOK. Die Bildagentur der Fotografen GmbH/Alamy

A Closer ▶ LOOK

◉─ View the Closer Look on MyHistoryLab.com

AN EIGHTEENTH-CENTURY ARTIST APPEALS TO THE ANCIENT WORLD

JACQUES-LOUIS DAVID completed *The Oath of the Horatii* in 1784. Like many of his other works, it used themes from the supposedly morally austere ancient Roman Republic to criticize the political life of his own day. David intended the painting to contrast ancient civic virtue with the luxurious aristocratic culture of contemporary France.

The Horatii take an oath their father administers to protect the Roman Republic against enemies even if it means sacrificing their own lives. One of these enemies is romantically involved with one of their sisters in the right of the painting. Patriotism must be upheld over other relationships.

The sharp division of the painting with a male world on the left and a female world on the right illustrates how eighteenth-century republican thinkers, such as Rousseau, excluded women from civic life and political participation.

The sisters and mother of the Horatii weep in a separate part of the scene. The emotion of the women and their uncertain political loyalty suggest that civic virtue pertains only to men.

Jacques-Louis David, *The Oath of the Horatii*. 1784–1785. © Réunion des Musees Nationaux, Paris, France/Art Resource, NY

What sort of social role did Enlightenment thinkers expect women to fulfill?

What kind of education would be required for a viewer to understand the symbolism of this painting fully?

What sort of values does this painting uphold?

the republic with their lives, the women in the scene appear too emotional to enter the masculine civic life of the republic. David painted many similar scenes from the ancient Roman Republic and later became an artistic champion of the French Revolution and Napoleon (who, ironically, made him a baron).

The philosophes themselves became the subjects of Neoclassical artists. French sculptor Jean-Antoine Houdon (1741–1828) produced numerous portraits in stone of leading philosophes including Voltaire and Rousseau as well as American representatives of the Enlightenment such as Benjamin Franklin (1706–1790) and Thomas Jefferson (1743–1826).

Even religious structures built in the Neoclassical style were, by the end of the century, transformed to monuments to the Enlightenment and Revolution. Modeled on its ancient pagan namesake in Rome, the Pantheon in Paris was begun in 1758 as a Jesuit church. During the French Revolution, the new government transformed it into a national monument where the remains of French heroes could be interred. Voltaire's remains were placed there in 1791 and Rousseau's in 1794.

View the Architectural Panorama *"Panthéon"* on **MyHistoryLab.com**

▼ Enlightened Absolutism

Most of the philosophes favored neither Montesquieu's reformed and revived aristocracy nor Rousseau's democracy as a solution to contemporary political problems. Like other thoughtful people of the day in other stations and occupations, they looked to the existing monarchies. Because of his personal clash with aristocrats as a young writer and his general distrust of democratic ideas, Voltaire was a strong monarchist. In 1759, he published a *History of the Russian Empire under Peter the Great*, which declared, "Peter was born, and Russia was formed."[16] Voltaire and other philosophes, such as Diderot, who visited Catherine II of Russia, and the physiocrats, some of whom were ministers to Louis XV and Louis XVI, did not wish to limit the power of monarchs. Rather, they sought to use their power to rationalize economic and political structures and liberate intellectual life. Most philosophes were not opposed to power if they could find a way to use it for their own purposes or if they could profit in one way or another from their personal relationships to strong monarchs. For this reason, it is important not to see Enlightenment political thought only as a source of modern liberal outlooks.

During the last third of the century, some observers believed that several European rulers had embraced many of the reforms the philosophes advocated. Historians use the term *enlightened absolutism* for this form of monarchical government in which the central absolutist administration was strengthened and rationalized at the cost of other, lesser centers of political power, such as the aristocracy, the church, and the parliaments or diets that had survived from the Middle Ages. The monarchs most closely associated with the Enlightenment are Frederick II (r. 1740–1786) of Prussia, Joseph II of Austria (r. 1765–1790), and Catherine II (r. 1762–1796) of Russia. Each had complicated relationships with the community of enlightened writers. Many other monarchs carried out similar reforms on a smaller scale.

Frederick II corresponded with the philosophes, gave Voltaire and others places at his court, and even wrote history, political tracts, literary criticism, and music. Catherine II, adept at what would later be called public relations, consciously sought to create the image of being an enlightened ruler. She read and cited the works of the philosophes, subsidized Diderot, and corresponded with Voltaire, lavishing compliments on him, all in the hope that she would receive favorable comments from them, as she indeed did. Joseph II continued numerous initiatives begun by his mother, Maria Theresa (r. 1740–1780). He imposed a series of religious, legal, and social reforms that contemporaries believed he had derived from the philosophes' suggestions.

The relationship between these rulers and the writers of the Enlightenment was, however, more complicated than these appearances suggest. The humanitarian and liberating zeal of the Enlightenment writers was only part of what motivated the policies of the rulers. Frederick II, Joseph II, and Catherine II were also determined to play major diplomatic and military roles in Europe. In no small measure, they adopted Enlightenment policies favoring the rational economic and social integration of their realms because these policies also increased their military strength and political power. As explained in Chapter 16, all the major European states had emerged from the Seven Years' War knowing they would need stronger armies for future wars and increased revenues to finance these armies. The search for new revenues and internal political support was one of the incentives prompting the enlightened reforms of the monarchs of Russia, Prussia, and Austria. Consequently, they and their advisers used rationality to pursue goals most philosophes admired, and also to further what some philosophes considered irrational militarism. The flattery of monarchs could bend the opinions of a philosophe. For example, Voltaire, who had written against war, could praise the military expansion of Catherine's Russia because it appeared in his mind to bring civilization to peoples he regarded as uncivilized and because he enjoyed being known as a literary confidant of the empress.

[16]Larry Wolff, *Inventing Eastern Europe: The Map of Civilization on the Mind of the Enlightenment* (Palo Alto, CA: Stanford University Press, 1994), p. 200.

Frederick the Great of Prussia

More than any other ruler of the age, Frederick the Great of Prussia embodied enlightened absolutism. Drawing upon the accomplishments of his Hohenzollern forebears, he forged a state that commanded the loyalty of the military, the Junker nobility, the Lutheran clergy, a growing bureaucracy recruited from an educated middle class, and university professors. Because the authority of the Prussian monarchy and the military were so strong and because the nobles, bureaucracy, clergy, and professors were so loyal, Frederick had the confidence to permit a more open discussion of Enlightenment ideas and to put into effect more Enlightenment values, such as extensive religious toleration, than any other continental ruler. Consequently, in marked contrast to France, Prussians sympathetic to the Enlightenment tended to support the state rather than criticize it.

View the Map "The Expansion of Prussia" on MyHistoryLab.com

Promotion Through Merit Reflecting an important change in the European view of the ruler, Frederick frequently described himself as "the first servant of the State," contending that his own personal and dynastic interests should always be subordinate to the good of his subjects. Like earlier Hohenzollern rulers, he protected the local social and political interests of the Prussian nobility as well as their role in the army, but he also required nobles who sought positions in his well-paid bureaucracy to qualify for those jobs by merit. By 1770, a Prussian Civil Service Commission oversaw the education and examinations required for all major government appointments. Frederick thus made it clear that merit rather than privilege of birth would determine who served the Prussian state.

During his reign Frederick created few new nobles, and those persons whom he did ennoble earned their titles by merit, for having served the king and the state well. This policy of ennobling only for merit and Frederick's protecting the nobility's local social interests and leadership of the army meant that Prussia did not experience the conflicts between the aristocracy and the monarchy that troubled other eighteenth-century European states.

Frederick felt comfortable in the intellectual life of his day and personally participated in the culture of the Enlightenment. He favored the Prussian universities and allowed professors wide latitude to discuss new ideas. In turn, Prussian professors were virtually unanimous in their praise and support of Frederick.

Because the Prussian state required academic training for appointment to positions of authority, nobles attended the universities. There they studied with middle-class Prussians who were training to serve the state either as Protestant clergy or bureaucrats. Consequently, nobles, clergy, and bureaucrats in Prussia shared a similar educational background that combined a moderate exposure to Enlightenment ideas with broadly shared religious values and loyalty to the state.

Religious Toleration No single policy so associated Frederick with the Enlightenment as that of full religious toleration. Continuing the Hohenzollern policy of toleration for foreign workers who brought important skills into Prussia, Frederick allowed Catholics and Jews to settle in his predominantly Lutheran country, and he

Frederick II of Prussia became known as Frederick the Great after his victories in the Seven Years' Wars. This portrait of 1763 shows him at the time of those triumphs when he had permanently secured the position of Prussia as a major European power. He was equally interested in the economic development of Prussia.   Erich Lessing/Art Resource, NY protected the Catholics living in Silesia after he conquered that province from the Habsburgs in the 1740s. (See Chapter 16.) He even stated that he would be willing to build mosques for Turks should they move into his country. His religious toleration won the strong support of philosophers, such as Immanuel Kant and Moses Mendelssohn. Frederick nonetheless tended to appoint Protestants to most key positions in the bureaucracy and army.

Administrative and Economic Reforms Frederick also ordered a new codification of Prussian law, which was completed after his death. His objective was to rationalize the existing legal system and make it more efficient, eliminating regional peculiarities, reducing aristocratic influence, abolishing torture, and limiting the number of capital crimes. The other enlightened monarchs shared this concern for legal reform, which they saw as a way to extend and strengthen royal power.

The midcentury wars had inflicted considerable economic damage on Prussia. Thereafter, Frederick used the power of the state to foster economic growth. He continued the long-standing Hohenzollern policy of importing workers from outside Prussia. He sought to develop Prussian agriculture. Under state supervision, swamps were drained, new crops introduced, and peasants encouraged and sometimes compelled to migrate where they were needed. For the first time in Prussia, potatoes and turnips became important crops. Frederick also established a land-mortgage credit association to help landowners raise money for agricultural improvements. Despite these efforts, however, most Prussians did not prosper under Frederick's reign, and the burden of taxation, reflecting his protection of the interests of the nobles, fell disproportionately on peasants and townspeople.

Joseph II of Austria

No eighteenth-century ruler so embodied rational, impersonal force as did the emperor Joseph II of Austria. He was the son of Maria Theresa and co-ruler with her from 1765 to 1780. Thereafter, he ruled alone until his death in 1790. Joseph was an austere and humorless person. During much of his life, he slept on straw and ate little but boiled beef. He prided himself on a narrow, passionless rationality, which he sought to impose by his own will on the various Habsburg domains. Despite his personal eccentricities and cold personality, Joseph II sincerely wished to improve the lot of his people. He was much less a political opportunist and cynic than either Frederick the Great of Prussia or Catherine the Great of Russia. Nonetheless, the ultimate result of his well-intentioned efforts was a series of aristocratic and

peasant rebellions extending from Hungary to the Austrian Netherlands.

Centralization of Authority As explained in Chapter 13, of all the rising states of the eighteenth century, Austria was the most diverse in its people and problems. To preserve the monarchy during the War of the Austrian Succession (1740–1748), Maria Theresa had guaranteed the aristocracy considerable independence, especially in Hungary.

During and after the conflict, however, she took steps to strengthen the power of the crown outside of Hungary, building more of a bureaucracy than had previous Habsburg rulers. In the Habsburgs' so-called core lands (corresponding roughly to today's Austria and Bohemia), the empress imposed a much more efficient system of tax collection that extracted funds even from the clergy and the nobles. She also established central councils to deal with governmental problems. To assure her government a supply of educated officials, she sought to bring all educational institutions into the service of the crown and expanded primary education on the local level.

Maria Theresa was concerned about the welfare of the peasants and serfs. She brought them some relief by expanding the authority of the royal bureaucracy over the local power of the nobility and limiting the amount of labor, or *robot*, landowners could demand from peasants. Her motives were less humanitarian than to assure a good pool from which to draw military recruits. In these policies and in her desire to stimulate prosperity and military strength by royal initiative, Maria Theresa anticipated the policies of her son.

Joseph II was more determined than his mother, and his projected reforms were more wide ranging. He aimed to extend his territories at the expense of Poland, Bavaria, and the Ottoman Empire. His greatest ambition, however, was to increase the authority of the Habsburg emperor over his various realms. He sought to overcome the pluralism of the Habsburg holdings by imposing central authority on areas of political and social life in which Maria Theresa had judiciously chosen not to interfere.

In particular, Joseph sought to reduce Hungarian autonomy. To avoid having to guarantee Hungary's existing privileges or extend new ones at the time of his coronation, he refused to have himself crowned king of Hungary and even had the Crown of Saint Stephen, symbol of the Hungarian state, sent to the Imperial Treasury in Vienna. He reorganized local government in Hungary to increase the authority of his own officials. He also required the use of German in all governmental matters.

Ecclesiastical Policies Another target of Joseph's royal absolutism was the church. Since the reign of Charles V (r. 1510–1558), the Habsburgs had been the most important dynastic champions of Roman Catholicism. Maria Theresa was devout, but she had not allowed the church to limit her authority. Although she had attempted to discourage certain of the more extreme modes of Roman Catholic popular religious piety, such as public flagellation, she was adamantly opposed to religious toleration. (See "Compare and Connect: Maria Theresa and Joseph II of Austria Debate Toleration," pages 542–543.)

Joseph II was also a practicing Catholic, but based on both Enlightenment values and pragmatic politics, he favored a policy of toleration. In October 1781, Joseph extended freedom of worship to Lutherans, Calvinists, and the Greek Orthodox. They were permitted to have their own places of worship, to sponsor schools, to enter skilled trades, and to hold academic appointments and positions in the public service. Joseph also granted the right of private worship to Jews and relaxed the financial and social burdens imposed on them, though he did not give Jews full equality with other Habsburg subjects.

Above all, Joseph sought to bring the Roman Catholic Church directly under royal control. He forbade the bishops of his realms to communicate directly with the pope. Since he considered religious orders that did not run schools or hospitals to be unproductive, he dissolved more than six hundred monasteries, confiscated their lands, and used some of their revenue to found new parishes in areas where there was a shortage of priests. He also reorganized the training of priests. The emperor believed that the traditional Roman Catholic seminaries, which were run by the various dioceses, instilled in priests too great a loyalty to the papacy and too little concern for their future parishioners. They were, therefore, replaced by eight general seminaries under government supervision whose training emphasized parish duties. In effect, Joseph's policies made Roman Catholic priests the employees of the state, ending the influence of the Roman Catholic Church as an independent institution in Habsburg lands. In many respects, his ecclesiastical policies, known as *Josephinism*, prefigured those of the French Revolution.

Economic and Agrarian Reform   Like Frederick of Prussia, Joseph sought to improve the economic life of his domains. He abolished many internal tariffs, encouraged road-building, and improved river transport. He personally inspected farms and manufacturing districts. Joseph also reconstructed the judicial system to make laws more uniform and rational and to lessen the influence of local landlords. All of these improvements were expected to bring new unity to the state and more taxes into the imperial coffers in Vienna.

Joseph's policies toward serfdom and the land were a far-reaching extension of those Maria Theresa had initiated. During his reign, he introduced reforms that touched the very heart of the rural social structure. He did not abolish the authority of landlords over their peasants, but he did seek to make that authority more moderate and subject to the oversight of royal officials. He abolished serfdom as a legally sanctioned state of servitude. He granted peasants a wide array of personal freedoms, including the right to marry, to engage in skilled work, and to have their children learn a skill without having to secure the landlord's permission.

Joseph reformed the procedures of the manorial courts and opened avenues of appeal to royal officials. He also encouraged landlords to change land leases, so that peasants could more easily inherit land or transfer it to other peasants. His goal in all of these efforts to reduce traditional burdens on peasants was to make them more productive and industrious farmers.

Near the end of his reign, Joseph proposed a new and daring system of land taxation. He decreed in 1789 that all proprietors of the land were to be taxed regardless of social status. No longer were the peasants alone to bear the burden of taxation. He commuted *robot* into a monetary tax, only part of which was to go to the landlord, the rest reverting to the state. Angry nobles blocked the implementation of this decree, and it died with Joseph in 1790. This and other of Joseph's earlier measures, however, brought turmoil throughout the Habsburg realms. Peasants revolted over disagreements with landlords about their newly granted rights. The nobles of the various Habsburg realms protested the taxation scheme. The Magyars resisted Joseph's centralization measures in Hungary and forced him to rescind them.

Joseph was succeeded by his brother Leopold II (r. 1790–1792). Although sympathetic to Joseph's goals, Leopold was forced to repeal many of the most controversial decrees, such as that on taxation. In other areas, Leopold considered his brother's policies simply wrong. For example, he returned political and administrative power to local nobles because he thought it expedient for them to have a voice in government. Still, he did not repudiate his brother's program wholesale. He retained, in particular, Joseph's religious policies and maintained as much political centralization as he thought possible. Joseph's own assessment of his reign was unforgiving: he wrote, "Such small reputation as I had and the political weight that the Monarchy had acquired—all down the drain" and "I am unfortunate in everything that I undertake." Nevertheless, one historian considers Joseph II to be the boldest of the enlightened absolutists: "he alone among these monarchs had to contend with a powerful, established and unreformed Roman Catholic Church within his dominions, and he alone seriously attempted reform across the board, including broad religious toleration and the abolition of serfdom."[17]

---

[17]Derek Beales, *Joseph II*. Volume 2, *Against the World, 1780–1790* (Cambridge, UK: Cambridge University Press, 2009), pp. 639, 661.

Maria Theresa and Joseph II of Austria Debate Toleration

📖 Read the **Compare and Connect** on **MyHistoryLab.com**

THE ISSUE OF religious toleration was widely debated throughout the age of Enlightenment. Many rulers feared that their domains would be overcome by religious turmoil and potential political unrest if their subjects could pursue religious freedom. The issue divided the Empress Maria Theresa and her son, Joseph II, who became her co-regent in 1765. In 1777 they exchanged important letters setting forth their sharply differing views of the subject.

Joseph believed some religious toleration should be introduced into the Habsburg realms. Maria Theresa refused to consider toleration. The toleration of Protestants that is in dispute related only to Lutherans and Calvinists. Maria Theresa died in 1780; the next year Joseph issued an edict of toleration.

QUESTIONS

1. How does Joseph define toleration, and why does Maria Theresa believe it is the same as religious indifference?

2. What does Joseph believe to be the advantages of toleration to Protestants? To Catholics? To the State?

3. Why does Maria Theresa fear that toleration will bring about political as well as religious turmoil?

I. Joseph to Maria Theresa, July 20, 1777

Dear Mother,

. . . The definition of the word "toleration" is to blame for our entire misunderstanding. You have taken it in an entirely different sense. God preserve me from thinking it is a matter of no consequence if your subjects become Protestant or remain Catholic, still less, if they do not believe in or at least observe the religion which they have been given by their fathers. I would give all I possess if all the Protestants of your lands would become Catholics!

As I use it, "tolerance" means only that, when it comes to purely temporal affairs, I would employ, allow to own property, pursue trades, be citizens, without regard to religion, all those who are capable and can bring advantage or industry to our lands. Those who unfortunately hold a false faith are even further from conversion if they remain in their own country than if they move to one in which they will see and hear the striking truths of the Catholic faith. At the same time, the undisturbed practice of their religion makes them far better subjects and causes them to avoid atheism, which is much more dangerous to our Catholics than the observation of other religions. ■

II. Maria Theresa to Joseph, Late July 1777

Without a dominant religion? Toleration and indifference are precisely the true means of undermining everything so that nothing remains. . . . It is no "friend of humanity," a phrase frequently used, who abandons each to his own ideas. I speak only politically, not as a Christian: nothing is as necessary and beneficial as religion. Would you have each create a religion according to his own imagination? No fixed religion, no submission to the church; what would become of us? Tranquility, contentment will not follow from that; the rule of force and more unfortunate times like those we have already seen. Such talk from you could cause the greatest misfortune and make you responsible for thousands of souls. But think of what I would suffer on account of your erroneous principles. Not only the welfare of the state is at stake, not only the preservation of a son who has been the sole object of my actions since his birth—but also your very salvation. . . . In combining your simultaneous desire to vex and to create, you lose yourself, but at the same time you carry away the entire monarchy. . . . No spirit of persecution, but still less one of indifference or "tolerantism," is the path I hope to follow as long as I live, and I do not wish to live unless I can descend in the company of my ancestors with the consolation that my son will be just as great, just as religious as his predecessors, and will turn away from his false thinking and from evil books and from those who let their wit sparkle at the expense of everything that is most holy and most respectable and who wish to introduce an imaginary liberty that can never exist and that will result in license and total upheaval. ■

From Alfred Arneth, ed., *Maria Theresia und Joseph II, Ihre Correspondenz* vol. II (Vienna: Carl Gerold's Sohn, 1867), 151–152, 157–158. [Translation by Alison Frank]

Joseph's coffin was placed in the Capuchin crypt directly in front of his parents' monument. Joseph had ordered that his sarcophagus be simple in design and constructed of copper, with no embellishment but a cross. The contrast with the elaborate sarcophagus of his parents, Maria Theresa and Francis Stephen, could not be more stark. Austrian National Library, Picture Archive, 118.173 STE

RUSSIA FROM PETER THE GREAT THROUGH CATHERINE THE GREAT

1725	Death of Peter the Great
1725–1727	Catherine I
1727–1730	Peter II
1730–1741	Anna
1740–1741	Ivan VI
1741–1762	Elizabeth
1762	Peter III
1762	Catherine II (the Great) becomes empress
1767	Legislative commission summoned
1769	War with Turkey begins
1773–1775	Pugachev's Rebellion
1772	First Partition of Poland
1774	Treaty of Kuchuk-Kainardji ends war with Turkey
1775	Reorganization of local government
1783	Russia annexes Crimea
1785	Catherine issues the Charter of the Nobility
1793	Second Partition of Poland
1795	Third Partition of Poland
1796	Death of Catherine the Great

Catherine the Great of Russia

Joseph II never grasped the practical necessity of forging political constituencies to support his policies. Catherine II, who had been born a German princess, but who became empress of Russia, understood only too well the fragility of the Romanov dynasty's base of power.

After the death of Peter the Great in 1725, the court nobles and the army repeatedly determined the Russian succession. As a result, the crown fell primarily into the hands of people with little talent. Peter's wife, Catherine I, ruled for two years (1725–1727) and was succeeded for three years by Peter's grandson, Peter II. In 1730, the crown devolved on Anna, a niece of Peter the Great. During 1740 and 1741, a child named Ivan VI, who was less than a year old, was the nominal ruler. Finally, in 1741, Peter the Great's daughter Elizabeth came to the throne. She held the title of empress until 1762, but her reign was not notable for new political departures or sound administration. Her court was a shambles of political and romantic intrigue. Much of the power the tsar possessed at the opening of the century had vanished.

At her death in 1762, Elizabeth was succeeded by her nephew Peter III. He was a weak ruler whom many contemporaries considered mad. He immediately exempted the nobles from compulsory military service and then rapidly made peace with Frederick the Great, whom he greatly admired. That decision probably saved Prussia

from military defeat in the Seven Years' War. The most significant event in Peter's life was his marriage in 1745 to a young German princess born in the Prussian city of Stettin, in Pomerania, to a member of the ruling dynasty of Anhalt-Zerbst. This was the future Catherine the Great.

For almost twenty years, Catherine lived in misery and frequent danger at the court of Elizabeth. During that time, she befriended important nobles and read widely the books of the philosophes. She was a shrewd person whose experience in a court crawling with rumors, intrigue, and conspiracy had taught her how to survive. She exhibited neither love nor fidelity toward her demented husband. A few months after his accession as tsar, Peter was deposed and murdered with Catherine's approval, although not her direct intervention, and she was immediately proclaimed empress.

Catherine's familiarity with the Enlightenment and the general culture of Western Europe convinced her Russia was backward and that it needed major reforms

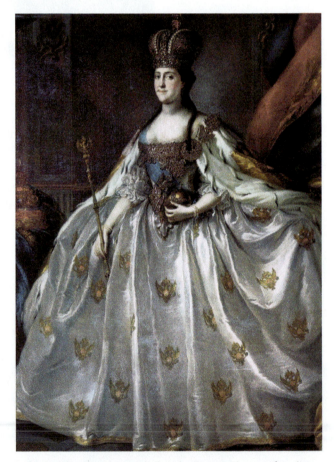

Catherine the Great ascended to the Russian throne after the murder of her husband. She tried initially to enact major reforms, but she never intended to abandon absolutism. She assured nobles of their rights and by the end of her reign had imposed press censorship. *The Granger Collection*

to remain a great power. She understood that any significant reform must have a wide base of political and social support, especially since she had assumed the throne through a palace coup. In 1767, she summoned a legislative commission to advise her on revising the law and government of Russia. There were more than five hundred delegates, drawn from all sectors of Russian life. Before the commission convened, Catherine issued a set of instructions, partly written by herself. They contained many ideas drawn from the political writings of the philosophes. The commission considered the instructions as well as other ideas and complaints its members raised.

Read the Document
"Catherine the Great, 'Instructions for a New Law Code' " on
MyHistoryLab.com

Russian law, however, was not revised for more than half a century. In 1768, Catherine dismissed the commission before several of its key committees had reported. Yet the meeting had not been useless, for it had gathered a vast amount of information about the conditions of local administration and economic life throughout Russia. The inconclusive debates and the absence of programs from the delegates themselves suggested that most Russians saw no alternative to an autocratic monarchy, and Catherine had no intention of departing from absolutism.

Limited Administrative Reform Catherine carried out limited reforms on her own authority. She gave strong support to the rights and local power of the nobility. In 1775, she reorganized local government to solve problems the legislative commission had brought to light. She put most local offices in the hands of nobles rather than creating a royal bureaucracy. In 1785, Catherine issued the Charter of the Nobility, which guaranteed nobles many rights and privileges. In part, the empress had to favor the nobles because they could topple her from the throne. Moreover, Russia's educated class was too small to provide an independent bureaucracy, and the treasury could not afford an army strictly loyal to the crown. Catherine wisely made a virtue of necessity: she strengthened her crown by making friends of her nobles.

View the Image
"Russian Charter Granted to the Nobility" on
MyHistoryLab.com

Economic Growth Part of Catherine's program was to continue the economic development begun under Peter the Great. She attempted to suppress internal barriers to trade. Exports of grain, flax, furs, and naval stores grew dramatically. She also favored the expansion of the small Russian urban middle class that was so vital to trade. Through all of these departures, Catherine tried to maintain ties of friendship and correspondence with the philosophes. She knew that if she treated them kindly,

they would be sufficiently flattered to give her a progressive reputation throughout Europe. At the same time, Catherine had a more realistic understanding of how to balance reform with maintaining the loyalty of the nobility than did Joseph II of Austria. While she considered emancipating serfs, she knew that to do so would infuriate her noble supporters, and left serfdom intact.

Territorial Expansion Catherine's limited administrative reforms and her policy of economic growth had a counterpart in the diplomatic sphere. The Russian drive for warm-water ports continued. (See Map 17–1.) This goal required warfare with the Turks. In 1769, in response to a minor Russian incursion, the Ottoman Empire declared war on Russia. Russia responded with a series of successful military strikes.

View the Map "Growth of Russia to 1914" on
MyHistoryLab.com

Map 17–1 **EXPANSION OF RUSSIA, 1689–1796** The overriding territorial aim of the two most powerful Russian monarchs of the eighteenth century, Peter the Great (in the first quarter of the century) and Catherine the Great (in the last half of the century), was to secure navigable outlets to the sea in both the north and the south for Russia's vast empire; hence Peter's push to the Baltic Sea and Catherine's to the Black Sea. Russia also expanded into Central Asia and Siberia during this time period.

During 1769 and 1770, the Russian fleet sailed all the way from the Baltic Sea into the eastern Mediterranean. The Russian army won several major victories that by 1771 gave Russia control of Ottoman provinces on the Danube River and the Crimean coast of the Black Sea. The conflict dragged on until 1774, when the Treaty of Kuchuk-Kainardji gave Russia a direct outlet on the Black Sea, free navigation rights in its waters, and free access through the Bosporus. Crimea became an independent state, which Catherine painlessly annexed in 1783. Finally, under this treaty, Catherine, as empress of Russia, was made the protector of the Orthodox Christians living in the Ottoman Empire. In the future this would cause conflict with France whose monarch had previously been recognized as the protector of Roman Catholic Christians in the empire.

The Partitions of Poland

The Russian military successes increased Catherine's domestic political support, but they made her neighbors, Prussia and Austria, uneasy. These anxieties were overcome by an extraordinary division of Polish territory known as the First Partition of Poland.

The Russian victories along the Danube River were most unwelcome to Austria, which also harbored ambitions of territorial expansion in that direction. At the same time, the Ottoman Empire was pressing Prussia for aid against Russia. Frederick the Great made a proposal to Russia and Austria that would give each something it wanted, prevent conflict among the powers, and save appearances. After long, complicated, secret negotiations, Russia agreed to abandon the conquered Danubian provinces. In compensation, it received a large portion of Polish territory with almost 2 million inhabitants. As a reward for remaining neutral, Prussia annexed most of the territory between East Prussia and Prussia proper. This land allowed Frederick to unite two previously separate sections of his realm. Finally, Austria took southern Poland, with its important salt mines, and other Polish territory with more than 2.5 million inhabitants. (See Map 17–2.)

View the Image "The Cake of Kings: First Partition of Poland, 1773—Engraving" on **MyHistoryLab.com**

In September 1772, the helpless Polish aristocracy, paying the price for maintaining internal liberties at the expense of developing a strong central government, ratified this seizure of nearly one-third of Polish territory. The loss was not immediately fatal to Poland's continued existence, and it inspired a revival of national feeling. Attempts were made to strengthen the Polish state and reform its feeble central government, but

they proved to be too little and too late. Poland was no match for its stronger, more ambitious neighbors. The partition of Poland clearly demonstrated that any nation without a strong monarchy, bureaucracy, and army could no longer compete within the European state system. It also demonstrated that the major powers in eastern Europe were prepared to settle their own rivalries at the expense of such a weak state. If Polish territory had not been available to ease tensions, international rivalries might have led to warfare among Russia, Austria, and Prussia.

As shall be seen in Chapter 18, the wars and social upheaval that followed the outbreak of the French Revolution gave Russia and Prussia an excuse to partition Poland again in 1793, and Russia, Prussia, and Austria partitioned it a third and final time in 1795, removing it from the map of Europe for more than a century. Each time, the great powers contended they were saving

Map 17–2 **PARTITIONS OF POLAND, 1772, 1793, AND 1795** The callous eradication of Poland from the map displayed eighteenth-century power politics at its most extreme. Poland, without a strong central government, fell victim to the strong absolute monarchies of central and eastern Europe.

themselves, and by implication the rest of Europe, from Polish anarchy.

The End of the Eighteenth Century in Central and Eastern Europe

During the last two decades of the eighteenth century, all three regimes based on enlightened absolutism became more conservative and politically repressive. In Prussia and Austria, rulers' innovations stirred resistance among the nobility. In Russia, fear of peasant unrest was the chief factor.

Frederick the Great of Prussia grew remote during his old age, leaving the aristocracy to fill important military and administrative posts. A reaction to Enlightenment ideas also set in among Prussian Lutheran writers.

In Austria, Joseph II's plans to restructure society and administration in his realms provoked growing frustration and political unrest, with the nobility calling for an end to innovation. In response, Joseph turned increasingly to censorship, which he had initially lessened, and his secret police.

Russia faced a peasant uprising, the Pugachev Rebellion, between 1773 and 1775, and Catherine the Great never fully recovered from the fears of social and political upheaval that it raised. Once the French Revolution broke out in 1789, the Russian empress censored books based on Enlightenment thought and sent offensive authors into Siberian exile.

By the close of the century, fear of, and hostility to, change permeated the ruling classes of central and eastern Europe. This reaction had begun before 1789, but the events in France bolstered and sustained it for almost half a century.

In Perspective

The writers of the Enlightenment, known as *philosophes*, charted a major new path in modern European and Western thought. They operated within a print culture that made public opinion into a distinct, cultural force. Admiring Newton and the achievements of physical science, they tried to apply reason and the principles of science to the cause of social reform. They also believed that passions and feelings are essential parts of human nature. Throughout their writings they championed reasonable moderation in social life. More than any other previous group of Western thinkers, they opposed the authority of the established churches. Most of them championed some form of religious toleration. They also sought to achieve a science of society that could discover how to maximize human productivity and material happiness. The great dissenter among them was Rousseau, who also wished to reform society, but in the name of virtue rather than material happiness.

The political influence of these writers was diverse and far-reaching. The founding fathers of the American republic looked to them for political guidance, as did moderate liberal reformers throughout Europe, especially within royal bureaucracies. The autocratic rulers of eastern Europe consulted the philosophes in the hope that Enlightenment ideas might allow them to rule more efficiently. The revolutionaries in France would honor them. This varied assortment of followers illustrates the diverse character of the philosophes themselves. It also shows that Enlightenment thought cannot be reduced to a single formula. Rather, it should be seen as an outlook that championed change and reform, giving central place to humans and their welfare on earth rather than to God and the hereafter.

KEY TERMS

deism (p. 518)
laissez-faire (p. 524)

Neoclassicism (p. 532)
philosophes (p. 515)

physiocrats (p. 524)
Rococo (p. 532)

REVIEW QUESTIONS

1. How did the Enlightenment change basic Western attitudes toward reform, faith, and reason? What were the major formative influences on the philosophes? How important were Voltaire and the *Encyclopedia* in the success of the Enlightenment?

2. Why did some philosophes consider organized religion to be their greatest enemy? What were the basic tenets of deism? How did Jewish writers contribute to Enlightenment thinking about religion? What are the similarities and differences between the

Enlightenment evaluation of Islam and its evaluations of Christianity and Judaism?

3. What were the attitudes of the philosophes toward women? What was Rousseau's view of women? What were the separate spheres he imagined men and women occupying? What were Mary Wollstonecraft's criticisms of Rousseau's view?

4. How did the views of the mercantilists about the earth's resources differ from those of Adam Smith in his book *The Wealth of Nations?* Why might Smith be regarded as an advocate of the consumer? How did his theory of history work to the detriment of less economically advanced non-European peoples? How

did some Enlightenment writers criticize European empires?

5. How did the political views of Montesquieu differ from those of Rousseau? Was Montesquieu's view of England accurate? Was Rousseau a child of the Enlightenment or its enemy? Which did Rousseau value more, the individual or society?

6. Were the enlightened monarchs true believers in the ideals of the philosophes, or was their enlightenment a mere veneer? Was their power really absolute? What motivated their reforms? What does the partition of Poland indicate about the spirit of enlightened absolutism?

SUGGESTED READINGS

D. D. Bien, *The Calas Affair: Persecution, Toleration, and Heresy in Eighteenth-Century Toulouse* (1960). The standard treatment of the famous case.

T. C. W. Blanning, *The Culture of Power and the Power of Culture: Old Regime Europe 1660–1789* (2002). A remarkable synthesis of the interaction of political power and culture in France, Prussia, and Austria.

P. Bloom, *Enlightening the World: Encyclopedie, The Book That Changed the Course of History* (2005). A lively, accessible introduction.

J. Buchan, *Crowded with Genius: The Scottish Enlightenment* (2003). A readable introduction.

L. Damrosch, *Rousseau: Restless Genius* (2007). The best recent biography.

I. De Madariaga, *Russia in the Age of Catherine the Great* (1981). The best discussion in English.

S. Feiner, *The Jewish Enlightenment* (2002). An extensive work, challenging pan-European treatment of the subject.

P. Gay, *The Enlightenment: An Interpretation*, 2 vols. (1966, 1969). A classic.

D. Goodman, *The Republic of Letters: A Cultural History of the French Enlightenment* (1994). Concentrates on the role of salons.

C. Hesse, *The Other Enlightenment: How French Women Became Modern* (2004). Explores the manner in which French women authors created their own sphere of thought and cultural activity.

J. Israel, *Enlightenment Contested: Philosophy, Modernity, and the Emancipation of Man 1670–1752* (2006). A challenging major revisionist history of the subject.

J. I. Israel, *Radical Enlightenment: Philosophy and the Making of Modernity* (2001). A controversial account of the most radical strains of thought in Enlightenment culture.

C. A. Kors, *Encyclopedia of the Enlightenment* (2002). A major reference work on all of the chief intellectual themes of the era.

J. P. Ledonne, *The Russian Empire and the World, 1700–1917* (1996). Explores the major reasons for Russian expansion from the eighteenth to the early twentieth centuries.

G. Macdonagh, *Frederick the Great* (2001). A thoughtful and accessible biography.

D. MacMahon, *Enemies of the Enlightenment: The French Counter-Enlightenment and the Making of Modernity* (2001). A fine exploration of French writers critical of the philosophes.

J. V. H. Melton, *The Rise of the Public in Enlightenment Europe* (2001). Explores the social basis of print culture with an excellent bibliography.

S. Muthu, *Enlightenment Against Empire* (2003). A challenging volume covering the critique of the empire.

R. Peason, *Voltaire Almighty: A Life in Pursuit of Freedom* (2005). An accessible biography.

R. Porter, *The Creation of the Modern World: The Untold Story of the British Enlightenment* (2000). Seeks to shift the center of the Enlightenment from France to England.

P. Riley, *The Cambridge Companion to Rousseau* (2001). Excellent accessible essays by major scholars.

E. Rothchild, *Economic Sentiments: Adam Smith, Condorcet, and the Enlightenment* (2001). A sensitive account of Smith's thought and its relationship to the social questions of the day.

J. Sheehan, *The Enlightenment Bible* (2007). Explores the Enlightenment treatment of the Bible.

S. Smith, *Spinoza, Liberalism, and the Question of Jewish Identity* (1997). A clear introduction to a challenging thinker.

A. M. Wilson, *Diderot* (1972). A splendid biography of the person behind the *Encyclopedia* and other major Enlightenment publications.

L. Wolff, *Inventing Eastern Europe: The Map of Civilization on the Mind of the Enlightenment* (1994). A remarkable study of how Enlightenment writers recast the understanding of this part of the Continent.

MyHistoryLab™ MEDIA ASSIGNMENTS

Find these resources in the Media Assignments folder for Chapter 17 on **MyHistoryLab**.

QUESTIONS FOR ANALYSIS

1. How does this painting illustrate the Enlightenment's relationship with the Classical past?

   Section: Rococo and Neoclassical Styles in Eighteenth-Century Art

   ◉ View the **Closer Look** An Eighteenth-Century Artist Appeals to the Ancient World, p. 537

2. How does Beccaria reflect Enlightenment ideals?

   Section: The Enlightenment and Society

   📖 Read the **Document** Cesare Beccaria, *On Crimes and Punishments*, p. 524

3. What political ideas of the 1700s does this image illustrate?

   Section: Enlightened Absolutism

   ◉ View the **Image** The Cake of Kings: First Partition of Poland, 1773—Engraving, p. 546

4. Are Voltaire's ideas ahead of his time, or part of the currents of Enlightenment thought?

   Section: The Enlightenment and Religion

   📖 Read the **Document** Voltaire, "On Universal Toleration," p. 519

5. Why does Diderot feel a new encyclopedia is required?

   Section: Formative Influences on the Enlightenment

   📖 Read the **Document** Denis Diderot, Preliminary Discourse from *The Encyclopedia*, p. 514

OTHER RESOURCES FROM THIS CHAPTER

Formative Influences on the Enlightenment

📖 Read the **Document** Immanuel Kant Defines the Enlightenment, 1784, p. 513

The Philosophes

📖 Read the **Document** Voltaire, on Social Conditions in Eighteenth-Century France, p. 515

📖 Read the **Document** Voltaire, *Letters on England*, p. 516

The Enlightenment and Religion

📖 Read the **Document** Lady Mary Wortley Montagu, Letters: (a) on Constantinople; (b) on Smallpox; (c) on Vaccination in Turkey, p. 519

Political Thought of the Philosophes

📖 Read the **Document** Baron de Montesquieu, Excerpt from *The Spirit of the Laws*, p. 526

Women in the Thought and Practice of the Enlightenment

📖 Read the **Document** Mary Wollstonecraft, Introduction to *A Vindication of the Rights of Woman*, p. 532

Rococo and Neoclassical Styles in Eighteenth-Century Art

◉ View the **Closer Look** Watteau's *The Signboard of Gersaint*, p. 532

◉ View the **Architectural Panorama**, Panthéon, p. 538

Enlightened Absolutism

◉ View the **Map** The Expansion of Prussia, p. 539

📖 Read the **Compare and Connect** Maria Theresa and Joseph II of Austria Debate Toleration, p. 542

📖 Read the **Document** Catherine the Great, "Instructions for a New Law Code," p. 545

◉ View the **Image** Russian Charter Granted to the Nobility, p. 545

◉ View the **Map** Growth of Russia to 1914, p. 545

On July 14, 1789, crowds stormed the Bastille, a prison in Paris. This event, whose only practical effect was to free a few prisoners, marked the first time the populace of Paris redirected the course of the revolution.   Anonymous, France, eighteenth century, Siege of the Bastille, 14 July, 1789. Musée de la Ville de Paris, Musée Carnavalet, Paris, France. Bridgeman—Giraudon/Art Resource, NY

((•—[**Listen** to the **Chapter Audio** on **MyHistoryLab.com**

18

The French Revolution

LEARNING OBJECTIVES

How did the financial weakness of the French monarchy lay the foundations of revolution in 1789?

How did the calling of the Estates General lead to revolution?

How did the National Constituent Assembly reorganize France?

What led to the radicalization of the French Revolution?

How did Europe respond to the French Revolution?

How did war and ideology combine to create the Reign of Terror?

What course did the French Revolution take after 1794?

I N THE SPRING of 1789 political turmoil erupted in France. By the summer it had led to a revolution that marked the beginning of a new political order in France and eventually throughout the West. The French Revolution brought to the foreground the principles of civic equality and popular sovereignty that challenged the major political and social institutions of Europe and that in evolving forms have continued to shape and reshape Western political and social life to the present day. During the

1790s the forces the revolution unleashed would cause small-town provincial lawyers and Parisian street orators to exercise more influence over the fate of the Continent than aristocrats, royal ministers, or monarchs. Citizen armies commanded by people of modest origin and filled by conscripted village youths would defeat armies composed of professional soldiers led by officers from the nobility. The king and queen of France, as well as thousands of French peasants and shopkeepers, would be executed. The existence of the Roman Catholic faith in France and indeed of Christianity itself would be challenged. Finally, Europe would embark on almost a quarter century of war that would eventually extend across the continent and result in millions of casualties.

▼ The Crisis of the French Monarchy

Although the French Revolution would shatter many of the political, social, and ecclesiastical structures of Europe, its origins lay in a much more mundane problem. By the late 1780s, thanks in large part to the expenditures associated with supporting the American revolution, the French royal government could not command sufficient taxes to finance itself. The monarchy's unsuccessful search for adequate revenues led it into ongoing conflicts with aristocratic and ecclesiastical institutions. Eventually, the resulting deadlock was so complete that Louis XVI and his ministers were required to summon the French Estates General, which had not met since 1614. Once the deputies to that body gathered, a new set of issues and problems quickly emerged that led to the revolution itself. Yet, none of this would have occurred if the monarchy had not reached a state of financial crisis that meant it could no longer function within the limits and practices of existing political institutions.

The Monarchy Seeks New Taxes

The French monarchy emerged from the Seven Years' War (1756–1763) defeated, deeply in debt, and unable thereafter to put its finances on a sound basis. French support of the American revolt against Great Britain further deepened the financial difficulties of the government. On the eve of the revolution, the interest and payments on the royal debt amounted to just over one-half of the entire budget. Given the economic vitality of France, the debt was neither overly large nor disproportionate to the debts of other European powers. The problem lay with the inability of the royal government to tap the nation's wealth through taxes to service and repay the debt. Paradoxically, France was a rich nation in which the inability to collect sufficient taxes led to an impoverished government. Peasants, who had the least to spare, bore the heaviest tax burden. They paid taxes not only to the king, but also to the church and their local lords. A bad harvest in 1788 meant that peasants were not only impoverished, but also in danger of starvation as bread prices soared. Without increased taxation on the aristocracy and the church, there was no way that taxation of peasants alone could resolve France's financial crisis.

The debt was symptomatic of the failure of the late-eighteenth-century French monarchy to come to terms with the political power of aristocratic institutions and, in particular, the *parlements*. As explained in Chapter 13, French absolutism had always involved a process of ongoing negotiation between the monarchy and local aristocratic interests. This process had become more difficult after the death of Louis XIV (r. 1643–1715) when the aristocracy had sought to reclaim parts of the influence it had lost. Nonetheless, for the first half of the century, the monarchy had retained most of its authority.

For twenty-five years after the Seven Years' War, however, a standoff occurred between the monarchy and the aristocracy, as one royal minister after another attempted to devise new tax schemes that would tap the wealth of the nobility, only to be confronted by opposition from both the *Parlement* of Paris and provincial *parlements*. Both Louis XV (r. 1715–1774) and Louis XVI (r. 1774–1792) lacked the character, resolution, and political skills to resolve the dispute. In place of a consistent policy for dealing with the growing debt and aristocratic resistance to change, the monarchy hesitated, retreated, and even lied.

Well-meaning, but weak and vacillating, Louis XVI (r. 1774–1792) stumbled from concession to concession until he finally lost all power to save his throne. Joseph Siffred Duplessis (1725–1802), *Louis XVI*. Versailles, France. Photograph copyright Bridgeman—Giraudon/Art Resource, NY

In 1770, Louis XV appointed René Maupeou (1714–1792) as chancellor. The new minister was determined to increase taxes on the nobility. He abolished the *parlements* and exiled their members to different parts of the country. He then began an ambitious program to make the administration more efficient. However, when Louis XV died of smallpox in 1774, his successor, Louis XVI, attempted to regain popular support by dismissing Maupeou, restoring all the *parlements*, and confirming their old powers.

Although the *parlements* spoke for aristocratic interests, they appear to have enjoyed public support. By the second half of the eighteenth century, many French nobles shared with the wealthy professional and commercial classes similar goals for administrative reforms that would support economic growth. Both groups regarded the lumbering institutions of monarchical absolutism as a burden. Moreover, throughout these initial and later disputes with the monarchy, the *parlements*, though completely dominated by the aristocracy, used the language of liberty and reform to defend their cause. They portrayed the monarchy as despotic—that is, as acting arbitrarily in defiance of the law. Here they drew on the ideas and arguments of many Enlightenment writers, such as Montesquieu and the physiocrats, discussed in Chapter 17.

● View the **Closer Look** "Challenging the French Political Order" on **MyHIstoryLab.com**

The monarchy was unable to rally public opinion to its side because it had lost much of its moral authority. Louis XVI was considered detached and ineffective. His wife, Marie Antoinette (1755–1793), was always suspect because of her Austrian background. She was viciously accused of sexual misconduct and personal extravagance in an underground pamphlet campaign that became increasingly prurient, misogynist, and xenophobic. Furthermore, Louis XVI and his family continued to live at Versailles, rarely leaving its grounds to mix with his subjects and with the aristocracy, who now, unlike in the days of Louis XIV, often dwelled in Paris or on their estates. Hence, the French monarch stood at a distinct popular disadvantage in his clashes first with the *parlements* and later with other groupings of the aristocracy.

In all these respects, the public image and daily reality of the French monarchy were much more problematical than those of other contemporary monarchs. Frederick II of Prussia and Joseph II of Austria genuinely saw themselves, and were seen by their subjects, as patriotic servants of the state. In central Europe, rulers were often themselves the generators of reform, which meant even criticism of current policy was generally combined with confidence in the monarchy's ability to correct any errors. George III of Great Britain, despite all his political difficulties, was regarded by most Britons as having a model character and as seeking the economic improvement of his nation. Frederick II, Joseph II, and George III all had reputations for personal frugality, and they moved frequently among the people they governed.

Necker's Report

France's successful intervention on behalf of the American colonists against the British only worsened the financial problems of Louis XVI's government. By 1781, as a result of the aid to America, its debt was larger, and its sources of revenues were unchanged. The new royal director-general of finances, Jacques Necker (1732–1804), did not want to admit that the situation was as bad as was feared. Necker, a Swiss banker, produced a public report in 1781 that used a financial sleight of hand to downplay France's financial difficulties. He argued that if the expenditures for the American war were removed, the budget was in surplus. Necker's report also revealed that a large portion of royal expenditures went to pensions for aristocrats and other royal court favorites. Necker was pressured to leave office not because of his dubious accounting, but because court aristocratic circles were embarrassed by his revelations. The damage had already been done: Necker's misleading assessment of French finances made it more difficult for government officials to claim a real need to raise new taxes.

Calonne's Reform Plan and the Assembly of Notables

The monarchy hobbled along without a plan for financial improvement until 1786. By this time, Charles Alexandre de Calonne (1734–1802) was the minister of finance. Calonne proposed to encourage internal trade, to lower some taxes, such as the *gabelle* on salt, and to transform the *corvée*, peasants' labor services on public works, into money payments. He also sought to remove internal barriers to trade and reduce government regulation of the grain trade. More importantly, Calonne wanted to introduce a new land tax that all landowners would have to pay regardless of their social status. If this tax had been imposed, the monarchy could have abandoned other indirect taxes. The government would also have had less need to seek additional taxes that required approval from the aristocratically dominated *parlements*. Calonne also intended to establish new local assemblies made up of landowners to approve land taxes; in these assemblies the voting power would have depended on the amount of land a person owned rather than on his social status. All these proposals would have undermined both the political and the social power of the French aristocracy. Other of his proposals touched the economic privileges of the French Church. These policies reflected much advanced economic and administrative thinking of the day.

The monarchy, however, had little room to maneuver. The creditors were at the door, and the treasury was nearly empty. Calonne needed public support for such bold new undertakings. In February 1787, he met with an Assembly of Notables, nominated by the royal ministry from the upper ranks of the aristocracy and the church, to seek support for his plan. The Assembly adamantly refused to give it. There was some agreement that reform and greater fairness in taxation were necessary, but the Assembly did not trust the information they had received from Calonne. In his place they called for the reappointment of Necker, who they believed had left the country in sound fiscal condition. Finally, they claimed that only the Estates General of France, a medieval institution that had not met since 1614, could consent to new taxes. The notables believed that calling the Estates General, which had been traditionally organized to allow aristocratic and church dominance, would actually allow the nobility to have a direct role in governing the country alongside the monarchy. The issue was less the nobility not wishing to reform tax structure than its determination to acquire power at the expense of the monarchy and to direct reforms itself.

Deadlock and the Calling of the Estates General

Again, Louis XVI backed off. He replaced Calonne with Étienne Charles Loménie de Brienne (1727–1794), archbishop of Toulouse and the chief opponent of Calonne at the Assembly of Notables. Once in office, Brienne found, to his astonishment, that the financial situation was as bad as his predecessor had asserted. Brienne himself now sought to reform the land tax. The *Parlement* of Paris, however, in its self-appointed role as the embodiment of public opinion, took the new position that it lacked authority to authorize the tax and that only the Estates General could do so. Shortly thereafter, Brienne appealed to the Assembly of the Clergy to approve a large subsidy to fund that part of the debt then coming due for payment. The clergy, like the *Parlement* dominated by aristocrats, not only refused the subsidy, but also reduced the voluntary contribution, or *don gratuit*, that it paid to the government in lieu of taxes.

As these unfruitful negotiations were taking place at the center of political life, local aristocratic *parlements* and estates in the provinces were making their own demands. They wanted to restore the privileges they had enjoyed during the early seventeenth century, before Richelieu and Louis XIV had crushed their independence. Furthermore, bringing the financial crisis to a new point of urgency, in the summer of 1788 bankers refused to extend necessary short-term credit to the government. Consequently, in July 1788, the king, through Brienne, agreed to convoke the Estates General the next year. Brienne resigned, and Necker replaced him. Some kind of political reform was coming, but what form it would take and how it would happen would be largely determined by the conflicts that emerged from summoning the Estates General.

▼ The Revolution of 1789

The Estates General Becomes the National Assembly

The Estates General had been called because of the political deadlock between the French monarchy and the vested interests of aristocratic institutions and the church. Almost immediately after it was summoned, however, the three groups, or estates, represented within it clashed with each other. The First Estate was the clergy, the Second Estate the nobility, and the **Third Estate** was, theoretically, all other adult men in the kingdom, although its representatives were drawn primarily from wealthy members of the commercial and professional middle classes. All the representatives in the Estates General were men. During the widespread public discussions preceding the meeting of the Estates General, representatives of the Third Estate made it clear they would not permit the monarchy and the aristocracy to decide the future of the nation.

A comment by a priest, the Abbé Siéyès (1748–1836), in a pamphlet published in 1789, captures the spirit of the Third Estate's representatives: "What is the Third Estate? Everything. What has it been in the political order up to the present? Nothing. What does it ask? To become something."[1] The spokesmen for the Third Estate became more determined to assert their role less from any preexisting conflicts with the nobility than from the conflicts that emerged during the debates and electioneering for the Estates General in late 1788 and early 1789.

Read the **Document** "Petition of Women of the Third Estate" on **MyHistoryLab.com**

Read the **Document** "Emmanuel Joseph Sieyès, *What Is the Third Estate?*" on **MyHistoryLab.com**

Debate Over Organization and Voting Before the Estates General gathered, a public debate over its proper organization drew the lines of basic disagreement. The aristocracy made two important attempts to limit the influence of the Third Estate. First, a reconvened Assembly of Notables demanded that each estate have an equal number of representatives. Second, in September 1788, the *Parlement* of Paris ruled that voting in the Estates General should be conducted by order, or estate, rather than by head—that is, each estate in the Estates General, rather than each individual member, should have

[1] Leo Gershoy, *The French Revolution and Napoleon* (New York: Appleton-Century-Crofts, 1964), p. 102.

one vote. This procedure would in all likelihood have ensured the aristocratically dominated First and Second Estates could always outvote the Third by a vote of two estates to one estate. Both moves raised doubt about the aristocracy's previously declared concern for French liberty. Spokesmen for the Third Estate immediately denounced the arrogant claims of the aristocracy, which seemed only concerned to protect its own privilege.

In many respects the interests of the aristocracy and the most prosperous and well-educated members of the Third Estate had converged during the eighteenth century, and many nobles had spouses from wealthy families of the Third Estate. Yet a fundamental social distance separated the members of the two orders. Many aristocrats were much richer than members of the Third Estate, and noblemen had all but monopolized the high command in the army and navy. The Third Estate had also experienced various forms of political and social discrimination from the nobility. The resistance of the nobility to voting by head confirmed the suspicions and resentments of the members of the Third Estate, who tended to be well-off, but not enormously rich, lawyers. The stance of both the reconvened Assembly of Notables and the *Parlement* of Paris regarding the composition and functioning of the forthcoming Estates General meant that the elected members of the Third Estate would approach the gathering with a newly awakened profound distrust of the nobility and of the aristocratically dominated church.

Doubling the Third   In the face of widespread public uproar over the aristocratic effort to dominate composition and procedures of the Estates General, the royal council eventually decided that strengthening the Third Estate would best serve the interests of the monarchy and the cause of fiscal reform. In December 1788, the council announced the Third Estate would elect twice as many representatives as either the nobles or the clergy. This so-called doubling of the Third Estate meant it could easily dominate the Estates General if voting proceeded by head rather than by order. The council correctly assumed that liberal nobles and clergy would support the Third Estate, confirming that, despite social differences, these groups shared important interests and reform goals. The method of voting had not yet been decided when the Estates General gathered at Versailles in May 1789.

The *Cahiers de Doléances*   When the representatives came to the royal palace, they brought with them *cahiers de doléances*, or lists of grievances, registered by the local electors, to be presented to the king. Many of these lists have survived and provide considerable information about the state of France on the eve of the revolution. The documents criticized government waste, indirect taxes, church taxes and corruption, and the hunting rights of the aristocracy. They included calls for periodic meetings

of the Estates General, more equitable taxes, more local control of administration, unified weights and measures to facilitate trade and commerce, and a free press. The overwhelming demand of the *cahiers* was for equality of rights among the king's subjects. Yet it is also clear that the *cahiers* that originated among the nobility were not radically different from those of the Third Estate. There was broad agreement that the French government needed major reform, that greater equality in taxation and other matters was desirable, and that many aristocratic privileges must be abandoned. (See the Document "The Third Estate of a French City Petitions the King," page 555.) The *cahiers* drawn up before May 1789 indicate that the three estates could have cooperated to reach these goals. But it became clear almost from the moment the Estates General opened that conflict among the estates, rather than cooperation, was to be the rule.

📖 **Read the Document**
"French Peasants, Cahiers de doléances (Grievances) (France), 1789" on **MyHistoryLab.com**

The Third Estate Creates the National Assembly   The complaints, demands, and hopes for reform expressed in the *cahiers* could not, however, be discussed until the questions of the organization and voting in the Estates General had been decided. From the beginning, the Third Estate, whose members consisted largely of local officials, professionals, and other persons of property, refused to sit as a separate order as the king desired. For several weeks there was a standoff. Then, on June 1, the Third Estate invited the clergy and the nobles to join them in organizing a new legislative body. A few priests did so. On June 17, that body declared itself the National Assembly, and on June 19 by a narrow margin, the Second Estate voted to join the Assembly.

The Tennis Court Oath   At this point, Louis XVI hoped to reassert a role in the proceedings. He intended to call a "Royal Session" of the Estates General for June 23 and closed the room where the National Assembly had been gathering. On June 20, finding themselves thus unexpectedly locked out of their usual meeting place, the National Assembly moved to a nearby indoor tennis court. There, its members took an oath to continue to sit until they had given France a constitution. This was the famous Tennis Court Oath. Louis XVI ordered the National Assembly to desist, but many clergy and nobles joined the Assembly in defiance of the royal command.

🔍 **View the Image** "Oath of the Tennis Court" on **MyHistoryLab.com**

On June 27, the king, now having completely lost control of the events around him, capitulated and formally requested the First and Second Estates to meet with the National Assembly, where voting would occur by head rather than by order. Because of the doubling of its membership, the Third Estate had twice

Document	THE THIRD ESTATE OF A FRENCH CITY PETITIONS THE KING

In the spring of 1789 representatives to the Estates General brought to Versailles cahiers de doléances *which were lists of grievances generated during the election process. (See page 554.) This particular* cahier *originated in Dourdan, a city in central France, and reflects the complaints of the Third Estate. The first two articles refer to the organization of the Estates General. The other articles ask the king to grant various forms of equality before the law and in taxation. Most of the* cahiers *of the Third Estate included these demands for equality.*

Which of the following petitions relate to political rights and which to economic equality? The slogan most associated with the French Revolution was "Liberty, Equality, Fraternity." Which of these petitions represents each of these values?

The order of the third estate of the City . . . of Dourdan . . . supplicates [the king] to accept the grievances, complaints, and remonstrances which it is permitted to bring to the foot of the throne, and to see therein only the expression of its zeal and the homage of its obedience.

It wishes:

1. That his subjects of the third estate, equal by such status to all other citizens, present themselves before the common father without other distinction which might degrade them.
2. That all the orders, already united by duty and common desire contribute equally to the needs of the State, also deliberate in common concerning its needs.
3. That no citizen lose his liberty except according to law: that, consequently, no one be arrested by virtue of special orders, or, if imperative circumstances necessitate such orders that the prisoner be handed over to regular courts of justice within forty-eight hours at the latest.
12. That every tax, direct or indirect, be granted only for a limited time, and that every collection beyond such term be regarded as peculation, and punished as such.
15. That every personal tax be abolished; that thus the capitation [a poll tax] and the taille [tax from which nobility and clergy were exempt] and its accessories be merged with the *vingtièmes* [an income tax] in a tax on land and real or nominal property.
16. That such tax be borne equally, without distinction, by all classes of citizens and by all kinds of property, even feudal . . . rights.
17. That the tax substituted for the *corvée* be borne by all classes of citizens equally and without distinction. That said tax, at present beyond the capacity of those who pay it and the needs to which it is destined, be reduced by at least one-half.

From John Hall Stewart, *Documentary Survey of the French Revolution*, 1st ed., © 1951. Reprinted by permission of Pearson Education, Inc., Upper Saddle River, NJ.

as many members as either of the other estates that joined them. Had nothing further occurred, the government of France would already have been transformed. Henceforth, the monarchy could govern only in cooperation with the National Assembly, and the National Assembly would not be a legislative body organized according to privileged orders. The National Assembly, which renamed itself the National Constituent Assembly because of its intention to write a new constitution, was composed of a majority of members drawn from all three orders, who shared liberal goals for the administrative, constitutional, and economic reform of the country. The revolution in France against government by privileged hereditary orders, however, rapidly extended beyond events occurring at Versailles.

This painting of the Tennis Court Oath, June 20, is by Jacques-Louis David (1748–1825). In the center foreground are members of different estates joining hands in cooperation as equals. The presiding officer is Jean-Sylvain Bailly, soon to become mayor of Paris. Jacques-Louis David, *Oath of the Tennis Court, the 20th of June 1789*. Chateaux de Versailles et de Trianon, Versailles, France. Bridgeman–Giraudon/Art Resource, NY

Fall of the Bastille

Two new forces soon intruded on the scene. First, Louis XVI again attempted to regain the political initiative by mustering royal troops near Versailles and Paris. On the advice of Queen Marie Antoinette, his brothers, and the most conservative aristocrats at court, he seemed to be contemplating the use of force against the National Constituent Assembly. On July 11, without consulting Assembly leaders, Louis abruptly dismissed Necker, his minister of finance. Louis's gathering troops and dismissal of Necker marked the beginning of a steady, but consistently poorly executed, royal attempt to undermine the Assembly and halt the revolution. Most of the National Constituent Assembly wished to establish some form of constitutional monarchy, but from the start, Louis's refusal to cooperate thwarted that effort. The king fatally decided to throw in his lot with the conservative aristocracy against the emerging forces of reform drawn from across the social and political spectrum.

The second new factor to impose itself on the events at Versailles was the populace of Paris, which numbered more than 600,000 people. The mustering of royal troops created anxiety in the city, where throughout the winter and spring of 1789 high prices for bread, which was the staple food of the poor, had produced riots. Those Parisians who had elected representatives to the Third Estate had continued to meet after the elections. By June they were organizing a citizen militia and collecting arms. They regarded the dismissal of Necker as the opening of a royal offensive against the National Constituent Assembly and the city. They intended to protect the Assembly and the revolution had begun.

On July 14, large crowds of Parisians, most of them small shopkeepers, tradespeople, artisans, and wage earners, marched to the Bastille to get weapons for the militia. This great fortress, with ten-foot-thick walls, had once held political prisoners. Through miscalculations and ineptitude by the governor of the fortress, the troops in the Bastille fired into the crowd, killing ninety-eight people and wounding many others. Thereafter, the crowd stormed the fortress. They released the seven prisoners inside, none of whom was a political prisoner, and killed several troops and the governor.

On July 15, the militia of Paris, by then called the National Guard, offered its command to a young liberal aristocrat, the Marquis de Lafayette (1757–1834). This hero of the American Revolution gave the guard a new insignia: the red and blue stripes from the colors of the coat of arms of Paris, separated by the white stripe of the royal flag. The emblem became the revolutionary *cockade* (badge) and eventually the tricolor flag of revolutionary France.

The attack on the Bastille marked the first of many crucial *journées*, days on which the populace of Paris redirected the course of the revolution. The fall of the fortress signaled that the National Constituent Assembly alone would not decide the political future of the nation. As the news of the taking of the Bastille spread, similar disturbances took place in provincial cities. A few days later, Louis XVI again bowed to the force of events and personally visited Paris, where he wore the revolutionary *cockade* and recognized the organized electors as the legitimate government of the city. The king also recognized the National Guard and thus implicitly admitted that he lacked the military support to turn back the revolution. The citizens of Paris were, for the time being, satisfied. They also had established themselves as an independent political force with which other political groups might ally for their own purposes.

The "Great Fear" and the Night of August 4

Simultaneous with the popular urban disturbances, a movement known as the "Great Fear" swept across much of the French countryside. Rumors that royal troops would be sent into the rural districts intensified the peasant disturbances that had begun during the spring. The Great Fear saw the burning of *châteaux*, the destruction of legal records and documents, and the refusal to pay feudal dues. The peasants were determined to take possession of food supplies and land that they considered rightfully theirs. They vented their anger against the injustices of rural life and reclaimed rights and property they had lost through administrative tightening of the collection of feudal dues during the past century. Their targets were both aristocratic and ecclesiastical landlords.

View the **Map**
"Map Discovery:
Revolutionary France" on
MyHistoryLab.com

On the night of August 4, 1789, aristocrats in the National Constituent Assembly attempted to halt the spreading disorder in the countryside. By prearrangement, several liberal nobles and clerics rose in the Assembly and renounced their feudal rights, dues, and tithes. In a scene of great emotion, they surrendered hunting and fishing rights, judicial authority, and legal exemptions. These nobles and clerics gave up what they had already lost and what they could not have regained without civil war in the rural areas. Many of them later received financial compensation for their losses. Nonetheless, after the night of August 4, all French citizens were subject to the same and equal laws. Furthermore, since the sale of government offices was also abolished, the events of that night opened political and military positions, careers, and advancement to talent rather than basing them exclusively on birth or wealth. This dramatic session of the Assembly effectively abolished the major social institutions of the Old Regime and created an unforeseen situation that required a vast legal and social reconstruction of the nation. Without those renunciations, the constructive work of the National Constituent Assembly would have been much more difficult and certainly much more limited. (See the Document "The National Assembly Decrees Civic Equality in France," page 560.)

Both the attack on the Bastille and the Great Fear displayed characteristics of the urban and rural riots that had occurred often in eighteenth-century France. Louis XVI first thought the turmoil over the Bastille was simply another bread riot. Indeed, the popular disturbances were only partly related to the events at Versailles. A deep economic downturn had struck France in 1787 and continued into 1788. The harvests for both years had been poor, and the food prices in 1789 were higher than at any time since 1703. Wages had not kept up with the rise in prices. Throughout the winter of 1788–1789, an unusually cold one, many people suffered from hunger. Wage and food riots had erupted in several cities. These economic problems fanned the fires of revolution.

The political, social, and economic grievances of many sections of the country became combined. The National Constituent Assembly could look to the popular forces as a source of strength against the king and the conservative aristocrats. When the various elements of the Assembly later quarreled among themselves, however, the resulting factions would appeal for support to the politically sophisticated and well-organized shopkeeping and artisan classes. They, in turn, would demand a price for their cooperation.

The Declaration of the Rights of Man and Citizen

In late August 1789, the National Constituent Assembly decided that before writing a new constitution, it should publish a statement of broad political principles. On August 27, the Assembly issued the Declaration of the Rights of Man and Citizen. This declaration drew on the political language of the Enlightenment and the Declaration of Rights that the state of Virginia had adopted in June 1776.

The French declaration proclaimed that all men were "born and remain free and equal in rights." The natural rights so proclaimed were "liberty, property, security, and resistance to oppression." Governments existed to protect those rights. All political sovereignty resided in the nation and its representatives. All citizens were to be equal before the law and were to be "equally admissible to all public dignities, offices, and employments, according to their capacity, and with no other distinction than that of their virtues and talents." There were to be due process of law and presumption of innocence until proof

A Closer LOOK

⚲ View the Closer Look on MyHistoryLab.com

CHALLENGING THE FRENCH POLITICAL ORDER

THIS LATE-EIGHTEENTH-CENTURY cartoon satirizes the French social and political structure as the events and tensions leading up to the outbreak of the French Revolution unfolded. This image embodies the highly radical critique of the French political structure that erupted from about 1787 when the nobility and church refused to aid the financial crisis of the monarchy. It is one of a series of similar cartoons, most of which depict men. The caption reads "Long Live the King, Long Live the Nation. I always knew we would have our turn!" The image shows the way in which women participated in creating the new order, without addressing any specific "women's rights" agenda.

The caption expresses the separation between loyalty to the king and criticism of the abuses of the peasants blamed on the clergy and the aristocracy. Only after the calling of the Estates General was Louis XVI seen as siding with the church and nobility against the people.

Vive le Roi, Vive la Nation.

Isavois ben Qu'jaurions not tour.

Library of Congress

A peasant woman holding a distaff (a tool used in spinning) and simultaneously nursing a baby rides on the back of a noble woman. Her attire is simple and her shoes are wooden, indicating her peasant background. Her hat is adorned with a cockade in revolutionary colors.

The noblewoman clutches onto a nun for support, suggesting the collusion of aristocracy and church.

Can you tell if this image is meant to celebrate the peasantry's newfound power or lament it? What hints does the artist provide as to his or her sympathy?

Similar images involving men were very common. What does this image suggest about the role of women in the ancien régime and in the revolution?

What is the symbolic significance of the suckling infant?

The women of Paris marched to Versailles on October 5, 1789. Although they did not make any demands specific to women's rights, the mere sight of so many women expressing political demands alarmed the king and his supporters. The following day the royal family was forced to return to Paris with them. Henceforth, the French government would function under the constant threat of mob violence. Anonymous, eighteenth century, *To Versailles, to Versailles. The women of Paris going to Versailles, 7 October, 1789.* French. Musée de la Ville de Paris, Musée Carnavalet, Paris, France. Photograph copyright Bridgeman—Giraudon/Art Resource, NY

of guilt. Freedom of religion was affirmed. Taxation was to be apportioned equally according to the capacity to pay. Property constituted "an inviolable and sacred right."[2]

The Declaration of the Rights of Man and Citizen was directed in large measure against specific abuses of the old French monarchical and aristocratic regime, but it was framed in abstract universalistic language applicable to other European nations. In this respect, the ideas set forth in the declaration like those of the Protestant reformers three centuries earlier could jump across national borders and find adherents outside France. The two most powerful, universal political ideas of the declaration were civic equality and popular sovereignty. The first would challenge the legal and social inequities of European life, and the second would assert that governments must be responsible to the governed. These two principles, in turn, could find themselves in tension with the declaration's principle of the protection of property.

It was not accidental that the Declaration of the Rights of Man and Citizen specifically applied to men and not to women. As discussed in Chapter 17, much of the political language of the Enlightenment, and especially that associated with Rousseau, separated men and women into distinct gender spheres. According to this view, which influenced

legislation during the revolution, men were suited for citizenship, women for motherhood and the domestic life. Nonetheless, in the charged atmosphere of the summer of 1789, many politically active and informed Frenchwomen hoped the guarantees of the declaration would be extended to them. They were particularly concerned with property, inheritance, family, and divorce. Some people saw in the declaration a framework within which women might eventually enjoy the rights and protection of citizenship. Those hopes would be disappointed during the years of the revolution and for many decades thereafter.

Nonetheless, over the succeeding two centuries the universalist language of the Declaration of the Rights of Man and Citizen would provide an intellectual framework for bringing into the realm of active civic life many groups who were excluded in the late eighteenth century. (See "Compare and Connect: The Declaration of the Rights of Man and Citizen Opens the Door for Disadvantaged Groups to Demand Equal Civic Rights," pages 564–565.)

The Parisian Women's March on Versailles

Louis XVI stalled before ratifying both the Declaration of the Rights of Man and Citizen and the aristocratic renunciation of feudalism. His hesitations fueled suspicions that he might again try to resort to

[2]Georges Lefebvre, *The Coming of the French Revolution,* trans. by R. R. Palmer (Princeton, NJ: Princeton University Press, 1967), pp. 221–223.

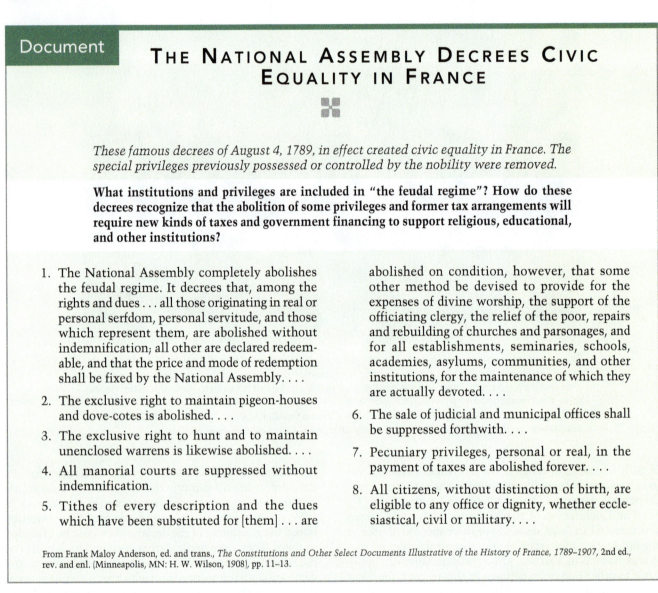

Document

THE NATIONAL ASSEMBLY DECREES CIVIC EQUALITY IN FRANCE

These famous decrees of August 4, 1789, in effect created civic equality in France. The special privileges previously possessed or controlled by the nobility were removed.

What institutions and privileges are included in "the feudal regime"? How do these decrees recognize that the abolition of some privileges and former tax arrangements will require new kinds of taxes and government financing to support religious, educational, and other institutions?

1. The National Assembly completely abolishes the feudal regime. It decrees that, among the rights and dues . . . all those originating in real or personal serfdom, personal servitude, and those which represent them, are abolished without indemnification; all other are declared redeemable, and that the price and mode of redemption shall be fixed by the National Assembly. . . .

2. The exclusive right to maintain pigeon-houses and dove-cotes is abolished. . . .

3. The exclusive right to hunt and to maintain unenclosed warrens is likewise abolished. . . .

4. All manorial courts are suppressed without indemnification.

5. Tithes of every description and the dues which have been substituted for [them] . . . are abolished on condition, however, that some other method be devised to provide for the expenses of divine worship, the support of the officiating clergy, the relief of the poor, repairs and rebuilding of churches and parsonages, and for all establishments, seminaries, schools, academies, asylums, communities, and other institutions, for the maintenance of which they are actually devoted. . . .

6. The sale of judicial and municipal offices shall be suppressed forthwith. . . .

7. Pecuniary privileges, personal or real, in the payment of taxes are abolished forever. . . .

8. All citizens, without distinction of birth, are eligible to any office or dignity, whether ecclesiastical, civil or military. . . .

From Frank Maloy Anderson, ed. and trans., *The Constitutions and Other Select Documents Illustrative of the History of France, 1789–1907*, 2nd ed., rev. and enl. (Minneapolis, MN: H. W. Wilson, 1908), pp. 11–13.

---

force. Moreover, bread remained scarce and expensive. On October 5, some 7,000 Parisian women armed with pikes, guns, swords, and knives marched to Versailles demanding more bread. They milled about the palace, and many stayed the night. Intimidated, the king agreed to sanction the decrees of the Assembly. The next day he and his family appeared on a balcony before the crowd. Deeply suspicious of the monarch and believing that he must be kept under the watchful eye of the people, the Parisians demanded that Louis and his family return to Paris with them. The monarch had no real choice. On October 6, 1789, his carriage followed the crowd into the city, where he and his family settled in the old palace of the Tuileries in the heart of Paris.

The National Constituent Assembly also soon moved to Paris. Thereafter, both Paris and France remained relatively stable and peaceful until the summer of 1792. A decline in the price of bread in late 1789 helped to calm the atmosphere.

▼ The Reconstruction of France

In Paris, the National Constituent Assembly set about reorganizing France. In government, it pursued a policy of constitutional monarchy; in administration, rationalism; in economics, unregulated freedom; and in religion, anticlericalism. Throughout its proceedings and following the principles of the Declaration of the Rights of Man and Citizen, the Assembly was determined to protect property in all its forms. The Assembly sought to limit the impact on the national life of those French people who had no property or only small amounts of it. Although championing civic equality before the law, the Assembly, with the aristocrats and middle-class elite united, spurned social equality and extensive democracy. It thus charted a general course that, to a greater or lesser degree, nineteenth-century liberals across Europe would follow.

Political Reorganization

In the Constitution of 1791, the National Constituent Assembly established a constitutional monarchy. The major political authority of the nation would be a unicameral Legislative Assembly, in which all laws would originate. The monarch was allowed a suspensive veto that could delay, but not halt, legislation. The Assembly also had the power to make war and peace.

Active and Passive Citizens The constitution provided for an elaborate system of indirect elections to thwart direct popular pressure on the government. The citizens of France were divided into active and passive categories. Only active citizens—that is, men paying annual taxes equal to three days of local labor wages—could vote. They chose electors, who then, in turn, voted for the members of the legislature. Further property qualifications were required to serve as an elector or member of the legislature. Only about 50,000 citizens of a population of about 25 million could qualify as electors or members of the Legislative Assembly. Women could neither vote nor hold office.

These constitutional arrangements effectively transferred political power from aristocratic wealth to all forms of propertied wealth in the nation. The accumulation of wealth from land and commercial property, not hereditary privilege or the purchase of titles or offices, would open the path to political authority. These new political arrangements based on property rather than birth reflected the changes in French society over the past century and allowed more social and economic interests to have a voice in governing the nation.

Olympe de Gouges's Declaration of the Rights of Woman The laws that excluded women from voting and holding office did not pass unnoticed. In 1791, Olympe de Gouges (d. 1793), a butcher's daughter from Montauban in northwest France who became a major revolutionary radical in Paris, composed a Declaration of the Rights of Woman, which she ironically addressed to Queen Marie Antoinette. Much of the document reprinted the Declaration of the Rights of Man and Citizen, adding the word *woman* to the various original clauses. That strategy demanded that women be regarded as citizens and not merely as daughters, sisters, wives, and mothers of citizens. Olympe de Gouges further outlined rights that would permit women to own property and require men to recognize the paternity of their children.

She called for equality of the sexes in marriage and improved education for women. She declared, "Women, wake up; the *tocsin* of reason is being heard throughout the whole universe; discover your rights."[3] Her declaration illustrated how the simple listing of rights in the Declaration of the Rights of Man and Citizen created a structure of universal civic expectations even for those it did not cover. The National Assembly had established a set of values against which it could itself be measured. It provided criteria for liberty, and those to whom it had not extended full liberties could demand to know why and could claim the revolution was incomplete until they too enjoyed those freedoms. (See "Compare and Connect: The Declaration of the Rights of Man and Citizen Opens the Door for Disadvantaged Groups to Demand Equal Civic Rights," pages 564–565.)

Read the Document
"Olympe de Gouges, Declaration of the Rights of Woman and the Female Citizen" on **MyHistoryLab.com**

Departments Replace Provinces In reconstructing the local and judicial administration, the National Constituent Assembly applied the rational spirit of the Enlightenment. It abolished the ancient French provinces, such as Burgundy and Brittany, and established in their place eighty-three administrative units called *départements* of generally equal size named after rivers, mountains, and other geographical features. The departments in turn were subdivided into districts, cantons, and communes. Elections for departmental and local assemblies were also indirect. This administrative reconstruction proved to be permanent. The departments still exist in twenty-first-century France. (See Map 18–1, p. 562.)

All the ancient judicial courts, including the seigneurial courts and the *parlements*, were also abolished and replaced by uniform courts with elected judges and prosecutors. Procedures were simplified, and the most degrading punishments, such as branding, torture, and public flogging, were outlawed.

Economic Policy

In economic matters, the National Constituent Assembly continued the policies Louis XVI's reformist ministers had formerly advocated. It suppressed the guilds and liberated the grain trade. The Assembly established the metric system to provide the nation with uniform weights and measures. (See "Encountering the Past: The Metric System," page 566.)

Workers' Organizations Forbidden The new policies of economic freedom and uniformity disappointed both peasants and urban workers. In 1789, the

[3]Sara E. Melzer and Leslie W. Rabine, eds., *Rebel Daughters: Women and the French Revolution* (New York: Oxford University Press, 1992), p. 88.

Map 18–1 **FRENCH PROVINCES AND THE REPUBLIC** In 1789, the National Constituent Assembly redrew the map of France. The ancient provinces were replaced with a larger number of new, smaller departments. This redrawing of the map was part of the Assembly's effort to impose greater administrative rationality in France.

Assembly placed the burden of proof on the peasants to rid themselves of the residual feudal dues for which compensation was to be paid. On June 14, 1791, the Assembly crushed the attempts of urban workers to protect their wages by enacting the Chapelier Law, which forbade workers' associations. The Assembly interpreted the efforts of workers to organize as a re-creation of the abolished guilds of the Old Regime and thus to oppose the new values of political and social individualism that the revolution championed. Peasants and workers were henceforth to be left to the freedom and mercy of the marketplace, without the protection of assocation.

Confiscation of Church Lands While these various reforms were being put into effect, the financial crisis that had occasioned the calling of the Estates General persisted. The Assembly did not repudiate the royal debt because it was owed to the bankers, the merchants, and the commercial traders of the Third Estate. The National Constituent Assembly had suppressed many of the old, hated indirect taxes (such as taxes on staples like salt, bread, and wine) and had substituted new land taxes, but these proved insufficient. Moreover, there

were not enough officials to collect the new taxes, and many people simply evaded them in the general confusion of the day. The continuing financial problem led the Assembly to take what may well have been, for the future of French life and society, its most decisive action. The Assembly decided to finance the debt by confiscating and then selling the land and property of the Roman Catholic Church in France. The results were further inflation, religious schism, and civil war. In effect, the National Constituent Assembly had opened a new chapter in the relations of church and state in Europe.

The *Assignats* Having chosen to plunder the church, the Assembly authorized the issuance of *assignats*, or government bonds, in December 1789. Their value was guaranteed by the revenue to be generated from the sale of church property. Initially, a limit was set on the quantity of *assignats* to be issued. The bonds, however, proved so acceptable to the public that they began to circulate as currency. The Assembly decided to issue an ever-larger number of them to liquidate the national debt and to create a large body of new property owners with a direct stake in the revolution. Within a few

The *assignats* were government bonds that were backed by confiscated church lands. They circulated as money. When the government printed too many of them, inflation resulted and their value fell. Bildarchiv Preussischer Kulturbesitz

months, however, the value of the *assignats* began to fall and inflation increased, putting new stress on the urban poor. Fluctuation in the worth of this currency would plague the revolutionary government throughout the 1790s.

The Civil Constitution of the Clergy

The confiscation of church lands required an ecclesiastical reconstruction. In July 1790, the National Constituent Assembly issued the Civil Constitution of the Clergy, which transformed the Roman Catholic Church in France into a branch of the secular state. This legislation reduced the number of bishoprics from 135 to 83, making one diocese for each of the new departments. It also provided for the election of pastors and bishops, who henceforth became salaried employees of the state. The Assembly, which also dissolved all religious orders in France except those that cared for the sick or ran schools, consulted neither Pope Pius VI (r. 1775–1799) nor the French clergy about these sweeping changes. The king approved the measure only with the greatest reluctance.

The Civil Constitution of the Clergy was the major blunder of the National Constituent Assembly. It embittered relations between the French church and the state, a problem that has persisted to the present day. The measure immediately created immense opposition within the French church, even from bishops who had long championed Gallican liberties over papal domination. In the face of this

resistance, the Assembly unwisely ruled that all clergy must take an oath to support the Civil Constitution. Only seven bishops and a little less than half the lower clergy did so. In reprisal, the Assembly designated those clergy who had not taken the oath as "refractory" and removed them from their clerical functions. Angry reactions were swift. Refractory priests celebrated Mass in defiance of the Assembly. In February 1791, Pope Pius VI condemned not only the Civil Constitution of the Clergy, but also the Declaration of the Rights of Man and Citizen. That condemnation marked the opening of a Roman Catholic offensive against the revolution and liberalism more broadly that continued throughout the nineteenth century. Within France itself, the pope's action created a crisis of conscience and political loyalty for all sincere Catholics. Religious devotion and revolutionary loyalty became incompatible for many people. French citizens were divided between those who supported the constitutional priests and those who, like the royal family, followed the refractory clergy.

Counterrevolutionary Activity

The revolution had other enemies besides the pope and devout Catholics. As it became clear that the old political and social order was undergoing fundamental and probably permanent change, many aristocrats, eventually over 16,000, left France. Known as the **émigrés**, they settled in countries near the French border, where they sought to foment counterrevolution. Among the most important of their number was the king's younger brother, the count of Artois (1757–1836). In the summer of 1791, his agents and the queen persuaded Louis XVI to attempt to flee the country.

Flight to Varennes On the night of June 20, 1791, Louis and his immediate family, disguised as servants, left Paris. They traveled as far as Varennes on their way to Metz in eastern France where a royalist military force was waiting for them. At Varennes the king was recognized, and his flight was halted. On June 24, a company of soldiers escorted the royal family back to Paris. Eventually the leaders of the National Constituent Assembly, determined to save the constitutional monarchy, announced the king had been abducted from the capital. This convenient public fiction could not cloak the reality that the king was now the chief counterrevolutionary in France and that the constitutional monarchy might not

The Declaration of the Rights of Man and Citizen Opens the Door for Disadvantaged Groups to Demand Equal Civic Rights

Read the **Compare and Connect** on **MyHistoryLab.com**

THE NATIONAL ASSEMBLY passed the Declaration of the Rights of Man and Citizen on August 26, 1789. The principles of the declaration were very broad and in theory could be extended beyond the domestic male French citizens to whom it applied. Within months various civically disadvantaged groups stepped forward to demand inclusion within the newly proclaimed realm of civic rights. These included free persons of color from the French Caribbean colony of St. Domingue and French women. It should be noted that during the same period French Jews also asked to have the principles of religious toleration proclaimed in the Declaration of the Rights of Man and Citizen extended to themselves.

QUESTIONS

1. How does Raymond portray himself as free but still clearly victimized by the Assembly in St. Domingue, composed only of white members?

2. How does Raymond invoke the principles of the Declaration of the Rights of Man and Citizen to apply pressure on the French National Assembly?

3. What are the specific parallels that de Gouges draws between the rights of man and the rights of woman?

4. How does her declaration suggest civic responsibilities for women as well as rights?

5. On what grounds might the same people who championed the Declaration of the Rights of Man and Citizen in 1789 deny the extension of those rights to the various groups that soon demanded inclusion under the ideals of the declaration?

I. A Free Person of Color from St. Domingue Demands Recognition of His Status

In the spring of 1791 Julian Raymond, a free person of color from the French Caribbean colony of St. Domingue (Haiti), petitioned the French National Assembly to recognize persons such as himself as free citizens. The National Assembly did so in May 1791 but later rescinded the decree. Only in March 1792 did the Assembly firmly recognize the civic equality of such persons. The background for the request and for the confusion of the French National Assembly over the matter was the eruption of the slave revolution in Haiti, which is discussed in Chapter 20.

Remaining to this day under the oppression of the white colonists, we dare hope that we do not ask the National Assembly in vain for the rights, which it has declared, belong to every man.

In our just protests, if the troubles, the calumnies that you have witnessed until today under the legislation of white colonists, and finally, if the truths which we had the honor of presenting yesterday to the bar of the Assembly do not overcome the unjust pretensions of the white colonial legislators who want to [proceed] without our participation, we beg the Assembly not to jeopardize the little remaining liberty we have, that of being able to abandon the ground soaked with the blood of our brothers and of permitting us to flee the sharp knife of the laws they will prepare against us.

If the Assembly has decided to pass a law which lets our fate depend on twenty-nine whites [in the colonial Assembly], our decided enemies, we demand to add an amendment to the decree which would be rendered in this situation, that free men of color can emigrate with their fortunes so that they can be neither disturbed nor hindered by the whites.

Mr. President, this is the last recourse which remains for us to escape the vengeance of the white colonists who menace us for not having given up our claims to the rights which the National Assembly has declared belong to every man. ■

From Laura Mason and Tracey Rizzo, *The French Revolution: A Document Collection* (Boston: Houghton Mifflin Company, 1999), p. 109.

II. Olympe de Gouges Issues a Declaration of the Rights of Woman

In September 1791 Olympe de Gouges published a Declaration of the Rights of Woman that paralleled in many respects the Declaration of the Rights of Man and Citizen proclaimed two years earlier. A self-educated woman and butcher's daughter, she had written widely on a number of reform topics. Radical as she was, she remained loyal to the monarchy and was eventually executed by the revolutionary government in 1793.

Mothers, daughters, sisters [and] representatives of the nation demand to be constituted into a national assembly. . . . Consequently, the sex that is as superior in beauty as it is in courage during the sufferings of maternity recognizes and declares in the presence and under the auspices of the Supreme Being, the following Rights of Woman and of Female Citizens.

ARTICLE I

Woman is born free and lives equal to man in her rights. Social distinctions can be based only on the common utility.

ARTICLE II

The purpose of any political association is the conservation of the natural and imprescriptible rights of woman and man; these rights are liberty, property, security, and especially resistance to oppression.

ARTICLE III

The principle of all sovereignty rests essentially with the nation, which is nothing but the union of woman and man. . . .

ARTICLE IV

Liberty and justice consist of restoring all that belongs to others; thus, the only limits on the exercise of the natural rights of woman are perpetual male tyranny; these limits are to be reformed by the laws of nature and reason. . . .

ARTICLE VI

The law must be the expression of the general will; all female and male citizens must contribute either personally or through their representatives to its formation; it must be the same for all: male and female citizens, being equal in the eyes of the law, must be equally admitted to all honors, positions, and public employment according to their capacity and without other distinctions besides those of their virtues and talents. . . .

ARTICLE X

No one is to be disquieted for his very basic opinions; woman has the right to mount the scaffold; she must equally have the right to mount the rostrum, provided that her demonstrations do not disturb the legally established public order. . . .

ARTICLE XI

The free communication of thoughts and opinions is one of the most precious rights of woman, since that liberty assures the recognition of children by their fathers. Any female citizen thus may say freely, I am the mother of a child which belongs to you, without being forced by a barbarous prejudice to hide the truth. . . .

ARTICLE XIII

For the support of the public force and the expenses of administration, the contributions of woman and man are equal; she shares all the duties and all the painful tasks; therefore, she must have the same share in the distribution of positions, employment, offices, honors, and jobs. . . .

ARTICLE XVII

Property belongs to both sexes whether united or separate; for each it is an inviolable and sacred right; no one can be deprived of it, since it is the true patrimony of nature, unless the legally determined public need obviously dictates it, and then only with a just and prior indemnity.

POSTSCRIPT

Woman, wake up; the *tocsin* of reason is being heard throughout the whole universe; discover your rights. ■

From Darline Gay Levy, Harriet Branson Applewhite, and Mary Durham Johnson, eds., *Women in Revolutionary Paris, 1789–1795* (Urbana: University of Illinois Press, 1980), pp. 87–96.

THE METRIC SYSTEM

MUCH ABOUT THE era of the French Revolution seems alien to us today. One French regime followed another amidst confusion, violence, and bloodshed. Yet one thing that the revolutionaries did still touches the lives of most people in the world. In 1795, the French revolutionary government decreed a new standard for weights and measures—the metric system. The United States, Myanmar, and Liberia are currently the only countries in the world that have not officially adopted the metric system.

Inspired by the rationalism of the eighteenth-century Enlightenment, the metric system was intended to bring the order and simplicity of a system based on 10 to the chaos of different weights and measures used in the various regions of pre-revolutionary France. For its adherents, the republic marked the dawn of a new era in human history in which the triumph of science would replace the reign of superstition and obscurity. A new system of uniform weights and measures would also further one of the revolutionaries' political goals: centralization. With one set of weights and measures in use throughout the country, France would be closer to becoming a single "indivisible" republic.

Astronomy, which relied on the rational application of mathematics to measure the heavens, provided the basis for the new system of distance or length. Astronomers had devised methods to measure the arch of meridians—the highest point reached by the sun—around the earth. The revolutionary authorities took the meridian in the latitude of Paris, which is 45°, as their standard for measuring the meter. The meter was to be one ten-millionth of one quarter of that meridian. All other measurements of length were then defined as decimal fractions or multiples of the meter.

1 centimeter (cm) = 10 millimeters (mm)
1 decimeter (dm) = 10 centimeters
1 meter = 100 centimeters
1 kilometer (km) = 1,000 meters

The standard for measuring weights was the gram, which constituted the weight of a cube of pure water measuring 0.01 meter on each side. Each measure of weight was defined as a decimal fraction or multiple of a gram. A kilogram is 1,000 grams.

The metric system was soon adopted by scientists, but in their everyday lives, the population of France clung to their old, familiar weights and measures. Change, however "rational," did not come easily and was resisted. In 1812, Napoleon, bowing to popular sentiment, brought back the old units, but in 1840, the French government reimposed the metric system. Thereafter, rationality—and convenience—triumphed, and by the close of the nineteenth century, the metric system was used throughout continental Europe and had been introduced into Latin America. In the twentieth century it was adopted throughout Asia and Africa.

Today, the United States remains the great exception. Despite efforts by scientists, engineers, and doctors, who all use the metric system in their work, people in the United States still prefer to measure in inches, feet, yards, and miles and to weigh in ounces and pounds.

Why did the French revolutionary government introduce the metric system?

How did the metric system reflect the ideas of the Enlightenment? Why has most of the world accepted this system?

This 1800 print introduces the new measures adopted by law in France: the liter (volume), the gram (weight), the meter (length), the are (area), the franc (currency), the stere (volume). L.F. Labrousse, "Usage des nouvelles mesures," © The Art Gallery Collection/Alamy

In June 1791, Louis XVI and his family attempted to flee France. They were recognized in the town of Varennes, where their flight was halted and they were returned to Paris. This ended any realistic hope for a constitutional monarchy. © Bettmann/CORBIS

last long. Profound distrust now dominated the political scene.

Declaration of Pillnitz Two months later, on August 27, 1791, under pressure from the *émigrés*, Emperor Leopold II (r. 1790–1792) of Austria, who was the brother of Marie Antoinette, and King Frederick William II (r. 1786–1797) of Prussia issued the Declaration of Pillnitz. The two monarchs promised to intervene in France to protect the royal family and to preserve the monarchy if the other major European powers agreed. This provision rendered the declaration practically meaningless because, at the time, Great Britain would not have given its consent. The declaration was, however, taken seriously in France, where the revolutionaries saw the nation surrounded by aristocratic and monarchical foes seeking to undo all that had been accomplished since 1789.

▼ The End of the Monarchy: A Second Revolution

The National Constituent Assembly drew to a close in September 1791, having completed its task of reconstructing the government and the administration of France. The Assembly had passed a measure that forbade any of its own members to sit in the Legislative Assembly the new constitution established. That new Assembly, filled with entirely new members, met on October 1 and immediately had to confront the challenges flowing from the resistance to the Civil Constitution of the

Clergy, the king's flight, and the Declaration of Pillnitz.

Emergence of the Jacobins

Ever since the original gathering of the Estates General, deputies from the Third Estate had organized themselves into clubs composed of politically like-minded persons. The most famous and best organized of these clubs were the **Jacobins** because the group met in a former Dominican priory dedicated to St. Jacques (James) in Paris. The Jacobins had also established a network of local clubs throughout the provinces. They had been the most advanced political group in the National Constituent Assembly and had pressed for a republic rather than a constitutional monarchy. They drew their political language from the most radical thought of the Enlightenment, most particularly Rousseau's emphasis on equality, popular sovereignty, and civic virtue. Such thought and language became all the more effective because the events of 1789 to 1791 had destroyed the old political framework, and the old monarchical political vocabulary was less and less relevant. The rhetoric of republicanism filled that vacuum and for a time supplied the political values of the day. The flight of Louis XVI in the summer of 1791 and the Declaration of Pillnitz led to renewed demands for a republic.

View the Image
"Death of Marat" on
MyHistoryLab.com

Factionalism plagued the Legislative Assembly throughout its short life (1791–1792). A group of Jacobins known as the *Girondists* (because many of them came from the department of the Gironde in southwest France) assumed leadership of the Assembly. They were determined to oppose the forces of counterrevolution. They passed one measure ordering the *émigrés* to return or suffer the loss of their property and another requiring the refractory clergy to support the Civil Constitution or lose their state pensions. The king vetoed both acts.

Furthermore, on April 20, 1792, the Girondists led the Legislative Assembly to declare war on Austria, by this time governed by Leopold II's son, Francis II (r. 1792–1835), and allied to Prussia. This decision launched a period of armed conflict across Western Europe that with only brief intervals of peace lasted until the final defeat of France at Waterloo in June 1815.

The Girondists believed the war would preserve the revolution from domestic enemies and bring the most advanced revolutionaries to power. Paradoxically, Louis XVI and other monarchists also favored the war. They thought the conflict would strengthen the executive power (the monarchy). The king also hoped that foreign armies might defeat French forces and restore the Old Regime. Both sides were playing a dangerous, deluded political game. The war radicalized French politics and within months led to what is usually called the second revolution, which overthrew the constitutional monarchy and established a republic.

With the outbreak of war, the country and the revolution seemed in danger. As early as March 1791, a group of women led by Pauline Léon had petitioned the Legislative Assembly for the right to bear arms and to fight to protect the revolution. Léon also wanted women to serve in the National Guard. These demands to serve, voiced in the universal language of citizenship, illustrated how the rhetoric of the revolution could be used to challenge traditional social roles and the concept of separate social spheres for men and women. Furthermore, the pressure of war raised the possibility that the nation could not meet its military needs if it honored the idea of separate spheres. Once the war began, some Frenchwomen did enlist in the army and served with distinction. Initially, the war effort went poorly. In July 1792, the duke of Brunswick, commander of the Prussian forces, issued a manifesto threatening to destroy Paris if the French royal family were harmed. This statement stiffened support for the war and increased distrust of the king.

Late in July, under radical working-class pressure, the government of Paris passed from the elected council to a committee, or *commune*, of representatives from the sections (municipal wards) of the city. Thereafter the Paris commune became an independent political force casting itself in the role of the protector of the gains of the revolution against both internal and external enemies. Its activities and forceful modes of intimidation largely accounted for the dominance of the city of Paris over many of the future directions of the revolutionary government for the next three years.

On August 10, 1792, a large crowd invaded the Tuileries palace and forced Louis XVI and Marie Antoinette to take refuge in the Legislative Assembly. The crowd fought with the royal Swiss guards. When Louis was finally able to call off the troops, several hundred of them and many Parisian citizens lay dead in the most extensive violence since the fall of the Bastille. Thereafter the royal family was imprisoned. Their quarters were comfortable, but the king was allowed to perform none of his political functions. The recently established constitutional monarchy no longer had a reigning monarch.

The Convention and the Role of the *Sans-culottes*

The September Massacres Early in September, the Parisian crowd again made its will felt. During the first week of the month, in what are known as the **September Massacres**, the Paris Commune summarily executed or murdered about 1,200 people who were in the city jails. Some of these people were aristocrats or priests, but most were simply common criminals. The crowd had mistakenly assumed the prisoners were all counterrevolutionaries. News of this event, the August massacre of the Swiss guards, and the imprisonment of the royal family spread rapidly across Europe, rousing new hostility toward the revolutionary government.

The Paris Commune then compelled the Legislative Assembly to call for the election by universal male suffrage of still another new assembly to write a democratic constitution. That body, called the **Convention** after the American Constitutional Convention of 1787, met on September 21, 1792. The previous day, the French army, filled with patriotic recruits willing to die for the revolution, had halted the Prussian advance at the Battle of Valmy in eastern France. Victory on the battlefield had confirmed the victory of democratic forces at home. As its first act, the Convention declared France a republic—that is, a nation governed by an elected assembly without a monarch.

Goals of the *Sans-culottes* The second revolution had been the work of Jacobins more radical than the Girondists and of the people of Paris known as the *sans-culottes.* The name of this group means "without breeches" and derived from the long trousers that, as working people, they wore instead of aristocratic knee breeches. The *sans-culottes* were shopkeepers, artisans, wage earners, and, in a few cases, factory workers. The persistent food shortages and the revolutionary inflation reflected in the ongoing fall of the value of the *assignats* had made their difficult lives even more burdensome. The politics of the Old Regime had ignored them, and the policies of the National Constituent Assembly had left them victims of unregulated economic liberty. The government, however, required their labor and their lives if the war was to succeed. From the summer of 1792 until the summer of 1794, their attitudes, desires, and ideals were the primary factors in the internal development of the revolution.

The *sans-culottes* generally knew what they wanted. The Parisian tradespeople and artisans sought immediate relief from food shortages and rising prices through price controls. The economic hardship of their lives made them impatient to see their demands met. They believed all people have a right to subsistence, and they resented most forms of social inequality. This attitude made them intensely hostile to the aristocracy and the original leaders of the revolution of 1789 from the Third Estate, who, they believed, simply wanted to share political power, social prestige, and economic security with the aristocracy. The *sans-culottes*' hatred of inequality did not take them so far as to demand the abolition of property. Rather, they advocated a community of small property owners who would also participate in the political nation.

In politics they were antimonarchical, strongly republican, and suspicious even of representative government. They believed the people should make the decisions of government to an extent as great as possible. In Paris, where their influence was most important, the *sans-culottes* had gained their political experience in meetings of the Paris sections. The Paris Commune organized the previous summer was their chief political vehicle and crowd action their chief instrument of action.

The Policies of the Jacobins The goals of the *sans-culottes* were not wholly compatible with those of the Jacobins, republicans who sought representative government. Jacobin hatred of the aristocracy and hereditary privilege did not extend to a general suspicion of wealth. Basically, the Jacobins favored an unregulated economy. From the time of Louis XVI's flight to Varennes onward, however, the more extreme Jacobins began to cooperate with leaders of the Parisian *sans-culottes* and the Paris Commune to overthrow the monarchy. Once the Convention began to deliberate, these Jacobins, known as the *Mountain* because their seats were high up in the assembly hall, worked with the *sans-culottes* to carry the revolution forward and to win the war. This willingness to cooperate with the forces of the popular revolution separated the Mountain from the Girondists, who were also members of the Jacobin Club.

Execution of Louis XVI By the spring of 1793, several issues had brought the Mountain and its *sans-culottes* allies to dominate the Convention and the revolution. In December 1792, Louis XVI was put on trial as "Citizen Capet," the original medieval name of the royal family. The Girondists looked for a way to spare his life, but the Mountain defeated the effort. An overwhelming majority convicted Louis of conspiring against the liberty of the people and the security of the state. Condemned to death by a smaller majority, he was beheaded on January 21, 1793. Marie Antoinette was subsequently tried and executed in October of the same year; their son died in 1795, in prison, of disease exacerbated by neglect.

View the **Image**
"Execution of Louis XVI"
on **MyHistoryLab.com**

In February 1793, the Convention declared war on Great Britain and Holland, and a month later on Spain. Soon thereafter, the Prussians renewed their offensive and drove the French out of Belgium. To make matters worse, General Dumouriez (1739–1823), the Girondist victor of Valmy, deserted to the enemy. Finally, in March 1793, a royalist revolt led by aristocratic officers and priests erupted in the Vendée in western France and roused much popular support. Thus, the revolution found itself at war with most of Europe and much of the French nation. The Girondists had led the country into the war but had been unable either to win it or to suppress the enemies of the revolution at home. The Mountain stood ready to take up the task.

▼ Europe at War with the Revolution

Initially, the rest of Europe had been ambivalent toward the revolutionary events in France. Those people who favored political reform regarded the revolution as wisely and rationally reorganizing a corrupt and inefficient government. The major foreign governments thought that the revolution meant France would cease to be an important factor in European affairs for years.

Edmund Burke Attacks the Revolution

In 1790, however, Irish-born writer and British statesman Edmund Burke (1729–1799) argued a different position in *Reflections on the Revolution in France*. Burke condemned the reconstruction of the French administration as the application of a blind rationalism that ignored the historical realities of political development and the concrete complexities of social relations. He also forecast further turmoil as people without political experience tried to govern France, predicted the possible deaths of Louis XVI and Marie Antoinette at the hands of the revolutionaries, and forecast that the revolution would end in military despotism. As the revolutionaries proceeded to attack the church, the monarchy, and finally the rest of Europe, Burke's ideas came to have many admirers.

Thomas Paine, the hero of the American Revolution, composed *The Rights of Man* (1791–1792) in direct response to Burke and in defense of the revolutionary principles. Paine declared, "From what we now see, nothing of reform on the political world ought to be held improbable. It is an age of revolutions, in which everything may be looked for."[4] Paine's volume sold more copies at the time in England, but Burke's was influential in the long run and was immediately published widely on the continent where it became a handbook of European conservatives.

By the outbreak of the war with Austria in April 1792, the other European monarchies recognized, along with Burke, the danger of both the ideas and the aggression of revolutionary France. In the United States, no amount of gratitude for France's assistance during the revolutionary war could move Washington to offer support to France;

[4]Thomas Paine, *Political Writings*, rev. student ed., Bruce Kuklick, ed. (Cambridge, UK: Cambridge University Press, 1997), p. 153.

After the execution of Louis XVI on January 21, 1793, the executioner displayed his severed head to the large crowd. *Execution of King Louis XVI of France, January 21, 1793,* engraving. Musée Carnavalet Paris. CCI/The Art Archive at Art Resource, NY

throughout his presidency, Washington insisted that the new republic must resist foreign entanglements. The increasing radicalism of the French Revolution alienated even those foreign statesmen initially sympathetic to its early reformist impulses. Instead of seeing in France a positive model, one European government after another turned to repressive domestic policies in order to forestall revolutionary activity at home. (See the Document "Burke Denounces the Extreme Measures of the French Revolution," page 571.)

Suppression of Reform in Britain

In Great Britain, William Pitt the Younger (1759–1806), the prime minister, who had unsuccessfully supported moderate reform of Parliament during the 1780s, turned against both reform and popular movements. The government suppressed the London Corresponding Society, founded in 1792 as a working-class reform group. In Birmingham, the government sponsored mob action to drive Joseph Priestley (1733–1804), a famous chemist and a radical political thinker, out of the country. In early 1793, Pitt secured parliamentary approval for acts suspending *habeas corpus* and making the writing of certain ideas treasonable. With less success, Pitt also attempted to curb

freedom of the press. All political groups who dared oppose the government faced being associated with sedition.

The Second and Third Partitions of Poland, 1793, 1795

The final two partitions of Poland, already noted in Chapter 17, occurred as a direct result of fears by the central and east European powers that the principles of the French Revolution were establishing themselves in Poland. After the first partition in 1772, Polish leaders had commenced reforms to provide for a stronger state. In 1791, a group of nobles known as the Polish Patriots issued a new constitution that substituted a hereditary for an elective monarchy, provided for real executive authority in the monarch and his council, established a new bicameral diet, and eliminated the *liberum veto*. Although this new constitution strengthened the monarch, it also asserted "all power in civil society should be derived from the will of the people."[5] The Polish government also adopted equality before the law and religious toleration. Frederick William II of Prussia (r. 1786–1797) promised to defend the new Polish constitutional order because he believed that a stronger Poland was in Prussia's interest against the growing Russian power. Catherine the Great of Russia also understood that a reformed Polish state would diminish Russian influence in Poland and eastern Europe.

View the **Map**
"Map Discovery: The Partitions of Poland" on
MyHistoryLab.com

In April 1792, conservative Polish nobles who opposed the reforms invited Russia to restore the old order. The Russian army quickly defeated the reformist Polish forces led by Tadeusz Kosciuszko (1746–1817), a veteran of the American Revolution. In response to the Russian invasion, Frederick William II moved his troops from the west where they were confronting the French revolutionary army to his eastern frontier with Poland. That transfer of Prussian troops proved crucial to the important later French victories in the autumn of 1792. However, rather than protecting Poland as he had promised, Frederick William reached an agreement with Catherine early in 1793 to carry out a second partition of Poland. The reformed constitution was abolished, and the new Polish government remained under the influence of Russia.

[5] *New Constitution of the Government of Poland, Established by the Revolution, the Third of May, 1791* (London: J. Debrett, 1791), Article V, p. 10.

Document

BURKE DENOUNCES THE EXTREME MEASURES OF THE FRENCH REVOLUTION

Edmund Burke was the most important foreign critic of the French Revolution. His first critique, Reflections on the Revolution in France, *appeared in 1790. In 1796, he composed* Letters on a Regicide Peace, *which opposed a proposed peace treaty between Great Britain and revolutionary France. In that work, he summarized what he regarded as the worst evils of the revolutionary government: the execution of the king, the confiscation of property of the church and nobles, and de-Christianization (see page 576).*

To which of the major events in the French Revolution does Burke refer? Why, by 1796, would Burke and others have emphasized the religious policies of the revolution? Did Burke exaggerate the evils of the revolution? Who was Burke trying to persuade?

A government of the nature of that set up at our very door has never been hitherto seen, or ever imagined in Europe. . . . France, since her revolution, is under the sway of a sect, whose leaders have deliberately, at one stroke, demolished the whole body of that jurisprudence which France had pretty nearly in common with other civilized countries. . . .

Its foundation is laid in regicide, in Jacobinism, and in atheism, and it has joined to those principles a body of systematic manners, which secures their operation. . . .

I call a commonwealth regicide, which lays it down as a fixed law of nature, and a fundamental right of man, that all government, not being a democracy, is an usurpation. That all kings, as such, are usurpers; and for being kings may and ought to be put to death, with their wives, families, and adherents. That commonwealth which acts uniformly upon those principles . . . —this I call regicide by establishment.

Jacobinism is the revolt of the enterprising talents of a country against its property. When private men form themselves into associations for the purpose of destroying the pre-existing laws and institutions of their country; when they secure to themselves an army, by dividing amongst the people of no property the estates of the ancient and lawful proprietors, when a state recognizes those acts; when it does not make confiscations for crimes, but makes crimes for confiscations; when it has its principal strength, and all its resources, in such a violation of property . . . —I call this Jacobinism by establishment.

I call it atheism by establishment, when any state, as such, shall not acknowledge the existence of God as a moral governor of the world; . . . —when it shall abolish the Christian religion by a regular decree;—when it shall persecute with a cold, unrelenting, steady cruelty, by every mode of confiscation, imprisonment, exile, and death, all its ministers;—when it shall generally shut up or pull down churches; when the few buildings which remain of this kind shall be opened only for the purpose of making a profane apotheosis of monsters, whose vices and crimes have no parallel amongst men. . . . When, in the place of that religion of social benevolence, and of individual self-denial, in mockery of all religion, they institute impious, blasphemous, indecent theatric rites, in honour of their vitiated, perverted reason, and erect altars to the personification of their own corrupted and bloody republic; . . . when wearied out with incessant martyrdom, and the cries of a people hungering and thirsting for religion, they permit it, only as a tolerated evil—I call this atheism by establishment.

When to these establishments of regicide, of Jacobinism, and of atheism, you add the correspondent system of manners, no doubt can be left on the mind of a thinking man concerning their determined hostility to the human race.

From *The Works of the Right Honourable Edmund Burke* (London: Henry G. Bohn, 1856), 5, pp. 206–208.

In the spring of 1794, Polish officers mutinied against efforts to unite their forces with the Russian army. Kosciuszko, who had been in France and Germany since his defeat in 1792, returned to Poland to lead these troops. Initially he was successful. As the rebellion expanded, the language and symbols of the French Revolution appeared in Polish cities. Before long, Prussia, Austria, and Russia sent troops into Poland. On November 4, 1794, in the single bloodiest day of combat in the decade, Russian troops killed well over 10,000 Poles outside Warsaw. Kosciuszko ended up in a Russian prison, and the next year the three partitioning empires divided what remained of Poland among them. Polish officers and troops who escaped Poland after the last partition later fought with the armies of the French Revolution and Napoleon against the forces of the partitioning powers.

▼ The Reign of Terror

War with Europe

The French invasion of the Austrian Netherlands (Belgium) and the revolutionary reorganization of that territory in 1792 roused the rest of Europe to active hostility. In November 1792, the Convention declared it would aid all peoples who wished to cast off aristocratic and monarchical oppression. The Convention had also proclaimed the Scheldt River in the Netherlands open to the commerce of all nations and thus had violated a treaty that Great Britain had made with Austria and Holland. The British were on the point of declaring war on France over this issue when the Convention issued its own declaration of hostilities against Britain in February 1793.

By April 1793, when the Jacobins began to direct the French government, the nation was at war with Austria, Prussia, Great Britain, Spain, Sardinia, and Holland. The governments of these nations, allied in what is known as the First Coalition, endeavored to protect their social structures, political systems, and economic interests against the aggression of the revolution.

This widening of the war in the winter and spring of 1792–1793 brought new, radical political actions within France as the revolutionary government mobilized itself and the nation for the conflict. (See the Document "A Nation at Arms," page 573.) Throughout France, there was the sense that a new kind of war had erupted. In this war the major issue was not protection of national borders as such, but rather the defense of the bold new republican political and social order that had emerged since 1789. The French people understood that the achievements of the revolution were in danger. To protect those achievements, the government took extraordinary actions that touched almost every aspect of national life. Thousands of people from all walks of life including peasants, nobles, clergy, business and professional people, and one-time revolutionary leaders, as well as the king and queen, were arbitrarily arrested and, in many cases, executed. The immediate need to protect the revolution from enemies, real or imagined, from across the spectrum of French political and social life was considered more important than the security of property or even of life. These actions to protect the revolution and silence dissent came to be known as the **Reign of Terror**. (See the Document "The Paris Jacobin Club Alerts the Nation to Internal Enemies of the Revolution," page 574.)

The Republic Defended

To mobilize for war, the revolutionary government organized a collective executive in the form of powerful committees. These, in turn, sought to organize all French national life on a wartime footing. The result was an immense military effort dedicated both to protecting and promoting revolutionary ideals.

The Committee of Public Safety In April 1793, the Convention established a Committee of General Security and a Committee of Public Safety to carry out the executive duties of the government. The latter committee eventually enjoyed almost dictatorial power. All of the revolutionary leaders who served on the Committee of Public Safety were convinced republicans who had long opposed the more vacillating policies of the Girondists. They saw their task as saving the revolution from mortal enemies at home and abroad. They enjoyed a working political relationship with the *sans-culottes* of Paris, but this was an alliance of expediency for the committee.

▶ **Read** the **Document**
"The National Convention, *Law on Suspects* (1793), and *Law of 22 Prairial Year II* (1794)" on
MyHistoryLab.com

The *Levée en Masse* The major problem for the Convention was to wage the war and at the same time to secure domestic support for the war effort. In early June 1793, the Parisian *sans-culottes* invaded the Convention and successfully demanded the expulsion of the Girondist members. That action further radicalized the Convention and gave the Mountain complete control. On June 22, the Convention approved a fully democratic constitution but delayed its implementation until the conclusion of the war. In fact, it was never implemented. On August 23, Lazare Carnot (1753–1823), the member of the Committee of Public Safety in charge of the military, began a mobilization for victory by issuing a **levée en masse,** a military requisition on the entire population, conscripting males into the army and directing economic production to military purposes.

Document

A NATION AT ARMS

On August 16, 1793, the National Convention called upon all French people, regardless of gender or age, to contribute to the war effort. Based on the notion that all citizens enjoyed political rights in the new France, the levée en masse asserted that they also all shared responsibilities to defend their nation. Different people could fulfill those responsibilities in different ways, but no one was exempt. Somewhere between 800,000 and 1 million men were conscripted into military service, creating an army that seized the attention of all European states. According to one historian, this constituted the "first declaration of total war" as "every man, woman, child, animal and inanimate object was conscripted for the war effort."[6]

What role are French citizens expected to play in defending France from its "enemies"? What other resources are considered rightful targets for the National Convention's call for support?

1. Henceforth, until the enemies have been driven from the territory of the Republic, the French people are in permanent requisition for army service. The young men shall go to battle; the married men shall forge arms and transport provisions; the women shall make tents and clothes, and shall serve in the hospitals; the children shall turn old linen into [bandages]; the old men shall repair to the public places, to stimulate the courage of the warriors and preach the unity of the Republic and hatred of kings.

2. National buildings shall be converted into barracks; public places into armament workshops; the soil of cellars shall be washed in lye to extract saltpeter therefrom.

3. Arms of caliber shall be turned over exclusively to those who march against the enemy. . . .

4. Saddle horses are called for to complete the cavalry corps; draught horses, other than those employed in agriculture, shall haul artillery and provisions.

5. The Committee of Public Safety is charged with taking all measures necessary for establishing, without delay, a special manufacture of arms of all kinds, in harmony with the *élan* and the energy of the French people. Accordingly, it is authorized to constitute all establishments, manufactories, workshops, and factories deemed necessary for the execution of such works, as well as to requisition for such purpose, throughout the entire extent of the Republic, the . . . workmen who may contribute to their success. . . .

7. No one may obtain a substitute in the service to which he is summoned. . . .

8. The levy shall be general. Unmarried citizens or childless widowers, from eighteen to twenty-five years, shall go first; they shall meet, without delay, at the chief town of their districts, where they shall practice manual exercise daily, while awaiting the hour of departure.

9. The representatives of the people shall regulate the musters and marches so as to have armed citizens arrive at the points of assembling only in so far as supplies, munitions, and all that constitutes the material part of the army exist in sufficient proportion. . . .

11. The battalion organized in each district shall be united under a banner bearing the inscription: *The French people risen against tyrants.* . . .

[6]Tim Blanning, *The Pursuit of Glory: The Five Revolutions that made Modern Europe, 1648–1815* (New York: Penguin, 2007), p. 628.

Document

THE PARIS JACOBIN CLUB ALERTS THE NATION TO INTERNAL ENEMIES OF THE REVOLUTION

By early 1793, the revolutionary groups in Paris stood sharply divided amongst themselves. The Girondists (also known as Brissotins), who had led the nation into war, faced military reversals. General Dumouriez, a former revolutionary commander, had changed sides and was leading an army against France. At this point, on April 5, the radical Jacobin Club of Paris sent a circular to its provincial clubs, painting a dire picture of the fate of the revolution. While Dumouriez was marching against Paris, they accused members of the government and its administrators of conspiring to betray the revolution. The circular suggested that some people were cooperating with England in the war against France. The Jacobins also portrayed as counterrevolutionaries all those political figures who had opposed the execution of Louis XVI. The Paris Jacobins then called on their allies in the provinces to defend the revolution and to take vengeance against its internal enemies. The distortion of the motives of political enemies, the appeal to a possible reversal of the revolution, and the accusations of internal conspiracy served to justify the demand for justice against enemies of the revolution. The accusations embodied in this circular and the fears it sought to arouse represented the kind of thinking that informed the suspension of legal rights and due process associated with the Reign of Terror.

How did the Jacobins use the war to call for actions against their own domestic political enemies? What real and imagined forces did they see threatening the revolution? How did this circular constitute a smear campaign by one group of revolutionaries against other groups? What actions did the Jacobins seek?

Friends, we are betrayed! To arms! To arms! The terrible hour is at hand when the defenders of the *Patrie* must vanquish or bury themselves under the bloody ruins of the Republic. Frenchmen, never was your liberty in such great peril! At last our enemies have put the finishing touch to their foul perfidy, and to complete it their accomplice Dumouriez is marching on Paris. . . .

But Brothers, not all your dangers are to be found there! . . . You must be convinced of a grievous truth! Your greatest enemies are in your midst, they direct your operations. O Vengeance !!! . . .

Yes, brothers and friends, yes, it is in the Senate that parricidal hands tear at your vitals! Yes, the counterrevolution is in the Government . . . , in the National Convention. It is there, at the center of your security and your hope, that criminal delegates hold the threads of the web that they have woven with the horde of despots who come to butcher us! . . . It is there that a sacrilegious cabal is directed by the English court . . . and others. . . .

Let us rise! Yes, let us rise! Let us arrest all the enemies of our revolution, and all suspected persons. Let us exterminate, without pity, all conspirators, unless we wish to be exterminated ourselves. . . .

Let the departments, the districts, the municipalities, and all the popular societies unite and concur in protesting to the Convention, by dispatching thereto a veritable rain of petitions manifesting the formal wish for the immediate recall of all unfaithful members who have betrayed their duty by not wishing the death of the tyrant, and, above all, against those who have led astray so many of their colleagues. Such delegates are traitors, royalists, or fatuous men. The Republic condemns the friends of kings! . . .

Let us all unite equally to demand that the thunder or indictments be loosed against generals who are traitors to the Republic, against prevaricating ministers, against postal administrators, and against all unfaithful agents of the government. Therein lies our most salutary means of defence; but let us repel the traitors and tyrants.

The center of their conspiracy is here: it is in Paris that our perfidious enemies wish to consummate their crime. Paris, the cradle, the bulwark of liberty, is, without doubt, the place where they have sworn to annihilate the holy cause of humanity under the corpses of patriots.

From John Hall Stewart, *Documentary Survey of the French Revolution*, 1st ed., © 1951. Reprinted by permission of Pearson Education, Inc., Upper Saddle River, NJ.

Following the *levée en masse*, the Convention on September 29, 1793, established a ceiling on prices in accord with *sans-culotte* demands. During these same months, the armies of the revolution also successfully crushed many of the counterrevolutionary disturbances in the provinces. Never before had Europe seen a nation organized in this way, nor one defended by a citizen army, which, by late 1794, with somewhere around a million men, had become larger than any ever organized in European history.

Other events within France astounded Europeans even more. The Reign of Terror had begun. Those months of quasi-judicial executions and murders stretching from the autumn of 1793 to the midsummer of 1794 are probably the most famous or infamous period of the revolution. They can be understood only in the context of the war on one hand and the revolutionary expectations of the Convention and the *sans-culottes* on the other.

The "Republic of Virtue" and Robespierre's Justification of Terror

The presence of armies closing in on the nation made it easy to dispense with legal due process. The people who sat in the Convention and those sitting on the Committee of Public Safety, however, did not see their actions simply in terms of expediency made necessary by war. They also believed they had created something new in world history, a "republic of virtue." In this republic, civic virtue largely understood in terms of Rousseau's *Social Contract*, the sacrifice of one's self and one's interest for the good of the republic, would replace selfish aristocratic and monarchical corruption. The republic of virtue manifested itself in many ways: in the renaming of streets from the egalitarian vocabulary of the revolution; in republican dress copied from that of the *sans-culottes* or the Roman Republic; in the absence of powdered wigs; in the suppression of plays and other literature that were insufficiently republican; and in a general attack against crimes, such as prostitution, that were supposedly characteristic of aristocratic society. Yet the core value of the republic of virtue in line with Rousseau's thought was the upholding of the public over the private good or the championing of the general will over individual interests. It was in the name of the public good that the Committee of Public Safety carried out the policies of the terror.

Read the Document "Maximilien Robespierre, 'Speech to National Convention: The Terror Justified'" on **MyHistoryLab.com**

The person who embodied this republic of virtue defended by terror was Maximilien de Robespierre (1758–1794), who, by late 1793, had emerged as the dominant figure on the Committee of Public Safety. This utterly selfless revolutionary figure has remained controversial from his day to the present. From the beginning of the revolution, he had favored a republic. The Jacobin Club provided his primary forum and base of power. A shrewd and sensitive politician, Robespierre had opposed the war in 1792 because he feared it might aid the monarchy. He depended largely on the support of the *sans-culottes* of Paris, but he continued to dress as he had before the revolution in powdered wig and knee breeches. For him, the republic of virtue meant whole-hearted support of the republican government, the renunciation of selfish gains from political life, and the assault on foreign and domestic enemies of the revolution. Portraying revolutionary France as endangered on all sides, he told the Convention early in 1794,

Without, all the tyrants encircle you; within, all the friends of tyranny conspire—they will conspire until crime has been robbed of hope. We must smother the internal and external enemies of the Republic or perish with them. Now, in this situation, the first maxim of your policy ought to be to lead the people by reason and the people's enemies by terror. If the mainspring of popular government in peacetime is virtue, amid revolution it is at the same time [both] virtue and *terror:* virtue, without which terror is fatal; terror, without which virtue is impotent. Terror is nothing but prompt, severe, inflexible justice; it is therefore an emanation of virtue. It is less a special principle than a consequence of the general principle of democracy applied to our country's most pressing needs.[7]

Robespierre and those who supported his policies were among the first of a succession of secular ideologues of the left and the right who, in the name of humanity, would bring so much suffering to Europe in the following two centuries. The policies associated with terror in the name of republican virtue included the exclusion of women from active political life, the de-Christianization of France, and the use of revolutionary tribunals to dispense justice to alleged enemies of the republic.

Repression of the Society of Revolutionary Republican Women

Revolutionary women established their own distinct institutions during these months. In May 1793, Pauline Léon and Claire Lacombe founded the Society of Revolutionary Republican Women. Its purpose was to fight the internal enemies of the revolution. Its members saw themselves as militant citizens. Initially, the Jacobin leaders welcomed the organization. Members of the society and other women filled the galleries of the Convention to hear the debates and cheer their favorite speakers. The society became increasingly radical, however. Its members sought stricter controls on the price of food and other commodities, worked to ferret out food hoarders, and brawled with working market women whom they thought to be insufficiently revolutionary. The women of the society also demanded the right to wear the revolutionary *cockade* that male citizens usually wore in their hats. By October 1793, the Jacobins in the Convention had begun to fear the turmoil the society was causing and banned all women's clubs and societies. The debates

[7]Richard T. Bienvenu, *The Ninth of Thermidor: The Fall of Robespierre* (New York: Oxford University Press, 1968), p. 38.

over these decrees show that the Jacobins believed the society opposed many of their economic policies, but the deputies used Rousseau's language of separate spheres for men and women to justify their exclusion of women from active political life.

There were other examples of repression of women in 1793. Olympe de Gouges, author of the Declaration of the Rights of Woman, opposed the Terror and accused Jacobins of corruption. She was guillotined in November 1793. The same year, women were formally excluded from serving in the French army and from the galleries of the Convention. The exclusion of women from public political life was part of the establishment of the Jacobin republic of virtue because in such a republic men would be active citizens in the military and political sphere and women would be active only in the domestic sphere.

De-Christianization

The most dramatic step taken by the republic of virtue, and one that illustrates its imposition of political values to justify the Terror, was the Convention's attempt to de-Christianize France. In November 1793, the Convention proclaimed a new calendar dating from the first day of the French Republic. There were twelve months of thirty days each, with names associated with the seasons and climate. Every tenth day, rather than every seventh, was a holiday. Many of the most important events of the next few years became known by their dates on the revolutionary calendar. From summer to spring, the months of the revolutionary calendar were Messidor, Thermidor, Fructidor, Vendémiaire, Brumaire, Frimaire, Nivose, Pluviose, Ventose, Germinal, Floreal, and Prairial. In November 1793, the Convention decreed the Cathedral of Notre Dame in Paris to be a "Temple of Reason."

The legislature then sent trusted members, known as deputies on mission, into the provinces to enforce de-Christianization by closing churches, persecuting clergy and believers (both Roman Catholic and Protestant), occasionally forcing priests to marry, and sometimes simply by killing priests and nuns. Churches were desecrated, torn down, or used as barns or warehouses. This radical religious policy attacking both clergy and religious property roused enormous popular opposition and alienated parts of the French provinces from the revolutionary government in Paris. Robespierre personally opposed de-Christianization because he was convinced it would prove a political blunder that would erode loyalty to the republic.

Revolutionary Tribunals

The Reign of Terror manifested itself in revolutionary tribunals that the Convention established during the summer of 1793. The mandate of these tribunals, the most prominent of which was in Paris, was to try the

enemies of the republic, but the definition of who was an "enemy" shifted as the months passed. It included those who might aid other European powers, those who endangered republican virtue, and, finally, good republicans who opposed the policies of the dominant faction of the government. The Terror of the revolutionary tribunals systematized and channeled the popular resentment that had manifested itself in the September Massacres of 1792. Those whom the tribunal condemned in Paris were beheaded on the guillotine, a recently invented instrument of efficient and supposedly humane execution. (The drop of the blade of the guillotine was certain to sever the head of the condemned at once, whereas beheading by axe or sword could, and often did, require multiple blows and cause unnecessary pain.) Other modes of execution, such as mass shootings and drowning, were used in the provinces.

The first victims of the Terror were Marie Antoinette, other members of the royal family, and aristocrats, who were executed in October 1793. Girondist politicians who had been prominent in the Legislative Assembly followed them. These executions took place in the same weeks that the Convention had moved against the Society of Revolutionary Republican Women, whom it had also seen as endangering Jacobin control.

On the way to her execution in 1793, Marie Antoinette was sketched from life by Jacques-Louis David as she passed his window. Note her cropped hair, which had recently been shorn as a symbol of her degradation. Jacques Louis David (1748–1825), Marie-Antoinette brought to the guillotine (after a drawing by David who witnessed the execution). Pen drawing. 1793. Bibliothèque Nationale, Paris, France. Bridgeman—Giraudon/Art Resource, NY

In early 1794, the Terror moved to the provinces, where the deputies on mission presided over the summary execution of thousands of people, most of whom were peasants, who had allegedly supported internal opposition to the revolution. One of the most infamous incidents occurred in Nantes on the west coast of France, where several hundred people, including many priests, were simply tied to rafts and drowned in the river Loire. The victims of the Terror now came from every social class, including the *sans-culottes*.

The End of the Terror

Revolutionaries Turn Against Themselves In Paris during the late winter of 1794, Robespierre began to orchestrate the Terror against republican political figures of the left and right. On March 24, he secured the execution of certain extreme *sans-culottes* leaders known as the *enragés*. They had wanted further measures to regulate prices, secure social equality, and press de-Christianization. Robespierre then turned against other republicans in the Convention. Most prominent among them was Jacques Danton (1759–1794), who had provided heroic national leadership in the dark days of September 1792 and who had later served briefly on the Committee of Public Safety before Robespierre joined the group. Danton and others were accused of being insufficiently militant on the war, profiting monetarily from the revolution, and rejecting the link between politics and moral virtue. Danton was executed in April 1794. Robespierre thus exterminated the leadership of both groups that might have threatened his position. Finally, on June 10, he secured passage of the Law of 22 Prairial, which permitted the revolutionary tribunal to convict suspects without hearing substantial evidence against them. The number of executions grew steadily.

Fall of Robespierre In May 1794, at the height of his power, Robespierre, considering the worship of "Reason" too abstract for most citizens, replaced it with the "Cult of the Supreme Being." This deistic cult reflected Rousseau's vision of a civic religion that would induce morality among citizens. (See the Document "The Convention Establishes the Worship of the Supreme Being," page 579.) Robespierre, however, did not long preside over his new religion.

View the Image "Cult of the Supreme Being, French Revolution" on **MyHistoryLab.com**

On July 26, Robespierre made an ill-tempered speech in the Convention, declaring that other leaders of the government were conspiring against him and the revolution. Similar accusations against unnamed persons had preceded his earlier attacks. No member of the Convention could now feel safe. On July 27—the Ninth of Thermidor on the revolutionary calendar—members of the Convention, by prearrangement, shouted him

Maximilien Robespierre (1758–1794) emerged as the most powerful revolutionary figure in 1793 and 1794, dominating the Committee of Public Safety. He considered the Terror essential for the success of the revolution. In this caricature, having already guillotined all the people in France, Robespierre must himself execute the executioner. © INTERFOTO/Alamy

down when he rose to make another speech. That night Robespierre was arrested, and the next day he and approximately eighty of his supporters were executed without trial. The revolutionary *sans-culottes* of Paris did not try to save him because he had deprived them of their chief leaders. He had also recently supported a measure to cap workers' wages. Other Jacobins turned against him because, after Danton's death, they feared they would be his next victims. Robespierre had destroyed rivals for leadership without creating supporters for himself. He had also for months tried to persuade the Paris populace that the Convention itself was harboring enemies of the revolution. Assured by the Convention that Robespierre had sought dictatorial powers, Parisians saw him as one more of those internal enemies. Robespierre was the unwitting creator of his own destruction.

▼ The Thermidorian Reaction

The fall of Robespierre might simply have been one more shift in the turbulent politics of the revolution, but instead it proved to be a major turning point. The members of the Convention used the event to reassert their authority over the executive power of the Committee of Public Safety. Within a short time, the Reign of Terror, which had claimed more than 25,000 victims, came to a close. It no longer seemed necessary since the war abroad was going well and the republican forces had crushed the provincial uprisings.

This tempering of the revolution, called the **Thermidorian Reaction** because of its association with the events of 9 Thermidor, consisted of the destruction of the machinery of terror and the establishment of a new constitutional regime. It resulted from a widespread feeling that the revolution had become too radical. In particular, it displayed a weariness of the Terror and a fear that the *sans-culottes* had become too powerful. The influence of generally wealthy middle-class and professional people soon replaced that of the *sans-culottes*.

In the weeks and months after Robespierre's execution, the Convention allowed the Girondists who had been in prison or hiding to return to their seats. A general amnesty freed political prisoners. The Convention restructured the Committee of Public Safety and diminished its power while repealing the notorious Law of 22 Prairial. Some, though by no means all, of the people responsible for the Terror were removed from public life. The Paris Commune was outlawed, and its leaders and deputies on mission were executed. The Paris Jacobin Club was closed, and Jacobin clubs in the provinces were forbidden to correspond with each other.

The end of the Reign of Terror did not mean the end of violence in France. Executions of former terrorists marked the beginning of "the white terror." Throughout the country, people who had been involved in the Reign of Terror were attacked and often murdered. Jacobins were executed with little more due process than they had extended to their victims a few months earlier. The Convention itself approved some of these trials. In other cases, gangs of youths who had aristocratic connections or who had avoided serving in the army roamed the streets, beating known Jacobins. In Lyons, Toulon, and Marseilles, these so-called "bands of Jesus" dragged suspected terrorists from prisons and murdered them

The Festival of the Supreme Being, which took place in June 1794, inaugurated Robespierre's new civic religion. Its climax occurred when a statue of Atheism was burned and another statue of Wisdom rose from the ashes. Pierre-Antoine Demachy, *Festival of the Supreme Being at the Champ de Mars on June 8, 1794.* Musée de la Ville de Paris, Musée Carnavalet, Paris, France. Bridgeman—Giraudon/Art Resource, NY

Document

THE CONVENTION ESTABLISHES THE WORSHIP OF THE SUPREME BEING

On May 7, 1794, the Convention passed an extraordinary piece of revolutionary legislation. It established the worship of the Supreme Being as a state cult. Although the law drew on the religious ideas of deism, the point of the legislation was to provide a religious basis for the new secular French state. Article 6 outlined the political and civic values that the Cult of the Supreme Being was supposed to nurture.

How does this declaration reflect the ideas of the Enlightenment? What personal and social values was this religion supposed to nurture? How might this declaration have led to Burke's criticism of the policies of the revolution?

1. The French people recognize the existence of the Supreme Being and the immortality of the soul.

2. They recognize that the worship worthy of the Supreme Being is the observance of the duties of man.

3. They place in the forefront of such duties detestation of bad faith and tyranny, punishment of tyrants and traiters, succoring of unfortunates, respect of weak persons, defence of the oppressed, doing to others all the good that one can, and being just towards everyone.

4. Festivals shall be instituted to remind man of the concept of the Divinity and of the dignity of his being.

5. They shall take their names from the glorious events of our Revolution, or from the virtues most dear and most useful to man, or from the greatest benefits of nature. . . .

6. On the days of *décade*, the name given to a particular day in each month of the revolutionary calendar, it shall celebrate the following festivals:

To the Supreme Being and to nature; to the human race; to the French people; to the benefactors of humanity; to the martyrs of liberty; to liberty and equality; to the Republic; to the liberty of the world; to the love of the *Patrie* [Fatherland]; to the hatred of tyrants and traitors; to truth; to justice; to modesty; to glory and immortality; to friendship; to frugality; to courage; to good faith; to heroism; to disinterestedness; to stoicism; to love; to conjugal love; to paternal love; to maternal tenderness; to filial piety; to infancy; to youth; to manhood; to old age; to misfortune; to agriculture; to industry; to our forefathers; to posterity; to happiness.

From John Hall Stewart, *Documentary Survey of the French Revolution*, 1st ed., © 1951. Reprinted by permission of Pearson Education, Inc., Upper Saddle River, NJ.

much as alleged royalists had been murdered during the September Massacres of 1792.

The republic of virtue gave way, if not to one of vice, at least to one of frivolous pleasures. The dress of the *sans-culottes* and the Roman Republic disappeared among the middle class and the aristocracy. New plays appeared in the theaters, and prostitutes again roamed the streets of Paris. Families of victims of the Reign of Terror gave parties in which they appeared with shaved necks, like the victims of the guillotine, and with red ribbons tied about them. Although the Convention continued to favor the Cult of the Supreme Being, it allowed Catholic services to be held. Many refractory priests returned to the country. One of the

unanticipated results of the Thermidorian Reaction was a genuine revival of Catholic worship.

The Thermidorian Reaction also saw the repeal of legislation that had been passed in 1792 making divorce more equitable for women. As the passage of that measure suggests, the reaction did not extend women's rights or improve their education. The Thermidorians and their successors had seen enough attempts at political and social change. They sought to return family life to its status before the outbreak of the revolution. Political authorities and the church were determined to reestablish separate spheres for men and women and to reinforce traditional gender roles. As a result, in at least some respects, Frenchwomen had less freedom after 1795 than before 1789.

Establishment of the Directory

The Thermidorian Reaction led to still another new constitution. The democratic constitution of 1793, which had never gone into effect, was abandoned. In its place, the Convention issued the Constitution of the Year III, which reflected the Thermidorian determination to reject *both* constitutional monarchy and democracy. In recognition of the danger of a legislature with only one chamber and unlimited authority, this new document provided for a legislature of two houses. Members of the upper body, or Council of Elders, were to be men over forty years of age who were either husbands or widowers. The lower Council of Five Hundred was to consist of men of at least thirty who could be either married or single. The executive body was to be a five-person Directory whom the Elders would choose from a list the Council of Five Hundred submitted. Property qualifications limited the franchise, except

((•─|**Listen** to the **Audio**
"The Directory" on
MyHistoryLab.com

for soldiers, who were permitted to vote whether they had property or not.

Historically, the term *Thermidor* has come to be associated with political reaction. That association requires considerable qualification. By 1795, the political structure and society of the Old Regime in France based on rank and birth had given way permanently to a political system based on civic equality and social status based on property ownership. People who had never been allowed direct, formal access to political power had, to different degrees, been granted it. Their entrance into political life had given rise to questions of property distribution and economic regulations that could not again be ignored. Representation was an established principle of politics. Henceforth, the question before France and eventually before all of Europe would be which new groups would be permitted representation. In the *levée en masse*, the French had demonstrated to Europe the power of the secular ideal of nationhood and of the willingness of citizen soldiers to embrace self-sacrifice.

The post-Thermidorian course of the French Revolution did not undo these stunning changes in the political and social contours of Europe. What triumphed in the Constitution of the Year III was the revolution of the holders of property. For this reason the French Revolution has often been considered a victory of the bourgeoisie, or middle class. The property that won the day, however, was not industrial wealth, but the wealth stemming from commerce, the professions, and land. The largest new propertied class to emerge from the revolutionary turmoil was the peasantry, who, as a result of the destruction of aristocratic privileges, now owned their own land. Unlike peasants liberated from traditional landholding in other parts of Europe during the next century, French peasants had to pay no monetary compensation either to their former landlords or to the state.

Removal of the *Sans-culottes* from Political Life

The most decisively reactionary element in the Thermidorian Reaction and the new constitution was the removal of the *sans-culottes* from political life. With the war effort succeeding, the Convention severed its ties with the *sans-culottes*. True to their belief in an unregulated economy, the Thermidorians repealed the ceiling on prices. As a result, the winter of 1794–1795 brought the worst food shortages of the period. There were many food riots, which the Convention suppressed to prove that the era of the *sans-culottes journées* had come to a close. Royalist agents, who aimed to restore the monarchy, tried to take advantage of their discontent. On October 5, 1795—13 Vendémiaire—the sections of Paris led by the royalists rose up against the Convention. The government turned the artillery against the royalist rebels. A general named Napoleon Bonaparte (1769–1821) commanded the cannon, and with a "whiff of grapeshot," he dispersed the crowd.

By the Treaties of Basel in March and June 1795, the Convention concluded peace with Prussia and Spain. The legislators, however, feared a resurgence of both radical democrats and royalists in the upcoming elections for the Council of Five Hundred. Consequently, the Convention ruled that at least two-thirds of the new legislature must have served in the Convention itself, thus rejecting the decision the National Constituent Assembly had made in 1791 when it forbade its members to be elected to the new Legislative Assembly. The Two-Thirds Law, which sought to foster continuity but also clearly favored politicians already in office, quickly undermined public faith in the new constitutional order.

The Directory faced almost immediate social unrest. During the spring of 1796 in Paris, Gracchus Babeuf (1760–1797) led the Conspiracy of Equals. He and his followers called for more radical democracy and for more equality of property. They declared at one point, "The aim of the French Revolution is to destroy inequality and to re-establish the general welfare. . . . The Revolution is not complete, because the rich monopolize all the property and govern exclusively, while the poor toil like slaves, languish in misery, and count for nothing in the state."[8] In a sense, they were correct. The Directory intended to resist any further social changes in France that might endanger property or political stability. Babeuf was arrested, tried, and executed. This minor plot became famous decades later, when European socialists attempted to find their historical roots in the French Revolution.

[8]John Hall Stewart, *A Documentary Survey of the French Revolution* (New York: Macmillan, 1966), pp. 656–657.

THE FRENCH REVOLUTION

1787

February–May	Unsuccessful negotiations with the Assembly of Notables

1788

August 8	Louis XVI summons the Estates General
December 27	Approval of doubling of the Third Estate membership

1789

May 5	The Estates General opens at Versailles
June 17	The Third Estate declares itself the National Assembly
June 20	The National Assembly takes the Tennis Court Oath
July 14	Fall of the Bastille in the city of Paris
Late July	The Great Fear spreads in the countryside
August 4	The nobles surrender their feudal rights at a meeting of the National Constituent Assembly
August 27	Declaration of the Rights of Man and Citizen
October 5–6	Parisian women march to Versailles and force Louis XVI and his family to return to Paris

1790

July 12	Civil Constitution of the Clergy adopted
July 14	A new political constitution is accepted by the king

1791

June 14	Chapelier Law
June 20–24	Louis XVI and his family attempt to flee France and are stopped at Varennes
August 27	The Declaration of Pillnitz
October 1	The Legislative Assembly meets

1792

April 20	France declares war on Austria
August 10	The Tuileries palace is stormed, and Louis XVI takes refuge with the Legislative Assembly
September 2–7	The September Massacres
September 20	France wins the Battle of Valmy
September 21	The Convention meets, and the monarchy is abolished

1793

January 21	King Louis XVI is executed
February 1	France declares war on Great Britain
March	Counterrevolution breaks out in the Vendée
April	The Committee of Public Safety is formed
June 22	The Constitution of 1793 is adopted but not implemented
July	Robespierre enters the Committee of Public Safety
August 23	*Levée en masse* proclaimed
September 29	Maximum prices set on food and other commodities
October 16	Queen Marie Antoinette is executed
October 30	Women's societies and clubs banned
November 10	The Cult of Reason is proclaimed; the revolutionary calendar, beginning on September 22, 1792, is adopted

1794

March 24	Execution of the leaders of the *sans-culottes* known as the *enragés*
April 6	Execution of Danton
May 7	Cult of the Supreme Being proclaimed
June 8	Robespierre leads the celebration of the Festival of the Supreme Being
June 10	The Law of 22 Prairial is adopted
July 27	The Ninth of Thermidor and the fall of Robespierre
July 28	Robespierre is executed
August 1	Repeal of the Law of 22 Prairial
August 10	Reorganization of the Revolutionary Tribunal
November 12	Closing of Jacobin Club in Paris

1795

May 31	Abolition of Revolutionary Tribunal
August 22	The Constitution of the Year III establishes the Directory
September 23	Two-Thirds Law adopted

1796

May 10	Babeuf's Conspiracy of Equals

1799

November 9	Napoleon's (18 Brumaire) *coup d'état* overthrows the Directory

The suppression of the *sans-culottes*, the narrow franchise of the constitution, the Two-Thirds Law, and the Catholic royalist revival presented the Directory with challenges that it was never able to overcome. Because France remained at war with Austria and Great Britain, it needed a broader-based active loyalty than it was able to command. Instead, the Directory came to depend on the power of the army to govern France. All soldiers could vote. Moreover, within the army that the revolution had created and sustained were ambitious officers who were eager for power. As will be seen in the next chapter, the instability of the Directory, the growing role of the army, and the ambitions of its leaders held profound consequences not only for France but for the entire Western world as well.

In Perspective

The French Revolution is the central political event of modern European history. It unleashed political and social forces that shaped Europe and much of the rest of the world for the next two centuries. The revolution began with a clash between the monarchy and the nobility. Once the Estates General gathered, however, the traditional boundaries of eighteenth-century political life could not contain the discontent. The Third Estate, in all of its diversity, demanded real influence in government. Initially, that meant the participation of middle-class members of the Estates General, but soon the people of Paris and the peasants made their own demands known. Thereafter, popular nationalism exerted itself on French political life and the destiny of Europe.

Revolutionary legislation and popular uprisings in Paris, the countryside, and other cities transformed the social as well as the political life of the nation. Nobles surrendered traditional social privileges. The church saw its property confiscated and its operations brought under state control. For a time, there was an attempt to de-Christianize France. Vast amounts of landed property changed hands, and France became a nation of peasant landowners. Urban workers lost the protection they had enjoyed under the guilds and became more subject to the forces of the marketplace.

Violence accompanied many of the revolutionary changes. Thousands died during the Reign of Terror. France also found itself at war with virtually the rest of Europe. Resentment, fear, and a new desire for stability eventually brought the Terror to an end. That desire for stability, combined with a determination to defeat the foreign enemies of the revolution and to carry it abroad, would, in turn, work to the advantage of the army. Eventually, Napoleon Bonaparte would claim leadership in the name of stability and national glory.

KEY TERMS

Convention (p. 568)
émigrés (p. 563)
Jacobins (p. 567)

levée en masse (p. 572)
Reign of Terror
   (p. 572)

sans-culottes (p. 568)
September Massacres
   (p. 568)

Thermidorian Reaction
   (p. 578)
Third Estate (p. 553)

REVIEW QUESTIONS

1. Why has France been called a rich nation with an impoverished government? How did the financial weaknesses of the French monarchy lay the foundations of the revolution of 1789?

2. What were Louis XVI's most serious mistakes during the French Revolution? Had he been a more able ruler, could the French Revolution have been avoided or a constitutional monarchy have succeeded? How much did the revolution have to do with the competence of the monarch?

3. How was the Estates General transformed into the National Assembly? How does the Declaration of the Rights of Man and Citizen reflect the social and political values of the eighteenth-century Enlightenment? How were France and its government reorganized in the early years of the revolution? Why has the Civil Constitution of the Clergy been called the greatest blunder of the National Assembly?

4. Why were some political factions dissatisfied with the constitutional settlement of 1791? What was the revolution of 1792 and why did it occur? Who were the *sans-culottes*, and how did they become a factor in the politics of the period? How influential were they during the Terror in particular? Why did the *sans-culottes* and the Jacobins cooperate at first? Why did that cooperation end?

5. Why did France go to war with Austria in 1792? What were the benefits and drawbacks for France of fighting an external war in the midst of a domestic political revolution?

6. What were the causes of the Terror? How did the rest of Europe react to the French Revolution and the Terror? How did events in France influence the last two partitions of Poland?

7. A motto of the French Revolution was "equality, liberty, and fraternity." How did the revolution both support and violate this motto? Did French women benefit from the revolution? Did French peasants benefit from it?

SUGGESTED READINGS

D. Andress, *The Terror: The Merciless War for Freedom in Revolutionary France* (2006). The best recent survey of the Reign of Terror.

N. Aston, *Christianity and Revolutionary Europe c. 1750–1830* (2002). Continent-wide survey of the impact of revolution on religion.

T. C. Blanning, *The Revolutionary Wars, 1787–1802* (1996). Essential for understanding the role of the army and the revolution.

S. Desan, *The Family on Trial in Revolutionary France* (2004). An important analysis of how the revolution impacted French domestic life.

W. Doyle, *The Oxford History of the French Revolution* (2003). A broad, complex narrative with an excellent bibliography.

A. Forrest, *Revolutionary Paris, the Provinces and the French Revolution* (2004). A clear presentation of the tensions between the center of the revolution and the provinces.

C. Hayden and W. Doyle, eds., *Robespierre* (1999). Essays evaluating Robespierre's ideas, career, and reputation.

P. Higonnet, *Goodness beyond Virtue: Jacobins During the French Revolution* (1998). An outstanding work that clearly relates political values to political actions.

D. Jordan, *The King's Trial: Louis XVI vs. the French Revolution* (1979). A gripping account of the event.

E. Kennedy, *A Cultural History of the French Revolution* (1989). An important examination of the role of the arts, schools, clubs, and intellectual institutions.

S. E. Melzer and L. W. Rabine, eds., *Rebel Daughters: Women and the French Revolution* (1997). Essays exploring the role and image of women in the revolution.

S. Neely, *A Concise History of the French Revolution* (2008). The best of the numerous brief accounts.

C. C. O'Brien, *The Great Melody: A Thematic Biography of Edmund Burke* (1992). A deeply thoughtful biography.

R. R. Palmer, *The Age of Democratic Revolution: A Political History of Europe and America, 1760–1800*, 2 vols. (1959, 1964). Still an impressive survey of the political turmoil in the transatlantic world.

M. Price, *The Road from Versailles: Louis XVI, Marie Antoinette, and the Fall of the French Monarchy* (2004). A lively narrative that brings the personalities of the king and queen into focus.

S. Schama, *Citizens: A Chronicle of the French Revolution* (1990). A lively account of the revolution that focuses on the personalities involved.

R. Scurr, *Fatal Purity: Robespierre and the French Revolution* (2007). A compelling analysis of a personality long difficult to understand.

T. Tackett, *Becoming a Revolutionary: The Deputies of the French National Assembly and the Emergence of a Revolutionary Culture (1789–1790)* (1996). The best study of the early months of the revolution.

MyHistoryLab™ MEDIA ASSIGNMENTS

Find these resources in the Media Assignments folder for Chapter 18 on **MyHistoryLab**.

QUESTIONS FOR ANALYSIS

1. How has this political cartoonist characterized the French king?

   Section: **The Crisis of the French Monarchy**
   View the **Closer Look** Challenging the French Political Order, p. 552

2. What were conditions like for working women around the time that this petition was written and what forms of redress do the petitioners seek from the king?

   Section: **The Revolution of 1789**
   Read the **Document** Petition of Women of the Third Estate, p. 553

3. What do you consider Robespierre's principal argument?

   Section: **The Reign of Terror**
   Read the **Document** Maximilien Robespierre, "Speech to National Convention: The Terror Justified," p. 575

4. Against whom is this complaint made?

   Section: **The Revolution of 1789**
   Read the **Document** French Peasants, Cahiers de doléances (Grievances) (France), 1789, p. 554

5. Why has de Gouges addressed this to Marie Antoinette?

   Section: **The Reconstruction of France**
   Read the **Document** Olympe de Gouges, Declaration of the Rights of Woman and the Female Citizen, p. 561

OTHER RESOURCES FROM THIS CHAPTER

The Revolution of 1789
Read the **Document** Emmanuel Joseph Sieyès, *What Is the Third Estate?*, p. 553

View the **Image** Oath of the Tennis Court, p. 554

View the **Map** Map Discovery: Revolutionary France, p. 557

The Reconstruction of France
Read the **Compare and Connect** The Declaration of the Rights of Man and Citizen Opens the Door for Disadvantaged Groups to Demand Equal Civic Rights, p. 564

The End of the Monarchy: A Second Revolution
View the **Image** Death of Marat, p. 567

View the **Image** Execution of Louis XVI, p. 569

Europe at War with the Revolution
View the **Map** Map Discovery: The Partitions of Poland, p. 570

The Reign of Terror
Read the **Document** The National Convention, *Law on Suspects* (1793) and *Law of 22 Prairial Year II* (1794), p. 572

View the **Image** Cult of the Supreme Being, French Revolution, p. 577

The Thermidorian Reaction
Listen to the **Audio** The Directory, p. 580

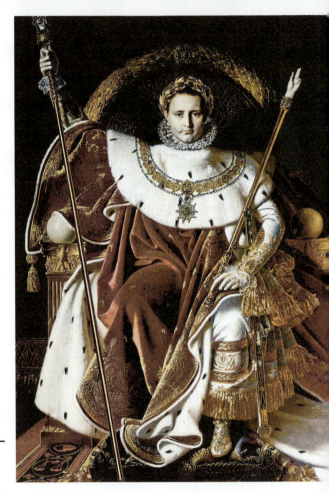

This portrait of Napoleon on his throne by Jean Ingres (1780–1867) shows him in the splendor of an imperial monarch who embodies the total power of the state. Jean Auguste Dominique Ingres (1780–1867), *Napoleon on His Imperial Throne*, 1806. Oil on canvas, 259 × 162 cm. Musée des Beaux-Arts, Rennes. Photograph © Erich Lessing/Art Resource, NY

((•—[**Listen** to the **Chapter Audio** on **MyHistoryLab.com**

19

The Age of Napoleon and the Triumph of Romanticism

LEARNING OBJECTIVES

How did Napoleon come to power in France?

How did the Consulate end the revolution in France?

How did Napoleon build an empire?

Why did Napoleonic rule breed resentment in Europe?

What were the consequences of the Congress of Vienna?

How did Rousseau and Kant contribute to the development of romanticism?

How were the ideals of romanticism reflected in English and German literature and in Romantic art?

How did Romantic religious thinkers view the religious experience?

What were the Romantic views of history and national identity?

BY THE LATE 1790s, the French people, especially property owners, who now included the peasants, longed for stability. The Directory was not providing it. Only the army was able to take charge of the nation as a symbol of both order and the popular values of the revolution. The most politically astute general was Napoleon Bonaparte, who had been a radical during the early revolution, a victorious commander in Italy, and a supporter of the repression of revolutionary disturbances after Thermidor.

Once in power, Napoleon consolidated many of the achievements of the revolution. He also repudiated much of it by establishing an empire. Thereafter, his ambitions drew France into wars of conquest and liberation across the Continent. For over a decade, Europe was at war, with only brief periods of armed truce. Through his conquests Napoleon spread many of the ideas and institutions of the revolution and overturned much of the old political and social order. He also provoked popular nationalism outside of France in opposition to French domination. This new force and the great alliances that opposed France eventually defeated Napoleon.

Throughout these Napoleonic years, new ideas and sensibilities, known by the term *Romanticism*, grew across Europe. Many of the ideas had originated in the eighteenth century, but they flourished in the turmoil of the French Revolution and the Napoleonic Wars. The revolution spurred the imagination of poets, painters, and philosophers. Some Romantic ideas, such as nationalism, supported the revolution; others, such as the emphasis on history and religion, opposed its values.

▼ The Rise of Napoleon Bonaparte

The chief threat to the Directory came from royalists, who hoped to restore the Bourbon monarchy by legal means. Many of the *émigrés* had returned to France. Their plans for a restoration drew support from devout Catholics and from those citizens horrified by the excesses of the revolution. Monarchy, they thought, promised a return to stability. The spring elections of 1797 replaced most incumbents with constitutional monarchists and their sympathizers, who now commanded a majority in the national legislature.

Read the Document "Madame de Remusat on the Rise of Napoleon" on **MyHistoryLab.com**

To preserve the republic and prevent a peaceful restoration of the Bourbons, the antimonarchist Directory staged a *coup d'état* on 18 Fructidor (September 4, 1797). They put their own supporters into the legislative seats their opponents had won. They then imposed censorship and exiled some of their enemies. At the request of the Directors, Napoleon Bonaparte, the general in charge of the French invasion of Italy, had sent a subordinate to Paris to guarantee the success of the coup. In 1797, as in 1795, the army and Bonaparte had saved the day for the government installed in the wake of the Thermidorian Reaction.

Napoleon Bonaparte was born in 1769 to a poor family of lesser nobles at Ajaccio, on the Mediterranean island of Corsica. Because France had annexed Corsica in 1768, he went to French schools and, in 1785, obtained a commission as a French artillery officer. He favored the revolution and was a fiery Jacobin. In 1793, he played a leading role in recovering the port of Toulon from the British. As a reward for his service, he was appointed a brigadier general. During the Thermidorian Reaction, his defense of the new regime on 13 Vendémiaire won him a command in Italy.

Early Military Victories

By 1795, French arms and diplomacy had shattered the enemy coalition, but France's annexation of Belgium guaranteed continued fighting with Britain and Austria. The invasion of the Italian peninsula aimed to deprive Austria of its rich northern Italian province of Lombardy. In a series of lightning victories, Bonaparte crushed the Austrian and Sardinian armies. On his own initiative, and against the wishes of the government in Paris, he concluded the Treaty of Campo Formio in October 1797. The treaty took Austria out of the war and crowned Napoleon's campaign with success. Before long, France dominated all of the Italian peninsula and Switzerland.

In November 1797, the triumphant Bonaparte returned to Paris as a hero and to confront France's only remaining enemy, Britain. He judged it impossible to cross the Channel and invade England at that time. Instead, he chose to attack British interests through the eastern Mediterranean by capturing Egypt from the Ottoman Empire. By this strategy, he hoped to drive the British fleet from the Mediterranean, cut off British communications with India, damage British trade, and threaten the British Empire.

Napoleon easily overran Egypt, but the invasion was a failure. Admiral Horatio Nelson (1758–1805) destroyed the French fleet at Abukir on August 1, 1798. The French army was cut off from France. To make matters worse, the situation in Europe was deteriorating. The invasion of Egypt had alarmed Russia, which had its own ambitions in the Near East. Russia, Austria, and the Ottomans joined Britain to form the Second Coalition against France. In 1799, the Russian and Austrian armies defeated the French in Italy and Switzerland and threatened to invade France.

Napoleon's venture into Egypt in 1798 and 1799 marked the first major Western European assault on the Ottoman Empire. It occurred less than a quarter century after Russia, under Catherine the Great, had taken control of the Crimea in the Treaty of Kuchuk-Kainardji. (See Chapter 17.) Significantly, British, not

Ottoman forces, drove the French out of Egypt. As shall be seen in Chapter 22, after Napoleon's invasion, the Ottoman Empire realized that it had to reform itself if it was to resist other European encroachments.

Read the **Document** "Louis Antoine Fauvelet de Bourrienne, *Memoirs of Napoleon Bonaparte*" on **MyHistoryLab.com**

The Constitution of the Year VIII

Economic troubles and the dangerous international situation eroded the Directory's fragile support. One of the Directors, the Abbé Siéyès (1748–1836), proposed a new constitution. The author of the pamphlet *What Is the Third Estate?* (1789) now wanted an executive body independent of the whims of electoral politics, a government based on the principle of "confidence from below, power from above." The change would require another *coup d'état* with military support. News of France's domestic troubles had reached Napoleon in Egypt. Without orders and leaving his army behind, he returned to France in October 1799 to popular acclaim. Soon he joined Siéyès. On 19 Brumaire (November 10, 1799), his troops ensured the success of the coup.

Siéyès appears to have thought that Napoleon could be used and then dismissed, but he misjudged his man. The proposed constitution divided executive authority among three consuls. Bonaparte quickly pushed Siéyès aside, and in December 1799, he issued the Constitution of the Year VIII. Behind a screen of universal male suffrage that suggested democratic principles, a complicated system of checks and balances that appealed to republican theory, and a Council of State that evoked memories of Louis XIV, the new constitution established the rule of one man—the First Consul, Bonaparte. In an age of widespread interest in classical analogies, Napoleon's takeover was reminiscent of Caesar and Augustus in ancient Rome, and to the Greek tyrants of the sixth century B.C.E. From the perspective of the twenty-first century, however, Bonaparte's career points forward to the dictators of the twentieth century. He was the first modern political figure to use the rhetoric of revolution and nationalism, to back it with military force, and to combine these elements into a mighty weapon of imperial expansion in the service of his own power.

▼ The Consulate in France (1799–1804)

The **Consulate** in effect ended the revolution in France. The leading elements of the Third Estate—that is, officials, landowners, doctors, lawyers, and financiers—had achieved most of their goals by 1799. They had abolished hereditary privilege, and the careers thus opened to talent allowed them to achieve wealth, status, and security for their property. The peasants were also satisfied. They had gained the land they had always wanted and had destroyed oppressive feudal privileges. The newly established dominant classes had little or no desire to share their new privileges with the lower social orders. Bonaparte seemed just the person to give them security. When he submitted his constitution to the voters in a plebiscite, they overwhelmingly approved it.

Suppressing Foreign Enemies and Domestic Opposition

Throughout much of the 1790s, the pressures of warfare, particularly conscription, had accounted for much French internal instability. Bonaparte justified the public's confidence in himself by making peace with France's enemies. Russia had already left the Second Coalition. A campaign in Italy brought another victory over Austria at Marengo in 1800. The Treaty of Luneville early in 1801 took Austria out of the war. Britain was now alone and, in 1802, concluded the Treaty of Amiens, which brought peace to Europe.

Bonaparte also restored peace and order at home. He used generosity, flattery, and bribery to win over enemies. He issued a general amnesty and employed men from all political factions, requiring only that they be loyal to him. Men who had been radicals during the Reign of Terror, or who had fled the Terror and favored constitutional monarchy, or who had been high officials under Louis XVI occupied some of the highest offices.

Bonaparte, however, ruthlessly suppressed opposition. He established a highly centralized administration in which prefects responsible to the government in Paris managed all departments. He employed secret police. He stamped out the royalist rebellion in the west and made the rule of Paris effective in Brittany and the Vendée for the first time in years.

Napoleon also invented and used opportunities to destroy his enemies. A plot on his life in 1804 provided an excuse to attack the Jacobins, though it was the work of the royalists. Also in 1804, he violated the sovereignty of the German state of Baden to seize and execute the Bourbon duke of Enghien (1772–1804). The duke was accused of participation in a royalist plot, though Bonaparte knew him to be innocent. The action was a flagrant violation of international law and of due process. Charles Maurice de Talleyrand-Périgord (1754–1838), Bonaparte's foreign minister, later termed the act "worse than a crime—a blunder" because it provoked foreign opposition. It was popular with the former Jacobins, however, for it seemed to preclude the possibility of a Bourbon restoration. The executioner of a Bourbon was not likely to restore the royal family. The execution also seems to have put an end to royalist plots.

Document

NAPOLEON ANNOUNCES HIS SEIZURE OF POWER

On November 10, 1799 (19 Brumaire, Year VIII), the day after his successful coup, Napoleon announced his own version of what had taken place. Although he was theoretically only one of three consuls, Napoleon's proclamation showed his assumption of personal responsibility for carrying out what he considered to be the true spirit of the Revolution, and laid the groundwork for his later assumption of sole imperial power.

Which of his personal qualities does Napoleon emphasize, and how does he expect the French people to evaluate them? How does Napoleon try to present his seizure of power as legitimate? Whom does he claim to represent? Do his actions, as he describes them, defend rule by majority, or undermine it?

On my return to Paris, I found a division reigning amongst all the constituted authorities. There was no agreement but on this single point—that the constitution was half destroyed, and could by no means effect the salvation of our liberties. All the parties came to me . . . and demanded my support. I refused to be a man of any party. A council of elders invited me, and I answered to their call. [Their] plan demanded a calm and liberal examination, free from every influence and every fear. The council of elders resolved, in consequence, that the sittings of the legislative body should be removed to St. Cloud, and charged me with the disposition of the force necessary to secure its independence, I owed it, my fellow-citizens, to the soldiers who are perishing in our armies, and the national glory, acquired at the price of their blood, to accept of this command. The councils being assembled at St. Cloud, the republican troops guaranteed their safety from without; but within, assassins had established the reign of terror. . . . The majority was disorganized, the most intrepid orators were disconcerted, and the inutility of every wise proposition was made evident. I bore my indignation and my grief to the council of elders, I demanded of them to ensure the execution of their generous designs. I represented to them the maladies of their country, from which those designs originated. . . . I then repaired to the council of five hundred without arms, and my head uncovered. . . . I wished to recall to the majority their wishes, and to assure them of their power. . . . Twenty assassins threw themselves upon me, and sought my breast. The grenadiers of the legislative body, whom I had left at the door of the hall, came up and placed themselves between me and my assassins. . . . They succeeded in bearing me away. I gave orders to rescue [the president, Napoleon's brother] from their power, and six grenadiers of the legislative body brought him out of the hall. . . . The factious were intimidated, and dispersed themselves. The majority, released from their blows, entered freely and peaceably into the hall of sitting, heard the propositions which were made to them for the public safety deliberated, and prepared the salutary resolution which is to become the new and provisional law of the republic. Frenchmen! you will recognize, without doubt, in this conduct, the zeal of a soldier of liberty, and of a citizen devoted to the republic. The ideas of preservation, protection, and freedom, immediately resumed their places on the dispersion of the faction who wished to oppress the councils, and who, in making themselves the most odious of men, never cease to be the most contemptible.

From The Annual Register, or, A View of the History, Politics, and Literature for the Year 1799 (London: Otridge & Sons, 1801), p. 253.

Concordat with the Roman Catholic Church

No single set of revolutionary policies had aroused as much domestic opposition as those regarding the French Catholic Church; nor were there any other policies to which fierce supporters of the revolution seemed so attached. When the French armies had invaded Italy, they had driven Pope Pius VI (r. 1775–1799) from Rome, and he eventually died in exile in France. In 1801, to the shock and dismay of his anticlerical supporters, Napoleon concluded a concordat with Pope Pius VII (r. 1800–1823). The agreement was possible because Pius VII, before becoming pope, had written that Christianity was compatible with the ideals of equality and democracy. The concordat gave Napoleon what he most wanted. The agreement required both the refractory clergy and those who had accepted the revolution to resign. Their replacements received their spiritual investiture from the pope, but the state named the bishops and paid their salaries and the salary of one priest in each parish. In return, the church gave up its claims to its confiscated property.

The concordat declared, "Catholicism is the religion of the great majority of French citizens." This was merely a statement of fact and fell far short of what the pope had wanted: religious dominance for the Roman Catholic Church. The clergy had to swear an oath of loyalty to the state. The Organic Articles of 1802, which the government issued on its own authority without consulting the pope, established the supremacy of state over church. Similar laws were applied to the Protestant and Jewish communities, reducing still further the privileged position of the Catholic Church.

The Napoleonic Code

In 1802, a plebiscite ratified Napoleon as consul for life, and he soon produced another constitution that granted him what amounted to full power. He thereafter set about reforming and codifying French law. The result was the Civil Code of 1804, usually known as the Napoleonic Code.

The Napoleonic Code safeguarded all forms of property and tried to secure French society against internal challenges. All the privileges based on birth that the revolution had overthrown remained abolished.

The conservative attitudes toward labor and women that had emerged during the revolution also received full support. Workers' organizations remained forbidden, and workers had fewer rights than their employers. Fathers were granted extensive control over their children and husbands over their wives. However, primogeniture— the right of an eldest son to inherit most or all of his parents' property— remained abolished, and property was distributed among all children, males and females. Married women needed their husbands' consent to dispose of their own property. Divorce remained more difficult for women than for men. Before this code, French law had differed from region to region. That confused set of laws had given women opportunities to protect their interests. The universality of the Napoleonic Code ended that.

Establishing a Dynasty

In 1804, Bonaparte seized on a bomb attack on his life to make himself emperor. He argued that establishing a dynasty would make the new regime secure and make further attempts on his life useless. Another new constitution declared Napoleon Bonaparte Emperor of the French, instead of First Consul of the Republic. A plebiscite also overwhelmingly ratified this constitution.

To conclude the drama, Napoleon invited Pope Pius VII to Notre Dame to take part in the coronation. At the last minute, however, Napoleon convinced the pope to agree that the new emperor should crown himself. Napoleon would not allow anyone to think his power and authority depended on the church. Henceforth, he was called Napoleon I.

▼ The Haitian Revolution (1791–1804)

Between 1791 and 1804, the French colony of Haiti achieved independence. This event was of key importance for two reasons. First, it was sparked by policies of

Toussaint L'Ouverture (1746–1803) began the revolt that led to Haitian independence in 1804. Library of Congress

A Closer ▶ LOOK

🔍 View the Closer Look on MyHistoryLab.com

THE CORONATION OF NAPOLEON

JACQUES-LOUIS DAVID recorded the elaborate coronation of Napoleon in a monumental painting that revealed the enormous political and religious tensions of that event, which involved the kind of ritual and ceremony associated with the monarchy of the ancien régime.

Napoleon's mother sits in a balcony-like setting and presides over her son's establishment of a new reigning dynasty in France and across Europe, through the placement of relatives on various thrones.

Napoleon is about to place a crown on the head of his wife Josephine whom he will later divorce because she and he were unable to conceive an heir for his new dynasty. He would then marry the daughter of his enemy, the Habsburg emperor Francis.

Jacques-Louis David (1748–1825), *Consecration of the Emperor Napoleon I and Coronation of Empress Josephine*, 1806–07. Louvre, (Museum), Paris, France/Scala/Art Resource, NY

To the right sits Pope Pius VII who observes the event but is not a real participant. Napoleon and the pope had signed a Concordat that restored much of the standing but by no means all of the prerevolutionary authority of the Roman Catholic Church in France. The pope understood that at that moment in France as well as throughout Europe his authority was largely subject to the wishes of the French emperor.

What tools does David use to make Napoleon's singular significance apparent?

Napoleon's mother did not actually attend the coronation. Why was it important to include her in the image?

the French Revolution overflowing into its New World Empire. Second, the Haitian Revolution demonstrated that slaves of African origins could lead a revolt against white masters and mulatto freemen. The example of the Haitian Revolution for years thereafter terrified slaveholders throughout the Americas.

The relationship between slaves and masters on Haiti had been filled with violence throughout the eighteenth century. The French colonial masters had frequently used racial divisions between black slaves and mulatto freemen to their own political advantage. Once the French Revolution had broken out in France, the French National Assembly in 1791 decreed that free property-owning mulattos on Haiti should enjoy the same rights as white plantation owners. The Colonial Assembly in Haiti resisted the orders from France.

In 1791, a full-fledged slave rebellion shook Haiti. The coordination that preceded the rebellion required that slaves place a tremendous amount of faith in one another: any conversation that could have been interpreted as advocating rebellion would have led to death if reported or overheard. François-Dominique Toussaint L'Ouverture (1743?–1803), himself a former slave, quickly emerged as its leader. The rebellion involved enormous violence and loss of life on both sides. Although the slave rebellion collapsed, mulattos and free black people in Haiti, who hoped to gain the rights the French National Assembly had promised, then took up arms against the white colonial masters. French officials sent by the revolutionary government in Paris soon backed them. Slaves now came to the aid of an invading French force and, in early 1793, the French abolished slavery in Haiti.

View the **Closer Look** "The Haitian Revolution: Guerilla Warfare" on **MyHistoryLab.com**

By this time both Spain and Great Britain were attempting to intervene in Haitian events to expand their own influence in the Caribbean. Both were opposed to the end of slavery and both coveted Haiti's rich sugar-producing lands. Toussaint L'Ouverture and his force of ex-slaves again supported the French against the Spanish and the British. By 1800, his army had achieved dominance throughout the island of Hispaniola. He imposed an authoritarian constitution on Haiti and made himself Governor-General for life, but he preserved formal ties with France.

The French government under Napoleon distrusted L'Ouverture and feared that his example would undermine French authority elsewhere in the Caribbean and North America. In 1802, Napoleon sent an army to Haiti and eventually captured L'Ouverture, who was sent back to France where he died in prison in 1803. Other Haitian military leaders of slave origin, the most important of whom was Jean-Jacques Dessalines (1758–1806), continued to resist. When Napoleon found himself again at war with Britain in 1803, he decided to abandon his American empire, selling Louisiana to the United States and withdrawing his forces from Haiti. The Haitian revolution had an anticolonial aspect, but it was most important as the first successful slave rebellion in modern history. France formally recognized Haitian independence in 1804.

▼ Napoleon's Empire (1804–1814)

Between his coronation as emperor and his final defeat at Waterloo (1815), Napoleon conquered most of Europe. France's victories changed the map of the Continent. The wars put an end to the Old Regime and its feudal trappings throughout Western Europe and forced those European states that remained independent to reorganize themselves to resist Napoleon's armies.

View the **Map** "Map Discovery: Napoleon's Empire" on **MyHistoryLab.com**

Everywhere, Napoleon's advance unleashed the powerful force of nationalism, discussed more fully in Chapter 20. His weapon was the militarily mobilized French nation, one of the achievements of the revolution. Napoleon could put 700,000 men under arms at one time, risk 100,000 troops in a single battle, endure heavy losses, and fight again. He could conscript citizen soldiers in unprecedented numbers, thanks to their loyalty to the nation and to him. No single enemy could match such resources. Even coalitions were unsuccessful, until Napoleon's own mistakes led to his defeat.

Conquering an Empire

The Peace of Amiens (1802) between France and Great Britain was merely a truce. Napoleon's unlimited ambitions shattered any hope that it might last. He sent an army to restore the rebellious colony of Haiti to French rule. This move aroused British fears that he was planning a new French empire in America because Spain had restored Louisiana to France in 1801. More serious were his interventions in the Dutch Republic, the Italian peninsula, and Switzerland and his reorganization of the German states. The Treaty of Campo Formio had required a redistribution of territories along the Rhine River, and the petty princes of the region engaged in a scramble to enlarge their holdings. Among the results were the reduction of Austrian influence and the emergence of fewer, but larger, German states in the West, all dependent on Napoleon.

British Naval Supremacy Alarmed by these developments, the British issued an ultimatum. When Napoleon ignored it, Britain declared war in May 1803. William Pitt the Younger returned to office as prime minister in 1804 and began to construct the Third Coalition. By

By the time this painting was completed in 1807, Nelson was already a hero in Britain. Here he is depicted on his deathbed aboard his ship the *Victory*, during the British defeat of French and Spanish fleets at the Battle of Trafalgar in 1805. The lighting that illuminates Nelson's suffering face evokes religious paintings and suggests martyrdom. Arthur William Devis, "The Death of Nelson." Oil on canvas. The Granger Collection, NYC—

August 1805, he had persuaded Russia and Austria to move once more against France. A great naval victory soon raised the fortunes of the allies. On October 21, 1805, the British admiral Lord Nelson destroyed the combined French and Spanish fleets at the Battle of Trafalgar off the Spanish coast. Nelson died in the battle, but the British lost no ships. Although it would take ten more years before Napoleon's final defeat, Trafalgar ended all French hope of invading Britain and ensured that Britain would be able to maintain its opposition to France for the duration of the war. Britain had endeavored to establish supremacy on the high seas for centuries; now the navy dominated global commercial shipping and seemed undefeatable in military confrontation as well. The Battle of Trafalgar not only foreshadowed Napoleon's ultimate defeat by exposing French vulnerability to British strength, but also seemed the proof of a longstanding British belief that, in the words of one historian, "concentrating resources upon the navy would render Britain 'the guardian of liberty' throughout Europe."[1] Britain's dominance of the seas would not be seriously challenged until World War I.

Napoleonic Victories in Central Europe On land the story was different. Even before Trafalgar, Napoleon had marched to the Danube River to attack his continental enemies. In mid-October he forced an Austrian army to

surrender at Ulm and occupied Vienna. On December 2, 1805, in perhaps his greatest victory, Napoleon defeated the combined Austrian and Russian forces at Austerlitz. The Treaty of Pressburg that followed won major concessions from Austria. The Austrians withdrew from Italy and left Napoleon in control of everything north of Rome. He was recognized as king of Italy.

📖 Read the Document
"Charles Parquin, 'Napoleon's Army' " on **MyHistoryLab.com**

Napoleon also made extensive political changes in the German states. In July 1806, he organized the Confederation of the Rhine, which included most of the western German princes. Their withdrawal from the Holy Roman Empire led the current Holy Roman Emperor, the Habsburg Francis II, to dissolve that ancient political body and henceforth to call himself Emperor Francis I of Austria.

Prussia, which had remained neutral up to this point, now foolishly went to war against France. Napoleon's forces quickly crushed the famous Prussian army at Jena and Auerstädt on October 14, 1806. Two weeks later, Napoleon was in Berlin. There, on November 21, he issued the Berlin Decrees, forbidding his allies from importing British goods. Napoleon, too, recognized the connection between Britain's commercial and military strength. On June 13, 1807, Napoleon defeated the Russians at Friedland and occupied East Prussia. Having occupied or co-opted the west German states, humbled and humiliated Austria, and defeated Prussia, the French emperor was master of all Germany.

[1]David Armitage, *The Ideological Origins of the British Empire* (Cambridge, UK: Cambridge University Press, 2000), p. 185.

In this 1806 caricature by the famous English artist James Gillray, Napoleon is shown as a baker who creates new kings as easily as gingerbread cookies. His new allies in the Rhine Confederation, including the rulers of Württemberg, Bavaria, and Saxony, are placed in the "New French Oven for Imperial Gingerbread." 'Tiddy-Doll, the Great French Gingerbread Maker, Drawing Out a New Batch of Kings. His Man, Hopping Talley, Mixing Up the Dough', pub. by Hannah Humphrey, 23rd January 1806 (aquatint), Gillray, James (1757–1815). Leeds Museums and Galleries (City Art Gallery) U.K./The Bridgeman Art Library International

TIDDY-DOLL the great French Gingerbread-Baker, drawing out a new Batch of Kings.—his Man, Hopping Talley, mixing up the Dough.

Treaty of Tilsit Unable to fight another battle and unwilling to retreat into Russia, Tsar Alexander I (r. 1801–1825) was ready to make peace. He and Napoleon met on a raft in the Niemen River while the two armies and the nervous king of Prussia watched from the bank. On July 7, 1807, they signed the Treaty of Tilsit, which confirmed France's gains. Prussia lost half its territory. Only the support of Alexander saved it from extinction. Prussia openly and Russia secretly became allies of Napoleon.

Napoleon established his family as the collective sovereigns of Europe. The great French Empire was ruled directly by the head of the clan, Napoleon. On its borders lay satellite states ruled by members of his family. His stepson ruled Italy for him, and three of his brothers and his brother-in-law were made kings of other conquered states. The French emperor expected his relatives to take orders without question. When they failed to do so, he rebuked and even punished them. The imposition of Napoleonic rule provoked political opposition that needed only encouragement and assistance to flare up into serious resistance.

The Continental System

After the Treaty of Tilsit, such assistance could come only from Britain, and Napoleon knew he must defeat the British before he could feel safe. Unable to compete with the British navy, he continued the economic warfare the Berlin Decrees had begun. He planned to cut off all British trade with the European continent and thus to cripple British commercial and financial power. He hoped to cause domestic unrest and drive Britain from the war. The Milan Decree of 1807 went further and attempted to stop neutral nations from trading with Britain. (See Map 19–1.) Britain responded with its own set of decrees, the Orders of Council, which in turn forbid British subjects, allies, or even neutral countries from trading with France.

Despite initial drops in exports, domestic unrest, and tension between Britain and neutral countries that resented the ban, the British economy survived. British control of the seas assured access to the growing markets of North and South America and of the eastern Mediterranean. At the same time, the Continental System badly hurt the European economies. Napoleon rejected advice to turn his empire into a free-trade area. Such a policy would have been both popular and helpful. Instead, his tariff policies favored France, increased the resentment of foreign merchants, and made them less willing to enforce the system and more ready to engage in smuggling. It was, in part, to prevent smuggling that Napoleon invaded Spain in 1808. The resulting peninsular campaign in Spain and Portugal helped bring on his ruin.

▼ European Response to the Empire

Wherever Napoleon ruled, he imposed the Napoleonic Code and abolished hereditary social distinctions. Feudal privileges disappeared, and the peasants were freed from serfdom and manorial dues. In the towns, the guilds and the local oligarchies that had been dominant for

Map 19–1 THE CONTINENTAL SYSTEM, 1806–1810 Napoleon hoped to cut off all British trade with the European continent and thereby drive the British from the war.

centuries were dissolved or deprived of their power. The established churches lost their traditional independence and were made subordinate to the state. Toleration replaced monopoly of religion by an established church. Despite these reforms, however, it was always clear that Napoleon's policies were intended first for his own glory and that of France. The Continental System demonstrated that Napoleon's rule was intended to enrich France, rather than Europe generally. Consequently, before long, the conquered states and peoples grew restive.

Read the Document
"Carl von Clausewitz, On War, 'Arming the Nation' " on **MyHistoryLab.com**

German Nationalism and Prussian Reform

The German response to Napoleon's success was particularly interesting and important. There had never been a unified German state. The great German writers of the Enlightenment, such as Immanuel Kant and Gotthold Lessing, were neither deeply politically engaged nor nationalistic.

At the beginning of the nineteenth century, the Romantic Movement had begun to take hold. One of its basic features in Germany was the emergence of nationalism, which went through two distinct stages there. Initially, nationalistic writers emphasized the unique and admirable qualities of German culture, which, they argued, arose from the history of the German people. Such cultural nationalism prevailed until Napoleon's humiliation of Prussia at Jena in 1806.

At that point many German intellectuals began to urge resistance to Napoleon on the basis of German nationalism. The French conquest endangered the independence and achievements of all German-speaking people. Many nationalists also criticized the German princes, who ruled selfishly and inefficiently and who seemed ever ready to lick Napoleon's boots. Only a people united through its language and culture could resist the French onslaught. No less important in forging a German national sentiment was the example of France itself, which had attained greatness by enlisting the active support of the entire people in the patriotic cause. Henceforth, many Germans sought to solve their internal political problems by attempting to establish a unified German state, reformed to harness the energies of the entire people.

After Tilsit, only Prussia could arouse such patriotic feelings. Elsewhere German rulers were either under Napoleon's thumb or collaborating with him. Defeated, humiliated, and diminished, Prussia continued to resist,

SAILORS AND CANNED FOOD

IN 1803, DURING the Napoleonic wars, the French navy undertook a secret experiment—provisioning a few of its naval vessels involved in long overseas voyages or blockades with food preserved by the then novel process of canning. The results were excellent: The crews thrived and the French government ordered more canned goods.

Until the discovery of canning, the chief methods for preserving food were drying, salting, pickling, smoking, fermenting, and condensing. Most of these techniques are still used, but they strongly alter the taste of food and destroy some of its nutritive value. Although vitamins were unknown in the eighteenth century, military authorities did know that something in fresh fruit and vegetables kept their men healthy. In the 1790s, the French government offered a reward to anyone who could invent a method of preserving food that would make it both nearer in taste and texture to fresh products and more nourishing for sailors and soldiers who often suffered from scurvy and malnutrition from their rations of dried bread and salted meat. The desired food would allow naval vessels to stay at sea longer without having to put into port for fresh food and armies to campaign without having to live off the land.

Nicholas Appert, a French chef, was determined to produce preserved food that would be both tasty and healthful. In 1795, he established what amounted to a small food preservation laboratory on the outskirts of Paris. He eventually discovered that if he filled glass jars with fresh vegetables, fruit, soups, or meat, added water or a sauce, sealed the jars with tight stoppers, and then cooked them in a hot water bath, the result was a tasty preserved food that lasted indefinitely as long as the jars remained sealed. Although Appert did not know it, one reason the food remained unspoiled was that his process killed any microbes in it.

Although many fine French foods are still canned in jars, the process quickly took a new turn in Great Britain where the navy as well as food producers were interested in it. Appert published a book on his method in 1810, and by 1813 an English company began canning in tins, which were less expensive and more durable than glass jars. Soon other canning companies appeared in Europe, including those that produced canned sardines. By midcentury, millions of people, particularly in Western Europe and North America, were eating canned food. By 1900, canned goods had become what they remain today—part of everyday life around the world. The basic process used in canning is still the one Appert devised in the 1790s.

From Sue Shephard, *Pickled, Potted, and Canned: How the Art and Science of Food Processing Changed the World* (New York: Simon & Schuster, 2000).

Nicholas Appert (1749–1841) invented canning as a way of preserving food nutritiously. Canned food could be transported over long distances without spoiling.   Private Collection/Bridgeman Art Library

What advantages did canning have over other methods of preserving food?

Why was the military interested in it?

How did canning become a part of everyday life?

however feebly. German nationalists from other states fled to Prussia. Once there, they called for reforms and unification that King Frederick William III (r. 1797–1840) and the Junker nobility feared and hated. Reforms came about despite such opposition because the defeat at Jena had shown that the Prussian state had to change to survive.

The Prussian administrative and social reforms were the work of Baron vom Stein (1757–1831) and Prince von Hardenberg (1750–1822). Neither of these reformers intended to reduce the autocratic power of the Prussian monarch or to end the dominance of the Junkers, who formed the bulwark of the state and of the officer corps. Rather, they wanted to fight French power with their own version of France's weapons. As Hardenberg declared,

Our objective, our guiding principle, must be a revolution in the better sense, a revolution leading directly to the great goal, the elevation of humanity through the wisdom of those in authority. . . . Democratic rules of conduct in a monarchical administration, such is the formula . . . which will conform most comfortably with the spirit of the age.[2]

Although the reforms came from the top, they wrought important changes in Prussian society.

Stein's reforms broke the Junker monopoly of landholding. Serfdom was abolished. However, unlike in the western German states where all remnants of serfdom disappeared, in Prussia the Junkers ensured that vestiges of the system survived. Former Prussian serfs were free to leave the land if they chose, but those who stayed had to continue to perform manorial labor. They could obtain the ownership of the land they worked only if they forfeited a third of it to the lord. The result was that Junker holdings grew larger. Some peasants went to the cities to find work, others became agricultural laborers, and some did actually become small freeholding farmers. In Prussia and elsewhere, serfdom had ended, but the rise in the numbers of landless laborers created new social problems.

Military reforms sought to increase the supply of soldiers and to improve their quality. Jena had shown that an army of free patriots commanded by officers chosen on merit rather than by birth could defeat an army of serfs and mercenaries commanded by incompetent nobles. To remedy the situation, the Prussian reformers abolished inhumane military punishments, sought to inspire patriotic feelings in the soldiers, opened the officer corps to commoners, gave promotions on the basis of merit, and organized war colleges that developed new theories of strategy and tactics.

View the **Map**
"Interactive Map: The Unification of Germany 1815–1871" on **MyHistoryLab.com**

[2]Geoffrey Brunn, *Europe and the French Imperium* (New York: Harper & Row, 1938), p. 174.

These reforms soon enabled Prussia to regain its former power. Because Napoleon strictly limited the size of its army to 42,000 men, however, Prussia could not introduce universal conscription until it broke with Napoleon in 1813. Before that date, the Prussians evaded the limit by training one group each year, putting them into the reserves, and then training a new group the same size. Prussia could thus boast an army of 270,000 by 1814.

The Wars of Liberation

Spain In Spain more than elsewhere in Europe, national resistance to France had deep social roots. Spain had achieved political unity as early as the sixteenth century. The Spanish peasants were devoted to the ruling dynasty and especially to the Roman Catholic Church. France and Spain had been allies since 1796. In 1807, however, a French army came into the Iberian Peninsula to force Portugal to abandon its traditional alliance with Britain. The army stayed in Spain to protect lines of supply and communication. Napoleon used a revolt that broke out in Madrid in 1808 as a pretext to depose the Spanish Bourbons and to place his brother Joseph (1768–1844) on the Spanish throne. Attacks on the privileges of the church were interpreted as attacks on Catholicism itself, and increased public outrage. Many members of the upper classes were prepared to collaborate with Napoleon, but the peasants, urged on by the lower clergy and the monks, rebelled.

In Spain, Napoleon faced a new kind of warfare. Guerrilla bands cut lines of communication, killed stragglers, destroyed isolated units, and then disappeared into the mountains. The British landed an army under Sir Arthur Wellesley (1769–1852), later the duke of Wellington, to support the Spanish insurgents. Thus began the long peninsular campaign that would drain French strength from elsewhere in Europe and hasten Napoleon's eventual defeat. (See "Compare and Connect: The Experience of War in the Napoleonic Age," pages 596–597.)

Austria France's troubles in Spain encouraged Austria to renew the war in 1809. Since their defeat at Austerlitz, they had sought a war of revenge. The Austrians counted on Napoleon's distraction in Spain, French war weariness, and aid from other German princes. Napoleon was fully in command in France, however, and the German princes did not move. The French army marched swiftly into Austria and won the Battle of Wagram. The resulting Peace of Schönbrunn deprived Austria of substantial territory and 3.5 million subjects.

Another spoil of victory was the Austrian archduchess Marie Louise (1791–1847), daughter of Emperor Francis I. Napoleon's first wife, Josephine de Beauharnais (1763–1814), was forty-six and had borne him no

The Experience of War in the Napoleonic Age

📖 Read the **Compare and Connect** on **MyHistoryLab.com**

THE NAPOLEONIC WARS spread violence across Europe. Different participants, writers, and artists portrayed the experience of war differently. William Napier reported his own heroism in a quite matter-of-fact manner. The German poet and historian Ernest Moritz Arndt recalled moments of intense nationalistic patriotism. The Spanish painter Goya portrayed a moment of enormous brutality suffered by the Spanish at the hands of French troops.

QUESTIONS

1. How was the warfare in Spain different from the classic battles of the eighteenth-century? What distinguished the new "guerilla" warfare?

2. Why does Arndt claim each of these various groups wanted war?

3. How does Arndt suggest the possibility of a united nation that did not yet actually exist?

4. How does Goya portray Spaniards as victims of harsh, unmerciful military violence?

5. How do Napier's memoir, Arndt's call to arms, and Goya's painting illustrate different points of view and ways of interpreting the violence of modern warfare?

I. A Polish Legionnaire Recalls Guerilla Warfare in Spain

Heinrich von Brandt (1789–1868), was a German-speaking Prussian who lived in territory that became part of the Duchy of Warsaw in 1807. Like many Germans his age, he was a great admirer of Napoleon's accomplishments, even if he resented his violation of Prussian sovereignty. Having first trained as a member of the Prussian military (in preparation to fight against Napoleon), he was subsequently enlisted to fight in the newly constituted Polish army, allied with Napoleon. As a member of the Vistula legion, he was sent to Spain in 1808. This excerpt from his memoirs refers to the siege of Saragossa in January and February 1809.

The more we advanced the more dogged resistance became. We knew that in order not to be killed, or to diminish that risk, we would have to take each and every one of these houses converted into redoubts and where death lurked in the cellars, behind doors and shutters—in fact, everywhere. When we broke into a house we had to make an immediate and thorough inspection from the cellar to the rooftop. Experience taught us that sudden and determined resistance could well be a trick. Often as we were securing one floor we would be shot at from point blank range from the floor above through loopholes in the floorboards. All the nooks and crannies of these old-fashioned houses aided such deadly ambushes. We also had to maintain a good watch on the rooftops. With their light sandals, the Aragonese could move with the ease of and as silently as a cat and were thus able to make surprise incursions well behind the front line. It was indeed aerial combat. We would be sitting peacefully around a fire, in a house occupied for some days, when suddenly shots would come through some window just as though they had come from the sky itself. . . .

The Spanish stopped at nothing to slow our advance down. Even when they were at last forced to abandon a building, they would scatter resin soaked faggots everywhere and set them alight. The ensuing fires would not destroy the stone buildings but served to give the besieged time to prepare their defences in neighboring houses. . . .

It was all over by the evening of 20 February. . . . [The next day] the vanguard of the famous defenders of Saragossa began to appear. A certain number of young men, aged between sixteen and eighteen, without uniforms and wearing grey cloaks and red cockades, lined up in front of us, nonchalantly smoking their cigarettes. Not long after we witnessed the arrival of the rest of the army: a strange collection composed of humanity of all shades and conditions. A few were in uniform but most were dressed like peasants. . . . Most of them were of such non-military bearing that our men were saying aloud that we should never have had so much trouble in beating such a rabble. ∎

From Heinrich von Brandt, *In the Legions of Napoleon: The Memoirs of a Polish Officer in Spain and Russia, 1808–1813*, trans. and ed. Jonathan North (London: Greenhill Books, 1999), pp. 58–63.

II. A German Writer Describes the War of Liberation

Although many Germans, including Ernst Moritz Arndt (1769–1860), initially greeted the French Revolution with enthusiasm, the French Army's invasion of German territory was met with a wave of nationalist resistance. As Napoleon's army retreated from Moscow in 1813, people from virtually all German-speaking lands overcame rivalry amongst themselves to join forces against a common enemy. Arndt described the excitement of that moment in a passage subsequently reprinted in German history textbooks for more than a century.

Fired with enthusiasm, the people rose, "with God for King and Fatherland." Among the Prussians there was only one voice, one feeling, one anger and one love, to save the Fatherland and to free Germany. . . . War, war, sounded the cry from the Carpathians to the Baltic, from the Niemen to the Elbe. War! cried the nobleman and landed proprietor who had become impoverished. War! that peasant who was driving his last horse to death. . . . War! the citizen who was growing exhausted from quartering soldiers and paying taxes. War! the widow who was sending her only son to the front. War! the young girl who, with tears of pride and pain, was leaving her betrothed. . . . Even young women, under all sorts of disguises, rushed to arms; all wanted to drill, arm themselves and fight and die for the Fatherland. . . .

The most beautiful thing about all this holy zeal and happy confusion was . . . that the one great feeling for the Fatherland, its freedom and honor, swallowed all other feelings, caused all other considerations and relationships to be forgotten. ■

From Louis L., Snyder, trans., *Documents of German History*. Copyright © 1958 by Rutgers, the State University. Reprinted by permission of Rutgers University Press.

III. Francisco Goya, *The Third of May, 1808* (painted 1814–1815)

Napoleon began to send troops into Spain in 1807 after the king of Spain had agreed to aid France against Britain's ally, Portugal. By early 1808 Spain had essentially become an occupied nation. The French troops included Islamic soldiers whom Napoleon had recruited in Egypt. Many Spaniards associated French soldiers with a threat to the Catholic faith. On May 2, riots took place in Madrid between French troops and Spanish civilians. In response, the French general Murat ordered the execution of numerous citizens of Madrid, which occurred the night of May 2 and 3. The events of these two days marked the opening of the Spanish effort to rid their peninsula of French rule.

After the restoration of the Spanish monarchy, Francisco Goya (1745–1828) depicted the savagery of those executions in the most memorable war painting of the Napoleonic era, The Third of May, 1808.

There is one group of humble Spaniards who have already been shot, another in the process of execution, and a third group, some of whom are hiding their eyes, who will be the next victims.

The painting illustrates two forces of Napoleonic warfare confronting each other: the professional solider and the guerilla (a term coined during the Spanish resistance of this era). The guerilla must fight with what few resources he finds at his command and with few advanced weapons. By contrast, in this painting, the well-disciplined soldiers, equipped with modern rifles, carry out the execution by the light of large technologically advanced lanterns fueled by either gas or oil with which Napoleon equipped his troops. Goya succeeds in making ordinary people and very poor clergy not only the victims, but also symbolic heroes of the national war of liberation. ■

Francisco de Goya y Lucientes recorded Napoleon's troops executing Spanish guerilla fighters who had rebelled against the French occupation in *The Third of May, 1808*.   PRISMA/VWPICS/© Visual&Written SL / Alamy children. His dynastic ambitions, as well as the desire for a royal marriage, led him to divorce Josephine and marry the eighteen-year-old Marie Louise. Napoleon had also considered marrying the sister of Tsar Alexander, but had received a polite rebuff. The emperor of Austria, however, was in no position to refuse the match.

The Invasion of Russia

The failure of Napoleon's marriage negotiations with Russia emphasized the shakiness of the Franco–Russian alliance concluded at Tilsit. Russian nobles disliked the alliance because of the liberal politics of France and because the Continental System prohibited timber sales to Britain. Only French aid in gaining Constantinople could justify the alliance in their eyes, but Napoleon gave them no help against the Ottoman Empire. The organization of the Polish Duchy of Warsaw as a Napoleonic satellite on the Russian doorstep and its enlargement with Austrian territory in 1809 after the Battle of Wagram angered Alexander. Napoleon's annexation of Holland in violation of the Treaty of Tilsit, his recognition of the French marshal Bernadotte (1763–1844) as the future King Charles XIV of Sweden, and his marriage to Marie Louise further disturbed the tsar. At the end of 1810, Russia withdrew from the Continental System and began to prepare for war. (See Map 19–2.)

Napoleon was determined to end the Russian military threat. He amassed an army of more than 600,000 men, including a core of Frenchmen and more than 400,000 other soldiers drawn from the rest of his empire. He intended the usual short campaign crowned by a decisive battle, but the Russians retreated before his advance. His vast superiority in numbers—the Russians had only about 160,000 troops—made it foolish for them to risk a battle. Instead, they followed a "scorched-earth" policy, destroying all food and supplies as they retreated. The so-called Grand Army of Napoleon could not live off the country, and the expanse of Russia made supply lines too long to maintain. Terrible rains, fierce heat, shortages of food and water, and the courage of the Russian rear guard eroded the morale of Napoleon's army. Napoleon's advisers urged him to abandon the venture, but he feared an unsuccessful campaign would undermine his position in the empire and in France. He pinned his faith on the Russians' unwillingness to abandon Moscow without a fight.

In September 1812, Russian public opinion forced the army to give Napoleon the battle he wanted despite the canny Russian general Mikhail Kutuzov's (1745–1813) wish to let the Russian winter defeat the invader. At Borodino, not far west of Moscow, the bloodiest battle of the Napoleonic era cost the French 30,000 casualties and the Russians almost twice as many. Yet the Russian army was not destroyed. Napoleon won nothing substantial, and the battle was regarded as a defeat for him.

Napoleon underestimated the Russians' willingness to sacrifice Moscow in the interests of victory. In order to deprive French troops of food, fuel, and housing, the Russians set fire to Moscow as they abandoned the city to the invading army. Napoleon was left far from home with a badly diminished army lacking adequate supplies as winter came to a vast and unfriendly country. After capturing the burned city, Napoleon addressed several peace offers to Alexander, but the tsar ignored them. By October, what was left of the Grand Army was forced to retreat. By December, Napoleon realized the Russian fiasco would encourage plots against him at home. He returned to Paris, leaving the remnants of his army to struggle westward. Perhaps only 100,000 of the original 600,000 survived their ordeal.

European Coalition

Even as the news of the disaster reached the West, the final defeat of Napoleon was far from certain. He was able to put down his opponents in Paris and raise another 350,000 men. Neither the Prussians nor the Austrians were eager to risk another contest with Napoleon, and even the Russians hesitated. The Austrian foreign minister, Prince Klemens von Metternich (1773–1859), would have preferred to make a negotiated peace that would leave Napoleon on the throne of a shrunken and chastened France rather than see Russia dominate Europe. Napoleon might have negotiated a reasonable settlement had he been willing to make concessions that would have split his jealous opponents. He would not consider that solution, however. As he explained to Metternich,

Your sovereigns born on the throne can let themselves be beaten twenty times and return to their capitals. I cannot do this because I am an upstart soldier. My domination will not survive the day when I cease to be strong, and therefore feared.[3]

In 1813, patriotic pressure and national ambition brought together the last and most powerful coalition against Napoleon. The Russians drove westward, and Prussia and then Austria joined them. Vast amounts of British money assisted them. From Spain, Wellington marched his army into France. Napoleon's new army was inexperienced and poorly equipped. His generals had lost confidence in him and were tired. The emperor himself was worn out and sick. Still, he waged a skillful campaign in central Europe and defeated the allies at Dresden. In October, however, the combined armies of the enemy decisively defeated him at Leipzig in what the Germans called the Battle of the Nations. In March 1814, the allied armies marched into Paris. A few days later, Napoleon abdicated and went into exile on the island of Elba, off the coast of central Italy.

---

[3]Felix Markham, *Napoleon and the Awakening of Europe* (New York: Macmillan, 1965), pp. 115–116.

Map 19–2 NAPOLEONIC EUROPE IN LATE 1812   By mid-1812 the areas shown in peach were incorporated into France, and most of the rest of Europe was directly controlled by or allied with Napoleon. But Russia had withdrawn from the failing Continental System, and the decline of Napoleon was about to begin.

▼ The Congress of Vienna and the European Settlement

Fear of Napoleon and hostility to his ambitions had held the victorious coalition together. As soon as he was removed, the allies pursued their separate ambitions. Nevertheless, Robert Stewart, Viscount Castlereagh (1769–1822), the British foreign secretary, brought about the signing of the Treaty of Chaumont on March 9, 1814. It provided for the restoration of the Bourbons to the French throne and the contraction of France to its frontiers of 1792. Even more importantly, Britain, Austria, Russia, and Prussia agreed

View the **Map** "Map Discovery: Europe After the Congress of Vienna, 1815" on **MyHistoryLab.com**

to form a Quadruple Alliance for twenty years to preserve whatever settlement they agreed on. Remaining problems—and there were many—and final details were left for a conference to be held at Vienna.

Territorial Adjustments

The Congress of Vienna assembled in September 1814, but did not conclude its work until November 1815. Although a glittering array of heads of state attended the gathering, the four great powers (Britain, Russia, Prussia, and Austria) conducted the important work of the conference. The only full session of the congress met to ratify the arrangements the big four made. The easiest problem the great powers faced was France. All the victors agreed that no single state should be allowed to dominate

Europe, and all were determined to prevent France from doing so again. The restoration of the French Bourbon monarchy, which was temporarily popular, and a nonvindictive boundary settlement were designed to keep France calm and satisfied.

The powers also strengthened the states around France's borders to serve as barriers to renewed French expansion. They established the kingdom of the Netherlands, which included Belgium and Luxembourg, in the north and added the important port of Genoa to strengthen Piedmont in the south. Prussia was given important new territories along the Rhine River to deter French aggression in the West. Austria gained full control of northern Italy to prevent a repetition of Napoleon's conquests there. As for the rest of the German states, most of Napoleon's territorial arrangements were left untouched. The venerable Holy Roman Empire, which had been dissolved in 1806, was not revived. (See Map 19–3.) In all these areas, the congress established the rule of legitimate monarchs and rejected any hint of the republican and democratic policies that had flowed from the French Revolution.

On these matters agreement was not difficult, but the settlement of eastern Europe sharply divided the victors. Alexander I of Russia wanted all of Poland under his rule. Prussia was willing to give it to him in return for all of Saxony, which had been allied with Napoleon. Austria, however, was unwilling to surrender its share of Poland or to see either Prussian or Russian power in central Europe grow. The Polish–Saxon question almost caused a new war among the victors, but defeated France

provided a way out. The wily Talleyrand, now representing France at Vienna, suggested the weight of France added to that of Britain and Austria might bring Alexander to his senses. When news of a secret treaty among the three leaked out, the tsar agreed to become ruler of a smaller Poland, and Prussia settled for only part of Saxony. Thereafter, France was included as a fifth great power in all deliberations.

The Hundred Days and the Quadruple Alliance

Napoleon's return from Elba on March 1, 1815, further united the victors. The French army was still loyal to the former emperor, and many of the French people preferred his rule to that of the restored Bourbons. Napoleon escaped to France, and soon regained power. He promised a liberal constitution and a peaceful foreign policy. The allies were not convinced. They declared Napoleon an outlaw (a new device under international law) and sent their armies to crush him. Wellington, with the crucial help of the Prussians under Field Marshal von Blücher (1742–1819), defeated Napoleon at Waterloo in Belgium on June 18, 1815. Napoleon again abdicated and was exiled on Saint Helena, a tiny Atlantic island off the coast of Africa, where he died in 1821.

Read the **Document**
"Napoleon's Exile to St. Helena (1815)" on
MyHistoryLab.com

The Hundred Days, as the period of Napoleon's return is called, frightened the great powers and made the peace settlement harsher for France. In addition to some

LE CONGRÈS.

In this political cartoon of the Congress of Vienna, Tallyrand simply watches which way the wind is blowing, Castlereagh hesitates, while the monarchs of Russia, Prussia, and Austria form the dance of the Holy Alliance. The king of Saxony holds on to his crown and the republic of Geneva pays homage to the kingdom of Sardinia.   bpk, Berlin/Art Resource, NY

Map 19–3   **THE GERMAN STATES AFTER 1815**   The German states continued to cooperate in a loose confederation, but maintained their independence. Independence was not restored to the small principalities that had been eliminated during the Napoleonic era.

minor territorial adjustments, the victors imposed a war indemnity and an army of occupation on France. Alexander proposed a Holy Alliance, whereby the monarchs promised to act together in accordance with Christian principles. Austria and Prussia signed, but Castlereagh thought it absurd, and Britain abstained. The tsar, who was then embracing mysticism, believed his proposal a valuable tool for international relations. The Holy Alliance soon became a symbol of extreme political reaction.

Britain, Austria, Prussia, and Russia renewed the Quadruple Alliance on November 20, 1815. Henceforth, it was as much a coalition for maintaining peace as for pursuing victory over France. A coalition for such a purpose had never existed in European diplomacy before. It represented an important new departure in European affairs. Unlike eighteenth-century diplomacy, certain powers were determined to prevent war. The statesmen at Vienna had seen the armies of the French Revolution and Napoleon overturning the political and social order of much of the Continent. Their nations had experienced unprecedented destruction and had had to raise enormous military forces. They

knew war affected not just professional armies and navies, but entire civilian populations as well. They were determined to prevent any more such upheaval and destruction.

Consequently, the chief aims of the Congress of Vienna were to prevent a recurrence of the Napoleonic nightmare and to arrange a lasting peace. The leaders of Europe had learned that a treaty should secure not victory, but peace. The diplomats aimed to establish a framework for stability, rather than to punish France. The great powers sought to ensure that each of them would respect the Vienna settlement and not use force to change it.

Though chastened by Prussia's power and its defeat by France, Austria continued to be a powerful player in European diplomacy. Much of the credit for this goes to Metternich, who emerged as the leading statesman of Europe at the Congress of Vienna. Metternich's commitment to preventing international war by preventing domestic revolution enabled him to take the lead in a new system of cooperative conservatism that would become known as the Concert of Europe.

The Congress of Vienna achieved its goals. France accepted the new situation without undue resentment, in part because the new international order recognized it as a great power. The victorious powers settled difficult problems reasonably. They established a new legal framework whereby treaties were made between states rather than between monarchs. The treaties remained in place when a monarch died. Furthermore, during the quarter century of warfare, European leaders had come to calculate the nature of political and economic power in new ways that went beyond the simple vision of gaining a favorable balance of trade that had caused so many eighteenth-century wars. They took into account their natural resources and economies, their systems of education, and the possibility that general growth in agriculture, commerce, and industry would benefit all states and not one at the expense of others.

The Congress has been criticized for failing to recognize and provide for the great forces that would stir the nineteenth century—nationalism and democracy. Such criticism is inappropriate. At the time nationalist pressures were relatively rare; the general desire was for peace. The settlement, like all such agreements, aimed to solve past ills, and in that it succeeded. The statesmen at Vienna could not have anticipated future problems and understandably refused to yield to forces of which they disapproved and that they believed threatened international peace and stability. The measure of the success of the Vienna settlement is that it remained essentially intact for almost half a century and prevented general war for a hundred years. (See Map 19–4.)

Map 19–4 EUROPE 1815, AFTER THE CONGRESS OF VIENNA   The Congress of Vienna achieved the post-Napoleonic territorial adjustments shown on the map. The most notable arrangements dealt with areas along France's borders (the Netherlands, Prussia, Switzerland, and Piedmont) and in Poland and northern Italy.

▼ The Romantic Movement

Reflecting on the social, political, and cultural changes within Europe from the mid-eighteenth century to the Congress of Vienna, one German writer asserted in 1818, "in the three generations alive today our own age has combined what cannot be combined. No sense of continuity informs the tremendous contrast inherent in the years 1750, 1789 and 1815."[4] The years of the French Revolution and the conquests of Napoleon saw the emergence of a new and important intellectual movement throughout Europe that has come to be called **Romanticism**. The Romantic movement was a reaction against much of the thought of the Enlightenment and the social transformation of the Industrial Revolution. Not surprisingly, given its emphasis on the individual, scholars have never been able to agree on a general definition of Romanticism. There is, however, a consensus that Romanticism represented a turn toward "absolute inwardness," in the words of Hegel: an emphasis on the artist over his or her work, on the subjective experience and potential heroism of the individual, and the inability to understand the external world through reason. Romantic writers and artists thought the imagination was superior to reason as a means to perceive the world. Instead of controlling nature, they believed, people would be awestruck by it. Many of them urged a revival of Christianity, so that it would once again permeate Europe. Unlike the philosophes, the Romantics liked

[4]Tim Blanning, *The Romantic Revolution: A History* (New York: Modern Library, 2010), p. ix.

NAPOLEONIC EUROPE

1797	Napoleon concludes the Treaty of Campo Formio
1798	Nelson defeats the French navy in the harbor of Abukir in Egypt
1799	Consulate established in France
1801	Concordat between France and the papacy
1802	Treaty of Amiens
1803	War renewed between France and Britain
1804	Execution of Duke d'Enghien
1804	Napoleonic Civil Code issued
1804	Napoleon crowned as emperor
1805 (October 21)	Nelson defeats French and Spanish fleet at Trafalgar
1805 (December 2)	Austerlitz
1806	Jena
1806	Continental System established by Berlin Decrees
1807	Friedland
1807	Treaty of Tilsit; Russia becomes an ally of Napoleon
1808	Beginning of Spanish resistance to Napoleonic domination
1809	Wagram
1809	Napoleon marries Archduchess Marie Louise of Austria
1812	Invasion of Russia and French defeat at Borodino
1813	Leipzig (Battle of the Nations)
1814 (March)	Treaty of Chaumont establishes Quadruple Alliance
1814 (September)	Congress of Vienna convenes
1815 (March 1)	Napoleon returns from Elba
1815 (June 18)	Waterloo
1815 (September 26)	Holy Alliance formed at Congress of Vienna
1815 (November 20)	Quadruple Alliance renewed at Congress of Vienna
1821	Napoleon dies on Saint Helena

the art, literature, and architecture of medieval times. They were also deeply interested in folklore, folk songs, and fairy tales. Dreams, hallucinations, sleepwalking, and other phenomena that suggested the existence of a world beyond that of empirical observation, sensory data, and discursive reasoning fascinated the Romantics. Although their specific interests, tools of expression, and priorities varied, Romantics shared an alienation from what they considered to be the cold rationalism that characterized the industrial economy and Enlightenment thought.

▼ Romantic Questioning of the Supremacy of Reason

The Romantic Movement had roots in the individualism of the Renaissance, Protestant devotion and personal piety, sentimental novels of the eighteenth century, and dramatic German poetry of the *Sturm und Drang* (literally, "storm and stress") movement, which rejected the influence of French rationalism on German literature. However, two writers who were also closely related to the Enlightenment provided the immediate intellectual foundations for Romanticism: Jean-Jacques Rousseau and Immanuel Kant raised questions about whether the rationalism so dear to the philosophes was sufficient to explain human nature and be the bedrock principle for organizing human society.

Rousseau and Education

Jean-Jacques Rousseau, though sharing in the reformist spirit of the Enlightenment, opposed many of its other facets (see Chapter 17). Rousseau's conviction that society and material prosperity had corrupted human nature profoundly influenced Romantic writers.

Rousseau set forth his view on how the individual could develop to lead a good and happy life uncorrupted by society in his novel *Émile* (1762). In *Émile*, Rousseau stressed the difference between children and adults. He distinguished the stages of human maturation and urged that children be raised with maximum individual freedom. Each child should be allowed to learn by trial and error what reality is and how best to deal with it. Beyond providing the basic necessities of life and warding off what was manifestly harmful, parents and teachers should stay completely out of the way.

> **Read** the **Document**
> "Jean-Jacques Rousseau, *Émile*" on **MyHistoryLab.com**

To Romantic writers, this concept of human development vindicated the rights of nature over those of artificial society. They thought such a form of open education would eventually lead to a natural society. In its fully developed form, this view of life led the Romantics to value the uniqueness of each individual and to explore childhood in great detail. The Romantics saw humankind, nature, and society as organically interrelated.

Kant and Reason

Immanuel Kant (1724–1804) wrote the two greatest philosophical works of the late eighteenth century: *The Critique of Pure Reason* (1781) and *The Critique of Practical Reason* (1788). He sought to accept the rationalism of the Enlightenment and to still preserve a belief in human freedom, immortality, and the existence of God. For Kant, the human mind does not simply reflect the world around it like a passive mirror; rather, the mind actively imposes on the world of sensory experience "forms of sensibility" and "categories of understanding." The mind itself generates these categories. This meant that human perceptions are as much the product of the mind's own activity as of sensory experience.

Kant found the sphere of reality that was accessible to pure reason to be limited. He believed, however, that beyond the phenomenal world of sensory experience, over which "pure reason" was master, there existed what he called the "noumenal" world. This world is a sphere of moral and aesthetic reality known by "practical reason" and conscience. Kant thought all human beings possess an innate sense of moral duty or an awareness of what he called a **categorical imperative**. This term refers to an inner command to act in every situation as one would have all other people always act in the same situation. On the basis of humankind's moral sense, Kant postulated the existence of God, eternal life, and future rewards and punishments. He believed that reason alone could not prove these transcendental truths. Still, he was convinced they were realities to which every reasonable person could attest.

To many Romantic writers, Kantian philosophy refuted the narrow rationality of the Enlightenment. Whether they called it "practical reason," "fancy," "imagination," "intuition," or simply "feeling," the Romantics believed that the human mind had the power to penetrate beyond the limits of largely passive human understanding.

▼ Romantic Literature

The term *Romantic* appeared in English and French literature as early as the seventeenth century. Neoclassical writers then used the word to describe literature they considered unreal, sentimental, or excessively fanciful. Later, in both England and Germany, the term came to be applied to all literature that did not observe classical forms and rules and gave free play to the imagination. The Romantic Movement had peaked in Germany and England before it became a major force in France under the leadership of Madame de Staël (1766–1817) and Victor Hugo (1802–1885). (See the Document "Madame de Staël Describes the New Romantic Literature of Germany," page 605.) The first French writer to declare himself a Romantic was Henri Beyle (1783–1842), who wrote under the pseudonym Stendhal.

English Romantic Writers

The English Romantics believed poetry was enhanced by freely following the creative impulses of the mind. For Samuel Taylor Coleridge (1772–1834), the artist's imagination was God at work in the mind. Poetry thus could not be considered idle play. Rather, it was the highest of

human acts, humankind's self-fulfillment in a transcendental world.

Coleridge was the master of Gothic poems of the supernatural, such as "The Rime of the Ancient Mariner," which relates the story of a sailor cursed for killing an albatross. The poem treats the subject as a crime against nature and God and raises the issues of guilt, punishment, and the redemptive possibilities of humility and penance. At the end of the poem, the mariner discovers the unity and beauty of all things. Having repented, he is delivered from his awful curse, which has been symbolized by the dead albatross hung around his neck:

O happy living things! no tongue
Their beauty might declare:
A spring of love gushed from my heart,
And I blessed them unaware . . .
The self-same moment I could pray;
And from my neck so free
The Albatross fell off, and sank
Like lead into the sea.

Wordsworth William Wordsworth (1770–1850) was Coleridge's closest friend. Together they published *Lyrical Ballads* in 1798 as a manifesto of a new poetry that rejected the rules of eighteenth-century criticism. Among Wordsworth's most important later poems is his "Ode on Intimations of Immortality" (1803). Its subject is the loss of poetic vision, something Wordsworth felt then in himself. Nature, which he had worshipped, no longer spoke freely to him, and he feared it might never speak to him again:

There was a time when meadow, grove, and stream,
The earth, and every common sight,
To me did seem
Appareled in celestial light,
The glory and the freshness of a dream.
It is not now as it hath been of yore—
Turn whereso'er I may,
By night or day,
The things which I have seen I now can
see no more.

He mourned the loss of his childlike vision and closeness to spiritual reality—a loss he believed was part of the necessary process of maturation. For Wordsworth and Coleridge, childhood was the bright period of creative imagination. Aging and urban living corrupt and deaden the imagination, making inner feelings and the beauty of nature less important.

Lord Byron A true rebel among the Romantic poets was Lord Byron (1788–1824). In Britain, even most of the other Romantic writers distrusted and disliked him. Outside England, however, Byron was regarded as the embodiment of the new person the French Revolution had created. He rejected old traditions (he was divorced

Document

MADAME DE STAËL DESCRIBES THE NEW ROMANTIC LITERATURE OF GERMANY

Anne-Louise-Germaine de Staël, known generally as Madame de Staël, was the daughter of Jacques Necker, the finance minister of Louis XVI. She was also the friend of major French political liberals and a critic of Napoleonic absolutism. More importantly for European literary life, Madame de Staël visited Germany, read the emerging German Romantic literature, and introduced it to both French- and English-speaking Europe in her book Concerning Germany *(1813). In the passage that follows, she endorses the new German literature. She points to the novelty of this Romantic poetry and then relates it to a new appreciation of Christianity and the Middle Ages. She praises the medieval troubadours, composers, and performers of lyric poetry in song.*

How does de Staël characterize the new Romantic school of poetry? How does she contrast it with the literature that had its roots in ancient Greece and Rome? What is the relationship of the Middle Ages to the new poetry and other examples of the fine arts touched by Romantic sensibilities?

The word *romantic* has been lately introduced in Germany, to designate that kind of poetry which is derived from the songs of the Troubadours; that which owes its birth to the union of chivalry and Christianity. If we do not admit that the empire of literature has been divided between paganism and Christianity, the north and the south, antiquity and the middle ages, chivalry and the institutions of Greece and Rome, we shall never succeed in forming a philosophical judgment of ancient and of modern taste.

Some French critics have asserted that German literature is still in its infancy; this opinion is entirely false: men who are best skilled in the knowledge of languages, and the works of the ancients, are certainly not ignorant of the defects and advantages attached to the species of literature which they either adopt or reject; but their character, their habits, and their modes of reasoning, have led them to prefer that which is founded on the recollection of chivalry, on the wonders of the middle ages, to that which has for its basis the mythology of the Greeks. The literature of romance is alone capable of further improvement, because, being rooted in our own soil, that alone can continue to grow and acquire fresh life: it expresses our religion; it recalls our history; its origin is ancient, although not of classical antiquity. Classic poetry, before it comes home to us, must pass through our recollections of paganism; that of the Germans is the Christian era of the fine arts; it employs our personal impressions to excite strong and vivid emotions; the genius by which it is inspired addresses itself immediately to our hearts; of all phantoms at once the most powerful and the most terrible....

The new school maintains the same system in the fine arts as in literature, and affirms that Christianity is the source of all modern genius; the writers of this school also characterize, in a new manner, all that in Gothic architecture agrees with the religious sentiments of Christians....It is only of consequence to us, in the present silence of genius, to lay aside the contempt which has been thrown on all the conceptions of the middle ages.

From Madame de Staël, *Concerning Germany* (London: John Murray, 1814) as quoted in Howard E. Hugo, ed., *The Romantic Reader* (New York: Viking, 1957), pp. 64–66.

and famous for his many love affairs) and championed the cause of personal liberty. Byron was outrageously skeptical and mocking, even of his own beliefs. In *Childe Harold's Pilgrimage* (1812), he created a brooding, melancholy Romantic hero. In *Don Juan* (1819), he wrote with ribald humor, acknowledged nature's cruelty as well as its beauty, and even expressed admiration for urban life.

Mary Godwin Shelley   Mary Godwin (1797–1851) was the daughter of Mary Wollstonecraft, author of *A Vindication of the Rights of Woman*. Wollstonecraft died of puerperal fever shortly after Godwin's birth. At the age of 16, Godwin fell in love with Romantic poet Percy Bysshe Shelley, who was already married. Fleeing ostracism and scandal in England, they traveled through Europe, and married after the suicide of Shelley's first wife. While spending the summer of 1816 on Lake Geneva with their mutual friend, Lord Byron, Godwin conceived of the idea behind *Frankenstein: or, The Modern Prometheus*, which she published in 1818. Often considered the first science fiction novel, it tells the story of a Swiss doctor, Frankenstein, who deliberately creates a living being out of components of dead bodies. Frankenstein finds he has created not a beautiful creature, but instead an abhorrent "monster." When Godwin, by then Mary Shelley, was revealed as the author, contemporary critics complained that the gruesome subject matter was inappropriate for a young female mind.

The German Romantic Writers

Almost all major German Romantics wrote at least one novel. Romantic novels often were highly sentimental and borrowed material from medieval romances. The

George Gordon, Lord Byron (1788–1824), chose Albanian attire for this portrait. A famous supporter of the Greek Revolution, which would cost him his life (he died of fever in Greece in 1824), Byron proudly suggested he was capable of embodying many different personalities and participating in different cultural traditions. In England, his personal life was considered scandalous.   The Granger Collection, New York

characters of Romantic novels were treated as symbols of the larger truth of life. Purely realistic description was avoided. Friedrich Schlegel (1767–1845) wrote the progressive early Romantic novel *Lucinde* (1799) that attacked prejudices against women as capable of being little more than lovers and domestics. Schlegel's novel reveals the ability of the Romantics to become involved in the social issues of their day. He depicted Lucinde as the perfect friend and companion, as well as the unsurpassed lover, of the hero. The work shocked contemporary morals by frankly discussing sexual activity and by describing Lucinde as equal to the male hero.

Goethe   Perhaps the greatest German writer of modern times, Johann Wolfgang von Goethe (1749–1832) defies easy classification. Part of his literary production fits into the Romantic mold, and part of it was a condemnation of Romantic excesses. The book that made his early reputation was *The Sorrows of Young Werther*, published in 1774. This novel, like many in the eighteenth century, is a series of letters. The hero falls in love with Lotte, who is married to another man. Eventually Werther and Lotte part, but in his grief, Werther takes his own life. This novel became popular throughout Europe. Romantic authors admired its emphasis on feeling and on living outside the bounds of polite society.

Read the **Document**
"Johann Wolfgang von Goethe, *Prometheus*, 1773" on
MyHistoryLab.com

Goethe's masterpiece was *Faust*, a long dramatic poem. Part I, published in 1808, tells the story of Faust, who makes a pact with the devil—he will exchange his soul for greater knowledge than other human beings possess. As the story progresses, Faust seduces a young woman named Gretchen. She dies but is received into heaven as the grief-stricken Faust realizes he must continue to live. At the conclusion of Part II, completed in 1832, Faust dedicates his life, or what remains of it, to the improvement of humankind. He feels this goal will allow him to overcome the restless striving that induced him to make the pact with the devil. That new knowledge breaks the pact. Faust dies and is received by angels.

▼ Romantic Art

The art of the Romantic Era, like its poetry and philosophy, stood largely in reaction to that of the eighteenth century. Whereas the Rococo artists had looked to Renaissance models and Neo-Classical painters to the art of the ancient world, Romantic painters often portrayed scenes from medieval life. For them, the Middle Ages represented the social stability and religious reverence that was disappearing from their own era.

Document

MARY SHELLEY REMEMBERS THE BIRTH OF A MONSTER

✜

Mary Wollstonecraft Godwin Shelley thought of the idea for her most famous novel, Frankenstein, *while spending a summer on Lake Geneva with her future husband, Percy Shelley, and their friend, Lord Byron. In the 1831 edition of the novel, published after Percy Shelley's death, she reflects on the genesis of the story in a manner that emphasizes the importance of imagination and the limits of enlightenment through science.*

How does Shelley describe the creative process? How can her message be interpreted as a criticism of the Enlightenment?

My imagination, unbidden, possessed and guided me, gifting the successive images that arose in my mind with a vividness far beyond the usual bound of reverie. I saw—with shut eyes, but acute mental vision—I saw the pale student of hallowed arts kneeling beside the thing he had put together. I saw the hideous phantasm of a man stretched out, and then, on the working of some powerful engine, show signs of life, and stir with an uneasy, half-vital motion. Frightful must it be; for supremely frightful would be the effect of any human endeavor to mock the stupendous mechanism of the Creator of the world. His success would terrify the artist; he would rush away from his odious handiwork, horror-stricken. He would hope that, left to itself, the slight spark of life which he had communicated, would fade, that this thing which had received such imperfect animation, would subside into dead matter; and he might sleep in the belief that the silence of the grave would quench for ever the transient existence of the hideous corpse which he had looked upon as the cradle of life. He sleeps: but he is awakened; he opens his eyes: behold the horrid thing stands at this beside, opening his curtains, and looking on him with yellow, watery, but speculative eyes.

I opened mine in terror.

From Mary W. Shelley, *Frankenstein; or, The Modern Prometheus* (Boston: Sever, Francis & Co, 1869), pp. 11–12.

PUBLICATION DATES OF MAJOR ROMANTIC WORKS

1762	Rousseau's *Émile*
1774	Goethe's *Sorrows of Young Werther*
1781	Kant's *Critique of Pure Reason**
1788	Kant's *Critique of Practical Reason**
1798	Wordsworth and Coleridge's *Lyrical Ballads*
1799	Schlegel's *Lucinde*
1799	Schleiermacher's *Speeches on Religion to Its Cultured Despisers*
1802	Chateaubriand's *Genius of Christianity*
1806	Hegel's *Phenomenology of Mind*
1808	Goethe's *Faust*, Part I
1812	Byron's *Childe Harold's Pilgrimage*
1819	Byron's *Don Juan*
1825	Scott's *Tales of the Crusaders*
1841	Carlyle's *On Heroes and Hero-Worship*

*Kant's books were not themselves part of the Romantic Movement, but they were fundamental to later Romantic writers.

The Cult of the Middle Ages and Neo-Gothicism

Like many early Romantic artists, English landscape painter John Constable (1776–1837) was politically conservative. In *Salisbury Cathedral from the Meadows*, he portrayed a stable world in which neither political turmoil nor industrial development challenged the traditional dominance of the church and the landed classes. Although the clouds and sky in the painting depict a severe storm, the works of both nature (the trees) and humankind (the cathedral) present a powerful sense of enduring order. Constable saw the church and the British constitution as intimately related. Like many English conservatives of his day, he expected religious institutions to deter political radicalism.

Constable and other Romantics tended to idealize rural life because they believed it opposed the increasingly urban, industrializing, commercial society that was developing around them. In fact, the rural landscape and rustic society that Constable depicted in his paintings had already largely disappeared from England.

View the **Closer Look** "Cult of the Unattainable" on **MyHistoryLab.com**

The Neo-Gothic revival in architecture dotted the European landscape with modern imitations of medieval structures. Many medieval cathedrals were restored during this era, and new churches were designed to resemble their medieval forerunners. The British Houses of Parliament built in 1836–1837 were the most famous public buildings in the Neo-Gothic style, but town halls, schools, and even railroad stations were designed to look like medieval buildings, while aristocratic country houses were rebuilt to resemble medieval castles.

Nature and the Sublime

Beyond their attraction to history, Romantic artists also sought to portray nature in all of its majestic power as no previous generation of European artists had ever done. Like Romantic poets, the artists of the era were drawn toward the mysterious and unruly side of nature rather than toward the rational Newtonian order that had prevailed during the Enlightenment. Their works often sought to portray what they and others termed *the sublime*—that is, subjects from nature that aroused strong emotions, such as fear, dread, and awe, and raised questions about whether and how much we control our lives. Painters often traveled to remote areas such as the Scottish Highlands or the Swiss Alps to portray dangerous scenes from nature

that would immediately grip and engage the viewer's emotions.

Romantics saw nature as a set of infinite forces that overwhelmed the smallness of humankind. For example, in 1824, the German artist Caspar David Friedrich (1774–1840) in *The Polar Sea* painted the plight of a ship trapped and crushed by the force of a vast polar ice field. In direct contrast to eighteenth-century artists' portrayal of sunny Enlightenment, Friedrich also painted numerous scenes in which human beings stand shrouded in the mysterious darkness of night where moonlight and torches cast only fitful illumination.

An artist who similarly understood the power of nature but also depicted the forces of the new industrialism that was challenging them was Joseph Mallord William Turner (1775–1851) whose painting *Rain, Steam and Speed—The Great Western Railway* of 1844 illustrated the recently invented railway engine barreling through an enveloping storm. In this scene the new technology is both part of the natural world and strong enough to dominate it.

Friedrich's and Turner's paintings taken together symbolize the contradictory forces affecting Romantic artists—the sense of the power, awe, and mastery of nature coupled with the sense that the advance of industry represented a new kind of awesome human power that could challenge or even surpass the forces of nature itself.

John Constable's *Salisbury Cathedral from the Meadows* displays the appeal of Romantic art to both medieval monuments and the sublime power of nature. Art Resource, NY. © The National Gallery, London

Caspar David Friedrich's *The Polar Sea* illustrated the power of nature to diminish the creations of humankind as seen in the wrecked ship on the right of the painting.   Kunsthalle, Hamburg, Germany/A.K.G., Berlin/ SuperStock

▼ Religion in the Romantic Period

During the Middle Ages, the foundation of religion had been the authority of the church. The Reformation leaders had appealed to the authority of the Bible. Then, many Enlightenment writers attempted to derive religion from the rational nature revealed by Newtonian physics, while others attacked it altogether. Romantic religious thinkers, in contrast, sought the foundations of religion in the inner emotions of humankind. Reacting to the anticlericalism of both the Enlightenment and the French Revolution, these thinkers also saw religious faith and institutions as central to human life. One of

the first great examples of a religion characterized by Romantic impulses—Methodism—arose in mid-eighteenth-century England during the Enlightenment itself and became one of the most powerful forces in transatlantic religion during the nineteenth century.

Methodism

Methodism originated in the middle of the eighteenth century as a revolt against deism and rationalism in the Church of England. The Methodist revival formed an important part of the background of English Romanticism.

Joseph Mallord William Turner's *Rain, Steam, and Speed—The Great Western Railway* captured the tensions many Europeans felt between their natural environment and the new technology of the industrial age.   Joseph Mallord William Turner, 1775–1851, *Rain, Steam, and Speed—The Great Western Railway 1844*. Oil on canvas, 90.8 × 121.9. The National Gallery, London/Art Resource, NY

The leader of the Methodist movement was John Wesley (1703–1791). His mother, Susannah Wesley, who bore eighteen children, had carefully supervised his education and religious development.

After studying at Oxford University to be an Anglican priest, Wesley left England for missionary work in the new colony of Georgia in America, where he arrived in 1735. While he was crossing the Atlantic, a group of German Moravians on the ship deeply impressed him with their unshakable faith and confidence during a storm. When he returned to England, Wesley began to worship with Moravians in London. There, in 1739, he underwent a conversion experience that he described in the words, "My heart felt strangely warmed."

Wesley began to preach in the open fields near the cities and towns of western England. Thousands of humble people responded to his message of repentance and good works. Soon he and his brother Charles (1707–1788), who became famous for his hymns, began to organize Methodist societies. By the late eighteenth century, the Methodists had become a separate church. They ordained their own clergy and sent missionaries to America.

Methodism stressed inward, heartfelt religion and the possibility of Christian perfection in this life. Methodist preachers emphasized the role of enthusiastic, emotional experience as part of Christian conversion. After Wesley, religious revivals became highly emotional in style and content.

New Directions in Continental Religion

Similar religious developments based on feeling appeared on the Continent. After the Thermidorian Reaction, a strong Roman Catholic revival took place in France. Its followers disapproved of both the religious policy of the revolution and the anticlericalism of the Enlightenment. The most important book to express these sentiments was *The Genius of Christianity* (1802) by Viscount François René de Chateaubriand (1768–1848). In this work, which became known as the "bible of Romanticism," Chateaubriand argued that the essence of religion is "passion." The foundation of faith in the church was the emotion that its teachings and sacraments inspired in the heart of the Christian.

Against the Newtonian view of the world and of a rational God, the Romantics found God immanent in nature. No one stated the Romantic religious ideal more eloquently or with greater impact on the modern world than Friedrich Schleiermacher (1768–1834). In 1799, he published a response to both Lutheran orthodoxy and Enlightenment rationalism, *Speeches on Religion to Its Cultured Despisers*. According to Schleiermacher, religion was an intuition or feeling of absolute dependence on an infinite reality.

Although Schleiermacher considered Christianity the "religion of religions," he also believed every world religion was unique in its expression of the primal intuition of the infinite in the finite. He thus turned against the universal natural religion of the Enlightenment, which he termed "a name applied to loose, unconnected impulses," and defended the meaningfulness of the numerous world religions. Schleiermacher interpreted the religions of the world in the same way that other Romantic writers interpreted the variety of unique peoples and cultures.

▼ Romantic Views of Nationalism and History

A distinctive feature of Romanticism, especially in Germany, was its glorification of both the individual person and individual cultures. Behind these views lay the philosophy of German idealism, which understood the world as the creation of subjective egos. J. G. Fichte (1762–1814), an important German philosopher and nationalist, identified the individual ego with the Absolute that underlies all existing things. According to Fichte, the world is as it is because especially strong persons conceive of it in a particular way and impose their wills on the world and other people. Napoleon served as the contemporary example of such a great person. This philosophy has ever since served to justify the glorification of great persons and their actions in overriding all opposition to their will and desires.

Herder and Culture

In addition to this philosophy, the influence of new historical studies lay behind the German glorification of individual cultures. German Romantic writers went in search of their own past in reaction to the copying of French manners in eighteenth-century Germany, the impact of the French Revolution, and the imperialism of Napoleon. An early leader in this effort was Johann Gottfried Herder (1744–1803), already discussed in Chapter 17 as a critic of European colonialism. In 1778, Herder published an influential essay, "On the Knowing and Feelings of the Human Soul." In it, he vigorously rejected the Enlightenment's mechanical explanation of nature. He saw human beings and societies as developing organically, like plants, over time.

Herder revived German folk culture by urging the collection and preservation of distinctive German songs and sayings. His most important followers in this work were the Grimm brothers, Jakob (1785–1863) and Wilhelm (1786–1859), famous for their collection of fairy tales. Believing each language and culture were the unique expression of a people, Herder opposed both the concept and the use of a "common" language, such as French, and "universal" institutions, such as those Napoleon had imposed on Europe. These, he believed, were forms of tyranny over the individuality of a people. Herder's writings led to a broad revival of interest in history and philosophy. Although initially directed toward identifying German origins, such work soon expanded to embrace other world cultures. Eventually the ability of the Romantic imagination to be at home in any age or culture spurred the study of non-Western religion, comparative literature, and philology.

Hegel and History

The most important philosopher of history in the Romantic period was the German Georg Wilhelm Friedrich Hegel (1770–1831). He is one of the most complicated and significant philosophers in the history of Western civilization.

Hegel believed ideas develop in an evolutionary fashion that involves conflict. At any given time, a predominant set of ideas, which he termed the *thesis*, holds sway. Conflicting ideas, which Hegel termed the *antithesis*, challenge the thesis. As these patterns of thought clash, a *synthesis* emerges that eventually becomes the new thesis. Then the process begins all over again. Periods of world history receive their character from the patterns of thought that predominate during them. (See the Document "Hegel Explains the Role of Great Men in History," page 612.)

Several important philosophical conclusions followed from this analysis. One of the most significant was the belief that all periods of history have been of almost equal value because each was, by definition, necessary to the achievements of those that came later. Also, all cultures are valuable because each contributes to the necessary clash of values and ideas that allows humankind to develop. Hegel discussed these concepts in *The Phenomenology of Mind* (1806), *Lectures on the Philosophy of History* (1822–1831), and other works, many of which were published only after his death. During his lifetime, his ideas became widely known through his university lectures at Berlin.

Islam, the Middle East, and Romanticism

The new religious, literary, and historical sensibilities of the Romantic period modified the European understanding of both Islam and the Arab world while at the same time preserving long-standing attitudes.

The energized Christianity associated with Methodist-like forms of Protestantism, on the one hand, and Chateaubriand's emotional Roman Catholicism, on the other, renewed the traditional sense of necessary conflict between Christianity and Islam. Chateaubriand wrote a travelogue of his journey from Paris to Jerusalem in 1811. A decade later, when he was a member of the French parliament, he invoked the concept of a crusade against the Muslim world in a speech on the danger posed by the Barbary pirates of North Africa.

The medieval Crusades against Islam fired the Romantic imagination. Nostalgic European artists painted from a Western standpoint the great moments of the Crusades including the bloody capture of Jerusalem. Stories from those conflicts filled historical novels such as *Tales of the Crusaders* (1825) by Sir Walter Scott (1771–1832). Although they presented heroic images of Muslim warriors, these paintings and novels ignored the havoc that the crusaders had visited on the peoples of the Middle East.

When Napoleon invaded Egypt in 1799, he met stiff resistance. On July 25, however, the French won a decisive victory. This painting of that battle by Baron Antoine Gros (1771–1835) emphasizes French heroism and Muslim defeat. Such an outlook was typical of European views of Arabs and the Islamic world. Antoine Jean Gros (1771–1835). Detail, *Battle of Aboukir, July 25, 1799*, c. 1806. Oil on canvas. Chateaux de Versailles et de Trianon, Versailles, France. Giraudon/Art Resource, NY

Document

HEGEL EXPLAINS THE ROLE OF GREAT MEN IN HISTORY

Hegel believed that behind the development of human history from one period to the next lay the mind and purpose of what he termed the World-Spirit, a concept somewhat like the Christian God. Hegel thought particular heroes from the past (such as Caesar) and in the present (such as Napoleon) were the unconscious instruments of that spirit. In this passage from his lectures on the philosophy of history, Hegel explained how these heroes could change history. All these concepts are characteristic of the Romantic belief that human beings and human history are always intimately connected with larger, spiritual forces at work in the world. The passage also reflects the widespread belief of the time that the world of civic or political action pertained to men and that of the domestic sphere belonged to women.

How might the career of Napoleon have inspired this passage? What are the antidemocratic implications of this passage? In this passage, do great men make history or do historical developments make great men? Why do you think Hegel does not associate this power of shaping history with women as well as men?

Such are all great historical men—whose own particular aims involve those large issues which are the will of the World-Spirit. They may be called Heroes, inasmuch as they have derived their purposes and their vocation, not from the calm, regular course of things, sanctioned by the existing order, but from a concealed fount—one which has not attained to phenomenal, present existence—from that inner Spirit, still hidden beneath the surface, which, impinging on the outer world as on a shell, bursts it in pieces, because it is another kernel than that which belonged to the shell in question. They are men, therefore, who appear to draw the impulse of their life from themselves; and whose deeds have produced a condition of things and a complex of historical relations which appear to be only their interest, and their work.

Such individuals had no consciousness of the general Idea they were unfolding, while prosecuting those aims of theirs; on the contrary, they were practical, political men. But at the same time they were thinking men, who had an insight into the requirements of the time—what was ripe for development. This was the very Truth for their age, for their world; the species next in order, so to speak, and which was already formed in the womb of time. It was theirs to know this nascent principle; the necessary, directly sequent step in progress, which their world was to take; to make this their aim, and to expend their energy in promoting it. World historical men—the Heroes of an epoch—must, therefore, be recognized as its clear-sighted ones; their deeds, their words are the best of that time.

From G. W. F. Hegel, *The Philosophy of History*, trans. by J. Sibree (New York: Dover, 1956), pp. 30–31. Reprinted by permission.

The general nineteenth-century association of nationalistic aspirations with Romanticism also cast the Ottoman Empire and with it Islam in an unfavorable political light. Romantic poets and intellectuals championed the cause of the Greek Revolution (see Chapter 20) and revived older charges of Ottoman despotism.

By contrast, other Romantic sensibilities induced Europeans to see the Muslim world in a more positive fashion. The Romantic emphasis on the value of literature drawn from different cultures and ages allowed many nineteenth-century European readers to enjoy the stories from

The Thousand and One Nights, which first appeared in English in 1778 from a French translation. In 1859, Edward FitzGerald (1809–1883) published his highly popular translation of the *Rubáiyát of Omar Khayyám* of Nishapur, a Persian poet of the twelfth century.

Read the Document
"The Rubaiyat (11th c. C.E.) Omar Khayyam" on
MyHistoryLab.com

Herder's and Hegel's concepts of history gave both the Arab peoples and Islam distinct roles in history. For Herder, Arab culture was one of the numerous communities that composed the human race and manifested the human spirit. The Prophet Muhammad, while giving voice to the ancient spirit of the Arab people, had drawn them from a polytheistic faith to a great monotheistic vision. For Hegel, Islam represented an important stage of the development of the world spirit. However, Hegel believed Islam had fulfilled its role in history and no longer had any significant part to play. These outlooks, which penetrated much nineteenth-century intellectual life, made it easy for Europeans to believe that Islam could, for all practical purposes, be ignored or reduced to a spent historical force.

British historian and social commentator Thomas Carlyle (1795–1881) attributed new, positive qualities to Muhammad himself. Carlyle disliked the Enlightenment's disparagement of religion and spiritual values and was drawn to German theories of history. In his book *On Heroes and Hero-Worship* (1841), Carlyle presented Muhammad as the embodiment of the hero as prophet. He repudiated the traditional Christian and general Enlightenment view of Muhammad as an impostor. (See Chapter 17.) To Carlyle, Muhammad appeared as a person who had experienced God subjectively and had communicated a sense of the divine to others. Although friendly to Muhammad from a historical standpoint, Carlyle nonetheless saw him as one of many great religious figures and not, as Muslims believed, as the last of the prophets through whom God had spoken.

The person whose actions in the long run did perhaps the most to reshape the idea of both Islam and the Middle East in the European imagination was Napoleon himself. With his Egyptian expedition of 1798, the first European military invasion of the Near East since the Crusades, the study of the Arab world became an important activity within French intellectual life. For his invasion of Egypt to succeed, Napoleon believed he must make it clear he had no intention of destroying Islam but rather sought to liberate Egypt from the military clique that governed the country in the name of the Ottoman Empire. To that end, he took with him scholars of Arabic and Islamic culture whom he urged to converse with the most educated people they could meet. Napoleon personally met with the local Islamic leaders and had all of his speeches and proclamations translated into classical Arabic. Such cultural sensitivity and the serious efforts of the French scholars to learn Arabic and study the Qur'an impressed Egyptian scholars. (When the French sought to levy new taxes, however, the Egyptians' enthusiasm waned.)

It was on this expedition that the famous Rosetta Stone was discovered. Now housed in the British Museum, it eventually led to the decipherment of ancient Egypt's hieroglyphic writing. Napoleon's scholars also published a twenty-three volume *Description of Egypt* (1809–1828), which concentrated largely on ancient Egypt. Their approach suggested the history of the Ottoman Empire needed to be related first to the larger context of Egyptian history and that Islam, although enormously important, was only part of a larger cultural story. The implication was that if Egypt and Islam were to be understood, it would be through European—if not necessarily Christian—categories of thought.

Two cultural effects in the West of Napoleon's invasion were an increase in the number of European visitors to the Middle East and a demand for architecture based on ancient Egyptian models. Perhaps the most famous example of this fad is the Washington Monument in Washington, D.C., which is modeled after ancient Egyptian obelisks.

In Perspective

Romantic ideas made a major contribution to the emergence of nationalism, which proved to be one of the strongest motivating forces of the nineteenth and twentieth centuries. The writers of the Enlightenment had generally championed a cosmopolitan outlook on the world. By contrast, the Romantic thinkers emphasized the individuality and worth of each separate people and culture. A people or a nation was defined by a common language, history, and customs and by the possession of a historical homeland. This cultural nationalism gradually became transformed into a political creed. It came to be widely believed that every people, ethnic group, or nation should constitute a separate political entity and that only when it so existed could the nation be secure in its own character.

France under the revolutionary government and Napoleon had demonstrated the power of nationhood. Other peoples came to desire similar strength and confidence. Napoleon's toppling of ancient political structures, such as the Holy Roman Empire, proved the need for new political organization in Europe. By 1815, only a few Europeans aspired to this, but as time passed, peoples from Ireland to Ukraine came to share these yearnings. The Congress of Vienna could ignore such feelings, but for the rest of the nineteenth century, as shall be seen in subsequent chapters, statesmen had to confront the growing power these feelings had unleashed.

KEY TERMS

categorical imperative (p. 604)

Consulate (p. 586)
Methodism (p. 609)

romanticism (p. 602)
Sturm und Drang (p. 603)

REVIEW QUESTIONS

1. How did Napoleon rise to power? What groups supported him? What were his major domestic achievements? Did his rule fulfill or betray the French Revolution? What sort of challenge did the Haitian Revolution pose to France's commitment to liberty, equality, and fraternity?
2. What regions made up Napoleon's realm, and what was the status of each region within it? Did his administration show foresight, or was the empire a burden he could not afford?
3. Why did Napoleon decide to invade Russia? Why did the operation fail?

4. What were the results of the Congress of Vienna? Was the Vienna settlement a success?
5. Why did Romantic writers champion feelings over reason? What questions did Rousseau and Kant raise about reason?
6. Why was poetry important to Romantic writers? How did the Romantic concept of religion differ from Reformation Protestantism and Enlightenment deism? How did Romantic ideas and sensibilities modify European ideas of Islam and the Middle East? What were the cultural results of Napoleon's invasion of Egypt?

SUGGESTED READINGS

E. Behler, *German Romantic Literary Theory* (1993). A clear introduction to a difficult subject.

D. Bell, *The First Total War: Napoleon's Europe and the Birth of Warfare as We Know It* (2007). A consideration of the Napoleonic conflicts and the culture of warfare.

G. E. Bentley, *The Stranger from Paradise: A Biography of William Blake* (2001). Now the standard work.

T. Blanning. *The Romantic Revolution: A History* (2010). A new synthesis.

N. Boyle, *Goethe* (2001). A challenging two-volume biography.

M. Broers, *Europe under Napoleon 1799–1815* (2002). Examines the subject from the standpoint of those Napoleon conquered.

T. Chapman, *Congress of Vienna: Origins, Processes, and Results* (1998). A clear introduction to the major issues.

P. Dwyer, *Napoleon: The Path to Power, 1769–1799* (2008). A major study of the subject.

P. Dwyer, *Talleyrand* (2002). A useful account of his diplomatic influence.

S. Englund, *Napoleon: A Political Life* (2004). A thoughtful recent biography.

C. Esdaile, *The Peninsular War: A New History* (2003). A narrative of the Napoleonic wars in Spain.

A. Forrest, *Napoleon's Men: The Soldiers of the Revolution and Empire* (2002). An examination of the troops rather than their commander.

H. Honour, *Romanticism* (1979). Still the best introduction to Romantic art, well illustrated.

F. Kagan, *The End of the Old Order: Napoleon and Europe, 1801–1805* (2006). A masterful narrative.

S. Körner, *Kant* (1955). A classic brief, clear introduction.

J. Lusvass, *Napoleon on the Art of War* (2001). A collection of Napoleon's own writings.

J. J. McGann and J. Soderholm, eds., *Byron and Romanticism* (2002). Essays on the poet who most embodied Romantic qualities to the people of his time.

R. Muir, *Tactics and the Experience of Battle in the Age of Napoleon* (1998). A splendid account of troops in battle.

T. Pinkard, *Hegel: A Biography* (2000). A long but accessible study.

N. Roe, *Romanticism: An Oxford Guide* (2005). A series of informative essays.

P. W. Schroeder, *The Transformation of European Politics, 1763–1848* (1994). A major synthesis of the diplomatic history of the period, emphasizing the new departures of the Congress of Vienna.

I. Woloch, *Napoleon and His Collaborators: The Making of a Dictatorship* (2001). A key study by one of the major scholars of the subject.

A. Zamoyski, *Rites of Peace: The Fall of Napoleon and the Congress of Vienna* (2007). A lively analysis and narrative.

MyHistoryLab MEDIA ASSIGNMENTS

Find these resources in the Media Assignments folder for Chapter 19 on **MyHistoryLab**.

QUESTIONS FOR ANALYSIS

1. What is the role of the pope in this ceremony?

   Section: **The Haitian Revolution (1791–1804)**
   View the **Closer Look** The Coronation of Napoleon, p. 589

2. Why do you think the author felt such loyalty toward Napoleon?

   Section: **Napoleon's Empire (1804–1814)**
   Read the **Document** Charles Parquin, "Napoleon's Army," p. 591

3. As the German lands became absorbed into a single state, what was the general direction of that state's growth?

Section: **European Response to the Empire**

View the **Map** Interactive Map: The Unification of Germany, 1815–1871, p. 595

4. How does this author describe and rationalize Napoleon's attitudes towards Muslims in Egypt?

Section: **The Rise of Napoleon Bonaparte**

Read the **Document** Louis Antoine Fauvelet de Bourrienne, *Memoirs of Napoleon Bonaparte*, p. 586

5. How does this passage illustrate some of the tendencies of romanticism?

Section: **Romantic Questioning of the Supremacy of Reason**

Read the **Document** Jean-Jacques Rousseau, *Émile*, p. 603

OTHER RESOURCES FROM THIS CHAPTER

The Rise of Napoleon Bonaparte

Read the **Document** Madame de Remusat on the Rise of Napoleon, p. 585

The Haitian Revolution (1791–1804)

View the **Closer Look** The Haitian Revolution: Guerilla Warfare, p. 590

Napoleon's Empire (1804–1814)

View the **Map** Map Discovery: Napoleon's Empire, p. 590

European Response to the Empire

Read the **Document** Carl von Clausewitz, On War, "Arming the Nation," p. 593

Read the **Compare and Connect** The Experience of War in the Napoleonic Age, p. 596

The Congress of Vienna and the European Settlement

View the **Map** Map Discovery: Europe After the Congress of Vienna, 1815, p. 599

Read the **Document** Napoleon's Exile to St. Helena (1815), p. 600

Romantic Literature

Read the **Document** Johann Wolfgang von Goethe, *Prometheus*, 1773, p. 606

Romantic Art

View the **Closer Look** Cult of the Unattainable, p. 607

Romantic Views of Nationalism and History

Read the **Document** The Rubaiyat (11th c. CE) Omar Khayyam, p. 612

GLOSSARY

Academy A center of philosophical investigation and a school for training statesmen and citizens that was founded by Plato in 386 B.C.E.

Acropolis (ACK-row-po-lis) The religious and civic center of Athens. It is the site of the Parthenon.

Act of Supremacy The declaration by Parliament in 1534 that Henry VIII, not the pope, was the head of the church in England.

agape (AG-a-pay) Meaning "love feast." A common meal that was part of the central ritual of early Christian worship.

agora (AG-o-rah) The Greek marketplace and civic center. It was the heart of the social life of the *polis*.

Agricultural Revolution The innovations in farm production that began in the eighteenth century and led to a scientific and mechanized agriculture.

Albigensians (Al-bi-GEN-see-uns) Thirteenth-century advocates of a dualist religion. They took their name from the city of Albi in southern France. Also called *Cathars*.

Anabaptists Protestants who insisted that only adult baptism conformed to Scripture.

anarchists Those who believe that government and social institutions are oppressive and unnecessary and society should be based on voluntary cooperation among individuals.

Anschluss (AHN-shluz) Meaning "union." The annexation of Austria by Germany in March 1938.

anti-Semitism Prejudice, hostility, or legal discrimination against Jews.

apartheid (a-PAR-tid) An official policy of segregation, assignment of peoples to distinct regions, and other forms of social, political, and economic discrimination based on race associated primarily with South Africa.

Apostolic Succession The Christian doctrine that the powers given by Jesus to his original disciples have been handed down from bishop to bishop through ordination.

appeasement The Anglo-French policy of making concessions to Germany in the 1930s to avoid a crisis that would lead to war. It assumed that Germany had real grievances and Hitler's aims were limited and ultimately acceptable.

Areopagus The governing council of Athens, originally open only to the nobility. It was named after the hill on which it met.

arete (AH-ray-tay) Manliness, courage, and the excellence appropriate to a hero. It was considered the highest virtue of Homeric society.

Arianism (AIR-ee-an-ism) The belief formulated by Arius of Alexandria (ca. 280–336 C.E.) that Jesus was a created being, neither fully man nor fully God, but something in between. It did away with the doctrine of the Trinity.

aristocratic resurgence Term applied to the eighteenth-century aristocratic efforts to resist the expanding power of European monarchies.

atomist School of ancient Greek philosophy founded in the fifth century B.C.E. by Leucippus of Miletus and Democritus of Abdera. It held that the world consists of innumerable, tiny, solid, indivisible, and unchangeable particles called *atoms*.

Attica (AT-tick-a) The region of Greece where Athens is located.

Augsburg Confession (AWGS-berg) The definitive statement of Lutheran belief made in 1530.

autocracy (AW-to-kra-see) Government in which the ruler has absolute power.

Axis The alliance between Nazi Germany and fascist Italy. Also called the *Pact of Steel*.

banalities Exactions that the lord of a manor could make on his tenants.

baroque (bah-ROWK) A style of art marked by heavy and dramatic ornamentation and curved rather than straight lines that flourished between 1550 and 1750. It was especially associated with the Catholic Counter-Reformation.

Beguines (bi-GEENS) Lay sisterhoods not bound by the rules of a religious order.

benefices Church offices granted by the ruler of a state or the pope to an individual. It also meant *fiefs* in the Middle Ages.

bishop Originally a person elected by early Christian congregations to lead them in worship and supervise their funds. In time, bishops became the religious and even political authorities for Christian communities within large geographical areas.

Black Death The bubonic plague that killed millions of Europeans in the fourteenth century.

blitzkrieg (BLITZ-kreeg) Meaning "lightning war." The German tactic early in World War II of employing fast-moving, massed armored columns supported by airpower to overwhelm the enemy.

Bolsheviks Meaning the "majority." Term Lenin applied to his faction of the Russian Social Democratic Party. It became the Communist Party of the Soviet Union after the Russian Revolution.

boyars The Russian nobility.

Brezhnev doctrine Statement by Soviet party chairman Brezhnev in 1968 that declared the right of the Soviet Union to interfere in the domestic policies of other communist countries.

Bronze Age The name given to the earliest civilized era, c. 4000 to 1000 B.C.E. The term reflects the importance of the metal bronze, a mixture of tin and copper, for the peoples of this age for use as weapons and tools.

Caesaropapism (SEE-zer-o-PAY-pi-zim) The direct involvement of the ruler in religious doctrine and practice as if he were the head of the church as well as the state.

caliphate (KAH-li-fate) The true line of succession to Muhammad.

categorical imperative According to Emmanuel Kant (1724–1804), the internal sense of moral duty or awareness possessed by all human beings.

catholic Meaning "universal." The body of belief held by most Christians enshrined within the church.

censor Official of the Roman republic charged with conducting the census and compiling the lists of citizens and members of the Senate. They could expel senators for financial or moral reasons. Two censors were elected every five years.

Chartism The first large-scale European working-class political movement. It sought political reforms that would favor the interests of skilled British workers in the 1830s and 1840s.

chiaroscuro (kyar-eh-SKEW-row) The use of shading to enhance naturalness in painting and drawing.

civilization A form of human culture marked by urbanism, metallurgy, and writing.

civilizing mission The concept that Western nations could bring advanced science and economic development to non-Western parts of the world that justified imperial administration.

clientage (KLI-ent-age) The custom in ancient Rome whereby men became supporters of more powerful men in return for legal and physical protection and economic benefits.

Cold War The ideological and geographical struggle between the United States and its allies and the USSR and its allies that began after World War II and lasted until the dissolution of the USSR in 1989.

collectivization The bedrock of Stalinist agriculture, which forced Russian peasants to give up their private farms and work as members of collectives, large agricultural units controlled by the state.

coloni (CO-loan-ee) Farmers or sharecroppers on the estates of wealthy Romans.

Commonwealthmen British political writers whose radical republican ideas influenced the American revolutionaries.

concentration camps Camps first established by Great Britain in South Africa during the Boer War to incarcerate non-combatant civilians; later, camps established for political prisoners and other persons deemed dangerous to the state in the Soviet Union and Nazi Germany. The term is now primarily associated with the camps established by the Nazis during the Holocaust.

Concert of Europe Term applied to the European great powers acting together (in "concert") to resolve international disputes between 1815 and the 1850s.

conciliar theory The argument that General Councils were superior in authority to the pope and represented the whole body of the faithful.

condottieri (con-da-TEE-AIR-ee) Military brokers who furnished mercenary forces to the Italian states during the Renaissance.

Congregationalists Congregationalists put a group or assembly above any one individual and prefer an ecclesiastical polity that allows each congregation to be autonomous, or self-governing.

congress system A series of international meetings among the European great powers to promote mutual cooperation between 1818 and 1822.

conquistadores (kahn-KWIS-teh-door-hez) Meaning "conquerors." The Spanish conquerors of the New World.

conservatism Support for the established order in church and state. In the nineteenth century, it implied support for legitimate monarchies, landed aristocracies, and established churches. Conservatives favored only gradual, or "organic," change.

Consulate French government dominated by Napoleon from 1799 to 1804.

consuls (CON-suls) The two chief magistrates of the Roman state.

consumer revolution The vast increase in both the desire and the possibility of consuming goods and services that began in the early eighteenth century and created the demand for sustaining the Industrial Revolution.

containment The U.S. policy during the Cold War of resisting Soviet expansion and influence in the expectation that the USSR would eventually collapse.

Convention French radical legislative body from 1792 to 1794.

Corn Laws British tariffs on imported grain that protected the price of grain grown within the British Isles.

Counter-Reformation The sixteenth-century reform movement in the Roman Catholic Church in reaction to the Protestant Reformation.

creed A brief statement of faith to which true Christians should adhere.

creoles (KRAY-ol-ez) Persons of Spanish descent born in the Spanish colonies.

Crusades Religious wars directed by the church against infidels and heretics.

cubism A radical new departure in early-twentieth-century Western art. This term was first coined to describe the paintings of Pablo Picasso and Georges Braque.

culture The ways of living built up by a group and passed on from one generation to another.

cuneiform (Q-nee-i-form) A writing system invented by the Sumerians that used a wedge-shaped stylus, or pointed tool, to write on wet clay tablets that were then baked or dried (*cuneus* means "wedge" in Latin). The writing was also cut into stone.

Curia (CURE-ee-a) The papal government.

Cynic School (SIN-ick) A fourth-century philosophical movement that ridiculed all religious observances and turned away from involvement in the affairs of the *polis*. Its most famous exemplar was Diogenes of Sinope (ca. 400–325 B.C.E.).

deacon Meaning "those who serve." In early Christian congregations, deacons assisted the presbyters, or elders.

decolonization The process of European retreat of colonial empires following World War II.

deism A belief in a rational God who had created the universe but then allowed it to function without his interference according to the mechanisms of nature and a belief in rewards and punishments after death for human action.

Delian League (DEE-li-an) An alliance of Greek states under the leadership of Athens that was formed in 478–477 B.C.E. to resist the Persians. In time the league was transformed into the Athenian Empire.

deme (DEEM) A small town in Attica or a ward in Athens that became the basic unit of Athenian civic life under the democratic reforms of Clisthenes in 508 B.C.E.

détente French for "relaxation," the easing of strained relations, especially in a political situation.

divine right of kings The theory that monarchs are appointed by and answerable only to God.

domestic system of textile production Method of producing textiles in which agents furnished raw materials to households whose members spun them into thread and then wove cloth, which the agents then sold as finished products.

Donatism The heresy that taught the efficacy of the sacraments depended on the moral character of the clergy who administered them.

Duce (DO-chay) Meaning "leader." Mussolini's title as head of the Fascist Party.

electors Nine German princes who had the right to elect the Holy Roman Emperor.

émigrés (em-ee-GRAYS) French aristocrats who fled France during the Revolution.

empiricism (em-PEER-ih-cism) The use of experiment and observation derived from sensory evidence to construct scientific theory or philosophy of knowledge.

enclosures The consolidation or fencing in of common lands by British landlords to increase production and achieve greater commercial profits. It also involved the reclamation of waste land and the consolidation of strips into block fields.

encomienda (en-co-mee-EN-da) The grant by the Spanish crown to a colonist of the labor of a specific number of Indians for a set period of time.

Enlightenment The eighteenth-century movement led by the *philosophes* that held that change and reform were both desirable through the application of reason and science.

Epicureans (EP-i-cure-ee-ans) School of philosophy founded by Epicurus of Athens (342–271 B.C.E.). It sought to liberate people from fear of death and the supernatural by teaching that the gods took no interest in human affairs and that true happiness consisted in pleasure, which was defined as the absence of pain. This could be achieved by attaining *ataraxia*, freedom from trouble, pain, and responsibility by withdrawing from business and public life.

equestrians (EE-quest-ree-ans) Literally "cavalrymen" or "knights." In the earliest years of the Roman Republic those who could afford to serve as mounted warriors. The equestrians evolved into a social rank of well-to-do businessmen and middle-ranking officials. Many of them supported the Gracchi.

Estates General The medieval French parliament. It consisted of three separate groups, or "estates": clergy, nobility, and commoners. It last met in 1789 at the outbreak of the French Revolution.

Etruscans (EE-trus-cans) A people of central Italy who exerted the most powerful external influence on the early Romans. Etruscan kings ruled Rome until 509 B.C.E.

Eucharist (YOU-ka-rist) Meaning "thanksgiving." The celebration of the Lord's Supper. Considered the central ritual of worship by most Christians. Also called *Holy Communion*.

euro The common currency created by the EEC in the late 1990s.

European Constitution A treaty adopted in 2004 by European Union member nations; it was a long, detailed, and highly complicated document involving a bill of rights and complex economic and political agreements among all the member states.

European Economic Community (EEC) The economic association formed by France, Germany, Italy, Belgium, the Netherlands, and Luxembourg in 1957. Also known as the *Common Market*.

European Union The new name given to the EEC in 1993. It included most of the states of Western Europe.

existentialism The post–World War II Western philosophy that holds human beings are totally responsible for their acts and that this responsibility causes them dread and anguish.

family economy The basic structure of production and consumption in preindustrial Europe.

fascism Political movements that tend to be antidemocratic, anti-Marxist, antiparliamentary, and often anti-Semitic. Fascists were invariably nationalists and exalted the nation over the individual. They supported the interests of the middle class and rejected the ideas of the French Revolution and nineteenth-century liberalism. The first fascist regime was founded by Benito Mussolini (1883–1945) in Italy in the 1920s.

fealty An oath of loyalty by a vassal to a lord, promising to perform specified services.

feudal society (FEW-dull) The social, political, military, and economic system that prevailed in the Middle Ages and beyond in some parts of Europe.

fiefs Land granted to a vassal in exchange for services, usually military.

foederati (FAY-der-ah-tee) Barbarian tribes enlisted as special allies of the Roman Empire.

Fourteen Points President Woodrow Wilson's (1856–1924) idealistic war aims.

Fronde (FROHND) A series of rebellions against royal authority in France between 1649 and 1652.

Führer (FYOOR-er) Meaning "leader." The title taken by Hitler when he became dictator of Germany.

Gallican Liberties The ecclesiastical independence of the French crown and the French Roman Catholic church from papal authority in Rome.

Gaul (GAWL) Modern France.

ghettos Separate communities in which Jews were required by law to live.

glasnost (GLAZ-nohst) Meaning "openness." The policy initiated by Mikhail Gorbachev (MEEK-hail GORE-buh-choff) in the 1980s of permitting open criticism of the policies of the Soviet Communist Party.

Glorious Revolution The largely peaceful replacement of James II by William and Mary as English monarchs in 1688. It marked the beginning of constitutional monarchy in Britain.

Golden Bull The agreement in 1356 to establish a seven-member electoral college of German princes to choose the Holy Roman Emperor.

Great Depression A prolonged worldwide economic downturn that began in 1929 with the collapse of the New York Stock Exchange.

Great Purges The imprisonment and execution of millions of Soviet citizens by Stalin between 1934 and 1939.

Great Reform Bill (1832) A limited reform of the British House of Commons and an expansion of the electorate to include a wider variety of the propertied classes. It laid the groundwork for further orderly reforms within the British constitutional system.

Great Schism The appearance of two and at times three rival popes between 1378 and 1415.

Great Trek The migration by Boer (Dutch) farmers during the 1830s and 1840s from regions around Cape Town into the eastern and northeastern regions of South Africa that ultimately resulted in the founding of the Orange Free State and Transvaal.

Green movement A political environmentalist movement that began in West Germany in the 1970s and spread to a number of other Western nations.

guilds Associations of merchants or craftsmen that offered protection to their members and set rules for their work and products.

hacienda (ha-SEE-hen-da) A large landed estate in Spanish America.

Hegira (HEJ-ear-a) The flight of Muhammad and his followers from Mecca to Medina in 622 C.E. It marks the beginning of the Islamic calendar.

heliocentric theory (HE-li-o-cen-trick) The theory, now universally accepted, that the earth and the other planets revolve around the sun. First proposed by Aristarchos of Samos (310–230 B.C.E.). Its opposite, the geocentric theory, which was dominant until the sixteenth century C.E., held that the sun and the planets revolved around the earth.

Hellenistic A term coined in the nineteenth century to describe the period of three centuries during which Greek culture spread far from its homeland to Egypt and deep into Asia.

Helots (HELL-ots) Hereditary Spartan serfs.

heretics (HAIR-i-ticks) People whose beliefs were contrary to those of the Catholic Church.

hieroglyphics (HI-er-o-gli-phicks) The complicated writing script of ancient Egypt. It combined picture writing with pictographs and sound signs. Hieroglyph means "sacred carvings" in Greek.

Holocaust The Nazi extermination of millions of European Jews between 1940 and 1945. Also called the "final solution to the Jewish problem."

Holy Roman Empire The revival of the old Roman Empire, based mainly in Germany and northern Italy, that endured from 870 to 1806.

home rule The advocacy of a large measure of administrative autonomy for Ireland within the British Empire between the 1880s and 1914.

Homo sapiens (HO-mo say-pee-ans) The scientific name for human beings, from the Latin words meaning "Wise man." *Homo sapiens* emerged some 200,000 years ago.

honestiores (HON-est-ee-or-ez) The Roman term formalized from the beginning of the third century C.E. to denote the privileged classes: senators, equestrians, the municipal aristocracy, and soldiers.

hoplite phalanx (FAY-lanks) The basic unit of Greek warfare in which infantrymen fought in close order, shield to shield, usually eight ranks deep. The phalanx perfectly suited the farmer-soldier-citizen who was the backbone of the *polis*.

hubris (WHO-bris) Arrogance brought on by excessive wealth or good fortune. The Greeks believed it led to moral blindness and divine vengeance.

Huguenots (HYOU-gu-nots) French Calvinists.

humanitas (HEW-man-i-tas) The Roman name for a liberal arts education.

humiliores (HEW-mi-lee-orez) The Roman term formalized at the beginning of the third century C.E. for the lower classes.

Hussites (HUS-Its) Followers of John Huss (d. 1415) who questioned Catholic teachings about the Eucharist.

iconoclasm (i-KON-o-kla-zoom) A heresy in Eastern Christianity that sought to ban the veneration of sacred images, or icons.

id, ego, superego The three entities in Sigmund Freud's model of the internal organization of the human mind. The id consists of the amoral, irrational instincts for self-gratification. The superego embodies the external morality imposed on the personality by society. The ego mediates between the two and allows the personality to cope with the internal and external demands of its existence.

Iliad and the *Odyssey*, **The** (ILL-ee-ad) (O-dis-see) Epic poems by Homer about the "Dark Age" heroes of Greece who fought at Troy. The poems were written down in the eighth century B.C.E. after centuries of being sung by bards.

imperialism The extension of a nation's authority over other nations or areas through conquest or political or economic hegemony.

Imperialism of Free Trade The advance of European economic and political interests in the nineteenth century by demanding that non-European nations allow European nations, most particularly Great Britain, to introduce their manufactured goods freely into all nations or to introduce other goods, such as opium into China, that allowed those nations to establish economic influence and to determine the terms of trade.

imperium (IM-pear-ee-um) In ancient Rome, the right to issue commands and to enforce them by fines, arrests, and even corporal and capital punishment.

indulgence Remission of the temporal penalty of punishment in purgatory that remained after sins had been forgiven.

Industrial Revolution Mechanization of the European economy that began in Britain in the second half of the eighteenth century.

Inquisition A tribunal created by the Catholic Church in the mid-twelfth century to detect and punish heresy.

insulae (IN-sul-lay) Meaning "islands." The multistoried apartment buildings of Rome in which most of the inhabitants of the city lived.

Intolerable Acts Measures passed by the British Parliament in 1774 to punish the colony of Massachusetts and strengthen Britain's authority in the colonies. The laws provoked colonial opposition, which led immediately to the American Revolution.

investiture controversy The medieval conflict between the church and lay rulers over who would control bishops and abbots, symbolized by the ceremony of "investing" them with the symbols of their authority.

Ionia (I-o-knee-a) The part of western Asia Minor heavily colonized by the Greeks.

Islam (IZ-lahm) Meaning "submission." The religion founded by the prophet Muhammad.

Jacobins (JACK-uh-bins) The radical republican party during the French Revolution that displaced the Girondins.

Jacquerie (jah-KREE) Revolt of the French peasantry.

Jansenism A seventeenth-century movement within the Catholic Church that taught that human beings were so corrupted by original sin that they could do nothing good nor secure their own salvation without divine grace. (It was opposed to the Jesuits.)

jihad Literally meaning "a struggle," but commonly interpreted as a religious war.

Junkers (YOONG-kerz) The noble landlords of Prussia.

jus gentium (YUZ GEN-tee-um) Meaning "law of peoples." The body of Roman law that dealt with foreigners.

jus naturale (YUZ NAH-tu-rah-lay) Meaning "natural law." The Stoic concept of a world ruled by divine reason.

Ka'ba (KAH-bah) A black meteorite in the city of Mecca that became Islam's holiest shrine.

Kristallnacht (KRIS-tahl-NAHKT) Meaning "crystal night" because of the broken glass that littered German streets after the looting and destruction of Jewish homes, businesses, and synagogues across Germany on the orders of the Nazi Party in November 1938.

Kulturkampf (cool-TOOR-cahmff) Meaning the "battle for culture." The conflict between the Roman Catholic Church and the government of the German Empire in the 1870s.

laissez-faire (lay-ZAY-faire) French phrase meaning "allow to do." In economics the doctrine of minimal government interference in the working of the economy.

Late Antiquity The multicultural period between the end of the ancient world and the birth of the Middle Ages, 250–800 C.E.

latifundia (LAT-ee-fun-dee-a) Large plantations for growing cash crops owned by wealthy Romans.

Latium (LAT-ee-um) The region of Italy in which Rome is located. Its inhabitants were called *Latins*.

League of Nations The association of sovereign states set up after World War I to pursue common policies and avert international aggression.

Lebensraum (LAY-benz-rauhm) Meaning "living space." The Nazi plan to colonize and exploit the Slavic areas of Eastern Europe for the benefit of Germany.

levée en masse (le-VAY en MASS) The French revolutionary conscription (1792) of all males into the army and the harnessing of the economy for war production.

liberal arts The medieval university program that consisted of the *trivium* (TRI-vee-um): grammar, rhetoric, and logic, and the *quadrivium* (qua-DRI-vee-um): arithmetic, geometry, astronomy, and music.

Logos (LOW-goz) Divine reason, or fire, which according to the Stoics was the guiding principle in nature. Every human had a spark of this divinity, which returned to the eternal divine spirit after death.

Lollards (LALL-erds) Followers of John Wycliffe (d. 1384) who questioned the supremacy and privileges of the pope and the church hierarchy.

Lower Egypt The Nile delta.

Luftwaffe (LUFT-vaff-uh) The German air force in World War II.

Lyceum The name of the school founded by Aristotle when he returned to Athens in 336 B.C.E.

Magna Carta (MAG-nuh CAR-tuh) The "Great Charter" limiting royal power that the English nobility forced King John to sign in 1215.

mandates The assigning of the former German colonies and Turkish territories in the Middle East to Britain, France, Japan, Belgium, Australia, and South Africa as de facto colonies under the vague supervision of the League of Nations with the hope that the territories would someday advance to independence.

mannerism A style of art in the mid- to late-sixteenth century that permitted artists to express their own "manner" or feelings in contrast to the symmetry and simplicity of the art of the High Renaissance.

manors Village farms owned by a lord.

Marshall Plan The U.S. program named after Secretary of State George C. Marshall of providing economic aid to Europe after World War II.

Marxism The theory of Karl Marx (1818–1883) and Friedrich Engels (FREE-drick ENG-ulz) (1820–1895) that history is the result of class conflict, which will end in the inevitable triumph of the industrial proletariat over the bourgeoisie and the abolition of private property and social class.

Mein Kampf (MINE KAHMFF) Meaning *My Struggle*. Hitler's statement of his political program, published in 1924.

Mensheviks Meaning the "minority." Term Lenin applied to the majority moderate faction of the Russian Social Democratic Party opposed to him and the Bolsheviks.

mercantilism Term used to describe close government control of the economy that sought to maximize exports and accumulate as much precious metals as possible to enable the state to defend its economic and political interests.

Mesopotamia (MEZ-o-po-tay-me-a) Modern Iraq. The land between the Tigris and Euphrates Rivers where the first civilization appeared around 3000 B.C.E.

Messiah (MESS-eye-a) The redeemer whose coming Jews believed would establish the kingdom of God on earth. Christians considered Jesus to be the Messiah (*Christ* means Messiah in Greek).

Methodism An English religious movement begun by John Wesley (1703–1791) that stressed inward, heartfelt religion and the possibility of attaining Christian perfection in this life.

Minoan (MIN-o-an) The Bronze Age civilization that arose in Crete in the third and second millennia B.C.E.

modernism The movement in the arts and literature in the late nineteenth and early twentieth centuries to create new aesthetic forms and to elevate the aesthetic experience of a work of art above the attempt to portray reality as accurately as possible.

Monasticism A movement in the Christian church that arose first in the East in the third and fourth centuries C.E. in which first individual hermits and later organized communities of men and women (monks and nuns) separated themselves from the world to lead lives in imitation of Christ. In the West the Rule of St. Benedict (c. 480–547) became the dominant form of monasticism.

Monophysites (ma-NO-fiz-its) Adherents of the theory that Jesus had only one nature.

monotheism The worship of one universal God.

Mycenaean (MY-cen-a-an) The Bronze Age civilization of mainland Greece that was centered at Mycenae.

nationalism The belief that one is part of a nation, defined as a community with its own language, traditions, customs, and history that distinguish it from other nations and make it the primary focus of a person's loyalty and sense of identity.

NATO North Atlantic Treaty Organization. An alliance of countries from North America and Europe committed to fulfilling the goals of the North Atlantic Treaty signed on April 4, 1949.

natural selection The theory originating with Darwin that organisms evolve through a struggle for existence in which those that have a marginal advantage live long enough to propagate their kind.

Nazis The German Nationalist Socialist Party.

Neoclassicism An artistic movement that began in the 1760s and reached its peak in the 1780s and 1790s. This movement was a reaction against the frivolously decorative Rococo style that had dominated European art from the 1720s on.

Neolithic Age (NEE-o-lith-ick) The shift beginning 10,000 years ago from hunter-gatherer societies to settled communities of farmers and artisans. Also called the Age of Agriculture, it witnessed the invention of farming, the domestication of plants and animals, and the development of technologies such as pottery and weaving. The earliest Neolithic societies appeared in the Near East about 8000 B.C.E. "Neolithic" comes from the Greek words for "new stone."

Neoplatonism (KNEE-o-play-ton-ism) A religious philosophy that tried to combine mysticism with classical and rationalist speculation. Its chief formulator was Plotinus (205–270 C.E.).

New Economic Policy (NEP) A limited revival of capitalism, especially in light industry and agriculture, introduced by Lenin in 1921 to repair the damage inflicted on the Russian economy by the Civil War and war communism.

New Imperialism The extension in the late nineteenth and early twentieth centuries of Western political and economic dominance to Asia, the Middle East, and Africa.

nomes Regions or provinces of ancient Egypt governed by officials called *nomarchs*.

Old Regime Term applied to the pattern of social, political, and economic relationships and institutions that existed in Europe before the French Revolution.

optimates (OP-tee-ma-tes) Meaning "the best men." Roman politicians who supported the traditional role of the Senate.

orthodox Meaning "holding the right opinions." Applied to the doctrines of the Catholic Church.

Paleolithic (PAY-lee-o-lith-ick) The earliest period when stone tools were used, from about 1,000,000 to 10,000 B.C.E. From the Greek meaning "old stone."

Panhellenic (PAN-hell-en-ick) ("all-Greek") The sense of cultural identity that all Greeks felt in common with each other.

Pan-Slavism The movement to create a nation or federation that would embrace all the Slavic peoples of Eastern Europe.

papal infallibility The doctrine that the pope is infallible when pronouncing officially in his capacity as head of the church on matters of faith and morals, enumerated by the First Vatican Council in 1870.

Papal States Territory in central Italy ruled by the pope until 1870.

parlements (par-luh-MAHNS) French regional courts dominated by hereditary nobility. The most important was the *Parlement* of Paris, which claimed the right to register royal decrees before they could become law.

parliamentary monarchy The form of limited or constitutional monarchy set up in Britain after the Glorious Revolution of 1689 in which the monarch was subject to the law and ruled by the consent of parliament.

patrician (PA-tri-she-an) The hereditary upper class of early Republican Rome.

Peloponnesian Wars (PELL-o-po-knees-ee-an) The protracted struggle between Athens and Sparta to dominate Greece between 465 and Athens's final defeat in 404 B.C.E.

Peloponnesus (PELL-o-po-knee-sus) The southern peninsula of Greece where Sparta was located.

peninsulares (pen-in-SUE-la-rez) Persons born in Spain who settled in the Spanish colonies.

perestroika (pare-ess-TROY-ka) Meaning "restructuring." The attempt in the 1980s to reform the Soviet government and economy.

petite bourgeoisie (peh-TEET BOOSH-schwa-zee) The lower middle class.

pharaoh (FAY-row) The god-kings of ancient Egypt. The term originally meant "great house" or palace.

Pharisees (FAIR-i-sees) The group that was most strict in its adherence to Jewish law.

philosophes (fee-lou-SOPHS) The eighteenth-century writers and critics who forged the new attitudes favorable to change. They sought to apply reason and common sense to the institutions and societies of their day.

Phoenicians (FA-nee-shi-ans) The ancient inhabitants of modern Lebanon. A trading people, they established colonies throughout the Mediterranean.

physiocrats Eighteenth-century French thinkers who attacked the mercantilist regulation of the economy, advocated a limited economic role for government, and believed that all economic production depended on sound agriculture.

Platonism Philosophy of Plato that posits preexistent Ideal Forms of which all earthly things are imperfect models.

plebeian (PLEB-bee-an) The hereditary lower class of early Republican Rome.

pogroms (PO-grohms) Organized riots against Jews in the Russian Empire.

polis (PO-lis) (plural, *poleis*) The basic Greek political unit. Usually, but incompletely, translated as "city-state," the Greeks thought of the *polis* as a community of citizens theoretically descended from a common ancestor.

political absolutism A model of political development embodied by France in the seventeenth century. The French monarchy was able to build a secure financial base that was not deeply dependent on the support of noble estates, diets, or assemblies, and so it achieved absolute rule.

politiques Rulers or people in positions of power who put the success and well-being of their states above all else.

polytheists (PAH-lee-thee-ists) Those who worship many gods.

pontifex maximus (PON-ti-feks MAK-suh-muss) Meaning "supreme priest." The chief priest of ancient Rome. The title was later assumed by the popes.

Popular Front A government of all left-wing parties that took power in France in 1936 to enact social and economic reforms.

populares (PO-pew-lar-es) Roman politicians who sought to pursue a political career based on the support of the people rather than just the aristocracy.

positivism The philosophy of Auguste Comte that science is the final, or positive, stage of human intellectual development because it involves exact descriptions of phenomena, without recourse to unobservable operative principles, such as gods or spirits.

Postimpressionism A term used to describe European painting that followed impressionism; the term actually applies to several styles of art all of which to some extent derived from impression or stood in reaction to impressionism.

Pragmatic Sanction The legal basis negotiated by the Emperor Charles VI (r. 1711–1740) for the Habsburg succession through his daughter Maria Theresa (r. 1740–1780).

predestination The doctrine that God had foreordained all souls to salvation (the "elect") or damnation. It was especially associated with Calvinism.

presbyters (PRESS-bi-ters) Meaning "elder." People who directed the affairs of early Christian congregations.

Presbyterians Scottish Calvinists and English Protestants who advocated a national church composed of semiautonomous congregations governed by "presbyteries."

proconsulship (PRO-con-sul-ship) In Republican Rome, the extension of a consul's imperium beyond the end of his term of office to allow him to continue to command an army in the field.

protectorates (pro-TEC-tor-ates) Non-Western territories administered by Western nations without formal conquest or annexation, usually de facto colonies.

Ptolemaic systems (tow-LEM-a-ick) The pre-Copernican explanation of the universe, with the earth at the center of the universe, originated in the ancient world.

Puritans English Protestants who sought to "purify" the Church of England of any vestiges of Catholicism.

Qur'an (kuh-RAN) Meaning "a reciting." The Islamic bible, which Muslims believe God revealed to the prophet Muhammad.

racism The pseudoscientific theory that biological features of race determine human character and worth.

realist The style of art and literature that seeks to depict the physical world and human life with scientific objectivity and detached observation.

Reformation The sixteenth-century religious movement that sought to reform the Roman Catholic Church and led to the establishment of Protestantism.

regular clergy Monks and nuns who belong to religious orders.

Reichstag (RIKES-stahg) The German parliament, which existed in various forms, until 1945.

Reign of Terror The period between the summer of 1793 and the end of July 1794 when the French revolutionary state used extensive executions and violence to defend the Revolution and suppress its alleged internal enemies.

Rococo An artistic style that embraced lavish, often lighthearted decoration with an emphasis on pastel colors and the play of light.

Romanitas (row-MAN-ee-tas) Meaning "Roman-ness." The spread of the Roman way of life and the sense of identifying with Rome across the Roman Empire.

romanticism A reaction in early-nineteenth-century literature, philosophy, and religion against what many considered the excessive rationality and scientific narrowness of the Enlightenment.

SA The Nazi parliamentary forces, or storm troopers.

sans-culottes (SAHN coo-LOTS) Meaning "without knee-breeches." The lower-middle classes and artisans of Paris during the French Revolution.

Scholasticism Method of study based on logic and dialectic that dominated the medieval schools. It assumed that truth already existed; students had only to organize, elucidate, and defend knowledge learned from authoritative texts, especially those of Aristotle and the Church Fathers.

scientific revolution The sweeping change in the scientific view of the universe that occurred in the sixteenth and seventeenth centuries. The new scientific concepts and the method of their construction became the standard for assessing the validity of knowledge in the West.

scutage Monetary payments by a vassal to a lord in place of the required military service.

Second Industrial Revolution The emergence of new industries and the spread of industrialization from Britain to other countries, especially Germany and the United States, in the second half of the nineteenth century.

secular clergy Parish clergy who did not belong to a religious order.

Sejm (SHEM) The legislative assembly of the Polish nobility.

September Massacres The executions or murders of about 1200 people who were in the Paris city jails (mostly common criminals) by the Parisian mob in the first week of September 1792 during the French Revolution.

serf A peasant tied to the land he tilled.

Shi'a (SHE-ah) The minority of Muslims who trace their beliefs from the caliph Ali who was assassinated in 661 C.E.

Social Darwinism The application of Darwin's concept of "the survival of the fittest" to explain evolution in nature to human social relationships.

socialist realism Established as the official doctrine of Soviet art and literature in 1934, it sought to create optimistic and easily intelligible scenes of a bold socialist future, in which prosperity and solidarity would reign.

spheres of influence A region, city, or territory where a non-Western nation exercised informal administrative influence through economic, diplomatic, or military advisors.

spinning jenny A machine invented in England by James Hargreaves around 1765 to mass-produce thread.

SS The chief security units of the Nazi state.

Stoic (STOW-ick) A philosophical school founded by Zeno of Citium (335–263 B.C.E.) that taught that humans could only be happy with natural law. Human misery was caused by passion, which was a disease of the soul. The wise sought *apatheia*, freedom from passion.

studia humanitatis (STEW-dee-a hew-MAHN-ee-tah-tis) During the Renaissance, a liberal arts program of study that embraced grammar, rhetoric, poetry, history, philosophy, and politics.

Sturm und Drang (SHTURM und DRAHNG) Meaning "storm and stress." A movement in German romantic literature and philosophy that emphasized feeling and emotion.

suffragettes British women who lobbied and agitated for the right to vote in the early twentieth century.

Sunnis Those who follow the "tradition" (sunna) of the Prophet Muhammad. They are the dominant movement within Islam to which the vast majority of Muslims adhere.

symposium (SIM-po-see-um) The carefully organized drinking party that was the center of Greek aristocratic social life. It featured games, songs, poetry, and even philosophical disputation.

syncretism (SIN-cret-ism) The intermingling of different religions to form an amalgam that contained elements from each.

Table of Ranks An official hierarchy established by Peter the Great in imperial Russia that equated a person's social position and privileges with his rank in the state bureaucracy or army.

taille (TIE) The direct tax on the French peasantry.

ten lost tribes The Israelites who were scattered and lost to history when the northern kingdom of Israel fell to the Assyrians in 722 B.C.E.

Tertiaries (TER-she-air-ees) Laypeople affiliated with the monastic life who took vows of poverty, chastity, and obedience but remained in the world.

tetrarchy (TET-rar-key) Diocletian's (r. 306–337 C.E.) system for ruling the Roman Empire by four men with power divided territorially.

Thermidorian Reaction The reaction against the radicalism of the French Revolution that began in July 1794. Associated with the end of terror and establishment of the Directory.

Third Estate The branch of the French Estates General representing all of the kingdom outside the nobility and the clergy.

Third Reich (RIKE) Hitler's regime in Germany, which lasted from 1933 to 1945.

Thirty-Nine Articles (1563) The official statement of the beliefs of the Church of England. They established a moderate form of Protestantism.

three-field system A medieval innovation that increased the amount of land under cultivation by leaving only one third fallow in a given year.

transubstantiation The doctrine that the entire substances of the bread and wine are changed in the Eucharist into the body and blood of Christ.

tribunes (TRIB-unes) Roman officials who had to be plebeians and were elected by the plebeian assembly to protect plebeians from the arbitrary power of the magistrates.

ulema (oo-LEE-mah) Meaning "persons with correct knowledge." The Islamic scholarly elite who served a social function similar to the Christian clergy.

Upper Egypt The part of Egypt that runs from the delta to the Sudanese border.

utilitarianism The theory associated with Jeremy Bentham (1748–1832) that the principle of utility, defined as the greatest good for the greatest number of people, should be applied to government, the economy, and the judicial system.

utopian socialists Early-nineteenth-century writers who sought to replace the existing capitalist structure and values with visionary solutions or ideal communities.

vassal A person granted an estate or cash payments in return for accepting the obligation to render services to a lord.

Vulgate The Latin translation of the Bible by Jerome (348–420 C.E.) that became the standard bible used by the Catholic Church.

War Communism The economic policy adopted by the Bolsheviks during the Russian Civil War to seize the banks, heavy industry, railroads, and grain.

war guilt clause Clause 231 of the Versailles Treaty, which assigned responsibility for World War I solely to Germany.

Warsaw Pact An alliance of East European socialist states, dominated by the Soviet Union.

water frame A water-powered device invented by Richard Arkwright to produce a more durable cotton fabric. It led to the shift in the production of cotton textiles from households to factories.

Weimar Republic (Why-mar) The German democratic regime that existed between the end of World War I and Hitler's coming to power in 1933.

Zionist The movement to create a Jewish state in Palestine (the Biblical Zion).

INDEX